Lecture Notes in Artificial Intelligence   6541

Edited by R. Goebel, J. Siekmann, and W. Wahlster

Subseries of Lecture Notes in Computer Science

W0246071

Marina De Vos   Nicoletta Fornara
Jeremy V. Pitt   George Vouros (Eds.)

Coordination, Organizations, Institutions, and Norms in Agent Systems VI

COIN 2010 International Workshops
COIN@AAMAS 2010, Toronto, Canada, May 2010
COIN@MALLOW 2010, Lyon, France, August 2010
Revised Selected Papers

 Springer

Series Editors

Randy Goebel, University of Alberta, Edmonton, Canada
Jörg Siekmann, University of Saarland, Saarbrücken, Germany
Wolfgang Wahlster, DFKI and University of Saarland, Saarbrücken, Germany

Volume Editors

Marina De Vos
University of Bath, Department of Computer Science,
Bath BA2 7AY, UK, E-mail: mdv@cs.bath.ac.uk

Nicoletta Fornara
Università della Svizzera Italiana
Via G. Buffi 13, 6900 Lugano, Switzerland, E-mail: nicoletta.fornara@usi.ch

Jeremy V. Pitt
Imperial College London, Department of Electrical & Electronic Engineering
London SW7 2BT, UK, E-mail: j.pitt@imperial.ac.uk

George Vouros
University of the Aegean
Department of Information and Communication Systems Engineering
Karlovassi, 83200 Samos, Greece, E-mail: georgev@aegean.gr

ISSN 0302-9743   e-ISSN 1611-3349
ISBN 978-3-642-21267-3   e-ISBN 978-3-642-21268-0
DOI 10.1007/978-3-642-21268-0
Springer Heidelberg Dordrecht London New York

Library of Congress Control Number: Applied for

CR Subject Classification (1998): I.2, D.2, C.2, H.4, H.5, H.3

LNCS Sublibrary: SL 7 – Artificial Intelligence

Typesetting: Camera-ready by author, data conversion by Scientific Publishing Services, Chennai, India

Printed on acid-free paper

Springer is part of Springer Science+Business Media (www.springer.com)

Preface

This volume is the sixth in a series that started in 2005, and it collects papers from the Coordination, Organizations, Institutions and Norms (COIN) workshops http://www.pcs.usp.br/~coin/. The papers in this volume are drawn from the two workshops that took place in 2010.

The development of complex distributed systems consisting of autonomous and heterogeneous agents with diverse knowledge is a challenge: System components must interact, coordinate and collaborate to solve problems that are intrinsically distributed, manage the complexity of task environments, targeting their well-being and persistence via adapted organization and regulation of behaviors. All this must happen in scalable ways. Autonomous and autonomic management of the scale and complexity of contemporary distributed systems requires intelligence; in particular an intelligence that is manifested by individual strategies and/or collective behavior. In such circumstances, system architects have to consider: the inter-operation of heterogeneously designed, developed or discovered components; inter-connection which cross-legal, temporal, or organizational boundaries; the absence of global objects or centralized controllers; the possibility that components will not comply with the given specifications; and embedding in an environment which is likely to change, with a possible impact on individual and collective objectives.

The convergence of the requirement for intelligence with these operational constraints demands: coordination—the collective ability of heterogeneous and autonomous components to arrange or synchronize the performance of specified actions in sequential or temporal order; organization—a formal structure supporting or producing intentional forms of coordination; institution—an organization where inter alia the performance of designated actions by empowered agents produces conventional outcomes; and norms—patterns of behavior in an institution established by decree, agreement, emergence, and so on.

The automation and distribution of intelligence is a crucial subject of study in autonomous agents and multi-agent systems; the automation and distribution of intelligence for coordination, organization, institutions and norms is the focus of the 2010 workshops.

The goal of these workshops is to bring together researchers in autonomous agents and multi-agent systems working on the scientific and technological aspects of organizational theory, electronic institutions and computational economies from an organizational or institutional perspective. Authors of the workshop papers were invited to extend their submitted work on the basis of reviewers' comments and the discussions during the meeting. These papers were reviewed again. The successful papers appear in this volume.

COIN@AAMAS 2010

COIN@AAMAS 2010 took place on May 11, 2010, as a satellite event of the 9th International Conference on Autonomous Agents and Multiagent Systems (AAMAS 2010), in Toronto, Canada. With about 30 participants in each session 35 registered participants, the workshop was an exciting and fruitful gathering where discussions followed the papers presented by an international group of speakers. We had participants from Australia, Italy, The Netherlands, Brazil, New Zealand, Portugal, Spain, UK and USA, to name a few. Of the 21 submissions, 14 were selected for presentation and, subsequently, included in the proceedings. Each paper was assigned three to five reviewers to provide constructive comments and to stimulate discussion.

COIN@MALLOW 2010

COIN@MALLOW 2010 took place on August 30, 2010, as one of the federated Multi-Agent Logics, Languages, and Organisations Workshops (MALLOW), in Lyon, France. This edition of COIN received 14 high-quality submissions, describing work by researchers coming from nine different countries; eight of the submissions were selected by the Program Committee as regular papers and two were selected by the Program Committee as position papers. Each paper received at least three reviews in order to supply the authors with helpful feedback that could stimulate the research as well as foster discussion. Seven of these papers appear in this volume.

The Papers

The papers in this volume are extended, revised versions of the best papers presented at the two workshops. The result is a balanced collection of high-quality papers that really can be called representative of the field at this moment. For this volume, the papers have been re-grouped around three themes: *Normative System Design and Modelling*, *Social Aspects* and *Norms at Run-time: Learning and Enforcing*. Here we summarize each of these themes and present a brief summary of the papers.

Normative System Design and Modelling

All the papers in this section model particular aspects of organizations, normative frameworks, or institutions at design time. The papers range from mechanisms for norm compliance and reputations, specification languages to mechanisms to assist the designer in the realization of prototypical implementation for offline verification of systems.

1. Criado et al., in "Rational Strategies for Norm Compliance in the n-BDI Proposal," present a BDI architecture in which agents can adopt norms autonomously allowing them to reason about the influence of norm compliance and violation with respect to their goals.

2. Köhler-Bußmeier et al., in "Generating Executable Multi-Agent System Prototypes from SONAR Specifications," provide a middleware, MULAN4SONAR,
   and its prototypical implementation for supporting organizational teamwork in
   all its various stages. The organizations are modelled using SONAR, a rich and
   elaborate formalism to provide all the necessary configuration information.
3. da Silva Figueiredo et al., in "Modelling Norms in Multi-agent Systems with
   NormML," propose a new normative modelling language to specify the main
   properties and characteristics of norms. Furthermore, they introduce a mechanism to validate the norm specification at design time with respect to possible conflicts.
4. Centeno et al., in "Building Reputation-Based Agreements: Collective Opinions as Information Sources," introduce a reputation mechanism that can be
   used by organizational models allowing agents to collaborate with better
   partners. The proposed mechanism collects opinions about agents and provides this information using different informative mechanisms.
5. Corapi et al., in "Norm Refinement and Design Through Inductive Learning," present an inductive logic programming approach for learning normative specifications on the basis of use cases. These use cases present the
   intended behavior of the system. If a specification does not satisfy the provided use cases, the system will provide the necessary rules or rule updates
   to satisfy these use cases.
6. Balke et al., in "Using a Normative Framework to Explore the Prototyping of
   Wireless Grids," present a case study of a normative framework to verify the
   usefulness of a technique proposed in the wireless grids community. Instead
   of having mobile phones obtain information only from a given base station,
   phones are encouraged (via norms) to share data with other handsets on a
   power-efficient channel.

Social Aspects

The papers in this section focus on the inter-relational aspects between agents
and/or agents and humans. They study models of interaction, commitment and
coherence within the context of MAS, or use mental models or human search
behavior to derive decision strategies for agents in a variety of contexts.

1. Martinez et al., in "Towards a Model of Social Coherence in Multi-Agent
   Organizations," study the dynamics of multi-agent organizations using a
   model based on social coherence and a simulation framework. The basic
   component of the model is the notion of social commitment, which is being
   used to describe all agents' interdependencies. A local coherence mechanism
   together with a sanctioning policy is then used to ensure social control and
   emergence of social coherence.
2. Jonker et al., in "Shared Mental Models: A Conceptual Analysis," investigate
   which concepts are relevant for shared mental models and model how they are
   related using UML. They develop a mental model ontology that formalizes a
   shared understanding of tasks between teams of agents and teams of human-
   agent teams.

3. Boella et al., in "Group Intention Is Social Choice with Commitment," propose a formalization of non-summative group intentions, using social choice theory to derive group goals. The framework combines judgement aggregation as a decision-mechanism with a multi-modal multi-agent logic derived from LTL to represent collective attitudes and all the aspects of group intentions.

4. Johnson et al., in "Coactive Design: Why Interdependence Must Shape Autonomy," introduce the fundamental principles of coactive design. This approach has been developed to highlight the interdependence between the various (groups of) actors, agents and humans, in a given system. The authors conjecture that the increased effectiveness of a human-agent system not only relies on the autonomy of agents but also on their capability of sophisticated interdependent joint activity with humans.

5. Traskas et al., in "A Probabilistic Mechanism for Agent Discovery and Pairing Using Domain-Specific Data," propose a mechanism for agent discovery and pairing using a probabilistic approach with domain-specific data. Agents employ a Bayesian inference model to control the search in a way akin to human disposition to give up after trying a certain number of alternatives and taking the best offer seen. The effectiveness of the proposed approach is demonstrated in identifing good enough solutions to satisfy holistic organizational service level objectives.

6. Wickramasinghe et al., in "An Adherence Support Framework for Service Delivery in Customer Life Cycle Management," propose a conceptual framework to model how deficits in mental attitudes can affect service delivery and propose an adherence support architecture to reduce failures due to such deficits. The effectiveness of this proposal is demonstrated in an MAS for chronic disease management.

Norms at Run-Time: Learning and Enforcing

The last group of papers looks at how norms emerge, are updated, discovered, reasoned about or monitored in a running system.

1. Griffiths and Luck, in "Norm Diversity and Emergence in Tag-Based Cooperation," investigate the problem of norm-emergence and group recognition using a tag-based cooperation for interaction. The paper explores the features that affect the longevity and adoption of norms in this type of system and empirically evaluates existing techniques for supporting cooperation when agents violate the norms.

2. Criado et al., in "Norm Enforceability in Electronic Institutions?", investigate the current shortcomings of the Electronic Institution approach for MAS. The proposed method supports enforcement mechanisms for norm execution and observance. The paper looks into complex situations where the system is unable to deal with norm observance in an appropriate manner.

3. Urovi et al., in "Initial Steps Towards Run-Time Support for Norm-Governed Systems," present an initial knowledge representation framework for run-time support of norm-governed systems. The system uses an Event Calculus

dialect for efficient temporal reasoning. The paper provides an experimental evaluation to demonstrate the scalability of the approach through distribution of the infrastructure.

4. Savarimuthu et al., in "Identifying Conditional Norms in Multi-Agent Societies," present a mechanism that allows agents to discover conditional norms in their society at run-time. The paper takes the reader through the algorithms and processes, and demonstrates how an agent could go about adding, modifying or deleting these conditional norms.

5. Campos et al., in "Using a Two-Level Multi-Agent System Architecture to Perform Norm Adaptation in a Peer-to-Peer Sharing Network," present an architecture that endows an organization with self-adaptation capabilities to adapt to the changing context in which it operates. Self-adaptation is proposed as an extra assistance layer on top of the (existing) organization layer.

6. Alvarez-Napagao et al., in "Normative Monitoring: Semantics and Implementation," present a formalism for monitoring both regulative (deontic) and substantive (constitutive) norms based on structural operational semantics. This formalism is reduced to production systems semantics and the authors demonstrate that their implementation is compliant with both semantics.

7. Koeppen et al., in "Generating New Regulations by Learning from Experience," propose an approach, based on utilitarianism, to enhance multi-agent systems with a regulatory authority that generates new norms based on the outcome of previous experiences. For the learning part of their system, the authors employ machine-learning techniques.

8. Boissier et al., in "Controlling Multi-Party Interaction Within Normative Multi-Agent Organizations," present an extension of the normative organization model MOISE to allow for the specification of different interaction modes: direct communication between roles and/or restricted to a group of agents. This allows organizations to monitor interactions between agents, and agents to reason on these modes as they do about norms. The paper focuses on the first point and demonstrates the capabilities provided with a crisis management application.

We would like to thank all authors for their contributions, the members of the Steering Committee for the valuable suggestions and support, and the members of the Program Committees for their excellent work during the reviewing phases. We would also like to thank the team behind EasyChair for providing us with an excellent system to run workshops/conference and produce proceedings in a more straightforward manner.

March 2011

Marina De Vos
Nicoletta Fornara
Jeremy Pitt
George Vouros

Organization

Workshop Organizers

COIN@AAMAS   Marina De Vos   Department of Computer Science
University of Bath, UK
mdv@cs.bath.ac.uk

Jeremy Pitt   Intelligent Systems and Networks
Group, Department of Electrical
and Electronic Engineering,
Imperial College London, UK
j.pitt@imperial.ac.uk

COIN@MALLOW   Nicoletta Fornara   Faculty of Communication
Sciences Universit della Svizzera
Italiana USI, Switserland
nicoletta.fornara@usi.ch

George Vouros   Department of Information and
Communication Systems
Engineering, School of Sciences,
University of the Aegean, Samos
axel.polleres@deri.org

Program Committee

COIN@AAMAS

Alexander Artikis	National Centre for Scientific Research Demokritos, Greece
Guido Boella	University of Turin, Italy
Olivier Boissier	ENS Mines Saint-Etienne, France
Dan Corkill	University of Massachusetts Amherst, USA
Antonio Carlos da Rocha Costa	UCPEL, Brazil
Stephen Cranefield	University of Otago, New Zealand
Virginia Dignum	Delft University of Technology, The Netherlands
Nicoletta Fornara	University of Lugano, Switzerland
Olivier Gutknecht	LPDL, France
Jomi Fred Hubner	Federal University of Santa Catarina, Brazil
Fuyuki Ishikawa	National Institute of Informatics, Japan

Catholijn Jonker	Delft University of Technology, The Netherlands
Christian Lemaitre	Universidad Autonoma Metropolitana, Mexico
Maite Lopez-Sanchez	University of Barcelona, Spain
Eric Matson	Purdue, USA
John-Jules Meyer	Utrecht University, The Netherlands
Daniel Moldt	University of Hamburg, Germany
Pablo Noriega	IIIA-CSI, Spain
Eugenio Oliveira	Universidade do Porto, Portugal
Sascha Ossowski	URJC, Spain
Julian Padget	University of Bath, UK
Eric Platon	National Institute of Informatics, Japan
Juan Antonio Rodriguez Aguilar	IIIA-CSIC, Spain
Christophe Sibertin-Blanc	IRIT, France
Jaime Sichman	University of Sao Paulo, Brazil
Catherine Tessier	ONERA, France
Luca Tummolini	ISTC/CNR, Italy
Leon van der Torre	University of Luxembourg, Luxembourg
Wamberto Vasconcelos	University of Aberdeen, UK
Javier Vazquez-Salceda	Universitat Politecnica de Catalunya, Spain
Harko Verhagen	Stockholm University, Sweden
George Vouros	University of the Aegean, Greece

COIN@MALLOW

Juan Antonio Rodriguez Aguilar	IIIA-CSIC, Spain
Alexander Artikis	National Centre for Scientific Research Demokritos, Greece
Guido Boella	University of Turin, Italy
Olivier Boissier	ENS Mines Saint-Etienne, France
Rafael Bordini	Federal University of Rio Grande do Sul, Brazil
Amit Chopra	University of Trento, Italy
Antonio Carlos da Rocha Costa	Universidade Federal do Rio Grande FURG, Brazil
Marina De Vos	University of Bath, UK
Virginia Dignum	Delft University of Technology, The Netherlands
Jomi Fred Hubner	Federal University of Santa Catarina, Brazil
Christian Lemaitre	Universidad Autonoma Metropolitana, Mexico
Henrique Lopes Cardoso	Universidade do Porto, Portugal

Eric Matson	Purdue, USA
John-Jules Meyer	Utrecht University, The Netherlands
Pablo Noriega	IIIA-CSI, Spain
Eugenio Oliveira	Universidade do Porto, Portugal
Andrea Omicini	University of Bologna, Italy
Sascha Ossowski	URJC, Spain
Julian Padget	University of Bath, UK
Jeremy Pitt	Imperial College, London, UK
Juan Antonio Rodriguez Aguilar	IIIA-CSIC, Spain
Jaime Sichman	University of Sao Paulo, Brazil
Munindar P. Singh	North Carolina State University, USA
Viviane Torres da Silva	Universidade Federal Fluminente, Brazil
Kostas Stathis	Royal Holloway, University of London, UK
Paolo Torroni	University of Bologna, Italy
Leon van der Torre	University of Luxembourg, Luxembourg
Birna van Riemsdijk	Delf University of Technology, The Netherlands
Wamberto Vasconcelos	University of Aberdeen, UK
Javier Vazquez-Salceda	Universitat Politecnica de Catalunya, Spain
Mario Verdicchio	University of Bergamo, Italy
Danny Weyns	Katholieke Universiteit Leuven, Belgium
Pinar Yolum	Bogazici University, Turkey

Additional Reviewers

Dmytro Tykhonov	Fernando J. M. Marcellino
Henrique Lopes Cardoso	Luis Gustavo Nardin
Luciano Coutinho	Moser Silva Fagundes
Inacio Guerberoff	Juan Antonio Rodriguez Aguilar
Valerio Genovese	Matteo Vasirani
Akin Gunay	Serena Villata
Ozgur Kafali	Matthias Wester-Ebbinghaus

COIN Steering Committee

Juan Antonio Rodriguez Aguilar	IIIA-CSIC, Spain
Guido Boella	University of Turin, Italy
Olivier Boissier	ENS Mines Saint-Etienne, France
Nicoletta Fornara	University of Lugano, Switzerland
Christian Lemaitre	Universidad Autonoma Metropolitana, Mexico
Eric Matson	Purdue University, USA
Pablo Noriega	Artficial Intelligence Research Institute, Spain

Table of Contents

Topic 3

Norms at Run-Time: Learning and Enforcing

Rational Strategies for Norm Compliance in the n-BDI Proposal

Natalia Criado, Estefania Argente, and Vicent Botti

Departamento de Sistemas Informáticos y Computación
Universidad Politécnica de Valencia
Camino de Vera s/n. 46022 Valencia (Spain)
{ncriado,eargente,vbotti}dsic.upv.es

Abstract. Norms represent an effective tool for achieving coordination and cooperation among members of open systems. However, agents must be able to adopt norms autonomously. In this sense, the n-BDI proposal is a BDI agent architecture which has been extended in order to allow agents to comply with norms autonomously. Compliance with norms can be explained by both rational and non-rational motivations. Rational motivations consider the influence of norm compliance and violation on agent's goals. In this work the implementation of rational strategies for making a decision about norm compliance in the n-BDI architecture is described.

1 Introduction

Maybe the most promising application of MAS technology is its usage for supporting Open Distributed Systems [21]. They are characterized by the heterogeneity of their participants, their limited trust, possible individual goals in conflict and a high uncertainty [2]. Norms represent an effective tool for achieving coordination and cooperation among members of open systems. However, norms, to become effective, must be dynamically adapted to the environmental changes and autonomously adopted by agents [10]. Therefore, autonomous agents need strategies for determining when and how complying with norms.

The question of norm compliance has been traditionally discussed by the sociology field. Taking as a basis the work on social norms presented in [16], the norm compliance process can be justified by: i) *Rational* motivations, i.e. a norm can be fulfilled by self-interest motivations (e.g. undesirability of the sanctions, interest in the rewards) or it can be considered as suitable for common interests; and (ii) *Non-Rational* reasons, which are related to emotions such as anxiety and shame which maintain social norms, honour and envy among others. Existing proposals of intelligent norm aware agents, like [6,1,19,27], tend to be concerned about the decision-making processes that are supported by a set of norms which are blindly followed by agents. In this paper, we discuss how agents are able to deliberate about whether to comply or violate a given norm according to their interests. Thus, several strategies for norm compliance based on rational motivations are described in this paper. More specifically, this

M. De Vos et al. (Eds.): COIN 2010 International Workshops, LNAI 6541, pp. 1–20, 2011.

work takes a normative BDI agent architecture, known as n-BDI [11,12], as basis. The n-BDI is a multi-context BDI agent architecture [7] which has been extended with recognition and normative reasoning capabilities in order to allow agents to consider norms in their decision making process. Thus, in this paper different rational strategies for norm compliance have been defined considering the facilities provided by the n-BDI architecture.

This paper is structured as follows: the first section describes the original multi-context BDI proposal. Next, the n-BDI proposal, that extends the multi-context BDI agent architecture with normative decision-making capabilities, is described. Rational strategies for norm compliance have been proposed in Section 4. In Section 5 this work has been applied into the m-Water case study, in which an irrigator agent must choose between respecting and not respecting norms employing these different norm compliance strategies. Discussion of related works is included in Section 6. Finally, conclusions and future works are detailed.

2   Preliminaries

A *multi-context system* [17] is formed by theoretical interrelationed components, named units or contexts. According to the multi-context proposal, a BDI agent architecture is defined as a set of interconnected contexts $\langle \{c_i\}_{i\in I}, \Delta \rangle$ which represent the mental modalities [23,26]. Each unit $c_i \in \{C_i\}_{i\in I}$ is a tuple $\langle L_i, A_i, \Delta_i \rangle$, where L_i, A_i and Δ_i are the language, axioms and inference rules defining the logic of each context, respectively. Δ is the set of bridge rules between the contexts; i.e. inference rules whose premises and conclusions belong to different contexts.

A general BDI agent is defined as a multi-context agent architecture in [24]. In [7] a general model of multi-context graded BDI is presented. The main idea beyond this work is to employ a weigh to represent the certainty or desirability degree of a mental proposition. According to these proposals, a multi-context graded BDI agent is mainly formed by (Figure 1 grey contexts): *mental* contexts that characterize beliefs (BC), intentions (IC) and desires (DC); and *functional* contexts for planning (PC) and communication (CC). Following, these contexts are explained:

- *Belief Context (BC)*. It is formed by propositions belonging to the BC-Logic [7]; i.e. logic propositions such as $(B\,\gamma, \beta_\gamma)$ where $B\,\gamma$ represents a belief of an agent, $\gamma \in \mathcal{L}_{\mathcal{DL}}$ is a dynamic logic [22] proposition and $\beta_\gamma \in [0,1]$ represents the certainty degree of this belief.
- *Intention Context (IC)*. It is formed by propositions belonging to the IC-Logic [7]; i.e. logic propositions such as $(I\,\gamma, \iota_\gamma)$ where $I\,\gamma$ represents an intention of an agent, $\gamma \in \mathcal{L}_{\mathcal{DL}}$ and $\iota_\gamma \in [0,1]$ represents the intention degree ascribed to this intention. The usage of degrees for representing intentions may be arguable, since it may seem confused that an agent intends to do an action at different degrees. However, as argued in [7] the truth degree

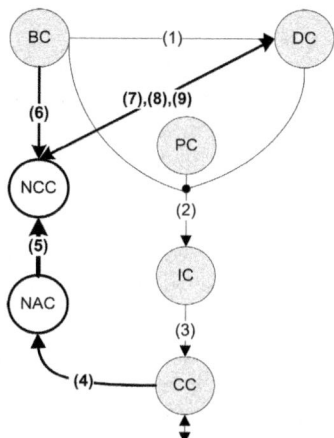

Fig. 1. n-BDI Architecture. Grey contexts and lines (bridge rules) correspond to the basic definition of a BDI agent. The normative contexts and normative bridge rules are the white circles (NCC, NAC) and bold lines, respectively.

(ι_γ) of the expression "γ is intended" is determined by the existence of a feasible plan that permits to achieve a state of the world where γ holds with a probability ι_γ.

- *Desire Context (DC)*. It is formed by propositions belonging to the DC-Logic [7]; i.e. logic propositions such as $(D^*\gamma, \delta_\gamma^*)$ where $D^*\gamma$ represents a desire of an agent; $\gamma \in \mathcal{L}_{\mathcal{DL}}$; $\delta_\gamma^* \in [0,1]$ represents the desirability degree; $* \in \{+, -\}$ represents positive desires and negative desires, respectively. Degrees of positive or negative desires allow setting different levels of preference or rejection. Thus, the expression $(D^+\gamma, \delta_\gamma^+)$ is read as "proposition γ is desired with a degree δ_γ^+", whereas $(D^-\gamma, \delta_\gamma^-)$ is read as "proposition γ is undesired with a degree δ_γ^-".

- *Planner Context (PC)*. It allows agents to determine sequence of actions that will be intended according to their desires [7]. The PC is formed by formulas such as $plan(\Sigma)$, where Σ is a set of actions that compose the plan. The process by which agents generate new plans for achieving their goals is beyond the scope of this paper and has not been described here.

- *Communication Context (CC)*. It communicates agents with their environment [7]. The CC is formed by expressions such as $(\mathcal{C} \gamma)$, where $\mathcal{C} \in \{\mathcal{P}, \mathcal{O}\}$. $\mathcal{O} \gamma$ represents that proposition γ has been perceived ($\mathcal{O}$bserved) whereas $\mathcal{P} \gamma$ means that γ has been $\mathcal{P}$erformed by the agent. Thus, propositions such as $(\mathcal{O} \gamma)$ are the inputs provided by the environment to the agent. The interaction with the environment is expressed using formulas as $(\mathcal{P} \gamma)$.

According to this notation, given a proposition γ: β_γ represents the belief degree assigned to $B \gamma$; ι_γ is the intentionality degree of $I \gamma$; $\delta_\gamma^!$ is the desirability degree of $D^+\gamma$; and δ_γ^- is the undesirability degree of $D^-\gamma$.

2.1 Bridge Rules

Several bridge rules, which connect both the mental and functional contexts, have been defined in the existing literature in order to determine different types of BDI agents (e.g. strong realism, realism and weak realism agents [25]). Next, only those bridge rules which have an impact on the normative reasoning process are described:

- The *Deriving Concrete Desires* bridge rule (Figure 1 Rule 1) allows abstract desires to be concreted into more realistic ones according to the agent beliefs:

$$\frac{DC : (D^*\varphi, \delta_\varphi^*),\, BC : (B([\alpha]\varphi), \beta_{[\alpha]\varphi})}{DC : (D^*[\alpha]\varphi, f_D(\delta_\varphi^*, \beta_{[\alpha]\varphi}))} \tag{1}$$

  Generic agent desires $(D^*\varphi, \delta_\varphi^*)$ derive more realistic desires $(D^*[\alpha]\varphi, f_D(\delta_\varphi^*, \beta_{[\alpha]\varphi}))$; taking into account the existence of actions that allow them to be reached $(B([\alpha]\varphi), \beta_{[\alpha]\varphi})$. Thus, the preference degree of the concrete desire relies on the original desirability (δ_φ^*) and the possibility of achieving it by means of action α $(\beta_{[\alpha]\varphi})$. This is calculated by f_D function; its concrete definition is problem dependent. However, in our proposal it is defined as the product of these two values for obtaining the expected satisfaction or disgust value.

- The *Deriving Agent Intentions From Positive Desires* bridge rule (Figure 1 Rule 2) derives the intended formulas of the agent from the set of preferred formulas which are reachable by some existing plan:

$$\frac{\begin{array}{c} DC : (D^+[\alpha]\varphi, \delta_{[\alpha]\varphi}^+),\, DC : (D^+\alpha, \delta_\alpha^+),\, PC : plan(\Sigma) \\ DC : (D^-[\alpha]\psi_1, \delta_{[\alpha]\psi_1}^-), ..., DC : (D^-[\alpha]\psi_n \delta_{[\alpha]\psi_n}^-), \\ \alpha \in \Sigma, (\delta_{[\alpha]\varphi}^+ + \delta_\alpha^+) \geq \sum_{k=1}^n \delta_{[\alpha]\psi_k}^- \end{array}}{IC : (I[\alpha]\varphi, f_I(\delta_{[\alpha]\varphi}^+ + \delta_\alpha^+, \sum_{k=1}^n \delta_{[\alpha]\psi_k}^-))} \tag{2}$$

  More specifically, those positive desires $(D^+[\alpha]\varphi, \delta_{[\alpha]\varphi}^+)$ which can be achieved by an action (α) belonging to a plan $(Plan(\Sigma))$ will generate a new intention $(I[\alpha]\varphi, f_I(\delta_{[\alpha]\varphi}^+ + \delta_\alpha^+, \sum_{k=1}^n \delta_{[\alpha]\psi_k}^-))$ if the desirability degree of both the proposition $(\delta_{[\alpha]\varphi}^+)$ and the action (δ_α^+) is greater than the sum of the negative effects of the action $(\sum_{k=1}^n \delta_{[\alpha]\psi_k}^-)$. Finally, f_I is a function that combines both positive and negative effects of an action; in this case it has been defined as: $f_I(a, b) = min(a - b, 1)$

- The *Deriving Actions From Intentions* bridge rule (Figure 1 Rule 3) defines the next action to be performed by the agent $(\mathcal{P}\,\alpha)$ as the intention which has the maximum degree $(I[\alpha]\varphi, \iota_{max})$:

$$\frac{IC : (I[\alpha]\varphi, \iota_{max})}{CC : (\mathcal{P}\,\alpha)} \tag{3}$$

3   Normative BDI Architecture (n-BDI)

Taking as a reference the multi-context graded BDI agent architecture [7], in [11,12] the n-BDI agent architecture has been proposed. Specifically, the n-BDI extends the multi-context graded BDI proposal by adding new contexts and bridge rules in order to allow agents to make decisions according to norms. These norms are classified into two groups [3]: *regulative* or *deontic* norms, which define the ideal behaviour of agents making use of deontic modalities; and *constitutive* norms, which are used for establishing social institutions which give rise to new types of facts that only make sense within the institution. This paper focus on compliance of deontic norms so constitutive norms have not been considered here.

In the n-BDI proposal two new functional contexts are defined (Figure 1, white contexts): the *Norm Acquisition Context* (NAC), which is responsible for the norm identification process; and the *Norm Compliance Context* (NCC), which allows agents to consider norms in their decision making processes.

Basically, the norm decision process starts when the NAC derives a new norm through analysing the environment (through the CC context). More specifically, the NAC allows agents to identify norms. These norms are translated into a set of inference rules which are included into the NCC. Then, the NCC derives new desires according to the current agent mental state and the inference rules which have been obtained from norms. These new desires may cause intentions to be updated and, as a consequence, normative actions might be carried out.

3.1   Norm Acquisition Context (NAC)

Norms can be explicitly created by the system designer or a representative agent which has been empowered to define the normative context. In addition, other types of norms such as commitments are created as a result of an interaction among agents. Finally, there are norms, such as social norms, which emerge in a society without being explicitly created by any agent. Whatever process norm creation is, any new norm must be spread in the society in order to be internalized and respected by agents. In this sense, agents are able to recognise norms which control their environment by two different manners [1]: they may be informed about the existing norms or, on the contrary, they are cognitive agents are capable of inferring norms from observation. Therefore, the NAC context receives the observed environmental facts, which include also those facts that have been communicated to the agent, by the CC context and identifies the set of norms which control the agent environment. In this proposal, recognised norms are defined as follows:

Definition 1 (Norm). *A norm n is defined as* $n = \langle D, C, A, E, S, R \rangle$ *where:*

- $D \in \{O, F\}$, *is the deontic operator. In this work only obligations (O) and prohibitions (F) which impose constraints on agent behaviours have been considered; whereas permissions have not been considered since they are defined as operators that invalidate the activation of obligations or prohibitions;*

- *C is a first order formula that represents the normative condition that must be carried out in case of obligations, or that must be avoided in case of prohibition norms;*
- *A, E are first order formulae that determine the norm activation and expiration conditions, respectively;*
- *S, R are expressions which describe the actions (sanctions and rewards) that will be carried out in case of norm violation or fulfilment, respectively.*

Thus, the NAC is formed by expressions defined as $(NAC\ n, \rho_n, \rho_S, \rho_R)$; where n is a first order formula which represents a norm. $\rho_n \in [0,1]$ is the probability of norm application; i.e. the trust degree of the communicated norm or the observed probability of norm compliance in case of an inferred norm. In this work we assume that agents are informed about norms which control their behaviours by a representative of the normative system. Thus, there is a total reliability on the recognised norm ($\rho_n = 1$). Finally, $\rho_S, \rho_R \in [0,1]$ are the probability values ascribed to the application of sanctions and rewards, respectively; i.e. the probability of being sanctioned or rewarded by the norm issuer. The estimation of these two probabilities is over the scope of this paper. However, they can be inferred by considering the number of times that the agent observes that norm violations and fulfilment have been sanctioned or rewarded, respectively.

This paper does not focus on the norm acquisition problem. In the following, the NAC will be considered as a black box that receives cues for detecting norms as input and generates norms as output.

3.2 Norm Compliance Context (NCC)

In our approach norms are not static constraints implemented on agents. On the contrary, agents are able to acquire and accept norms dynamically in an autonomous way. Performance of the NCC is: i) mental contexts inject formulas inside the NCC; ii) the NCC carries out an inference process in order to reason about norms considering the current mental state; and iii) BDI contexts are modified according to the new mental propositions which have been derived from norms.

In this paper a simplistic approximation to the norm internalization process [9] has been considered. However, it will be object of future work extensions. In particular, we have only considered the internalization of norms as goals. In this sense, the process of norm internalization has been described by the self-determination theory [15] as a dynamic relation between norms and desires. This shift would represent the assumption that internalized norms become part of the agent's sense of identity. Thus, the NCC updates the DC with the new normative desires.

The NCC is formed by expressions like $NCC(\lceil\gamma\rceil)$; where γ is a first-order logic expression which is defined as an inference rule which corresponds to a translated norm from the NAC. In particular, these inference rules relate belief propositions with desires. The expression $\lceil\gamma\rceil$ means that γ is embedded in the normative context as a term; i.e. modal logic expressions modelled as first order theories.

The normative context logic consists of the axiom schema K, closure under implication, together with the consistency axiom. Therefore, contradictory norms are allowed; i.e. it is possible to define $NCC(\lceil\gamma\rceil) \wedge NCC(\lceil\neg\gamma\rceil)$. This fact is interesting for our work since agents are usually controlled by conflicting norms addressed at the different roles played by the agent or there may be a conflict among agent goals and norms. However, contradictory predicates such as $NCC(\lceil\gamma\rceil) \wedge \neg NCC(\lceil\gamma\rceil)$ are not allowed, i.e. expressions that claim that a certain norm exists and not exits simultaneously.

3.3   Bridge Rules

Normative BDI Agents require the definition of additional bridge rules for allowing norms to be recognised and normative decisions to be taken.

Updating the NAC. Agent observations and communications which it perceives from its environment ($\mathcal{O}\ \beta$) are included into the norm acquisition context as a new term or theory ($\lceil\beta\rceil$) (see Figure 1 Rule 4):

$$\frac{CC : (\mathcal{O}\ \beta)}{NAC : (\lceil\beta\rceil)} \tag{4}$$

Norm Transformation Rules. Inside the norm acquisition context new norms are acquired. Those recognised norms ($NAC\ n, \rho_n, \rho_S, \rho_R$) are transformed into terms inside the normative context ($NCC(\lceil\gamma\rceil)$) (see Figure 1 Rule 5):

$$\frac{NAC : (NAC\ n, \rho_n, \rho_S, \rho_R)}{NCC : (NCC(\lceil\gamma\rceil))} \tag{5}$$

As previously argued, each norm is translated into an inference rule ($\gamma = \varphi \rightarrow \psi$) belonging to the normative context. The definition of this inference rule depends on the concrete deontic type of the norm which is being translated.

– *Obligation Norm.*

$$\frac{NAC : (NAC\ \langle O, C, A, E, S, R\rangle, \rho_n, \rho_S, \rho_R)}{NCC : NCC(\lceil\gamma\rceil)}$$

where:

$$\gamma = \varphi \rightarrow \psi$$
$$\varphi = (B\ A, \beta_A) \wedge (B\neg E, \beta_{\neg E})$$
$$\psi = (D^+C, f(\theta_{activation}, \theta_{compliance}))$$

If an agent considers that the obligation is currently active ($(B\ A, \beta_A) \wedge (B\neg E, \beta_{\neg E})$) then a new positive desire corresponding to the norm condition is inferred:

$$(D^+C, f(\theta_{activation}, \theta_{compliance}))$$

– *Prohibition Norm.*

$$\frac{NAC : (NAC \langle F, C, A, E, S, R \rangle, \rho_n, \rho_S, \rho_R)}{NCC : NCC(\lceil \gamma \rceil)}$$

where:

$$\gamma = \varphi \rightarrow \psi$$
$$\varphi = (B\ A, \beta_A) \wedge (B\neg E, \beta_{\neg E})$$
$$\psi = (D^- C, f(\theta_{activation}, \theta_{compliance}))$$

Similarly to obligation norms, a prohibition related to a condition C is transformed into an inference rule which asserts a negative desire if the norm is active.

The certainty degree related to the norm activation ($\theta_{activation}$), together with the certainty or desirability of norm compliance ($\theta_{compliance}$) are employed by the function f in order to assign a degree to the normative desire. The concrete definition of f is problem dependent. However, in this work it has been implemented as:

$$f(\theta_{activation}, \theta_{compliance}) = \theta_{activation} \times \theta_{compliance}$$

The norm activation ($\theta_{activation}$) is defined as a $f_{activation}$ function that combines the belief degrees related to the norm activation and expiration conditions (β_A and $\beta_{\neg E}$) and the certainty degree of the norm (ρ_n):

$$\theta_{activation} = f_{activation}(\beta_A, \beta_{\neg E}, \rho_n) = \beta_A \times \beta_{\neg E} \times \rho_n$$

If the agent has not any belief related to occurrence of any of these conditions, then the belief degree is defined as zero.

The norm compliance ($\theta_{compliance}$) is defined as a $f_{compliance}$ function that takes as input the positive/negative degrees of the norm condition (δ_C^*), sanction (δ_S^*) and reward (δ_R^*); and the possibilities of being sanctioned and rewarded (ρ_S and ρ_R). With this information, the compliance function will determine if the agent fulfils the norm.

$$\theta_{compliance} = f_{compliance}(\delta_C^*, \delta_S^*, \delta_R^*, \rho_S, \rho_R)$$

were $\delta_C^* = (\delta_C^+, \delta_C^-); \delta_S^* = (\delta_S^+, \delta_S^-); \delta_R^* = (\delta_R^+, \delta_R^-)$

Updating the NCC. Besides the definition of bridge rules for connecting the NAC with the NCC; additional bridge rules are needed in order to allow normative BDI agents to consider norms in their decision making process. More specifically, both agent desires and beliefs (γ) are included into the normative context as first order formulas ($\lceil \gamma \rceil$) in order to determine when a norm is active (Figure 1 Rules 6 and 7):

$$\frac{BC : \gamma}{NCC : NCC(\lceil \gamma \rceil)} \tag{6}$$

$$\frac{DC : \gamma}{NCC : NCC(\lceil \gamma \rceil)} \tag{7}$$

Updating the DC: Coherence Maintenance. In addition, after performing the inference process for creating new desires ($\lceil (D^* \ \gamma, \delta) \rceil$) derived from norm application; the normative context must update the DC (Figure 1 Rules 8 and 9). The addition of these propositions into this mental context may cause an inconsistency with the current mental state. Next, the problem of coherence maintenance among desires is faced.

In this proposal of BDI architecture, the maintenance of coherency among desires has been achieved by means of two different schemas (i.e. DC_1 and DC_2) which have been previously defined in [7]. These schemas impose some constraints between the positive and negative desires of a formula and its negation. Next, each schema is explained.

On the one hand, the DC_1 schema avoids having contradictory desires; i.e. to desire $(D^+\gamma, \delta_\gamma^+)$ and $(D^+\neg\gamma, \delta_{\neg\gamma}^+)$ simultaneously. Thus, this constraint and the corresponding for negative desires impose the next constraint over propositions belonging to the DC:

$$min(\delta_\gamma^*, \delta_{\neg\gamma}^*) = 0$$

where δ_γ^* and $\delta_{\neg\gamma}^*$ are the desirability or undesirability degrees assigned to proposition γ and its negation, respectively.

On the other hand, schema DC_2 imposes a restriction over positive and negative desires for a same goal. In particular, it claims that an agent cannot desire to be in world more than it is tolerated (i.e. not rejected). Therefore, it determines that:

$$\delta_\gamma^+ + \delta_\gamma^- \leq 1$$

According to DC_1 and DC_2 schemas, bridge rule for updating the DC with the positive desires derived from norms is defined as follows (Figure 1 Rule 8):

$$\frac{NCC : NCC(\lceil (D^+ \ \gamma, \delta) \rceil), \delta > \delta_{thres}, DC : (D^- \ \gamma, \delta^-), DC : (D^+ \ \gamma, \delta^+)}{\begin{array}{c} DC : (D^+ \ \gamma, max(\delta, \delta^+)), DC : (D^+\neg\gamma, 0), \\ DC : (D^- \ \gamma, min(\delta^-, 1 - max(\delta, \delta^+))) \end{array}} \quad (8)$$

Thus, the desire degree assigned to the new proposition γ is defined as the maximum between the new desirability and the previous value $(max(\delta, \delta^+))$. In order to follow DC_1 schema, desirability of $\neg\gamma$ is updated to 0. According to DC_2 schema, the undesirability assigned to γ is updated as the minimum between the previous value of undesirability assigned to γ (δ^-) and its maximum coherent undesirability, which is defined as $1 - max(\delta, \delta^+)$. Moreover, in order to avoid the propagation of insignificant terms, only these new terms whose degree exceeds δ_{thres} will be transformed into mental objects. The definition of this threshold is also problem dependent.

Similarly, bridge rule for updating the DC with negative desires is defined as follows (Figure 1 Rule 9):

$$\frac{NCC : NCC(\lceil (D^- \ \gamma, \delta) \rceil), \delta > \delta_{thres}, DC : (D^- \ \gamma, \delta^-), DC : (D^+ \ \gamma, \delta^+)}{\begin{array}{c} DC : (D^- \ \gamma, max(\delta, \delta^-)), DC : (D^-\neg\gamma, 0), \\ DC : (D^+ \ \gamma, min(\delta^+, 1 - max(\delta, \delta^-))) \end{array}} \quad (9)$$

Along this section, our proposal of Normative Graded BDI architecture has been explained. Through the norm compliance function different strategies for norm compliance can be implemented. Strategies for norm compliance have been classified into rational and non-rational motivations. The next section illustrates how the former type of norm compliance strategies is implemented in our architecture.

4   Rational Strategies for Norm Compliance

Several proposals [8,10,20] have been made with the aim of defining rational strategies for norm compliance. One of the first works on analysing motivations for norm compliance from an agent perspective was presented in [8]. Here it is claimed that norms not only require a *behaviour* but also a *mental* attitude. According to this work, strategies for norm compliance are classified into: i) *unconditional* compliance, which implies that agents do not have capabilities for considering norms and they always fulfil norms; ii) *instrumental* compliance, which implies a greater level of autonomy since agents adopt norms if they consider them as beneficial to their goals; iii) *cooperative* agents adopt norms whenever they consider them being beneficial for the whole society; and iv) *benevolent* agents fulfil those norms which benefit other agents which they want to favour. In [20] these strategies were revised and extended.

This section illustrates how different norm compliance strategies can be easily implemented by our proposal of multi-context BDI agent. Mainly, the norm compliance strategy determines the certainty degree assigned to the new mental attributes created by the inference rules inside the normative context. Specifically, the $f_{compliance}$ function implements the different norm compliance strategies.

4.1   Traditional Strategies for Norm Compliance

Taking as a reference the classification of strategies for norm compliance described in [20], we propose to implement each strategy as follows:

- *Simple Strategies*, these ones do not consider the effects that compliance with a norm might have on agent's goals. They are classified into:
  - Agents which follow the *Automatic* strategy will accept all norms:

$$f_{compliance}(\delta_C^*, \delta_S^*, \delta_R^*, \rho_S, \rho_R) = 1$$

  - Agents which follow the *Rebellious* strategy will reject all norms systematically:

$$f_{compliance}(\delta_C^*, \delta_S^*, \delta_R^*, \rho_S, \rho_R) = 0$$

  - Agents which follow a *Fearful* strategy will accept those norms which have a sanction. Thus, these agents do not consider whether the sanction is beneficial or detrimental to their goals, but they only consider if the norm has a sanction:

$$f_{compliance}(\delta_C^*, \delta_S^*, \delta_R^*, \rho_S, \rho_R) = \begin{cases} 1 \text{ if } \delta_S^+ + \delta_S^- > 0 \\ 0 \text{ otherwise} \end{cases}$$

- Finally, *Greedy* agents adopt all norms whose compliance is rewarded, without considering the utility of the reward:

$$f_{compliance}(\delta_C^*, \delta_S^*, \delta_R^*, \rho_S, \rho_R) = \begin{cases} 1 \text{ if } \delta_R^+ + \delta_R^- > 0 \\ 0 \text{ otherwise} \end{cases}$$

– *Motivated Strategies* are more complex strategies which consider the possible effects on goals of both the norm condition and the rewards in the case a norm is fulfilled, and the effects of punishments if it is not. These strategies are based on the *utilitarian* view which defines the utility as the good to be maximized. Thus, the desirability of both norm fulfilment and violation is considered as criteria for norm compliance.
  - An *Egoist* agent will accept only those norms which benefit its goals:

$$f_{compliance}(\delta_C^*, \delta_S^*, \delta_R^*, \rho_S, \rho_R) = \begin{cases} 1 \text{ if } \delta_C^+ > 0 \\ 0 \text{ otherwise} \end{cases}$$

  - *Pressure* can be a motivation for norm compliance. More concretely, an agent which follows the *Pressure* strategy will respect all norms whose sanction is more undesired than the norm condition:

$$f_{compliance}(\delta_C^*, \delta_S^*, \delta_R^*, \rho_S, \rho_R) = \begin{cases} 1 \text{ if } \delta_S^- > \delta_C^- \\ 0 \text{ otherwise} \end{cases}$$

  - An *Opportunist* agent will accept all norms whose reward is more preferred to the negative effects of the norm:

$$f_{compliance}(\delta_C^*, \delta_S^*, \delta_R^*, \rho_S, \rho_R) = \begin{cases} 1 \text{ if } \delta_R^+ > \delta_C^- \\ 0 \text{ otherwise} \end{cases}$$

– *Social Strategies.* In the existing literature different social strategies for norm compliance have been defined:
  - *Cooperative* agents accept norms which are considered as beneficial for the whole society. This strategy can be implemented by defining social goals as agent desires.
  - A *benevolent* agent adopts those norms which are desirable for another agent which it wants to favour.
    In order to implement this strategy, it is necessary to determine if a target agent j would be favoured from norm application; i.e. if target agent j has a positive desire of C. Therefore, any agent should be able to represent other's mental attitudes as beliefs (i.e. nested mental propositions such as $(B(D_j^+ C), \beta) \in BC$). This represents a problem since desire formulas as $(D_j^+ C)$ are many-valued formulae (they have a truth value belonging

to [0,1]). Taking as a reference the solution proposed in [7], this problem can be solved by means of the definition of a projection operator (∇) defined as true if the mental proposition has a positive degree. In this sense, $\nabla(D_j^+ C)$ would be true when target agent j had a positive desire related to proposition C whose degree was greater than 0. Thus, norms will be adopted if the agent has the belief $(B \nabla(D_j^+ C), \beta)$, which means that an agent beliefs that another agent j desires occurrence of C with an intensity higher than 0.

4.2   Complex Strategies for Norm Compliance

Besides these well known strategies for norm compliance, more complex ones can be defined taking advance of the possibilities which the proposed Normative BDI architecture provides. The main idea beyond complex strategies is to consider both positive and negative effects derived from norm fulfilment and violation.

– *Mixed Strategy.* It accepts a norm if the effect of norm compliance is higher than the effect of norm violation. On the one hand, consequences of norm fulfilment are the desirability of both the norm condition (δ_C^+) and the reward (δ_R^+) and the undesirability of the norm sanction (δ_S^-), which will be avoided if the norm is respected. On the other hand, the effects of norm violation are the desirability of the sanction (δ_S^+) and the undesirability of both the norm condition (δ_C^-) and reward (δ_R^-), that will be avoided if the norm is not respected.

$$f_{compliance}(\delta_C^*, \delta_S^*, \delta_R^*, \rho_S, \rho_R) = \begin{cases} 1 \text{ if } \delta_R^+ + \delta_C^+ + \delta_S^- > \\ \quad \delta_R^- + \delta_C^- + \delta_S^+ \\ 0 \text{ otherwise} \end{cases}$$

– *Mixed Pondered Strategy.* This strategy is very similar to the previous one, since it accepts a norm if the effect of norm compliance is higher than the effect of norm violation. However, both desirability and undesirability of sanctions and rewards are pondered with their observed probabilities (ρ_S and ρ_R) when calculating the effects of the norm.

$$f_{compliance}(\delta_C^*, \delta_S^*, \delta_R^*, \rho_S, \rho_R) = \begin{cases} 1 \text{ if } (\rho_R * \delta_R^+) + \delta_C^+ + \\ \quad (\rho_S * \delta_S^-) > (\rho_R * \delta_R^-) \\ \quad + \delta_C^- + (\rho_S * \delta_S^+) \\ 0 \text{ otherwise} \end{cases}$$

These are discrete strategies in the sense they determine if the norm will be adopted or not. However, continuous functions can be easily defined by employing the difference between norm compliance and violation effects.

As being illustrated, the proposed Normative BDI agent architecture is general enough for implementing well known strategies for norm compliance as well as more complex strategies or a combination of different strategies. Next, our proposal of normative agent architecture is applied into a case study which illustrates the differences among the norm compliance strategies.

5 The m-Water Problem

The m-Water [4] is a water right market which is implemented as a regulated open multi-agent system. It is a challenging problem, specially in countries like Spain, since scarcity of water is a matter of public interest. The m-Water framework is a somewhat idealized version of current water-use regulations that articulate the interactions of those individual and collective entities that are involved in the use of water in a closed basin. This is a regulated environment which includes the expression and use of regulations of different sorts: from actual laws and regulations issued by governments, to policies and local regulations issued by basin managers, and to social norms that prevail in a given community of users [13]. For these reasons, we consider the m-Water problem as a suitable case study for evaluating performance of the n-BDI agent architecture, since agents' behaviour is affected by different sorts of norms which are controlled by different mechanisms such as regimentation, enforcement and grievance and arbitration processes.

As argued in [5], the use of water in a basin can be seen as a MAS controlled by norms. In this section an example scenario of the m-Water problem is illustrated. According to the Spanish Water Law, the *irrigators* which belong to the same area of a basin can be organized forming *irrigator communities*. These communities act on behalf of their members by defending their rights and interests. However, each community can impose some norms or restrictions to their members.

5.1 Basic Scenario

The *irrigator* agent represents a farmer who wants to obtain high quality vegetables from its plantation. Since this is its main goal, this desire has the highest degree of desirability:

$$(D^+ highQuality, 1)$$

In order to achieve its goal of picking high quality vegetables it has two different irrigation possibilities: to irrigate daily or every two days. Logically, it is more possible to obtain a good crop if the land is frequently irrigated:

$$(B\ [dailyIrrigation]highQuality, 0.75)$$
$$(B\ [alternateDaysIrrigation]highQuality, 0.5)$$

Thus, there are, at least, two different cultivation plans: one which contains the daily irrigation action and another which performs the action corresponding to the irrigation in alternative days:

$$PC : (plan(dailyIrrigation))$$
$$PC : (plan(alternateDaysIrrigation))$$

Finally, he avoids being fined: $(D^- payFine, 0.8)$. The undesirability degree has been defined by means of an utility function whose definition is over the scope of this paper.

Bridge Rule Application Realistic Desires. The first step performed by the BDI architecture consists in applying Bridge Rule 1 in order to refine abstract desires into more realistic ones:

$$\frac{(D^+ \ highQuality, 1), (B \ [dailyIrrigation]highQuality, 0.75)}{DC : (D^+ \ [dailyIrrigation]highQuality, f_D(1, 0.75))}$$

$$\frac{(D^+ \ highQuality, 1), (B \ [alternateDaysIrrigation]highQuality, 0.5)}{DC : (D^+ \ [alternateDaysIrrigation]highQuality, f_D(1, 0.5))}$$

Function f_D is implemented as the product of both degrees.

Deriving Intentions. These more specific desires allow the agent to determine which actions will be intended according to the existing plans (Bridge Rule 2):

$$\frac{DC : (D^+ \ [dailyIrrigation]highQuality, 0.75), \quad PC : plan(dailyIrrigation), 0.75 > 0}{IC : (I[dailyIrrigation]highQuality, 0.75)}$$

$$\frac{DC : (D^+ \ [alternateDaysIrrigation]highQuality, 0.5), \quad PC : plan(alternateDaysIrrigation), 0.5 > 0}{IC : (I[alternateDaysIrrigation]highQuality, 0.5)}$$

Action Selection. Finally, the action which is more intended will be performed by the agent (Bridge Rule 3):

$$\frac{IC : (I[dailyIrrigation]highQuality, 0.75), \quad IC : (I[alternateDaysIrrigation]highQuality, 0.5), 0.75 > 0.5}{CC : (\mathcal{P} \ dailyIrrigation)}$$

5.2   Normative Decision Making

Before making a decision about joining an irrigator community, the *irrigator* agent is advertised by a representative about the main norms imposed by the community. In this example the community forbids agents to irrigate daily if a drought state has been declared in this area. Once the agent decides to become a member of the community it includes this norm advertised by the representative since it affect it. Thus, the agent assigns the maximum certainty degree to the recognised norm:

$$(NAC \ \langle F, drought, -, dailyIrrigation, payFine, candidateGov \rangle, \rho_n, \rho_S, \rho_R)$$
$$\rho_n = 1, \rho_S = 0.25, \rho_R = 1$$

If the *irrigator* respects the norm then it would become a candidate to the *governor board* of the community. However, being a governor implies a lot of responsibilities. Because of this the *irrigator* is not interested on becoming a candidate to the *governors board* $((D^- candidateGov, 0.5))$.

In this example, the irrigator agent is not sure if a drought state has been declared. However, according to the meteorological conditions it thinks it is possible that there is a drought situation. Hence it has a belief $(B \ drought, 0.6)$ in order to represent this drought possibility.

Norm Transformation. Once the norm is been recognised by the NAC it is transformed into an inference rule inside the NCC (Bridge Rule 5):

$$\frac{NAC : (NAC \; \langle F, drought, -, dailyIrrigation, payFine, candidateGov \rangle, 1, 0.25, 1)}{NCC : NCC(\lceil \varphi \rightarrow \psi \rceil)}$$

where:

$$\varphi = (B \; drought, 0.6)$$
$$\psi = (D^- dailyIrrigation, f(f_{activation}(0.6, -, 1)),$$
$$f_{compliance}(\delta^*_{dailyIrrigation}, \delta^*_{payFine}, \delta^*_{candidateGov}, 0.25, 1))$$

On the one hand, the norm activation function takes as input the certainty value assigned to the occurrence of the norm activation condition (0.6) and the confidence value assigned to the norm acquisition (1). In particular, this agent has implemented the $f_{activation}$ as the product of its not empty parameters:

$$f_{activation}(\delta_A, \delta_{\neg E}, \delta_{nr}) = \delta_A \times \delta_{\neg E} \times \delta_{nr} = 0.6$$

Norm Compliance. Regarding the norm acceptance, different results can be obtained depending on the compliance strategy that has been employed.

$$f_{compliance}(\delta^*_C, \delta^*_S, \delta^*_R, \rho_S, \rho_R)$$

where:

$\delta^+_C = \delta^+_{dailyIrrigation} = 0; \delta^-_C = \delta^-_{dailyIrrigation} = 0$ since there is no (positive or negative) desire on the norm condition (i.e. *dailyIrrigation*);
$\delta^+_S = \delta^+_{payFine} = 0; \delta^-_S = \delta^-_{payFine} = 0.8$, since the irrigator agent avoids being fined ($(D^- payFine, 0.8)$);
$\delta^+_R = \delta^+_{candidateGov} = 0; \delta^-_R = \delta^-_{candidateGov} = 0.5$, as he is not interested on becoming a candidate to governor ($(D^- candidateGov, 0.5)$);
$\rho_S = 0.25$, which implies that there is a low probability of being sanctioned when not following this norm;
$\rho_R = 1$, which implies that the reward action will be always applied when following this norm;

Next, results obtained with each strategy are shown:

- *Automatic Strategy.* In this case the *irrigator* agent always accepts the norm, thus $f_{compliance} = 1$. Then the f function multiplies the values obtained by the $f_{activation}$ and $f_{compliance}$ functions. Therefore, a new normative desire ($D^- dailyIrrigation, 0.6$) is inserted into the DC (Bridge Rule 8), being $\delta_{threshold} = 0.25$:

$$\frac{NCC : NCC(\lceil (D^- dailyIrrigation, 0.6) \rceil), 0.6 > 0.25}{DC : (D^- dailyIrrigation, 0.6)}$$

Then the IC is updated through Bridge Rule 2:

$$DC : (D^+[dailyIrrigation]highQuality, 0.9),$$
$$\frac{DC : (D^- dailyIrrigation, 0.6), PC : plan(dailyIrrigation), 0.9 > 0.6}{IC : (I[dailyIrrigation]highQuality, f_I(0.9, 0.6))}$$

Thus, a new intention related to the $dailyIrrigation$ action ($I[dailyIrriga$-$tion]highQuality, 0.3$) is created. Its intentionality has been reduced since the action has a negative desire. Finally, the intention update implies the modification of the agent behaviour. The intention related to the $alternate$-$DaysIrrigation$, whose degree is 0.5, is the most intended. Thus, the action performed is $alternateDaysIrrigation$, since the $irrigator$ has adopted the norms of its irrigation community.

- $Rebellious\ Strategy.$ This strategy implies that the $irrigator$ rebuts respecting norms systematically, so then $f_{compliance} = 0$ for any norm. In this case a new intention will be created in the NCC ($D^+ alternateDaysIrrigation, 0$). However, this normative desire is not inserted into the DC since its degree does not exceed δ_{thres}. Consequently, the norm is not followed and the agent maintains the daily irrigation.

- $Fearful\ Strategy.$ Since the norm has a sanction which punishes $agents$ that do not respect the prohibition, the $irrigator$ would follow the social norm ($f_{compliance} = 1$). Consequently, it will adopt an $alternateDaysIrrigation$ action, similarly as in the case of an automatic strategy.

- $Greedy\ Strategy.$ This strategy implies following the norm whenever there is a reward. In this case, since $\delta_R^+ + \delta_R^- = 1 > 0$ the $irrigator$ agent will adopt the norm and, thus, it will perform the $alternateDaysIrrigation$ action.

- $Egoist\ Strategy.$ With this strategy, the $irrigator$ will respect the norm only if it benefits its goals ($\delta_C^+ > 0$). In this case $\delta_{dailyIrrigation}^+ = 0$ and then $f_{compliance} = 0$.

- $Pressure\ Strategy.$ This strategy defines that the agent adopts the norm only if its sanction is more undesired than the norm condition ($\delta_S^- > \delta_C^-$). Since $\delta_{payFine}^- = 0.8$ and $\delta_{dailyIrrigation}^- = 0$, then $f_{compliance} = 1$.

- $Opportunistic\ Strategy.$ This strategy defines that the agent will adopt the norm only if its reward is more desired than the undesirability of the norm condition ($\delta_R^+ > \delta_C^-$). $\delta_R^+ = 0$, since the irrigator agent does not desire the reward at all, so then $f_{compliance} = 0$.

- $Mixed\ Strategy.$ With this strategy the agent would consider both positive and negative effects derived from norm respect or norm violation. The norm is adopted if:

$$\delta_R^+ + \delta_C^+ + \delta_S^- > \delta_R^- + \delta_C^- + \delta_S^+$$

According to the current mental state its value is:

$$0 + 0 + 0.8 > 0.5 + 0 + 0$$

which is true. Then $f_{compliance} = 1$.

 − *Mixed Pondered Strategy*. This strategy is defined as the previous one but
   the reward and sanction desirability and undesirability are pondered with
   their possibilities; i.e. the norm is respected if:

$$(\rho_R * \delta_R^+) + \delta_C^+ + (\rho_S * \delta_S^-) > (\rho_R * \delta_R^-) + \delta_C^- + (\rho_S * \delta_S^+)$$

In this example this formula is:

$$(1 \times 0) + 0 + (0.25 \times 0.8) > (1 \times 0.5) + 0 + (0.25 \times 0)$$

Then, the comparison is not true and $f_{compliance} = 0$.

Along this section, a case study of an autonomous normative agent has been
illustrated. More specifically, it consists of an *irrigator* agent which must choose
whether respecting and not respecting norms. In its decision making process it
employs different norm compliance strategies which have been defined for the
proposed Normative BDI architecture.

6   Discussion

Autonomous normative agents are defined as agents which have explicit knowledge about norms and are able to decide about norm compliance convenience;
i.e. they have capabilities for recognizing, representing and accepting norms, and
for solving possible conflicts among them [8]. Several proposals have been made
in order to define agents provided with some of these capabilities. However, the
definition of an agent architecture and the reasoning processes over this architecture which overcome all of the challenges raised by autonomous normative
agents stays an open issue.

Regarding recent works on normative reasoning, the BOID architecture [6]
represents obligations as mental attributes and analyses the relationship and influence of such obligations on agent beliefs, desires and intentions. This approach
is very similar to the work proposed here. However, our approach overlaps the
main drawbacks of the BOID proposal in different ways: i) our normative model
does not only consider obligation norms but it gives support to constitutive and
regulative norms [11]; ii) it employs graded BDI logics for representing mental attitudes, which allows agents to face with uncertain and conflicting mental
sates; and iii) it consider norms as dynamic entities that agents should acquire
from their environment. In relation with this last feature, the EMIL proposal
[1], which has developed a framework for autonomous norm acquisition, might
be employed for complementing the NAC component of our normative BDI architecture. Thus, agents would be able to acquire new norms by observing the
behaviour of other agents which are situated in their environments. The main
disadvantage of EMIL with respect to the n-BDI is that the EMIL agents obey
all recognised norms blindly by deriving new normative goals. Thus, they do
not consider their own motivations and interests. This drawback is also present
in the NoA [19] architecture. Mainly, this architecture allows agents to make

decisions about what action to execute according to a set of contracts imposed on them. Another interesting issue not considered by none of these works is how the behaviour can be modified for respecting unforeseen norms. Regarding this matter, in [27] the KGP (*Knowledge-Goal-Plan*) model of agency is augmented with normative notions such as obligations, prohibitions and roles.

Finally, the normative reasoning problem requires sophisticated techniques in order to allow agents to consider convenience of norm compliance according to their current mental state. In this sense, norms may be inconsistent with the mental state of agents. The *cognitive coherence theory* evaluates the truth of cognitions in relation with a set of cognitions [28]. Its main purpose is the study of associations; i.e. how pieces of information influence each other by imposing a positive or negative constraint over the rest of information. The problem of coherence among agent cognitions has been superficially addressed in this paper and will be object of future work. Regarding more elaborated solutions to the coherence problem, in [18] a formalization of deductive coherence theory has been used as a criterion for rejecting or accepting norms. This work is based on a very simple notion of norm as an unconditional obligation. In addition, the problem of norm conflict has not been faced. Finally the process by which agents' desires are updated according to norms have also been defined in a simple way. In particular, this proposal only considers coherence as the one rational criterion for norm acceptance. Thus, the effect of these normative desires on the previous existing desires is not considered.

In this paper we have focused on the definition of rational criteria for determining norm compliance. The usage of coherence theory as a criterion for determining *which* and *how* to comply with norms is over the scope of this paper. However, it is explained in [14]. In this paper, it is proposed to calculate the coherence maximization process in order to determine which norm instances are consistent and must be taken into account when updating the desire theory.

7   Conclusions

The n-BDI architecture allows agents to acquire new norms from their environment and consider them in their decision making process. The fact that mental attitudes of agents are quantified allows them to reason in open environments which are controlled by norms. In this sense, graded modalities allow agents to represent uncertain knowledge about the current state of the world. Moreover, graded intentions and desires enable agents to make decisions according to their satisfaction criterion. This is specially interesting when designing normative agents whose behaviour can be affected by conflicting norms. Thus, the desirability degrees of desires and intentions allow agents to decide between norm violation or fulfilment according to their priorities.

As been illustrated, the n-BDI architecture: i) allows the definition of those strategies which had been defined in previous works; ii) the fact that mental attitudes are represented as graded propositions allows agents to consider not only whether norms are beneficial to their goals and motivations but also the intensity in which they will be affected; and iii) it overlaps previous works since it allows the definition of complex strategies which consider both positive and negative effects of norm fulfilment and violation.

In this paper, no evaluation has been included. However, works describing the previous versions of the n-BDI agent architecture provide an evaluation of the proposal. Thus, in [12] results of a set of simulations belonging to the m-Water case study can be found. However, we are working on the implementation of a fully functional prototype of the n-BDI architecture. Our aim is to evaluate empirically our proposal through the design and implementation of more complex and elaborated scenarios. As future work, we plan to continue by working on the analysis of non-rational motivations for norm compliance. In this sense, we are working on extending the n-BDI agent architecture with an emotion model which will allow agents to take into consideration phenomena such as shame, honour, gratitude, etc. when adopting norms.

Acknowledgements

This work was partially supported by the Spanish government under grants CONSOLIDER-INGENIO 2010 CSD2007-00022, TIN2009-13839-C03-01 and TIN2008-04446 and by the FPU grant AP-2007-01256 awarded to N. Criado.

References

1. Andrighetto, G., Campenní, M., Cecconi, F., Conte, R.: How agents find out norms: A simulation based model of norm innovation. In: Proc. of NORMAS, pp. 16–30 (2008)
2. Artikis, A., Pitt, J.: A formal model of open agent societies. In: Proc. of AGENTS, pp. 192–193. ACM, New York (2001)
3. Boella, G., Van Der Torre, L.: Regulative and constitutive norms in normative multiagent systems. In: Procs. of KR 2004, pp. 255–265 (2004)
4. Botti, V., Garrido, A., Giret, A., Igual, F., Noriega, P.: On the design of mWater: a case study for Agreement Technologies. In: Proc. of EUMAS, pp. 1–15 (2009)
5. Botti, V., Garrido, A., Giret, A., Noriega, P.: Managing water demand as a regulated open mas. In: MALLOW Workshop on COIN, pp. 1–10 (2009)
6. Broersen, J., Dastani, M., Hulstijn, J., Huang, Z., van der Torre, L.: The boid architecture – conflicts between beliefs, obligations, intentions and desires. In: Proc. of AAMAS, pp. 9–16. ACM Press, New York (2001)
7. Casali, A.: On Intentional and Social Agents with Graded Attitudes. PhD thesis, Universitat de Girona (2008)
8. Castelfranchi, C.: Prescribed mental attitudes in goal-adoption and norm-adoption. Artif. Intell. Law 7(1), 37–50 (1999)
9. Conte, R., Andrighetto, G., Campenni, M.: On norm internalization. a position paper. In: Proc. of EUMAS (2009)
10. Conte, R., Castelfranchi, C., Dignum, F.: Autonomous norm acceptance. In: Papadimitriou, C., Singh, M.P., Müller, J.P. (eds.) ATAL 1998. LNCS (LNAI), vol. 1555, pp. 99–112. Springer, Heidelberg (1999)

11. Criado, N., Argente, E., Botti, V.: A BDI Architecture for Normative Decision Making (Extended Abstract). In: Proc. of AAMAS, pp. 1383–1384 (2010)
12. Criado, N., Argente, E., Botti, V.: Normative Deliberation in Graded BDI Agents. In: Dix, J., Witteveen, C. (eds.) MATES 2010. LNCS, vol. 6251, pp. 52–63. Springer, Heidelberg (2010)
13. Criado, N., Argente, E., Garrido, A., Igual, F., Botti, V., Noriega, P., Giret, A.: Norm enforceability in Electronic Institutions? In: De Vos, M., et al. (eds.) COIN 2010. LNCS (LNAI), vol. 6541, pp. 250–267. Springer, Heidelberg (2011)
14. Criado, N., Argente, E., Noriega, P., Botti, V.: Towards a Normative BDI Architecture for Norm Compliance. In: De Vos, M., et al. (eds.) COIN 2010. LNCS (LNAI), vol. 6541, pp. 1–20. Springer, Heidelberg (2011)
15. Deci, E., Ryan, R.: The" what" and" why" of goal pursuits: Human needs and the self-determination of behavior. Psychological Inquiry 11(4), 227–268 (2000)
16. Elster, J.: Social norms and economic theory. Journal of Economic Perspectives 3(4), 99–117 (1989)
17. Giunchiglia, F., Serafini, L.: Multilanguage hierarchical logics, or: How we can do without modal logics. Artificial Intelligence 65(1), 29–70 (1994)
18. Joseph, S., Sierra, C., Schorlemmer, M., Dellunde, P.: Deductive coherence and norm adoption. Logic Journal of the IGPL 18, 118–156 (2010)
19. Kollingbaum, M., Norman, T.: Noa-a normative agent architecture. In: Proc. of IJCAI, vol. 18, pp. 1465–1466. Citeseer (2003)
20. López y López, F.: Social Power and Norms: Impact on agent behaviour. Citeseer (2003)
21. Luck, M., McBurney, P.: Computing as interaction: Agent and agreement technologies. In: Proc. of EUMAS, pp. 1–15 (2008)
22. Meyer, J.: Dynamic logic for reasoning about actions and agents. In: Minker, J. (ed.) Logic-Based Artificial Intelligence, pp. 281–311. Kluwer Academic Publishers, Dordrecht (2000)
23. Noriega, P., Sierra, C.: Towards layered dialogical agents. In: Jennings, N.R., Wooldridge, M.J., Müller, J.P. (eds.) ECAI-WS 1996 and ATAL 1996. LNCS, vol. 1193, pp. 173–188. Springer, Heidelberg (1997)
24. Parsons, S., Jennings, N.R., Sabater, J., Sierra, C.: Agent specification using multi-context systems. In: d'Inverno, M., Luck, M., Fisher, M., Preist, C. (eds.) UKMAS Workshops 1996-2000. LNCS (LNAI), vol. 2403, pp. 205–226. Springer, Heidelberg (2002)
25. Parsons, S., Sierra, C., Jennings, N.R.: Agents that reason and negotiate by arguing. JLC: Journal of Logic and Computation 8(3), 261–292 (1998)
26. Perrussel, L.: Contextual reasoning. In: ECAI, pp. 366–367 (1998)
27. Sadri, F., Stathis, K., Toni, F.: Normative KGP agents. Computational & Mathematical Organization Theory 12(2), 101–126 (2006)
28. Thagard, P.: Coherence in Thought and Action. The MIT Press, Cambridge (2000)

Generating Executable Multi-agent System Prototypes from SONAR Specifications

Michael Köhler-Bußmeier, Matthias Wester-Ebbinghaus, and Daniel Moldt

University of Hamburg, Department for Informatics
Vogt-Kölln-Str. 30, D-22527 Hamburg
{koehler,wester,moldt}@informatik.uni-hamburg.de

Abstract. This contribution presents the MULAN4SONAR middleware and its prototypical implementation for a comprehensive support of organisational teamwork, including aspects like team formation, negotiation, team planning, coordination, and transformation. Organisations are modelled in SONAR, a Petri net–based specification formalism for multi-agent organisations. SONAR models are rich and elaborated enough to automatically generate all necessary configuration information for the MULAN4SONAR middleware.

Keywords: middleware, MULAN4SONAR, multi-agent systems, organisations, Petri nets, RENEW, SONAR.

1 Introduction

Organisation-oriented software engineering is a discipline which incorporates research trends from distributed artificial intelligence, agent-oriented software engineering, and business information systems (cf. [1,2] for an overview). The basic metaphors are built around the interplay of the macro level (i.e. the organisation or institution) and the micro level (i.e. the agent). Organisation-oriented software models are particularly interesting for self- and re-organising systems since the system's organising principles (structural as well as behavioural) are taken into account explicitly by representing (in terms of reifying) them at run-time.

The following work is based on the platform independent organisation model SONAR (Self-Organising Net Architecture) which we have presented in [3,4]. In this paper we turn to a middleware concept and its prototypical implementation for the complete organisational teamwork that is induced by SONAR.

First of all we aim at a rapid development of our middleware prototype. Therefore we need a specification language that inherently supports powerful high-level features like pattern matching and synchronisation patterns. The second requirement is a narrow gap between the specification and implementation of the middleware prototype. Ideally, middleware specifications are directly executable. As a third requirement, we are interested in well established analysis techniques to study the prototype's behaviour. As a fourth requirement we want

M. De Vos et al. (Eds.): COIN 2010 International Workshops, LNAI 6541, pp. 21–38, 2011.

the middleware specifications to be as close as possible to the supported SONAR-model of an organisation. Related to this, the fifth requirement results as the possibility to be able to directly generate the middleware specifications from the SONAR-model automatically. The sixth requirement is that we want an easy translation of the prototype into an agent programming language.

Since SONAR-models are based on Petri nets we have chosen high-level Petri nets [5] as the specification language for our middleware prototype. This choice meets the requirements stated above: We can reuse SONAR-models by enriching them with high-level features, like data types, arc inscription functions etc. Petri nets are well known for their precise and intuitive semantics and their well established analysis techniques, including model checking or linear algebraic techniques. We particularly choose the formalism of *reference nets*, a dialect of high-level nets which supports the nets-in-nets concept [6] and thus allows to immediately incorporate ("program") micro-macro dynamics into our middleware. Reference nets receive tool support with respect to editing and simulation by the RENEW tool [7]. Additionally, RENEW has been extended by the agent-oriented development framework MULAN [8,9], which allows to program multi-agent systems in a language that is a hybridisation of reference nets and Java. We make use of MULAN and provide a middleware for SONAR-models. Consequently, our middleware is called MULAN4SONAR and we present a fully-functional prototype in this paper.

The paper is structured as follows: Section 2 briefly sketches our formal specification language for organisational models, called SONAR. Section 3 addresses our MULAN4SONAR middleware approach on a rather abstract and conceptual level. It illustrates the structure of our target system: SONAR-models are compiled into a multi-agent system consisting of so called position agents, i.e. agents that are responsible for the organisational constraints. Section 4 describes our implemented middleware prototype in detail and how it is generated from SONAR-models. The middleware serves integration and control of all organisational activities, like team formation, negotiation, team planning, coordination, and transformation. In Section 5 we evaluate the strength of our approach and discuss ongoing and future work. We consider related work in Section 6 before we close the paper with a conclusion in Section 7.

2   The Underlying Theoretical Model: SONAR

In this section we give a short introduction into our modelling formalism, called SONAR. A SONAR-model encompasses (i) a data ontology, (ii) a set of interaction models (called *distributed workflow nets, DWFs*), (iii) a model, that describes the team-based delegation of tasks (called *role/delegation nets*), (iv) a network of organisational positions, and (v) a set of transformation rules. A detailed discussion of the formalism can be found in [3], its theoretical properties are studied in [4].

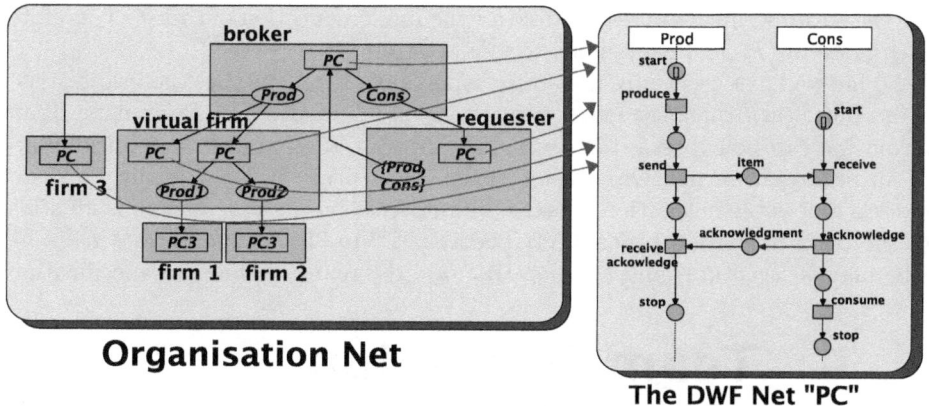

Organisation Net

The DWF Net "PC"

Fig. 1. A simplified SONAR-Model

In SONAR a formal organisation is characterised as a delegation network of sub-systems, called *positions*. Each position is responsible for the execution or delegation of several tasks. Figure 1 illustrates the relationship between the SONAR interaction model, the delegation model and the position network – i.e. the aspects (ii) to (iv)[1]. The left side of the figure describes the relationship between the positions (here: *broker*, *virtual firm*, *requester*, etc.) in terms of their respective roles (here: *Producer*, *Consumer*, *Producer1* and *Producer2* – *Prod*, *Cons*, *Prod1* and *Prod2* for short) and their associated delegation links. In this scenario, we have a requester and two suppliers of some product. Coupling between them is provided by a broker. From a more fine-grained perspective, some positions form a delegation network themselves. For example, in the case of the supplier, we can identify a management level: the *virtual firm*, and two subcontractors: *firm 1* and *firm 2*. The two subcontractors may be legally independent firms that integrate their core competencies in order to form a virtual enterprise (e.g. separating fabrication of product parts from their assembly). The coupling between the firms constituting the virtual enterprise is apt to be tighter and more persistent than between requester and supplier at the next higher system level, which provides more of a market-based and on-the-spot connection.

SONAR relies on the formalism of Petri nets. Each task is modelled by a place p and each task implementation (delegation/execution) is modelled by a transition t. Each task place is inscribed by the set of roles which are needed to implement it, e.g. the set $\{Prod, Cons\}$ for the place in the position *requester*. Each transition t is inscribed by the DWF net $D(t)$ that specifies the interaction between the roles. In the example we have two inscriptions: *PC* and *PC3* where the former is show on the right of Figure 1. The latter is a refinement which replaces the behaviour of *Prod* by the interaction of *Prod1* and *Prod2*. Positions

---

[1] To keep the model small we we have omitted all data-related aspects and transformation rules – i.e. the aspects (i) and (v) – in this figure.

are the entities which are responsible for the implementation of tasks[2]. Therefore, each node in $(P \cup T)$ is assigned to one position O[3].

So far we have used only the static aspects of Petri nets, i.e. the graph structure. But SONAR also benefits from the dynamic aspects of Petri nets: Team formation can be expressed in a very elegant way. If one marks one initial place of an organisation net *Org* with a token, each firing process of the Petri net models a possible delegation process. More precisely, the *token game* is identical to the team formation process (cf. Theorem 4.2 in [4]). It generates a *team net* (the team's structure) and a *team DWF*, i.e. the team's behaviour specification.

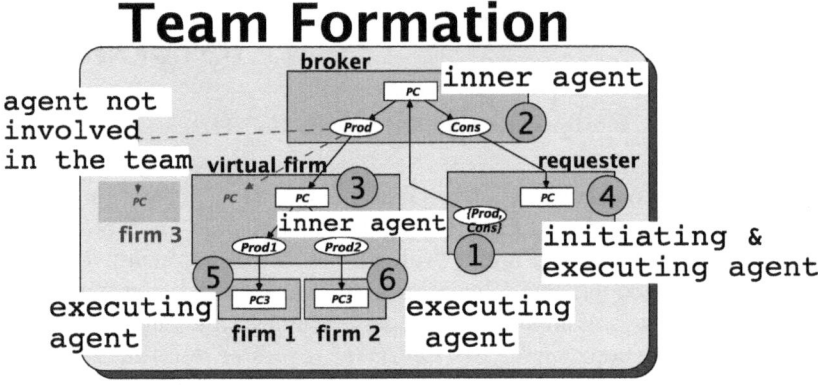

Fig. 2. The formation of a team generated by the Petri net token game

An example is given in Figure 2 where the *requester* starts the team formation (step #1). The team formation process is generated from the net where the initial place inside the *requester* is marked with a token. According to the Petri net firing rule control is given over to the *broker* (step #2) which becomes an inner agent of the team. Concurrently, the *broker* delegates the role *Prod* to the *virtual firm* (step #3) and the role *Cons* to the *requester* (step #4) where the former becomes an inner team agent while the latter becomes an executing agent (i.e. a final agent). The *virtual firm* further delegates to *firm 1* (step #5) and to *firm 2* (step #6) which are executing agents, too. So, the team has three executing agents which implement one role in the team DWF, each. While the delegation

---

[2] The main distinction between roles and position is that positions – unlike roles – are situated in the organisational network. Positions implement roles and are equipped with resources.

[3] Organisation nets can be considered as enriched organisation charts. Organisation nets encode the information about delegation structures – similar to charts – and also about the delegation/execution choices of tasks, which is not present in charts. If one fuses all nodes of each position into one single node, one obtains a graph which represents the organisation's chart. Obviously, this construction removes all information about the organisational processes.

process from *broker* back to the *requester* does not change the role interaction description (it stil is the role *Cons*) the delegation from the *virtual firm* to *firm 1* and *firm 2* refines the role *Prod* into the interplay of the roles *Prod1* and *Prod2*. The refinement is specified by the DWF *PC3*.

The resulting team net is shown in Figure 3 together with its team DWF net. The team DFW net is a composition of the *Prod1* and *Prod2* related part of *PC3* and the *Cons* part of *PC*. (Since the concrete behaviour refinement of the role *Prod* into the interplay of the roles *Prod1* and *Prod2* is irrelevant for the purpose of this paper, it is hidden inside the "black box" area of the team DWF in Figure 3.) Each team net induces a clear assignment of the roles in the team DWF to executing agents: Here, position *firm 1* implements the role *Prod1*, *firm 2* implements *Prod2*, and *requester* implements *Cons*.

As another aspect, SONAR-models are equipped with transformation rules. Transformation rules describe which modifications of the given model are allowed. They are specified as graph rewrite rules [10]. As a minimal requirement the rules must preserve the correctness of the given organisational model. In SONAR transformations are not performed by the modeller – they are part of

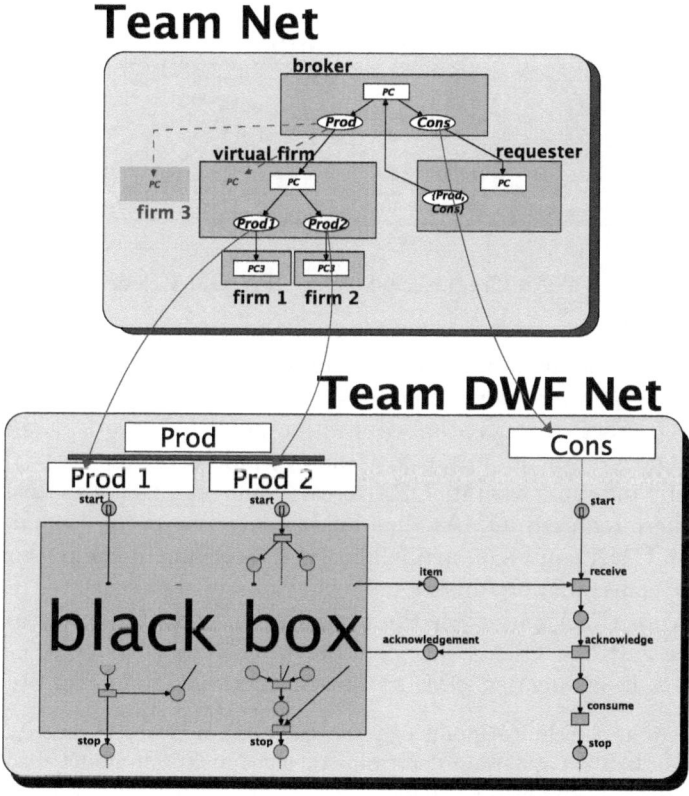

Fig. 3. *Team Net* and *Team DWF* generated from the formation process in Fig. 2

the model itself. Therefore a SONAR model is *stratified* by models of different levels. The main idea is that the activities of DWF nets that belong to the level n are allowed to modify those parts that belong to levels $k < n$ but not to higher ones.

3 Organisational Position Network Activities

We now elaborate on the activities of a multi-agent system behaving according to a SONAR-model.

3.1 Conceptual Overview

The basic idea is quite simple: With each position of a SONAR-model we associate one dedicated agent, called an *organisational position agent* (OPA). This is illustrated in Figure 4 where the OPAs associated with a SONAR-model together embody a middleware layer.

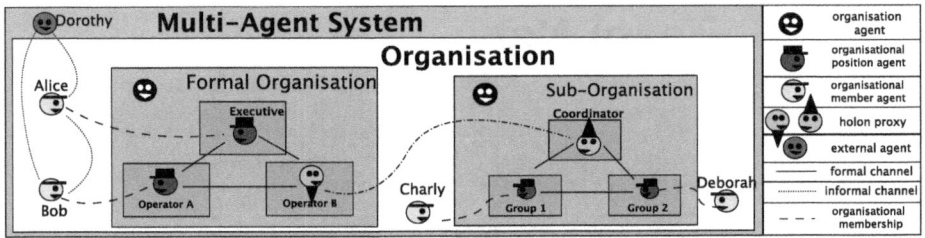

Fig. 4. An Organisation as an OPA/OMA Network

An OPA network embodies a formal organisation. An OPA represents an organisational *artifact* and not a *member/employee* of the organisation. However, each OPA represents a conceptual connection point for an *organisational member agent* (OMA). An organisation is not complete without its OMAs. Each OMA actually interacts with its OPA to carry out organisational tasks, to make decisions where required. OMAs thus implement/occupy the formal positions[4]. Note that an OMA can be an artificial as well as a human agent. An OPA both enables and constrains organisational behaviour of its associated OMA. Only via an OPA an OMA can effect the organisation and only in a way that is in conformance with the OPA's specification. In addition, the OPA network as a whole relieves its associated OMAs of a considerable amount of organisational

---

[4] Note that from a technical point of view, the OPA network *is* already a complete MAS. This MAS is highly non-deterministic since a SONAR-model specifies what is allowed and what is obligatory, so many choices are left open. Conceptually, the OPA network represents the *formal organisation* while the OMAs represent its *informal* part which in combination describe the whole organisation.

overhead by automating coordination and administration. To put it differently, an OPA offers its OMA a "behaviour corridor" for organisational membership. OMAs might of course only be partially involved in an organisation and have relationships to multiple other agents than their OPA (like Alice and Bob in Figure 4) or even to agents completely external to the organisation (like Alice and Dorothy). From the perspective of the organisation, all other ties than the OPA-OMA link are considered as informal connections.

To conclude, an OPA embodies two conceptual interfaces, the first one between micro and macro level (one OPA versus the complete network of OPAs) and the second one between formal and informal aspects of an organisation (OPA versus OMA). We can make additional use of this twofold interface. Whenever we have a system of systems setting with multiple scopes or domains of authority (e.g. virtual organisations, strategic alliances, organisational fields), we can let an OPA of a given (sub-)organisation act as a member towards another OPA of another organisation. This basically combines the middleware perspective with a holonic perspective (cf. [11]). We have developed this approach for SONAR in [12].

3.2   Organisational Teamwork

SONAR-models of organisations induce *teamwork activities*. We distinguish between organisational teamwork activities of first- and of second-order. First-order activities target at carrying out "ordinary" business processes to accomplish business tasks:

- *Team Formation:* Teams are formed in the course of an iterated delegation procedure in a top-down manner. Starting with an initial organisational task to be carried out, successive task decompositions are carried out and subtasks are delegated further. A team net according to Section 2 consists of the positions that were involved in the delegation procedure.
- *Team Plan Formation/Negotiation:* After a team has been formed, a compromise has to be found concerning how the corresponding team DWF net (cf. Section 2) is to be executed as it typically leaves various alternatives of going one way or the other. A compromise is found in a bottom-up manner with respect to the team structure. The "leaf" positions of the team net tell their preferences and the intermediary, inner team positions iteratively seek compromises between the preferences/compromise results of subordinates. The final compromise is a particular process of the team DWF net and is called the team plan.
- *Team Plan Execution:* As the team plan is a DWF net process that describes an interaction between team positions, team plan execution follows straightforward[5].

---

[5] For the time being, we do not address the topic that team plan execution might fail and what rescue efforts this might entail.

- *Hierarchic propagation:* If a holonic approach as illustrated in Figure 4 is chosen, team activities that span multiple organisations are propagated accordingly.

Second-order activities describe reorganisation efforts:

- *Evaluation:* Organisational performance is monitored and evaluated in order to estimate prospects of transformations. To estimate whether an organisational transformation would improve organisational performance, we introduce *metrics* that assign a multi-dimensional assessment to a formal organisation. In addition to the Petri net-based specifications of the previous section, there may exist additional teamwork constraints and parameters that may be referred to. How to measure the quality of an organisational structure is generally a very difficult topic and highly contingent. We will not pursue it further in this paper.
- *Organisational Transformations:* As described in Section 2, transformations can either be applied to a formal organisation externally or be carried out by the positions themselves as transformation teams (cf. exogenous versus endogenous reorganisation [13]). In the latter case, transformations are typically triggered by the above mentioned evaluations. But it might also be the case that a new constraint or directive has been imposed and the organisation has to comply.

3.3   Organisation Agents

As shown in Figure 4 all the OPAs of an organisation are within the context of an *organisation agent* which represents the OPA network as a whole. The organisation agent is responsible for the management of the organisational domain data (e.g. customer databases etc.) but also for the management of the organisational *meta data* which includes the data ontology, the interaction protocols (i.e. the process ontology), and also a representation of the SONAR-model itself. This is illustrated in the top half of Figure 5.

Additionally, the organisation agent is responsible for the network wide framing of the organisational teamwork efforts, i.e. team formation, negotiation, and team plan execution (as illustrated in the bottom half of Figure 5). The organisation agent is responsible for monitoring the *abstract* aspects on the teamwork (i.e. the OPA network perspective), while the OPAs are responsible for the *concrete* decisions (i.e. the OPA perspective)[6]. For example, the organisation agent abstractly specifies that during the team formation the OPA O may delegate

---

[6] Note that the existence of a single agent representing the organisation has not to be confused with a monolithic architecture. The main benefit of the existence of an organisation agent is that it allows to provide a network-wide *view* on the team activities. The abstract aspects could as well be implemented by the OPAs themselves and thus be totally distributed. In fact the concurrency semantics of Petri nets perfectly reflects this aspect: In the mathematical sense the processes of an organisation agent are in fact distributed, even if generated from one single net.

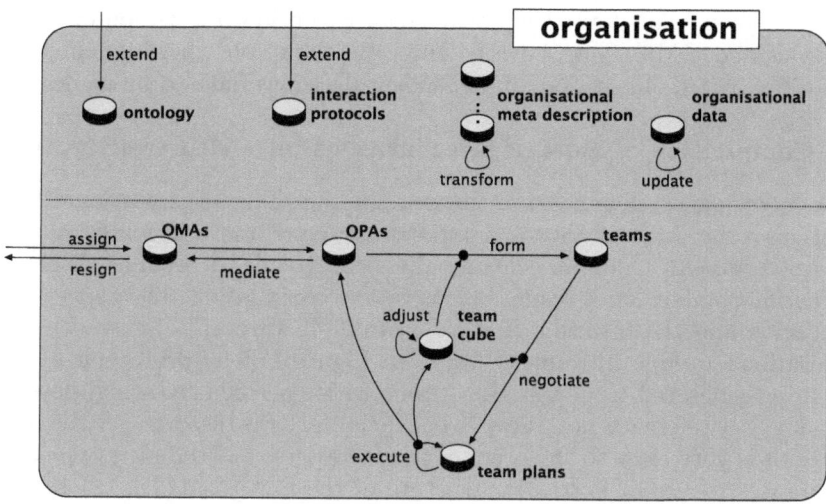

Fig. 5. The Organisation Agent

some task to another agent which must belong to a certain set of OPAs[7], but the concrete choice for a partner is left to the OPA O which in turn coordinates its decision with its associated OMA.

In our architecture the concrete choices of the OPAs are framed by the so called *team cube* (cf. Figure 5). The notation *cube* is due to the fact that we have three dimensions of teamwork: team formation, negotiation, and team plan execution. For each dimension we can choose between several mechanisms. For example in the team formation phase the delegation of tasks to subcontractors can either be implemented by a market mechanism (i.e. choosing the cheapest contractor), by a round-robin scheduling (i.e. choosing contractors in cyclic order), or even by some kind of "affection" between OPAs/OMAs. Given a concrete situation that initiates a teamwork activitiy, the organisation chooses an appropriate mechanism for each of the three dimensions. During the execution phase of the team plans the team cube evaluates the process to improve the assignment of mechanisms.

4 The MULAN4SONAR Middleware

Each position of a SONAR-organisation consists of a formal part (the OPA as an organisational artifact) and an informal part (the OMA as a domain member). An organisation together with the OPA network relieves its associated OMAs of a great part of the organisational overhead by automation of administrative and coordination activities. It is exactly the *generic* part of the teamwork activities from Section 3.2 that is automated by the organisation/OPA network: Team

---

[7] This set of possible delegation partners is calculated from the SONAR-model.

formation, team plan formation, team plan execution always follow the same mechanics and OMAs only have to enter the equation where domain actions have to be carried out or domain-dependent decisions have to be made.

4.1   Compilation of SONAR Specifications into MULAN4SONAR

In the following we demonstrate the compilation of an organisational SONAR-model into the MULAN4SONAR middleware layer for automated teamwork support. A SONAR-model is semantically rich enough to provide all necessary information to allow an automated generation/compilation. The aspects of this compilation and the resulting prototypical middleware are discussed using the organisation example introduced above in Figure 1. The prototypical middleware layer generated from this SONAR-model is specified by a high-level Petri net, namely a reference net. This is beneficial for two reasons: (1) the translation result is very close to the original specification, since the prototype directly incorporates the main Petri net structure of the SONAR-model; (2) the prototype is immediately functional as reference nets are directly executable using the open-source Petri net simulator RENEW [7] and we can easily integrate the prototype into MULAN [8,9], our development and simulation system for MAS based on Java and reference nets. Therefore we have chosen to implement the compiler as a RENEW-plugin.

In the context of OMG's model driven architecture (MDA) the SONAR-organisation is the platform independent model (PIM), while the MULAN4SONAR middleware adds those aspects that are part of the platform specific model (PSM). The simulation engine RENEW is the code target:

$$\frac{\textbf{PIM}}{\text{SONAR}} \quad \rightarrow \quad \frac{\textbf{PSM}}{\text{MULAN4SONAR}} \quad \rightarrow \quad \frac{\textbf{code}}{\text{RENEW}}$$

The plugin implements a compiler that is based on graph rewriting. The compiler searches for a net fragment in the SONAR-model that matches the pattern on the left hand side of a rewrite rule and translates it into a reference net fragment which is obtained as the instantiation of the rule's right hand side. An example rule with the parameter n is given in Figure 6: The rule attaches a place for the OPA a to the transition.

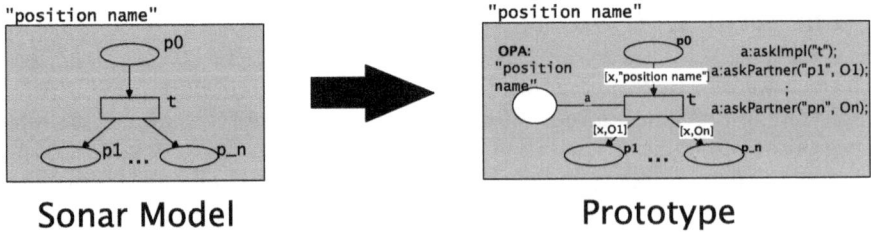

Fig. 6. A transformation rule for Phase 1

In the final model this place contains the OPA that represents the position "position name". The rule also adds inscriptions that describe that OPA a is willing to implement the task t (denoted by the inscription a:askImpl("t")) and a list of inscriptions a:askPartner($"p_i"$, O_i) (one for each p_i, $1 \leq i \leq n$) describing that a delegates the subtask p_i to the OPA O_i. The variable x denotes the identifier of the teamwork process.

We consider teamwork in six phases. For each phase, the original SONAR-model (in our case the one from Figure 1) is taken and transformation rules generate an executable reference net fragment. For example, the transformation rule from Figure 6 is used for the first phase, *selection of team members* (see below). Finally, the fragments for the phases 1 to 6 are linked sequentially and the resulting overall net represents the main (organisation-specific) middleware component that is used in the (generic) MULAN4SONAR middleware layer to coordinate the organisational teamwork. The six teamwork phases are the following:

1. *Selection of team members:* By agents receiving tasks, refining them and delegating sub-tasks, the organisation is explored to select the team agents. This way, a team tree is iteratively constructed but the overall tree is not globally known at the end of this phase.
2. *Team assembly:* The overall team tree is assembled by iteratively putting sub-teams together. At the end of this phase, only the root agent of the team tree knows the overall team.
3. *Team announcement:* The overall team is announced among all team member agents.
4. *Team plan formation:* The executing team agents (i.e. the leaves of the team tree) construct partial local plans related to the team DWF net. These partial plans are iteratively processed by the ancestors in the team tree. They seek compromises concerning the (possibly conflicting) partial plans until the root of the team tree has build a global plan with a global compromise.
5. *Team plan announcement and plan localisation:* The global team plan is announced among all team member agents. The executing team agents have to localise the global plan according to their respective share of the plan.
6. *Team plan execution:* The team generates an instance of the team DWF net, assigns all the local plans to it, and starts the execution.

Here, we will only discuss first-order organisational teamwork. However, our MULAN4SONAR middleware approach features a recursive system architecture in order to support reorganisation, including second-order activities (a presentation of the whole model can be found in [14]).

Before the six phases are discussed in more detail, we illustrate how a MULAN multi-agent system that incorporates our MULAN4SONAR middleware layer looks like.

4.2 Multi-agent System with MULAN4SONAR Middleware Layer

In Section 3, we have described our general vision of a multi-agent system that incorporates SONAR organisations: The formal part of each SONAR organisation is explicitly represented by a distributed middleware layer consisting of OPAs for each position and one organisation agent as an additional meta-level entity. In our current prototypical implementation of the MULAN4SONAR middleware layer, the organisation agent is actually not yet fully included, at least not as an *agent*. Instead, the organisation agent of a SONAR organisation manifests itself in terms of the generated six-phase reference net explained in the previous subsection (together with possible DWF nets). This concept is illustrated in Figure 7.

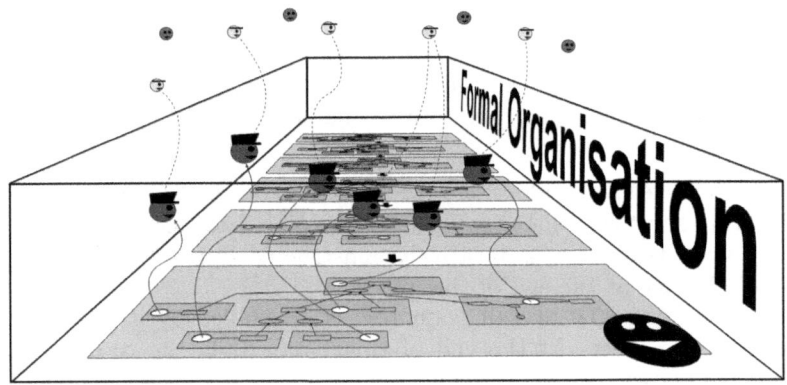

Fig. 7. MULAN4SONAR middleware layer in the current prototype

It is shown that the formal part of a SONAR organisation is embodied by the generated middleware net and the position agents that are hosted on the *agent places* of the net. Here we do not elaborate on the internal structure of the agents as we would have to go into the details of multi-agent system programming with MULAN which is out of the scope of the paper. All OPAs share the same generic OPA architecture (GOPA) that we have presented in [15]. Note that in the current prototype, the OPAs are *directly embedded* on the agent places of the middleware net. This is justified as they are actually reified *parts* of the formal organisation and we assume that the whole middleware (and thus the formal organisation) is executed on the same MULAN platform. The OMAs however are external agents that have chosen to act as members of the organisation. Consequently, they can be hosted on remote platforms and communicate with their respective OPAs via message passing.

For future developments of our MULAN4SONAR middleware we plan to have the organisation agent to be actually realized as a MULAN agent (see Section 5).

4.3   Explanation of the Six Teamwork Phases

As explained in Subsection 4.1, a SONAR-model of an organisation is compiled into executable reference nets for each of the six teamwork phases. Afterwards,the reference nets for the phases 1 to 6 are combined in one reference net and linked sequentially. This linkage is achieved via synchronisation inscriptions. Thus, the end of a phase is synchronised with the start of the succeeding phase.

The reference nets for the six phases share the same net structure but have different inscriptions. This reflects the fact that all teamwork is generated from the same organisational SONAR-specification, but in different phases different information is needed. Figure 8 shows the generated reference net for the first phase, *selection of team members*[8].

Before any teamwork can occur, the system setup has to be carried out. Six position agents (OPAs) – one for each position – are initialized and registered. The position agents are hosted on the **agent** places of the generated middleware net. After this step the initialisation is finished and teamwork may ensue.

For our given SONAR-model we have only one position that is able to start a team, namely O_4 since it is the only position having a place with an empty preset (i.e. the place p_0). Whenever the position agent O_4 decides to begin teamwork, it starts the first phase, *team member selection*. The only possibility for task p_0 is to delegate it to O_1. Here, O_1 has only one implementation possibility for this task, namely t_1. This entails to generate the two subtasks p_1 and p_2. O_1 selects the agents these subtasks are delegated to. For p_2 there is the only possibility O_4 but for p_1 there is the choice between O_2 and O_3. Partner choices occur via the synchronisation a:askPartner(p, O) between the middleware net and the position agents: Agent a provides a binding for the partner O when the task p has to be delegated. Assume that the agent O_1 decides in favour of O_3, then the control is handed over to O_3 which has a choice how to implement the task: either by t_2 or by t_5. This decision is made by the position agent a of O_3 which is synchronised with the middleware net via the channel a:askImpl(t) which is activated by the agent a only if t has to be used for delegation/implementation.

After this iterated delegation has come to an end – which is guaranteed for well-formed SONAR-models – all subtasks have been assigned to team agents and the first phase ends. At this point the agents know that they are team members, but they do not know each other yet. To establish such mutual knowledge the second phase starts.

We cannot cover every phase in detail. The general principle has been shown for phase one, namely enriching the original SONAR model of an organisation with (1) connections to position agents and (2) execution inscriptions along the purpose of the respective teamwork phase.

The purpose of the remaining five phases has been covered in Subsection 4.1. Here, we want to cover one technical aspect specifically. The description of the first phase has made clear that it is a top-down phase. Following the delegation relationships of the original SONAR-model, a team tree is built from the root down to the leaves. It is also clear that the second phase has to be a bottom-up phase. The overall team is not yet known to any position agent. Thus, beginning with the leaves of the team tree and the corresponding "one-man sub-teams",

---

[8] Note that the rule from Figure 6 has been applied several times.

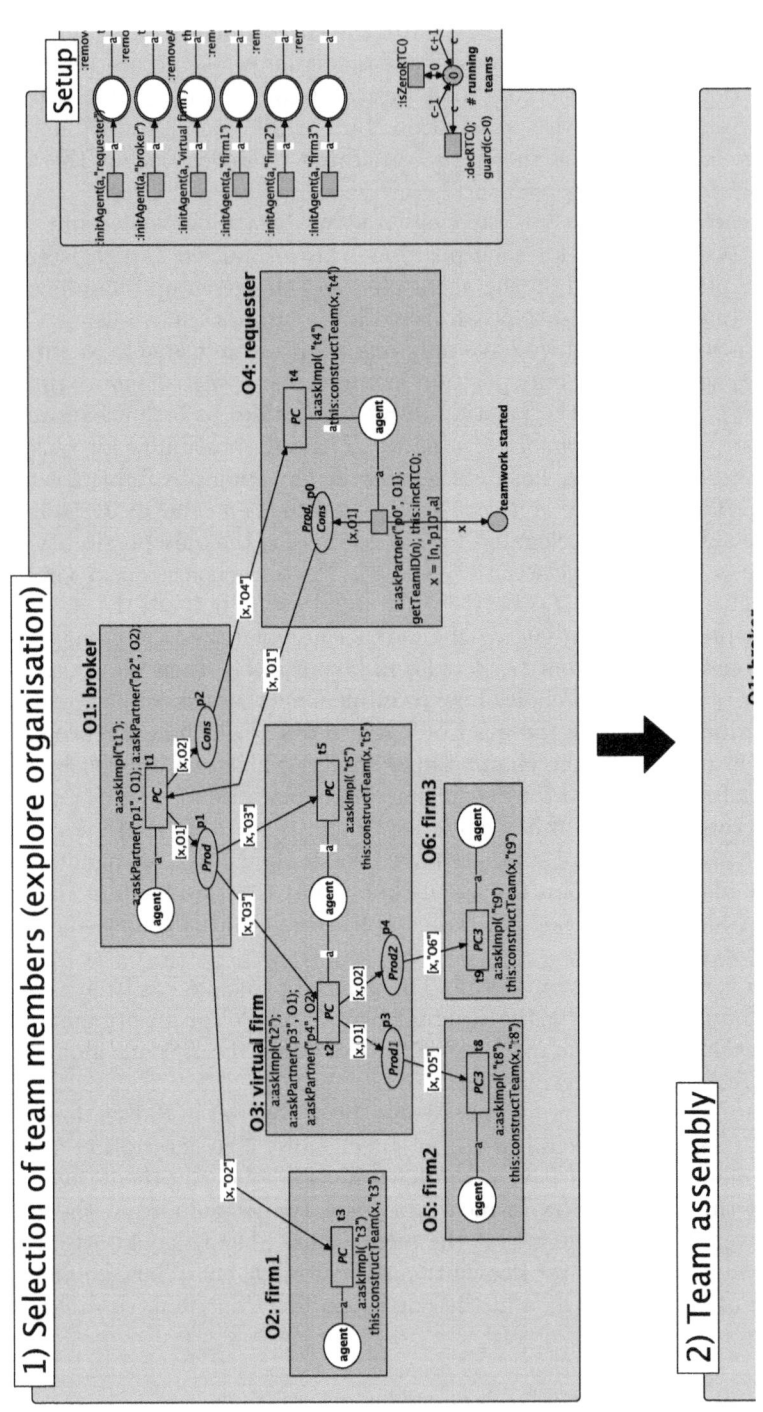

Fig. 8. Zoom: First Phase of the MULAN4SONAR-middleware

sub-teams are iteratively assembled until the complete team is finally known at the root node. Consequently, for the second phase, the direction of the arrows has to be reversed compared to the original SONAR model. Analogous observations hold for the remaining four phases. Phases 3 and 5 are top-down phases while phases 4 and 6 are bottom-up phases.

5   Strengths, Weaknesses and Future Work

In this section, we give a brief qualitative evaluation of the approach taken in this paper. SONAR is a formal model of organisations based on Petri nets. It is often difficult to initially come up with an approach to deploy formal specifications in a software environment. In the case of the Petri net specifications, one can take advantage of the inherent operational semantics. In this sense, Petri nets often allow for a rapid prototyping approach to go from abstract models (requiring only simple Petri net formalisms) to fully functional, executable models (requiring high-level Petri net formalism, in our case reference nets). Consequently, our first approach was to take a SONAR-specification of an organisation and derive an executable prototype by manually attaching inscriptions and add some auxiliary net elements.

While manually crafting an executable reference net for each specific SONAR-model is of course not worthwhile in the long run, it provided us with very early lessons learned and running systems from the beginning on. The work presented in this paper was the next step. Based on our experiences from the handcrafted prototypes we were able to clearly denominate and devise the transformation rules that were needed for automated generation of executable reference net fragments from SONAR-models.

Consequently, we see the conceptual as well as operational closeness between an underlying SONAR-model and its generated middleware net as a crucial advantage for our fast progress in deploying SONAR-organisations. In addition, formal properties like well-formedness (cf. [3,4]) of a SONAR-model directly carry over to the implementation level.

Because of the mentioned problems, we are working on further improving the MULAN4SONAR middleware. Current efforts target at keeping the organisational specification as a more accessible and mutable data structure at the level of the middleware layer. Although it is no longer necessarily represented as a reference net itself, the organisational activities and dynamics allowed by the middleware layer are still directly derived from the underlying Petri net semantics of SONAR.

6   Related Work

Our work is closely related to other approaches that propagate middleware layers for organisation support in multi-agent systems like $\mathcal{S}$-$\mathcal{M}$OISE$^+$ [16], AMELI [17] or TEAMCORE/KARMA [18]. The specifics of each middleware layer depends on the specifics of the organisational model that is supported.

What all approaches have in common is that domain agents are granted access
to the middleware layer via *proxies* that constrain, guide and support an agent
in its function as a member of the organisation, cf. *OrgBox* in $\mathcal{S}$-$\mathcal{M}$OISE$^+$, *Governor* in AMELI, *Team Wrapper* in TEAMCORE/KARMA. Our organisational
position agents, the OPAs, serve a similar purpose. They are coupled with organisational member agents, the OMAs, which are responsible for domain-level
actions and decisions.

However, in the case of $\mathcal{S}$-$\mathcal{M}$OISE$^+$ and AMELI, management of organisational dynamics is mainly taken care of by middleware manager agents (the
OrgManager for $\mathcal{S}$-$\mathcal{M}$OISE$^+$ and the *institution, scene* and *transition managers*
for AMELI). The proxies mainly route communication between the domain level
agents and the middleware managers. Consequently, middleware management is
to some degree centralised[9]. In our case, the OPAs are both proxies and middleware managers. They manage all six phases of organisational teamwork in a
completely distributed way. This is quite similar to the function of the Team
Wrappers in TEAMCORE/KARMA. The KARMA middleware component can
be compared to the organisational agent in our approach. It is a meta-level
entity that is responsible for setting up the whole system and for monitoring
performance. In [20], we additionally study the conceptual fit between different
middleware approaches (in combination with the supported organisational models) and their application on different levels of a large-scale system of systems.

7   Conclusion

In this paper, we have built upon our previous work SONAR on formalising organisational models for MAS by means of Petri nets [4,3]. In particular, the paper
is dedicated to a prototypical MULAN4SONAR middleware layer that supports
the deployment of SONAR-models. As SONAR-specifications are formalised with
Petri nets, they inherently have an operational semantics and thus already lend
themselves towards immediate implementation. We have taken advantage of this
possibility and have chosen the reference net formalism as an implementation
means. Reference nets implement the nets-in-nets concept [6] and thus allow us
to deploy SONAR-organisations as nested Petri net systems. The reference net
tool RENEW [7] offers comprehensive support, allowing us to refine/extend the
SONAR specifications into fully executable prototypes.

This leaves us with a close link between a SONAR specification of an organisation and its accompanying MULAN4SONAR middleware support. The structure
and behaviour of the resulting software system is directly derived and compiled
from the underlying formal model. For example, we have explicitly shown how
the organisation net of a formal SONAR-specification can be utilised for the middleware support of six different phases of teamwork. In each phase, the original

---

[9] However, in the case of $\mathcal{S}$-$\mathcal{M}$OISE$^+$, the new middleware approach ORA4MAS [19]
(*organizational artifacts for MAS*) has been devised, resulting in a more decentralised approach.

net is used differently (with different inscriptions and arrow directions). This approach of deploying SONAR-models does not only relieve the developer of much otherwise tedious programming. It also allows to preserve desirable properties that can be proven for the formal model and that now carry over to the software technical implementation.

Finally, although we have introduced the idea of SONAR-organisations acting in the context of other SONAR-organisations, we have not addressed the topic in detail here. We study this subject in [12,21], but on a more abstract/generic level than SONAR offers. Nevertheless, we have already begun to transfer the results to SONAR.

References

1. Carley, K.M., Gasser, L.: Computational organisation theory. In: Weiß, G. (ed.) Multiagent Systems, pp. 229–330. MIT Press, Cambridge (1999)
2. Dignum, V. (ed.): Handbook of Research on Multi-Agent Systems: Semantics and Dynamics of Organizational Models. IGI Global, Information Science Reference (2009)
3. Köhler-Bußmeier, M., Wester-Ebbinghaus, M., Moldt, D.: A formal model for organisational structures behind process-aware information systems. In: Jensen, K., van der Aalst, W.M.P. (eds.) Transactions on Petri Nets and Other Models of Concurrency II. LNCS, vol. 5460, pp. 98–114. Springer, Heidelberg (2009)
4. Köhler, M.: A formal model of multi-agent organisations. Fundamenta Informaticae 79, 415–430 (2007)
5. Girault, C., Valk, R. (eds.): Petri Nets for System Engineering – A Guide to Modeling, Verification, and Applications. Springer, Heidelberg (2003)
6. Valk, R.: Object Petri nets: Using the nets-within-nets paradigm. In: Desel, J., Reisig, W., Rozenberg, G. (eds.) Advanced Course on Petri Nets. LNCS, vol. 3098, pp. 819–848. Springer, Heidelberg (2004)
7. Kummer, O., Wienberg, F., Duvigneau, M., Schumacher, J., Köhler, M., Moldt, D., Rölke, H., Valk, R.: An extensible editor and simulation engine for Petri nets: Renew. In: Cortadella, J., Reisig, W. (eds.) ICATPN 2004. LNCS, vol. 3099, pp. 484–493. Springer, Heidelberg (2004)
8. Köhler, M., Moldt, D., Rölke, H.: Modeling the behaviour of Petri net agents. In: Colom, J.M., Koutny, M. (eds.) ICATPN 2001. LNCS, vol. 2075, pp. 224–241. Springer, Heidelberg (2001)
9. Cabac, L., Dörges, T., Duvigneau, M., Moldt, D., Reese, C., Wester-Ebbinghaus, M.: Agent models for concurrent software systems. In: Bergmann, R., Lindemann, G. (eds.) MATES 2008. LNCS (LNAI), vol. 5244, pp. 37–48. Springer, Heidelberg (2008)
10. Ehrig, H., Ehrig, K., Prange, U., Taentzer, G.: Fundamentals of algebraic graph transformation. Springer, Heidelberg (2006)
11. Fischer, K., Schillo, M., Siekmann, J.: Holonic multiagent systems: A foundation for the organisation of multiagent systems. In: Mařík, V., McFarlane, D.C., Valckenaers, P. (eds.) HoloMAS 2003. LNCS (LNAI), vol. 2744, pp. 71–80. Springer, Heidelberg (2003)

12. Wester-Ebbinghaus, M., Moldt, D., Köhler-Bußmeier, M.: Modelling an open and controlled system unit as a modular component of systems of systems. In: Jensen, K., Donatelli, S., Koutny, M. (eds.) Transactions on Petri Nets and Other Models of Concurrency IV. LNCS, vol. 6550, pp. 174–198. Springer, Heidelberg (2010)

13. Boissier, O., Hübner, J.F., Sichman, J.S.: Organization oriented programming: From closed to open organizations. In: O'Hare, G., Ricci, A., O'Grady, M., Dikenelli, O. (eds.) ESAW 2006. LNCS (LNAI), vol. 4457, pp. 86–105. Springer, Heidelberg (2007)

14. Köhler-Bußmeier, M., Wester-Ebbinghaus, M.: A Petri net based prototype for MAS organisation middleware. In: Moldt, D. (ed.) Workshop on Modelling, object, components, and agents (MOCA 2009), University of Hamburg, Department for Computer Science, pp. 29–44 (2009)

15. Köhler-Bußmeier, M., Wester-Ebbinghaus, M.: Sonar: A multi-agent infrastructure for active application architectures and inter-organisational information systems. In: Braubach, L., van der Hoek, W., Petta, P., Pokahr, A. (eds.) MATES 2009. LNCS, vol. 5774, pp. 248–257. Springer, Heidelberg (2009)

16. Hübner, J.F., Sichman, J.S., Boissier, O.: S-MOISE: A middleware for developing organised multi-agent systems. In: Boissier, O., Padget, J., Dignum, V., Lindemann, G., Matson, E., Ossowski, S., Sichman, J.S., Vázquez-Salceda, J. (eds.) ANIREM 2005 and OOOP 2005. LNCS (LNAI), vol. 3913, pp. 64–78. Springer, Heidelberg (2006)

17. Esteva, M., Rodriguez-Aguilar, J., Rosell, B., Arcos, J.: Ameli: An agent-based middleware for electronic institutions. In: Sierra, C., Sonenberg, L., Tambe, M. (eds.) Proceedings of the 3rd International Joint Conference on Autonomous Agents and Multi-Agent Systems (AAMAS 2004), pp. 236–243 (2004)

18. Pynadath, D., Tambe, M.: An automated teamwork infrastructure for heterogeneous software agents and humans. Autonomous Agents and Multi-Agent Systems 7, 71–100 (2003)

19. Hübner, J.F., Boissier, O., Kitio, R., Ricci, A.: Instrumenting multi-agent organisations with organisational artifacts and agents. Autonomous Agents and Multi-Agent Systems 20, 369–400 (2010)

20. Wester-Ebbinghaus, M., Köhler-Bußmeier, M., Moldt, D.: From multi-agent to multi-organization systems: Utilizing middleware approaches. In: Artikis, A., Picard, G., Vercouter, L. (eds.) ESAW 2008. LNCS, vol. 5485, pp. 46–65. Springer, Heidelberg (2009)

21. Wester-Ebbinghaus, M., Moldt, D.: Structure in threes: Modelling organization-oriented software architectures built upon multi-agent systems. In: Proceedings of the 7th International Conference an Autonomous Agents and Multi-Agent Systems (AAMAS 2008), pp. 1307–1311 (2008)

Modeling Norms in Multi-agent Systems with NormML*

Karen da Silva Figueiredo, Viviane Torres da Silva,
and Christiano de Oliveira Braga

Computer Science Department, Universidade Federal Fluminense (UFF),
Rua Passos da Pátria 156, Bloco E, 24210-240, Niterói, Brazil
{kfigueiredo,viviane.silva,cbraga}@ic.uff.br

Abstract. Norms in multi-agent systems are a mechanism used to restrict the behavior of agents by defining what agents are obligated, permitted or prohibited to do and by stating stimulus to their fulfillment by defining rewards and discouraging their violation by pointing out punishments. In this paper we propose a normative modeling language called NormML that makes possible the modeling of the main properties and characteristics of the norms. In addition, we also propose a mechanism to validate the norms at design time, i.e., to check if the norms respect the constraints defined by the language and also their possible conflicts.

Keywords: Norm, Modeling, Validation, Conflict, Metamodel.

1 Introduction

Norms in multi-agent systems are mechanism used to restrict the behavior of agents by describing the actions that must be performed or states that must be achieved (*obligations*), actions that can be performed or states that can be achieved (*permissions*) and actions that cannot be performed or states that cannot be achieved (*prohibitions*). They represent a way for agents to understand their responsibilities and the responsibilities of the others. Norms are used to cope with the autonomy, different interests and desires of the agents that cohabit the system.

Norms can be defined at design time together with the modeling of the system, or created at runtime by agents that have the power to do so [1]. In this paper we focus on the description of norms at design time. The modeling of norms is an important part of the specification of a system and should be treated as an important task of Multiagent System (MAS) design. The alignment of the norms with the elements that represent the system, such as its entities and the actions that they execute, is a fundamental activity because the

---

* The present work has been partially funded by the Spanish project "Agreement Technologies" (CONSOLIDER CSD2007-0022, INGENIO 2010), by the Spanish Ministry of Education and Science under project TIN2009-13839-C03-02 and by the Brazilian research councils CNPq under grant 135891/2009-4 and 303531/2009-6 and FAPERJ under grant E-26/110.959/2009.

M. De Vos et al. (Eds.): COIN 2010 International Workshops, LNAI 6541, pp. 39–57, 2011.

norms specification relates such entities, their actions and the period during while the actions are being regulated. Thus, the redesign of the system may affect the specification of the norms and the redesign of the norms may influence the set of elements that represent the system.

Another important issue that must be considered while specifying the norms is the conflicts that may arise between them. A clear example of such conflicts occurs when there is a norm that prohibits an agent to perform a particular action and another that requires the same agent to perform the same action at the same period of time. When norms are defined at design time some of those conflicts can be detected and solved by, for instance, amending the conflicting norms, which might cause the system's redesign (by the inclusion of new actions, actors and roles, for example). By solving at least part of the conflicts at design time, it is possible to reduce the time the agents will spend executing this task at runtime.

Due to the interdependency between the modeling of norms and the modeling of the elements of the system and the importance of finding out conflicts and solving them at design time, it is important that the modeling languages and the notations used by methodologies and organizational models to model MAS make possible the modeling of the norms together with the modeling of the whole system and also provide mechanism for solving the conflicts at design time.

Taking this into account, the goals of this paper are: (i) to investigate if the elements that compose norms can be modeled by using the MAS modeling languages and notations provided by methodologies and organizational models; and (ii) to explore the languages, methodologies and organizational models in order to find out if they give support to the checking of conflicts at design time. The paper also aims to present a normative modeling language called NormML, which is an extension of its preliminary version presented in [2] and that is able to model the main elements that compose the norms and to check the conflicts between them.

The paper is organized as follows. In Section 2 we identify the main elements that compose the norms. In Section 3 we discuss the support given by the modeling languages and the notations provided by the methodologies and organizational models analyzed to model such elements and to check norm conflicts. Section 4 describes the case study used in this paper. Section 5 provides some background material and Section 6 presents the normative modeling language NormML and details the mechanism used to check for conflicts between the modeled norms. Section 7 concludes the paper with final remarks and discusses future work.

2 Main Elements of a Norm

In this section we stress the key static aspects of a norm, i.e., the main elements that compose a norm: *deontic concept, involved entities, actions, activation constraints, sanctions* and *context*. Such elements were found out after investigating ten specification and implementation languages used to describe and implement norms [1, 3-11]. The elements that compose a norm are based on the premise that *norms restrict the behavior of system entities during a period of time and define the sanctions applied when they are violated or fulfilled.*

Deontic Concept. Deontic logic refers to the logic of requests, commands, rules, laws, moral principles and judgments [13]. In multi-agent systems, such concepts have been used to describe behavior restrictions for the agents in the form of obligations (what the agent must execute), permissions (what the agent can execute) and prohibitions (what the agent cannot execute). Thus, one of the main elements of a norm is the identification of the type of restriction being defined, i.e., the identification of the deontic concept associated with the norm.

Involved Entities. Since norms are always defined to restrict the behavior of entities, the identification of such entities whose behavior is being restricted is fundamental. A norm may regulate the behavior of individuals (e.g., a given agent, or an agent while playing a given role) or the behavior of a group of individuals (e.g., all agents playing a given role, groups of agents, groups of agents playing roles or all agents in the system).

Actions. Since a norm defines restriction over the execution of entities, it is important to clearly represent the action being regulated. Such actions can be communicative ones, typically represented by the sending and receiving of a message, or non-communicative actions (such as to access and modify a resource, to enter in an organization, to move to another environment, etc.). In this paper we have not taken into account norms applied to states yet.

Activation Constraints. Norms have a period during which they are active, i.e., during while their restrictions must be fulfilled. Norms can be activated by one constraint or a set of constraints that can be: the execution of actions, the specification of time intervals (before, after, between), the achievement of systems states or temporal aspects (such as dates), and also the activation / deactivation of another norm and the fulfillment / violation of a norm.

Sanctions. When a norm is violated the entity that has violated this norm may suffer a punishment and when a norm is fulfilled the entity who has followed the norm may receive a reward. Such rewards and punishments are called sanctions and should be described together with the norm specification.

Context. Norms are usually defined in a given context that determines the area of their application. A norm can, for instance, be described in the context of a given environment and should be fulfilled only by the agents executing in the environment or can be defined in the context of an organization and fulfilled only by the agents playing roles in the organization.

3   Related Work

Although there are some works, such as the modeling languages AUML [13] and ANote [14] and the methodology MESSAGE [15] that do not support the modeling of norms, there are already many others that make possible the modeling of several elements of a norm. From the set of two modeling languages [16, 17], seven methodologies [6, 18-23] and three organization models [24-26] analyzed, no one is able to model all the properties of the elements described in the previous section. In this section we discuss those modeling languages, methodologies and organization models showing how they represent the concepts related to the norms and employ these elements when they are modeling norms (we summarize it in Table 1). We compare such works with NormML, the modeling language being proposed in this paper.

Deontic Concept. Most modeling languages and methodologies make available the deontic concept of obligation in order to describe the actions that agents must execute. Methodologies such as Secure Tropos (ST) [22], SODA [23], Prometheus [20] and the organization model proposed in MOISE+ [25] only offer the concepts of obligation and permission since they consider that everything that is not permitted is automatically prohibited. In the ST methodology the concept of obligation can be represented by the delegation relationship and the concept of permission by the ownership and trust relationships. NormML, different from the majority, includes all the three deontic concepts (obligation, permission and prohibition) in the modeling of norms.

Involved Entities. All works analyzed propose a way to describe the entities to which the norm applies (elements checked in Table 1). The majority provides support to describe a norm for a particular role. Some works [18, 19, 21, 25] do not allow the description of norms that apply to a group of individuals. This fact does not imply that the work analyzed do not support the modeling of such entities, however the work cannot provide ways to the description of norms related to them. The ST methodology also allows the designer to describe the system itself as an entity and to define norms that can be applied to the system as a whole. By using NormML it is possible to describe norms to individuals, groups of individuals or all the entities of the system (see the "Context" item).

Actions. All the modeling languages, methodologies and models analyzed provide a way to restrict non-communicative actions. In ROADMAP [21], that is one of the proposed extensions for Gaia, the user can only restrict the access to objects, roles and protocols of the system. NormML supports the modeling of both kinds of actions, communicative and non-communicative.

Activation Constraints. The works analyzed present several ways to describe the period during while a norm is active, i.e., to describe the restrictions for their activation and deactivation (see more details in Table 1). According to [27], the SODA formalism is still being developed so we cannot affirm the types of restrictions that such methodology will support. By using NormML all these activation constraints can be modeled.

Sanctions. A small number of languages and methodologies consider that norms can be violated, and only a few of them provide a way for describing sanctions. The AORML [17] language assumes that commitments (or obligations) between entities of the system can be violated, and, as consequence, a sanction should be applied. But the language does not offer a way to describe this sanction. The organizational models OperA [26], MASQ [24] and MOISE+ consider that norms can be violated, and, excluding MOISE+, they have mechanisms to describe sanctions. The O-MaSE [6] methodology groups norms into two kinds of policies: law policies and guidance

Table 1. Main elements of a norm

		AML [16]	AORML [17]	Gaia [18]	O-MaSE [6]	PASSI [19]	Prometheus [20]	ROADMAP [21]	ST [22]	SODA [23]	MASQ [24]	MOISE+ [25]	OperA [26]	NormML
Deontic Concept	Permission	•	•	•			•	•	•	•	•	•	•	•
	Prohibition	•	•	•	•						•		•	•
	Obligation	•	•	•	•	•	•		•	•	•	•	•	•
Involved Entities	Agent	•	•		•				•	•			•	•
	Role	•	•	•		•	•	•	•	•		•	•	•
	Agent playing role	•			•						•			•
	Groups of individuals	•	•		•		•		•	•	•		•	•
	All in the system				•		•		•	•			•	•
Actions	Communicative Actions	•		•	•	•	•		•		•		•	•
	Non-communicative Actions	•	•	•	•	•	•	•	•	•	•	•	•	•
Activation Constraints	Execution of actions	•		•	•	•	•				•		•	•
	Time intervals	•		•	•	•	•	•			•		•	•
	Achievement of states	•		•	•	•	•				•		•	•
	Temporal aspects	•	•	•	•	•	•				•	•	•	•
	Activation, deactivation, fulfillment and violation of a norm										•		•	•
Sanctions	Punishment										•		•	•
	Reward													•
Context	Environment													•
	Organization	•	•	•	•	•	•	•	•	•	•	•	•	•
	Interaction	•		•			•		•				•	
	Transition of scene			•									•	

policies. Only the guidance policies can be violated but there is not a way to define sanctions for such violations. The Gaia [18] and PASSI [19] methodologies express norms as organization rules that cannot be violated, and so there is no need to define a sanction mechanism. None of the analyzed languages or methodologies allows the description of rewards in case of the fulfillment of a norm. However, NormML supports the definition of both punishments and rewards.

Context. All languages, methodologies and organizational models define the norms in an organizational context. The AORML language offers support to express obligations between two agents (as commitments) in the context of an interaction. Besides AORML, methodologies such as PASSI, Prometheus, Gaia and the organizational model OperA also allow the description of norms in such a context. Moreover, in OperA and Gaia it is possible to describe a norm in a context that represents the transition of scenes. Besides describing norms in an organizational context, NormML also provides the environmental context.

In addition to the elements presented, another interesting characteristic to be considered when analyzing the modeling languages, methodologies and organizational models is the ability to detect conflicts between the norms of the system at design phase.

Check Conflict. The AORML language assumes that there is a normative inconsistency when there is at the same time a permission and a prohibition, or a prohibition and an obligation to the same action. It considers that obligations already have a permission embedded, so there is no conflict in this sense. Although the language considers that conflicts can occur, it does not have an automatic mechanism to detect these conflicts.

The ST methodology defines eight properties to be used in an automatic verification of conflicts, including the validation of conflicts between the system's obligations and permissions. Although norms can be defined in different contexts, they do not check conflicts between norms in different contexts. Moreover, since all the norms are applied to roles and norms have no activation constraints, they do not take these characteristics into account when checking for conflicts.

The OperA organizational model allows the automatic verification of conflicts between the norms that apply to a given entity. However, such mechanism does not give support to the checking of conflicts between norms applied to different entity types, i.e., between the norms applied to a group and the norms applied to roles or agents themselves. In addition, it also does not give support for checking conflicts among norms defined in different contexts and considering different activation conditions.

Besides the support provided by the modeling languages, methodologies, and organizational models to model norms, we have also investigated the support to the checking of conflicts between norms in the literature. In [28] the authors point out that there are conflicts between obligations and prohibitions, and permissions and prohibitions to the same agent or role to execute actions over the same states. They also consider that there are conflicts between obligations related to states that are mutually exclusive. The norms analyzed in this work do not have any kind of activation constraint.

In [11, 29, 30] they consider that there is a normative conflict when one norm states an obligation or a permission and the other norm states a prohibition on the same agent to execute the same action at time intervals that intersect. In [29] only communicative actions are mentioned. None of the works reviewed considers the special case of conflicts between obligations and permissions that may occur when an agent is obliged to execute an action when it has not a permission to do so.

4 Case Study

In order to exemplify our approach, we define a set of ten norms that govern a simplified version of a *web store*. The web store is being modeled as an organization that
inhabits the *market place* environment and defines two roles to be played by the
agents: *seller* or *buyer*. The sellers of the web store can advertise goods while the
buyers can buy the goods that are announced on the store by the sellers. For some of
the norms we have specified the sanctions (punishments or rewards) the agent should
receive if it violates or fulfills the norm. Note that those sanctions are also norms that
are activated when the related norm is violated or fulfilled.

N1. All agents executing in the context of the environment MarketPlace are prohibited to read and update the price of the goods.

N2. Sellers are permitted, in the context of the organization WebStore that inhabits
the environment MarketPlace, to update the price of the goods before it opens for
sale.

N3. Sellers are obliged, in the context of the organization WebStore that inhabits the
environment MarketPlace, to delete the good's advertisement if the stock of the good
is empty.

N4. Buyers are obliged, in the context of the organization WebStore that inhabits the
environment MarketPlace, to pay for the good that they have bought.
    Punishment: N5. Buyers are prohibited, in the context of the organization Web-
Store that inhabits the environment MarketPlace, to buy goods.

N6. Buyers are obliged, in the context of the organization WebStore that inhabits the
environment MarketPlace, to pay off their debts.
    Reward: N7. Buyers are permitted, in the context of the organization WebStore
that inhabits the environment MarketPlace, to buy goods.

N8. Buyers are prohibited, in the context of the organization WebStore that inhabits
the environment MarketPlace, to return a good that they have bought.

N9. Sellers are obliged, in the context of the organization WebStore that inhabits the
environment MarketPlace, to give the good to the buyer after the given buyer pays for it.
    Punishment: N10. Sellers are prohibited, in the context of the organization Web-
Store that inhabits the environment MarketPlace, to advertise goods.
    In Section 6 the set of norms above are used to illustrate the use of the NormML
modeling language.

5 Background

In this section we briefly provide background material for the rest of this paper.
NormML is a UML-based modeling language for the specification of norms. The

choice for UML as metalanguage allows for an easy integration of NormML with UML-based MAS modeling languages such as AUML, AML and MAS-ML [31]. Moreover, metamodel-based validation techniques may be applied to norms specified in NormML. Therefore, Section 5.1 introduces basic notions of models and metamodels, necessary to understand the design of NormML.

Our modeling language was designed with the perception that norm specification in MAS design and security policy specification in RBAC (role based access control) [32] design are closely coupled issues. RBAC security policies specify the *permissions* that a *user* has under a given *role*, while trying to access system *resources*. In MAS we specify the *norms* that regulate the behavior (or *actions*) of a *role*, an *agent* or an *agent playing a given role,* for instance. Although we consider security policies and norms coupled issues, norms can be violated since they only define how agents *should* behave.

In Section 5.2 we introduce SecureUML [33], a Domain-specific Language (DSL) for modeling RBAC policies. It has been applied successfully both in academic projects [33] and industrial ones [34]. The reasons why SecureUML was chosen are: it has a well-defined syntax, given by its metamodel; it has a formal semantics [35]; and it is designed specifically for RBAC modeling. In this paper we want to explore the modeling of norms using RBAC concepts.

5.1 Models and Metamodels

A modeling language provides a vocabulary (concepts and relations) for creating *models*. Such vocabulary is described by the *metamodel* of the modeling language which elements formalize the language concepts and their relationships. A metamodel may include invariants that specify additional properties that the models must fulfill as instances of the metamodel. Such invariants specify the *well-formedness* conditions (or *well-formed rules*) of a model with respect to its metamodel and the *consistency* conditions between metamodel concepts.

When UML is chosen as metalanguage, a metamodel is represented by a class diagram and its invariants are written in OCL (Object Constraint Language) [36]. This is the choice followed in this paper.

5.2 SecureUML

SecureUML provides a language for modeling *Roles, Permissions, Actions, Resources,* and *Authorization Constraints*, along with the relationships between permissions and roles, actions and permissions, resources and actions, and constraints and permissions. The actions described in the language can be either *Atomic* or *Composite*. The atomic actions are intended to map directly onto actual operations of the modeled system (delete, update, read, create and execute). The composite actions are used to hierarchically group atomic ones.

SecureUML leaves open what the protected resources are and which actions they offer to clients. ComponentUML [32] is a simple language for modeling component-based systems that provides provides a subset of UML class models: entities can be related by associations and may have attributes and methods. Therefore, *Entity, Attribute, Method, Association* and *AssociationEnd* are the possible protected resources.

By using SecureUML+ComponentUML[1] it is possible, for instance, to specify the permissions a user playing a given role must have to execute a method (or to update an attribute) of a resource. In order to do so, it is necessary to instantiate the meta-classes *User, Role, Permission, ActionExecute* (or *ActionUpdate*), and *Method* (or *Attribute*).

6   NormML: A Normative Modeling Language

As stated before, norms are viewed as security policies. While in SecureUML it is possible to define the *permissions* a *user* has, i.e., the constraints that a user, in a given role, must fulfill to perform actions over the system resources, in NormML it is possible to define the *norms* an *entity* must obey, i.e., it is possible to describe the set of *actions* that the *agents, roles, agents playing roles* or a *group of agents* in an particular context (*organization* or *environment*) are *obliged, permitted* or *prohibited* to execute conditioned by the execution of other *actions* and the achievement of *dates* and *states*. The language also permits the definition of *sanctions*, i.e., *rewards* and *punishments*, to be applied in case of fulfillment or violation of the norms.

The preliminary version of the NormML metamodel [2] extends the SecureUML metamodel with the following basic elements: *Norm, NormConstraint, Agent* and *AgentAction* to model norms, activation constraints, agents whose behavior is being restricted by the norm and the actions representing such behavior. The metamodel of the current version of the language extends the preliminary version by including the following new elements: (i) *Organization* (to model contexts and groups of agents); (ii) *Environment* (to model contexts); (iii) *Protocol, AtomicSend, AtomicReceive* and *Message* (to model norms that restrict the sending and receiving of messages); and (iv) *If* and *Date* (to model activation constraints using deadlines and states); and (v) *Sanction, Punishment* and *Reward* (to model rewards and punishments) (see Section 6.1 for details). The NormML metamodel also includes a set of invariants that guarantees the well-formedness of a norm and several operations that are used to identify conflicts between two given norms (Section 6.3).

6.1   The NormML Metamodel

A norm corresponds to an instance of the NormML metamodel, i.e., it is defined by instantiating several metaclasses and their relationships. In this section, we present the NormML metamodel[2] focusing on the definition of the main elements of a norm.

Deontic Concept. A norm is either an obligation (represented by the metaclass *NormObligation*), a permission (represented by the metaclass *NormPermission*) or a prohibition (represented by the metaclass *NormProhibition*), as illustrated in Fig. 1.

---

[1] The metamodel of SecureUML+ComponentUML (from now referred as SecureUML metamodel) is available at http://www.ic.uff.br/~viviane.silva/normML/secureUML.pdf

[2] The whole picture of the NormML metamodel is available in http://www.ic.uff.br/~kfigueiredo/normML/metamodel.pdf

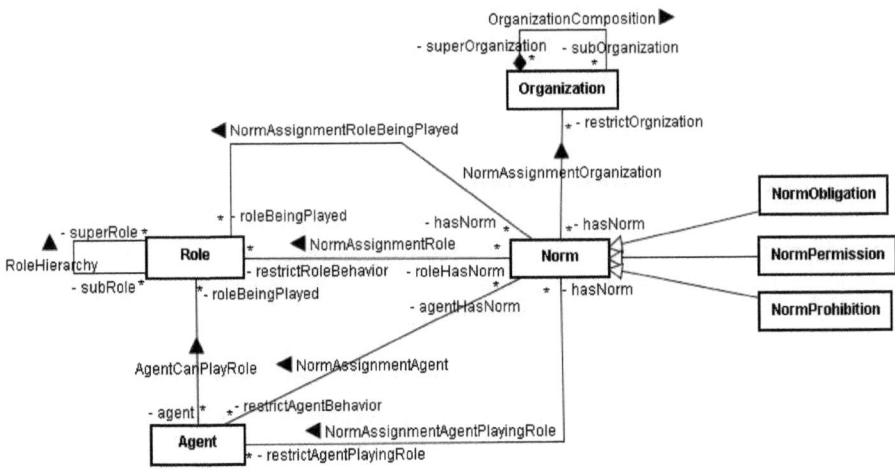

Fig. 1. Deontic concept and involved entities related metaclasses at the NormML Metamodel

Involved Entities. In the preliminary version of the language, a norm could only be described to regulate the behavior of *Agents*, the behavior of all agents that play a given *Role*, or the behavior of a specific agent when it is playing a given role. Nowadays, it is also possible to define a norm for a group of agents by using the metaclass *Organization* (as shown in Fig. 1). In this paper, we do not make any distinction among the definition of group, team and organization.

A norm can also be defined for all agents executing in a given context. In such case, it is only necessary to relate the norm to a context without specifying the entities whose behavior is being regulated (see norm N1 in Fig. 6 for an example).

Actions. NormML inherits four resource kinds from SecureUML: *Attribute*, *Method*, *Entity* and *AssociationEnd*. It extends the set of resources with agent and roles' actions represented by the metaclass *AgentAction* and with roles' messages represented by the metaclass *Message* that is part of a communication protocol of a role (*Protocol* metaclass). Thus, it is possible to describe norms to control the access to attributes, methods, objects and association ends, to control the execution of the actions of agents and roles, and also to control the sending and the receiving of messages by roles (Fig. 2).

Each resource kind has a set of actions that can be used to control the access to the resource. For instance, the actions *read*, *update* and *full access* (*read+update*) can be used to regulate the access to attributes. In the case of restrictions applied to actions of agents and roles (*AgentAction* metaclass), the behavior that must be used is the *execution* of the action (*AtomicExecute*). Note that *AgentAction* is the resource and *AtomicExecute* is the action being used to control or restrict the access to the resource. In the case of restrictions applied to messages (*Message* metaclass), the behavior that must be used is the *sending* of the message (*AtomicSend*), the *receiving* of the message (*AtomicReceive*) or the *full access* (*send+receive*) of the message (*MessageFullAccess*). Fig. 2 illustrates all metaclasses that define the resources and the actions.

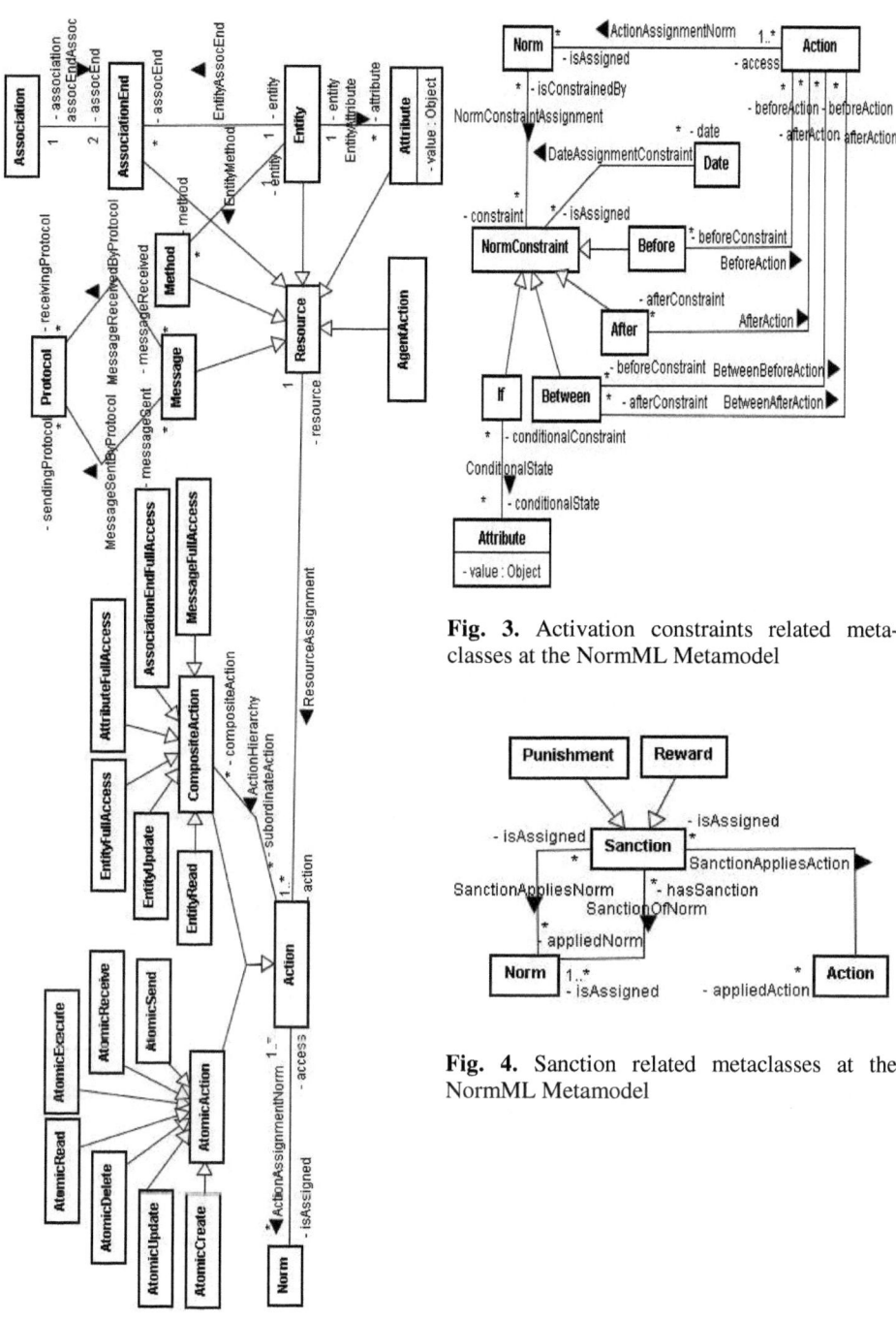

Fig. 3. Activation constraints related metaclasses at the NormML Metamodel

Fig. 4. Sanction related metaclasses at the NormML Metamodel

Fig. 2. Actions related metaclasses at the NormML Metamodel

Activation Constraints. The preliminary version of NormML allows for the specification of the time period that a norm is *active* based on the execution of actions. The language was extended to define activation constraints also based on the definition of dates and predicates (i.e., values associated with attributes), as shown in Fig. 3.

The activation constraints are represented by the metaclass *NormConstraint*. If a norm is conditioned by a *Before* clause, it means that the norm is active before the execution of the action(s) and/or the achievement of the date(s) described in the *Before* clause. If a norm is conditioned by an *After* clause, it means that the norm is active only after the execution of the action(s) and/or the achievement of the date(s) described in the *After* clause. In the case of a *Between* clause, the norm is only active during the period delimited by two groups of actions and dates. In the case of a norm conditioned by an *If* clause, the norm is only active when the value(s) of the attribute(s) described in the *If* clause is (are) achieved (see norm N3 in Fig. 8 for an example).

Sanctions. The current version of NormML supports the description of sanctions (*Sanction* metaclass) for the norms, as shown in Fig. 4. A sanction may be a reward applied when the norm is fulfilled (by instantiating the metaclass *Reward*) or a punishment applied when the norm is violated (by instantiating the metaclass *Punishment*). A sanction can state an action or a set of actions to be executed after the fulfillment/violation of the norm (represented by the *SanctionAppliesAction* relationship) or can activate other norms to restrict the behavior of some particular entities (represented by the *SanctionAppliesNorm* relationship). For instance, in case an agent violates a norm, another norm is activated to prohibit the agent from executing a particular action (see norms N9 and N10 in Fig. 9 for an example).

Context. The recent version of NormML makes possible the definition of norms in two different contexts, as illustrated in Fig. 5: *Organization* and *Environment*. Organizations define roles played by agents and both organizations and agents inhabit environments.

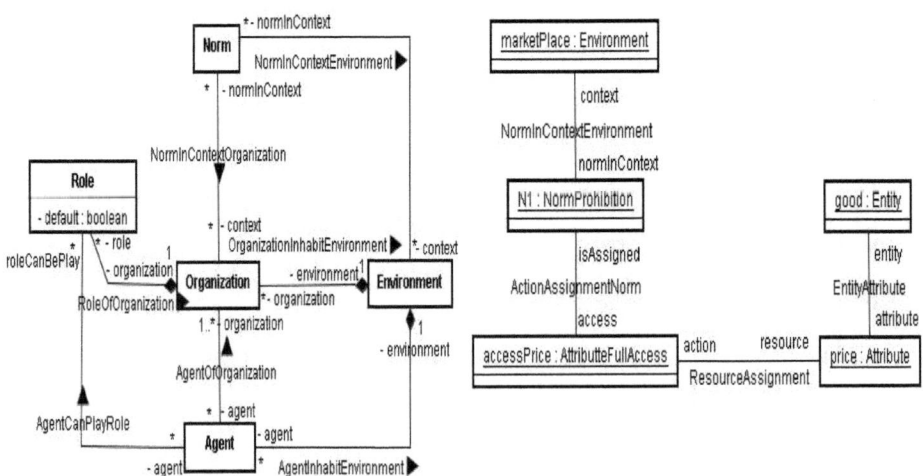

Fig. 5. Context related metaclasses at the
NormML Metamodel   **Fig. 6.** Norm N1

6.2 Modeling Norms with NormML

In order to exemplify the use of NormML to model the norms of a MAS, consider the set of norms presented in Section 3. Norm N1 states a prohibition (*the deontic concept*) on all agents executing (*the involved entities*) in the environment MarketPlace (*the context*) to read and update (*non-communicative action attributeFullAccess*) the price of goods (*the resource of the action*). Fig. 6 shows the model of the norm N1 by instantiating the classes of the NormML metamodel.

N2 (Fig. 7) states a permission (*deontic concept*) to the sellers (*involved entities*) of the organization WebStore (*context*) to update (*non-communicative action atomicUpdate*) the price of the goods (*resource of the action*) before it opens for sale (*activation constraint*).

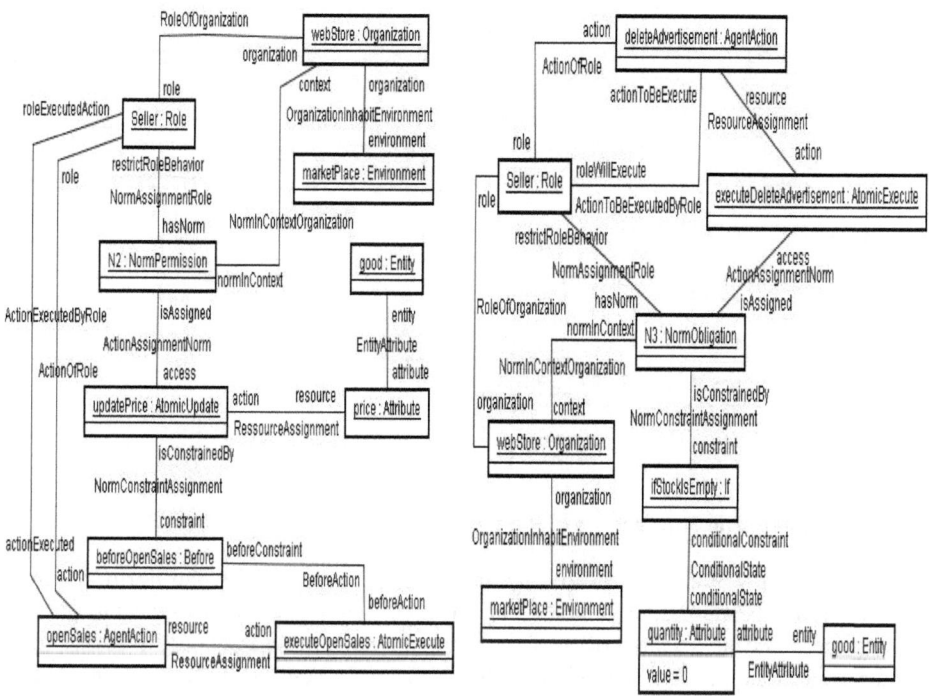

Fig. 7. Norm N2   **Fig. 8.** Norm N3

Norm N3 (Fig. 8) applies an obligation (*deontic concept*) to the sellers of the organization WebStore (as norm N2) to delete the good's advertisement (*non-communicative action atomicExecute*) if the stock of the good is empty (*activation constraint*).

N9 also states an obligation to the sellers of the organization WebStore to give the good to the buyer (an *atomicExecute* of an *AgenAction*) after the given buyer pays for it (*activation constraint*). Norm N9 applies a punishment as a sanction that is a norm too (norm N10). If a seller violates N9, N10 states to the given seller (*related entity*) a prohibition (*deontic concept*) to advertise goods (an *atomicExecute* of an *AgenAction*). Fig. 9 shows the model of norm N9 and N10.

Similar to norms N9 and N10, norms N4 and N5, and N6 and N7 can be modeled. The same occurs to the norm N8 that can be modeled following the approach used to model N2.

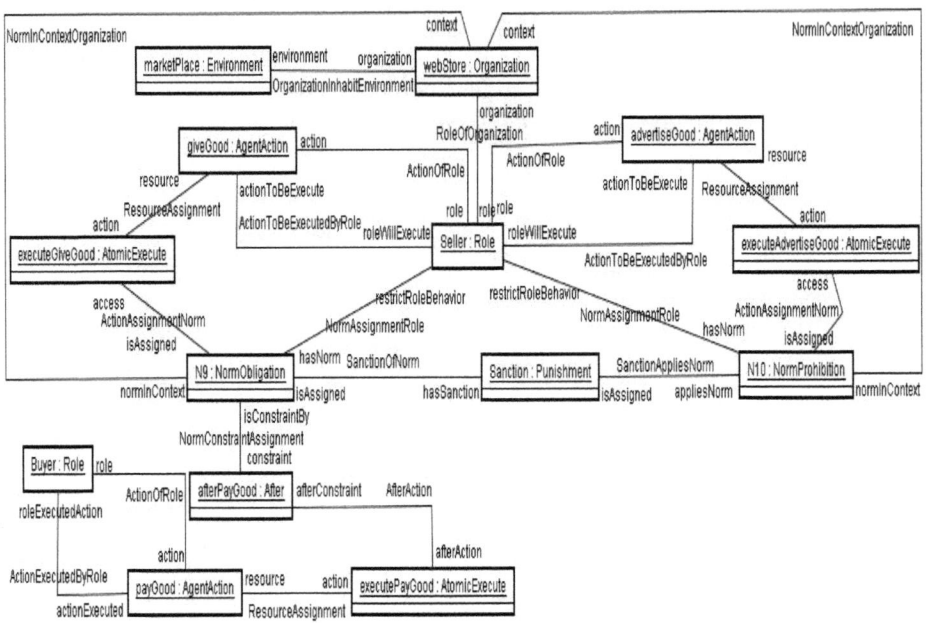

Fig. 9. Norm N9 and N10

6.3   Validating the Norms

The process of validating a norm encompasses two steps. First, the norm, as an instance of the NormML metamodel, is checked according to the invariants of the metamodel. The invariants check if the norm is well-formed according to the metamodel specification. The second step checks if any given two norms are in conflict. The current version of NormML has a set of operations described in OCL to check the invariants and conflicts of the norms[3].

6.3.1   Well-Formed Rules
Not all the norms that can be instantiated from the metamodel are well-formed. Below we describe two examples of well-formed rules of the NormML metamodel. Those were chosen since they represent rules that are related to the specification of the norms themselves and discuss some of the new elements included in the actual version of the language.

---

[3] The OCL operations are available at http://www.ic.uff.br/~kfigueiredo/normML/OCL.zip

WFR1. *The action to be executed by an entity that is defined in the before clause of a Between cannot also be defined in the after clause of such Between to be executed by the same entity in the same context.* If the actions in the before of a Between and in the after of a Between are the same, are related to the same entity (an agent, a role or an agent playing a role) and executed in the same context, this situation does not constitute a time period, but a moment in the time.

WFR2. *If the norm applied to an entity is constrained by an If whose condition is the value of an attribute, the entity of the norm must have permission to read this attribute.* The entity related to a norm that states an If constraint must be able to read the attribute associated with the constraint (by a permission of read or full access to the *Attribute* or to the *Entity* which the attribute belongs), otherwise the entity will not be capable of knowing when the norm is active.

6.3.2 Checking for Conflicts

After verifying the well-formedness of the norms, it is important to check if there are conflicts between the norms. As stated in Sections 2 and 6, a norm in NormML is composed of the following elements: *context, entities involved, deontic concept, actions, activation constraints* and *sanction*. Therefore, the checking for conflicts between two norms should consider the following situations related to these elements. In order to exemplify the checking for conflicts, let's consider norms N1 and N2 presented in Section. 4.

Context. (i) It is important to check for conflicts if the norms are defined in the same context; (ii) whenever a norm is defined in the context of an environment, it is necessary to check if the norms defined in the context of organizations that inhabit such an environment are in conflicts with the norms of the environment; and (iii) it is also important to check for conflicts between norms defined in the same hierarchy of organizations. *E.g. of case (i):* N1 is defined in the context of an environment and N2 is defined in the context of an organization that inhabits such an environment. Therefore, it is important to check if these norms are in conflicts. The operation below is able to check if an organization inhabits an environment.

```
context Organization::isInEnvironment(env:Environment):Boolean
body: self.environment=env
```

Entities Involved. It is necessary to check for conflicts: (i) between norms applied to the same entity; (ii) between a norm defined to a role and a norm defined to an agent that can play a role; (iii) between norms applied to different roles played by the same agent; (iv) between the norms applied to roles in a hierarchy of roles; and (v) between the norms of an organization and norms of the roles, agents and sub-organizations of this organization.

E.g. of case (ii): N1 is applied to all agents and N2 is applied to a given role that can be played by one of the agents. Since both norms are in related contexts and applied to related subjects, these two norms can be in conflict. The operation below can be used to check if there is an agent playing a role. If there is not any agent linked to the seller role, these norms are not in conflict.

```
context Role::isAgentPlayingRole():Boolean
body: self.agentPlayingRole->size()>0
```

Deontic Concept. Two norms may be in conflict if: (i) one norm states a permission and another states a prohibition; (ii) one norm states an obligation and another states a prohibition; and (iii) one norm states a permission and another one states an obligation in the period the permission is not activated. *E.g. of case (iii):* N1 states a prohibition and N2 states a permission applied to related subjects executing in related contexts. The operation below checks if two norms define deontic concepts that may characterize a conflict.

```
Context Set{Norm}::checkDeonticConcept
                              (n1:Norm,n2:Norm):Boolean
body: if((n1.oclIsTypeOf(NormProhibition))
                and (n2.oclIsTypeOf(NormObligation)))
then(true)
else(if((n1.oclIsTypeOf(NormProhibition))
                and (n2.oclIsTypeOf(NormPermission)))
    then(true)
    else(if((n1.oclIsTypeOf(NormObligation))
                and (n2.oclIsTypeOf(NormPermission)))
        then (true)
        else (false)endif)endif)endif
```

Actions. In case the deontic concepts of the norms are in one of the above situations, it is important to check for conflicts if: (i) the actions being regulated by the norms are of the same type on the same resource; (ii) one norm states an EntityRead, an EntityUpdate or an EntityFullAccess to one Entity and another one states an AtomicRead or an AtomicUpdate to the attributes or association ends of the same Entity; (iii) one norm states an EntityUpdate or an EntityFullAccess to one Entity and another one states an AtomicExecute to the methods of the same Entity; (iv) between an AttributeFullAccess and an AtomicRead or an AtomicUpdate to the same attribute of the same Entity; (v) between an AssociationEndFullAccess and an AtomicRead or an AtomicUpdate to the same association end of the same Association; (vi) between an AtomicRead and an AtomicUpdate to the same attribute of an Entity or the same association end of an Association, (vii) between an EntityRead and an EntityUpdate to the same Entity, and (viii) between a MessageFullAccess and a MessageSend or a MessageReceive to the same message.

Moreover, a special case needs to be considered: an AtomicCreate and an AtomicDelete to the same Entity may be in conflict if the deontic concepts associated with the norms are the same (contrasting to the cases mentioned in the previous item), i.e., if one norm states an obligation to create a particular Entity and another one states an obligation to delete the same Entity, these norms may be in conflict. The same is valid to prohibitions.

E.g. of case (iv): N1 regulates the reading and updating of an attribute and N2 regulates the reading of the same attribute of the same entity. Both norms can be in conflict since they are applied to related subjects, executing in related contexts and regulating related actions. The operation below checks if a norm is restricting the reading and updating (i.e., fullAccess) of an attribute and if the other is restricting the reading of an attribute.

```
context Set{Norm}::checkAttributeFullAccessAndRead
                            (n1:Norm,n2:Norm):Boolean
body: if((n1.access.oclIsTypeOf(AttributeFullAccess))
                and(n2.access.oclIsTypeOf(AttributeRead))))
then (true)      else (false)endif
```

Activation Constraints. Finally, two norms may be in conflict if: (i) the periods established by the invariants Before, After, Between (considering the actions and dates associated) and If (considering the dates associated) intersect, or (ii) in case of two If conditions, the values related to the same attribute intersects (e.g.: x>10 and x=15). *E.g. of case (v):* N1 and N2 are defined in time periods that intersects because N1 is always activated, i.e., it is not restricted to any condition. The operation below checks if one of the norms is not constrained to any period of time.

```
context Norm::isConstrained():Boolean
body: self.constraint->size()>0
```

N1 and N2 are in conflict because both norms are applied to related subjects, executing in related context, regulating related actions and defined in time periods that intersects. Similarly, norms N5 and N7 presented in Section 4 are also in conflict if the buyer violates N4 and after it fulfills N6. The current version of NormML is able to check the conflicts between the norms by using a set of operations described in OCL that verifies each case described in this section.

7 Conclusion and Future Work

We have presented the main elements that compose a norm and discussed how several MAS modeling languages and the notations provide by methodologies and organizational models give support to the modeling of these elements and to the checking of conflicts between norms. And we also have emphasized the contributions of the normative modeling language NormML when compared with other modeling languages and notations used by methodologies and organization models.

With the preliminary version of NormML [2] it was possible (i) to model permissions, prohibitions and obligations; (ii) to regulate the behavior of agents and roles; (iii) to define norms that restrict the execution of non-dialogical actions; (iv) to define activation constraints based on the execution of actions. By using the current version of NormML it is also possible (i) to model norms associated with different contexts; (ii) to regulate the behavior of groups of individuals (or organizations); (iii) to define norms that restrict the execution of dialogical actions; (iv) to define activation constraints based on the definition of deadlines and predicates (values associated with attributes); and (v) to define sanctions associated with the norms. We are in the process of extending the language to define norms that restrict the achievement of states.

The language also gives support to the checking of conflicts among norms. In order to do so, we have used EOS, a Java component which implements OCL2.0 evaluation on model scenarios [37]. The NormML metamodel was described as a UML class diagram together with its operations that implement the conflict rules. Norms are modeled as instances in object diagrams that are validated by executing the operations over such diagrams.

In this paper we focus on the modeling of the static aspects of the norms. However, it is our intension to define a sequence diagram for NormML to describe the sequence of the executed actions. By using such diagram it will be possible to: (i) represent dynamic aspects as the creation, cancellation and delegation of a norm; (ii) define norms in an interaction context; (iii) check conflicts that depend on the sequence of the executed actions; and (iv) identify the norms that are active and the ones that were violated. It is also our aim to develop a graphical tool for modeling and validating norms using NormML.

References

1. López y López, F.: Social power and norms: impact on agent behavior. PhD thesis, Univ. of Southampton, Department of Electronics and Computer Science (2003)
2. Silva, V., Braga, C., Figueiredo, K.: A Modeling Language to Model Norms. In: De Vos, M., et al. (eds.) COIN 2010. LNCS (LNAI), vol. 6541, pp. 39–57. Springer, Heidelberg (2011)
3. Aldewereld, H., Dignum, F., Garcia-Camino, A., Noriega, P., Rodriguez-Aguilar, J., Sierra, C.: Operationalisation of norms for usage in electronic institutions. In: Proc. 5th AAMAS, pp. 223–225 (2006)
4. Cranefield, S.: Modelling and monitoring social expectations in multi-agent systems. In: Noriega, P., Vázquez-Salceda, J., Boella, G., Boissier, O., Dignum, V., Fornara, N., Matson, E. (eds.) COIN 2006. LNCS (LNAI), vol. 4386, pp. 308–321. Springer, Heidelberg (2007)
5. García-Camino, A., Noriega, P., Rodríguez-Aguilar, J.: Implementing norms in electronic institutions. In: Proc. 4th AAMAS, pp. 667–673. ACM Press, New York (2005)
6. Garcia-Ojeda, J., DeLoach, S., Robby, O., Valenzuela, J.: O-maSE: A customizable approach to developing multiagent development processes. In: Luck, M., Padgham, L. (eds.) AOSE VIII. LNCS, vol. 4951, pp. 1–15. Springer, Heidelberg (2008)
7. Governatori, G., Rotolo, A.: Defeasible logic: Agency, intention and obligation. In: Lomuscio, A., Nute, D. (eds.) DEON 2004. LNCS (LNAI), vol. 3065, pp. 114–128. Springer, Heidelberg (2004)
8. Lomuscio, A., Sergot, M.: A formalization of violation, error recovery, and enforcement in the bit transmission problem. Journal of Applied Logic 2(1), 93–116 (2004)
9. López y López, F., Luck, M., d'Inverno, M.: Constraining autonomy through norms. In: Proceedings of the 1st AAMAS, pp. 674–681. ACM Press, New York (2002)
10. Silva, V.: From the specification to the implementation of norms: an automatic approach to generate rules from norms to govern the behaviour of agents. In: IJAAMAS, Special Issue on Norms in Multi-Agent Systems, pp. 113–155 (2008)
11. Vasconcelos, W., Kollingbaum, M. and Norman, T.: Resolving conflict and inconsistency in norm-regulated virtual organizations. In Proc. AAMAS 2007 (2007)
12. Meyer, J.J., Wieringa, R.J.: Deontic logic in computer science: normative system specification. John Wiley and Sons, Chichester (1991)
13. Odell, J., Parunak, H., Bauer, B.: Extending UML for agents. In: Proc. Agent-Oriented Information Systems Workshop at National Conf. of AI, pp. 3–17 (2000)
14. Choren, R., Lucena, C.: The ANote Modeling Language for Agent-Oriented Specification. In: Choren, R., Garcia, A., Lucena, C., Romanovsky, A. (eds.) SELMAS 2004. LNCS, vol. 3390, pp. 198–212. Springer, Heidelberg (2005)
15. Caire, G., Coulier, W., Garijo, F., Gomez, J., Pavon, J., Leal, F., Chainho, P., Kearney, P., Stark, J., Evans, R., Massonet, P.: Agent Oriented Analysis Using Message/UML. In: Wooldridge, M.J., Weiß, G., Ciancarini, P. (eds.) AOSE 2001. LNCS, vol. 2222, pp. 119–135. Springer, Heidelberg (2002)
16. Danc, J.: Formal specification of AML. Department of Computer Science, Comenius University, Master's Thesis (2008)

17. Wagner, G.: The Agent-Object-Relationship meta-model: towards a unified view of state and behavior. Information Systems, 475–504 (2003)
18. Zambonelli, F., Jennings, N.R., Wooldridge, M.J.: Developing multiagent systems: the Gaia methodology. ACM TSEM, 417–470 (2003)
19. Cossentino, M.: From requirements to code with the PASSI methodology. In: Agent-oriented Methods, pp. 79–106. Idea group, USA (2005)
20. Padgham, L., Winikoff, M.: Developing intelligent agent systems: a practical guide, 225 pages. John Wiley and Sons, Chichester (2004)
21. Juan, T., Pierce, A., Sterling, L.: ROADMAP: extending the Gaia methodology for complex open systems. In: Proc. 1st AAMAS, pp. 3–10 (2002)
22. Giorgini, P., Mouratidis, H., Zannone, N.: Modelling security and trust with Secure Tropos. In: Integrating Security Soft. Eng.: Advances and Future Vision (2006)
23. Zhang, S.-W.: SODA: Societies and infrastructures in the analysis and design of agent-based systems. In: Ciancarini, P., Wooldridge, M.J. (eds.) AOSE 2000. LNCS, vol. 1957, pp. 185–193. Springer, Heidelberg (2001)
24. Ferber, J., Stratulat, T., Tranier, J.: Towards an integral approach of organizations: the MASQ approach in multi-agent systems. In: Multi-agent Systems: Semantics and Dynamics of Organizational Models. IGI (2009)
25. Hübner, J.F., Sichman, J.S., Olivier, B.: A model for the structural, functional, and deontic specification of organizations in multiagent systems. In: Bittencourt, G., Ramalho, G.L. (eds.) SBIA 2002. LNCS (LNAI), vol. 2507, pp. 118–128. Springer, Heidelberg (2002)
26. Dignum, V.: A model for organizational interaction: based on agents, founded in logic. PhD dissertation, Universiteit Utrecht, SIKS dissertation series 2004-1 (2004)
27. Molesini, A., Denti, E., Omicini, A.: RBAC-MAS & SODA: experimenting RBAC in AOSE engineering societies in the agents world. In: Artikis, A., Picard, G., Vercouter, L. (eds.) ESAW 2008. LNCS, vol. 5485, pp. 69–84. Springer, Heidelberg (2009)
28. Oren, N., Luck, M., Miles, S., Norman, T.J.: An argumentation inspired heuristic for resolving normative conflict. In: Proc. of Workshop COIN at AAMAS, pp. 41–56 (2008)
29. Kagal, L., Finin, T.: Modeling Conversation Policies using Permissions and Obligations. In: van Eijk, R., Huget, M., Dignum, F. (eds.) AC 2004. LNCS (LNAI), vol. 3396, pp. 120–133. Springer, Heidelberg (2005)
30. García-Camino, A., Noriega, P., Rodríguez-Aguilar, J.A.: An Algorithm for Confict Resolution in Regulated Compound Activities. In: O'Hare, G.M.P., Ricci, A., O'Grady, M.J., Dikenelli, O. (eds.) ESAW 2006. LNCS (LNAI), vol. 4457, pp. 193–208. Springer, Heidelberg (2007)
31. Silva, V., Choren, R., Lucena, C.: MAS-ML: a multi-agent system modelling language. In: IJAOSE, Modeling Lang. for Agent Systems, pp. 382–421 (2008)
32. Ferraiolo, D.F., Kuhn, D.R., Chandramouli, R.: Role-based access control, 2nd edn. Artech House Publishers, Boston (2007)
33. Basin, D., Doser, J., Lodderstedt, T.: Model driven security: from UML models to access control infrastructures. ACM TSEM, 39–91 (2006)
34. Clavel, M., Silva, V., Braga, C., Egea, M.: Model-driven security in practice: An industrial experience. In: Schieferdecker, I., Hartman, A. (eds.) ECMDA-FA 2008. LNCS, vol. 5095, pp. 326–337. Springer, Heidelberg (2008)
35. Basin, D., Clavel, M., Doser, J., Egea, M.: Automated analysis of security-design models. Inf. Software Technology, 815–831 (2009)
36. Object Management Group: OCL Specification, OMG, http://www.omg.org/docs/ptc/03-10-14.pdf (accessed: May 1, 2010)
37. EOS, http://maude.sip.ucm.es/eos/ (accessed: May 1, 2010)

Building Reputation-Based Agreements: Collective Opinions as Information Sources*

Roberto Centeno[1], Ramón Hermoso[1], and Viviane Torres da Silva[2]

[1] Centre for Intelligent Information Technology (CETINIA),
University Rey Juan Carlos, Madrid, Spain
[2] Universidade Federal Fluminense (UFF), Rio de Janeiro, Brazil
{roberto.centeno,ramon.hermoso}@urjc.es,
viviane.silva@ic.uff.br

Abstract. Reputation mechanisms, which can be used in organisational environments, have been developed during last few years as valid methods to allow agents to better select their partners. In most of works presented in the literature, reputation is summarised as a value, typically a number, that represents an opinion sent by an agent to another about a certain third party. In this work, we put forward a novel concept of *reputation-based agreement* in order to support the reputation definition, as well as, some desirable properties about it. We define a reputation service that collects opinions from agents, so creating *agreements* over *situations*. This service will also be in charge of presenting the information by using different *informative mechanisms*. On the other hand, we analyse how to enforce agents to send their opinions to the reputation service by adding *incentive mechanisms*. Finally, two different case studies are presented to exemplify our work.

Keywords: Agreement, Reputation, Organisation, Trust.

1 Introduction

Reputation mechanisms have been proved to be successful methods to build multi-agent systems where agents' decision-making processes to select partners are crucial for the system functioning [5][6][12]. In models such as in [6][12] the authors focus on letting the agent the duty of requesting opinions, aggregating replies and inferring conclusions from the gathered information. Although reputation gathering process from the agent's point of view is an important issue, in this work we propose a complementary approach that endows organisations with a reputation service that may help agents to make decisions when their own information is scarce.

* The present work has been partially funded by the Spanish Ministry of Education and Science under project TIN2006-14630-C03-02 (FPI grants program) and TIN2009-13839-C03-02 and by the Spanish project "Agreement Technologies" (CONSOLIDER CSD2007-0022, INGENIO 2010).

M. De Vos et al. (Eds.): COIN 2010 International Workshops, LNAI 6541, pp. 58–76, 2011.
© Springer-Verlag Berlin Heidelberg 2011

In this paper we introduce the concept of *reputation-based agreement* as the cornerstone of the reputation service in an organisational multi-agent system. An *agreement* is usually defined as a meeting of minds between two or more parties, about their relative duties and rights regarding current or future performance. Around this concept new paradigms have emerged [1][2] aimed at increasing the reliability and performance of agents in organisations by introducing in such communities these well-known human social mechanisms. With this in mind, we propose a novel approach for the meaning of reputation. From a global point of view, a *reputation-based agreement* is a meeting point on the behaviour of an agent, participating within an organisation, with regard to its reputation. Agreements are evaluated by aggregating opinions sent by participants about the behaviour of agents. Notice that this notion of agreement bases on a passive process instead of on an active one, since agreement is reached without any dialogue among agents, but with the opinions gathered from them. We also define some properties that describe different types of agreements. Besides, information about reached agreements will be provided to agents by using the concept of informative mechanism [3].

The second part of the paper tackles the problem of how to make agents to collaborate sending their opinions to the reputation service in a pro-active manner. We will examine the concept of incentive mechanism [3] as a way of manipulating participants, in order to get more collaboration sending their opinions about different situations they have been involved in.

The paper is organised as follows: Section 2 formalises the reputation service, supported by the idea of reputation-based agreements. In Section 3 we illustrate all concepts introduced by means of a case study. Section 4 puts forward an incentive mechanism that enforces agents to collaborate with the reputation service. Section 5 elaborates a second case study using an incentive mechanism to enforce agents to collaborate sending their opinions to the reputation service. Section 6 discusses some related work and, finally, Section 7 summarises the paper and presents the future work.

2   A Service Based on Reputation-Based Agreements

As we have previously pointed out, the current work faces with the task of formalising a reputation service working on organisational multi-agent systems. It is motivated because the reputation of an agent participating within an organisation varies as consequence of its behaviour with regard to the norms of such a system. That is, the violation of norms within an organisation affects the reputation of an agent. We adhere the definition of organisation given in [4]. Summarising, an organisation is defined as a tuple $\langle \mathcal{Ag}, \mathcal{A}, \mathcal{X}, \phi, x_0, \varphi, \{\mathcal{ON}^{om}, \mathcal{R}^{om}\}\rangle$ where $\mathcal{Ag}$ represents the set of agents participating within the organisation; $\mathcal{A}$ is the set of actions agents can perform; $\mathcal{X}$ stands for the environmental states space; ϕ is a function describing how the system evolves as a result of agents actions; x_0 represents the initial state of the system; φ is the agents' capability function describing the actions agents are able to perform in a given state of

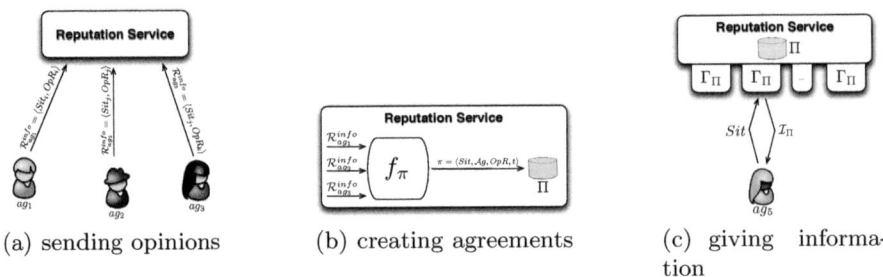

(a) sending opinions   (b) creating agreements   (c) giving information

Fig. 1. Dynamics of the Reputation Service

the environment; $\mathcal{ON}^{om}$ is an organisational mechanism based on organisational norms; and $\mathcal{R}^{om}$ is an organisational mechanism based on roles that defines the positions agents may enact in the organisation (see [4] for more details).

By introducing a reputation mechanism in an organization regulated by norms that may have its own sanctioning mechanism, we are proposing a complementary decentralized sanctioning mechanism implemented by each agent in the organization. The agent is able to evaluate the behavior of its partners according to the norms they violate and to its own opinion about the importance of complying with such norms. The reputations are the results of such evaluation and are used by each agent to sanction their partners according to their own will.

2.1 How Agents Send Their Opinions

During an agent lifetime within an organisation, it is involved in several different *situations*. A situation is defined as a tuple $\langle \mathcal{Ag}, \mathcal{R}, \mathcal{A}, \mathcal{T} \rangle$, that represents an agent $\mathcal{Ag}$, playing the role $\mathcal{R}$, while performing the action $\mathcal{A}$, through a time period $\mathcal{T}$. As detailed in [4], different types of situations can be defined following this definition. For instance, situations in which an agent performs an action, regardless of the role it is playing – $\langle \mathcal{Ag}, \_, \mathcal{A}, \mathcal{T} \rangle$ –, or situations in which an agent is playing a role during a time period, regardless the action it performs – $\langle \mathcal{Ag}, \mathcal{R}, \_, \mathcal{T} \rangle$. Agents usually evaluate those situations in order to compile reliable information that allows them to predict the result of future situations. The rationale of the current work is that if agents share their knowledge about the situations they are involved in, this information might be useful when other agents have not enough information to select partners to interact with. This problem becomes hard when new participants join an organisation and they do not have not strong opinions yet.

Situations are evaluated from an agent's individual point of view. Thus, an evaluation may reflect the experience of the agent performing the evaluation – direct way – or the opinions provided by third parties about the evaluated situation – indirect way.

At any time, an agent can send its opinion about a particular situation to the reputation service. We call this information *reputation information message*:

Definition 1. *A reputation information message $\mathcal{R}_{ag_i \in \mathcal{Ag}}^{info}$ is a tuple, representing an opinion sent by the agent ag_i to the reputation service containing an evaluation about a particular situation:*

$$\mathcal{R}_{ag_i}^{info} = \langle Sit_{ag_i}, N_{ag_i}, OpR_{ag_i} \rangle,$$

where ag_i stands for the agent which sends the opinion; Sit_{ag_i} is the situation being evaluated by ag_i; N_{ag_i} states the set of norms violated by the partner and reported by ag_i, and OpR_{ag_i} represents ag_i's opinion about the behaviour of its partner in the situation (typically a number). The set of norms violated are used to justify the evaluation of the agent behaviour, i.e., it represents the reasons for such evaluation. Therefore, an agent, by using this kind of messages, is somehow making public its opinions – evaluations – about different situations: agents, roles, etc.

2.2   Creating Reputation-Based Agreements

In this section we intend to face the task of giving a novel approach for the meaning of reputation tackling this concept as a partial agreement about a certain situation. When the reputation service receives reputation information messages from agents, it aggregates them creating what we have called *reputation-based agreements*. That is, the aggregation of all the opinions regarding a particular situation is 'per se' what a set of agents – as a whole – actually think about the aforesaid situation. Thus, a reputation-based agreement represents the consensus reached in the reputation opinions space sent by a set of agents about a particular situation.

Definition 2. *A reputation-based agreement π for a particular situation, is a tuple:*

$$\pi = \langle Sit, \mathcal{Ag}, N, OpR, t \rangle$$

where:

- Sit is the situation about the agreement is reached;
- $\mathcal{Ag}$ is the set of agents that contributed to the agreement;
- N is the set of all norms reported by the agents that contributed to the agreement: $N = \{N_{ag_1}, ..., N_{ag_n}\}$ where $ag_i \in \mathcal{Ag}$;
- OpR represents the opinion rating – whatever its representation is (qualitative, quantitative, etc.) – reached as a consequence of all opinions sent about Sit;
- t stands for the time when the agreement was reached.

Therefore, an agreement means a global opinion that a set of agents have on a certain situation. This agreement, as we put forward in the next section, can be used as a generalist expectation for a situation in which agents have no (or little) previous information about.

As we have claimed, a reputation-based agreement is reached as consequence of the aggregation of all opinions sent about a particular situation. Thus, the

reputation service requires a function that is able to aggregate information reputation messages sent by agents. The aim of such a function is to create agreements
from reputation opinions that agents send to the service by means of reputation
information messages. We formally define the function as follows:

Definition 3. *Let f_π be a function that given all the reputation information
messages sent by agents and a particular situation creates a reputation-based
agreement for that situation:*

$$f_\pi : |\mathcal{R}^{info}_{ag_i \in Ag}| \times Sit \to \Pi$$

where:

- $|\mathcal{R}^{info}_{ag_i \in Ag}|$ stands for the set of reputation information messages received by
  the reputation service;
- Sit is the set of situations;
- Π represents the set of reputation-based agreements.

Some desirable characteristics should be taken into account when a function
is designed. Therefore, we propose the following guidelines:

- an agreement about a situation should be updated when new reputation
  information messages are sent to the reputation service about the same situation;
- the function should take into account the temporality of the messages received, that is, two opinions should not have the same importance if they
  were sent in different moments;
- when an agreement about a specific situation is being created, the function should also consider opinions about a more general situation. Let us
  illustrate it by an example. If a reputation-based agreement is being created about the situation $\langle Harry, seller, sellingShoes, t \rangle$, the function should
  take into account opinions about situations such as: $\langle Harry, seller, \_, t \rangle$ or
  $\langle Harry, \_, \_, t \rangle$.

Following these guidelines the reputation service might use any function that
is able to aggregate values. It could use a simple function to calculate the average
of all opinions, or a more elaborated one that aggregates the opinions by means
of complex calculation, i.e., weighting the assessment by taking into account who
is giving the information.

2.3   Reputation-Based Agreements: Properties

From previous definitions (2 and 3) it is possible to define some desirable properties about reputation-based agreements. These properties should be taken into
account when agreements are created and may also provide useful extra information when informing about different issues.

Property 1. *A reputation-based agreement π is **complete** iff all agents participating in an organisation, at time t, contribute to reach that agreement:*

$$\pi^* \Leftrightarrow \begin{cases} \mathcal{O} = \langle \mathcal{Ag}, \mathcal{A}, \mathcal{X}, \phi, x_0, \varphi, \{\mathcal{ON}^{om}, \mathcal{R}^{om}\} \rangle \; \wedge \\ \pi = \langle Sit, \mathcal{Ag}', N, OpR, t \rangle \quad \wedge \\ (\mathcal{Ag} = \mathcal{Ag}') \end{cases}$$

That is, given a time t every participant $ag \in \mathcal{Ag}$ in the organisation $\mathcal{O}$ has necessarily sent a reputation information message indicating its opinion about the situation concerning the agreement ($\mathcal{Ag} = \mathcal{Ag}'$). More complete agreements mean more reliable the information in the system.

Property 2. *A reputation-based agreement π is α-**consistent** iff. the reputation value of π differs, at most, $1 - \alpha$ from the reputation value sent by every agent that contributed to reach that agreement:*

$$\pi^\alpha \Leftrightarrow \begin{cases} \pi = \langle Sit, \mathcal{Ag}, N, OpR, t \rangle \quad \wedge \\ \forall ag_i \in \mathcal{Ag} \; [\forall r \in Rep_{ag_i}^{info}[(r = \langle Sit_{ag_i}, N_{ag_i}, OpR_{ag_i} \rangle) \; \wedge \\ (Sit_{ag_i} = Sit) \; \wedge \; (|OpR_{ag_i} - OpR| \leq 1 - \alpha)]] \end{cases}$$

This property represents how agents sending their opinions about a situation agree in a certain extent. Therefore, the higher α is, the more similar the opinions are.

Property 3. *A reputation-based agreement π is β-**norm consistent** iff. the difference between size of union set of those norms reported by agents involved in π and the intersection set of sets of norms reported by each agent over the union of all norms in π is 1-β.*

$$\pi^\beta \Leftrightarrow \begin{cases} \pi = \langle Sit, \mathcal{Ag}, N, OpR, t \rangle \quad \wedge \\[2mm] ag_i \in \mathcal{Ag} \; \wedge \; N_{ag_i} \in N \; \wedge \\[2mm] \dfrac{|\bigcup\limits_{ag_i} N_{ag_i}| - |\bigcap\limits_{ag_i} N_{ag_i}|}{|\bigcup\limits_{ag_i} N_{ag_i}|} = (1 - \beta) \end{cases}$$

It means that if β is 1 then the agent whose behaviour is being evaluated has exactly violated the same set of norms when participating in the very same situation with different partners. This property is rather than important when an agent wants to know if the behaviour of its future partner in a given situation is usually the same or if it is unpredictable. The latter would be totally unpredictable in the case in which β is 0.

Property 4. *A reputation-based agreement π is **partially-full** iff it is complete and 1-consistent:*

$$\pi^\phi \Leftrightarrow (\pi^* \; \wedge \; \pi^\alpha \; \wedge \; \alpha = 1)$$

In the case α is 1 every agent has the very same opinion about a given situation.

Property 5. *A reputation-based agreement π is **full** iff. it is complete, 1-consistent and 1-normConsistent:*

$$\pi^{\phi} \Leftrightarrow (\pi^{*} \ \wedge \ \pi^{\alpha} \ \wedge \ \alpha = 1 \ \wedge \ \pi^{\beta} \ \wedge \ \beta = 1)$$

In the case α is 1 and β is 1 all agents have the same opinion about a given situation and the agent whose behaviour is being evaluated has violated exactly the same norms. Note that, $\beta = 1$ does not implies $\alpha = 1$ since different agents can evaluate exactly the same behaviour (i.e., the same set of norms have been violated in the same situation) in different ways.

This property is very desirable when seeking reputation-based agreements, because (i) the more agents contribute to the agreement, the stronger validity the latter gets, and (ii) the more similar is the behaviour of the agent when interacting with different partner, the more predictable it is. Thus, the likelihood of capturing what is actually happening in the organisation tends to be higher.

Property 6. *A reputation-based agreement π is $\mathcal{R}$-**consistent** iff all the agents participating in the agreement play the same role in the system:*

$$\pi_{\mathcal{R}} = \langle Sit, \mathcal{Ag}, N, OpR, t \rangle \Leftrightarrow \forall ag_i \in \mathcal{Ag} \ play(ag_i, \mathcal{R})$$

where $\mathcal{R}$ stands for the role the consistency is based on, $\mathcal{Ag}$ is the set of agents that contribute to reach the agreement, and $play : \mathcal{Ag} \times \mathcal{R} \rightarrow [true, false]$ is a function that returns *true* if the agent $\mathcal{Ag}$ plays the role $\mathcal{R}$.

This property is useful in cases in which a new agent, joining an organisation, wants to know what other agents – that are executing in the organisation and playing the same role – think about a given situation. For instance, someone who is thinking of *buying* something would like to know which are the opinions of those who have previously played the role *buyer*.

Property 7. *A reputation-based agreement π is $\mathcal{R}$-**complete** iff it is $\mathcal{R}$-consistent and is complete for all the agents that play the role $\mathcal{R}$ at time t:*

$$\pi_{\mathcal{R}}^{*} = \langle Sit, \mathcal{Ag}', N, OpR, t \rangle \Leftrightarrow \begin{cases} \pi_{\mathcal{R}} \wedge \mathcal{O} = \langle \mathcal{Ag}, \mathcal{A}, \mathcal{X}, \phi, x_0, \varphi, \{\mathcal{ON}^{om}, \mathcal{R}^{om}\} \rangle \wedge \\ \forall ag \in \mathcal{Ag} \ (play(ag, \mathcal{R}) \rightarrow ag \in \mathcal{Ag}') \end{cases}$$

Property 8. *A reputation-based agreement π is $\mathcal{R}$-**full** iff it is $\mathcal{R}$-complete and is 1-consistent:*

$$\pi_{\mathcal{R}}^{\phi} \Leftrightarrow (\pi_{\mathcal{R}}^{*} \ \wedge \ \pi^{\alpha} \ \wedge \ \alpha = 1)$$

Although properties 1 and 5 are desirable, they are not achievable in systems that have a significant number of agents, for instance, in electronic marketplaces. However, many systems have those properties, such as closed organisational systems where the number of participants is not huge.

2.4   Providing Information About Reputation-Based Agreements

Once we have defined an agreement as a distributed consensus-based expectation for a set of agents on a certain situation, we now describe how the reputation service can present the relevant information about the reached agreements to the agents participating in the organisation. Reputation-based agreements somehow capture the general thinking about a particular situation – the more α-consistent the agreement is the more reliable it is. Thus, information about the agreements reached until that moment may be very useful for agents. In particular, when agents have recently joined the organisation, they do not have any hint about situations in which they might be involved in, so if the reputation service provides information about agreements, agents may improve their utility from the very beginning.

With this in mind, we deal with the problem of how the reputation service may provide such information. To that end, we part from the notion of *informative mechanism* [3]. Those types of mechanisms are in charge of providing some kind of information to agents in order to regulate a multi-agent system. Thus, an *informative mechanism* $\Gamma : S' \times X' \to I$ is a function that given a partial description of an internal state of an agent (S') and, taking into account the partial view that the service has of the current environmental state (X'), provides certain information (I). We formally define them as follows:

Definition 4. *An informative mechanism providing information about reputation-based agreements is:*

$$\Gamma_\Pi : Sit \times X' \to I_\Pi$$

where Sit and X' are already defined and I_Π stands for the information provided by the mechanism by using the set of agreements Π reached over the situation Sit.

We have chosen a very general definition of information in order to cover all possible types of information the reputation service could offer taking into account the reputation-based agreements reached. The information provided may consist of (i) a ranking sorting the best agents for a particular situation, such as $\langle \_, \mathcal{R}, \mathcal{A}, \_ \rangle$, created from the agreements reached for that situation, (ii) a value representing the reputation value for a situation plus the reasons (i.e., the set of norms violated), reached as a consequence of the agreement for that situation, (iii) an information about the properties of the agreement reached for a particular situation, if it is full, complete, etc.

Notice that we consider agents as rational entities capable of choosing which informative mechanisms to ask for information depending of, e.g. its own preferences or basing on past requests.

3   Case Study: Pubs Area

In this section, we illustrate the proposed model by means of a simple case study. The scenario we use involves five different agents: *Anna, John, Jessica, Albert* and *Harry* participating within an organisation. In this organisation agents can *order* and *delivery* drinks, so the action space of agents is composed of actions such as, *order-1000-drink-a, delivery-2000-drink-b*, where a and b represent the type of the drink agents order/deliver. That organisation is created with the aim of getting in touch pubs' owners and providers of drinks. Thus, agents join the organisation playing the roles of *pub* and *provider*, representing a pub's owner and a company provider of drinks, respectively. In our particular example, agents are playing the following roles: *Anna - pub, John - pub, Jessica - pub, Albert - provider* and *Harry - provider*.

In this scenario, agents representing pubs' owners are interested in collaborating by sharing information about providers. The pubs are situated in the same area and they collaborate with each other so as to foster the attraction customers to that area. That is, although they try to maximise their own benefits, one of their goals is to foster the pubs area where they are, even if that entails to exchange information about drink providers.

Therefore, after several interactions among them – performing actions of ordering and delivering different types of drinks – *Anna* decides to make public her opinion about *Albert* and *Harry* as providers. Thus, she uses the reputation information messages to send to the reputation service her opinions, as follows:

$$\mathcal{R}_{Anna}^{info} = \langle\langle Albert, provider, \_, \_\rangle, \{N_a, N_b\}, 0.2\rangle$$
$$\mathcal{R}_{Anna}^{info} = \langle\langle Harry, provider, \_, \_\rangle, \{N_c\}, 0.9\rangle$$

This information shows that *Anna* has had bad experiences while she was ordering drinks from *Albert* (0.2)[1] because *Albert* always delivers all drinks later than the agreed date (violating norm N_a) and frequently forget to delivery part of the drinks ordered (violating norm N_b). Otherwise, the second message shows that she has had good experiences with *Harry* (0.9) because *Harry*, for instance, never violates contracts and offers low prices. Similarly, *John* and *Jessica* send their opinions about *Albert* and *Harry* as providers, by using the following messages:

$$\mathcal{R}_{John}^{info} = \langle\langle Albert, provider, \_, \_\rangle, \{N_a, N_b\}, 0.2\rangle$$
$$\mathcal{R}_{John}^{info} = \langle\langle Harry, provider, \_, \_\rangle, \{N_c\}, 0.8\rangle$$
$$\mathcal{R}_{Jessica}^{info} = \langle\langle Albert, provider, \_, \_\rangle, \{N_a, N_d\}, 0.2\rangle$$

On the one hand, it seems that both *John* and *Jessica* agree that *Albert* is not a reliable provider. However, they partially disagree about the reasons represented by the different sets of norms reported. On the other hand, *Harry* is quite reliable delivering drinks, from *John*'s point of view.

When the reputation service receives this information, it is able to create reputation-based agreements by using a function that aggregates the reputation information messages. Let us suppose that it aggregates the messages by calculating the average of reputation values sent by agents over exactly the same situation and by putting together all the reported violated norms[2]:

$$f_\pi(Sit) = \frac{\sum_{i=1}^{n} \mathcal{R}_{ag_i}^{info} = \langle Sit, N_{ag_i}, OpR_{ag_i}\rangle}{n}$$

---

[1] We suppose that reputation values – denoted by OpR – are in the range $[0..1]$.
[2] It could be used whatever other function that is able to aggregate the information received from agents.

Therefore, from the set of messages sent by the agents, so far, the reputation service can create two reputation-based agreements regarding two different situations:

$$\pi_1 =$$
$$\langle\langle Albert, provider, \_, \_\rangle, \{Anna, John, Jessica\}, 0.2, \{\{N_a, N_b\}, \{N_a, N_b\}, \{N_a, N_c\}\}, t\rangle$$
$$\pi_2 = \langle\langle Harry, provider, \_, \_\rangle, \{Anna, John\}, \{\{N_c\}, \{N_c\}\}, 0.85, t\rangle$$

π_1 represents that there exists an agreement within the organisation regarding to *Albert* as *provider* – regardless the action he performs – is evaluated as 0.2, and such an agreement is reached by the collaboration of *Anna, John* and *Jessica*, at time t. Besides, π_2 shows that there exists an agreement in which Harry is evaluated 0.85 – it is calculated as the mean of all opinions sent – as *provider* and that the agreement is reached by *Anna* and *John*, at time t.

In order to provide information about agreements the reputation service offers following different informative mechanisms:

- $\Gamma_\Pi^1(\langle Ag, \mathcal{R}, \_, \_\rangle)$ given a situation where an agent and a role are specified, it returns the meta-information about the *consistency* of the agreement reached regarding that situation;
- $\Gamma_\Pi^2(\langle Ag, \mathcal{R}, \_, \_\rangle)$ given a situation where an agent and a role are specified, it returns the reputation-based agreement reached. In particular, it returns the reputation value in the agreement of that situation;
- $\Gamma_\Pi^3(\langle \_, \mathcal{R}, \_, \_\rangle)$ given a situation where a role is specified, it returns a ranking of agents playing that role, sorted by the reputation value they have as consequence of the reputation-based agreements reached until the current time t.
- $\Gamma_\Pi^4(\langle Ag, \mathcal{R}, \_, \_\rangle)$ given a situation where an agent and a role are specified, it returns the meta-information about the *norm consistency* of the agreement reached regarding that situation;

Let us suppose that a new pub is opened in the same area by *Alice*, so she joins the organisation playing the role *pub*. Since the pub is recently open, she needs to order drinks. Thus, she should select a provider of drinks but she does not know any provider yet. One solution could be asking to another agent about a particular provider – distributed reputation mechanism. However, this process could be very costly because she would require many queries sent to different agents to ask about different providers. Another solution is to use informative mechanisms to get information about other participants, in this case about providers. Thus, *Alice* searches for an informative mechanism that provides a ranking of "best" providers[3]. She finds Γ_Π^3 that returns a ranking of agreements when it is queried based on a situation and a role. So, *Alice* performs the following query to Γ_Π^3: $\Gamma_\Pi^3(\langle \_, provider, \_, \_\rangle) \Rightarrow \{Harry, Albert\}$ and the informative mechanism returns a ranking of agents, sorted by the reputation values according to

---

[3] We suppose that informative mechanisms are publicly available to all participants within the organisation.

all reputation-based agreements reached at that moment, by matching the situation specified in the query with the situation of agreements. By using this information *Alice* knows that there exists an agreement within the organisation showing that *Harry* is a better provider than *Albert*. But, how good are they? To answer this question *Alice* queries the informative mechanism Γ_{Π}^2 as follows:

$$\Gamma_{\Pi}^2(\langle Harry, provider, \_, \_\rangle) \Rightarrow 0.85$$
$$\Gamma_{\Pi}^2(\langle Albert, provider, \_, \_\rangle) \Rightarrow 0.2$$

In that moment, *Alice* is quite sure that *Harry* is much better provider than *Albert* and there exists an agreement, within the organisation, that *Harry*'s reputation delivering drinks is 0.85 and another one that *Albert* as provider is 0.2. However, *Alice* is still doubting about which provider could be the best, because she is wondering how consistent those agreements are. Thus, she queries the informative mechanism that provides the α-meta-information about the agreement reached regarding a given situation. Therefore, she performs the following queries:

$$\Gamma_{\Pi}^1(\langle Harry, provider, \_, \_\rangle) \Rightarrow \pi^{0.95}$$
$$\Gamma_{\Pi}^1(\langle Albert, provider, \_, \_\rangle) \Rightarrow \pi^1$$

With this information *Alice* knows that all opinions sent about *Albert* are coincident because the reputation-based agreement reached is 1-consistent (π^1). Besides, she knows that the opinions sent by the agents that have interacted with *Harry* are almost the same since their variability is low (0.95-consistent). With this in mind, the last information that *Alice* wants to know is about the predictability of *Harry*'s behaviour. Therefore, *Alice* queries the informative mechanism Γ_{Π}^4 as follows:

$$\Gamma_{\Pi}^4(\langle Harry, provider, \_, \_\rangle) \Rightarrow \pi^{0.33}$$

Although *Alice* decides to selects *Harry* as her provider since he has the best reputation-based agreement, she knows that his behaviour is not very predictable since he has a 0.33-*norm consistency* value for the referred situation.

In this domain, the reputation service has been an useful mechanism allowing *Alice* to select the provider, when she did not have any previous information about providers. The mechanism worked perfectly due to agents participating in the organisation collaborated by sending their opinions to the reputation service. They were motivated to send opinions because of the own nature of the domain – pub's owners wants to create a pubs area to attract customers. Thus, pubs get benefits individually from making public their opinions about providers. But what happens when agents are not motivated by the domain to send opinions to the reputation service? Next section deals with that problem.

4   How to Motivate Agents to Send Their Opinions

As we have mentioned before, this section deals with the problem of motivating agents to send their reputation information messages to the system. Thus, we propose to endow the reputation system with an *incentive mechanism* [3] so as to face this task. The model presented in [3] assumes that the system evolves at discrete time steps. In each step, all agents in the system perform one action, that is, the new state of the environment is produced through the joint actions of all agents. Besides, it is assumed that agents can take a "skip" action, which allows for modelling asynchronous behaviours. From the point of view of an individual agents, the consequences of doing an action depends not only on the action, but also on the actions of other agents, the characteristics of the resources embedded in the system, and possibly on other external influences. In this regard, the evolution of the system is formalised as a transition probability distribution $\Phi : \mathcal{X} \times \mathcal{A}^{|Ag|} \times \mathcal{X} \to [0..1]$ so as to allow for existing additional external influences on the environment. As consequence, an incentive mechanism is formalised as a function that, given a possibly partial description of an environmental state of a multiagent system, produces changes in the transition probability distribution of the system: $\Upsilon_{inc} : \mathcal{X}' \to [\mathcal{X} \times \mathcal{A}^{|Ag|} \times \mathcal{X} \to [0..1]]$, where $\mathcal{X}'$ stands for the partial description of an environmental state; and $\mathcal{X} \times \mathcal{A}^{|Ag|} \times \mathcal{X} \to [0..1]$ is the transition probability distribution of the system, that describes how the environment ($\mathcal{X}$) evolves as a result of agents' actions ($\mathcal{A}^{|Ag|}$) with certain probability in $[0..1]$. Hence, an incentive mechanism, producing changes in the transition probability distribution of the system, is equivalent to introduce rewards and/or penalties. That is, when a mechanism is able to modify the consequences of an action, such a modification might become in a reward or a penalty for the agent, hence, rational agents would change their decisions accordingly (if they know of such incentives). For instance, a mechanism that installs radars over a road, is an incentive mechanism, since the probability of a car – an agent – to get fined (and, thus, the probability to change to a state with less money) is higher if the car passes at prohibited velocity than without the radar. Thus, the mechanism changes the consequences of the action *passing a road at high velocity*.

Any incentive mechanism must tackle the following requirements: *i)* to choose the agents that will be affected by the mechanism; *ii)* to select the actions in which the incentive will be applied; *iii)* to find out, at least one attribute and a possible modification of this, that affects the preferences of each selected agent[4]; and finally, *iv)* to apply the modification of the parameters selected in the step *iii)* as a consequence of the selected actions in the step *ii)*, giving in such a way a reward or a penalty to these agents. Formally, an incentive mechanism is composed of $\Upsilon_{inc} = \langle Ag_{inc}, \nabla, \omega_{inc} \rangle$, where Ag_{inc} is the set of agents that will be applied for the incentive mechanism, ∇ stands for the set of actions in which the incentive will be applied and ω_{inc} represents the set of attributes and their selected modification to tune up the preferences of agents Ag_{inc}. Each attribute is formalised as a tuple $\langle attribute, value \rangle$.

In our particular case, we are interested in motivating all agents participating in the organisation, because the more information the system has, the more complete the reputation-based agreements will be, and consequently, the more useful

---

[4] It means that this attribute affects to the utility function of the agent. Because we assume that such preferences are expressed by means of an utility function.

the information provided will be as well. Thus, all agents within the organisation will be affected by the incentive mechanism: $Ag_{inc} = Ag$ (requirement *i*)). As we have pointed out, all agents should be motivated to send their opinions to the system. Thus, the action of *sending reputation information messages* to the system has to be affected by the incentive mechanism (requirement *ii*)). Therefore, $\bigtriangledown = \{send(\mathcal{R}_{ag_i}^{info})\}$. In order to find out the attributes that affect agents' preferences – requirement *iii*) – there exist two different alternatives: *a)* discover the attributes by observing the performance of agents, by modifying – the mechanism – attributes randomly, what could be very costly; and *b)* introduce a new attribute in the system, becoming an attribute that influences the agents' preferences. We tend to favour the second option, introducing a new attribute to the organisation: *points*. That is, each agent is assigned with an amount of points when it joins the organisation and the incentive mechanism will modify their amont. Formally: $\omega_{inc} = \langle points_{ag_i}, value \rangle$

Furthermore, agents within an organisation must select partners to interact with, so whatever the domain of the organisation is, such agentes are interested in selecting the best partners. Thus, their utility is influenced by the selection of such partners. So, since the reputation system might provide them useful information to that end, if we associate the new attribute with the action of querying that information, the new attribute somehow becomes in an attribute that influences the agents' preferences. Therefore, the action of querying an informative mechanism has to be affected by the incentive mechanism as well. Formally: $\bigtriangledown = \{send(\mathcal{R}_{ag_i}^{info}), query(\Gamma_\Pi)\}$.

In order to complete requirement *iv*) the mechanism must decide how to modify the attribute introduced – the points each agent has – as a consequence of the actions selected to receive an incentive – to send opinions and to query information. If the incentive mechanism does not exist, agents will be interested in performing the action of querying an informative mechanism – because they might get useful information –, but they will not be interested in performing the action of sending their opinions – because they might lose utility if they make public such opinions. Hence, the mechanism has to get the opposite effect, that is, it should make more attractive the sending of opinions and less attractive the querying for information. In this way, the new attribute becomes an attribute whose modification affects the agents' preferences.

In the case of the action $send(\mathcal{R}_{ag_i}^{info})$, the mechanism should make more attractive the state in which an agent will be, when it performs that action, since they are not interested in performing it. Thus, when an agent $ag_i \in Ag_{inc}$ performs the action $send(\mathcal{R}_{ag_i}^{info})$ the consequence of such an action will be a modification of the value of the attribute $\omega_{inc} = \langle points_{ag_i}, value \rangle$, such that:

$$value = value + (\alpha_1 x + \alpha_2)$$

where x is the number of new reputation-based agreements that will be created with the new opinion sent and α_1, α_2 are parameters to weight the incentive $(\alpha_1 > 0, \alpha_2 > 0)$.

We are inspired by the market and the law of demand and offer, that is, the price of a service/product is fixed based on the demand and offer this service/product has. Thus, the points an agent gets when it sends an opinion depends on how further the new opinion is. This is measured by calculating the number of reputation-based agreements it creates – parameter x in the equation. It fluctuates between 0 and 1, when an agent sends an opinion about a situation that an agreement was not reached so far, it creates as maximum one new agreement. In such a way, when more new opinions are sent, more points agents get, so consequently, agents will be motivated to send new opinions.

On the other hand, when an agent $ag_i \in Ag_{inc}$ performs the action $query(\Gamma_{\Pi})$, the attribute $w_{inc} = \langle points_{ag_i}, value \rangle$ is modified as a consequence in the following way:

$$value = value - (\alpha_3 y + \alpha_4)$$

where y stands for the demand the informative mechanism being queried by the agent has. It is calculated by the number of times such a mechanism is queried; and α_3, α_4 are parameters to weight the incentive, such that $\alpha_3 > 0$ and $\alpha_4 > 0$.

Following the simile of the law of offer and demand, the more an informative mechanism is queried, the more points agents lose querying it. Therefore, it supposes that the more an informative mechanism is queried, the more useful is the information it provides. Thus, its price will be risen and consequently, agents will need more points to query. Since the only way to get points is sending opinions, agents are definitely motivated to send information. Hence, a market of points is created giving incentives to agents to share their opinions. It is important to notice that the attribute $points_{ag_i}$ cannot be negative. That is, if the consequence of performing the action $query(\Gamma_{\Pi})$ was a negative value the information will not be provided.

In order to solve a deadlock produced when agents join the organisation without any points, the incentive mechanism assigns to agents an amount of "trial" points. It should assign, at least, a minimum quantity of points to make them able to query the informative mechanism, since the available information might be useful for them. Therefore, the attributes will be initialised as follows: $w_{inc} = \langle points_{ag_i}, value \rangle$ where $value = \alpha_3 n + \alpha_4$ such that, α_3 and α_4 are the same as the modification of the attribute when agents query an informative mechanism; and n is the number of "free" queries the incentive mechanism assigns when agents join the organisation.

Finally, it is important to remark that those incentives should be published so as to be effective. We suppose that the organisation also publishes them together with the informative mechanisms. In Section 5 we illustrate how the reputation service, coupled with this incentive mechanism, works in domains in which agents are not motivated to share their opinions.

5   Case Study: Tasks Servers

In this section we put all together by illustrating the dynamics of the reputation service working with the incentive mechanism introduced in the same system.

This scenario involves the same five agents: *Anna, John, Jessica, Albert* and *Harry* participating within another organisation. In this organisation, agents can execute different tasks when another agent requests it. Thus, agents can join the organisation playing two different roles: *servers* and *customers*. The formers are able to execute the tasks that customers request them. This domain is characterised by the following aspects: *i)* when a tasks server is overload it is not able to execute more tasks; *ii)* each server has different capabilities to execute a task, i.e., the quality of the executed task may be different; and *iii)* when a task is assigned to a server and the quality of the executed task is not good enough, the task could be required to be executed again by another server. With this characteristics agents are not motivated to send their opinions, because if all agents discover the best server, the latter will unrelentingly be overload. On the other hand, if agents do not have any hint about the best servers for each task, they will select the partners – the servers – randomly, and it could imply a loss of utility, because they could need to repeat the request to a different server. Obviously, the reputation service, without the incentive mechanism, will not work in this domain, because agents will not send their opinions and, as a result, reputation-based agreements will not be created. Therefore, the organisation will be endowed with an incentive mechanism set up as follows:

$$\Upsilon_{inc} : \langle \mathcal{Ag}_{inc} = \{Anna, John, Jessica, Albert, Harry\},$$
$$\nabla = \{send_{ag_i}(\mathcal{R}_{ag_i}^{info}), query_{ag_i}(\Gamma_\Pi)\},$$
$$\omega_{inc} = \{\langle points_{ag_i}, 130\rangle\}\rangle$$

where ag_i stands for an agent in the set $\mathcal{Ag}_{inc}$; and the number 130 represents the initial points, calculated by the equation $value = \alpha_3 n + \alpha_4$ with $n = 2$ and α_3, α_4 as we will detail next. In order to modify the value of the attributes, as consequence of the execution of actions in ∇, the mechanism is configured with the following parameters: $\alpha_1 = 200 \quad \alpha_2 = 100 \quad \alpha_3 = 10 \quad \alpha_4 = 50$.

In addition, agents join the organisation playing the following roles: *Anna - customer*; *John - customer*; *Jessica - customer*; *Albert - server* and *Harry - server*. Within the organisation there are many agents playing the server role as well, but for the sake of simplicity we do not detail them.

After this point, agents start to interact by selecting their partners randomly, because although they have enough points to query informative mechanisms, there are not agreements available yet, since agents have not send their opinions. Since bootstrapping of the incentive mechanism is out of the scope of the paper we decided to assign no points to agents forming the initial state of the scenario. Thus, initial agents will have a value of 0 in the corresponding attribute of points. Otherwise, newcomers will have a value of 130, calculated as we have explained before.

When several interactions have been carried out, *customer* agents are aware of some useful information about *servers*. Once agents run out of points they need to send their opinions, so as to get some points in order to keep on querying. Thus, the following reputation information messages are sent to the service:

$$\mathcal{R}^{info}_{Anna} = \langle\langle Albert, server, \_, \_\rangle, \{N_a\}, 0.9\rangle$$
$$\mathcal{R}^{info}_{John} = \langle\langle Albert, server, \_, \_\rangle, \{N_a\}, 0.9\rangle$$
$$\mathcal{R}^{info}_{Jessica} = \langle\langle Albert, server, \_, \_\rangle, \{N_a\}, 0.9\rangle$$
$$\mathcal{R}^{info}_{John} = \langle\langle Harry, server, \_, \_\rangle, \{N_b\}, 0.9\rangle$$
$$\mathcal{R}^{info}_{Anna} = \langle\langle Harry, server, \_, \_\rangle, \{N_b\}, 0.2\rangle$$

As a consequence of executing those actions, the incentive mechanism modifies the values of the attribute $points_{ag_i}$ by using the equation explained in Section 4, as follows: $\langle points_{Anna}, 400\rangle$, $\langle points_{John}, 400\rangle$ and $\langle points_{Jessica}, 100\rangle$, since Anna and John contributed to create a new agreement when they sent their opinions. However, Jessica did not contribute to any new agreement.

When the reputation service receives those messages, the following reputation-based agreements are created, by using the same function – the average function – that in the case study explained in Section 3:

$$\pi_1 = \langle\langle Albert, server, \_, \_\rangle, \{Anna, John, Jessica\}, \{\{N_a\}, \{N_a\}, \{N_a\}\}, 0.9, t_1\rangle$$
$$\pi_2 = \langle\langle Harry, server, \_, \_\rangle, \{Anna, John\}, \{\{N_b\}, \{N_b\}\}, 0.55, t_1\rangle$$

These agreements show that all agents playing the role *customer* think the same about *Albert* as server and that Harry is evaluated with 0.55 as *server*, from the point of view of *Anna* and *John*. We suppose that the reputation service has the same informative mechanisms as in the example of Section 3: $\Gamma^1_\Pi(\langle Ag, \mathcal{R}, \_, \_\rangle)$, $\Gamma^2_\Pi(\langle Ag, \mathcal{R}, \_, \_\rangle)$, $\Gamma^3_\Pi(\langle \_, \mathcal{R}, \_, \_\rangle)$ and $\Gamma^4_\Pi(\langle Ag, \mathcal{R}, \_, \_\rangle)$.

At this point, our agents could query any informative mechanism because they have enough points to do it. However, we will focus on a new agent – *Alice* – that joins the organisation at this moment. Since she is a newcomer, she will be assigned 130 points – two "free" queries to an informative mechanism. Then, she performs the following queries:

$$\Gamma^3_\Pi(\langle \_, server, \_, \_\rangle) \Rightarrow \{Albert, Harry\}$$
$$\Gamma^2_\Pi(\langle Albert, server, \_, \_\rangle) \Rightarrow 0.9$$

After these queries *Alice* knows that the best server, according to the reputation-based agreements reached, so far, is *Albert*, with 0.9 evaluation. Then, the value of the attribute $points_{Alice}$ will be modified to 10, following the equation explained in Section 3. Since she cannot query again due to the lack of points, she will select *Albert* as server even though she does not know if his behaviour can be predicted or not. When she performs the interaction with Albert, she wants to get more information about how the agreement about *Albert* is, because she is wondering if such an agreement is not consistent enough, she could have problems if she assigns a different task to *Albert*. Thus, she needs to send her opinion in order to get more points. After that, she gets 310 points (10 that she already had plus 300 that she gets sending an opinion about a situation that does not form part of an agreement yet). Now, she can perform a new query: $\Gamma^1_\Pi(\langle Albert, server, \_, \_\rangle) \Rightarrow \pi^*_{customer}$. With this new information, she knows that *Albert* is the best server and all customers evaluate him exactly with the same reputation ($\pi^*_{customer}$ is *customer-complete*). This information is worthy for *Alice* because she will not need to change of server.

6 Related Work

In this paper we do not propose another reputation mechanism but a reputation service that generates agreements based on collected opinions about the reputations of agents in a given situation. Such service can be used by the centralised part of an hybrid reputation model [15] or by an agent participating in a distributed mechanism that is interested in aggregate the opinions it has received about its behaviour or in aggregate the opinions it has about the behaviour of another agent, for instance.

One of the main advantages of having a centralised reputation service is the feasibility for an individual to know a more consistent reputation about another agent based on numeral experiences. In the case of distributed mechanisms (such as [13][6][12]), the agent itself would need to participate in several interactions with the given agent and also to ask other agents for their experiences with others. In the case of a centralised mechanism, the agent can easily get information about the reputation showing the behaviour of other agents within the system. In [14], Sabater et al. present a technological framework that allows virtual cognitive agents and humans to participate in the same Electronic Institution (EI). The authors claim that a centralised reputation mechanism has to be implemented as a service in an EI. The conceptual idea is similar to ours, but they do not study in depth neither how to collect opinions from the participants nor present a formal approach to incorporate such reputation service. They only present a very vague notion of how to incorporate a centralised reputation mechanism into EIs, while we present a formal approach that fits not only in EIs but in any organisational environment.

Another known example of centralised reputation mechanism is the Beta Reputation System, presented by Josang and Ismail in [8]. This system is based on using beta probability density functions to combine feedback and derive reputation ratings from the participants. The main differences with our approach is that the former does not have an organisational flavour, so important properties from aggregation process cannot be derived. Furthermore, Josang and Ismail does not take into account important concepts as, for instance, norms or roles, what makes our system more flexible, above all, when presenting different type of information from the same original data regarding different participants' requests.

Although there exist many distributed reputation mechanisms that try to ensure more reliable interactions among agents, such as [13][6][11], we cannot compare our work with them, since we claim that distributed approaches are fully complementary to our conception of reputation based-agreements. In fact, since it is out of the scope of this paper, we do not get into details of how agents calculate and maintain their reputation assessments for other agents.

Regarding the incentive mechanisms existing in literature to drive agents to collaborate by sending their truthfully opinions a well known work is the one by Jurca and Faltings [9]. They use a mechanism of buy/sell information using credits. The main difference is that they use it in a distributed environment, where agents send opinions among them, but not to a central repository as in our case. In [7] the authors present an approach to create rankings able not only to provide the most trustful agents but also a probabilistic evidence of such reputation values. Those rankings are also computed by a centralised system by aggregating the reputations reported by the agents. This approach and the one presented in our paper could be complementary, since that paper focuses on defining the ranking algorithms and ours focuses on describing the mechanism that allows to receive the reputation information and to provide the already evaluated agreements (for instance by using rankings). Another work that could be also complementary to the approach presented here, is the one presented in [10]. They describe the algorithm *NodeRanking* that creates rankings of reputation ratings. Therefore, our reputation service could use this algorithm so as to provide information about the reputation-based agreements reached within the organisation.

7   Conclusions and Future Work

Summarising, this work puts forward a novel approach of reputation-based agreement concept by supporting on a reputation service that creates reputation-based agreements as aggregations of opinions sent by participants within an organisation. The organizational mechanism defines the norms that the agents must fulfil by pointing out the situations being regulated and the reputation mechanisms aggregate reputations provided by agents based on the evaluations of the behaviour of their partners according to the violation of the norms that regulate a given situation. Thus, we have added to the reputation mechanism the notion of reputations based on norms and situations and the ability of receiving reputations, aggregating then and providing information about such aggregation.

Besides, we also define some desirable properties that can be derived and should be taken into account when providing the information they contain. Furthermore, we also propose to use the agreements by utilising the concept of informative mechanisms [3], so providing agents with useful information. On the other hand, we propose an incentive mechanism [3] to deal with the problem of lack of collaboration from agents to send their opinions to the service. Finally, different examples have been analysed so that they illustrate how the reputation service works in two different domains: the former represents a collaborative domain where agents are interested in sharing their opinions, and the later shows a competitive domain in which the reputation service must be coupled with an incentive mechanism to motivate agents to send their opinions.

In future work we plan to experimentally test our approach by implementing a case study presented here, as well as, running several experiments comparing our approach with similar ones. We also intend to investigate new properties about reputation-based agreements to provide agents participating in an organisation with more useful information. Finally, we plan to extend the concept of reputation-based agreement by creating agreements aggregating "similar" situations, so we must go into the concept of similar situations in depth. Moreover, it is our intention to provide agreements based on more abstract (or general) situations. The agreements of a generic situation can be created based on the agreements of its specific situations. In order to do so, an ontology of action/situation could be used to represent the generic situations and the more specific ones.

References

1. Billhardt, H., Centeno, R., Fernández, A., Hermoso, R., Ortiz, R., Ossowski, S., Pérez, J., Vasirani, M.: Organisational structures in next-generation distributed systems: Towards a technology of agreement. Multiagent and Grid Systems: An International Journal (2009)
2. Carrascosa, C., Rebollo, M.: Modelling agreement spaces. In: Proc. of WAT@IBERAMIA 2008, pp. 79–88 (2008)
3. Centeno, R., Billhardt, H., Hermoso, R., Ossowski, S.: Organising mas: A formal model based on organisational mechanisms. In: Proc. of SAC 2009, pp. 740–746 (2009)
4. Centeno, R., da Silva, V.T., Hermoso, R.: A reputation model for organisational supply chain formation. In: Proc. of the COIN@AAMAS 2009, pp. 33–48 (2009)
5. Dellarocas, C.: Reputation Mechanisms. In: Handbook on Economics and Information Systems. Elsevier, Amsterdam (2005)
6. Huynh, T., Jennings, N., Shadbolt, N.: Fire: An integrated trust and reputation model for open multi-agent systems. In: Proc. of the ECAI 2004, pp. 18–22 (2004)
7. Ignjatovic, A., Foo, N., Lee, C.: An analytic approach to reputation ranking of participants in online transactions. In: Proc. of the WI-IAT 2008, pp. 587–590 (2008)
8. Josang, A., Ismail, R.: The beta reputation system. In: 15th Bled Electronic Commerce Conference (2002)
9. Jurca, R., Faltings, B.: An incentive compatible reputation mechanism. In: Proceedings of the AAMAS 2003, pp. 1026–1027. ACM, New York (2003)
10. Pujol, J., Sangüesa, R., Delgado, J.: Extracting reputation in multi agent systems by means of social network topology. In: Proc. of the AAMAS 2002, pp. 467–474. ACM, New York (2002)
11. Ramchurn, S., Sierra, C., God, L., Jennings, N.: A computational trust model for multi-agent interactions based on confidence and reputation. In: Proceedings of 6th International Workshop of Deception, Fraud and Trust in Agent Societies, pp. 69–75 (2003)
12. Sabater, J., Sierra, C.: Reputation and social network analysis in multi-agent systems. In: Proc. of the AAMAS 2002, pp. 475–482. ACM Press, New York (2002)
13. Sabater, J., Sierra, C.: Review on computational trust and reputation models. Artificial Intelligence Review 24(1), 33–60 (2005)
14. Sabater-Mir, J., Pinyol, I., Villatoro, D., Cuní, G.: Towards hybrid experiments on reputation mechanisms: Bdi agents and humans in electronic institutions. In: XII Conference of the Spanish Association for Artificial Intelligence (CAEPIA 2007), vol. 2, pp. 299–308 (2007)
15. Silva, V., Hermoso, R., Centeno, R.: A hybrid reputation model based on the use of organizations. In: Hübner, J.F., Matson, E., Boissier, O., Dignum, V. (eds.) COIN@AAMAS 2008. LNCS, vol. 5428, pp. 111–125. Springer, Heidelberg (2009)

Norm Refinement and Design through Inductive Learning*

Domenico Corapi[1], Marina De Vos[2], Julian Padget[2],
Alessandra Russo[1], and Ken Satoh[3]

[1] Department of Computing, Imperial College London
{d.corapi,a.russo}@imperial.ac.uk
[2] Department of Computer Science, University of Bath
{mdv,jap}@cs.bath.ac.uk
[3] National Institute of Informatics
ksatoh@nii.ac.jp

Abstract. In the physical world, the rules governing behaviour are debugged by observing an outcome that was not intended and the addition of new constraints to prevent the attainment of that outcome. We propose a similar approach to support the incremental development of normative frameworks (also called institutions) and demonstrate how this works through the validation and synthesis of normative rules using model generation and inductive learning. This is achieved by the designer providing a set of *use cases*, comprising collections of event traces that describe how the system is used along with the desired outcome with respect to the normative framework. The model generator encodes the description of the current behaviour of the system. The current specification and the traces for which current behaviour and expected behaviour do not match are given to the learning framework to propose new rules that revise the existing norm set in order to inhibit the unwanted behaviour. The elaboration of a normative system can then be viewed as a semi-automatic, iterative process for the detection of incompleteness or incorrectness of the existing normative rules, with respect to desired properties, and the construction of potential additional rules for the normative system.

1 Introduction

Norms and regulations play an important role in the governance of human society. Social rules such as laws, conventions and contracts prescribe and regulate our behaviour. However it is possible for us to break these rules at our discretion and face the consequences. By providing the means to describe and reason about norms in a computational context, normative frameworks (also called institutions or virtual organisations) may be applied to software systems allowing for automated reasoning about the consequences of socially acceptable and unacceptable behaviour. This can be achieved by monitoring the permissions, empowerment and obligations of the participants and generating violations when norms are not followed.

* This work is partially supported through the EU Framework 7 project *ALIVE (FP7-IST-215890)*, and the EPSRC PRiMMA project (EP/F023294/1).

M. De Vos et al. (Eds.): COIN 2010 International Workshops, LNAI 6541, pp. 77–94, 2011.
© Springer-Verlag Berlin Heidelberg 2011

The formal model put forward in [11] and its corresponding operationalisation through Answer Set Programming (ASP) [3, 26] aims to support the top-down design of normative frameworks. *AnsProlog* is a knowledge representation language that allows the programmer to describe a problem and required properties on the solutions in an intuitive way. Programs consist of rules interpreted under the answer set semantics. Answer set solvers, like CLASP [25] or SMODELS [35], can be used to reason about the given *AnsProlog* specification, by returning *acceptable solutions* in the form of traces, as answer sets. In a similar way, the correctness of the specification with respect to given properties can be verified.

Currently, the elaboration of behavioural rules and norms is an error-prone process that relies on the manual efforts of the designer and would, therefore, benefit from automated support. In this paper, we present an inductive logic programming (ILP) [33] approach for the extraction of norms and behaviourial rules from a set of use cases. The approach is intended as a design support tool for normative frameworks. Complex systems are hard to model and even if testing of properties is possible, sometimes it is hard to identify missing or incorrect rules. In some cases, e.g. legal reasoning, the abstract specification of the system can be in part given in terms of specific instances and use cases that ultimately drive the design process and are used to assess it. We propose a design support tool that employs *use-cases*, i.e. traces together with their expected normative behaviour, to assist in the revision of a normative framework. The system is correct when none of the traces are considered *dysfunctional*, i.e. they match the expected normative behaviour. When a dysfunctional trace is encountered the normative specification needs to be adjusted: the task is to refine the given description by learning missing norms and/or behavioural rules that, added to the description, entail the expected behaviour over the traces. We show how this task can be naturally represented as a non-monotonic ILP problem in which the partial description of the normative system provides the background knowledge and the expected behaviour comprises the examples. In particular, we show how a given *AnsProlog* program and traces can be reformulated into an ILP representation that makes essential use of negation in inducing missing parts of the specification. As the resulting learning problem is inherently non-monotonic, we use a non-monotonic ILP system, called TAL [14], to compute the missing specification from the traces and the initial description.

Given the declarative nature of ASP, the computational paradigm used for our normative frameworks, we needed to adopt a declarative learning approach as we aim to learn declarative specifications. This differs from other approaches, such as reinforcement learning whereby norms or policies are learned as outcomes of estimation and optimisation processes. Such types of policies are not directly representable in a declarative format and are quite different in nature from the work reported here.

The paper is organised as follows. Section 2 presents some background material on the normative framework, while Section 3 introduces the non-monotonic ILP system used in our proposed approach. Section 4 describes the *AnsProlog* modelling of normative frameworks. Section 5 illustrates how the revision task can be formulated into an ILP problem, and how the generated ILP hypothesis can be reformulated as norms and behaviour rules within the *AnsProlog* representation. In Section 6 we illustrate the flexibility and expressiveness of our approach through a number of different partial specifications of a reciprocal file sharing normative framework. Section 7 relates our approach to existing work on learning norms with respects to changing/improved requirements. We conclude with a summary and remarks about future work.

2 Normative Frameworks

The concept of normative frameworks has become firmly embedded in the agent community as a necessary foil to the essential autonomy of agents, in just the same way as societal conventions and legal frameworks have grown up to constrain people. In both the physical and the virtual world, and the emerging combination of the two, the arguments in favour centre on the minimisation of disruptive behaviour and supporting the achievement of the goals for which the normative framework has been conceived and thus also the motivation for submission to its governance by the participants. While the concept remains attractive, its realisation in a computational setting remains a subject for research, with a wide range of existing logics [40, 2, 7, 11, 43] and tools [37, 18, 27].

2.1 Formal Model

To provide context for this paper, we give an outline of a formal event-based model for the specification of normative frameworks that captures all the essential properties, namely empowerment, permission, obligation and violation. Extended presentations appear in [11] and [12].

   The essential elements of our normative framework are: (i) events ($\mathcal{E}$), that bring about changes in state, and (ii) fluents ($\mathcal{F}$), that characterise the state at a given instant. The function of the framework is to define the interplay between these concepts over time, in order to capture the evolution of a particular institution through the interaction of its participants. We distinguish two kinds of events: normative events ($\mathcal{E}_{norm}$), that are the events defined by the framework and exogenous ($\mathcal{E}_{ex}$), that are outside its scope, but whose occurrence triggers normative events in a direct reflection of the "counts-as" principle [30]. We further partition normative events into normative actions ($\mathcal{E}_{act}$) that denote changes in normative state and violation events ($\mathcal{E}_{viol}$), that signal the occurrence of violations. Violations may arise either from explicit generation, from the occurrence of a non-permitted event, or from the failure to fulfil an obligation. We also distinguish two kinds of fluents: *normative fluents* that denote normative properties of the state such as permissions $\mathcal{P}$, powers $\mathcal{W}$ and obligations $\mathcal{O}$, and *domain fluents* $\mathcal{D}$ that correspond to properties specific to the normative framework itself. The set of all fluents is denoted as $\mathcal{F}$. A normative state is represented by the fluents that hold true in this state. Fluents that are not presented are considered to be false. Conditions on a state are therefore expressed by a set of fluents that should be true or false. The set of possible conditions is referred to as $\mathcal{X} = 2^{\mathcal{F} \cup \neg \mathcal{F}}$.

   Changes in state are achieved through the definition of two relations: (i) the generation relation, which implements counts-as by specifying how the occurrence of one (exogenous or normative) event generates another (normative) event, subject to the empowerment of the actor and the conditions on the state, and (ii) the consequence relation. This latter specifies the initiation and termination of fluents subject to the performance of some action in a state matching some expression. The generation relation is formally defined as $\mathcal{G} : \mathcal{X} \times \mathcal{E} \to 2^{\mathcal{E}_{norm}}$, and the consequence relation as $\mathcal{C} : \mathcal{X} \times \mathcal{E} \to 2^{\mathcal{F}} \times 2^{\mathcal{F}}$. The fluents to be initiated as a result of an event E are often denoted by $\mathcal{C}^{\uparrow}(\phi, e)$ while the ones to be terminated are denoted by $\mathcal{C}^{\downarrow}(\phi, e)$.

The semantics of our normative framework is defined over a sequence, called a *trace*, of exogenous events. Starting from the initial state, each exogenous event is responsible for a state change, through initiation and termination of fluents. This is achieved by a three-step process: (i) the transitive closure of $\mathcal{G}$ with respect to a given exogenous event determines all the generated (normative) events, (ii) to this all violations of events not permitted and obligations not fulfilled are added, giving the set of all events whose consequences determine the new state, (iii) the application of $\mathcal{C}$ to this set of events identifies all fluents that are initiated and terminated with respect to the current state so giving the next state. For each trace, we can therefore compute a sequence of states that constitutes the model of the normative framework for that trace. This process is realised as a computational model through Answer Set Programming (see Section 4) and it is this representation that is the subject of the learning process described in Section 5.

3   Learning

Inductive Logic Programming (ILP) [33] is a machine learning technique concerned with the induction of logic theories from (positive and negative) examples and has been successfully applied to a wide range of problems [19]. Automatic induction of hypotheses represented as logic programs is one of the distinctive features of ILP. Moreover, the use of logic programming as representation language allows a principled representation of background information relevant to the learning. To refine normative theories we employ an ILP learning system, called TAL [14], that is able to learn non-monotonic theories, and can be employed to perform learning of new rules and the revision of existing rules. The TAL approach is based on mapping a given inductive problem into an abductive reasoning process. The current implementation of TAL relies on an extension of the abductive procedure SLDNFA [17] and preserves its semantics.

Definition 1. *A* non-monotonic ILP task *is defined as* $\langle E, B, S \rangle$ *where E is a set of ground positive or negative literals, called* examples, *B is a* background *normal theory and S is a set of clauses called* language bias. *The normal theory $H \in ILP\langle E, B, S \rangle$, called* hypothesis, *is an inductive solution for the task* $\langle E, B, S \rangle$, *if $H \subseteq S$, H is consistent with B and $B \cup H \models E$.*

B and H are normal theories and thus support negation as failure. The choice of an appropriate language bias is critical. In TAL the language bias S is specified by means of *mode declarations* [34].

Definition 2. *A mode declaration is either a head or body declaration, respectively* $modeh(s)$ *and* $modeb(s)$ *where s is called a* scheme. *A scheme s is a ground literal containing place-markers. A* place-marker *is a ground function whose functor is one of the three symbols '+' (input), '-' (output), '#' (constant) and the argument is a constant called* type.

Given a schema s, s^* is the literal obtained from s by replacing all place-markers with different variables $X_1, ..., X_n$. A rule r is *compatible* with a set M of mode declarations iff (a) there is a mapping from each head/body literal l in r to a head/body declaration $m \in M$ with schema s such that each literal is subsumed by its corresponding s^*; (b) each output place-marker is bound to an *output variable*; (c) each input place-marker is bound to an output variable appearing in the body or to a variable in the head; (d) every constant place-marker is bound to a constant; (e) all variables and constants are of the corresponding type. From a user perspective, mode declarations establish how rules in the final hypotheses are structured, defining literals that can be used in the head and in the body of a well-formed hypothesis. Although we show M in the running example of this paper for reference, the mode declarations can be concealed from the user and derived automatically. They can be optionally refined to constrain the search whenever the designer wants to employ useful information on the outcome of the learning to reduce the number of alternative hypotheses or improve performance.

4 Modelling Normative Frameworks

While the formal model of a normative framework allows for clear specification of a normative system, it is of little support to designers or users of these systems. In order to be able to do so, computational tools are needed. The first step is a computational model equivalent to the formal model. We have opted for a form of logic programming, called Answer Set Programming (ASP) [26]. Here we only present a short flavour of the language *AnsProlog*, and the interested reader is referred to [3] for in-depth coverage.

AnsProlog is a knowledge representation language that allows the programmer to describe a problem and the requirements on the solutions in an intuitive way, rather than the algorithm to find the solutions to the problem. The basic components of the language are atoms, elements that can be assigned a truth value. An atom can be negated using *negation as failure* so creating the *literal* not a. We say that not a is true if we cannot find evidence supporting the truth of a. If a is true then not a is false and vice versa. Atoms and literals are used to create rules of the general form: $a \leftarrow B$, not C, where a is an atom and B and C are set of atoms. Intuitively, this means *if all elements of B are known/true and no element of C is known/true, then a must be known/true*. We refer to a as the head and $B \cup$ not C as the body of the rule. Rules with empty body are called *facts; A* program in *AnsProlog* is a finite set of rules.

The semantics of *AnsProlog* are defined in terms of *answer sets*, i.e. assignments of true and false to all atoms in the program that satisfy the rules in a minimal and consistent fashion. A program has zero or more answer sets, each corresponding to a solution.

4.1 Mapping the Formal Model into *AnsProlog*

In this section we only provide a summary description of how the formal institutional model is translated in to *AnsProlog* . A full description of the model can be found in [11] together with completeness and correctness of model with respect to traces. Each program models the semantics of the normative framework over a sequence of n time instants such that $t_i : 0 \leq i \leq n$. Events are considered to occur *between* these snapshots, where for simplicity we do not define the intervals at which events occur explicitly, and instead refer to the time instant at the start of the interval at which an event is considered to occur. Fluents may be true or false at any given instant of time, so we use atoms of the form $\mathtt{holdsat(f,t_i)}$ to indicate that fluent $\mathtt{f}$ holds at time instant $\mathtt{t_i}$. In order to represent changes in the state of fluents over time, we use atoms of the form $\mathtt{initiated(f,t_i)}$ and $\mathtt{terminated(f,t_i)}$ to denote the fact that fluent $\mathtt{f}$ was initiated or terminated, respectively, *between* time instants i and $i + 1$. We use atoms of the form $\mathtt{occurred(e,t_i)}$ to indicate that event $\mathtt{e} \in \mathcal{E}$ is considered to have occurred between instant $\mathtt{t_i}$ and $\mathtt{t_{i+1}}$. These atoms denote events that occur in an external context or are generated by the normative framework. For exogenous events we additionally use atoms of the form $\mathtt{observed(e,t_i)}$ to denote the fact that e has been observed.

The mapping of a normative framework consists of three parts: a base component which is independent of the framework being modelled, the time model and the framework specific component. The independent component deals with inertia of the fluents, the generation of violation events of un-permitted actions and unsatisfied obligations. The time model defines the predicates for time and is responsible for generating a single observed event at every time instance. In this paper we will focus solely on the representation of the specific features of the normative framework.

In order to translate rules the relations $\mathcal{G}$ and $\mathcal{C}$, we must first define a translation for expressions which may appear in these rules. The valuation of a given expression taken from the set $\mathcal{X}$ depends on which fluents may be held to be true or false in the current state (at a give time instant). We translate expressions into ASP rule bodies as conjunctions of extended literals using negation as failure for negated expressions.

With all these atoms defined, mapping the generation function and the consequence relation of a specific normative framework becomes rather straightforward. The generation function specifies that an normative event e occurs at a certain instance ($\mathtt{occurred(e,t)}$) when an another event e' occurs ($\mathtt{occurred(e',t)}$), the event e is empowered ($\mathtt{holdsat(pow(e),t)}$ and a set of conditions on the state are satisfied ($\mathtt{holdsat(f,t)}$ or **not** $\mathtt{holdsat(f,t)}$). The rules for initiation ($\mathtt{initiated(f,t)}$) and termination ($\mathtt{terminated(f,t)}$ of a fluent f are triggered when a certain event e occurs ($\mathtt{occurred(e,t)}$) and a set of conditions on the state are fulfilled. The initial state of our normative framework is encoded as simple facts ($\mathtt{holdsat(f,i00)}$).

Fig. 1 gives a summary of all *AnsProlog* rules that are generated for a specific normative framework, including the definition of all the fluents and events as facts. For a given expression $\phi \in \mathcal{X}$, we use the term $EX(\phi,T)$ to denote the translation of ϕ into a set of ASP literals of the form $\mathtt{holdsat(f,T)}$ or **not** $\mathtt{holdsat(f,T)}$.

In situations where the normative system consists of a number of agents whose actions can be treated in the same way (e.g. the rules for borrowing a book are the same for every member of a library) or where the state consists of fluents that can be treated in a similar way (e.g. the status of book), we can parametrise the events and fluents. This is represented in the *AnsProlog* program by function symbols (e.g $\mathtt{borrowed(Agent,Book)}$) rather than terms. To allow for grounding, extra atoms to ground these variables need to be added. Grounded versions of the atoms also need to be added to the program. An example of this can be found in Section 6.

$$p \in \mathcal{F} \Leftrightarrow \texttt{ifluent(p)}.$$
$$e \in \mathcal{E} \Leftrightarrow \texttt{event(e)}.$$
$$e \in \mathcal{E}_{ex} \Leftrightarrow \texttt{evtype(e, obs)}.$$
$$e \in \mathcal{E}_{act} \Leftrightarrow \texttt{evtype(e, act)}.$$
$$e \in \mathcal{E}_{viol} \Leftrightarrow \texttt{evtype(e, viol)}.$$
$$\mathcal{C}^{\uparrow}(\phi, e) = P \Leftrightarrow \forall p \in P \cdot \texttt{initiated(p, T)} \leftarrow \texttt{occurred(e, T)}, EX(\phi, T).$$
$$\mathcal{C}^{\downarrow}(\phi, e) = P \Leftrightarrow \forall p \in P \cdot \texttt{terminated(p, T)} \leftarrow \texttt{occurred(e, T)}, EX(\phi, T).$$
$$\mathcal{G}(\phi, e) = E \Leftrightarrow g \in E, \texttt{occurred(g, T)} \leftarrow \texttt{occurred(e, T)},$$
$$\texttt{holdsat(pow(e), T)}, EX(\phi, T).$$
$$p \in S_0 \Leftrightarrow \texttt{holdsat(p, i00)}.$$

Fig. 1. The translation of normative framework specific rules into $AnsProlog$

5 Learning Normative Rules

5.1 Methodology

The development process is supported by a set of *use cases* U. Use cases represent instances of executions that are known to the designer and that drive the elaboration of the normative system. If the current formalisation of the system does not match the intended behaviour in the use case then the formalisation is still not complete or incorrect. Each use case $u \in U$ is a tuple $\langle T, C, O \rangle$ where T is a *trace* that specifies *all* the exogenous events occurring at all the time points considered (observed(e, T)); C are ground holdsat or occurred facts that the designer believes to be important and represents the *conditional expected output*; O are ground holdsat and occurred literals that represent the *expected output* of the use case.

The design process is iterative. A current formalisation of the model in $AnsProlog$ is tested against a set of use cases. Together with the $AnsProlog$ specification of the normative framework we add the observed events and a constraint that no answer set that does not satisfy O is acceptable. The latter is done by adding a constraint containing the negation of all the elements in O. If for some use cases the solver is not able to find an answer set (returns unsatisfiable), then a revision step is performed. All the use cases and the current formalisation are given as input to TAL. Possible revisions are provided to the designer who ultimately chooses which is the most appropriate. The success of the revision step depends on the state of the formalisation of the model. The set of supporting use cases can be extended as the design progresses to more accurate models.

In this paper we focus on the learning step and we show how a non-monotonic ILP system can be used to derive new rules. Refining existing rules (i.e. deleting rules or adding and deleting conditions in rules) is a straightforward extension of the current framework. Though we do not discuss it in this paper, revision can be performed by extending the original rules with additional predicates that extend the search to deletion of conditions in rules and to exceptions as shown in [13].

5.2 Mapping ASP to ILP

The differences between the $AnsProlog$ program and the translation into a suitable representation for TAL is procedural and only involves syntactic transformations. Thus

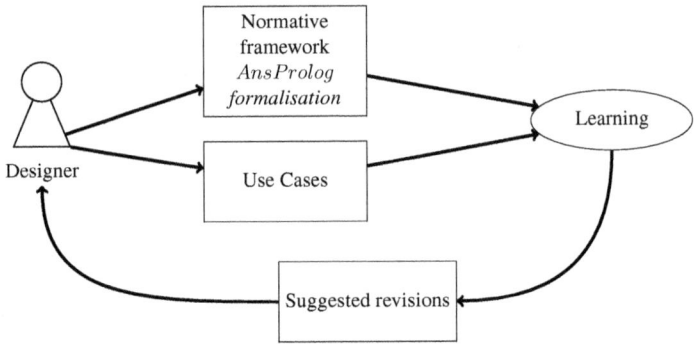

Fig. 2. Iterative design driven by use cases

the difference in the two representations only consists in how the inference is performed. The two semantics coincide since the same logic program is encoded and, as shown in [10], the mapping of a normative framework has exactly one answer set when given a trace. If conditions are added this can be reduced to zero.

A normative model $\mathcal{F}$ corresponds to a $AnsProlog$ program $P_{\mathcal{F}}$ as described in Section 4. All the normal clauses contained in $P_{\mathcal{F}}$ are part of B; the only differences involve time points, that are handled in B by means of a finite domain constraint solver. B also contains all the facts in C and T (negated facts are encoded by adding exceptions to the definitions of holdsat and occurred). The set of examples E contains the literals in O. Each $H \in ILP\langle E, B, S \rangle$ represents a possible revision for $\mathcal{P}$ and thus for the original normative model.

6   Example

To illustrate the capabilities of the norm learning mechanism, we have developed a relatively simple scenario that, at the same time, is complicated enough to demonstrate the key properties with little extraneous detail.

The active parties—agents—of the scenario each find themselves initially in the situation of having ownership of several (digital) objects—the blocks—that form part of some larger composite (digital) entity—a file. An agent may give a copy of one its blocks in exchange for a copy of another block with the aim of acquiring a complete set of all the blocks. For simplicity, in the situation we analyse here, we assume that initially each agent holds the only copy of a given block, and that is there is only one copy of each block in the agent population. Furthermore, we do not take into account the possibility of exchanging a block for one that the agent already has. We believe that neither of these issues does more than complicate the situation by adding more states that would obscure the essential properties that we seek to demonstrate. Thus, we arrive at a statement of the example: two agents, Alice and Bob, each holding two blocks from a set of four and each having the goal of owning all four by downloading the blocks they lack from the other while sharing, with another agent, the ones it does.

We model this as a simple normative framework, where the brute event [29] of downloading a block initiates several normative events, but the act of downloading revokes

% Normative and Domain Rules

$initiated(hasBlock(Agent, Block), I) \leftarrow$
      $occurred(myDownload(Agent, Block), I), holdsat(live(filesharing), I).$
$initiated(perm(myDownload(Agent, Block)), I) \leftarrow$
      $occurred(myShare(Agent), I), holdsat(live(filesharing), I).$
$terminated(pow(filesharing, myDownload(Agent, Block)), I) \leftarrow$
      $occurred(myDownload(Agent, Block), I), holdsat(live(filesharing), I).$
$terminated(needsBlock(Agent, Block), I) \leftarrow$
      $occurred(myDownload(Agent, Block), I), holdsat(live(filesharing), I).$
$terminated(pow(filesharing, myDownload(Agent, Block)), I) \leftarrow$
      $occurred(misuse(Agent), I), holdsat(live(filesharing), I).$
$terminated(perm(myDownload(Agent, Block)), I) \leftarrow$
      $occurred(myDownload(Agent, Block), I), holdsat(live(filesharing), I).$
$occurred(myDownload(AgentA, Block), I) \leftarrow$
      $occurred(download(AgentA, AgentB, Block), I),$
      $holdsat(hasBlock(AgentB, Block), I),$
      $holdsat(pow(filesharing, myDownload(AgentA, Block)), I),$
      $AgentA! = AgentB.$
$occurred(myShare(AgentB), I) \leftarrow$
      $occurred(download(AgentA, AgentB, Block), I),$
      $holdsat(hasBlock(AgentB, Block), I),$
      $holdsat(pow(filesharing, myDownload(AgentA, Block)), I),$
      $AgentA! = AgentB.$
$occurred(misuse(Agent), I) \leftarrow occurred(viol(myDownload(Agent, Block)), I), i).$

% Initial state

$holdsat(pow(filesharing, myDownload(Agent, Block)), i0).$
$holdsat(pow(filesharing, myShare(Agent)), i0).$
$holdsat(perm(download(AgentA, AgentB, Block)), i0)).$
$holdsat(perm(myDownload(Agent, Block)), i0).$
$holdsat(perm(myShare(Agent)), i0).$
$holdsat(hasBlock(alice, x1), i0).$ $holdsat(hasBlock(alice, x2), i0).$
$holdsat(hasBlock(bob, x3), i0).$ $holdsat(hasBlock(bob, x4), i0).$
$holdsat(needsBlock(alice, x3), i0).$ $holdsat(needsBlock(alice, x4), i0).$
$holdsat(needsBlock(bob, x1), i0).$ $holdsat(needsBlock(bob, x2), i0).$
$holdsat(live(filesharing), i0).$

% fluent rules

$holdsat(P, J) \leftarrow holdsat(P, I), not\ terminated(P, I), next(I, J).$
$holdsat(P, J) \leftarrow initiated(P, I), next(I, J).$
$occurred(E, I) \leftarrow evtype(E, ex), observed(E, I).$
$occurred(viol(E), I) \leftarrow$
      $occurred(E, I), not\ holdsat(perm(E), I), holdsat(live(X), I), evinst(E, X).$
$occurred(viol(E), I) \leftarrow$
      $occurred(E, I), evtype(E, inst), not\ holdsat(perm(E), I), event(viol(E)).$

Fig. 3. Translation of the "sharing" normative framework into $AnsProlog$ (types omitted)

the permission of that agent to download another block until it has shared (this the complementary action to download) a block with another agent. Violation of this norm results in the download power being revoked permanently. In this way reciprocity is assured by the normative framework. Initially, each agent is empowered and permitted to share and to download, so that either agent may initiate a download operation.

Fig. 3 shows the $AnsProlog$ representation of the complete normative framework representing this scenario. In the following examples a variety of normative rules will be deliberately removed and re-learned.

6.1 Learning Setting

To show how different parts of the formal model can be learned we start from a correct specification and, after deleting some of the rules, we use TAL to reconstruct the missing parts based on a single use case. In our example TAL is set to learn hypotheses of at most three rules with at most three conditions. The choice of an upper bound on the complexity (number of literals) of the rule ultimately rests on the final user. Alternatively, TAL can iterate on the complexity or perform a best first search that returns increasingly more complex solutions. We use the following mode declarations, M:

$m1 : modeh(terminated(perm(myDownload(+agent,+block)),+instant)).$
$m2 : modeh(initiated(perm(myDownload(+agent,+block)),+instant)).$
$m3 : modeb(occurred(myDownload(+agent,+block),+instant)).$
$m4 : modeb(occurred(myDownload(+agent,-block),+instant)).$
$m5 : modeb(occurred(myShare(+agent),+instant)).$
$m6 : modeb((+agent!= +agent)).$
$m7 : modeb(holdsat(hasblock(+agent,+block),+instant)).$
$m8 : modeb(holdsat(powfilesharing(myDownload(+agent,+block)),+instant)).$

The first two mode declarations state that terminate and initiate permission rules for the normative fluent $myDownload$ can be learned. The other declarations constrain the structure of the body. The difference between $m3$ and $m4$ is that the former must refer to the same block as the one in the head of the rule while the latter introduces a possibly different block. $m8$ is an inequality constraint between agents. In general more mode declarations should be considered (e.g. initiation and termination of all types of fluents should be included) but the revision can be guided by the designer. For example new changes to a stable theory are more likely to contain errors and thus can be isolated in the revision process. The time to compute all the reported hypotheses ranges from 30 to 500 milliseconds on a 2.8 GHz Intel Core 2 Duo iMac with 2 GB of RAM.

The background knowledge B contains the rules in Fig. 3 together with the traces T given in the use cases. C in this example is empty to allow for the demonstration of the most general types of learning.

Learning a single terminate/initiate rule. We suppose one of the *initiate* rules is missing from the current specification:

$$initiated(perm(myDownload(Agent, Block)), I) \leftarrow$$
$$occurred(myShare(Agent), I).$$

The designer inputs the following observed events that show how in a two agent scenario, one of the agents loses permission to download after downloading a block and reacquires it after providing a block for another agent. The trace T looks like:

$$observed(download(alice, bob, x3), 0).$$
$$observed(download(bob, alice, x1), 1).$$

The expected output O is:

$$not\ holdsat(perm(myDownload(alice, x4)), 1).$$
$$holdsat(perm(myDownload(alice, x4)), 2).$$

The trace is dysfunctional if the expected output is not true in the answer set of $T \cup B$. The ILP task is thus to find a set of rules H within the language bias specified by mode declarations in M such that given the background knowledge B in Fig. 3 and the given expected output O as conjunction of literals, O is true in the only answer set of $B \cup T \cup H$ (if one exists). TAL produces the following hypotheses:

$$initiated(perm(myDownload(A, \_)), C) \leftarrow \quad (H_1)$$
$$occurred(myShare(A), C).$$

and

$$terminated(perm(myDownload(\_, \_)), \_). \quad (H_2)$$
$$initiated(perm(myDownload(A, \_)), C) \leftarrow$$
$$occurred(myShare(A), C).$$

The second solution is not the one intended but it still supports the use case. Note that according to current implementation, whenever a fluent f is both initiated and terminated at the same time point, f still holds at the subsequent time point.

Learning multiple rules. In this scenario two rules are missing from the specification:

$$initiated(perm(myDownload(Agent, Block)), I) \leftarrow$$
$$occurred(myShare(Agent), I).$$
$$terminated(perm(myDownload(Agent, Block2)), I) \leftarrow$$
$$occurred(myDownload(Agent, Block1), I).$$

We use the same T and O as previously. TAL produces the following hypotheses:

$$terminated(perm(myDownload(A, \_)), C) \leftarrow \quad (H_1)$$
$$occurred(myDownload(A, \_), C).$$
$$initiated(perm(myDownload(A, \_)), C) \leftarrow$$
$$occurred(myShare(A), C).$$
$$terminated(perm(myDownload(\_, \_)), \_). \quad (H_2)$$
$$initiated(perm(myDownload(A, \_)), C) \leftarrow$$
$$occurred(myShare(A), C).$$

The second solution is consistent with the use case, but the designer can easily discard it, since the rule is not syntactically valid with respect to the normative framework: a fluent can only be terminated as a consequence of the occurrence of an event. Using more advanced techniques for the language bias specification it would be possible to rule out such a hypothesis.

Learning of undesired violation. We assume the following rule is missing:

$$initiated(perm(myDownload(Agent, Block)), I) \leftarrow$$
$$occurred(myShare(Agent), I).$$

This time we provide a different trace T:

$$observed(download(alice, bob, x3), 0).$$
$$observed(download(bob, alice, x1), 1).$$
$$observed(download(alice, bob, x4), 2).$$

As a result of the trace, a violation at time point 2 is implied that the designer knows to be undesired. The expected output is:

$$not\ occurred(viol(myDownload(alice, x4)), 2).$$

The outcome of the learning consists of the following two possible solutions:

$$initiated(perm(myDownload(A, \_)), C) \leftarrow \quad (H_1)$$
$$occurred(myShare(A), C).$$
$$initiated(perm(myDownload(\_, \_)), \_). \quad (H_2)$$

that show how the missing rule is derived from the undesired violation. As in the previous scenario the designer can easily dismiss the second candidate.

Learning a generate rule. To account for the different type of rules that need to be learned, the language bias is extended to consider learning of generate rules. The new

$$occurred(myShare(A), B) \leftarrow \quad (H1)$$
$$occurred(download(C, A, E), B), A! = C,$$
$$holdsat(pow(filesharing, myDownload(A, E)), B).$$

$$occurred(myShare(A), B) \leftarrow \quad (H2)$$
$$occurred(download(C, A, E), B), A! = C,$$
$$holdsat(pow(filesharing, myDownload(A, E)), B),$$
$$holdsat(hasblock(A, E), B).$$

$$occurred(myShare(A), B) \leftarrow \quad (H3)$$
$$occurred(download(C, A, E), B), A! = C,$$
$$holdsat(pow(filesharing, myDownload(C, E)), B).$$

$$occurred(myShare(A), B) \leftarrow \quad (H4)$$
$$occurred(download(C, A, E), B), A! = C,$$
$$holdsat(pow(filesharing, myDownload(C, E)), B),$$
$$holdsat(hasblock(A, E), B).$$

$$occurred(myShare(A), B) \leftarrow \quad (H5)$$
$$occurred(download(C, A, E), B), A! = C,$$
$$holdsat(hasblock(A, E), B).$$

$$occurred(myShare(A), B) \leftarrow \quad (H6)$$
$$occurred(download(C, A, E), B),$$
$$holdsat(pow(filesharing, myDownload(C, E)), B).$$

Fig. 4. Proposals to revise the generate rule

mode declarations are:

$$modeh(occurred(myShare(+agent),+instant)).$$
$$modeb(occurred(download(-agent,+agent,-block),+instant)).$$

We use the same trace and expected output as in the previous scenario (three observed events). The following rule is eliminated from the specification:

$$occurred(myShare(AgentB),I) \leftarrow$$
$$\quad AgentA! = AgentB,$$
$$\quad occurred(download(AgentA, AgentB, Block), I),$$
$$\quad holdsat(hasblock(AgentB, Block), I),$$
$$\quad holdsat(pow(filesharing, myDownload(AgentA, Block)), I).$$

This is the most complicated case for the designer as a set of six different hypotheses are returned by TAL (see Fig. 4). Knowing the semantics of the function symbol `download(AgentA, AgentB, Block)` as `AgentA` downloads from `AgentB` the designer should be able to select the most appropriate rule.

7   Related Work

The motivation behind this paper is the problem of how to converge upon a complete and correct normative framework *with respect to the intended range of application*, where in practice these properties may be manifested by incorrect or unexpected behaviour in use. Additionally, we would observe, from practical experience with our particular framework, that it is often desirable, as with much software development, to be able to develop and test incrementally—and regressively—rather than attempt verification once the system is (notionally) complete.

The literature seems to fall broadly into three categories:

1. Concrete language frameworks (OMASE [23], Operetta [36], InstSuite [27], MOISE [28], Islander [20], OCeAN [21] and the constraint approach of Garcia-Camino [22]) for the specification of normative systems, that are typically supported by some form of model-checking, and in some cases allow for change in the normative structure;
2. Logical formalisms, such as [24], that capture consistency and completeness via modalities and other formalisms like [6], that capture the concept of norm change, or [44] and [8];
3. Mechanisms that look out for (new) conventions and handle their assimilation into the normative framework over time and subject to the current normative state and the position of other agents [1, 9].

Essentially, the objective of each of the above is to realize a transformation of the normative framework to accommodate some form of shortcoming. These shortcomings can be identified in several ways:

1. By observing that a particular state is rarely achieved, which can indicate there is insufficient normative guidance for participants, or

2. A norm conflict occurs, such that an agent is unable to act consistently under the governing norms [32], or
3. A particular violation occurs frequently, which may indicate that the violation conflicts with an effective course of action that agents prefer to take, the penalty notwithstanding.

All of these can be viewed as characterising emergent [39] approaches to the evolution of normative frameworks, where some mechanism, either in the framework, or in the environment, is used to revise the norms. In the approach taken here, the designer presents use cases that effectively capture their behavioural requirements for the system, in order to 'fix' bad states. This has an interesting parallel with the scheme put forward by Serrano and Saugar [41], where they propose the specification of incomplete theories and their management through incomplete normative states identified as "pending". The framework lets designated agents resolve this category through the speech acts *allow* and *forbid* and scheme is formalised using an action language.

A useful categorisation of normative frameworks appears in [4]. Whether the norms here are 'strong' or 'weak' —the first guideline— depends on whether the purpose of the normative model is to develop the system specification or additionally to provide an explicit representation for run-time reference. Likewise, in respect of the remaining guidelines, it all depends on how the framework we have developed is actually used: we have chosen, for the purpose of this presentation, to stage norm refinement so that it is an off-line (in the sense of prior to deployment) process, while much of the discussion in [4] addresses run-time issues. Whether the process we have outlined here could effectively be a means for on-line mechanism design, is something we have yet to explore.

From an ILP perspective, we employ an ILP system that can learn logic programs with negation (stratified or otherwise). Though recently introduced and in its early stages of development *TAL* is the most appropriate choice to support this work for two main reasons: it is supported by completeness results, unlike other existing non-monotonic ILP systems ([38], [31]), and it can be tailored to particular requirements (e.g. different search strategies can address performance requirements). The approach presented in this paper is related to other recently proposed frameworks for the elaboration of formal specifications via inductive learning. Within the context of software engineering, [16] has shown how examples of desirable and undesirable behaviour of a software system can be used by an ILP system, together with an incomplete background knowledge of the envisioned system and its environment, to compute missing requirements specifications. A more general framework has been proposed [15] where desirable and undesirable behaviours are generated from counterexamples produced by model checking a given (incomplete) requirements specification with respect to given system properties. The learning of missing requirements has in this case the effect of eliminating the counterexamples by elaborating further the specification.

8   Conclusions and Future Work

We have presented an approach for learning norms and behavioural rules, via inductive logic programming, from example traces in order to guide and support the synthesis of a normative framework. This addresses a crucial problem in normative systems as the development of such specifications is in general a manual and error-prone task. The approach deploys an established inductive logic programming system [14] that takes in input an initial (partial) description of a normative system and use cases of expected behaviours provided by the designer and generates hypothesis in the form of missing norms and behavioural rules that together with the given description explain the use cases. Although the approach presented in this paper has been tailored for learning missing information, it can also be applied to computing revisions over the existing description. In principle this can be achieved by transforming the existing normative rules into defeasible rules with exceptions and using the same ILP system to compute exception rules. These exceptions would in essence be prescriptions for changes (i.e. addition and/or deletion of literals in the body of existing rules) in the current specification. An appropriate refactoring of the defeasible rules based on the learned exception rules would give a revised (non-defeasible) specification. In this case, the revision would be in terms of changes over the rules of a normative framework instead of changes over its belief state, as would be the case if a TMS approach were adopted.

There are several criticisms that can be levelled at the approach as it stands. Firstly, the design language is somewhat unfriendly: a proper tool would have a problem-oriented language, like InstAL/QL [12,27]. A system designer would then start from an initial description of their normative framework with some use cases and receive automated suggestions of additional norms to include in the framework written in the same high-level language. The machinery described here, based on $AnsProlog$ syntax and ILP formulation, would then be used as a sound "back- end" computation to a formalism familiar to the system designer. Secondly, better control is needed over the rules that are learned and over the filtering of incorrect rules; at present this depends on specialised knowledge of the learning process. This can to some extent be controlled through careful choice of and limits on the size of use cases—probably involving heuristics—to improve the effectiveness of the learning process in the search for relevant hypotheses and pruning of those potential solutions that cannot be translated back into the canonical form of the normative framework. Despite these issues, we believe we have identified an interesting path for automation, development and debugging of practical normative specifications and perhaps, in the long term, a mechanism for on-line norm evolution.

In this paper, we assume that a use case contains a complete trace. With the underlying system, TAL, being capable of non-monotonic reasoning, there is no reason why the designer should not be able to give a partial trace or even specify conditions on the states that should be considered during the learning. This would make specifying use cases easier for the designer. Of course, having to specify the conditions in $AnsProlog$ could be a hurdle, bringing us back to the case for a more domain-specific language to express institutional information and queries.

The examples examined in this paper always suggest learning one rule for a given use case. This does not have to be so in general. TAL is capable learning any number of rules in one go. Unfortunately, with large number of rules to be added or revised, it becomes difficult for the designer to find the desired (sub)set of rules. In the future, we aim to look at methodologies to support the designer in this process. The most obvious solution is to opt for an incremental approach, but this would require re-computation, which in large examples could be expensive unless we can exploit the structure of the learning algorithm to learn incrementally.

At the moment, our system is set up for the designer of a normative framework to support the debugging and verification. However, the same approach could also be used for a running normative system where the rules need to be updated. The challenge in such a system is how to provide the learning system with appropriate automatically generated use case. Without human intervention, the system will need to provide rules that the system can use immediately.

References

1. Artikis, A.: Dynamic protocols for open agent systems. In: Sierra, C., et al. (eds.) [42], pp. 97–104
2. Artikis, A., Sergot, M., Pitt, J.: Specifying electronic societies with the Causal Calculator. In: Giunchiglia, F., Odell, J.J., Weiss, G. (eds.) AOSE 2002. LNCS, vol. 2585, pp. 1–15. Springer, Heidelberg (2003)
3. Baral, C.: Knowledge Representation, Reasoning and Declarative Problem Solving. Cambridge Press, Cambridge (2003)
4. Boella, G., Pigozzi, G., van der Torre, L.: Normative Systems in Computer Science – Ten Guidelines for Normative Multiagent Systems. In: Normative Mult-Agent Systems (2009)
5. Boella, G., Noriega, P., Pigozzi, G., Verhagen, H. (eds.): Normative Mult-Agent Systems. Dagstuhl Seminar Proceedings, vol. 09121. Schloss Dagstuhl - Leibniz-Zentrum fuer Informatik, Germany (2009)
6. Boella, G., Pigozzi, G., van der Torre, L.: Normative framework for normative system change. In: Sierra, C., et al. (eds.) [42], pp. 169–176
7. Boella, G., van der Torre, L.: Constitutive Norms in the Design of Normative Multiagent Systems. In: Toni, F., Torroni, P. (eds.) CLIMA 2005. LNCS (LNAI), vol. 3900, pp. 303–319. Springer, Heidelberg (2006)
8. Cardoso, H.L., Oliveira, E.C.: Norm defeasibility in an institutional normative framework. In: Ghallab, M., Spyropoulos, C.D., Fakotakis, N., Avouris, N.M. (eds.) ECAI. Frontiers in Artificial Intelligence and Applications, vol. 178, pp. 468–472. IOS Press, Amsterdam (2008)
9. Christelis, G., Rovatsos, M.: Automated norm synthesis in an agent-based planning environment. In: Sierra, C., et al. (eds.) [42], pp. 161–168
10. Cliffe, O.: Specifying and Analysing Institutions in Multi-Agent Systems using Answer Set Programming. PhD thesis, University of Bath (2007)
11. Cliffe, O., De Vos, M., Padget, J.: Answer set programming for representing and reasoning about virtual institutions. In: Inoue, K., Satoh, K., Toni, F. (eds.) CLIMA 2006. LNCS (LNAI), vol. 4371, pp. 60–79. Springer, Heidelberg (2007)
12. Cliffe, O., De Vos, M., Padget, J.A.: Embedding landmarks and scenes in a computational model of institutions. In: Sichman, J.S., Padget, J., Ossowski, S., Noriega, P. (eds.) COIN 2007. LNCS (LNAI), vol. 4870, pp. 41–57. Springer, Heidelberg (2008)
13. Corapi, D., Ray, O., Russo, A., Bandara, A.K., Lupu, E.C.: Learning rules from user behaviour. In: 5th Aritificial Intelligence Applications and Innovations (AIAI 2009) (April 2009)
14. Corapi, D., Russo, A., Lupu, E.: Inductive logic programming as abductive search. In: 26th International Conference on Logic Programming, Leibniz International Proceedings in Informatics. Schloss Dagstuhl Research Online Publication Server (2010)

15. Alrajeh, D., Kramer, J., Russo, A., Uchitel, S.: Learning operational requirements from goal models. In: Proceedings of the 31st International Conference on Software Engineering (ICSE 2009), pp. 265–275. IEEE Computer Society, Los Alamitos (2009)
16. Alrajeh, D., Ray, O., Russo, A., Uchitel, S.: Extracting requirements from Scenarios using ILP. In: Muggleton, S.H., Otero, R., Tamaddoni-Nezhad, A. (eds.) ILP 2006. LNCS (LNAI), vol. 4455, pp. 64–78. Springer, Heidelberg (2007)
17. Denecker, M., De Schreye, D.: SLDNFA: An Abductive Procedure for Abductive Logic Programs. J. Log. Program. 34(2), 111–167 (1998)
18. Dignum, V.: A model for organizational interaction: based on agents, founded in logic. PhD thesis, University of Utrecht (2004)
19. Džroski, S., Lavrač, N. (eds.): Relational Data Mining. Relational data mining applications: an overview, vol. ch. 14, pp. 339–360. Springer Verlag, New York, Inc., New York (2000)
20. Esteva, M., de la Cruz, D., Sierra, C.: Islander: an electronic institutions editor. In: AAMAS, pp. 1045–1052. ACM, New York (2002)
21. Fornara, N., Viganò, F., Verdicchio, M., Colombetti, M.: Artificial institutions: a model of institutional reality for open multiagent systems. Artif. Intell. Law 16(1), 89–105 (2008)
22. García-Camino, A., Rodríguez-Aguilar, J.A., Sierra, C., Vasconcelos, W.W.: Constraint rule-based programming of norms for electronic institutions. Autonomous Agents and Multi-Agent Systems 18(1), 186–217 (2009)
23. Garcia-Ojeda, J.C., DeLoach, S.A., Robby, Oyenan, W.H., Valenzuela, J.L.: O-maSE: A customizable approach to developing multiagent development processes. In: Luck, M., Padgham, L. (eds.) Agent-Oriented Software Engineering VIII. LNCS, vol. 4951, pp. 1–15. Springer, Heidelberg (2008)
24. Garion, C., Roussel, S., Cholvy, L.: A modal logic for reasoning on consistency and completeness of regulations. In: Boella, G., et al. (eds.) [5]
25. Gebser, M., Kaufmann, B., Neumann, A., Schaub, T.: Conflict-Driven Answer Set Solving. In: Proceeding of IJCAI 2007, pp. 386–392 (2007)
26. Gelfond, M., Lifschitz, V.: Classical negation in logic programs and disjunctive databases. New Generation Computing 9(3-4), 365–386 (1991)
27. Hopton, L., Cliffe, O., De Vos, M., Padget, J.: Instql: A query language for virtual institutions using answer set programming. In: Dix, J., Fisher, M., Novák, P. (eds.) CLIMA X. LNCS, vol. 6214, pp. 102–121. Springer, Heidelberg (2010)
28. Hübner, J.F., Sichman, J.S., Boissier, O.: Developing organised multiagent systems using the moise. IJAOSE 1(3/4), 370–395 (2007)
29. Searle, J.R.: The Construction of Social Reality. Allen Lane, The Penguin Press (1995)
30. Jones, A.J.I., Sergot, M.: A Formal Characterisation of Institutionalised Power. ACM Computing Surveys 28(4cs), 121 (1996) (read 28/11/2004)
31. Kimber, T., Broda, K., Russo, A.: Induction on failure: Learning connected horn theories. In: Erdem, E., Lin, F., Schaub, T. (eds.) LPNMR 2009. LNCS, vol. 5753, pp. 169–181. Springer, Heidelberg (2009)
32. Kollingbaum, M., Norman, T., Preece, A., Sleeman, D.: Norm conflicts and inconsistencies in virtual organisations. In: Noriega, P., Vázquez-Salceda, J., Boella, G., Boissier, O., Dignum, V., Fornara, N., Matson, E. (eds.) COIN 2006. LNCS (LNAI), vol. 4386, pp. 245–258. Springer, Heidelberg (2007)
33. Lavrač, N., Džeroski, S.: Inductive Logic Programming: Techniques and Applications. Ellis Horwood (1994)
34. Muggleton, S.: Inverse entailment and progol. New Gen. Comp. 13(3&4), 245–286 (1995)
35. Niemelä, I., Simons, P.: Smodels: An implementation of the stable model and well-founded semantics for normal LP. In: Fuhrbach, U., Dix, J., Nerode, A. (eds.) LPNMR 1997. LNCS, vol. 1265, pp. 420–429. Springer, Heidelberg (1997)

36. Okouya, D., Dignum, V.: Operetta: a prototype tool for the design, analysis and development of multi-agent organizations. In: AAMAS (Demos), pp. 1677–1678. IFAAMAS (2008)
37. Rodriguez-Aguilar, J.A.: On the Design and Construction of Agent-mediated Institutions. PhD thesis, Universitat Autonomá de Barcelona (2001)
38. Sakama, C.: Nonmonotonic inductive logic programming. In: Eiter, T., Faber, W., Truszczyński, M. (eds.) LPNMR 2001. LNCS (LNAI), vol. 2173, p. 62. Springer, Heidelberg (2001)
39. Savarimuthu, B.T.R., Cranefield, S.: A categorization of simulation works on norms. In: Boella, G., et al. (eds.) [5]
40. Sergot, M.: (C+)++: An Action Language For Representing Norms and Institutions. Technical report, Imperial College, London (August 2004)
41. Serrano, J.M., Saugar, S.: Dealing with incomplete normative states. In: Padget, J., Artikis, A., Vasconcelos, W., Stathis, K., da Silva, V.T., Matson, E., Polleres, A. (eds.) COIN@AAMAS 2009. LNCS, vol. 6069, pp. 304–319. Springer, Heidelberg (2010)
42. Sierra, C., Castelfranchi, C., Decker, K.S., Sichman, J.S. (eds.): AAMAS. IFAAMAS (2009)
43. Singh, M.P.: A social semantics for agent communication languages. In: Dignum, F.P.M., Greaves, M. (eds.) Issues in Agent Communication. LNCS, vol. 1916, pp. 31–45. Springer, Heidelberg (2000)
44. Vasconcelos, W., Kollingbaum, M., Norman, T.: Resolving conflict and inconsistency in norm-regulated virtual organizations. In: Durfee, E.H., Yokoo, M., Huhns, M.N., Shehory, O. (eds.) AAMAS, p. 91. IFAAMAS (2007)

Using a Normative Framework to Explore the Prototyping of Wireless Grids

Tina Balke[1], Marina De Vos[2] Julian Padget[2], and Frank Fitzek[3]

[1] University of Bayreuth, Chair of Information Systems Management
`tina.balke@uni-bayreuth.de`
[2] University of Bath, Dept. of Computer Science
`{mdv,jap}@cs.bath.ac.uk`
[3] University of Aalborg, Multimedia Information and Signal Processing
`ff@es.aau.dk`

Abstract. The capacity for normative frameworks to capture the essential features of interactions between components in open architectures suggests they might also be of assistance in an early, rapid prototyping phase of system development, helping to refine concepts, identify actors, explore policies and evaluate feasibility. As an exercise to examine this thesis, we investigate the concept of the wireless grid. Wireless grids have been proposed to address the energy issues arising from a new generation of mobile phones, the idea being that local communication with other mobile phones, being cheaper, can be used in combination with network communication to achieve common goals while at the same time extending the battery duty cycle. This results in a social dilemma, as it is advantageous for rational users to benefit from the energy savings without any contribution to the cooperation, as every commitment has its price. We present a necessarily simplified model, whose purpose is to provide us with the foundation to explore issues in the management of such a framework, policies to encourage collaborative behaviour, and the means to evaluate the effects on energy consumption.

1 Introduction

This article reports on a feasibility study into how and whether institutional models can help in evaluating the concept of wireless grids. While that is the specific topic of the article, the broader contribution is that of asking the question of how such normative model building can be of use in an early design phase, long before hardware or software is available, in order to evaluate both principles and alternative policies — that might have significant consequences subsequently.

In technology neutral terms, the problem we consider is of some digital content to be distributed to a collection of nodes that support an expensive (in terms of power and money) connection via a structured network and a cheaper connection via an ad-hoc network. The task is to minimise the cost of the distribution of this digital content by using a combination of the structured and ad-hoc networks. The model can essentially be parameterised by the cost functions for the (un)structured network technology. The particular case that interests us is the forthcoming 4G mobile phone network where the

M. De Vos et al. (Eds.): COIN 2010 International Workshops, LNAI 6541, pp. 95–113, 2011.
© Springer-Verlag Berlin Heidelberg 2011

structured network uses a traditional cellular link and the ad-hoc network uses IEEE 802.11 (wireless LAN) with the ethernet transport protocol. The motivation for the idea of such a "wireless grid" is that local communication over (wireless) ethernet uses significantly less power per unit of data than communicating with the network base-station and that duration of the battery duty cycle is a major usability factor for users.

The deployment of third generation (3G) of mobile network systems is in progress, but a quite different next generation network (called Fourth Generation or 4G) is under development that is intended to cause a paradigm shift in the cooperation architecture of wireless communication [14]. While for 3G the industry focused on technology for enabling voice and basic data communications (technology-centric-view), the emphasis in 4G is more user-centric [24]. Consequently, studies to find possible drivers for consumer demand for mobile devices, such as the one by TNS [21] across 15 countries in mid-2004, have been conducted. This study revealed that it was not high performance that was attractive to consumers, but rather useful, convenient and enjoyable services coupled with ubiquitous infrastructures for constant connection. In addition, "two days of battery life during active use" topped the wish list of key features in 14 of the 15 countries surveyed.

Batteries have fixed capacity that puts limits on the operational time for a device in one charge cycle. The increasing sophistication of mobile phones and their evolution into smart phones offering Internet access, imaging (still and video), audio and access to new services, has had a significant impact on power consumption, leading to shorter stand-by times, as well as the problem of rising battery temperature unless there is active cooling [19].

Fitzek and Katz [9] have proposed a way around some of these issues with the concept of a wireless grid, in which users share resources in a peer-to-peer fashion that uses less power but this requires a difficult to obtain collaboration between the users. The contribution of this article is to build an institutional model of the interactions between handsets and base-station and between handsets in order to provide a foundational model from which to be able to explore policies, identify suitable sanctions and evaluate potential gains from reduced power consumption.

The remainder of the article is structured as follows: in the next section (2) we cover three aspects of the background, namely (i) normative frameworks, (ii) a detailed discussion of the wireless grid scenario, and (iii) the energy model: what different agent actions cost in terms of power consumption. Then, in section 3 we describe the action model—what the agents may do—before presenting some results from its analysis. We conclude in section 4 with a discussion of the related work, results and future directions.

2   Technical Context

The first section here serves to provide a brief description of the event-based normative framework that is used later for the model. The second provides a detailed description of some technical issues surrounding the wireless grid idea, highlighting in particular, actual energy costs and the risk of free-loading, which has some elements that echo issues with public pool resource problems.

2.1   Normative Frameworks

The concept of the normative framework—sometimes also called an institution, some-times a virtual organisation—has become firmly embedded in the agent community as a necessary foil to the essential autonomy of agents, in just the same way as societal conventions and legal frameworks have been developed to constrain people. In both the physical and the virtual worlds—and the emerging combination of the two—the arguments in favour centre on the minimization of disruptive behaviour and supporting the achievement of the goals for which the normative framework has been conceived and thus also the motivation for submission to its governance by the participants.

While the concept remains attractive, its realization in a computational setting remains a subject for research, with a wide range of logics [1,4,6] and tools [20,22,12], to cite but a few. We do not include an extensive and detailed case for the purpose and value of normative frameworks here—this can be found in [23,5], for example.

Formal Model.   To provide context for this article, we give an outline of a formal event-based model for the specification of normative frameworks that captures all the essential properties, namely empowerment, permission, obligation and violation. Extended presentations can be found in the citations above.

The essential elements of our normative framework are:

1.   Events ($\mathcal{E}$), that bring about changes in state, and
2.   Fluents ($\mathcal{F}$), that characterise the state at a given instant.

The function of the framework is to define the interplay between these concepts over time, in order to capture the evolution of a particular framework through the interaction of its participants. We distinguish two kinds of event: normative events ($\mathcal{E}_{inst}$), that are the events defined by the framework and exogenous ($\mathcal{E}_{ex}$), that are outside its scope, but whose occurrence triggers normative events in a direct reflection of the "counts-as" principle [13]. We further partition normative events into normative actions ($\mathcal{E}_{act}$) that denote changes in the normative state and violation events ($\mathcal{E}_{viol}$) that signal the occurrence of violations. Violations may arise either from explicit generation, from the occurrence of a non-permitted event, or from the failure to fulfil an obligation. We also distinguish two kinds of fluents: *normative fluents* that denote normative properties of the state such as permissions, powers and obligations, and *domain fluents* that correspond to properties specific to the normative framework itself.

The evolution of the state of the framework is achieved through the definition of two relations:

1.   The generation relation: this implements counts-as, in that it specifies how the occurrence of one (exogenous or normative) event generates another (normative) event, subject to the empowerment of the actor. Formally, this can be expressed as $\mathcal{G} : \mathcal{X} \times \mathcal{E} \rightarrow 2^{\mathcal{E}_{inst}}$, where $\mathcal{X}$ denotes a formula over the (normative) state and $\mathcal{E}$ an event, whose confluence results in an institutional event, and
2.   The consequence relation, that specifies the initiation and termination of fluents subject to the performance of some action in a state matching some expression, or formally $\mathcal{C} : \mathcal{X} \times \mathcal{E} \rightarrow 2^{\mathcal{F}} \times 2^{\mathcal{F}}$.

Again, for the sake of context, we summarize the semantics of our framework and cite [7] for an in-depth discussion. The semantics are defined over a sequence, called a trace, of exogenous events. Starting from the initial state, each exogenous event is responsible for a state change, through initiation and termination of fluents, that is achieved by a three-step process:

1. The transitive closure of $\mathcal{G}$ with respect to a given exogenous event determines all the (normative) events that result,
2. To this we add all violations of events not permitted and all obligations not fulfilled, giving the set of all events whose consequences determine the new state, so that
3. The application of $\mathcal{C}$ to this set of events, identifies all fluents to initiate and terminate with respect to the current state in order to obtain the next state.

So for each trace, we can obtain a sequence of states that constitutes the model of the normative framework. As with human regulatory settings, normative frameworks become useful when it is possible to *verify* that particular properties are satisfied for all possible scenarios. In order to do so, we need to incorporate a computational model in our formal representation.

Implementation. This formalisation is realized as a computational model through Answer Set Programming [3,11] and it is this representation that is the subject of the evaluation process described in Section 3.2. In [7] it was shown that the formal model of an normative framework could be translated to an $AnsProlog$ program—a logic program under answer set semantics—such that the answer sets of the program correspond to the traces of the framework. A detailed description of the mapping can be found there.

$AnsProlog$ is a declarative knowledge representation language that allows the programmer to describe a problem and the requirements on the solutions. Answer set solvers like CLASP [10] or SMODELS [16] process the $AnsProlog$ specification and return the solutions, in this case the traces, as answer sets. Answer set programming, a logic programming paradigm, permits, in contrast to related techniques like the event calculus [15] and C+ [8], the specification of both problem and query as an executable program, thus eliminating the gap between specification and verification language. But perhaps more importantly, both languages are identical, allowing for more straightforward verification and validation.

A level of abstraction can be added using a domain-specific action language, like InstAL [7], and query language, InstQL [12] for example, which can be both translated into $AnsProlog$ in order to specify not only the valid traces, but those that exhibit features of interest. We use InstAL to describe our scenario in Section 3. The action language uses semi-natural language to describe the various components of the normative framework and allows type definitions to avoid grounding problems when translating to $AnsProlog$. For example, events are defined by `typeOfEvent event namOfEvent;` with type being one of `exogenous`, `create`, `inst` or `violation`, while fluents are defined by `fluent nameofFluent(ParameterType, ...);`. Generation of normative events from exogenous events is specified using the `generates` statement, while `initiates` and `terminates` define the two parts of the consequence relation. Conditions on the state are expressed using `if`. The `initially` statement serves to specify the set of fluents that characterise the initial state after the

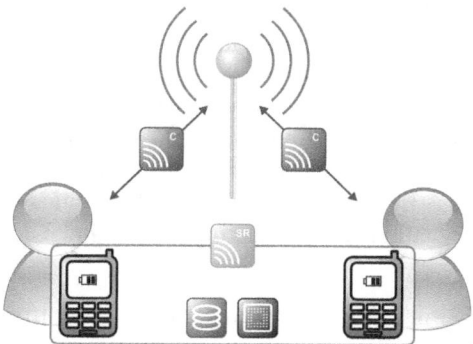

Fig. 1. Wireless Grid Communication Architecture

normative framework is created. For our model we are interested in all traces that lead to success, so we do not require the additional facilities of the query language InstQL. Instead we specify the fluents or events we want to show or hide directly in *AnsProlog* using the directives #show and #hide.

2.2   The Wireless Grid Scenario

The Wireless Grid Architecture. As described in the introduction, to overcome the energy problems of 4th generation mobile phones, Fitzek and Katz [9] proposed the establishment of *wireless grids* as shown in Figure 1 [9].

In these wireless grids, ubiquitous mobile devices with potentially different capabilities are expected to create ad-hoc connections and to cooperate and share their limited resources for the benefit of the community. Cooperation between mobile devices is achieved by short range communication link technologies, such as WLAN or Bluetooth. Compared to the traditional cellular 3G communication with the base-station, the advantage of the short-range communication is much higher bandwidth while using much less power, which we quantify latet in this section. Thus, the battery and CPU power needed on the short link is significantly lower than it would be needed on the cellular one [19]. In this article we will focus on the IEEE802.11 WLAN specification, that allows mobile devices to communicate directly with each other and according to Perrucci et al. [19] has the highest energy saving potential.

For a better understanding of the wireless grid idea we briefly present a scenario that we can refer back to later. This scenario is set in a football stadium: while watching one game, the fans are very likely to be interested in games that take place at the same time at another place. As they cannot watch two games live at the same time, they might use mobile phones in order to get information about other games. A likely problem for the infrastructure provider is that once a goal has been scored in another game, fans want to watch the other goal on their mobile phones and all try to stream the video file from the base station at the same time, thus overloading it. The bandwidth of the base station connection is divided into several channels that are sent out sequentially within one time frame. Thereby—up to a certain technical maximum—each mobile phone is allocated one slot. As the total bandwidth of a base station is fixed, the more mobile phone users are given a slot, the smaller the bandwidth that can be assigned to each channel gets. As a result the download times increase, leading both to more battery consumption and lower quality in the streaming service.

In contrast to the normal "non-cooperative" scenario in which a single mobile phone user would need to receive all sub-streams over the cellular link resulting in the above mentioned problems, using the cooperation envisioned in the wireless grid scenario, users could share the task by receiving a subset of the multicast channels over the cellular link from the base station and exchanging the missing pieces over the short range link.

The Energy Advantage in IEEE802.11. To understand the IEEE802.11 WLAN wireless grid scenario and its energy implications better, this section examines the technical aspects of WLAN transmission in more detail. We use A to denote the set of agents in the scenario. In considering the energy implications of the wireless grid scenario, we observe the following basic definition of energy $[E]$, that states that energy consumption in terms of battery depends on two factors: the power $[P]$ consumed per connection type and the time $[t]$ needed for the actual transmission:

$$Energy = Power * Time \ [Joules] \tag{1}$$

So what is the energy consumption in this scenario? The total energy consumption is the energy consumed over the tradition cellular 3G connection (E_{3G}) plus that over the short link (i.e. WLAN) connection (E_{WLAN}) plus the idle time for both links (E_{idle}). In case of no cooperation the shortlink costs are 0, i.e. it is assumed that the WLAN connection is turned off and the football fan has to stream the complete video using the 3G connection. In case of wireless grid cooperation it is assumed that both connections (WLAN and 3G) are turned on and the devices help one another in a peer-to-peer-like fashion. Assuming $|A_{Coop}|$ cooperating agents in the scenario for example, each agent only needs to stream only a part of the total video from the base station (i.e. $\frac{1}{|A_{Coop}|}$ in an ideal scenario) and obtain the missing chunks from the other cooperation partners using the short link connection. Therefore the energy consumption in the cooperation case (E_{Coop}) comprises the amounts for:

1. **Streaming** part of the video from the base station using the 3G link ($E_{3G,rx}$) (plus the energy consumed while the 3G connection is idle ($E_{3G,i}$)),
2. **Receiving** the remaining chunks of the video on the WLAN connection ($E_{WLAN,rx}$),
3. **Sending** own chunks to the other participants via the WLAN connection ($E_{WLAN,tx}$), and
4. **Idling** (i.e. when not transmitting or receiving anything but waiting for the next interaction) ($E_{WLAN,i}$).

With reference to equation 1, by replacing the E with the respective $P*t$-values, one can analyse the power consumption as well as the transmission times for the scenario in the cooperative and non-cooperative case in detail. Representative power and time values for the transmission in the different states using 3G and WLAN connection can be found in [19, p.D10] for example, which are based on measurements from a Nokia

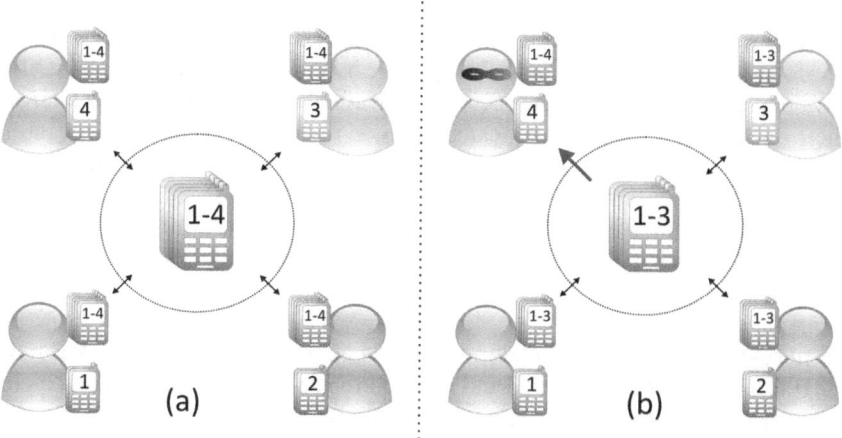

Fig. 2. The Reciprocity Problem in Wireless Grids

N95. These numbers indicate that although the power needed for the WLAN and the 3G state are about the same, for a point-to-point communication, the data rate for the 3G link (0.193 Mbit/s for the receiving state) is significantly lower than that of WLAN (5.115 Mbit/s, receiving state, 30m distance) leading to significantly worse transmission times and consequently a much worse energy per bit ratio for the 3G link. The energy consumed in the idle states is of secondary importance and therefore neglected here.

This suggests that the cooperation scenario has a significant potential advantage in energy consumption, compared to the conventional cellular communication architecture, especially if the number of cooperating mobile phones is high and a large proportion of the data transmission can be done via the short-link connection.

The Reciprocity Problem in Wireless Grids. Although the wireless grid may have a huge advantage with regard to the battery consumption, it also has the intrinsic weakness of distributed cooperative architectures: it relies on cooperation to succeed. The cooperation idea in the wireless grid, as shown in Figure 2(a), is as follows:

1. The participants volunteer their resources, forming a common pool which can be used by all of them in order to achieve a common goal, such as file streaming. The utility which users can obtain from the pooled resources is much higher than they can obtain on their own. For example, in the football stadium scenario, both download time and battery consumption are reduced. However, the problem is that commitment comes at a cost, in the form of battery consumption for sending file chunks, i.e. $E_{WLAN,tx}$. As a consequence, (bounded) rational users would prefer to access the resources without any commitment of their own, as shown in figure 2.
2. Thus, as shown in (b), the grey agent in the top left corner (with blindfold) can enjoy the full benefits from the common pool without committing anything itself, hence cheating on the three other agents.

However, if a substantial number of users follows this selfish strategy, the network itself would be at stake, depriving all users of the benefits [17]. The reason for this is straightforward: network users can have strategic behaviour and are not necessarily obediently cooperating by making their resources available without the prospect of rewards for their good behaviour. Unreciprocated, there is no inherent value to cooperation for a user. A lone cooperating user draws no benefit from its cooperation, even if the rest of the network does. Guaranteed cost paired with uncertainty or even lack of any resulting benefit does not induce cooperation in a (bounded) rational, utility-maximising user. Without any further incentives, rational users therefore would not cooperate in such an environment and all be worse off than if they cooperated [2].

The Energy Model. Utility quantification is being used by the (bounded rational) agents (i.e. agents that only have partial information about their environment, including other agents) to determine the utility of the different possible actions and choose their actions in such as way that maximises their utility. Concerning the knowledge that they can rely on when calculating utilities, we assume the agents do not have knowledge of the whole system, but only the small part of it in their vicinity.

We now explain how the agents determine the utility of an action, using the football stadium scenario described earlier. However, to keep the example simple, for the utility considerations we consider the interaction of two agents only and formulate the costs in such a way that they can easily be expanded to any number of agents.

The two agents both want to stream the same file G in the stadium. In order to get the complete file, they can cooperate and thereby reduce their energy consumption or stream the file themselves using a cellular link connection. The exchange is done in chunks ($g \in G$).

As described above, the issue in the particular wireless grid scenario that we consider here is that the different agents have different subsets of G (i.e. parts of the file) already and each is trying to obtain the full set by exchanging parts of their subsets of G with one another. Thus, looking at a potential exchange, from the perspective of an agent a_i, for each chunk only two mutually exclusive situations can occur: either the agent does, or does not, have a given chunk. This can be expressed in terms of the set H_{a_i} (the set of chunks agent a_i has; $H_{a_i} \subseteq G$) and the corresponding complement set (with respect to G) H'_{a_i} that represents the set of chunks agent a_i has not.

In an exchange, an agent a_1 will try to obtain the set of the missing chunks H'_1 and in turn can potentially provide the set H_1. Let H_2 being the chunks agent a_2 possesses and let agent a_1 and a_2 enter an exchange process ($H_1 \cup H_2 \subseteq G$). In order to reflect the local connectivity properties, we write $\overline{A}_{a_1}$ ($\subseteq A$) to denote those $a_j \in A, j \neq i$ that are within communication range of a_i. The local radius of each agent is determined by the transaction protocol dependent signal radius of its mobile phone.

What is important to the agent now are the utilities of the different action alternatives. Thus, an agent needs to consider the utility of using the short-link cooperation (including the costs for searching short-link cooperation partners in the first place) compared to the cellular link as well as the utility of reciprocating in contrast to cheating on other agents.

The search costs are those that accumulate as a result of the agents searching for the missing chunks. We assume that the costs of sending out a request message for cooperation using WLAN transmission are fixed and independent of the number of chunks requested. However, the number of messages an agent has to send before it finds an agent that is willing to cooperate and one that can supply at least one missing chunks depends on the success probability $p = f(|\overline{A}|, H'); p \in [0, 1]$ for a single message. We define "success" to mean finding a cooperation partner with at least one missing chunk. As stated above, the probability p is a result of the function of the number of agents in the neighbourhood $|\overline{A}|$ and of the number of chunks missing H'. As yet, we have no measure of how these two quantities are related, but we can make some general observations about their correlation. Thus, for the missing chunks, we contend, without evidence at this point, that p has a proportional relation with the missing chunks of the form $H'_{a_i} \propto p$. Our rationale starts from the assumption that the chunks are distributed uniformly over all agents. Thus, if missing many chunks an agent is more likely to find another agent that can offer any of the missing chunks, whereas the probability is lower if it is only missing a small number of specific chunks. Besides the number of missing chunks, p is furthermore dependent on the number of agents in the neighbourhood, i.e. the number of other agents $|\overline{A}_{a_i}|$ an agent a_i can see locally[1]. The probability p is proportional to $|\overline{A}|$ as well. The intuition is that the higher the agent population density, the higher the probability of finding an agents that responds positively to the request when searching for the chunks.

To give an example for p, in a football-stadium where many people are in one place and want to download the same file (e.g. a replay of a goal), it will approach 1 as there are many people searching for and offering the same chunks, while it tends to approach 0 when there are fewer people searching for and offering the same chunks. Once an agent has found a transaction partner, they can exchange chunks. Thus the maximum number of chunks available for exchange is the intersection of the set an agent can offer to the transaction partner (i.e. all the chunks it has) and that the transaction partner needs; and vice versa, i.e. $H_1 \cap H'_2$ & $H_2 \cap H'_1$.

Returning to the example, in the course of the exchange both agents have the option to cooperate (i.e. deliver what they promised) or defect and not send their chunks. As a consequence of this, two different utility situations can occur. Thus, in the cooperation case, based on opportunity cost considerations, the utility is calculated by taking into account what it would have cost for an agent to download the chunks from the base station using the 3G connection ($E_{3G,rx}$) reduced by the costs of receiving the chunks on a short range WLAN link from another agent ($E_{WLAN,rx}$) minus the costs for sending its own chunks ($E_{WLAN,tx}$). The latter cost can be saved by the agent if it defects. However, assuming that the transaction partner stops the transaction if being cheated and no further chunks are be exchanged (tit-for-tat), in this case the agent will have search for a new transaction partner for the remaining missing chunks. This results in search costs that could otherwise have been saved. The specific energy cost $E_{a,b}$ where $a \in WLAN, 3G; b \in tx, rx, idle$ have already been determined by Perrucci et al. [18] for single bits. As a first approximation, using a constant bpc (i.e. bits per chunk) these could be mapped to the chunks in the model.

---

[1] For reasons of simplicity it is assumed that the number of agents in the neighbourhood has no volatility, but remains the same throughout the process.

Using the *bpc* mapping and the figures by Perrucci et al. and substituting them with the variables of our utility considerations an agent is able to compute a utility for all the actions available and decide on the action to take as a consequence.

3   Formalizing the Wireless Grid Scenario

Now that we have explained the wireless grid scenario in some detail from the technological perspective, we now shift focus to the normative framework.

We observe three perspectives to the wireless grid scenario:

1. The actions that agents may take, as prescribed by the normative framework,
2. The utility functions that quantify battery costs for a given action, and
3. The agents that populate the normative frameworks and choose which action to take, informed by the utility functions.

In this article, our focus is on the (normative) actions and the utility functions (see Section 2.2): we will address their integration through the agents that participate in the normative framework in future work.

3.1   The Normative Framework

The model is preliminary in that it focusses on the essential interactions and the communication costs that arise from those interactions. Although a more elaborate model is desirable from a realistic point of view, more details would also distract and complicate while not adding to the presentation.

The features of the the prototypical scenario are:

- 1 × base-station: B
- m × agents: $A = \{a_1, \ldots, a_m\}$
- 1 × digital good: G divided into
- n × chunks: $\{g_1, \ldots, g_n\}$

We further assume that $n|m$, which is to say the number of chunks is a multiple of the number of agents.

Negotiation, obtaining and sharing. We identify three phases to the interactions for handset to base-station and handset to handset:

- **Negotiation:** assign g_i to a_j s.t. $f : G \to A$ and

$$f^{-1} : A \to G^{n|m} \text{ s.t. } f^{-1}(a_i) = \{g_j, f(g_j) = a_i\}$$

- **Obtaining:** agent a_i receives chunks $f^{-1}(a_i)$ from B
- **Sharing:** agent a_i sends chunks $f^{-1}(a_i)$ to and receives chunks $G \setminus f^{-1}(a_i)$ from other agents.

These three phases are distinct, but although negotiation must come first, obtaining and sharing can be interleaved as soon as downloading has commenced. In the following paragraphs we discuss each phase in more detail and how each is encoded in InstAL.

Each InstAL specification starts with the identification of the normative framework, the different types of variables it will use (their values can be specified in a domain file) and the fluents and events it will recognise. The full definition can be seen in Figure 3. The meaning of the various elements is explained as we progress through the different phases.

Negotiation Phase: We are not particularly concerned with the technicalities of the negotiation phase—any off-the-shelf protocol could be employed—as long as the post-condition is satisfied: that each chunk is assigned to exactly one agent and that each agent is assigned the same number of chunks—although these conditions can readily be relaxed at the cost of a lengthier specification. An allocation satisfying these conditions is given in the initial state of the model (see Figure 6, lines 104–105) via the obtainChunk fluents indicating which agents are tasked with obtaining which blocks from the base-station. Together with their chunk assignment the agents receive the necessary permission to do so (lines 102–103).

Obtaining Phase: This is where each agent downloads its assigned chunks from the base-station. This process should result in each agent holding $n|m$ distinct chunks. Because the base-station uses several different frequencies (frequency division multiplexing), many agents may download chunks simultaneously. We refer to a frequency division in the model as a channel. Of course, there is a physical limit to the number of frequency divisions and hence the number of simultaneous agent connections. The full specification of this phase can be seen in Figure 4. Each agent can only physically obtain one chunk at a time from the base station, while each channel can only be used to obtain one chunk. This is modelled by the fluent cbusy. The first InstAL rule (lines 34–36) indicates that a request to obtain a chunk is granted (intObtain) whenever there is an available channel and the agent is not busy obtaining another chunk. When a block is obtained the agent and the channel will become busy for a fixed amount of time — 2 time steps in this case (lines 42–43). From the first instant of the agent interacting with the base station, it is deemed to have obtained the block, so parts can be shared (line 41). As soon as a channel and an agent become engaged, the framework takes away the power from the agent and from the channel to engage in any other interactions (lines 53–54), stops the agent from needing the chunk and cancels the permission to obtain the chunk again later on (lines 55 and 56, respectively).

Each exogenous event generates a transition to mark the passing of time (lines 38–39). The clock event indicates that no agent was interacting with the normative framework. The transition event reduces the duration of the interaction between the channel and agent (line 46). When the interaction comes to an end, transition restores the power for agents to obtain chunks via the channel and for the agent to obtain more chunks (lines 48–51). The event also terminates any busy fluents that are no longer needed (line 58).

Sharing Phase: In this phase each agent shares its chunks with another agent, with the goal that at the end of the process, each agent has a complete set of the chunks. The full specification can be found in Figure 5. The principle here is more or less the same as with obtaining blocks, only that we build in a mechanism to encourage agents to share their chunks with others rather than just downloading them. To be able to monitor the

```
1    institution grid;
2
3    type Agent;
4    type Chunk;
5    type Time;
6    type Channel;
7    type ConnectionPoint;
8
9    exogenous event clock;
10   exogenous event obtain(Agent,Chunk,Channel);
11   exogenous event download(Agent,Agent,Chunk);
12
13   create event creategrid;
14
15   inst event intObtain(Agent,Chunk,Channel);
16   inst event intShare(Agent);
17   inst event intDownload(Agent,Chunk);
18   inst event transition;
19
20   violation event misuse(Agent);
21
22   fluent obtainChunk(Agent,Chunk);
23   fluent hasChunk(Agent,Chunk);
24   fluent abusy(Agent,Time);
25   fluent cbusy(ConnectionPoint,Time);
26
27   fluent previous(Time,Time);
28   fluent matchA(Agent,ConnectionPoint);
29   fluent matchC(Channel,ConnectionPoint);
```

Fig. 3. Declaration of types and events in the model

```
34   obtain(A,X,C) generates intObtain(A,X,C)
35     if not cbusy(C1,T1), not cbusy(A1,T2),
36       matchA(A,A1), matchC(C,C1);
37
38   obtain(A,X,C) generates transition;
39   clock generates transition;
40
41   intObtain(A,X,C) initiates hasChunk(A,X);
42   intObtain(A,X,C) initiates
43     cbusy(A1,2), cbusy(C1,2)
44     if matchA(A,A1), matchC(C,C1);
45
46   transition initiates cbusy(A,T2)
47     if cbusy(A,T1), previous(T1,T2);
48   transition initiates pow(intObtain(A,X,C))
49     if cbusy(A1,1), matchA(A,A1);
50   transition initiates pow(intObtain(A,X,C))
51     if cbusy(C1,1), matchC(C,C1);
52
53   intObtain(A,X,C) terminates pow(intObtain(A,X1,C1));
54   intObtain(A,X,C) terminates pow(intObtain(B,X1,C));
55   intObtain(A,X,C) terminates obtainChunk(A,X);
56   intObtain(A,X,C) terminates perm(obtain(A,X,C1));
57
58   transition terminates cbusy(A,Time);
```

Fig. 4. Generation and consequence relations for obtaining

different costs of obtaining a chunk from the base-station or from a peer, we introduced the fluent abusy. When a chunk is downloaded from a peer, the agent loses permission to download another chunk until it has shared a chunk with another agent (lines 85 and 73 respectively). Continuous downloading without sharing (no permission is granted to download) results in a violation event named misuse (line 70). The penalty we chose to implement in our model is that the violation agent loses the power to intDownload (Line 91), which means that for all intents and purposes it has been expelled from the peer group. Initially, agents are given the permission and power to download one chunk (Figure 6 lines 112-114).

```
63    download(A,B,X) generates
64      intDownload(A,X), intShare(B)
65      if hasChunk(B,X), not abusy(A,T1), not abusy(B,T2);
66
67    download(A,B,X) generates transition;
68    clock generates transition;
69
70    viol(intDownload(A,X)) generates misuse(A);
71
72    intDownload(A,X) initiates hasChunk(A,X);
73    intShare(B) initiates perm(intDownload(B,X));
74    intDownload(A,X) initiates abusy(A,3);
75    intShare(B) initiates abusy(B,3);
76
77
78    transition initiates abusy(A,T2)
79      if abusy(A,T1), previous(T1,T2);
80    transition initiates pow(intDownload(A,X))
81      if abusy(A,1);
82    transition initiates pow(intShare(B))
83      if abusy(B,1);
84
85    intDownload(A,X) terminates perm(intDownload(A,X));
86    intDownload(A,X) terminates pow(intDownload(A,X));
87    intDownload(A,X) terminates pow(intShare(A));
88    intShare(B) terminates pow(intDownload(B,X));
89    intShare(B) terminates pow(intShare(B));
90
91    misuse(A) terminates pow(intDownload(A,X)),abusy(A,T);
92    intDownload(A,X) terminates perm(intDownload(A,Y));
93
94    transition terminates abusy(A,Time);
```

Fig. 5. Generation and consequence relations for sharing

```
98    initially
99      pow(transition), perm(transition),
100     perm(clock),
101     pow(intObtain(A,B,C)),perm(intObtain(A,B,C)),
102     perm(obtain(alice,x1,C)), perm(obtain(alice,x3,C)),
103     perm(obtain(bob,x2,C)), perm(obtain(bob,x4,C)),
104     obtainChunk(alice,x1), obtainChunk(alice,x3),
105     obtainChunk(bob,x2), obtainChunk(bob,x4);

109   initially
110     pow(transition), perm(transition),
111     perm(clock),
112     pow(intDownload(Agent,Chunk)), pow(intShare(Agent)),
113     perm(download(Agent,Agent1,Chunk)),
114     perm(intDownload(Agent,Chunk)), perm(intShare(Agent));
```

Fig. 6. Initial state of the model, post negotiation

Figures 3 to 6 give the complete characterisation of our wireless grid scenario. When translated to *AnsProlog* and combined with the non-framework-dependent program components, we obtain all the possible traces over a specified number of time instances. A successful trace makes sure that at the end all agents have all chunks and are no longer engaged. Figure 7 shows a graphical representation of a successful trace for a scenario with two agents (bob and alice), four chunks (x1, x2, x3 and x4) and a base-station with two channels (c1 and c2). The circles indicate the time steps. Light grey fill means the device is cbusy while dark grey indicates abusy. The arrows indicate which block goes to which agent. The labels on the left-hand side indicate the exogenous event and the current distribution of chunks. The observed event clock is not shown to avoid cluttering the diagram.

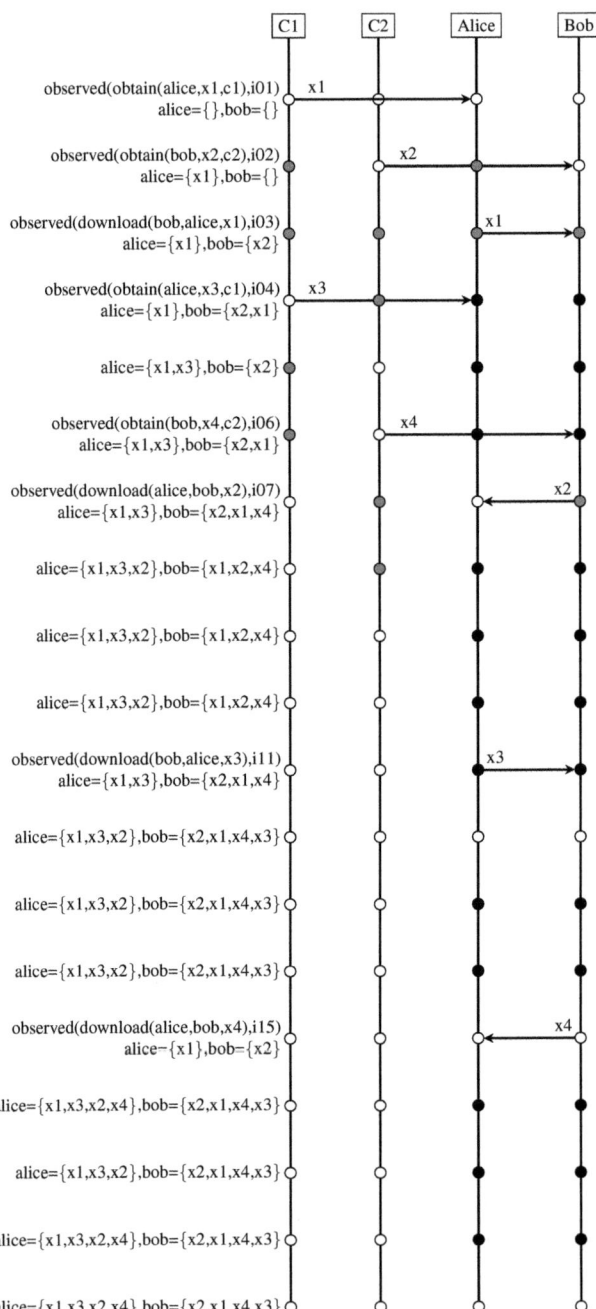

Fig. 7. One trace of the interaction between alice, bob and the channels of base-station

Sanctioning. The model as presented in Figure 5 takes a rather harsh position on sanctioning, in that the violating agent is expelled—the power to get chunks from other agents is rescinded. In fact, this is both harsh and counter-productive, because given the initial state shown in Figure 6, the chunk assignment is not 1-resilient—meaning the distribution cannot be achieved following the expulsion of one agent, unless in the very special case where the expulsion occurs after the other agent no longer requires any chunks from this agent. Full 1-resilient assignment can be achieved with two chunks for each of three agents, in which each chunk is assigned to two agents and of course, n-resilience can be achieved by each agent downloading all the chunks from the base-station. In terms of the effect on the group goal, the ejection scenario is equivalent to one of the agents leaving the ad-hoc network. In either case, for an a-priori solution there is a trade-off to be explored in delivering i-resilience, based on the estimated number agent failures and on the additional cost of replicated base-station downloads. Alternatively, some agents may engage autonomously in additional base-station downloads for the sake of the group goal.

A more practical sanction may be to lock the offending agent out of the sharing process for a number of time steps, but as with the above scenario, this is only effective if it does not impact the group goal.

3.2   Evaluation

Now that we have set out the normative framework and how to quantify communication costs for the particular situation of a 3G structured network and an ethernet ad-hoc network (see Section 2.2), we can use the model to examine the traces for expected, but also unexpected behaviour and, simply by counting the number of cbusy and abusy states, get an estimate for battery consumption under different initial conditions.

Each of the models of our framework contains information about the energy consumption of each of agents in the form of the messages they have been passing signalled by the exogenous events obtain and download and the amount of time they have been spending communicating with the base-station, by the number of occurrences of cbusy, and communicating with the other agents by the number of times abusy occurs.

The model is presently being used as an off-line tool and generates all possible traces. The likelihood of a high proportion of these trace occurring in practice, depends on the relative intelligence and (bounded) rationality of the agents participating in the normative framework, e.g. continuously trying the download a chunk when you are busy. Our model purposely avoids modelling handset behaviour—we believe that is the responsibility of the handset designer—because our objective is the exploration of the design of the space in which the handsets interact. However, these unsuccessful or unnatural traces can easily be filtered out by adding the filters displayed in Figures 8 and 9 to the *AnsProlog* specification. The first filter only admits those traces that lead to success: all agents have all the chunks and are no longer busy. When adding the filter, we obtain the first traces after nine time steps. To be more precise we obtain 142368 different traces satisfying the criteria. CLINGO returns these in 22.96 second, excluding printing, on a standard laptop. When the second filter is added to the first, we only obtain successful traces that contain no violations and where each exogenous event leads to its corresponding normative event (e.g. download leads to intdownload). This reduces

```
1    % success criteria
2    success :- holdsat(hasChunk(alice,x1),T),holdsat(hasChunk(alice,x2),T),
3               holdsat(hasChunk(alice,x3),T),holdsat(hasChunk(alice,x4),T),
4               holdsat(hasChunk(bob,x1),T),holdsat(hasChunk(bob,x2),T),
5               holdsat(hasChunk(bob,x3),T),holdsat(hasChunk(bob,x4),T),
6               not holdsat(cbusy(dbob,T),F),not holdsat(cbusy(dalice,T),F),
7               not holdsat(cbusy(dc1,T),F), not holdsat(cbusy(dc2,T),F),
8               not holdsat(abusy(alice,T),F),not holdsat(abusy(bob,T),F),final(F).
```

Fig. 8. A filter to remove unsuccessful traces

```
10    % only interested in successful traces
11    :- not success.
12
13    % indication that a violation has occurred
14    viol :- occured(viol(X),I).
15
16    :- viol.
17
18    % exogenous event should be follow by corresponding normative event
19    :- occured(download(H1,H2,Chunk),T), not occured(intDownload(H1,Chunk),T).
20    :- occured(obtain(Handset,Chunk,Channel),T),
21       not occured(intObtain(Handset,Chunk,Channel),T).
```

Fig. 9. A filter to remove unsuccessful violation traces with unintuitive events

the number of traces significantly. Traces are only returned after fifteen time steps, after which 5280 of them are returned in 3.58 seconds. If we do not constrain each download and obtain to be followed by its normative equivalent, we get over three million traces.

By changing the durations for obtaining and sharing chunks and altering the penalties imposed on agents not conforming to the norms, we are able to study a variety of situations and finding the most appropriate enforcement mechanisms.

Furthermore some model assumption need to be reconsidered. The model at the moment demands that sending and receiving alternate. In reality this is might not always be the case. Handsets should be allowed to take advantages of chunks being sent even when the same number of chunks have not yet been shared. Thus, it would be more realistic to evaluate a handset's willingness to collaborate over a larger time period.

4   Discussion

We have presented a normative framework as a mechanism to help understand and to model the economic challenges that might arise in the context of a wireless grid. We have developed a model for the actions of the agents that participate in such a grid and hence provide us with a basic energy model, that may be used by the agents as part of a utility maximization decision-making process.

This was the first time we had modelled a complete, but simplified, realistic scenario of a normative framework. While InstAL is very intuitive and makes the task significantly more approachable it still lacks certain features that would make the modelling process easier. To model that channels and handsets were busy during a given period we had to resort to introducing the fluent previous, as InstAL does not allow arithmetic in its rules (which the underlying *AnsProlog* does allow). The current version of InstAL also does not allow hierarchies in its type structure or polymorphic propositions. Ideally we would have liked Device to be a superset of both Channel and

`Agent`, such that we would not have had to resort to the `matchC` and `matchA` fluents, which are a technical artifice to overcome a linguistic weakness. The answer sets representing the traces contain significant numbers of atoms, making debugging difficult. Neither InstAL nor InstQL have built-in mechanisms to filter the output. So for debugging purposes we often referred to the underlying *AnsProlog* program and its `#show` and `#hide` functionalities, although those are not very flexible. Thus, the exercise has identified a number of practical issues that need to be addressed to make InstAL more usable.

The modelling of the wireless grid scenario also gave us a good insight into our formal model. The model does not allow us to expel an agent completely from a normative framework, as all the observed events are automatically empowered. While this can be partially remedied by removing the empowerment of consequent normative events, as we have done in the sharing phase, it raises interesting issues on how membership of a normative framework should be handled.

The traces of the normative framework give an indication of how much energy each of the handsets will be using if the trace would be executed. It also allows us to test different sanctioning techniques and compare their efficacy. However, a number of the traces that are produced by our simple model, while valid, stand very little chance of being executed by rational agents. Agents are not going to download the same block repeatedly, or try to download/obtain a block when they are busy. While this can be easily added to the model, we believe it is more properly viewed as an aspect of agent behaviour and should therefore be encoded in the agent rather than the normative framework. From a normative perspective we are only interested in correct, valid traces.

A particularly intriguing line of research, arising from the capacity to compute such traces, is to explore those (economic) mechanisms that might alleviate the effects of free-loading, in a more subtle, and less draconian way, than the simple sanction of expelling, that has been applied here.

Both the wireless grid scenario and the energy model are necessarily simplified and demand expansion. As stated earlier in the article some functions such as the one defining p, i.e. the probability of finding a cooperation partner that has the right chunks, have to be specified. Further aspects of interest to be included in the model are error rates on the different communication links as well as the aspect that agents are moving within the environment and as a consequence the neighbourhood of an agent is constantly changing.

Furthermore, our current model has very simple penalty mechanisms for violating agents. It does not allow for more elaborate forms of sanctions as was demonstrated in Section 3.1, when we blocked agents that obtained unallocated chunks from the base-station. However, with regard to future work we plan to develop several enforcement mechanisms in order to address the reciprocity problem in more detail. Thus, our intention is to take the existing model as a reference point and analyse the additional benefits and costs resulting from different normative mechanisms.

Acknowledgements. Tina Balke is partially supported by a grant from the German Academic Exchange Service (DAAD).

References

1. Artikis, A., Sergot, M., Pitt, J.: Specifying electronic societies with the causal calculator. In: Giunchiglia, F., Odell, J., Weiss, G. (eds.) AOSE 2002. LNCS, vol. 2585, pp. 1–15. Springer, Heidelberg (2003)
2. Axelrod, R.: The emergence of cooperation among egoists. The American Political Science Review 75(2), 306–318 (1981)
3. Baral, C.: Knowledge Representation, Reasoning and Declarative Problem Solving. Cambridge Press, Cambridge (2003)
4. Boella, G., van der Torre, L.: Constitutive Norms in the Design of Normative Multiagent Systems. In: Toni, F., Torroni, P. (eds.) CLIMA 2005. LNCS (LNAI), vol. 3900, pp. 303–319. Springer, Heidelberg (2006)
5. Cliffe, O.: Specifying and Analysing Institutions in Multi-Agent Systems using Answer Set Programming. PhD thesis, University of Bath (2007)
6. Cliffe, O., De Vos, M., Padget, J.: Answer set programming for representing and reasoning about virtual institutions. In: Inoue, K., Satoh, K., Toni, F. (eds.) CLIMA 2006. LNCS (LNAI), vol. 4371, pp. 60–79. Springer, Heidelberg (2007)
7. Cliffe, O., De Vos, M., Padget, J.: Specifying and reasoning about multiple institutions. In: Noriega, P., Vázquez-Salceda, J., Boella, G., Boissier, O., Dignum, V., Fornara, N., Matson, E. (eds.) COIN 2006. LNCS (LNAI), vol. 4386, pp. 67–85. Springer, Heidelberg (2007)
8. Giunchiglia, E., Lee, J., Lifschitz, V., McCain, N., Turner, H.: Nonmonotonic causal theories. Artificial Intelligence 153, 49–104 (2004)
9. Fitzek, F.H.P., Katz, M.D.: Cellular controlled peer to peer communications: Overview and potentials. In: Fitzek, F.H.P., Katz, M.D. (eds.) Cognitive Wireless Networks, pp. 31–59. Springer, Heidelberg (2007)
10. Gebser, M., Kaufmann, B., Neumann, A., Schaub, T.: Conflict-Driven Answer Set Solving. In: Proceeding of IJCAI 2007, pp. 386–392 (2007)
11. Gelfond, M., Lifschitz, V.: Classical negation in logic programs and disjunctive databases. New Generation Computing 9(3-4), 365–386 (1991)
12. Hopton, L., Cliffe, O., De Vos, M., Padget, J.: InstQL: A query language for virtual institutions using answer set programming. In: Dix, J., Fisher, M., Novák, P. (eds.) CLIMA X. LNCS, vol. 6214, pp. 102–121. Springer, Heidelberg (2010)
13. Jones, A.J., Sergot, M.: A Formal Characterisation of Institutionalised Power. ACM Computing Surveys 28(4es), 121 (1996)
14. Katz, M.D., Fitzek, F.H.P.: Cooperation in 4g networks - cooperation in a heterogenous wireless world. In: Fitzek, F.H.P., Katz, M.D. (eds.) Cooperation in Wireless Networks: Principles and Applications, pp. 463–496. Springer, Heidelberg (2006)
15. Kowalski, R.A., Sadri, F.: Reconciling the event calculus with the situation calculus. Journal of Logic Programming 31(1-3), 39–58 (1997)
16. Niemelä, I., Simons, P.: Smodels: An implementation of the stable model and well-founded semantics for normal LP. In: Dix, J., Furbach, U., Nerode, A. (eds.) LPNMR 1997. LNCS (LNAI), vol. 1265, pp. 420–429. Springer, Heidelberg (1997)
17. Ostrom, E.: Coping with tragedies of the commons. Annual Review of Political Science 2, 493–535 (1999); Workshop in Political Theory and Policy Analysis; Center for the Study of Institutions, Population, and Environmental Change
18. Perrucci, G.P., Fitzek, F.: Measurements campaign for energy consumption on mobile phones. Technical report, Aalborg University (2009)
19. Perrucci, G.P., Fitzek, F.H., Petersen, M.V.: Energy saving aspects for mobile device exploiting heterogeneous wireless networks. In: Heterogeneous Wireless Access Networks. Springer, US (2009)

20. Sergot, M.: (C+)++: An Action Language for Representing Norms and Institutions. Technical report, Imperial College, London (2004)
21. TNS. Two-day battery life tops wish list for future all-in-one phone device. Technical report, Taylor Nelson Sofres, 004
22. Vázquez-Salceda, J., Dignum, V., Dignum, F.: Organizing multiagent systems. AAMAS 11(3), 307–360 (2005)
23. Dignum, V.: A Model for Organizational Interaction Based on Agents, Founded in Logic. PhD thesis, Utrecht University (2004)
24. Wrona, K., Mähönen, P.: Analytical model of cooperation in ad hoc networks. Telecommunication Systems 27(2-4), 347–369 (2004)

Towards a Model of Social Coherence in Multi-agent Organizations

Erick Martínez[1], Ivan Kwiatkowski[2], and Philippe Pasquier[1]

[1] School of Interactive Arts and Technology
Simon Fraser University, Vancouver, Canada
{emartinez,pasquier}@sfu.ca
http://www.metacreation.net/
[2] Institut Supérieur d'Informatique, de Modélisation et de leurs Applications
Clermont-Ferrand, France

Abstract. We propose a *social coherence*-based model and *simulation framework* to study the dynamics of multi-agent organizations. This model rests on the notion of *social commitment* to represent all the agents' explicit inter-dependencies including *roles* and *organizational structures*. A local coherence-based approach is used that, along with a *sanction policy*, ensures *social control* in the system and the *emergence* of *social coherence*. We illustrate the model and the simulator with a simple experiment comparing two *sanction policies*.

Keywords: Social and organizational structure, social commitments, agent reasoning, social control

1 Introduction and Motivations

Research in the area of Computational Organization Theory [4,3] and multi-agent systems (MAS) has resulted in a large number of models capturing different aspects of organizational behaviour [21,22,1,7]. This paper presents a model and *simulation framework* to study the social dynamics of multi-agent organizations. The model uses the notion of *social commitment* (defined in Section 2) as the main building block to represent all the inter-dependencies between *social entities*. *Sanction policies* provide *social control* mechanisms (defined in Section 3) to regulate the enforcement of *social commitments*. Our model extends previous work on *cognitive coherence* [17,19] by showing how the *coherence principle* can drive the emergence of *social behaviour*. In particular, by organizing agent behaviour in a way that makes global *social coherence* (formalized in Section 4) emerge from the local *cognitive coherence* of interacting agents.

We strive to build a simple minimalist model, where *social behaviour* emerges from local *coherence-driven behaviour*, enabling us to study some of the social dynamics of multi-agent organizations. This paper advances the state of the art by proposing a unified yet computational and operational view of some of the social aspects of multi-agent systems. More specifically, we propose a knowledge transfer from results in cognitive science and social psychology into the area

M. De Vos et al. (Eds.): COIN 2010 International Workshops, LNAI 6541, pp. 114–131, 2011.
© Springer-Verlag Berlin Heidelberg 2011

of multi-agent organizations. At the core of our proposal is a model of agent rationality based on the unification of the cognitive coherence [24] and cognitive dissonance [9] theories. We also present a sample pizza delivery domain (Section 5), and illustrate the use of the model and simulator with a simple experiment (Section 6) to investigate *social control* mechanisms while comparing two *sanction policies*. Then, we discuss our work while relating it to other research (Section 7). Finally, we conclude and discusses future work (Section 8).

2 Social Modelling

2.1 Handling Actions

We represent atomic actions as (possibly) parametrized predicate formulas with unique names. We use a discreet instant-based sequential model of time where actions are assumed to be instantaneous. However, each action requires a *preparation time* expressed in time steps.

Definition 1. *(**Primitive or Atomic Action**) Given the non-empty set $\mathcal{X}$ of all atomic actions in the system, a **primitive action** $\alpha \in \mathcal{X}$ is represented as a tuple $\alpha = \langle \alpha(\boldsymbol{x}), \Delta_\alpha \rangle$, where:*

- $\alpha(\boldsymbol{x})$ *is a predicate formula s.t.* $\alpha(\boldsymbol{x}) \neq \beta(\boldsymbol{x})$*, and* $\alpha(\boldsymbol{x}) = \alpha(\boldsymbol{y}) \Rightarrow \boldsymbol{x} = \boldsymbol{y}$*; and*
- $\Delta_\alpha > 0$ *specifies the* preparation time *of action* $\alpha(\boldsymbol{x})$ *measured in time steps.*

In our model, *exogenous* events are treated as actions not necessarily performed by agents in the system. Therefore, in the rest of the paper events and actions are used interchangeably. We model an *exogenous* event as an action recurring within certain period of time.

Definition 2. *(**Exogenous Action**) Given the set $\hat{\mathcal{X}}$ of all exogenous actions in the system, an **exogenous action** $\hat{\alpha} \in \hat{\mathcal{X}}$ is represented as a tuple $\hat{\alpha} = \langle \alpha^{exog}(\boldsymbol{x}), \varepsilon \rangle$, where:*

- $\alpha^{exog}(\boldsymbol{x})$ *is a predicate formula s.t.* $\alpha^{exog}(\boldsymbol{x}) \neq \beta^{exog}(\boldsymbol{x})$*, and* $\alpha^{exog}(\boldsymbol{x}) = \alpha^{exog}(\boldsymbol{y}) \Rightarrow \boldsymbol{x} = \boldsymbol{y}$*; and*
- $\varepsilon \geq 0$ *specifies the maximum period within which the event* $\alpha^{exog}(\boldsymbol{x})$ *will occur once.*

2.2 Social Commitment

This section briefly presents a formal model of social commitment (henceforth abbreviated s-commitment). Concretely, commitments have proven useful to represent all the agent inter-dependencies: social norms, roles, authority relations and the semantics of agent communication [5,23]. Conceptually, commitments are oriented responsibilities contracted by a *debtor* towards a *creditor*[1]. One can distinguish *action commitments* from *propositional commitments* [29]. Propositional

---

[1] Social commitments share a great deal with the notion of directed obligation as defined in deontic logic and as also used by some researchers in the context of agent communication.

commitments entail complications and for that reason, following a number of other researchers [5,11,10], we will only consider action commitments in the rest of this paper. That is, commitments where a *debtor* is committed towards a *creditor* to bring about the effects of some *atomic action*. We adopt the model of Pasquier et al. [19] in which the dynamics of social commitments is formalized as a finite state machine (FSM). Figure 1 illustrates the different ways s-commitments can be manipulated. Note that update and delegation will not be considered in the rest of this paper.

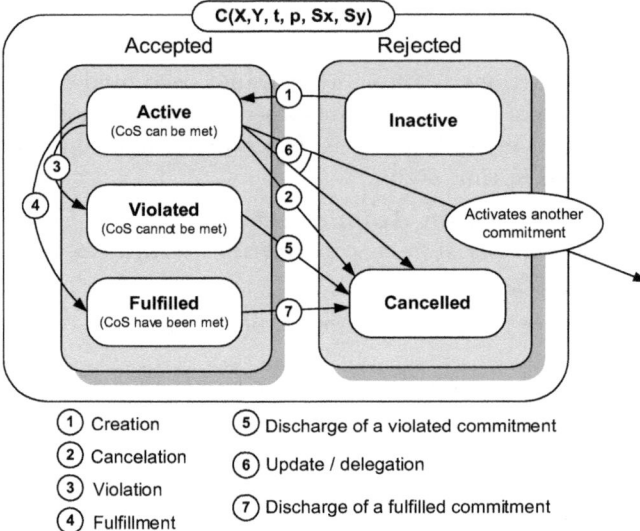

Fig. 1. Social commitment finite state transition machine

Definition 3. *(Social Commitment Schema) A **social commitment schema** is represented as a* unique *rule of the form:*

$$s\bar{c}s = \phi \Rightarrow C(\mathfrak{r}_x, \mathfrak{r}_y, \alpha, t_d, \mathcal{S}_{\mathfrak{r}_x}, \mathcal{S}_{\mathfrak{r}_y}) \tag{1}$$

where:

- *The antecedent ϕ is a formula representing any general trigger condition, i.e. a primitive action, an exogenous action, or any other complex condition[2];*
- *The consequent $C(\mathfrak{r}_x, \mathfrak{r}_y, \alpha, t_d, \mathcal{S}_{\mathfrak{r}_x}, \mathcal{S}_{\mathfrak{r}_y})$ is a predicate formula; representing the fact that debtor $\mathfrak{r}_x$ is committed towards creditor $\mathfrak{r}_y$ to achieve the effects of action α within $t_d > 0$ time steps of the creation time $(t_d \geq \Delta_\alpha)$ –under the sanctions sets $\mathcal{S}_{\mathfrak{r}_x}$ and $\mathcal{S}_{\mathfrak{r}_y}$, which specify the different sanctions that will be applied to $\mathfrak{r}_x$ and $\mathfrak{r}_y$ according to the states and transitions applicable to this commitment; and*
- *$\alpha = \langle \alpha(\boldsymbol{x}), \Delta_\alpha \rangle$.*

---

[2] For now we restrict the antecedent formula ϕ to be either a primitive or exogenous event.

Note that, *action commitment schema* (1) can only be valid, if its total duration time t_d is at least as long as the *preparation time* (i.e. Δ_α) of the *atomic action* α. In this paper, we only consider action commitments involving atomic actions. We can look at *action commitment schemes* as *abstract* place holders describing generic oriented responsibilities contracted by a *debtor* towards a *creditor*. Social commitment *schemes* are ultimately instantiated by agents.

Definition 4. *(Instantiated Social Commitment)*
Given a social commitment schema $\bar{scs}$ *as defined in Formula (1) where the trigger condition ϕ is satisfied, an **instantiation** of $\bar{scs}$ is represented as a unique grounded predicate formula of the form:*

$$isc = C(\mathfrak{ag}_i : \mathfrak{r}_x, \mathfrak{ag}_j : \mathfrak{r}_y, \alpha, [t_s, t_f], \mathcal{S}_{\mathfrak{ag}_i}, \mathcal{S}_{\mathfrak{ag}_j}) \qquad (2)$$

where debtor *agent* $\mathfrak{ag}_i$ *(resp.* creditor *agent* $\mathfrak{ag}_j$*) enacts role* $\mathfrak{r}_x$ *(resp. role* $\mathfrak{r}_y$*). Formula (2) results from:*

- *Removing the (satisfied) antecedent ϕ from Formula (1); and*
- *Replacing parameter t_d from Formula (1) with interval $[t_s, t_f]$, where: t_s represents the creation time when ϕ occurs and schema $\bar{scs}$ gets instantiated; and t_f represents the instantiated commitment's deadline $(t_f = t_s + t_d)$.*

Note that both *schemes* and *instantiated action commitments* must be distinctly identified in the system. *Accepted* action commitments take the form of a grounded predicate formula: $C(\mathfrak{ag}_i : \mathfrak{r}_x, \mathfrak{ag}_j : \mathfrak{r}_y, \alpha, [t_s, t_f], \mathcal{S}_{\mathfrak{ag}_i}, \mathcal{S}_{\mathfrak{ag}_j})$. *Rejected* commitments, meaning that *debtor* $\mathfrak{ag}_i$ is not committed towards *creditor* $\mathfrak{ag}_j$ to achieve the effects of action α, take the form $\neg C(\mathfrak{ag}_i : \mathfrak{r}_x, \mathfrak{ag}_j : \mathfrak{r}_y, \alpha, [t_s, t_f], \mathcal{S}_{\mathfrak{ag}_i}, \mathcal{S}_{\mathfrak{ag}_j})$. Our model also accounts for *time interval overlap* between *instantiated* social commitments.

Definition 5. *(Disjoint & Overlapping Commitments)* *Given two* distinct instances *of social commitments*

$$isc_1 = C(\mathfrak{ag}_i : \mathfrak{r}_x, \mathfrak{ag}_j : \mathfrak{r}_y, \alpha, [t_{s_1}, t_{f_1}], \mathcal{S}_{\mathfrak{ag}_i}, \mathcal{S}_{\mathfrak{ag}_j})$$
$$isc_2 = C(\mathfrak{ag}_i : \mathfrak{r}_p, \mathfrak{ag}_k : \mathfrak{r}_q, \beta, [t_{s_2}, t_{f_2}], \mathcal{S}_{\mathfrak{ag}_i}, \mathcal{S}_{\mathfrak{ag}_k}) \qquad (3)$$

where: $t_{f_1} < t_{s_2}$ (resp. $t_{f_2} < t_{s_1}$); we use the notation $isc_1 \prec isc_2$ (resp. $isc_2 \prec isc_1$) to represent disjoint time intervals between isc_1 and isc_2, where isc_1 (resp. isc_2) temporally precedes isc_2 (resp. isc_1). Otherwise, we use the notation $isc_1 \preccurlyeq isc_2$ (resp. $isc_2 \preccurlyeq isc_1$) to represent a time interval overlap between isc_1 and isc_2.

Active social commitments raise action expectations, and the enforcement of social commitments can take place through various *social control* mechanisms instead of through assumptions of sincerity and cooperativeness [19]. Social commitments, when modelled with their enforcement mechanism [19], are not necessarily sincere and do not require the agents to be cooperative. From this perspective, social commitments serve to coordinate the agents whether or not they are cooperative and whether or not they are sincere.

2.3   Social Entities

In this paper, we only consider three types of social entities: agents, social roles, and social organizations. While numerous refinements are possible, we take a minimalist approach to define these entities. Formally:

Definition 6. *(Social Entity)* *Given the non-empty set* $\mathfrak{SE} = \mathfrak{Ag} \cup \mathfrak{Role} \cup \mathfrak{Org}$, *a **social entity** $\mathfrak{e}$ is represented as $\mathfrak{e} \in \mathfrak{SE}$ where:*

- $\mathfrak{Ag}$, $\mathfrak{Role}$, $\mathfrak{Org}$ *are sets that stand for all the agents, social roles, and organizations respectively; and*
- $\mathfrak{Ag} \cap \mathfrak{Role} = \emptyset$, $\mathfrak{Ag} \cap \mathfrak{Org} = \emptyset$, $\mathfrak{Role} \cap \mathfrak{Org} = \emptyset$.

Definition 7. *(Organization)* *An **organization** is represented as a tuple* $\mathfrak{o} = \langle \mathfrak{Ag}_\mathfrak{o}, \mathfrak{Role}_\mathfrak{o}, \rho_\mathfrak{o} \rangle$ *where:*

- $\mathfrak{Ag}_\mathfrak{o}$ *is the non-empty set of agents that belongs to organization $\mathfrak{o}$;*
- $\mathfrak{Role}_\mathfrak{o}$ *is the non-empty set of social roles relevant to the organization; and*
- $\rho_\mathfrak{o}$ *is a binary relation (or enactment function) that assigns to each agent that belongs to organization $\mathfrak{o}$, one or several roles from $\mathfrak{Role}_\mathfrak{o}$, noted $\rho_\mathfrak{o}$: $\mathfrak{Ag}_\mathfrak{o} \longrightarrow \mathfrak{Role}_\mathfrak{o}^n$ $(1 \leq n \leq |\mathfrak{Role}_\mathfrak{o}|)$, s.t. $\forall \mathfrak{ag} \in \mathfrak{Ag}_\mathfrak{o}$ $\rho_\mathfrak{o}(\mathfrak{ag}) \neq \emptyset$.*

Definition 8. *(Social Role)* *A **social role** is represented as a tuple* $\mathfrak{r} = \langle \mathcal{X}_\mathfrak{r}, SComm_\mathfrak{r} \rangle$ *where:*

- $\mathcal{X}_\mathfrak{r}$ *is the non-empty set of* primitive actions *that define the functions of role* $\mathfrak{r}$ *; and*
- $SComm_\mathfrak{r}$ *is the non-empty set of* s-commitment schemes *specifying the interdependencies between role $\mathfrak{r}$ and every other* debtor *or* creditor.

Definition 9. *(Agent)* *An **agent** is represented as a tuple* $\mathfrak{ag} = \langle \mathfrak{Role}_\mathfrak{ag}, \varkappa_\mathfrak{ag} \rangle$ *where:*

- $\mathfrak{Role}_\mathfrak{ag}$ *is the non-empty set of social roles agent $\mathfrak{ag}$ is assigned to; and*
- $\varkappa_\mathfrak{ag}$ *is a binary relation that assigns a probabilistic* reliability *value to each primitive action $\alpha_i \in \mathcal{X}_\mathfrak{ag}$ within the capabilities of agent $\mathfrak{ag}$, capturing the probability of agent $\mathfrak{ag}$ succeeding at performing primitive action α_i, noted $\varkappa_\mathfrak{ag} : \mathcal{X}_\mathfrak{ag} \longrightarrow [0,1]$, with $\mathcal{X}_\mathfrak{ag} = \bigcup \{ \mathcal{X}_{\mathfrak{r}_j} \mid \langle \mathcal{X}_{\mathfrak{r}_j}, SComm_{\mathfrak{r}_j} \rangle \in \mathfrak{Role}_\mathfrak{ag} \}$.*

Organizations and roles are abstract constructs enacted by actual agents. The *capabilities* of an agent are determined by all the primitive actions which define the functions of each *role* the agent is assigned to. For example, besides being a *cook* within organization Ω, an agent $\mathfrak{ag}$ could also play the role of a *volunteer firefighter* within a different organization. In such a case, the individual capabilities of the agent $\mathfrak{ag}$ will clearly span beyond the functions determined by the scope of his/her role within organization Ω.

There might be instances where the same agent plays several roles within an organization. There might be other instances where several agents play the same role within an organization. In the latter case, we follow a *fair allocation principle* so that (on average) all agents have a similar chance to enact the same role they were assigned to. In our implementation of the model, the Agent Allocation Manager (AAM) module handles the system-wide allocation of agents. It is actually implemented as a wrapper to the *Mersenne Twister* (MT19937 implementation) pseudo-random number generator, which provides fast generation of high-quality pseudo-random numbers. For each role $\mathfrak{r}$ the AAM keeps track of which agents are available (resp. unavailable). When instantiating a s-commitment, the AAM will randomly pick an agent from the *pool* of available agents enacting role $\mathfrak{r}$ until all agents have been allocated a s-commitment and the *pool* is empty. Then, the AAM 'replenishes' the *pool* by flagging all agents enacting role $\mathfrak{r}$ as available and repeats the same process again.

3   Social Control Mechanisms

Theories of *social control* [15,12] focus on the strategies and techniques that help to regulate agent behaviour, and lead to conformity and compliance with the rules of society (at both the macro and the micro level). In the remainder of this section, we detail the main elements used in the enforcement of social commitments: *sanctions*, which are considered in their general sense of positive or negative incentives.

Most s-commitment-based approaches assume that the agents will respect their social commitments (thus applying regimentation). This assumption is unrealistic since unintended commitment violation is likely to occur and unilateral commitment cancellation as well as commitment modification are desirable. Intuitively, sanctions should meet the following base criteria. Violation and *cancellation* are either associated with (possibly) *negative* sanctions, *fulfilment* is associated with a (possibly) *positive* sanction and *violation* carries either a harsher or similar sanction than *cancellation*.

In previous work [19], we have proposed an ontology of sanction types and punishment policies. Here we will only present the basic mechanism by which the enforcement of s-commitment is ensured in our model of *social coherence*. A *sanction policy* determines the type of sanctions (and their magnitude) that are assigned to social commitments at creation time. For simplicity, we assume that sanctions are not delayed through time and are applied at the time of occurrence as specified in the sanction policy. That is, we rely on a strict liability principle where all violations in the system are assumed to be detected and dealt with.

Definition 10. *(Organizational Sanction Policy) Given the non-empty set $SComm_{o}$ of all social commitment schemes relevant to organization* o; *and the set $\mathbb{T}$ of all the transitions applicable to s-commitments. For every schema $s\bar{c}s \in SComm_{o}$ of the form $s\bar{c}s = \phi \Rightarrow C(\mathfrak{r}_{x}, \mathfrak{r}_{y}, \alpha, t_{d}, \mathcal{S}_{\mathfrak{r}_{x}}, \mathcal{S}_{\mathfrak{r}_{y}})$, we specify the sanction sets $\mathcal{S}_{\mathfrak{r}_{x}} = \{s^{f}_{\mathfrak{r}_{x}}, s^{c}_{\mathfrak{r}_{x}}, s^{v}_{\mathfrak{r}_{x}}\}$, and $\mathcal{S}_{\mathfrak{r}_{y}} = \{s^{c}_{\mathfrak{r}_{y}}\}$ using the following function:*

$$\sigma_{o}(s\bar{c}s, z) = \begin{cases} s_{\mathfrak{r}_x}^{f} & \text{if } z = \textcircled{7}, \text{ // discharge of fulfilment} \\ s_{\mathfrak{r}_x}^{v} & \text{if } z = \textcircled{5}, \text{ // discharge of violation,} \\ s_{\mathfrak{r}_x}^{c} & \text{if } z = \textcircled{2}, \text{ // cancellation by debtor,} \\ s_{\mathfrak{r}_y}^{c} & \text{if } z = \textcircled{2}, \text{ // cancellation by creditor} \\ nil & \text{if } z \notin \{\textcircled{2}, \textcircled{5}, \textcircled{7}\} \end{cases} \qquad (4)$$

where:

- $z \in \mathbb{T}$ *is the transition consumed in the FSM from Figure (1), with* σ_{sc} :
  $\mathbb{T} \longrightarrow [-1, 1]$;
- $s_{\mathfrak{r}_x}^{f} \in [0, 1]$ *represents the sanction value applied to debtor* $\mathfrak{r}_x$ *when* fulfilling
  commitment $s\bar{c}s$;
- $s_{\mathfrak{r}_x}^{v} \in [-1, 0]$ *represents the sanction value applied to debtor* $\mathfrak{r}_x$ *when* violating *commitment* $s\bar{c}s$;
- $s_{\mathfrak{r}_x}^{c} \in [-1, 0]$ *represents the sanction value applied to debtor* $\mathfrak{r}_x$ *when can-*
  celling commitment $s\bar{c}s$; *and*
- $s_{\mathfrak{r}_y}^{c} \in [-1, 0]$ *represents the sanction value applied to creditor* $\mathfrak{r}_y$ *when can-*
  celling commitment $s\bar{c}s$.

4   Social Coherence

In cognitive sciences and social psychology most cognitive theories appeal to a homeostatic principle which puts coherence as the main organizing mechanism: *the individual is more satisfied with coherence than with incoherence.* Our main contribution is applying a model of agent rationality, based on the unification of the cognitive dissonance [9] and cognitive coherence [24] theories, to multi-agent organizations. In this section, we extend previous work on *cognitive coherence* [17,19] by showing how to use the *coherence principle* as the driving force that makes *social behaviour* emerge from the local *cognitive coherence* of interacting agents. For simplicity, s-commitments are the only type of cognition considered by agents.

4.1   Formal Characterization of Social Coherence

We present a constraint satisfaction based model of social coherence resulting in a symbolic-connexionist hybrid formalism. In our approach, the cognitions of a social entity are represented through the notion of elements (i.e. instantiated s-commitments). We denote $\mathbb{E}$ the set of all elements. *Elements* are divided in two sets: the set $\mathcal{A}$ of *accepted elements* and the set $\mathcal{R}$ of *rejected elements*. We adopt a closed-world assumption which states that *every non-explicitly accepted element is rejected*. Since not all s-commitments are equally modifiable, a *resistance to change* is associated to each element. Formally:

Definition 11. (Resistance to Change) *We specify the **resistance to change** of cancelling an accepted element (i.e. instantiated s-commitment) through the function:*

$$Res^{c} : \mathcal{A} \longrightarrow \mathbb{R} \equiv \sigma(x, z = \textcircled{2}) \qquad (x \in \mathcal{A}) \qquad (5)$$

where: $\mathcal{A}$ is the set of all accepted instantiated s-commitments, and σ is the sanction policy.

Note that, we equate the *resistance to change* with the penalty corresponding to the *cancellation* of an instantiated s-commitment as specified in the *sanction policy* (Formula (4)). The higher the punishment for cancelling a s-commitment, the higher the *resistance to change* will be.

S-commitments can be related or unrelated. When they are related, positive compatibility relations like facilitation and entailment are represented as *positive constraints*. Negative incompatibility relations like mutual exclusion (e.g. critical time overlap), hindering, and disabling are represented as *negative constraints*. We use C^+ (resp. C^-) to denote the set of positive (resp. negative) constraints and $\mathbb{C} = C^+ \cup C^-$ to refer to the set of all constraints. For each of these constraints, a weight reflecting the importance degree for the underlying relation is attributed (our constraint generation mechanism is described in Section 4.2). Those weights can be accessed through the function $Weight : \mathbb{C} \longrightarrow \mathbb{R}$. Constraints can be satisfied or not.

Definition 12. *(Constraint Satisfaction) A positive constraint is satisfied if and only if the two elements that it binds are both accepted or both rejected, noted $Sat^+(x,y) \equiv (x,y) \in C^+ \wedge [(x \in \mathcal{A} \wedge y \in \mathcal{A}) \vee (x \in \mathcal{R} \wedge y \in \mathcal{R})]$. On the contrary, a negative constraint is satisfied if and only if one of the two elements that it binds is accepted and the other one rejected, noted $Sat^-(x,y) \equiv (x,y) \in C^- \wedge [(x \in \mathcal{A} \wedge y \in \mathcal{R}) \vee (x \in \mathcal{R} \wedge y \in \mathcal{A})]$. Satisfied constraints within a set of elements $\mathcal{E}$ are accessed through the function:*

$$Sat : \mathcal{E} \subseteq \mathbb{E} \longrightarrow \left\{ \begin{array}{l} (x,y) \mid x,y \in \mathcal{E} \wedge \\ (Sat^+(x,y) \vee Sat^-(x,y)) \end{array} \right\} \tag{6}$$

In that context, two elements are said to be *coherent* (resp. *incoherent*) if and only if they are connected by a relation to which a satisfied (resp. non-satisfied) constraint corresponds. The main interest of this type of modelling is to allow defining a metric of cognitive coherence that permits the reification of the coherence principle in a computational calculus.

Given a partition of elements among $\mathcal{A}$ and $\mathcal{R}$, one can measure the *coherence degree* of a non-empty set of elements $\mathcal{E}$. We use $Con()$ to denote the function that gives the constraints associated with a set of elements $\mathcal{E}$. $Con : \mathcal{E} \subseteq \mathbb{E} \longrightarrow \{(x,y) \mid x,y \in \mathcal{E}, (x,y) \in \mathbb{C}\}$.

Definition 13. *(Coherence Degree) The **coherence degree** $\mathcal{C}(\mathcal{E})$, of a non-empty set of elements, $\mathcal{E}$ is obtained by adding the weights of constraints linking elements of $\mathcal{E}$ which are satisfied divided by the total weight of concerned constraints. Formally:*

$$\mathcal{C}(\mathcal{E}) = \frac{\sum_{(x,y) \in Sat(\mathcal{E})} Weight(x,y)}{\sum_{(x,y) \in Con(\mathcal{E})} Weight(x,y)} \tag{7}$$

Note that $\mathcal{C}(\mathcal{E}) \in [0,1]$ since $Sat(\mathcal{E}) \subseteq Con(\mathcal{E})$. The general social coherence problem is then:

Definition 14. *(**Coherence Problem**) The general **coherence problem** is to find a partition of the set of elements $\mathcal{E} \subseteq \mathbb{E}$ (i.e. instantiated s-commitments) into the set of accepted elements $\mathcal{A}$ and the set of rejected elements $\mathcal{R}$, such that, it maximizes the coherence degree $\mathcal{C}(\mathcal{E})$ of the set of elements $\mathcal{E}$.*

The coherence problem is a constraint optimization problem shown to be NP-complete [25]. The state of an agent can be defined as follows:

Definition 15. *(**Agent's State**) An **agent's state** is characterized by a tuple $W = \langle Agenda, \mathcal{C}^+, \mathcal{C}^-, \mathcal{A}, \mathcal{R} \rangle$, where:*

- *Agenda is a set of elements that stand for the agent's social agenda, that stores all the instantiated social commitments from which the agent is either the debtor or the creditor;*
- *$\mathcal{C}^+$ (resp. $\mathcal{C}^-$) is a set of non-ordered positive (resp. negative) binary constraints over Agenda such that $\forall (x, y) \in \mathcal{C}^+ \cup \mathcal{C}^-$, $x \neq y$;*
- *$\mathcal{A}$ is the set of accepted elements and $\mathcal{R}$ the set of rejected elements and $\mathcal{A} \cap \mathcal{R} = \emptyset$ and $\mathcal{A} \cup \mathcal{R} = Agenda$.*

For now, s-commitments are the only type of cognition considered by agents. More specifically, active s-commitments are treated as public cognitions because they raise shared action expectations between debtors and creditors. However, the state of an agent can be extended to accommodate other types of (private) cognitions e.g. perceptions, believes, intentions –as shown in previous work [18]. Finally, the overall degree of *social coherence* of an organization can be formally defined as follows:

Definition 16. *(**Organization's Social Coherence**)*
*The degree of **social coherence** of an organization o is calculated over the set of elements $\mathcal{E}_{int} \cup \mathcal{E}_{ext} \subseteq \mathbb{E}$, where:*

- *$\mathcal{E}_{int}$ is the set of instantiated s-commitments where both the debtor and the creditor are members of organization o; and*
- *$\mathcal{E}_{ext}$ is the set of instantiated s-commitments where either the debtor or the creditor (XOR) is member of organization o.*

4.2   Constraints Generation

Our social coherence model does provide a systematic mechanism for generating the constraints between social commitments. Our approach draws from TÆMS [8], a domain-independent framework for environment centred analysis and design of coordination mechanisms. This well studied framework [27,28,30], provides a comprehensive taxonomy of elements (i.e. tasks, methods, resources) and their interrelationships for modelling open MAS. We adapted their taxonomy of constraints between tasks and constraint precedence to generate constraints between action commitments, as follows:

1. *Disabling.* Given two disjoint instantiated social commitments $isc_i \prec isc_j$ involving distinct primitive actions α_i, α_j respectively, such that the execution of α_i disables α_j, we say there is a negative *disabling constraint* $c^-_{ij}(isc_i, isc_j, w^D) \in \mathcal{C}^-$ between isc_i and isc_j, with weight w^D.

Table 1. Weights and precedence order between *hard* and *soft* constraints

Hard Constraints		Soft Constraints	
Disabling	$w^D = 3$	Hindering	$w^H = 1$
Overlapping	$w^O = 2.5$	Facilitating	$w^F = 1$
Enabling	$w^E = 2$		

2. *Overlapping (duration)*. Given two overlapped instantiated social commitments $isc_i \preccurlyeq isc_j$ involving the same *debtor*, we say there is a negative *overlapping constraint* $c_{ij}^-(isc_i, isc_j, w^O) \in \mathcal{C}^-$ between isc_i and isc_j, with weight w^O.

3. *Enabling*. Given two disjoint instantiated social commitments $isc_i \prec isc_j$ involving distinct primitive actions α_i, α_j respectively, such that the execution of α_i enables α_j, we say there is a positive *enabling constraint* $c_{ij}^+(isc_i, isc_j, w^E) \in \mathcal{C}^+$ between isc_i and isc_j, with weight w^E.

4. *Hindering*. Given two disjoint instantiated social commitments $isc_i \prec isc_j$ involving distinct primitive actions α_i, α_j respectively, such that the execution of α_i somewhat *diminishes* the way (e.g. cost, duration) α_j can get executed; we say there is a negative *hindering constraint* $c_{ij}^-(isc_i, isc_j, w^H) \in \mathcal{C}^-$ between isc_i and isc_j, with weight w^H.

5. *Facilitating*. Given two disjoint instantiated social commitments $isc_i \prec isc_j$ involving distinct primitive actions α_i, α_j respectively, such that the execution of α_i somewhat *improves* the way (e.g. cost, duration) α_j can get executed; we say there is a positive *facilitating constraint* $c_{ij}^+(isc_i, isc_j, w^F) \in \mathcal{C}^+$ between isc_i and isc_j, with weight w^F.

We assign weights to *hard* (i.e. *disabling, overlapping, enabling*) and *soft* (i.e. *hindering, facilitating*) constraints to capture the precedence ordering between constraints. (Table 1). The constraints are generated automatically at instantiation time based on the relationships between actions (See Example 1, Formula 11). As in TÆMS *hard* constraints have a higher precedence than *soft* ones. Note that, *hard* constraints have a strict ordering (i.e. $w^D > w^O > w^E$) while *soft* constraints have the same precedence (i.e. $w^H = w^F$).

4.3   Local Search Algorithm

Decision theories as well as micro-economical theories define utility as a property of some valuation functions over some states of interest (e.g. consumption bundles, outcome of actions, state of the world). A function is a *utility function* if and only if it reflects the agent's preferences over these states. In our model, according to the afore-mentioned *coherence principle*, *social coherence* is preferred to *incoherence* which allows us to define the following expected utility function:

Definition 17. *(Expected Utility Function) The **expected utility** for an agent to attempt to reach the state W' from the state W^3 (which only differs by the change of state of **one** instantiated s-commitment x from accepted to cancelled) is expressed as the difference between the incoherence before and after*

---

[3] See Definition 15.

this change plus the cost of the change (expressed in term of the resistance to change of the modified s-commitment , that is in term of sanctions). Formally:

$$G(W') = (C(W') - C(W)) + Res^c(x) \qquad (8)$$

Note that, our expected utility function does not include any probabilities. This reflects the case of equi-probability in which the agent has no information about the probabilities that an actual change of the social commitment will occur. For now, agents do not take into account any uncertainty measures into their coherence calculus. For example, they do not have knowledge of their own *reliability*, nor about others'. Since *sanction policies* provide the *social control* mechanisms to regulate the enforcement of social commitments; Formula (8) explicitly integrates *social control* into the coherence calculus.

At each step of his reasoning, an agent will search for a cognition acceptance state change which maximizes this expected utility. That is, the agent will attempt to change an instantiated social commitment that maximizes the utility value through dialogue. A recursive version of the local search algorithm the agents use to maximize their *social coherence* is presented in Algorithm 1. While this is an approximation algorithm for solving the *coherence problem* (Def. 14), it behaved optimally on tested examples. Since it does not make any backtracking, the worst-case complexity of this algorithm is polynomial: $\mathcal{O}(mn^2)$, where n is the number of elements considered and m the number of constraints that bind them[4].

Algorithm 1. Recursive Local Search Algorithm

Function LocalSearch(W)

Require: $W = \langle \mathcal{Agenda}, \mathcal{C}^+, \mathcal{C}^-, \mathcal{A}, \mathcal{R} \rangle$; // current agent state
Ensure: List: $Change$; // ordered list of elements to change

    Local:
    Float: $G, Gval, C, Cval$; // expected utility value of best move
    Set: $\mathcal{A}', \mathcal{R}'$;
    Element: y, x;
    State: J; // agent state buffer

1: **for all** $x \in \mathcal{Agenda}$ **do**
2:     **if** $x \in \mathcal{A}$ **then**
3:         $\mathcal{A}' \leftarrow \mathcal{A} - \{x\}$; $\mathcal{R}' \leftarrow \mathcal{R} \cup \{x\}$;
4:     **end if**
5:     $W' \leftarrow \langle \mathcal{Agenda}, \mathcal{C}^+, \mathcal{C}^-, \mathcal{A}', \mathcal{R}' \rangle$;
       // expected utility of cancelling x
6:     $G \leftarrow C(W') - C(W) - Res^c(x)$;
7:     $C \leftarrow C(W') - C(W)$; // pure coherence gain
8:     **if** $G > Gval$ **then**
9:         $J \leftarrow W'$; $y \leftarrow x$; $Gval \leftarrow G$; $Cval \leftarrow C$;
10:    **end if**
11: **end for**
12: **if** ($Cval < 0$ and $Gval < 0$) **then**
13:    **return** $Change$; // stop when coherence is not raising anymore and the expected utility is not positive
14: **else**
15:    $Dialogue(y)$;
16:    Update ($Res(y)$); Add ($J, Change$);
17:    LocalSearch(J); // recursive call
18: **end if**

---

[4] n coherence calculus (sum over m constraints) for each level and a maximum of n levels to be searched.

Note that, we have no need to encode agents' behaviour as it automatically emerges from the coherence calculus. Although the model provides a computational metric for measuring organizational coherence (Def. 16), the overall behaviour of the system is solely driven by the local (coherence-driven) behaviour of agents. That is, macro-level social order is a coherence-driven emergent phenomena resulting from the local *cognitive coherence* of interacting agents.

5 Example: Pizza Delivery Domain

Example 1. Lets consider a domain involving a pizza delivery organization Ω; social roles $\{r_k = cook\}$, $\{r_{dp} = delivery\text{-}person\}$, $\{r_{mt} = maintenance\text{-} technician\}$, and $\{r_c = customer\}$; and agents $\{ag_1, ag_2, ag_3, ag_4, ag_5\}$ as follows:

- Primitive actions *(Def. 1)*:

$$\mathcal{X} = \left\{ \begin{array}{l} \alpha_1 = \langle \textbf{\textit{order-pizza}}(ag_i : r_c, pid), 1\rangle, \\ \alpha_2 = \langle \textbf{\textit{cook-pizza}}(ag_i : r_k, pid), 7\rangle, \\ \alpha_3 = \langle \textbf{\textit{clean-oven}}(ag_i : r_k, oid), 5\rangle, \\ \alpha_4 = \langle \textbf{\textit{pack-pizza}}(ag_i : r_{dp}, pid), 2\rangle, \\ \alpha_5 = \langle \textbf{\textit{deliver-pizza}}(ag_i : r_{dp}, c, pid), 20\rangle, \\ \alpha_6 = \langle \textbf{\textit{pay-order}}(ag_i : r_c, ag_j : r_{dp}, price, pid), 1\rangle, \\ \alpha_7 = \langle \textbf{\textit{repair-oven}}(ag_i : r_{mt}, oid), 30\rangle, \end{array} \right\} \tag{9}$$

- Exogenous events *(Def. 2)*:

$$\hat{\mathcal{X}} = \left\{ \begin{array}{l} \hat{\alpha}_8 = \langle \textbf{\textit{break-oven}}^{exog}(oid), 200\rangle, \\ \hat{\alpha}_9 = \langle \textbf{\textit{make-oven-dirty}}^{exog}(oid), 100\rangle, \\ \hat{\alpha}_{10} = \langle \textbf{\textit{become-hungry}}^{exog}, 20\rangle \end{array} \right\} \tag{10}$$

- Constraints between actions *(Section 4.2)*:

$$\mathcal{X}_{cons} = \left\{ \begin{array}{l} \textbf{\textit{order-pizza}} \text{ enables } \textbf{\textit{cook-pizza}}, \\ \textbf{\textit{break-oven}}^{exog} \text{ disables } \textbf{\textit{cook-pizza}}, \\ \textbf{\textit{make-oven-dirty}}^{exog} \text{ hinders } \textbf{\textit{cook-pizza}}, \\ \textbf{\textit{clean-oven}} \text{ disables } \textbf{\textit{cook-pizza}}, \\ \textbf{\textit{repair-oven}} \text{ disables } \textbf{\textit{cook-pizza}}, \\ \textbf{\textit{cook-pizza}} \text{ enables } \textbf{\textit{delivery-pizza}}, \\ \textbf{\textit{delivery-pizza}} \text{ enables } \textbf{\textit{pay-order}}, \end{array} \right\} \tag{11}$$

Organization *(Def. 7)*:

$$\Omega = \left\langle \begin{array}{l} \{ag_1, ag_2, ag_3, ag_4\}, \\ \{r_k, r_{dp}, r_{mt}\}, \\ \{(ag_1, r_k), (ag_2, r_{dp}), \\ (ag_3, r_{dp}), (ag_4, r_{mt})\} \end{array} \right\rangle \tag{12}$$

- Social roles *(Def. 8)*:[5]

$$Roles = \left\{ \begin{array}{l} r_k = \langle \{\alpha_2, \alpha_3\}, \{\bar{c}_1, \bar{c}_2, \bar{c}_5, \bar{c}_6\}\rangle, \\ r_{dp} = \langle \{\alpha_4, \alpha_5\}, \{\bar{c}_1, \bar{c}_2, \bar{c}_3, \bar{c}_4, \bar{c}_6\}\rangle, \\ r_{mt} = \langle \{\alpha_7\}, \{\bar{c}_4\}\rangle, \\ r_c = \langle \{\alpha_1, \alpha_6\}, \{\bar{c}_3, \bar{c}_4\}\rangle \end{array} \right\} \tag{13}$$

---

[5] Roles $\{r_k = cook\}$, $\{r_{dp} = delivery\text{-}person\}$, and $\{r_{mt} = maintenance\text{-}technician\}$ are part of Ω, but role $\{r_c = customer\}$ is external to the organization.

– Agents *(Def. 9)*:

$$Ag = \begin{cases} ag_1 = \langle \{r_k\}, \{(\alpha_2, 1), (\alpha_3, 1)\} \rangle, \\ ag_2 = \langle \{r_{dp}\}, \{(\alpha_4, 1), (\alpha_5, 1)\} \rangle, \\ ag_3 = \langle \{r_{dp}\}, \{(\alpha_4, 1), (\alpha_5, 1)\} \rangle, \\ ag_4 = \langle \{r_{mt}\}, \{(\alpha_7, 1)\} \rangle, \\ ag_5 = \langle \{r_c\}, \{(\alpha_1, 1), (\alpha_6, 1)\} \rangle \end{cases} \tag{14}$$

– Social commitment schemes *(Def. 3)*:

$$SComm = \begin{cases} \bar{c}_1 = \alpha_1 \Rightarrow C(r_k, r_{dp}, \alpha_2, 8, [0, 0, 0], [0]) \\ \bar{c}_2 = \alpha_2 \Rightarrow C(r_{dp}, r_k, \alpha_4, 3, [0, 0, 0], [0]) \\ \bar{c}_3 = \alpha_4 \Rightarrow C(r_{dp}, r_c, \alpha_5, 21, [0, 0, 0], [0]) \\ \bar{c}_4 = \alpha_5 \Rightarrow C(r_c, r_{dp}, \alpha_6, 2, [0, 0, 0], [0]) \\ \bar{c}_5 = \hat{\alpha_8} \Rightarrow C(r_{mt}, r_k, \alpha_7, 31, [0, 0, 0], [0]) \\ \bar{c}_6 = \hat{\alpha_9} \Rightarrow C(r_k, r_{mt}, \alpha_3, 6, [0, 0, 0], [0]) \end{cases} \tag{15}$$

This example comprises 1 *cook* agent (ag_1), 2 *delivery-person* agents (ag_2, ag_3), 1 *maintenance-technician* agent (ag_4), and 1 *customer* agent (ag_5). Note that, the social commitment schemes in Formula (15) implicitly define the following pizza delivery workflow: **order-pizza** → **cook-pizza** → **pack-pizza** → **deliver-pizza** → **pay-order**; which is initiated when exogenous event **become-hungry**^{exog} occurs, making the *customer* agent perform the action **order-pizza**.

6 Initial Validation

A *SC-sim* simulator has been implemented as a Java applet, which provides some flexibility in terms of deployment and facilitates sharing results with the research community. To illustrate the use of the model and the simulator, we introduce a simple experiment involving two *sanctions policies*:

– **SPol ∅**. $\mathcal{S}_d = \{0, 0, 0\}$, and $\mathcal{S}_c = \{0\}$. Debtors receive no rewards. Both debtors and creditors have no penalties. This policy entails no social control; and
– **SPol 1**. $\mathcal{S}_d = \{0, -1, -1\}$, and $\mathcal{S}_c = \{-1\}$. Debtors receive no rewards and high violation penalties. Both debtors and creditors have high cancellation penalties.

Experiment. We ran the experiment on the pizza delivery domain presented in Example 1. We varied the *periodicity* (Def. 2) of the exogenous event **become-hungry**^{exog} (starting from 80 time steps, down to 40, 20, 10, 5, 2, and 1 time steps). As a result, the *customer* agent starts placing orders more frequently. Note that we assume neither agents, nor actions can fail. We measured the overall *efficiency* (i.e. percentage of s-commitments fulfilled) of the system. For each parametrization, we ran 15 simulations of 750 time steps each and computed the standard sample mean. Figure 2 presents the results.

Observation 1. As expected, the *efficiency* of the organization degraded from nearly optimal as the *frequency* of orders and the corresponding *level of activity* (i.e. number of s-commitments per agent per time step, not shown here) was increased.

Observation 2. We can observe drastic differences between the evaluated policies. These two *sanction policies* had a distinct effect on the performance of the system. Under policy **SPol 1** the organization was more *efficient* than without having any *social control* (i.e., **SPol ∅**).

Observation 3. Desirable (sometimes nearly optimal) agent behaviour results from local *coherence maximization*, without explicitly encoding agents behaviour. More importantly, macro-level *social coherence* does emerge from local *coherence maximization*.

Although this paper focuses on presenting the model, we think these experimental results are encouraging as they provide some preliminary validation. Of course, there is still much work to be done in terms of running more experiments, analyzing results and evaluating the scalability of the model. Our work takes on the problem of modelling *desirable and (relatively) predictable emergent social behaviour* from the local (coherence-driven) actions of the agents [6]. Observation 3 provides some preliminary evidence to support the suitability of our model for running social simulations, where complex *emergent social patterns* can be obtained and reproduced from the dynamics of local interactions among agents. There is complexity happening that cannot be fully explained analytically, thus justifying an empirical simulation-based approach. Similarly, Observation 2 provides some evidence to support the effectiveness of integrating *social control* mechanisms (for the enforcement of *s-commitments*), into the coherence calculus. Note that, when agents have neither positive, nor negative incentives their local *coherence-driven deliberation* might eventually lead them to unilaterally cancelling, or even violating *social commitments* as there are no consequences. Some authors have suggested [6] that *social cooperation* does not necessarily require an agent's understanding, agreement, nor even awareness. Our proposal aligns with this view, and Observation 2 shows that we are able to re-produce *desirable cooperation-like behaviour*, through the implementation of an appropriate *sanction policy* (e.g., **SPol 1**).

7 Discussion and Related Work

There have been several approaches [5,23,19,2] to formalizing *social commitments*. The proposal of Carabelea and Boissier [2] relies on *social commitments* for coordinating agents within the context of organizational interactions. Like us, they do define *social entities* and *organizational structures* entirely based on *social commitments*. However, in our proposal all the dynamics of *social commitments* are captured by a generic state-transition model which is associated with *social control* mechanisms for the enforcement of *social commitments*. In addition, we choose not to explicitly specify *authority relations* between roles. Instead, we capture them as implicitly resulting from *social commitments schema* associated with roles. Thus, we can get a more compact representation without compromising expressiveness.

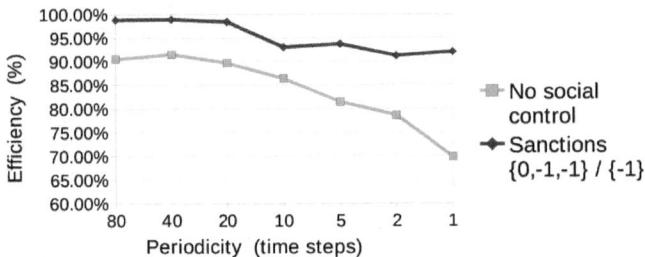

Fig. 2. Experimental Results (Efficiency %)

One other coherence-based framework inspired by early work on cognitive coherence in MAS [17] has been proposed by Joseph et al. [21,22]. Their framework builds on the BDI model of agency and the coherence theory [24]. Their approach, is also based on a *coherence maximization* model of agent rationality implemented as a constraint satisfaction problem. However, their proposal substantially differs from ours as (i) their main motivation seems to be the study of the interactions between the agent's internal cognitions (BDI) and some social aspects of MAS such as: norm evaluation [22], and the behaviour of institutional agents [21]; and (ii) their approach uses coherence graphs to represent each BDI modality resulting in a more complex model that has not been validated nor implemented and thus does not allow to derive new knowledge. In contrast, we are interested in modelling and evaluating the general dynamics of social systems. We claim that our model not only is more compact and decreases the computational overhead incurred when calculating coherence, but also is expressive enough to represent complex social systems. Although, in this paper, we do not consider *social norms*, we can certainly model them by representing s-commitments from a role towards an organization[6].

Other organizational approaches to social modelling have been reported in the literature [20,26]. The former, is a knowledge-based approach to automated organizational design, which enables efficient role selection to match organizational goals, as well as agent-to-role allocation. Like us, they define organizational structures in terms of *agents* enacting *roles* in *organizations*. However, their focus is on designing effective organizations which can change forms depending of varying performance requirements. Instead, our *simulation framework* focuses on evaluating the emergent social dynamics and performance of multi-agent organizations from the local *coherence*-driven interactions among agents. The latter proposal [26], presents an agent-oriented language (endowed with an operational semantics) for developing multi-agent organizations. *Organizations* are defined in terms of *roles*, *norms*, and *sanctions*. Although structurally close from an abstract organizational standpoint; our models also differ as theirs specify *roles* in terms of the same mental attitudes attributed to BDI agents. Instead, we define *roles* in terms of *capabilities* which can be enacted by *agents*. Moreover, the *state* of a *role* makes no reference to mental attitudes.

---

[6] An *institution* can be seen as a particular type of organization.

8   Conclusions and Future Work

In this paper, we presented a simple operational model capturing some of the dynamics of social systems. Our work advances the state of the art by proposing a unified yet computational view of some of the social aspects of multi-agent organizations. More specifically, our proposal relies on applying a local coherence maximization model of agent rationality to multi-agent organizations. In previous work [17], we proposed a constraint satisfaction-based model of *cognitive coherence* within the context of agent communication pragmatics. Here, we built on this work and extended it to consider *social coherence*. We introduced the notion of local *cognitive coherence* as the main social organizing principle in MAS. Moreover, our model relies on the notion of *social commitment* to represent all the inter-dependencies between *social entities*. Together with the notion of *sanction policy*, *social coherence* reify the notion of *social control*. In our model, *social control* is actually integrated into the coherence calculus (Def. 17). In addition, sanctions are embedded into the life-cycle of s-commitments. Local *coherence maximization* is the driving force that organizes agents' behaviour and from which *social coherence* emerges. For now, agents only do constraint optimization over the network of instantiated s-commitment stored in their individual agendas. However, our model could also accommodate other type of cognitions (and constraints between them) beside s-commitments e.g. perceptions, believes, and intentions. Finally, we illustrated our model and simulator by running a simple experiment to investigate the effects sanction-based *social control* mechanisms (reified in the form of two different *sanction policies*) on a sample domain.

As future work, we will refine our model using an action language such as *event calculus* [14]. We want to evaluate the benefits of introducing a more comprehensive treatment of *time*, as well as reasoning about *actions*. We also plan to address the issue of handling *complex actions*. Another immediate extension to our model will be the introduction of *uncertainty reasoning* into the *coherence calculus*. For now, agents do not take into account any uncertainty measures. Since both *actions* and *agents* can fail (as reflected by the *reliability* probability value in Def. 9), agents should be able to incorporate these information into their expected utility calculus. Agents with different levels of knowledge should also be modelled, such as: agents with no knowledge, with partial knowledge, or with complete/shared knowledge. Furthermore, various machine learning mechanisms would allow agents to progressively learn these probabilities. In addition, uncertainty measures such as an agent's reliability could be used to compute dynamic weights of constraints between s-commitments. This would allow different agents to generate similar types of constraints with different weights.

Finally, we want to run more experiments and evaluate the scalability of our model. For instance, we should model social domains with multiple organizations and greater number of agents, where agents can play several roles possibly in different organizations. We also want to investigate how our coherence-based approach might be used to evaluate the functionality and behaviour of typical *organizational structures* reported in the literature (e.g., hierarchies, holarchies, societies, federations [13]). Furthermore, since no single organizational design is suitable for all domain applications we want to cross-validate our model by running simulations involving different organizational structures. Last but not least, we want to continue studying the effects of other sanction-based *social control* mechanisms. For instance, by introducing (i) dynamic sanctions which increase over time, or increase as the number of violations increases; and (ii) decommitment sanctions specifying the penalty that either a debtor or creditor (or both) have to the other party in case of unilateral decommitment. Furthermore, we want to investigate how to design sanctions policies that bring desirable global properties into the system. In particular, determining which sanction policy is the optimal one for a particular system.

Acknowledgments

The authors would like to thank Marek Hatala and the anonymous reviewers for their useful comments.

References

1. Bandini, S., Manzoni, S., Vizzari, G.: Agent based modeling and simulation. In: Meyers, R.A. (eds.) [16], pp. 184–197
2. Carabelea, C., Boissier, O.: Coordinanting Agents in Organizations Using Social Commitments. In: Proceedings of the 1st International Workshop on Coordination and Organisation, Namur (April 2005)
3. Carley, K.M., Gasser, L.: Computational Organization Theory. In: Multiagent Systems: A Modern Approach to Distributed Artificial Intelligence, pp. 299–330. MIT Press, Cambridge (2001)
4. Carley, K.M., Prietula, M.J. (eds.): Computational Organization Theory. L. Erlbaum Associates Inc., Hillsdale (1994)
5. Castelfranchi, C.: Commitments: from Individual Intentions to Groups and Organizations. In: Proceedings of ICMAS 1995, pp. 41–48 (June 1995)
6. Castelfranchi, C.: Engineering Social Order. In: Zhang, S.-W., Tolksdorf, R., Zambonelli, F. (eds.) ESAW 2000. LNCS (LNAI), vol. 1972, pp. 1–18. Springer, Heidelberg (2000)
7. Davidsson, P., Verhagen, H.: Social phenomena simulation. In: Meyers, R.A. (eds.) [16], pp. 8375–8379
8. Decker, K., Lesser, V.: Quantitative Modeling of Complex Environments. International Journal of Intelligent Systems in Accounting, Finance and Management. Special Issue on Mathematical and Computational Models and Characteristics of Agent Behaviour 2, 215–234 (1993)
9. Festinger, L.: A Theory of Cognitive Dissonance. Stanford University Press, Stanford (1957)
10. Flores, R.A., Kremer, R.C.: To Commit or Not to Commit: Modeling Agent Conversations for Action. Computational Intelligence 18(2), 120–173 (2002)
11. Fornara, N., Colombetti, C.: Operational Specification of a Commitment-Based Agent Communication Language. In: Castelfranchi, C., Johnson, W.L. (eds.) Proceeding of the First Autonomous Agents and Multi-Agents Systems Joint Conference (AAMAS 2002), vol. 2, pp. 535–543. ACM Press, New York (2002)

12. Hechter, M., Opp, K.D.: Introduction. Social Norms, pp. xi–xx (2001)
13. Horling, B., Lesser, V.: A Survey of Multi-Agent Organizational Paradigms. The Knowledge Engineering Review 19(4), 281–316 (2005)
14. Kowalski, R.A., Sergot, M.: A Logic-Based Calculus of Events. New Generation Computing 4, 67–95 (1986)
15. Martindale, D.: The Theory of Social Control. In: Social Control for the 1980s: A Handbook for Order in a Democratic Society, pp. 46–58. Greenwood Press, New York (1978)
16. Meyers, R.A. (ed.): Encyclopedia of Complexity and Systems Science. Springer, Heidelberg (2009)
17. Pasquier, P., Chaib-draa, B.: The Cognitive Coherence Approach for Agent Communication Pragmatics. In: Proceedings of The Second International Joint Conference on Autonomous Agent and Multi-Agents Sytems (AAMAS 2003), Melbourne, pp. 544–552 (2003)
18. Pasquier, P., Dignum, F., Rahwan, I., Sonenberg, L.: Argumentation and Persuasion in the Cognitive Coherence Theory. In: Proceedings of the First International Conference on Computational Model of Argumentation (COMMA 2006), Liverpool. Frontier in Artificial Intelligence. IOS Press, Amsterdam (2006)
19. Pasquier, P., Flores, R.A., Chaib-draa, B.: Modelling Flexible Social Commitments and their Enforcement. In: Gleizes, M.-P., Zhang, S.-W., Zambonelli, F. (eds.) ESAW 2004. LNCS (LNAI), vol. 3451, pp. 139–151. Springer, Heidelberg (2005)
20. Sims, M., Corkill, D., Lesser, V.: Automated Organization Design for Multi-agent Systems. Autonomous Agents and Multi-Agent Systems 16(2), 151–185 (2008)
21. Sindhu, J., Sierra, C., Schorlemmer, M.: A Coherence Based Framework for Institutional Agents. In: Proceedings of the Fifth European Workshop on Multi-Agent Systems (EUMAS 2007) (December 2007)
22. Sindhu, J., Sierra, C., Schorlemmer, M., Delunde, P.: Formalizing Deductive Coherence: An Application to Norm Evaluation. Logic Journal of the Interest Group in Pure and Applied Logic (IGPL) (2008)
23. Singh, M.P.: An Ontology for Commitments in Multiagent Systems: Toward a Unification of Normative Concepts. Artificial Intelligence and Law 7, 97–113 (1999)
24. Thagard, P.: Coherence in Thought and Action. MIT Press, Cambridge (2000)
25. Thagard, P., Verbeurgt, K.: Coherence as Constraint Satisfaction. Cognitive Science 22, 1–24 (1998)
26. Tinnemeier, N., Dastani, M., Meyer, J.-J.: Roles and Norms for Programming Agent Organizations. In: Proceedings of the 8th International Conference on Autonomous Agents and Multiagent Systems, Richland, SC, pp. 121–128 (2009)
27. Vincent, R., Horling, B., Lesser, V.: Experiences in Simulating Multi-Agent Systems Using TÆMS. International Conference on Multi-Agent Systems, vol. 0, pp. 04–55 (2000)
28. Wagner, T., Raja, A., Lesser, V.: Modeling Uncertainty and its Implications to Sophisticated Control TÆMS Agents. Autonomous Agents and Multi-Agent Systems 13, 463 (2006)
29. Walton, D.N., Krabbe, E.: Commitment in Dialogue: Basic Concepts of Interpersonal Reasoning. Suny Press (1995)
30. Wu, J., Durfee, E.H.: Solving Large TÆMS Problems Efficiently by Selective Exploration and Decomposition. In: Proceedings of the 6th International Joint Conference on Autonomous Agents and Multiagent Systems, AAMAS 2007, pp. 56:1–56:8. ACM, New York (2007)

Shared Mental Models

A Conceptual Analysis

Catholijn M. Jonker[1], M. Birna van Riemsdijk[1], and Bas Vermeulen[2]

[1] EEMCS, Delft University of Technology, Delft, The Netherlands
{m.b.vanriemsdijk,c.m.jonker}@tudelft.nl
[2] ForceVision, Den Helder, The Netherlands
bas.vermeulen@forcevision.nl

Abstract. The notion of a shared mental model is well known in the literature regarding team work among humans. It has been used to explain team functioning. The idea is that team performance improves if team members have a shared understanding of the task that is to be performed and of the involved team work. We maintain that the notion of shared mental model is not only highly relevant in the context of human teams, but also for teams of agents and for human-agent teams. However, before we can start investigating how to engineer agents on the basis of the notion of shared mental model, we first have to get a better understanding of the notion, which is the aim of this paper. We do this by investigating which concepts are relevant for shared mental models, and modeling how they are related by means of UML. Through this, we obtain a mental model ontology. Then, we formally define the notion of shared mental model and related notions. We illustrate our definitions by means of an example.

1 Introduction

The notion of a shared mental model is well known in the literature regarding team work among humans [6,3,22,21]. It has been used to explain team functioning. The idea is that team performance improves if team members have a shared understanding of the task that is to be performed and of the involved team work.

We maintain that shared mental model theory as developed in social psychology, can be used as an inspiration for the development of techniques for improving team work in (human-)agent teams. In recent years, several authors have made similar observations. In particular, in [27] agents are implemented that use a shared mental model of the task to be performed and the current role assignment to proactively communicate the information other agents need. Also, [25] identify "creating shared understanding between human and agent teammates" as the biggest challenge facing developers of human-agent teams. Moreover, [20,19] identify common ground and mutual predictability as important for effective coordination in human-agent teamwork.

In this paper, we aim to lay the foundations for research on using shared mental model theory as inspiration for the engineering of agents capable of effective teamwork. We believe that when embarking on such an undertaking, it is important to get a better understanding of the notion of shared mental model. In this paper, we do this by investigating which concepts are relevant for shared mental models (Section 2), and

M. De Vos et al. (Eds.): COIN 2010 International Workshops, LNAI 6541, pp. 132–151, 2011.
© Springer-Verlag Berlin Heidelberg 2011

modeling how they are related by means of UML (Section 3). Through this, we obtain a mental model ontology. Then, we formally define the notion of shared mental model using several related notions (Section 4). We illustrate our definitions by means of an example in Section 5 and discuss related work in Section 7.

2 Exploration of Concepts

This section discusses important concepts related to the notion of shared mental models.

2.1 Working in a Team

An abundance of literature has appeared on working in teams, both in social psychology as well as in the area of multi-agent systems. It is beyond the scope of this paper to provide an overview. Rather, we discuss briefly how work on shared mental models distinguishes aspects of teamwork. Since we are interested in shared mental models, we take their perspective on teamwork for the analyses in this paper. We do not suggest that it is the only (right) way to view teamwork, but it suffices for the purpose of this paper.

An important distinction that has been made in the literature on shared mental models, is the distinction between *task work* and *team work* (see, e.g., [6,22]). Task work concerns the task or job that the team is to perform, while team work concerns what has to be done only because the task is performed by a team instead of an individual agent. In particular, task work mental models concern the equipment (equipment functioning and likely failures) and the task (task procedures and likely contingencies). Team work mental models concern team interaction (roles and responsibilities of team members, interaction patterns, and information flow), and team members (knowledge, skills, and preferences of teammates).

2.2 Mental Models

In order to be able to interact with the world, humans must have some internal representation of the world. The notion of *mental model* has been introduced to refer to these representations. A mental model can consist of knowledge about a physical system that should be understood or controlled, such as a heat exchanger or an interactive device [11]. The knowledge can concern, e.g., the structure and overall behavior of the system, and the disturbances that act on the system and how these affect the system. Such mental models allow humans to interact successfully with the system.

Different definitions of mental models have been proposed in the literature (see, e.g., [9] for a discussion in the context of system dynamics). In this paper, we use the following often cited, functional definition as proposed in [24]:

> Mental models are the mechanisms whereby humans are able to generate descriptions of system purpose and form, explanations of system functioning and observed system states, and predictions of future system states.

Central to this definition is that mental models concern a *system* and that they serve the purpose of *describing, explaining, and predicting the behavior of the system.*

Another important view of mental models was proposed in [17]. The idea proposed there focuses on the way people reason. It is argued that when people reason, they do not use formal rules of inference but rather think about the possibilities compatible with the premises and with their general knowledge. In this paper, we use the definition of [24] because as we will show, it is closely related to the definition of shared mental model that we discuss in the next section.

2.3   Shared Mental Models

Mental models have not only been used to explain how humans interact with physical systems that they have to understand and control, but they have also been used in the context of team work [6,22]. There the *system that mental models concern is the team.* The idea is that mental models help team members predict what their teammates are going to do and are going to need, and hence they facilitate coordinating actions between teammates. In this way, mental models help explain team functioning.

Mental models have received a lot of attention in literature regarding team performance. Several studies have shown a positive relation between team performance and similarity between mental models of team members (see, e.g., [3,22,21]). That is, it is important for team performance that team members have a shared understanding of the team and the task that is to be performed, i.e., that team members have a *shared mental model*. The concept of shared mental model is defined in [6] as:

> knowledge structures held by members of a team that enable them to form accurate explanations and expectations for the task, and, in turn, coordinate their actions and adapt their behavior to demands of the task and other team members.

Shared mental models thus help *describe, explain and predict the behavior of the team,* which allows team members to coordinate and adapt to changes. In [6], it is argued that shared mental model theory does not imply identical mental models, but "rather, the crucial implication of shared mental model theory is that team members hold compatible mental models that lead to common expectations for the task and team."

In correspondence with the various aspects of teamwork as discussed above, it has been argued that multiple different types of shared mental models are relevant for team performance: shared mental models for task work (equipment model and task model) and for team work (team interaction model and team member model) [6,22].

In this paper, we are interested in the notion of shared mental model both in humans and in software agents, but at this general level of analysis we do not distinguish between the two. Therefore, from now on we use the term "agent" to refer to either a human or a software agent.

3   Mental Model Ontology

We start our analysis of the notion of shared mental model by analyzing the notion of mental model. We do this by investigating the relations between notions that are essential for defining this concept, and provide UML[1] models describing these relations. The UML models thus form a mental model ontology. This means that the models are not meant as a design for an implementation. As such, attributes of and navigability between concepts is not specified. For example, we model that a model concerns a system by placing a relation between the concepts. But that does not mean that if one would build an agent with a mental model of another agent, that the first would be able to navigate to the contents of the mind of the other agent. We have devided the ontology in three figures for reasons of space and clarity of presentation. We have not duplicated all relations in all diagrams to reduce the complexity of the diagrams.

We use UML rather than (formal) ontology languages such as frames [23] or description logics [2], since it suffices for our purpose. We develop the ontology not for doing sophisticated reasoning or as a design for a multi-agent system, but rather to get a better understanding of the essential concepts that are involved and their relations. Also, the developed ontologies are relatively manageable and do not rely on involved concept definitions. We can work out more formal representations in the future when developing techniques that allow agents to reason with mental models.

We present the UML models in three steps. First, since the concept of a mental model refers to systems, we discuss the notion of *system*. Then, since shared mental models are important in the context of teams, we show how a *team* can be defined *as a system*. Following that, we introduce the notion of agent into the picture and show how the notions of agent, system, and mental model are related.

In UML, classes (concepts) are denoted as rectangles. A number of relations can be defined between concepts. The generalization relation is a relation between two concepts that is denoted like an arrow. This relation represents a relationship between a general class and a more specific class. Every instance of the specific class is also an instance of the general class and inherits all features of the general class. A relationship from a class A to class B with an open diamond at side one of the ends is called a shared aggregate, defined here as a part-whole relation. The end of the association with the diamond is the whole, the other side is the part. Because of the nature of this relationship it cannot be used to form a cycle. A composite aggregation is drawn as an association with a black diamond. The difference with a shared aggregation is that in a composite aggregation, the whole is also responsible for the existence, persistence and destruction of the parts. This means that a part in a composite aggregation can be related to only one whole. Finally, a relationship between two concepts that is represented with a normal line, an association, can be defined. The nature of this relationship is written along the relationship. This can either be done by placing the name of the association in the middle of the line or by placing a role name of a related concept near the concept. The role name specifies the kind of role that the concept plays in the relation. Further, numbers can be placed at the ends of the shared aggregation, composite aggregation and associations. They indicate how many instances of the related concepts can be related in one instance of the relationship. Note that we have not duplicated all relations and concepts in all figures. This is done to keep the figures of the separate parts of our conceptualization clean.

---

[1] http://www.omg.org/spec/UML/2.2/

3.1 System

The previous section shows that the concept of a mental model refers to systems. In this section, we further analyze the notion of system in order to use it to define a team as a system. For this purpose, the basic definition provided by Wikipedia[2] suffices as a point of departure: *A system is a set of interacting or independent entities, real or abstract, forming an integrated whole.* This definition captures the basic ingredients of the notion of system found in the literature (see, e.g., [10]), namely static structures within the system as well as the dynamic interrelations between parts of the system.

Our conceptualization of systems is supported by the UML diagram in Figure 1.

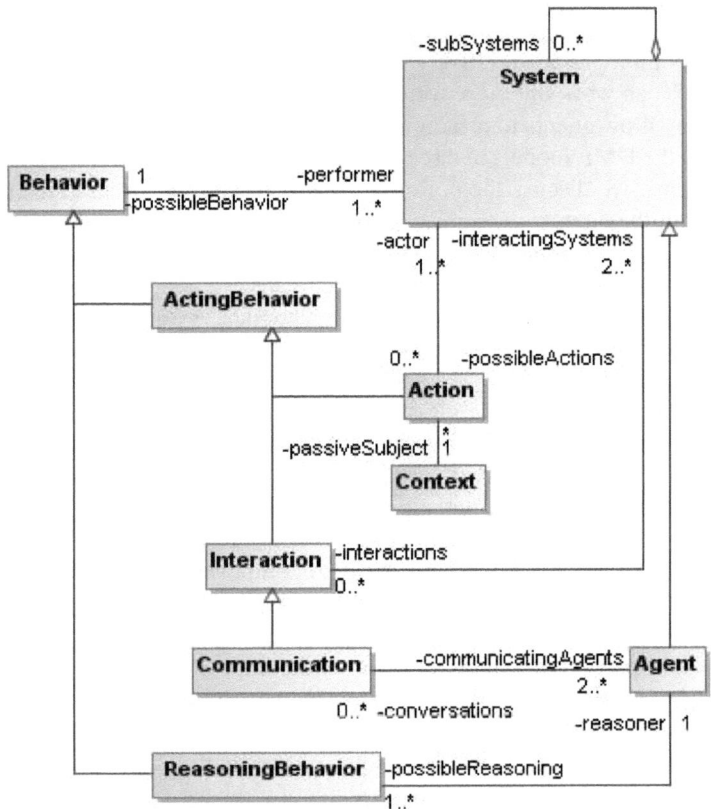

Fig. 1. System

The upper-right corner of the diagram depicts that a system may be a composite, i.e., it may be composed of other systems. This modeling choice makes it easier to define in the following section the notion of team as a system. In particular, the compositionality of the concept system in terms of other systems makes the compositionality of mental

---

[2] http://en.wikipedia.org/wiki/System

models straightforward in the next sections. Regarding the definition, this part addresses the sub-phrase that a system is a set of entities.

The system forms an integrated whole, according to the definition. Therefore, the whole shows behavior. As we do not distinguish between natural or designed systems, living or otherwise, we chose behavior to represent the dynamics of the system as a whole. Note that we further distinguish between reasoning behavior and acting behavior. Not all systems will show both forms of behavior. Acting behavior refers to either actions or interactions. An action is a process that affects the environment of the system and/or the composition of the system itself. Interaction is a process with which a sub-system of the system (or the system as a whole) affects another sub-system of the system. Communication is a special form of interaction, in which the effect of the interaction concerns the information state of the other element. Communication is a term we restricted for the information-based interaction between two agents. The term reasoning behavior is also reserved for agents. The concept "context" refers to both the environment of the system as well as the dynamics of the situation the system is in. The system executes its actions in its context. Thus one context is related to multiple actions.

3.2 Team as a System

The notion of system is central to the definition of mental model. In the context of shared mental models we are especially interested in a certain kind of system, namely a team. According to the definition of system, a team can be viewed as a system: it consists of a set of interacting team members, forming an integrated whole.

As noted above, several aspects are relevant for working in a team. We take as a basis for our model the distinction made in [6,22]. As noted in Section 2.1, we by no means claim that this is the only suitable definition of a team or that it captures all aspects. We start from this research since it discusses teams in the context of shared mental models. The most important realization for the sequel is that we define a team as a system and that it has as a set of team members that are agents. Other aspects of the team definition can be varied if nessecary.

The following aspects are distinguished: *equipment* and *task* (related to task work), and *team interaction* and *team members* (related to team work). In our model, we include these four aspects of working in a team. However, we divide them not into team work and task work, but rather into *physical components* and *team activity*, where team members and equipment are physical components and task and team interaction are team activities The reason for making this distinction is that we argue that physical components can in turn be viewed as systems themselves, while team activities cannot, as reflected by the link from physical components to system in Figure 2 below. Moreover, we make another refinement and make a distinction between a task and *task execution*. We argue that task execution is a team activity, even though a task might be performed by only one team member. The task itself describes what should be executed. The concept task is also linked to equipment, to express the equipment that should be used for executing the task, and to team member, to describe which team members are responsible for a certain task.

We link this conceptualization of the notion of team to the general notion of system of Figure 1 by defining a team activity as a kind of acting behavior, and more specifically team interaction as a kind of interaction[3]. We see team interaction as interaction induced by executing the team activity. Moreover, by defining that physical components are systems, we can deduce from Figure 1 that they can have interactions with each other. Moreover, by defining a team member as an agent, we can deduce from Figure 1 that team members can have reasoning behavior and that they can communicate. The reasoning of a team is built up from the interaction between team members and the individual reasoning of these team members during the interaction. A fully specified example of two agents Arnie and Bernie that have to cooperate to solve an identification task is provided in [18]. It contains examples of team reasoning.

These considerations are reflected in the UML model of Figure 2.

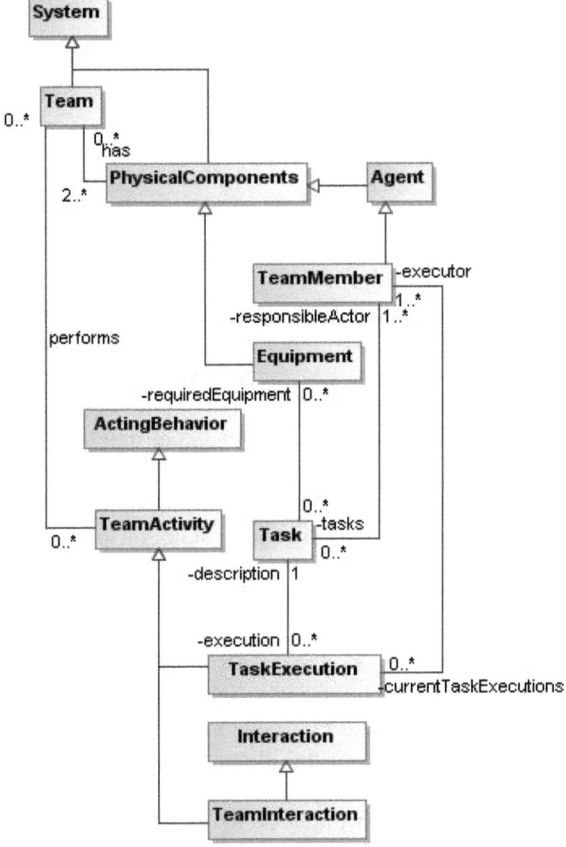

Fig. 2. Team

---

[3] We could have distinguished "interaction" as a description of an activity from the "performance of the interaction", similarly to the distinction between task and task execution. This is done in the case of task (execution) to be able to express that a team member is responsible for a task, which when executed becomes a team activity. We omit this distinction for interaction for reasons of simplicity.

3.3   Mental Model

Now that we have conceptualized in some detail the notion of system and of a team as a system, we are ready to zoom in on the notion of mental model.

As noted above, mental models are used by humans, i.e., humans have mental models. However, since in this paper we use the notion of agent as a generalization of human and software agent, here we consider that agents have mental models. Moreover, a mental model concerns a system. The basic structure of how mental models are related to systems and agents is thus that an agent has mental models and a mental model concerns a system.

However, we make several refinements to this basic view. First, we would like to express where a mental model resides, namely in the *mind* of an agent. As such, mental models can be contrasted with *physical models*. In order to do this, we introduce the notion of a *model*, and define that physical models and mental model are kinds of models. Both kinds of models can concern any type of system. A nice feature of this distinction is that it allows us to easily express how the notion of *extended mind* [7] is related. The notion of extended mind is being developed in research on philosophy of mind, and the idea is that some objects in the external environment of an agent, such as a diary to record a schedule of meetings or a shared display, are utilized by the mind in such a way that the objects can be seen as extensions of the mind itself. The notion is relevant to research on shared mental models because agents in a team may share an extended mind, and through this obtain a shared mental model [3].

Another aspect that we add to the conceptualization, is the notion of *goal* to express that a mental model is used by an agent for a certain purpose, expressed by the goal of the model.

This is captured in the UML model of Figure 3.

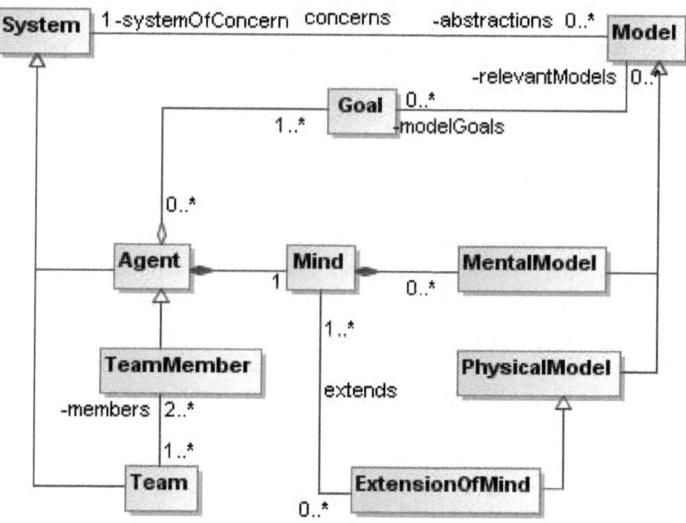

Fig. 3. Mental Model

Given this conceptualization, we can express that an agent can have a mental model of a team. An agent can have a mental model, since it has a mind and a mind can have mental models. A mental model can concern a team, since a mental model is a model and a model concerns a system, and a team is a kind of system. However, since team interaction is not by itself a system (see previous subsection), our model does not allow to express, for example, that the agent has a team interaction mental model. What our conceptualization does allow to express, is that the team mental model has a part that describes team interaction, since the team mental model concerns a team, and a team has team interaction. According to our model, we thus cannot call this part a mental model. However, we will for the sake of convenience refer to that part as a team interaction model (and similarly for the other parts of a team mental model). This is in line with [6,22], where the parts of a team mental model are called mental models themselves. We have modelled the relation between team and team member as a normal association instead of by an aggregation because modelling this relation as an aggregation would mean that an agent's mind is part of a team, which does not conform to intuition.

3.4   Accuracy of Models

In research on shared mental models, the relation of both *accuracy*[4] and *similarity* of mental models to team performance has been investigated [21]. As noted in [22], "similarity does not equal quality - and teammates may share a common vision of their situation yet be wrong about the circumstances that they are confronting".

We suggest that the notions of accuracy and similarity not only have different meanings, but play a different role in the conceptualization of shared mental models. That is, the notion of accuracy of a mental model can be defined by comparing the mental model against some standard or "correct" mental model, i.e., it does not (necessarily) involve comparing mental models of team members. Depending on what one views as a correct model one gets a different notion of accuracy. We have defined two such notions below. The notion of similarity, on the other hand, *does* involve comparing mental models of team members. Although both accuracy and similarity affect team performance [21], we maintain that conceptually, only similarity is to be used for defining the notion of shared mental model. We therefore discuss accuracy informally, and omit the formalizations. We discuss accuracy and similarity with respect to models in general, rather than to only mental models.

We identify two kinds of accuracy, depending on what one takes to compare the model with. The first is what we call *system accuracy*, which assumes that one has a "bird's eye view" of the system and can see all relevant aspects, including the mental models of agents in the system. In general, this is only of theoretical relevance, since one typically has limited access to the various parts of a system[5]. Another notion of accuracy that is easier to operationalize, is *expert accuracy*. In expert accuracy, the idea is to compare a model to an expert model (see e.g. [21] for an example of how to obtain an expert model). Expert accuracy may be defined as the extent to which the model agrees

---

[4] Here, accuracy is meant in the sense of "freedom from errors", not in the sense of exactness.

[5] In a multi-agent system where one has access to the environment and internal mental states of all agents, one *would* be able to obtain all necessary information.

(see Section 4.2) with the expert model. This then assumes that the expert has a correct model. In research on shared mental models, this is the approach taken to determine accuracy of mental models of team members [21]. That work also describes how this can be operationalized. If the questions we pose to the model should result in a set of answers, then the measures of precision, defined as the number of relevant documents retrieved by a search divided by the total number of existing relevant documents, defined as the number of relevant documents retrieved by a search divided by the total number of existing relevant documents and recall from the field of information retrieval are good ways to measure the accuracy of the answers [5]. However, in this paper we have only considered questions with single answers.

4 Similarity of Models

As we suggested in the previous section, the essence of the concept of shared mental model is the extent to which agents have *similar* mental models. The word "shared" suggests full similarity, but this is typically not the case. Rather, we propose that *measures* of similarity should be used, which allow the investigation of when models are similar enough for a good team performance, or, in general, good enough for achieving certain goals. We introduce a formal framework in order to be able to express several definitions of notions of similarity. We define sharedness in terms of those notions.

4.1 Formal Framework

The definitions of similarity are based on the concepts and their relations as discussed above. The basic concept that we use in all definitions is *model* (Figure 3). We denote a model typically as M. In this paper, we abstract from the knowledge representation language used for representing the model. Depending on the context, different languages may be chosen. For example, when investigating shared mental models in the context of cognitive agent programming languages (see, e.g., [14]), the knowledge representation language of the respective language can be used. In that context, following Figure 3, the agent is programmed in an agent programming language, it has a mind which is represented by the agent program, this mind can contain mental models which would typically be represented in the so-called mental state of the agent, these mental models concern systems, which can in particular be the team of which the agent is a part.

In order to define to what extent a model is similar to another model, we need to express the content of the model. Depending on which system the model concerns, the content may differ. In particular, in case of mental models concerning a team, the content would represent information about the physical components and activity of the team, which in turn consist of information about equipment and team members, and about task execution and team interaction (Figure 2).

In order to compare models, one could (in principle) inspect the content of these models and compare this content directly. However, this is not always practicable, in particular when considering people: one cannot open up the mind of people to inspect the content of their mental models. Moreover, not all content of a model is always relevant. Depending on what one wants to use the model for, i.e., depending on the *goal* for which the model is to be used (Figure 3), different parts of the model may be relevant, or different levels of detail may be needed. For these reasons we propose to use a set of *questions* Q that can be posed to the model in order to determine its contents, thereby treating the model as a black box. For example, a mental model that is to be used for weather predictions should be able to answer a question such as what the weather will be tomorrow in a certain city. A physical model of our solar system should be able to answer a question such as whether the Earth or Mars is closer to the sun.

Choosing an appropriate set of questions is critical for obtaining useful measures of similarity. For example, posing questions about the solar system to a model for weather predictions will not be useful for measuring the similarity of the weather prediction model to another such model. Moreover, posing only questions about whether it will rain to a weather prediction model, will not provide a useful measure of the weather model's similarity to another model in predicting the weather in general. If the model concerns a team, the questions will have to concern the team's physical components and the team activity (Figure 2). With some mental flexibility one can use questions both for mental as well as for physical models, as illustrated by the examples provided above (cf. Figure 3).

Designing a set of questions is also done in research on shared mental models in social psychology. In that work, researchers commonly assess mental models by presenting respondents with a list of concepts and asking them to describe the strength of relationships among the concepts [21,22]. These concepts are carefully chosen based on, for example, interviews with domain experts. The operationalization of our definitions thus requires methods and techniques to determine the appropriate sets of questions Q for the team tasks, respecting the characteristics of the domain/environment in which the team has to function. The methods and techniques we consider important are those for knowledge engineering and elicitation and should take into account social theories about team building and team performance (as partly conceptualized in Figure 2). In the definitions that follow, we abstract from the content of models and assume a set of relevant questions is given. A more thorough investigation of how to define the set of questions is left for future work.

We write $M \vdash answer(a, q)$ to express that M answers a to question q. As usual, we use $|s|$ to denote the number of elements of a set s. If the model is represented using a logical knowledge representation language, $\vdash$ can be taken to be the entailment relation of the logic. If this is not the case, $\vdash$ should be interpreted more loosely.

4.2   Definitions

In the following, let M_1 and M_2 be models concerning the same system, and let Q be the set of questions identified as relevant for the goal for which M_1 and M_2 are to be used. Let T be a background theory used for interpreting answers. In particular, equivalence is defined with respect to T. For example, the answers "1,00 meter" and "100 centimeter" are equivalent with respect to the usual definitions of units of length.

The first definition of similarity that we provide, is what we call *subject overlap*. Subject overlap provides a measure for the extent to which models provide answers to the set of relevant questions Q. These answers may be different, but at least an answer should be given. We assume that if the answer is not known, no answer is provided.

For example, posing a question about the weather in a certain city to a model of the solar system would typically not yield an answer. Also, we assume that answers are individually consistent.

Definition 1 (subject overlap). *Let the set of questions for which the models provide answers (not necessarily similar answers) be* $OverAns(M_1, M_2, Q) = \{q \in Q \mid \exists a_1, a_2 : M_1 \vdash answer(a_1, q) \text{ and } M_2 \vdash answer(a_2, q)\}$. *Then, we define the level of subject overlap between the model* M_1 *and* M_2 *with respect to set of questions* Q *as* $SO(M_1, M_2, Q) = |OverAns(M_1, M_2, Q)| / |Q|$.

Since the literature (see Section 2.3) says that shared mental model theory implies that team members hold compatible mental models, we define a notion of compatibility of models. It is defined as the extent to which models do not provide contradictory answers.

Definition 2 (compatibility). *Let the set of questions for which the models provide incompatible answers be* $IncompAns(M_1, M_2, Q) = \{q \in Q \mid \exists a_1, a_2 : M_1 \vdash answer(a_1, q) \text{ and } M_2 \vdash answer(a_2, q) \text{ and } T, a_1, a_2 \vdash \bot\}$. *Then, we define the level of compatibility between the model* M_1 *and* M_2 *with respect to set of questions* Q *as:* $C(M_1, M_2, Q) = 1 - (|IncompAns(M_1, M_2, Q)| / |Q|)$.

Note that our definition of compatibility does not investigate more complex ways in which the set so determined might lead to inconsistencies. Also note that non-overlapping models are maximally compatible. This is due to the fact that we define incompatibility based on inconsistent answers. If the models do not provide answers to the same questions, they cannot contradict, and therefore they are compatible.

Next, we define *agreement* between models, which defines the extent to which models provide *equivalent* answers to questions.

Definition 3 (agreement). *Let the set of questions for which the models agree be* $AgrAns(M_1, M_2, Q) = \{q \in Q \mid \exists a_1, a_2 : M_1 \vdash answer(a_1, q) \text{ and } M_2 \vdash answer(a_2, q) \text{ and } a_1 \equiv_T a_2\}$. *Then, we define the level of agreement between the model* M_1 *and* M_2 *with respect to set of questions* Q *as:* $A(M_1, M_2, Q) = |AgrAns(M_1, M_2, Q)| / |Q|$.

These measures of similarity are related in the following way.

Proposition 1 (relations between measures). *We always have that* $A(M_1, M_2, Q) \leq SO(M_1, M_2, Q)$. *Moreover, if* $SO(M_1, M_2, Q) = 1$, *we have* $A(M_1, M_2, Q) \leq C(M_1, M_2, Q)$.

Proof. The first part follows from the fact that $AgrAns(M_1, M_2, Q) \subseteq OverAns(M_1, M_2, Q)$. The second part follows from the fact that if $SO(M_1, M_2, Q) = 1$, all questions are answered by both models. Then we have $AgrAns(M_1, M_2, Q) \subseteq (Q \setminus IncompAns(M_1, M_2, Q))$, using the assumption that answers are consistent.

Next we define what a shared mental model is in terms of the most important characteristics. The model is a mental model, thus it must be in the mind of an agent. Sharedness is defined with respect to a relevant set of questions Q. Furthermore, we have to indicate by which agents the model is shared. The measure of sharedness is defined in terms of the aspects of similarity as specified above.

Definition 4 (shared mental model). *A model M is a mental model that is shared to the extent θ by agents A_1 and A_2 with respect to a set of questions Q iff there is a mental model M_1 of A_1 and M_2 of A_2, both with respect to Q, such that*

1. *$SO(M, M_1, Q) = 1$, and $SO(M, M_2, Q) = 1$*
2. *$A(M, M_1, Q) \geq \theta$, and $A(M, M_2, Q) \geq \theta$*

The definition is easily extendable for handling an arbitrary number n of agents. The definition allows for two important ways to tune it to various situations: varying θ gives a measure of sharedness, varying Q allows to adapt to a specific usage of the model. For example, for some teamwork it is not necessary for every team member to know exactly who does what, as long as each team member knows his own task. This is possible if the amount of interdependencies between sub-tasks is relatively low. For other teamwork in which the tasks are highly interdependent and the dynamics is high, e.g., soccer, it might be fundamental to understand exactly what the others are doing and what you can expect of them. This can also be expressed more precisely by defining expectations and defining sharedness as full agreement of expectations. Making this precise is left for future research.

5   Example: BW4T

In this section, we illustrate the concepts defined in the previous sections using an example from the Blocks World for Teams (BW4T) domain [16]. BW4T is an extension of the classic blocks world that is used to research joint activity of heterogeneous teams in a controlled manner. A team of agents have to deliver colored blocks from a number of rooms to the so-called drop zone in a certain color sequence. The agents are allowed to communicate with each other but their visual range is limited to the room they are in.

We distinguish questions on three levels: *object level*, which concerns the environment (e.g., which blocks are in which rooms, which other agents are there, etc.), *informational and motivational level*, which concerns, e.g., beliefs of agents about the environment, and task allocation and intentions, and *strategic level*, which concerns the reasoning that agents are using to solve problems. These levels correspond to physical components and team activity in Figure 2, and reasoning behavior of agents in Figure 1, respectively.

For the object level, we constructed a set Q of questions regarding, e.g., the number of blocks per color per room, the required color per position in the required color sequence. For example, one can formulate questions such as "How many red blocks are there in room 1?". The answer to such a question is a number that can easily be compared to the answer given by another model. Assuming that there are 12 rooms and 3 colors (white, blue, and red), one can formulate 36 questions of the atomic kind for rooms and the number of blocks per color. Similarly, assuming that the required color sequence (the team task) has 9 positions, one can formulate questions such as "What is the required color at position 1?", leading to 9 questions of this kind (in BW4T the team task is displayed in the environment). In this way, we constructed 36 + 9 questions that refer to the current state of the environment. Note that over time, the situation changes, because the agents move the blocks around.

Suppose room 1 contains 2 red blocks, 2 white blocks and no blue blocks. Further-more assume, that agent A, having just arrived in room 1 has been able to observe the blocks in this room, whereas agent B is still en route to room 2 and has no idea about the colors of the blocks in the various rooms as yet. Assume that both agents have an accurate picture of the team task (which color has to go to which position). Taking this set of 45 question Q, then we have that the mental model of agent A, M_A, answers 12 questions out of a total of 45, while M_B, the model of agent B only an-swers 9 questions. The subject overlap is then $SO(M_A, M_B, Q) = 9/45$, and the com-patibility is $C(M_A, M_B, Q) = 1$. Also the level of agreement between the models is $A(M_A, M_B, Q) = 9/45$, which in this case equals the subject overlap since the answers do not differ. In order to identify a shared mental model between these agents, we have to restrict the questions to only the part concerning the team task. This model is shared to extent 1. Now, if agent A communicates his findings to agent B, then somewhat later in time the overlap and agreement could grow to 12/45, and the shared mental model would grow when modifying the set of questions accordingly. As the agents walk through the environment, they could achieve the maximum number on measures for these models, as long as they keep informing each other. If this is not done effec-tively, it may be the case that an agent believes a block to be in a room, while another agent believes it is not there anymore. This would lead to a decreased agreement.

For the informational and motivational level, one may, e.g., formulate the following questions: "Under which conditions should agents inform other agents?" which regards what each agent thinks is the common strategy for the team, and For the task level, one may formulate for each agent A the questions like "What is the preferred task order of agent A?", "Which task does agent A have?", "What is the intention of agent A?", and "What information was communicated by agent A at time X?". Note that the intention of agents changes over time during the task execution, and also X varies over time, thus leading to an incremental number of questions as the team is at work.

For the strategic level, one may consider questions like "Under which conditions should agents inform other agents?". Agent A might answer "An agent communicates when it knows something it knows other agents need to know and everything it intends itself", while B's response may be "An agent communicates when it knows something it knows other agents need to know". The formalizations of these statements could be:

belief(hasTask(Agent,Task)) ∧ belief(requires(Task,Info)) ∧
hasInfo(self,Info) ∧ Agent ≠ self ∧ belief(¬ hasInfo(Agent,Info))
→ toBeCommunicatedTo(Info,Agent))

intends(self, X) ∧ belief(¬ hasInfo(Agent,hasTask(self,X)))
→ toBeCommunicatedTo(hasTask(self,X),Agent)

This implies higher order aspects of the mental models that these agents need to have, i.e., a good image of what other agents know about the current situation, knowledge about the tasks and their dependence on information, and information about who has what task. For this example domain, this means that the questions need to be extended to include, e.g., "What information is relevant for task T?", and either informational and motivational level questions of the form "How many red blocks does agent A believe to be in room 1?" or strategic questions of the form "When can you be sure that an agent knows something?", to which an answer could be *observed(Info, self)* ∨ *communicatedBy(Info, Agent)*. Note that the complexity of computing the measures of similarity depends heavily on the complexity of the logic underlying the questions and thus the answers to the questions. The operationalization of testing these measures might require advanced logical theorem proving tools or model checkers.

6   Agent Reasoning with Shared Mental Models

The concepts introduced in Section 4 which were illustrated in Section 5, consider similarity between mental models from a *bird's eye* perspective. One could say that questions are posed to the mental models by an outside observer. However, this does not demonstrate how the notion of shared mental model can be *operationalized* and used in agents' reasoning. In this section we sketch the latter, using the Two Generals' Problem [1] (see also http://en.wikipedia.org/wiki/Two_Generals%27_Problem). The operationalization is done on the strategic level, with shared mental models in the lower two levels as a result. The aim is not to argue that the way this problem is solved using shared mental models is better than other solutions. The example is used only for illustration purposes.

> Two armies, each led by a general, are preparing to attack a fortified city. The armies are encamped near the city, each on its own hill. A valley separates the two hills, and the only way for the two generals to communicate is by sending messengers through the valley. Unfortunately, the valley is occupied by the city's defenders and there's a chance that any given messenger sent through the valley will be captured. Note that while the two generals have agreed that they will attack, they haven't agreed upon a time for attack before taking up their positions on their respective hills.
>
> The two generals must have their armies attack the city at the same time in order to succeed. They must thus communicate with each other to decide on a time to attack and to agree to attack at that time, and each general must know that the other general knows that they have agreed to the attack plan. Because acknowledgement of message receipt can be lost as easily as the original message, a potentially infinite series of messages is required to come to consensus.

The problem the generals face is that they are aware that they do not have a mental model of the attack time that is shared between them. Thus, the communication stream that they initiate is an attempt to come to a shared mental model and to know that they have a shared mental model.

By introducing the concept of a shared mental model, the problem can be formulated internally within the code of the agents (gen_a and gen_b) as follows. The notation we use resembles that of the agent programming language GOAL [14], giving an indication of how the reasoning can be programmed in an agent. GOAL uses Prolog for expressing the agent's knowledge, which represents general (static) knowledge of the domain and environment. Goals represent what agents want to achieve. The program section has rules of the form if <condition> then <action>, where the condition refers to the beliefs and/or goals of the agent. Percept rules are used to process percepts and/or execute multiple send actions. In each cycle of the agent's reasoning, all instantiations of percept rules are applied (meaning that the actions in the consequent are executed if the conditions in the antecedent hold), after which one action rule of which the condition holds is applied.

```
knowledge{
  conquer(city) :-
    simultaneous_attack.
  simultaneous_attack :-
    attacks_at(gen_a, T), attacks_at(gen_b, T).
  requires(shared_mental_model(attack_planned_at),
           hasInfo(A, attack_planned_at(B, T))).

}

goals{ conquer(city). }

program{
  if a-goal(conquer(city)) then
    adopt(simultaneous_attack) +
    adopt(shared_mental_model(attack_planned_at)).

  if a_goal(G) then insert(hasGoal(self,G)).

  <code to determine attack time T>

  if bel(hasInfo(gen_a, attack_planned_at(gen_a, T))),
     bel(hasInfo(gen_a, attack_planned_at(gen_b, T))),
     bel(hasInfo(gen_b, attack_planned_at(gen_a, T))),
     bel(hasInfo(gen_b, attack_planned_at(gen_b, T)))
  then do(attack_at(T)).
}

perceptrules{
  % the agents perceive the predicate "attacks_at(A,T)"
  % for any agent at the T the attack is performed.

  % Generic reflection rule for informing teammates
  if bel(hasGoal(Agent,Goal)),
     bel(requires(Goal,Info)),
     bel(Info),
     not(Agent = self),
     not(bel(hasInfo(Agent,Info)))
  then sendonce(Agent, Info) + insert(hasInfo(Agent,Info)).

}
```

The knowledge line about conquer city expresses that the city will be successfully conquered if the generals simultaneously attack at some time T and share a mental model with respect to the predicate attacks_at. The knowledge line about the requirement of a shared mental model about attacks_at explains that all agents A (thus both gen_a and gen_b) should have information about when all agents B (thus both gen_a and gen_b) will attack.

The initial goal of conquer city will lead to subsequent goals for the agents to attack simultaneously and to have a shared mental model with respect to the attack time, by applying the first rule in the program section.

The generic reflection rule in the perceptrules section cannot be executed by GOAL directly, but has to be interpreted as a scheme of rules that should be instantiated with concrete predicates for the kind of information to be sent in a specific domain. Using (instantiations of) this rule, the generals will start to inform each other of choices they made regarding the time to attack. This is done based on the goal of having a shared mental model concerning the attack plan (adopted through applying the first action rule), and the fact that for this certain information is required (as specified in the knowledge base).

The rest of the code of the agents, which is omitted here for brevity, should consist of code to get to the same time T at which they will attack. A simple solution is that e.g., gen_a is the boss, and gen_b will accept his proposal for the attack time. Once a common time has been established, the generals attack as specified in the last action rule.

Note that the formulation chosen does not require the infinite epistemic chain of hasInfo that is part of the thought experiment that the Two Generals' Problem is. Simply put, each of the agents will attack if it believes that it has the same idea about the attack time as the other agent. The agents as formulated above do not reflect again, that both should also share a mental model with respect to the predicate hasInfo. This would of course be interesting to model, but will lead to the long, infinitely long, process of informing each other of their plans as is explained in the literature on the Two Generals' Problem. We choose to stop here to explain a possible explicit use of the concept of a shared mental model.

7   Related Work

In this section, we discuss how our work is related to existing approaches to (human-)agent teamwork. An important difference between our work and other approaches is that to the best of our knowledge, few other approaches are based directly on shared mental model theory (see below for an exception). Moreover, our focus is on a conceptualization of the involved notions rather than on reasoning techniques that can be applied directly when developing agent teams, since this is one of the first papers that aims at bringing shared mental model theory to agent research. We believe it is important to get a better understanding of the concepts, thereby developing a solid foundation upon which reasoning techniques inspired by shared mental model theory can be built.

Although most existing approaches to (human-)agent teamwork are not based *directly* on shared-mental model theory, similar ideas have been used for developing these approaches. Many of these approaches advocate an explicit representation of teamwork knowledge (see, e.g., [15,12,26,4]). Such teamwork knowledge may concern, e.g., rules for communication to team members, for example if the execution of a task is not going according to plan, and for establishing a joint plan or recipe on how to achieve the team goal. By making the teamwork representations explicit and implementing agents that behave according to them, agents inherently have a shared understanding of teamwork. Moreover, these representations often incorporate strategies for obtaining a shared view on the concrete team activity that the agents engage in. Jennings [15] and Tambe [26] propose work that is based on joint intentions theory [8]. A joint intention is defined as "a joint commitment to perform a collective action while in a certain shared mental state". The latter refers to an important aspect of a joint intention, which is that team members mutually believe they are committed to a joint activity.

These approaches thus already provide concrete techniques for establishing shared mental models to some extent. However, the notion of shared mental model is implicit in these approaches. We believe that considering (human-)agent teamwork from the perspective of shared mental models could on the one hand yield a unifying perspective on various forms of shared understanding that are part of existing teamwork frameworks, and on the other hand could inspire new research by identifying aspects related to shared mental models that are not addressed by existing frameworks. An example of the latter is the development of techniques for dealing with an observed lack of sharedness. Existing approaches provide ways of trying to prevent this from occurring, but in real-word settings this may not always be possible. Therefore, one needs techniques for detecting and dealing with mental models that are not shared to the needed extent. This is important, for example in human-agent teamwork where humans cannot be programmed to always provide the right information at the right time.

An approach for agent teamwork that incorporates an explicit notion of shared mental model is [27]. The paper presents an agent architecture that focuses on proactive information sharing, based on shared mental models. An agent in this architecture is composed of several models, including an individual mental model and a shared mental model. The individual mental model stores beliefs (possibly including beliefs about others) and general world knowledge. The shared mental model stores information and knowledge shared by all team members. This concerns information about the team structure and process, and dynamic information needs such as the progress of teammates.

This notion of shared mental model differs from ours. In particular, while we do consider mental models to be part of agents' minds (Figure 3), we do not consider a shared mental model to be a component of an agent. Rather, we suggest that the essence of the notion of shared mental model is the extent to which agents have similar mental models, i.e., a shared mental model is a mental model that is shared to some extent between agents. We thus consider shared mental model a derived concept which expresses a property of the relation between mental models, rather than an explicit component inside an agent. This makes our notion fundamentally different from the one proposed by [27].

An approach for representing mental models of other agents in agent programming is proposed in [13]. In that work, mental states of agent are represented by means of beliefs and goals, as is common in cognitive agent programming languages. Besides the agent's own mental state, an agent has mental models for the other agents in the system, which consist of the beliefs and goals the agent thinks other agents have. These are updated through communication. For example, if an agent A informs another agent B of some fact p, agent B will update its model of A to include that agent A believes p (assuming agents do not send this information if they do not believe it). A similar mechanism applies to goals. This approach can be extended by applying similarity measures on the mental state of the agent and of the mental models it has of other agents, to determine what should be communicated.

8   Conclusion

In this paper, we have studied the notion of shared mental model, motivated by the idea of taking shared mental model theory as inspiration for the engineering of agents capable of effective teamwork. We have analyzed the notion starting from an analysis of the notion of mental model, and continuing with definitions of similarity of models, leading to a definition of shared mental model. We have illustrated how these definitions can be operationalized using an example in the BW4T domain.

As for future work, there are conceptual as well as engineering challenges. We aim to investigate how theory of mind (agents that have mental models about other agents) fits into this framework. We will study in more detail models of agent teamwork in which a notion of sharedness plays a role (e.g., [15,12,26,4]), and analyze how these approaches compare to our notion of shared mental model. As in joint intentions theory, awareness of sharedness may be relevant for effective teamwork and worth investigating from the perspective of shared mental models. From an engineering perspective, a main challenge for future research is the investigation of mechanisms that lead to a shared mental model that is shared to the extent needed for effective teamwork, which may also depend on the kind of task and environment. A thorough comparison of existing approaches for agent teamwork with our notion of shared mental model will form the basis for this.

References

1. Akkoyunlu, E., Ekanadham, K., Huber, R.: Some constraints and tradeoffs in the design of network communications. In: Proceedings of the Fifth ACM Symposium on Operating Systems Principles (SOSP 1975), pp. 67–74. ACM, New York (1975)
2. Baader, F., Calvanese, D., McGuinness, D.L., Nardi, D., Patel-Schneider, P.F.: The description logic handbook: Theory, implementation, and applications. Cambridge University Press, Cambridge (2003)
3. Bolstad, C., Endsley, M.: Shared mental models and shared displays: An empirical evaluation of team performance. Human Factors and Ergonomics Society Annual Meeting Proceedings 43(3), 213–217 (1999)
4. Bradshaw, J., Feltovich, P., Jung, H., Kulkami, S., Allen, J., Bunch, L., Chambers, N., Galescu, L., Jeffers, R., Johnson, M., Sierhuis, M., Taysom, W., Uszok, A., Hoof, R.V.: Policy-based coordination in joint human-agent activity. In: Proceedings of the IEEE International Conference on Systems, Man, and Cybernetics, pp. 2029–2036 (2004)
5. Buckland, M., Gey, F.: The relationship between recall and precision. Journal of the American Society for Information Science 45(1), 12–19 (1994)
6. Cannon-Bowers, J.A., Salas, E., Converse, S.: Shared mental models in expert team decision making. In: Castellan, N.J. (ed.) Individual and Group Decision Making, pp. 221–245. Lawrence Erlbaum Associates, Mahwah (1993)
7. Clark, A., Chalmers, D.J.: The extended mind. Analysis 58, 10–23 (1998)
8. Cohen, P., Levesque, H.: Teamwork. Nous, 487–512 (1991)
9. Doyle, J., Ford, D.: Mental models concepts for system dynamics research. System Dynamics Review 14(1), 3–29 (1998)
10. Francois, C.: Systemics and cybernetics in a historical perspective. Systems Research and Behavioral Science 16, 203–219 (1999)
11. Gentner, D., Stevens, A.: Mental Models. Lawrence Erlbaum Associates, New Jersey (1983)
12. Grosz, B., Kraus, S.: Collaborative plans for complex group action. Journal of Artifical Intelligence 86(2), 269–357 (1996)
13. Hindriks, K., van Riemsdijk, M.B.: A computational semantics for communicating rational agents based on mental models. In: Braubach, L., Briot, J.-P., Thangarajah, J. (eds.) ProMAS 2009. LNCS (LNAI), vol. 5919, pp. 31–48. Springer, Heidelberg (2010)

14. Hindriks, K.V.: Programming rational agents in GOAL. In: Bordini, R.H., Dastani, M., Dix, J., El Fallah Seghrouchni, A. (eds.) Multi-Agent Programming: Languages, Tools and Applications. Springer, Berlin (2009)

15. Jennings, N.: Controlling cooperative problem solving in industrial multi-agent systems using joint intentions. Artificial Intelligence Journal 74(2) (1995)

16. Johnson, M., Jonker, C., van Riemsdijk, M.B., Feltovich, P.J., Bradshaw, J.M.: Joint activity testbed: Blocks world for teams (BW4T). In: Aldewereld, H., Dignum, V., Picard, G. (eds.) ESAW 2009. LNCS, vol. 5881, pp. 254–256. Springer, Heidelberg (2009)

17. Johnson-Laird, P.N.: Mental Models: Towards a Cognitive Science of Language, Inference, and Consciousness. Cambridge University Press, Cambridge (1983)

18. Jonker, C., Treur, J.: Compositional verification of multi-agent systems: a formal analysis of pro-activeness and reactiveness. International Journal of Cooperative Information Systems 11, 51–92 (2002)

19. Klein, G., Feltovich, P., Bradshaw, J., Woods, D.: Common ground and coordination in joint activity. In: Organizational Simulation, pp. 139–184 (2004)

20. Klein, G., Woods, D.D., Bradshaw, J.M., Hoffman, R.R., Feltovich, P.J.: Ten challenges for making automation a "team player" in joint human-agent activity. IEEE Intelligent Systems 19(6), 91–95 (2004)

21. Lim, B., Klein, K.: Team mental models and team performance: A field study of the effects of team mental model similarity and accuracy. Journal of Organizational Behavior 27(4), 403 (2006)

22. Mathieu, E., Heffner, T.S., Goodwin, G., Salas, E., Cannon-Bowers, J.: The influence of shared mental models on team process and performance. The Journal of Applied Psychology 85(2), 273–283 (2000)

23. Minsky, M.: A framework for representing knowledge. The Psychology of Computer Vision (1975)

24. Rouse, W., Morris, N.: On looking into the black box: Prospects and limits in the search for mental models. Psychological Bulletin 100(3), 349–363 (1986)

25. Sycara, K., Sukthankar, G.: Literature review of teamwork models. Technical Report CMU-RI-TR-06-50, Carnegie Mellon University (2006)

26. Tambe, M.: Towards flexible teamwork. Journal of Artificial Intelligence Research 7, 83–124 (1997)

27. Yen, J., Fan, X., Sun, S., Hanratty, T., Dumer, J.: Agents with shared mental models for enhancing team decision makings. Decision Support Systems 41(3), 634–653 (2006)

Group Intention Is Social Choice with Commitment

Guido Boella[1], Gabriella Pigozzi[2], Marija Slavkovik[2], and Leendert van der Torre[2]

[1] guido@di.unito.it
[2] {gabriella.pigozzi,marija.slavkovik,leon.vandertorre}@uni.lu

Abstract. An agent intends g if it has chosen to pursue goal g an is committed to pursuing g. How do groups decide on a common goal? Social epistemology offers two views on collective attitudes: according to the summative approach, a group has attitude p if all or most of the group members have the attitude p; according to the non-summative approach, for a group to have attitude p it is required that the members together agree that they have attitude p. The summative approach is used extensively in multi-agent systems. We propose a formalization of non-summative group intentions, using social choice to determine the group goals. We use judgment aggregation as a decision-making mechanism and a multi-modal multi-agent logic to represent the collective attitudes, as well as the commitment and revision strategies for the groups intentions.

1 Introduction

Within the context of multi-agent systems, the concept of collective intentions is studied and formalized in (Chapter 3, [12]) and also in [17,21,36,41]. All of these theories and formalizations use the summative approach to define group beliefs and goals: a group has attitude p if all or most of the group members have the attitude p [13,18,30]. Alternatively, collective attitudes can be specified using the non-summative approach: a group has an attitude p if the members together agree that they have that attitude p. To the best of our knowledge, there is no formalization of non-summative collective attitudes within multi-agent systems. We consider the following research question:

How can a group agree on what to believe, pursue and what to intend?

This paper summarizes our initial efforts towards formalizing non-summative group intentions using the conceptualizations proposed by Gilbert [13,14,15,16].

How can a group decide which goals to pursue? A rational agent makes decisions based on what he believes, what he knows and what he desires. Each group member can express whether he is for or against a candidate group goal. An agent can rationalize his goal decision by expressing opinions on relevant reasons for adopting (or rejecting) that candidate group goal. To reach non-summative group attitudes, a group can use a decision making mechanism that aggregates the members' opinions to produce the group agreement of what to believe and, based on those beliefs, which goals to pursue. A group that jointly decided on a course of action is jointly committed to uphold that decision [15].

In practical reasoning, the roles of intentions can be summarized as: intentions drive means-end-reasoning, intentions constrain future deliberation, intentions persist long enough, according to a reconsideration strategy, and intentions influence beliefs upon

M. De Vos et al. (Eds.): COIN 2010 International Workshops, LNAI 6541, pp. 152–171, 2011.
© Springer-Verlag Berlin Heidelberg 2011

which future practical reasoning is based [12]. A formalization of group intentions should be completed with a formalization of group intention persistence and reconsideration strategies.

Our research question thus breaks down to the following sub-questions:

1. How to aggregate the individual opinions into group beliefs and goals?
2. How to represent individual opinions and non-summative group attitudes?
3. How can groups persist in their intentions?
4. How can groups reconsider their attitudes?

We need a mechanism for generating group beliefs and goals that aggregates individual opinions into collective attitudes, as studied in voting, merging and judgment aggregation [5,19,22,24].

The relation between individual goals and beliefs can be specified and analyzed in modal agent logics like BDI_{LTL} [35]. The challenge is to find an adequate representation for the individual opinions and the non-summative beliefs, goals and intentions into multi-agent logic. We give an extension logic AGE_{LTL} that fuses existing modal logics to provide the adequate modalities. We use this logic to represent the group intention and reconsideration strategies.

We require that the group has a set of candidate group goals, a relevance order over this set, as well as a set of decision rules, one for each candidate goal, in the form of logic formulas, that express what is the relation between a goal and a given set of reasons. The members are required to have the ability to form and communicate "yes" or "no" judgments regarding a candidate goal and associated reasons. There are two modes of communicating the individual judgments: a centralized and a decentralized mode. In the decentralized mode, every individual judgment is communicated to all the agents in the group. Each agent then aggregates the individual judgments using the known mechanism and generates the group beliefs, goals and thus intentions. In the centralized mode, one of the members acts as an administrator for the group. All individual judgments are sent to the administrator who aggregates them and notifies the rest of the members what the group beliefs and goals are.

We assume that all members are aware of the judgment aggregation mechanism (and possibly tie breaking rule), the commitment and the revision strategy that are in use. We also assume that group membership does not change; neither does the aggregation mechanism, the commitment and revision strategy for each goal. The group members can communicate with each other. We further assume that all members accept the decision rules and give opinions that are logically consistent with them. Lastly, we assume that each agent is able to revise his individual judgments, on a given goal and reasons, with given information.

The generation and revision of decision rules is outside the scope of this paper. Agents of the group may have individual goals in addition to the group ones. It is not a requirement that the group attitudes are individual attitudes of the members.

Cohen and Levesque, in their seminal paper [7], proclaimed that intentions are choice (of a goal) with commitment. Judgment aggregation is a social choice mechanism. Following the intuition of Cohen and Levesque, (a non-summative) group intention is (a group goal determined by) social choice with commitment.

The layout of the paper is as follows. In Section 2 we discuss how to choose group goals. We first summarize the non-summative view on collective attitudes. We then extend BDI_{LTL} with the necessary modalities for representing these group attitudes and the concepts from judgment aggregation. We introduce a judgment aggregation framework using this logic extension and, in Section 3, show how it can be used. Sections 4 and 5 respectively study the commitment and reconsideration strategies. Related work, conclusions and outlines for future work are in Section 6.

2   Non-summative Group Attitudes Obtained by Judgment Aggregation

First we discuss how non-summative goals and beliefs are determined and then introduce the logic AGE_{LTL} which is used for representing these attitudes. The formal model of judgment aggregation, using this logic, is given in Section 2.3.

2.1   From Individual Opinions to Group Attitudes

According to existing theories [12,21,23], the intention of the group is formalized using the summative approach, following Bratman [3] and Rao *et al.* [32]: g is the intention of the group is equivalent to g being the individual intention of all the group members. Unlike the joint intention of, for example, Dunin-Keplicz and Verbrugge [12], our group intention is not necessarily decomposable into individual intentions: "an adequate account of shared intention is such that it is not necessarily the case that for every shared intention, on that account, there be correlative personal intentions of the individual parties" (pg.172, [16]).

Example 1. Let $C = \{w_1, w_2, w_3\}$ be a crew of cleaning robots. We denote the group goal to clean the meeting room with g_1, and the reasons to adopt this goal with: there are no people in the room (p_1), the room is dirty (p_2), the garbage bin in it is full (p_3). The individual beliefs of the robots on whether g_1 should be the group goal are justified by individual beliefs on p_1, p_2, p_3 using the decision rule $(p_1 \wedge (p_2 \vee p_3)) \leftrightarrow g_1$.

The group goal g_1 is not necessarily decomposable to individual goals g_1. Assume that robot w_1 in Example 1 is a mopper, the robot w_2 is a garbage collector and the robot w_3 sprays adequate cleaning chemicals. It can be that the individual goals of w_1 and w_2 are to clean the room. The goal of w_3 may be others, but the group agreed to pursue g_1 and he, being committed to g_1 as part of the group, will spray the cleaner as an act towards accomplishing g_1.

We formalize only goals that can be achieved by the group as a whole. Whether these goals can be achieved by joint actions or by a combination of individual actions is out of the scope. We define group intention to be the goal, which the members agreed on, and by that, are committed to pursuing.

The robots in Example 1 can disagree on various issues when reaching a decision for a group goal. Assume that one robot believes the room is occupied and thus, according to it, the group should not pursue g_1. According to the other two robots, the group should pursue g_1. The second robot is of the opinion that the garbage bin is full and the floor is clean, while the third believes that the floor is dirty. According to the non-summative view of collective beliefs, a group believes p if the group members together agree that as a group they believe p. The question is how should the beliefs of the robots be aggregated to reach an agreement.

Voting and preference aggregation theories [1] study the problem of aggregating individual preferences over a set of independent issues, candidates or alternatives. The robots need to aggregate their individual opinions on the set of issues $\{p_1, p_2, p_3, g_1\}$. However the issues in this set are logically related. The problem of aggregating individual "yes" or "no" opinions, a.k.a. judgments, over a set of logically related issues is studied by judgment aggregation [24]. Judgment aggregation is modeled in general logic and it is an abstract framework that allows for various desirable social properties to be specified.

To use judgment aggregation for aggregating the opinions of the robots, one needs to represent the individual and collective judgments. A logic of belief-desire-intention is insufficient to model these doxastic attitudes. According to Gilbert, "it is not logically sufficient for a group belief that p either that most group members believe that p, or that there be common knowledge within the group that most members believe that p" (pg.189 [13]). Furthermore, "it is not necessary that any members of the group personally believe p" (pg.191 [13]). A w_1 robots judgment "yes" on $\neg p_1$ is not implied by nor it implies that robot's belief $B_{w_1} \neg p_1$.

Hakli [18] summarizes the difference between beliefs and acceptances as: (1) beliefs are involuntary and acceptances are voluntary; (2) beliefs aim at truth and acceptances depend on goals; (3) beliefs are shaped by evidence and acceptances need not be; (4) beliefs are independent of context and acceptances are context-dependant; and (5) beliefs come in degrees and acceptances are categorical. We find that an individual judgment is closer to an acceptance than to a belief and therefore represent it with an acceptance. There is a debate among social epistemologists on whether collective believes are proper believes or they are in essence acceptances [14,27,18]. Since we use acceptances for individual judgments, we deem most adequate to use acceptances to represent the collective judgments as well.

The set of collective acceptances is the agreed upon group goal and group beliefs. Having group beliefs in support of group goals is in line with Castelfrachi and Paglieri who argue [4] that the goals should be considered together with their supporting "belief structure". In Example 1, the decision rule $(p_1 \wedge (p_2 \vee p_3)) \leftrightarrow y_1$ is nothing else but the "belief structure" for g_1. We use the group beliefs to define commitment strategies in Section 4.

2.2   The Logic AGE_{LTL}

The logic we introduce to represent non-summative group attitudes is a fusion of two K-modal logics [6], the logic of acceptance [26] and the linear temporal logic [29]. As such, it inherits the decidability properties of the [40]. The syntax of AGE_{LTL} is presented in Definition 1. The semantics is as that given by Schield [35] for BDI_{CTL}.

To model the considered group goals we use a single K modal operator G. Thus Gg, where g is a propositional formula, is to be interpreted as "g is a group goal". Since we are interested in modeling the change upon new information, we also need to model these observations of new information. To this end we add the K modal operator E, reading $E\phi$ as "*it is observed that ϕ*".

To model the individual and collective judgments we use the modal operator of acceptance A_S, where S is a subset of some set of agents N. $A_S\phi$ allows us to represent both individual judgments, $S = \{i\}$, for $i \in N$ and collective judgments with $S = N$.

Definition 1 (Syntax). *Let Agt be a non-empty set of agents, with $S \subseteq Agt$, and L_P be a set of atomic propositions. The admissible formulae of AGE_{LTL} are formulae ψ_0, ψ_1 and ψ_2 of languages $\mathcal{L}_{prop}$, $\mathcal{L}_G$ and $\mathcal{L}_{AE_{LTL}}$ correspondingly:*

$\psi_0 ::= p \mid (\psi_0 \wedge \psi_0) \mid \neg\psi_0$
$\psi_1 ::= \psi_0 \mid G\psi_0$
$\psi_2 ::= \psi_0 \mid A_S\psi_1 \mid E\psi_2 \mid X\psi_2 \mid (\psi_2 U\psi_2)$
where p ranges over L_P and S over 2^{Agt}. Moreover, $\Diamond\phi \equiv \top U\phi$, $\Box\phi \equiv \neg\Diamond\neg\phi$, and $\phi R\phi' \equiv \neg(\neg\phi U\neg\phi')$. X, U and R are standard operators of LTL.

Example 2. Consider Example 1. "Cleaning the room is a group goal" is represented by Gg_1. "The group C has the group goal to clean the room is represented with A_CGg_1. "Agent w_3 does is of the opinion that the group does not need to achieve g_1" is represented by $A_{\{w_3\}}g_1$. "It is observed the there are no people in the meeting room" is represented by Ep_1. "It is observed to be impossible to clean the meeting room" is represented with $E\Box\neg p_1$.

We use the linear temporal logic to model the change of group attitudes. By using LTL we do not need to distinguish between path formulas and state formulas. BDI_{LTL} uses, for example $B\Box a$ to quantify over traces. We can use E for that purpose.

We define the intention of the group of agents S to be their acceptance of a goal, where S ranges over 2^{Agt} as

$$I_S\psi \equiv_{def} A_SG\psi.$$

Semantics of AGE_{LTL}. As mentioned, the semantics of AGE_{LTL} follows the semantics of BDI_{LTL} presented in Schild [35]. A Kripke structure is defined as a tuple $\mathcal{M} = \langle W, \mathcal{R}, \mathcal{G}, \mathcal{E}, \mathcal{A}, L \rangle$. The set W is a set of possible situations. The set $\mathcal{R}$ is a set of pairs identifying the temporal relation over situations $\mathcal{R} \subseteq W \times W$. The set $\mathcal{G}$ is a set of pairs identifying the goal relation over situations $\mathcal{G} \subseteq W \times W$. Lastly, the set $\mathcal{E}$ is a set of pairs identifying the observation relation over situations $\mathcal{E} \subseteq W \times W$. The element $\mathcal{A}$ is a map $\mathcal{A} : 2^N \mapsto W \times W$. The mapping $\mathcal{A}$ assigns to every set of agents $S \in 2^N$ a relation $\mathcal{A}_S$ between possible situations. L is a truth assignment to the primitive propositions of L_P for each situation $w \in W$, i.e., $L(w) : Prop \mapsto \{true, false\}$.

Given a structure $\mathcal{M} = \langle W, \mathcal{R}, \mathcal{G}, \mathcal{E}, \mathcal{A}, L \rangle$ and $s \in W$, the truth conditions for the formulas of AGE_{LTL} (in a situation s) are:

- $\mathcal{M}, s \nvDash \bot$;
- $\mathcal{M}, s \models p$ if and only if $p \in L(p)$;
- $\mathcal{M}, s \models \neg\phi$ if and only if $\mathcal{M}, s \nvDash \neg\phi$;
- $\mathcal{M}, s \models \phi \wedge \psi$ if and only if $\mathcal{M}, s \models \phi$ and $\mathcal{M}, s \models \psi$;
- $\mathcal{M}, s \models A_S\phi$ if and only if $\mathcal{M}, s' \models \phi$ for all $(s, s') \in \mathcal{A}(S)$;
- $\mathcal{M}, s \models G\phi$ if and only if $\mathcal{M}, s' \models \phi$ for all $(s, s') \in \mathcal{G}$;

- $\mathcal{M}, s \models E\phi$ if and only if $\mathcal{M}, s' \models \phi$ for all $(s, s') \in \mathcal{E}$;
- $\mathcal{M}, s \models \mathbf{X}\phi$ if and only if $\mathcal{M}, s' \models \phi$ for the s', $(s, s') \in \mathcal{R}$.
- $\mathcal{M}, s \models \phi\mathbf{U}\psi$ if and only if $\mathcal{M}, s \models \phi$; $\mathcal{M}, s^i \models \phi$ for all s^i, $i \in \{1, 2, \ldots, k\}$ such that $\{(s, s^1), (s^1, s^2), \ldots (s^{k-1}, s^k)\} \in \mathcal{R}$ and for s^{k+1} such that $(s^k, s^{k+1}) \in \mathcal{R}$ it holds $\mathcal{M}, s^{k+1} \not\models \phi$ and $\mathcal{M}, s^{k+1} \models \psi$.

A formula ϕ is true in a AGE_{LTL}model $\mathcal{M}$ if and only if $\mathcal{M}, s \models \phi$ for every situation $s \in W$. The formula ϕ is valid (noted $\models_{AGE_{LTL}}$) if and only if ϕ is true in all AGE_{LTL}models. The formula ϕ is AGE_{LTL}-satisfiable if and only if the formula $\neg\varphi$ is not AGE_{LTL}valid.

For the purposes of constructing the formal judgment aggregation model, we emphasize that a set of sentences $M \subseteq AGE_{LTL}$ is called consistent if $M \not\models \bot$ and inconsistent otherwise. The logic AGE_{LTL} satisfies the following properties: for each pair $\{\phi, \neg\phi\} \in AGE_{LTL}$, $\{\phi, \neg\phi\} \models \bot$ and, $\emptyset \not\models \bot$.

(C_1) For each set $\{a, \neg a\} \in AGE_{LTL}$ it holds $\{a, \neg a\} \models \bot$.
(C_2) Given a set $M \subseteq AGE_{LTL}$ such that $AGE_{LTL} \not\models \bot$, it holds that $M' \not\models \bot$ for every $M' \subset M$.
(C_3) For the empty set $\emptyset$ it holds that $\emptyset \not\models \bot$.
(C_4) For each set M such that $M \subseteq AGE_{LTL}$, there exists a superset $T \in AGE_{LTL}$ such that $T \not\models \bot$ and either $a \in T$ or $\neg a \in T$ for every pair $\{a, \neg a\} \in AGE_{LTL}$.

Axiomatization of AGE_{LTL}. In our logic we model only individual acceptances which are "declared" to all the agents in the group and we do not model the private mental states, since this is done by the BDI_{LTL} logic which we extend. We include the axioms and the semantics for LTL, since we use LTL to define the commitment strategies of the agents in Section 4.

The modal operator $A_S\phi$ we use is equivalent to the modal operator $A_{S:x}\phi$ of the *acceptance logic* of [26] with one syntactic and one semantic exception. These exceptions do not infringe on the decidability properties of the logic, as it can be observed by the decidability proof for acceptance logic provided in [26].

The operator $A_{S:x}\phi$ uses x ranging over a set of labels to describe the context under which the acceptance is made. In our case the context is that of the group and since we deal with only one group, we have no use of these labels. The context labels play no role in the semantics of the acceptance logic formulas.

On the semantic level, the axioms for $A_S\phi$ are all the axioms of $A_{S:x}\phi$ except two: the axiom inclusion ($Inc.$) and the axiom unanimity ($Un.$). Dropping ($Un.$) and ($Inc.$) does not affect the decidability of the logic of acceptance. ($Un.$)[1] states that if $A_{N:x}\phi$, then $\forall i \in N$, $A_{\{i\}:x}\phi$. In our case, it is the aggregation of individual acceptances that determines the collective acceptance and we do not require that the group accepting p entails that all the members accept p, a property of non-summative collective belief indicated by Gilbert in [13]. The opposite property, *i.e.*, all the agents accepting p implies that the group accepts p, is ensured via the judgment aggregation mechanism. ($Inc.$) states that if a group C accepts φ, so will any subgroup $B \subset C$. In our case, the judgment aggregation over the input from group B can produce different group attitudes than the judgment aggregation over the input from a larger group C.

---

[1] Not to be confused with unanimity introduced in judgment aggregation in Section 3.

The axiomatization of the AGE_{LTL} logic is thus:

(ProTau) All principles of propositional calculus
(LTLTau) All axioms and derivation rules of LTL
(K-G) $G(\phi \rightarrow \psi) \rightarrow (G\phi \rightarrow G\psi)$
(K-E) $E(\phi \rightarrow \psi) \rightarrow (E\phi \rightarrow E\psi)$
(K-A) $A_S(\phi \rightarrow \psi) \rightarrow (A_S\phi \rightarrow A_S\psi)$
(PAccess) $A_S\phi \rightarrow A_M A_S\phi$ if $M \subseteq S$
(NAccess) $\neg A_S\phi \rightarrow A_M \neg A_S\phi$ if $M \subseteq S$
(Mon) $\neg A_S\bot \rightarrow \neg A_M\bot$ if $M \subseteq S$
(MP)   From $\vdash \phi$ and $\vdash (\phi \rightarrow \psi)$ infer $\vdash \psi$
(Nec-A) From $\vdash \phi$ infer $\vdash A_S\phi$
(Nec-G) From $\vdash \phi$ infer $\vdash G\phi$
(Nec-E) From $\vdash \phi$ infer $\vdash E\phi$

2.3   The Judgment Aggregation Framework

Our judgment aggregation model in AGE_{LTL} follows the judgment aggregation (JA) model in general logics of Dietrich [11]. For a general overview of JA see [24].

We presume that all the goals which the group considers to adopt are given in a set of candidate group goals $\mathcal{G} = \{Gg \mid g \in \mathcal{L}_{prop}\}$. The decision problem in judgment aggregation, in our case choosing or not a given group goal, is specified by an agenda. An agenda is a pre-defined consistent set of formulas, each representing an issue on which an agent casts his judgments. An agenda is *truth-functional* if it can be partitioned into premises and conclusions. In our case, the agendas consist of one conclusion, which is the group goal $g \in \mathcal{G}$ being considered. The relevant reasons for this group goal are premises.

Definition 2 (Agenda). *An agenda $\mathcal{A} \subseteq \mathcal{L}_G$ is a consistent set of formulas, such that $\mathcal{A} = \mathcal{A}^p \cup \mathcal{A}^c$. The sets $\mathcal{A}^p$ and $\mathcal{A}^c$ are such that $\mathcal{A}^p \subseteq \mathcal{L}_{prop}$, $\mathcal{A}^c \subseteq \mathcal{L}_G$ and $\mathcal{A}^p \cap \mathcal{A}^c = \emptyset$.*

We remark that in judgment aggregation models, as the one of Dietrich [11], the distinction between conclusions and premises is only indicated by the partition but not formalized in the language of the agenda. In our AGE_{LTL} model, we explicitly formalize this distinction trough the modal operator G.

For a given agenda $\mathcal{A}$, each agent in the group N expresses his judgments by accepting (or not) the agenda issues. We define judgments formally in Definition 3.

Definition 3 (Judgment). *Given a set of agents N and an agenda $\mathcal{A}$, for each issue $a \in \mathcal{A}$ the individual judgment of agent $i \in N$ is one element of the set $\{A_{\{i\}}a, A_{\{i\}}\neg a\}$. The collective judgment of N is one element of the set $\{A_N a, A_N \neg a\}$.*

The formula $A_{\{i\}}a$ is interpreted as agent i judges a to be true, while the formula $A_{\{i\}}\neg a$ is interpreted as agent i judges a to be false. In theory, an agent, or a group can also express the judgment of "do not know how to judge a" via the formula $\neg A_{\{i\}}a \wedge \neg A_{\{i\}}\neg a$, or respectively $\neg A_N a \wedge \neg A_N \neg a$. In the scenarios we consider, for simplicity, we do not allow the agents to be unopinionated, thus a judgment $\neg A_{\{i\}}a$ is taken to be the same as judgment $A_{\{i\}}\neg a$, and the judgments $\neg A_N a$ the same as judgments $A_N \neg a$.

The goal and the reasons are logically related. These relations are represented by the decisions rules. In our model, we assume that the decision rules are a set of formulas $\mathcal{R} \subseteq \mathcal{L}_G$. For each goal $Gg \in \mathcal{G}$ there is, provided together with the agenda, a set of decision rules $\mathcal{R}_g \subseteq \mathcal{R}$. The decision rules contain all the constraints that the agent should observe when casting judgments. These constraints contain three types of information: rules describing how the goal depends on the reasons (justification rules $\mathcal{R}_g^{just}$), rules describing the constraints of the world inhabited by the agents (domain knowledge $\mathcal{R}_g^{DK}$) and rules that describe how g interacts with other candidate goals of the group (coordination rules $\mathcal{R}_g^{coord}$). Hence, the decision rules for a group goal g are $\mathcal{R}_g = \mathcal{R}_g^{just} \cup \mathcal{R}_g^{DK} \cup \mathcal{R}_g^{coord}$.

We want the reasons for a goal to rationalize, not only the choice of a goal, but also its rejection. Having collective justifications for rejecting a goal enables the agents to re-consider adopting a previously rejected group goal. To this end, we require that the justification rules have the schema $Gg \leftrightarrow \Gamma$, where $\{Gg\} = \mathcal{A}_g^c$ and $\Gamma \in \mathcal{L}_{Prop}$ is a formula such that all the non-logical symbols of Γ occur in $\mathcal{A}_g^p$ as well.

The agents express their judgments on the agenda issues, but they accept the decision rules *in toto*.

Example 3 (Example 1 revisited). Consider the cleaning crew from Example 1. $\mathcal{R}_{g_1}^{just}$ is $(p_1 \wedge (p_2 \vee p_3)) \leftrightarrow Gg_1$ and $\mathcal{A}_{g_1} = \{p_1, p_2, p_3, Gg_1\}$. Suppose that the crew has the following candidate group goals as well: place the furniture in its designated location (g_2) and collect recyclables from garbage bin (g_3). The agendas are $\mathcal{A}_{g_2} = \{p_4, p_5, p_6, p_7, Gg_2\}$, $\mathcal{A}_{g_3} = \{p_3, p_8, p_9, Gg_3\}$. The justification rules are $\mathcal{R}_{g_2}^{just} \equiv (p_4 \wedge p_5 \wedge (p_6 \vee p_7)) \leftrightarrow Gg_2$ and $\mathcal{R}_{g_3}^{just} \equiv (p_8 \wedge p_9 \wedge p_3) \leftrightarrow Gg_3$. The formulas $p_4 - p_9$ are: the furniture is out of place (p_4), the designated location for the furniture is empty (p_5), the furniture has wheels (p_6) , the furniture has handles (p_7), the agents can get revenue for recyclables (p_8), there is a container for the recyclables (p_9).
An example of a domain knowledge could be $\mathcal{R}_{g_2}^{DK} \equiv \neg p_4 \rightarrow \neg p_5$, since it cannot happen that the designated location for the furniture is empty while the furniture is not out of place. Group goal Gg_3 can be pursued at the same time as Gg_1, however, Gg_2 can only be pursued alone. Thus the coordination rule for all three goals is $\mathcal{R}_{g_1}^{coord} = \mathcal{R}_{g_2}^{coord} = \mathcal{R}_{g_3}^{coord} \equiv ((Gg_2 \wedge (Gg_1 \vee Gg_3)) \vee \neg Gg_2)$.

To ensure that the judgments provided by the agents are usable for generating group goals, we impose certain conditions on the set of individual judgments.

Definition 4 (Admissible judgment set). *Let $\varphi = \{A_M \bar{a} \mid \bar{a} = a \text{ or } \bar{a} = \neg a, a \in \mathcal{A}\}$ be the set of all judgments from agents $M \subseteq N$ for agenda $\mathcal{A}$. We define the set of accepted decision rules $\mathcal{R}_M = \{A_M r \mid r \in \mathcal{R}\}$. The set of judgments φ is admissible if it satisfies the following conditions:*

- *for each $a \in \mathcal{A}$, either $A_M a \in \varphi$ or $A_M \neg a \in \varphi$ (completeness), and*
- *$\varphi \cup \mathcal{R}_M \nvDash \bot$ (consistency).*

A profile is a set of every judgment rendered for an agenda $\mathcal{A}$ by an agent in N.

Definition 5 (Profile). *A profile π is a set $\pi = \{A_{\{i\}}\bar{a} \mid i \in N, \bar{a} = a \text{ or } \bar{a} = \neg a, a \in \mathcal{A}\}$. We define two operators over profiles:*
The judgment set for agent i is $\pi \rhd i = \{\bar{a} \mid A_{\{i\}}\bar{a} \in \pi\}$.
The set of all the agents who accepted $\bar{a}$ is $\pi \triangledown \bar{a} = \{i \mid A_{\{i\}}\bar{a} \in \pi\}$.
A profile is admissible if the judgment set $\pi \rhd i$ is admissible for every $i \in N$.

We introduce the operators $\rhd$ and $\triangledown$ to facilitate the explanation of the aggregation properties we present in Section 3. To get a better intuitive grasp on these operators, the reader should envision the profile as a two-dimensional object with the agenda items identifying the columns and the agents identifying the rows:

$$\pi = \begin{array}{c} \\ w_1 \\ w_2 \\ w_3 \end{array} \overset{\displaystyle p_1 p_2 \; p_3 \; Gg_1}{\left\{\begin{array}{cccc} 1 & 1 & 0 & 1 \\ 0 & 1 & 1 & 1 \\ 1 & 0 & 0 & 0 \end{array}\right\}}$$

$\pi = \{A_{\{w_1\}}p_1, A_{\{w_1\}}p_2, A_{\{w_1\}}\neg p_3, A_{\{w_1\}}Gg_1, A_{\{w_2\}}\neg p_1, A_{\{w_2\}}p_2, A_{\{w_2\}}p_3, A_{\{w_2\}}Gg_1, A_{\{w_3\}}p_1, A_{\{w_3\}}\neg p_2, A_{\{w_3\}}\neg p_3, A_{\{w_3\}}\neg Gg_1\}$ is a possible profile for Example 1. We identify $\pi \rhd w_2$ as the row labeled w_2 and $\pi \triangledown p_2$ as the 1 entries in the column labeled p_2, which identify the agents who casted judgment "yes" on p_2.

In the model of Dietrich [11], the profile is defined as a set of judgment sets. Using the acceptance operator to model judgments, we can make a distinction between the individual judgments directly thus simplifying the profile structure.

In judgment aggregation, the collective judgment set of a group of agents is obtained by applying a judgment aggregation function to the profile. Judgment aggregation functions are defined in Definition 6.

Definition 6 (Judgment aggregation function). *Let Π be the set of all profiles π that can be defined for $\mathcal{A}$ and N and let $\overline{\mathcal{A}} = \mathcal{A} \cup \{\neg a \mid a \in \mathcal{A}\}$. A judgment aggregation function f is a mapping $f : \Pi \mapsto 2^{\overline{\mathcal{A}}}$.*

The definition of aggregation function we propose here is identical to that commonly given in the literature [11,24]. In [11,24], a judgment aggregation function is defined as $F(J_1, J_2, \ldots J_n) = J$, where J_i, $i \in N$ are the judgment sets of the agents in N and $J \in 2^{\overline{\mathcal{A}}}$. For $J_i = \pi \rhd i$ it holds $F(J_1, J_2, \ldots J_n) = f(\pi)$.

Let $\mathcal{A}_g$ be the agenda corresponding to a goal g considered by a group of agents N and let π_g be the profile of the members judgment regarding $\mathcal{A}_g$. We define the group attitudes regarding a goal g, *i.e.*, the *decision*, to be the collective judgment set of the group.

Definition 7 (Decision). *Given a profile π_g for a considered goal g and a judgment aggregation function f, the group $N's$ decision regarding g is $\mathcal{D}_g = \{A_N a \mid a \in f(\pi)\}$.*

Proposition 1. *Every group member accepts the group decision.*

*Proof. As a direct consequence of axiom (**PAccess**), when the group has intention $I_N g$, every agent in N accepts that this is the group's intention, regardless of what their individually accepted regarding Gg. Also, as a consequence of axiom (**NAccess**), when the group rejects a goal, $A_N \neg Gg$, every agent i accepts this group decision. The same holds for the group beliefs.*

3   Generating Group Goals with Judgment Aggregation

We introduced the language in which we model group goals, intentions and the information the group accepts as valid, as well as the judgment aggregation framework. We defined a family of functions that can be used for aggregation of judgments. Which specific judgment aggregation function is used to reach a group decision depends on the properties of the decision it is applied to. In the next section we discuss the desirable properties for judgment aggregation used for group goal generation. Our framework allows the agents to decide on one goal at a time. Since groups can have more than one goal, in Section 3.2 we propose a procedure for handling multiple goals.

3.1   Desirable Properties of Judgment Aggregation

The properties of judgment aggregation (JA) are defined in terms of properties of the judgment aggregation function. The typical focus of the judgment aggregation theory is to study which properties can be accepted together (avoiding impossibility results). Given a JA function f, we describe the most common properties found in the literature.

Universal domain. A JA function f satisfies universal domain if and only if all the admissible profiles for a given $\mathcal{A}$, $\mathcal{R}$ and N are in the domain of f. The judgment aggregation function as defined in Definition 6 satisfies universal domain by construction.

Anonymity. Given a profile $\pi \in \Pi$, let $\widehat{\pi} = \{\pi \triangleright 1, \ldots, \pi \triangleright n\}$, be the multiset of all the individual judgment sets in π. Two profiles $\pi, \pi' \in \Pi$ are permutations of each other if and only if $\widehat{\pi} = \widehat{\pi}'$. f satisfies anonymity if and only if $f(\pi) = f(\pi')$ for all permutation π and π'.

Unanimity on $a \in \mathcal{A}$. Let $\overline{a} = a$ or $\overline{a} = \neg a$, where $a \in \mathcal{A}$. The JA function f satisfies unanimity on $a \in \mathcal{A}$ if and only if for every profile $\pi \in \Pi$ it holds: if for all $i \in N$, $A_i \overline{a} \in \pi$, then $\overline{a} \in f(\pi)$.

Collective rationality. f satisfies collective rationality if and only if for all $\pi \in \Pi$, and a given $\mathcal{R}$, $f(\pi) \cup \mathcal{R} \nvdash \bot$.

Constant. f is constant when there exists $\varphi \in 2^{\overline{A}}$ such that for every $\pi \in \Pi$, $f(\pi) = \varphi$.

Independence. Given $\mathcal{A} = \{a_1, \ldots, a_m\}$ and $\pi \subset \Pi$, let $f_1, \ldots, f_m$ be functions defined as $f_j(\pi \triangledown a_j) \in \{a_j, \neg a_j\}$. The JA function f satisfies independence if and only if there exists a set of functions $\{f_1, \ldots, f_m\}$ such that $f(\pi) = \{f_1(\pi \triangledown a_1), \ldots f_m(\pi \triangledown a_m)\}$ for each $\pi \in \Pi$.

The best known example of a judgment aggregation function that satisfies independence is the issue-wise majority function f_{maj}, defined as

$$f_{maj}(\pi) = \{f_j(\pi \triangledown a_j) \mid a_j \in \mathcal{A}, f_j(\pi \triangledown a_j) = a_j \text{ if } |\pi \triangledown a_j| \geq \lceil \frac{n}{2} \rceil,$$

$$\text{otherwise } f_j(\pi \triangledown a_j) = \neg a_j\}.$$

The function f_{maj} satisfies *universal domain, anonymity, unanimity* (on each $a \in \mathcal{A}$), *completeness*, and *independence* but it does not satisfy *collective rationality*, as it can be seen on Figure 1.

All judgment aggregation functions that satisfy *universal domain, anonymity, independence* and *collective rationality* are *constant* [24]. *Independence* is the most debated property [5,24]. The reason why it is convenient to have independence is because it is a necessary condition to guarantee the non-manipulability of f [10]. An aggregation function is non-manipulable if no agent can obtain his sincere judgment set φ selected as the collective judgment set by submitting another judgment set φ'.

We define two more properties of JA function, the premise- and conclusion-based aggregation function. In the literature [24], premise- and conclusion-based are procedures are specified in terms of issue-wise majority. These aggregation functions violate independence, but can be designed to guarantee *collective rationality*.

Premise- and conclusion-based aggregation

Let $\pi^p = \{A_{\{i\}}\overline{a} \mid A_{\{i\}}\overline{a} \in \pi, \overline{a} = a \text{ or } \overline{a} = \neg a, a \in \mathcal{A}^p\}$ and $\pi^c = \{A_{\{i\}}\overline{a} \mid A_{\{i\}}\overline{a} \in \pi, \overline{a} = a \text{ or } \overline{a} = \neg a, a \in \mathcal{A}^c\}$. We define Π^p and Π^c to be the sets of all π^p, π^c, defined for a given N and given $\mathcal{A}^p, \mathcal{A}^c$ correspondingly. Let $\overline{\mathcal{A}^p} = \mathcal{A}^p \cup \{\neg a \mid a \in \mathcal{A}^p\}$ and $\overline{\mathcal{A}^c} = \mathcal{A}^c \cup \{\neg a \mid a \in \mathcal{A}^c\}$ and $f^p : \Pi^p \mapsto 2^{\overline{\mathcal{A}^p}}/\emptyset$ and $f^c : \Pi^c \mapsto 2^{\overline{\mathcal{A}^c}}/\emptyset$. The JA function f is premise-based if and only if there exists a f^p such that $f^p(\pi^p) \subseteq f(\pi)$ for every $\pi \in \Pi$. The function f is conclusion-based if and only if there is a f^c such that $f^c(\pi^c) \subseteq f(\pi)$ for every $\pi \in \Pi$.

The completeness of the collective judgment set is obtained by extending the outcome of f^p (or that of f^c correspondingly) to a consistent collective judgment set. The example in Figure 1 illustrates the premise-based and conclusion-baded procedure when issue-wise majority is used. As the example there shows, the conclusion-based procedure can produce multiple collective judgment sets. Multiple sets can be obtained via the premise-based procedure as well.

The JA function we can use for obtaining group goals should produce decisions that are complete and it should satisfy *collective rationality*. If $f(\pi)$ is not complete we cannot revise the group intentions. For example, if the decision contains only a group goal acceptance, then we do not know why the goal was (not) adopted and consequently when to revise it. For example, the cleaning crew decides for the goal g_3 (to collect recyclables), without having the reasons like p_9 (a container where to put them). If the world changes and $\neg p_9$ holds, the robots will continue to collect recyclables. If the aggregation of an admissible profile is not consistent with the decision rules, we

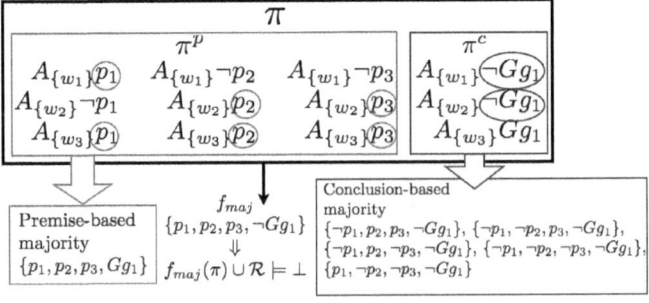

Fig. 1. A profile, issue-wise majority aggregation, premise-based and conclusion-based majority

would not be generating reasons for the group goal. The JA function we can use for obtaining group goals should produce decisions that are complete and it should satisfy *collective rationality*. If the decision contains only a group goal acceptance, the group does not know why the goal was (not) adopted and consequently when to revise it. If the aggregation of an admissible profile were not consistent with the decision rules, reasons for the group goal would not be generated.

We have to choose between a conclusion-based and a premise-based procedure. In the profile in Figure 1, a premise-based procedure leads the group to adopting a conclusion that the majority of the group does not endorse. There are cases in which the premise-based procedure leads the group to adopting a goal that neither of the agents endorses individually. The conclusion is the goal and a premise-based aggregation may establish a group goal which none of the agents is interested in pursuing. To avoid this, we need to aggregate using a conclusion-based procedure that satisfies *unanimity on Gg*. Since we have only one goal per agenda, we use issue-based majority to aggregate the group goal judgments.

Our decision rules are of the form $g \leftrightarrow \Gamma$. Hence, there exist profiles for which a conclusion-based procedure will not produce complete collective set of judgments. The conclusion-based aggregation can be supplemented with an additional procedure that completes the produced set of judgments when necessary. Such aggregation procedure is the complete conclusion-based procedure (CCBP) developed in [28]. This CCBP is *collectively rational*.

CCBP produces a unique collective judgment for the goal, but it can generate more than one set of justifications for it. This is an undesirable, especially if the agents are in a decentralized communication mode. To deal with ties, as it is the practice with voting procedures, the group determines a default set of justifications for adopting/rejecting each candidate goal. A lexicographic order on the judgment sets can be used to this end. In the centralized communication mode, the administrator can also break the ties.

The CCBP from [28] also satisfies *anonimity*. Whether this is a desirable property for a group of artificial agents depends entirely on whether the group is democratic or the opinions of some agents are more important. CCBP can be adjusted to take into consideration different weights on different agents' judgment sets.

3.2   The Generation of Multiple Group Goals

The mental state of the group is determined by the mental states of the members and the choice of judgment aggregation function. We represent the mental state of the group by a set χ of AGE_{LTL} formulas. The set χ contains the set of all candidate goals for the group $\mathcal{G} \subseteq \mathcal{L}_G/\mathcal{L}_{prop}$ and, for each $Gg \in \mathcal{G}$, the corresponding decision rules $\mathcal{R}_g$, as well as the individual and collective acceptances made in the group regarding agenda $\mathcal{A}_g$. The set χ is common knowledge for the group members. An agent uses χ when it acts as a group member and its own beliefs and goals when it acts as an individual.

To deal with multiple, possibly mutually inconsistent goals, the group has a priority order $\succsim_x$ over the group goals $\mathcal{G} \subset \chi$. To avoid overburdening the language with a $\succsim_x$ operator, we incorporate the priority order within the decision rules $\mathcal{R}_{g_i}^{just} \equiv l_i' \leftrightarrow Gg_i$. We want the decision rules to capture that if Gg_i is not consistent (according to the coordination rules) with some higher priority goals $Gg_1, \ldots, Gg_m$, then the group can accept Gg_i if and only if none of $Gg_1, \ldots, Gg_m$ is accepted. Hence, we replace the justification rule $\mathcal{R}_{g_i}^{just} \in \chi$ with $\mathcal{R}_{g_i}^{pjust} \equiv (\Gamma_i \wedge \bigwedge_j^m (A_N \neg Gg_j)) \leftrightarrow Gg_i$, where $Gg_j \in \mathcal{G}$, $Gg_j \succsim_x Gg_i$ and $Gg_i \wedge Gg_j \wedge \mathcal{R}_{g_i}^{coord} \models \bot$.

Example 4. Consider the goals and rules of the robot crew C from Example 3. Assume the crew has been given the priority order $Gg_1 >_\chi Gg_2 >_\chi Gg_3$. χ contains: $\mathcal{G} = \{Gg_1, Gg_2, Gg_3\}$, one background knowledge rule, one coordination rule, three justification rules, out of which two are new priority modified rules:

$\{\mathcal{G}, \neg p_4 \to \neg p_5, (Gg_2 \wedge \neg(Gg_1 \vee Gg_3)) \vee \neg Gg_2, Gg_1 \leftrightarrow (p_1 \wedge (p_2 \vee p_3)),$
$Gg_2 \leftrightarrow (p_4 \wedge p_5 \wedge (p_6 \vee p_7) \wedge A_C \neg Gg_1), Gg_3 \leftrightarrow (p_8 \wedge p_9 \wedge p_3 \wedge (A_C \neg Gg_2))\}.$

The agents give their judgments on one agenda after another starting with the agenda for the highest priority candidate goal. Once the profile π and the decision $\mathcal{D}_g$ for a goal g are obtained, they are added to χ. To avoid the situation in which the group casts judgments on an issue that has already been decided, we need to remove decided issues from $\mathcal{A}_g$ before eliciting the profile for this agenda.

The group goals are generated by executing **GenerateGoals**(χ, N).

```
function GenerateGoals (χ,  S) :
for each Ggᵢ ∈ 𝒢 s.t. [∀Ggⱼ ∈ 𝒢: (Ggⱼ ≳ Ggᵢ) ⇒ (A_N Ggⱼ ∈ χ or A_N ¬Ggⱼ ∈ χ)]
    { B := ({a | A_N a ∈ χ} ∪ {¬a | A_N ¬a ∈ χ}) ∩ 𝒜_{gᵢ};
    𝒜*_{gᵢ} := 𝒜_{gᵢ}/B;
    π_{gᵢ} := elicit(S, 𝒜*_{gᵢ}, χ);
    χ := χ ∪ π_{gᵢ} ∪ fᵃ(π_{gᵢ});   }
return χ.
```

GenerateGoals does not violate the candidate goal preference order and it terminates if *elicit* terminates. *elicit* requests the agents to submit complete judgment sets for $\pi_{g_i} \subset \chi$. We require that *elicit* is such that for all returned π it holds: $\chi \cup f(\pi)) \not\models \bot$ and $\chi \cup \pi \triangleright i \not\models \bot$ for every $i \in N$. When a higher priority goal Gg_i is accepted by the group, a lower priority incompatible goal Gg_j cannot be adopted regardless of the judgments on the issues in $\mathcal{A}_{g_j}$. Nevertheless, *elicit* will provide individual judgments for the agenda $\mathcal{A}_{g_j}$. If the acceptance of Gg_i is reconsidered, we can obtain a new decision on Gg_j because the profile for Gg_j is available.

Example 5. Consider the χ for robots given in Example 4. The following calls to *elicit* are made in the given order. First, $\pi_{g_1} = elicit(N, \mathcal{A}_{g_1}^*, \chi)$ with the $GenerateGoals(\chi) = \chi' = \chi \cup \pi_{g_1} \cup f^a(\pi_{g_1})$. Second, $\pi_{g_2} = elicit(N, \mathcal{A}_{g_2}^*, \chi')$, with $GenerateGoals(\chi') = \chi'' = \chi' \cup \pi_{g_2} \cup f^a(\pi(g_2))$. Last, $\pi_{g_3} = elicit(N, \mathcal{A}_{g_3}^*, \chi'')$, with $GenerateGoals(\chi'') = \chi''' = \chi'' \cup \pi_{g_3} \cup f^a(\pi_{g_3})$. Since there is no overlapping between agendas $\mathcal{A}_{g_2}$ and $\mathcal{A}_{g_1}$, $\mathcal{A}_{g_1}^* \equiv \mathcal{A}_{g_1}$ and $\mathcal{A}_{g_2}^* \equiv \mathcal{A}_{g_2}$. However, since $\mathcal{A}_{g_2} \cap \mathcal{A}_{g_3} = p_3$, then $\mathcal{A}_{g_3}^* = \{p_8, p_9, Gg_3\}$.

4 Commitment Strategies

The group can choose to reconsider the group goal in presence of new information – "a joint commitment must be *terminated* jointly" (pg. 143, [15]). Whether the group chooses to reconsider depends on how committed it is to the group intention corresponding to that goal. We defined the group intention to be $I_N g \equiv A_N Gg$, *i.e.* the decision to accept g as the group goal. The level of persistence of a group in their collective decision depends on the choice of commitment strategy.

These are the three main commitment strategies (introduced by Rao and Georgeff [31]):

Blind commitment: $I_i g \rightarrow (I_i g \mathbf{U} B_i g)$
Single-minded commitment: $I_i g \rightarrow (I_i g \mathbf{U} (B_i g \vee B_i \Box \neg g))$
Open-minded commitment: $I_i g \rightarrow (I_i g \mathbf{U} (B_i g \vee \neg G_i g))$

These commitment strategies only consider the relation between the intention and the beliefs regarding g and Gg. In our model of group intentions, a commitment is to a goal acceptance. This enables intention reconsideration upon new information on either one of the agenda issues in $\mathcal{A}_g$, as well as on a higher priority goal.

The strength of our framework is exhibited in its ability to describe the groups' commitment not only to its decision to adopt a goal, but also to its decision to reject a goal. Namely, if the agents decided $I_N g_i$ and $A_N \neg Gg_j$, they are committed to both $I_N g_i$ and $A_N \neg Gg_j$. Commitment to reject g allows for g to be reconsidered and eventually adopted if the state of the world changes.

Let N be a set of agents with a set of candidate goals $\mathcal{G}$. Let $Gg_i, Gg_j \in \mathcal{G}$ have agendas $\mathcal{A}_{g_i}, \mathcal{A}_{g_j}$. We use $p \in \overline{\mathcal{A}}_{g_i}^p$ and $q_i \in \overline{\mathcal{A}}_{g_i}^c$, $q_j \in \overline{\mathcal{A}}_{g_j}^c$. The profiles and decisions are π_{g_i} and $f(\pi_{g_i})$; $Gg_j > Gg_i$, and Gg_j cannot be pursued at the same time as Gg_i.

We use the formulas $(\alpha_1) - (\alpha_5)$ to refine the blind, single-minded and open-minded commitment. Instead of the *until*, we use the temporal operator *release*: $\psi \mathbf{R} \phi \equiv \neg(\neg \psi \mathbf{U} \neg \phi)$, meaning that ϕ has to be true until and including the point where ψ first becomes true; if ψ never becomes true, ϕ must remain true forever. Unlike the *until* operator, the *release* operator does not guarantee that the right hand-side formula will ever become true, which in our case translates to the fact that an agent could be forever committed to a goal.

$(\alpha_1)\ E g_i \mathbf{R} I_N g_i$
$(\alpha_2)\ \bot \mathbf{R} A_N \neg Gg_i$
$(\alpha_3)\ (E \Box \neg g_i \vee E g_i) \mathbf{R} A_N q_i$
$(\alpha_4)\ A_N \neg q_j \mathbf{R} A_N q_i$
$(\alpha_5)\ A_N p \rightarrow (E \neg p \mathbf{R} A_N q_i)$

Blind commitment: $\alpha_1 \wedge \alpha_2$.
Only the observation that the goal is achieved ($E g_i$) can release the intention to achieve the goal $I_N g_i$. If the goal is never achieved, the group is always committed to it. If a goal is not accepted, then the agents do not reconsider accepting it.

Single-minded commitment: α_3.
Only new information on the goal (either that the goal is achieved or had become impossible) can release the decision of the group to adopt /reject the goal. Hence, new information is only regarded if it concerns the conclusion, while information on the remaining agenda items is ignored.

Extended single-minded commitment: $\alpha_3 \wedge \alpha_4$.
Not only new information on Gg_i, but also the collective acceptance to adopt a more important incompatible goal Gg_j can release the intention of the group to achieve Gg_i. Similarly, if Gg_i is not accepted, the non-acceptance can be revised, not only if Gg_j is observed to be impossible or achieved, but also when the commitment to pursue Gg_j is dropped (for whatever reason).

Open-minded commitment: $\alpha_3 \wedge \alpha_5$.
A group maintains its collective acceptances to adopt or reject a goal as long as the new information regarding all collectively accepted agenda items is consistent with $f(\pi_{g_i})$.

Extended open-minded commitment: $\alpha_3 \wedge \alpha_4 \wedge \alpha_5$.
Extending on the single-minded commitment, a change in intention to pursue a higher priority goal Gg_j can also release the acceptance of the group on Gg_i.

Once an intention is dropped, a group may need to reconsider its collective acceptances. This may cause for the dropped goal to be re-affirmed, but a reconsideration process will be invoked nevertheless.

5   Reconsideration of Group Attitudes

In Section 3.2 we defined the mental state of the group χ. We can now define what it means for a group to be *coherent*.

Definition 8 (Group coherence). *Given a Kripke structure $\mathcal{M}$ and situations $s \in W$, a group of N agents is coherent if the following conditions are met:*
(ρ_1): $\mathcal{M} \models \neg(A_S a \wedge A_S \neg a)$ *for any $S \subseteq N$ and any $a \in \mathcal{A}_g$.*
(ρ_2): *If $\mathcal{M}, s \models \chi$ then $\chi \not\models \bot$.*
(ρ_3): $\mathcal{M}, s \models \bigwedge \mathcal{G} \rightarrow \neg \Box \neg g$ *for all $Gg \in \mathcal{G}$.*
(ρ_4): *Let $Gg \in \mathcal{G}$ and $\mathcal{G}' = \mathcal{G}/\{Gg\}$, then $\mathcal{M} \models (\bigwedge \mathcal{G} \wedge E \Box \neg g) \rightarrow X(\neg Gg)$.*
(ρ_5): *Let $p \in \mathcal{A}_g^p$ and $q \in \{Gg, \neg Gg\}$. $Ep \wedge (Ep \, \boldsymbol{R} \, A_N q) \rightarrow XA_N p$*

The first condition ensures that no contradictory judgments are given. The second condition ensures that the mental state of the group is logically consistent in all situations. The third and fourth conditions ensure that impossible goals cannot be part of the set of candidate goals and if g is observed to be impossible in situation s, then it will be removed from $\mathcal{G}$ in the next situation. ρ_5 enforces the acceptance of the new information on the group level, when the commitment strategy so allows – after a is observed and that led the group to de-commit from g, the group necessarily accepts a.

A coherent group accepts the observed new information on a premise. This may cause the collective acceptances to be inconsistent with the justification rules. Consequently, the decisions and/or the profiles in χ need to be changed in order to ensure that ρ_1 and ρ_2 are satisfied. If, however $\Box \neg g$ or g is observed, the group reconsiders χ by removing Gg from $\mathcal{G}$. In this case, the decisions and profiles are not changed.

For simplicity, at present we work with a world in which the agents' knowledge can only increase, namely the observed information is not a fluent. A few more conditions need to be added to the definition of group coherence for our model to be able to be applicable to fluents. For example, we need to define which observation is accepted when two subsequent contradictory observations happen.

5.1   Reconsideration Strategies

For the group to be coherent at all situations, the acceptances regarding the group goals need to be reconsidered after de-commitment. Let $\mathcal{D}_g \subset \chi$ contain the group acceptances for a goal g, while $\pi_g \subset \chi$ contain the profile for g. There are two basic ways in which a collective judgment set can be reconsidered. The first way is to elicit a new profile for g and apply judgment aggregation to it to obtain the reconsidered $\mathcal{D}_g^*$. The second is to reconsider only $\mathcal{D}_g$ without re-eliciting individual judgments. The first approach requires communication among agents. The second approach can be done by each agent reconsidering χ by herself. We identify three reconsideration strategies available to the agents. The strategies are ordered from the least to the most demanding in terms of agent communication.

Decision reconsideration ($\mathcal{D}$-r). Assume that Ea, $a \in \overline{\mathcal{A}}_g^p$, $q \in \{Gg, \neg Gg\}$ and the group de-committed from $A_N q$. The reconsidered decision $\mathcal{D}_g^*$ is such that a is accepted, i.e., $A_N a \in \mathcal{D}_g^*$, and the entire decision is consistent with the justification rules, namely $\mathcal{R}_g^{pjust} \cup \mathcal{D}_g^* \not\vdash \bot$. If the $\mathcal{D}$-r specifies a unique $\mathcal{D}_g^*$, for any observed information and any $\mathcal{D}_g$, then χ can be reconsidered without any communication among the agents. Given the form of $\mathcal{R}_g^{pjust}$ (see Section 3.2), this will always be the case.

   However $\mathcal{D}$-r is not always an option when the de-commitment occurred due to a change in collective acceptance of a higher priority goal g'. Let $q' \in \{Gg', \neg Gg'\}$. Let the new acceptance be $A_N \neg q'$. $\mathcal{D}$-r is possible if and only if $\mathcal{D}_g^* = \mathcal{D}_g$ and $\mathcal{R}_g^{pjust} \cup \mathcal{D}_g \cup \{A_N \neg q'\} \not\vdash \bot$. Recall that $A_N q'$ was not in $\mathcal{A}_g$ and as such the acceptance of q' or $\neg q'$ is never in the decision for π_g.

Partial reconsideration of the profile (Partial π-r). Assume that Ea, $a \in \overline{\mathcal{A}}_g$, $Gg \in \mathcal{G}$. Not only the group, but also the individual agents need to accept a. The *Partial π-r* asks for new individual judgments to be elicited. This is done to ensure the logical consistency of the individual judgment sets with the observations. New judgments are only elicited from the agents i which $A_{\{i\}} \neg a$.

   Let $W \subseteq N$ be the subset of agents i s.t. $A_{\{i\}} \neg a \in \chi$. Agents i are s.t. $A_{\{i\}} a \in \chi$ when the observation is $E \neg a$. Let $\pi_g^W \subseteq \pi_g$ be the set of all acceptances made by the agents in W. We construct $\chi' = \chi / \pi_g^W$. The new profile and decision are obtained by executing $GenerateGoals$ (χ', W).

Example 6. Consider Example 3. Assume that $\mathcal{D}_{g_1} = \{A_C p_1, A_C \neg p_2, A_C p_3, A_C Gg_1\}$, $\mathcal{D}_{g_2} = \{A_C p_4, A_C p_5, A_C p_6, A_C p_7, A_C \neg Gg_2\}$ and $\mathcal{D}_{g_3} = \{A_C p_8, A_C p_9, A_C Gg_3\}$ are the group's decisions. Assume the group de-commits on Gg_1 because of $E \neg p_2$. If the group is committed to Gg_3, the commitment on Gg_3 will not allow for $A_N p_3$ to be modified when reconsidering Gg_1. Since $A_N p_3$ exists in χ', p_3 will be excluded from the (new) agenda for g_1, although it was originally in it. *elicit* calls only on the agents in W to complete $\pi_{g_1} \in \chi'$ with their judgment sets.

Full profile reconsideration (Full π-r). The full profile reconsideration is the same as the partial reconsiderations except now $W = N$. Namely, within the full profile revision strategy, each agent is asked to revise his judgment set by accepting the new information, regardless of whether he had already accepted it.

5.2 Combining Revision and Commitment Strategies

Unlike the Rao and Georgeff commitment strategies [31], in our framework the commitment strategies are not axioms of the logic. We require that the commitment strategy is valid in all the models of the group and not in all the models of AGE_{LTL}. This allows the group to define different commitment strategies and different revision strategies for different goals. It might even choose to revise differently depending on which information triggered the revision. Choosing different revision strategies for each goal, or each type of new information, should not undermine the coherence of the group record χ. The conditions of group coherence of the group ensures that, after every reconsideration, χ must remain consistent. However, some combinations of commitment strategies can lead to incoherence of χ.

Example 7. Consider the decisions in Example 6. Assume that initially the group chose open-minded commitment for $I_C g_1$ and blind commitment for $I_C g_3$, with goal open-minded commitment for $A_C \neg G g_2$. If $E g_1$ and thus $I_C g_1$ is dropped, then the extended open-minded commitment would allow $A_C \neg G g_2$ to be reconsidered and eventually $I_C g_2$ established. However, since the group is blindly committed to $I_C g_3$, this change will not cause reconsideration and as a result both $I_C g_2$ and $I_C g_3$ will be in χ, thus making χ incoherent.

Problems arise when $sub(\mathcal{R}_{g_i}^{pjust}) \cap sub(\mathcal{R}_{g_j}^{pjust}) \neq \emptyset$, where $sub(\mathcal{R}_{g}^{pjust})$ denotes the set of atomic sub-formulas of some goal g and $G g_i, G g_j \in \mathcal{G}$. Proposition 2 summarizes under which conditions these problems are avoided.

Proposition 2. *Let α' and α'' be the commitment strategies selected for g_i and g_j correspondingly. $\chi \cup \alpha' \cup \alpha'' \nvdash \bot$ (in all situations):*
a) if $\phi \in sub(\mathcal{R}_{g_i}^{pjust}) \cap sub(\mathcal{R}_{g_j}^{pjust})$ and $p \in \mathcal{A}_{g_i} \cap \mathcal{A}_{g_j}$, then α_5 is either in both α' and α'' or in none;
b) if $G g_i$ is more important than $G g_j$ while $G g_j$ and $G g_i$ cannot be accepted at the same time, then $\alpha_4 \in \alpha''$.

Proof. The proof is straightforward. If the change in the group (non)acceptance of $G g_i$ causes the $A_N G g_j$ to induce group incoherence, then we are able to de-commit from $A_N G g_j$. If we would not able to de-comit from $A_N G g_j$ then group coherence would be blocked. If the change in the group (non)acceptance of $G g_i$ is caused by an observation on a premise $p \subset \mathcal{A}_{g_i} \cap \mathcal{A}_{g_j}$ then condition a) ensures that the commitment to $A_N G g_j$ does not block group coherence. If the change on $A_N G g_j$ is caused by a change in commitment to a higher priority goal, the condition b) ensures that a commitment regarding $G g_j$ does not block group coherence. Condition b) allows only "goal sensitive" commitments to be selected for lower level goals.

6 Conclusions

We presented a formalization of non-summative beliefs, goals and intentions in AGE_{LTL} and showed how they can be generated using judgment aggregation. Our multi-agent AGE_{LTL} logic extends BDI_{LTL}. In accordance with the non-summative view, having a group intention $I_N g$ in our framework does not imply $I_{\{i\}} g$ for each the

Table 1. $Gg_j > Gg$ and can not be pursued at the same time with Gg. $\circledast\mathcal{D}_g$ denotes: collective attitudes for g are reconsidered. $\circledast\ \pi_g$ denotes: the profile (all or some parts of it) is re-elicited.

Commitment to	Release on				Change	How		
$A_N(\neg)Gg$	$\Box\neg g$	g	Gg_j	$\mathcal{A}_g^p$	χ	$\circledast\mathcal{D}_g$	$\circledast\pi_g$	JA
Blind	✓							
Single-minded	✓	✓			$\mathcal{D}$-r	✓		
Extended	✓	✓	✓		Partial π-r		✓	✓
Open-minded	✓	✓		✓	Full π-r		✓	✓
Extended	✓	✓	✓	✓				

member i. We extended the commitment strategies of Rao and Georgeff [31] to increase the reactivity of the group to new information. Now the commitment strategies are not axioms of the representation logic; instead they are a property of a group. Groups can have different levels of commitment to different goals. We showed how the group can combine different commitments to different goals.

Our framework is intended for groups that engage in joint activity and it is applicable when it cannot be assumed that the agents persuade each other on a single position and goal, and yet it is necessary that the group presents itself as a single whole from the point of view of beliefs and goals. The requirement that the group presents itself as a rational entity that has goals justified by the beliefs it holds, and is able to revise these goals under the light of new information, was held by Tuomela [37] and adopted in agent theory by Boella and van der Torre [2] and Lorini [25]. The proposal of the paper can be applied, for example, in an opensource project, where several people have to discuss online to agree on which is their position on issues and which is their goal.

An advantage of our framework is its ability to allow groups to commit to a decision to reject a goal, thus having the option to reconsider rejected goals. Furthermore, we do not only show when to reconsider, but also how, by defining reconsideration strategies. Table 1 summarizes our commitment and reconsideration strategies.

We assume that the group has an order of importance for its candidate goals. Alternatively, the group can also agree on this order by expressing individual preferences. Uckelman and Endriss [38] show how individual (cardinal) preferences over goals can be aggregated. In [39] the reconsideration of individual intentions and associated plans is considered. Intentions and their role in deliberation for individual agents have been studied in a game theoretic framework by Roy [33,34]. Icard et al. [20] consider the joint revision of individual attitudes, with the revision of beliefs triggering intention revision. We allow for both the change in epistemic and in motivational attitudes to be the cause for reconsideration.

In our framework, the entire group observes the new information. In the future we intend to explore the case when only some members of the group observe the new information. The only assumptions we make regarding the connectivity of the members is that they are able to communicate their acceptances and receive the aggregation result. The problem of elicitation and communication complexity in voting is a nontrivial one [8,9] and in the future we intend to study these properties of our framework.

In the work we presented, we do not consider how an individual constructs his judgments. We can take that $B_i\phi \rightarrow A_{\{i\}}\phi$, but this is not a requirement for all agents. We would expect "honest" agents to follow this rule, but we can also define dishonest agents for which $B_i\phi \rightarrow A_{\{i\}}\phi$ does not hold. In the latter case, the agent might declare $A_{\{i\}}\phi$ while it does not believe ϕ. Given that the group attitudes are established by an aggregation procedure that is, as almost all but the most trivial procedures, manipulable, the question is whether there are scenarios in which an agent can have the incentive to behave strategically in rendering judgments. Furthermore, given that some of the reconsideration strategies call for re-elicitation of judgments, can an agent have the incentive to behave strategically in rendering judgments that would lead to sooner re-elicitation? We intend to devote more attention to answering these questions as well as studying the manipulability properties of our framework.

References

1. Arrow, K., Sen, A.K., Suzumura, K.: Handbook of Social Choice and Welfare, vol. 1. Elsevier, Amsterdam (2002)
2. Boella, G., van der Torre, L.: The ontological properties of social roles in multi-agent systems: Definitional dependence, powers and roles playing roles. Artificial Intelligence and Law Journal (AILaw) 15(3), 201–221 (2007)
3. Bratman, M.E.: Shared intention. Ethics 104(1), 97–113 (1993)
4. Castelfranchi, C., Paglieri, F.: The role of beliefs in goal dynamics: Prolegomena to a constructive theory of intentions. Synthese 155, 237–263 (2007)
5. Chapman, B.: Rational aggregation. Politics, Philosophy and Economics 1(3), 337–354 (2002)
6. Chellas, B.F.: Modal Logic: An Introduction. Cambridge University Press, Cambridge (1980)
7. Cohen, P.R., Levesque, H.: Intention is choice with commitment. Artificial Intelligence 42(2-3), 213–261 (1990)
8. Conitzer, V., Sandholm, T.: Vote elicitation: Complexity and strategy-proofness. In: AAAI/IAAI, pp. 392–397 (2002)
9. Conitzer, V., Sandholm, T.: Communication complexity of common voting rules. In: ACM Conference on Electronic Commerce, pp. 78–87 (2005)
10. Dietrich, F., List, C.: Strategy-proof judgment aggregation. STICERD - Political Economy and Public Policy Paper Series, (09). Suntory and Toyota International Centres for Economics and Related Disciplines, LSE (August 2005)
11. Dietrich, F., List, C.: Arrow's theorem in judgment aggregation. Social Choice and Welfare 29(1), 19–33 (2007)
12. Dunin-Keplicz, B., Verbrugge, R.: Teamwork in Multi-Agent Systems: A Formal Approach. Wiley and Sons, Chichester (July 2010)
13. Gilbert, M.P.: Modeling Collective Belief. Synthese 73, 185–204 (1987)
14. Gilbert, M.P.: Belief and acceptance as features of groups. Protosociology: An International Journal of Interdisciplinary Research 16, 35–69 (2002)
15. Gilbert, M.P.: Acting together, joint commitment, and obligation. Philosophische Analyse/Philosophical Analysis (2007)
16. Gilbert, M.P.: Shared Intention and Personal Intentions. Philosophical Studies (2009)
17. Grosz, B., Hunsberger, L.: The dynamics of intention in collaborative activity. Cognitive Systems Research 7(2-3), 259–272 (2007)
18. Hakli, R.: Group beliefs and the distinction between belief and acceptance. Cognitive Systems Research 7(2-3), 286–297 (2006); Cognition, Joint Action and Collective Intentionality

19. Hartmann, S., Pigozzi, G., Sprenger, J.: Reliable methods of judgment aggregation. Journal of Logic and Computation (forthcoming)
20. Icard, T., Pacuit, E., Shoham, Y.: Joint revision of belief and intention. In: Proc.of the 12th International Conference on Principles of Knowledge Representation and Reasoning (KR 2010) (2010)
21. Jennings, N.R.: Controlling cooperative problem solving in industrial multi-agent systems using joint intentions. Artif. Intell. 75(2), 195–240 (1995)
22. Konieczny, S., Pino-Pérez, R.: Merging with integrity constraints. In: Hunter, A., Parsons, S. (eds.) ECSQARU 1999. LNCS (LNAI), vol. 1638, pp. 233–244. Springer, Heidelberg (1999)
23. Levesque, H.J., Cohen, P.R., Nunes, J.H.T.: On acting together. In: AAAI, pp. 94–99 (1990)
24. List, C., Puppe, C.: Judgment aggregation: A survey. In: Anand, P., Puppe, C., Pattanaik, P. (eds.) Oxford Handbook of Rational and Social Choice, Oxford (2009)
25. Lorini, E., Longin, D.: A logical account of institutions: From acceptances to norms via legislators. In: KR, pp. 38–48 (2008)
26. Lorini, E., Longin, D., Gaudou, B., Herzig, A.: The logic of acceptance. Journal of Logic and Computation 19(6), 901–940 (2009)
27. Meijers, A.: Collective agents and cognitive agents. Protosociology. Special Issue Understanding the Social: New Perspectives from Epistemology 16, 70–86 (2002)
28. Pigozzi, G., Slavkovik, M., van der Torre, L.: A complete conclusion-based procedure for judgment aggregation. In: Rossi, F., Tsoukias, A. (eds.) ADT 2009. LNCS, vol. 5783, pp. 1–13. Springer, Heidelberg (2009)
29. Pnueli, A.: The temporal logic of programs. In: SFCS 1977: Proceedings of the 18th Annual Symposium on Foundations of Computer Science, pp. 46–57. IEEE Computer Society, Washington, DC, USA (1977)
30. Quinton, A.: The presidential address: Social objects. Proceedings of the Aristotelian Society 76, 1–27+viii (1975)
31. Rao, A.S., Georgeff, M.P.: Intentions and rational commitment. In: Proceedings of the First Pacific Rim Conference on Artificial Intelligence (PRICAI 1990), pp. 94–99 (1993)
32. Rao, A.S., Georgeff, M.P., Sonenberg, E.A.: Social plans: a preliminary report (abstract). SIGOIS Bull. 13, 10 (1992)
33. Roy, O.: A dynamic-epistemic hybrid logic for intentions and information changes in strategic games. Synthese 171, 291–320 (2009)
34. Roy, O.: Intentions and interactive transformations of decision problems. Synthese 169, 335–349 (2009)
35. Schild, K.: On the relationship between bdi logics and standard logics of concurrency. Autonomous Agents and Multi-Agent Systems 3(3), 259–283 (2000)
36. Singh, M.P.: Group intentions. In: Proceedings of the Tenth International Workshop on Distributed Artificial Intelligence (IWDAI 1990) (1990)
37. Tuomela, R., Miller, K.: Groups beliefs. Synthese 91, 285–318 (1992)
38. Uckelman, J., Endriss, U.: Compactly representing utility functions using weighted goals and the max aggregator. Artif. Intell. 174, 1222–1246 (2010)
39. van der Hoek, W., Jamroga, W., Wooldridge, M.: Towards a theory of intention revision. Synthese 155(2), 265–290 (2007)
40. Wolter, F.: Fusions of modal logics revisited. In: Kracht, M., de Rijke, M., Zakharyaschev, M. (eds.) Advances in Modal Logic 96, pp. 361–379. CSLI Lecture Notes (1998)
41. Wooldridge, M., Jennings, N.: The cooperative problem-solving process. Journal of Logic and Computation 9(4) (1999)

The Fundamental Principle of Coactive Design: Interdependence Must Shape Autonomy

Matthew Johnson[1,2], Jeffrey M. Bradshaw[1], Paul J. Feltovich[1], Catholijn M. Jonker[2], Birna van Riemsdijk[2], and Maarten Sierhuis[2,3]

[1] Florida Institute for Human and Machine Cognition (IHMC), Pensacola, Florida, USA
[2] EEMCS, Delft University of Technology, Delft, The Netherlands
[3] PARC, Palo Alto, California, USA
{mjohnson,jbradshaw,pfeltovich}@ihmc.us,
{c.m.jonker,m.b.vanriemsdijk}@tudelft.nl,
maarten.sierhuis@parc.com

Abstract. This article presents the fundamental principle of *Coactive Design*, a new approach being developed to address the increasingly sophisticated roles for both people and agents in mixed human-agent systems. The fundamental principle of Coactive Design is that the underlying *interdependence* of participants in joint activity is a critical factor in the design of human-agent systems. In order to enable appropriate interaction, an understanding of the potential interdependencies among groups of humans and agents working together in a given situation should be used to shape the way agent architectures and individual agent capabilities for autonomy are designed. Increased effectiveness in human-agent teamwork hinges not merely on trying to make agents more independent through their autonomy, but also in striving to make them more capable of sophisticated *interdependent* joint activity with people.

Keywords: Coactive, autonomy, interdependence, joint activity.

1 Introduction

Researchers and developers continue to pursue increasingly sophisticated roles for agents.[1] Envisioned roles include caretakers for the homebound, physician assistants, coworkers and aides in factories and offices, and servants in our homes. Not only are the agents themselves increasing in their capabilities, but also the composition of human-robot systems is growing in scale and heterogeneity. All these requirements showcase the importance of robots transitioning from today's common modes of reliance, where they are frequently operated as mere teleoperated tools, to more sophisticated partners or teammates [1, 2].

Direct teleoperation and complete autonomy are often thought of as two extremes on a spectrum. Researchers in human-agent interaction have typically seen themselves as investigating the middle ground between these extremes. Such research has gone

---

[1] Throughout the article we will use the terms "agent" and "robot" interchangeably to mean any artificial actor.

M. De Vos et al. (Eds.): COIN 2010 International Workshops, LNAI 6541, pp. 172–191, 2011.

under various names, including mixed-initiative interaction [3], adjustable autonomy [4], collaborative control [5], and sliding autonomy [6]. Each of these approaches attempts to keep the human-agent system operating at a "sweet spot" between the two extremes. As the names of these approaches suggest, researchers understand that the ideal is not a fixed location along this spectrum but may need to vary dynamically along the spectrum as context and resources change. Of importance to our discussion is the fact that these approaches, along with traditional planning technologies at the foundation of intelligent systems, typically take an autonomy-centered perspective, focusing mainly on the problems of control and task allocation when agents and humans attempt to work together.

In contrast to these autonomy-centered approaches, Coactive Design is a teamwork-centered approach. The concept of teamwork-centered autonomy was addressed by Bradshaw *et al.* [7]. It takes as a beginning premise that joint activity of a consequential nature often requires people to work in close and continuous interaction with autonomous systems, and hence adopts the stance that the processes of understanding, problem solving and task execution are necessarily incremental, subject to negotiation, and forever tentative.

The overall objective of our work in Coactive Design is to describe and, insofar as possible, empirically validate design principles and guidelines to support joint activity in human-agent systems. Though these principles and guidelines are still under development, our research has progressed to the point where we are ready to present the fundamental principle that serves as the foundation for our approach. The fundamental principle of Coactive Design recognizes that the underlying *interdependence* of participants in joint activity is a critical factor in the design of human-agent systems. In order to enable appropriate interaction, an understanding of the potential interdependencies among groups of humans and agents working together in a given situation should be used to shape the way agent architectures and individual agent capabilities for autonomy are designed. We no longer look at the primary problem of the research community as simply trying to make agents more independent through their autonomy. Rather, in addition, we strive to make them more capable of sophisticated interdependent joint activity with people.

This article will begin by an overview of different usages of the term *autonomy* in the agent and robot literature. We provide a rationale for our belief that a new approach to human-agent system design is needed in the context of prior research and its associated challenges. Next we introduce some of the concepts important to the Coactive Design approach and present different aspects of its fundamental principle. We discuss relevant experimental work to date that has begun to demonstrate our claims. Finally, we close with a summary of the work.

2 Defining Autonomy

Autonomy has two basic senses in everyday usage. The first sense, self-sufficiency, is about the degree to which an entity is able to take care of itself. Bradshaw [8] refers to this as the *descriptive dimension* of autonomy. Similarly, Castelfranchi [9] referred to this as one of the two aspects of *social autonomy* that he called *independence*. People usually consider robot autonomy in this sense in relation to a particular task. For example, a robot may be able to navigate autonomously, but only in an office environment. The second sense refers to the quality of self-directedness, or the degree of freedom from outside constraints (whether social or environmental), which Bradshaw calls the *prescriptive dimension* of autonomy. Castelfranchi referred to this as autonomy of delegation and considered it another form of *social autonomy*. For robots, this usually means freedom from human input or intervention during a particular task.

In the following section, we will describe some of the more prominent approaches to improve human-robot system effectiveness.[2] To avoid the ambiguity often found in the agent literature, we will use the terms *self-sufficiency* and *self-directedness* in our discussion.

3 Prior Work

3.1 Function Allocation and Supervisory Control

The concept of automation—which began with the straightforward objective of replacing whenever feasible any task currently performed by a human with a machine that could do the same task better, faster, or cheaper—became one of the first issues to attract the notice of early human factors researchers. These researchers attempted to systematically characterize the general strengths and weaknesses of humans and machines [10]. The resulting discipline of *Function Allocation* aimed to provide a rational means of determining which system-level functions should be carried out by humans and which by machines. Sheridan proposed the concept of *Supervisory Control* [11], in which a human oversees one or more autonomous systems, statically allocating tasks to them. Once control is given to the system, it is ideally expected to complete the tasks without human intervention. The designer's job is to determine what needs to be done and then provide the agent the capability (i.e., self-sufficiency) to do it. Therefore, this approach to achieving autonomy is shaped by a system's self-sufficiency.

3.2 Adaptive, Sliding, or Adjustable Autonomy

Over time it became plain to researchers that things were not as simple as they first appeared. For example, the suitability of a particular human or machine to take on a particular task may vary by time and over different situations; hence the need for methods of function allocation that are dynamic and adaptive. Dorais [12] defines "adjustable autonomy" as "the ability of autonomous systems to operate with dynamically varying levels of independence, intelligence and control." Dias [13] uses a similar definition for the term "sliding autonomy." Sheridan discusses "adaptive automation," in which the system must decide at runtime which functions to automate and to what extent. We will use the term *adjustable autonomy* as a catch-all to refer to this concept, namely, a change in agent autonomy—in this case the self-directedness aspect—to some appropriate level, based on the situation. The action of adjustment may be initiated by the human, by the agent framework, or by the agent itself.

---

[2] Parts of our discussion of this topic are adapted from [8].

It is evident that such approaches are autonomy-centered, with the focus being on task assignment, control, and level of independence. Autonomy, in this case, is shaped exclusively by varying levels of self-directedness. One very important concept emphasized by these approaches is adaptivity, a quality that will be important in the operation of increasingly-sophisticated intelligent systems.

3.3 Mixed-Initiative Interaction

Mixed-initiative approaches evolved from a different research community, but share some similar ideas and assumptions. Allen defines mixed-initiative as "a flexible interaction strategy, where each agent can contribute to the task what it does best" [3]. In Allen's work, the system is able to reason about which party should initiate action with respect to a given task or communicative exchange. In a similar vein, Myers and Morley describe a framework called "Taskable Reactive Agent Communities (TRAC) [14] that supports the directability of a team of agents by a human supervisor by modifying task guidance." Directability or task allocation is once again the central feature of the approach. Murphy [15] also uses the term "mixed-initiative" to describe their attention-directing system, the goal of which is to get the human to assume responsibility for a task when a robot fails.

Mixed-initiative interaction is also essentially autonomy-centered. Its usual focus is on task assignment or the authority to act and, as such, varying self-directedness is used to shape the operation of the autonomous system. Mixed-initiative interaction contributes the valuable insight that joint activity is about interaction and negotiation, and that dynamic shifts in control may be useful.

3.4 Collaborative Control

Collaborative Control is an approach proposed by Fong [5] that uses human-robot dialogue (i.e., queries from the robot and the subsequent presence or absence of a responses from the human), as the mechanism for adaptation. As Fong states, "Collaborative control... allows robots to benefit from human assistance during perception and cognition, and not just planning and command generation" [5]. Collaborative Control is a first step toward Coactive Design, introducing the idea that both parties may participate simultaneously in the same action. Here the ongoing interdependence of the human and the robot in carrying out a navigation task is used to shape the design of autonomous capabilities. The robot was designed to enable the human to provide assistance in the perceptual and cognitive parts of the task. The robotic assistance is not strictly required, so we are not merely talking about self-sufficiency. The key point is that the robotic assistance in this case is an integral part of the robot design and operation. We have adopted and extended some of the ideas from Collaborative Control as we have developed the Coactive Design approach.

3.5 How Autonomy Has Been Characterized in Former Research

One way to gain insight into the predominant perspectives in a research community is to review how it categorizes and describes its own work. This provides a test of our claim that prior work in agents and robots has been largely autonomy-centered.

The general drift is perhaps most clearly seen in the work of researchers who have tried to describe different "levels" of autonomy. For example, Yanco [16] characterized autonomy in terms of the amount of intervention required. For example, full teleoperation is 100% intervention and 0% automation. On the other hand, tour guide robots are labelled 100% autonomous and 0% intervention. The assumption in this model is that intervention only occurs when the robot lacks self-sufficiency. However, identifying the "percentage" of intervention is a very subjective matter except when one is at the extreme ends of the spectrum. Similarly Parasuraman and Sheridan [17] provide a list of levels of autonomy shown in figure 1.

HIGH	10. The computer decides everything, acts autonomously, ignoring the human.
	9. informs the human only if it, the computer, decides to
	8. informs the human only if asked, or
	7. executes automatically, then necessarily informs the human, and
	6. allows the human a restricted time to veto before automatic execution, or
	5. executes that suggestion if the human approves, or
	4. suggests on alternative
	3. narrows the selection down to a few, or
	2. The computer offers a complete set of decision/action alternatives, or
LOW	1. The computer offers no assistance: human must take all decisions and actions

Fig. 1. Levels of Automation [17]

Sheridan's scale is clearly autonomy-centered, as noted by Goodrich and Schultz [18]. Specifically it focused on the self-directedness aspect of autonomy. In response to the limitations of Sheridan's scale, Goodrich and Schultz [18] developed a scale that attempts to focus on levels of interaction rather than of automation (figure 2).

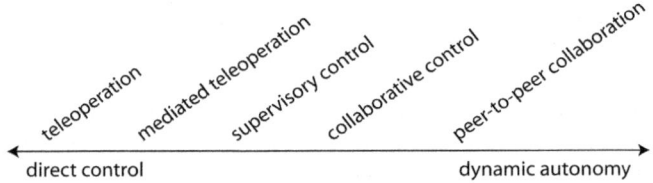

Fig. 2. Levels of autonomy with an emphasis on human interaction [18]

Though Goodrich and Schultz rightfully recognized that something more than the previous autonomy-centered characterizations of the field needed to be captured, in reality the left-to-right progress of the scale provides little more than a historical summary of robot research, with peer-to-peer collaboration as the next step. The label of the right end of the spectrum, "dynamic autonomy," reveals that this scale is, like the others discussed previously, autonomy-centered.

Bradshaw has characterized autonomy in terms of multiple dimensions rather than a single one-dimensional scale of levels [8]. The descriptive and prescriptive aspects of autonomy discussed above capture two of these primary dimensions. He also argues that the measurement of these dimensions should be specific to task and situation, since an agent may be self-directed or self-sufficient in one particular task or situation, but not in another.

Castelfranchi suggested dependence as the complement of autonomy [9] and attempts to capture several dimensions of autonomy in terms of the autonomy vs. dependence of various capabilities in a standard Procedural Reasoning System (PRS) architecture. These include information, interpretation, know-how, planning, plan discretion, goal dynamics, goal discretion, motivation, reasoning, monitoring, and skill autonomy. Like Bradshaw, Castelfranchi recognizes that autonomy is not a monolithic property, but should be measured with respect to different aspects of the agent. Castelfranchi put it this way: "any needed resource or power within the action-perception loop of an agent defines a possible dimension of dependence or autonomy" [9].

3.6 Challenges of Autonomy-Centered Approaches

We now describe the most common challenges faced by autonomy-centered approaches in the context of both senses of autonomy. Since the capability to perform a task and the authority to perform a task are orthogonal concepts, we separate these two dimensions onto separate axes, as in figure 3. Together these two axes represent an autonomy-centered plane of robotic capabilities. The *self-sufficiency* axis represents the degree to which a robot can perform a task by itself. "Low" indicates that the robot is not capable of performing the task without significant help. "High" indicates that the robot can perform the task reliably without assistance. The *self-directedness* axis is about freedom from outside control. Though a robot may be sufficiently competent to perform a range of actions, it may be constrained from doing so by a variety of social and environmental factors. "Low" indicates that, although possibly capable of performing the task, the robot is not permitted to do so. "High" indicates the robot has the authority over its own actions, though it does not necessarily imply sufficient competence.

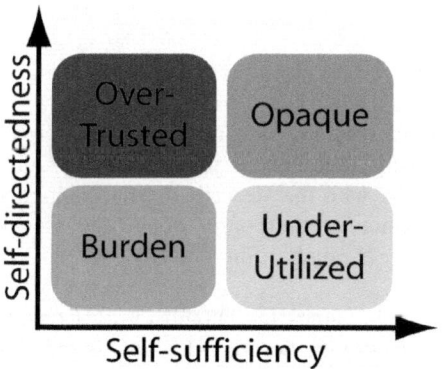

Fig. 3. Common system issues mapped against an autonomy-centered plane

Direct teleoperation, in which both self-sufficiency and self-directedness are absent, corresponds to the region labeled *Burden*. Increasing the self-directedness without a corresponding level of self-sufficiency will result in a system that is *over-trusted*, as shown in the upper left of the figure. Many systems fall in this category, including, for example, every entry in the DARPA robotic vehicle Grand Challenge that failed to complete the task. When autonomous capabilities are seen as insufficient, particularly in situations where the consequences of robot error may be disastrous, it is common for self-directedness to be limited. When the system self-directedness is reduced significantly below the potential of its capabilities the result is an *underutilized* system, as shown in the lower right corner of the figure. An example of this would be the first generations of Mars rovers which, due to the high cost of failure, were not trusted with autonomous action, but rather were subject to the decisions of a sizable team of NASA engineers. Here is the key point, however:

> *Even when self-directedness and self-sufficiency are reliable, matched appropriately to each other, and sufficient for the performance of the robot's individual tasks, human-robot teams engaged in consequential joint activity frequently encounter the potentially debilitating problem of opacity, meaning the inability for team members to maintain sufficient awareness of the state and actions of others to maintain effective team performance.*

The problem of *opacity* in robotics was highlighted recently by Stubbs [19] but had been previously identified as a general challenge more than two decades ago by Norman [20]. Norman cites numerous examples of opacity, most of which come from aviation where silent (opaque) automation has led to major accidents. This opacity often leads to what Woods calls "automation surprises" [21] that may result in catastrophe. An example is an autopilot that silently compensates for ice build-up on the airplane wings, while pilots remain unaware. Then, when the limits of control authority are reached and it can no longer compensate for extreme conditions, the automation simply turns off, forcing the pilots to try to recover from a very dangerous situation.

In the next section, we discuss the importance of interdependence in joint activity, and highlight opportunities for addressing it.

4   Interdependence

Coactive Design takes *interdependence* as the central organizing principle among people and agents working together in joint activity. Our sense of joint activity parallels that of Clark [22], who has described what happens in situations when one party does depends on what another party does (and vice-versa) over a sustained sequence of actions [23]. In such joint activity, we say that team members are "interdependent."

In his seminal 1967 book, James D. Thompson [24] recognized the importance of interdependence in organizational design. He also noted that there was a lack of understanding about interdependence. Similarly, we feel that understanding interdependence is critical to the design of human-agent systems. Understanding the nature of the interdependencies involved provides insight into the kinds of coordination that will be required among groups of humans and agents. Indeed, we assert that coordination mechanisms in skilled teams arise largely because of such interdependencies [25]. For this reason, understanding interdependence is an important requirement in designing agents that will be required to work as part of human-agent systems engaged in joint activity. Below, we introduce three new concepts that are important extensions to previous work on interdependence, particularly in the context of Coactive Design of human-agent systems.

4.1 Hard vs. Soft Interdependence

In their interdisciplinary study of coordination, Malone and Crowston [26] summarized prior work on coordination from many fields. Like us, they view coordination as required for managing dependencies (though we would say interdependencies—more on that below). They also characterize some of the most common types of dependencies, e.g., use of shared resources, producer/consumer relationships, simultaneity of processes, and task/subtask roles. These types of dependencies have received considerable attention in the literature. Unfortunately, they are insufficient to capture the necessary types of interdependence in human-agent systems.

In his research, Malone specifically was concerned with dependency as a matter of understanding how the results of one task enable the performance of another. However, in joint activity, we are not exclusively interested in the hard constraints that enable or prevent the possibility of an activity, but also in the idea of "soft interdependence," which includes a wide range of "helpful" things that a participant may do to facilitate team performance. The difference between strict dependence and soft interdependence is illustrated in the contrast between the two situations shown in figure 4—one in which a train car is completely dependent on the engine to pull it, and the other in which two friends provide mutual support of a helpful nature that is optional and opportunistic rather than strictly required. Indeed, our observations to date suggest that good teams can often be distinguished from great ones by how well they support requirements arising from soft interdependencies.

Dependence   Interdependence

vs.

Fig. 4. Dependence vs. Interdependence

Examples of such forms of interdependence often seen among effective human teams include progress appraisals [27] ("I'm running late"), warnings ("Watch your step"), helpful adjuncts ("Do you want me to pick up your prescription when I go by the drug store?"), and observations about relevant unexpected events ("It has started to rain"). They can also be physical actions, such as opening a door for someone who has their hands full. Though social science research on teamwork clearly demonstrates their importance, soft interdependencies have been relatively neglected by agent researchers.

Although some previous human-agent systems have succeeded in supporting various aspects of teamwork that relate to soft interdependence, they have often lacked convincing general principles relating to their success. We are hopeful that the concept of interdependence can eventually provide such principles. In the meantime, we have at least become convinced that human-agent systems defined solely in terms of traditional notions of hard dependence and autonomy limit the potential for effective teamwork, as the preliminary experimental results discussed in a later section seem to indicate.

4.2 Inter-activity Dependence vs. Intra-activity Interdependence

Thompson [24] suggested three types of interdependence: *pooled, sequential and reciprocal*. Pooled interdependence describes a situation in which each entity contributing (independently) a discrete part to the whole, with each in turn being supported by the whole. Sequential interdependence occurs when one entity directly depends on the output of another—to us this would be better described as simple *dependence*. Reciprocal interdependence is a bidirectional sequential interdependence or what we would call mutual dependence.

Thompson's three types of interdependence are described in terms of how the output or product of an entity affects other entities engaged in independent activities. They do not, however, adequately model the full range of interdependencies involved in joint activity. Thompson's types can be viewed as *inter*-activity dependence. For human-agent systems engaged in joint activity there remain other types that can be considered *intra*-activity interdependence. For example, progress appraisal (determining and sharing with others how one's task "is going") and notifying others of unexpected events [27] are usually performed *within* an ongoing activity. We will call this *supportive interdependence*. In future research, this type of interdependence will be further elaborated, and additional types of interdependence in joint activity will be identified.

4.3 Monitoring As a Requirement for Handling Supportive Interdependence

The problem of monitoring for conditions that relate directly to an assigned agent task, apart from the vagaries of sensing itself, presents a few challenges for agent developers. If, for example, an agent needs an elevator (resource dependence), the agent can monitor the elevator doors to see when they open. Alternatively, the agent could be notified of availability (sequential interdependence) through signaling (e.g. up arrow light turns on, audible bell, or an elevator operator telling you "going up").

However, handling supportive interdependence often requires groups of agents and people to monitor the ongoing situation, to "look out for each other," even when the aspects of the situation being monitored do not relate directly to a given individual's assigned tasks. For example, in order to provide back-up behavior to compensate for a teammate's frail self-sufficiency, other team members might decide to monitor the teammate to know when it is appropriate to provide assistance. Monitoring interdependence also highlights the reciprocal nature of the activity. Not only does the monitoring entity need to monitor, but the monitored entity may need to make certain aspects of its state and behavior observable.

5 Coactive Design

The fundamental principle of Coactive Design is that interdependence must shape autonomy. Certainly joint activity of any consequence requires a measure of autonomy (both self-sufficiency and self-directedness) of its participants. Without a minimum level of autonomy, an agent will simply be a burden on a team, as noted by Stubbs [19]. However, it can be shown that in some situations simply adding more autonomy can hinder rather than help team performance. The means by which that agent realizes the necessary capabilities of self-sufficiency and self-directedness must be guided by an understanding of the interdependence between team members in the types of joint activity in which it will be involved. This understanding of interdependence can be used to shape the design and implementation of the agent's autonomous capabilities, thus enabling appropriate interaction with people and other agents.

In contrast to autonomous systems designed to take humans out of the loop, we are specifically designing systems to address requirements that allow close and continuous interaction with people. As we try to design more sophisticated systems, we move along a maturity continuum [28] from dependence to independence to interdependence. The process is a continuum because at least some level of independence of agents through autonomous capabilities is a prerequisite for interdependence. However, independence is not the supreme achievement in human-human interaction [28], nor should it be in human-agent systems. Imagine a completely capable autonomous human possessing no skills for coactivity—how well would such a person fit in most everyday situations?

The dictionary gives three meanings [29] to the word "coactive": 1) Joint action, 2) An impelling or restraining force; a compulsion, 3) Ecology; any of the reciprocal actions or effects, such as symbiosis, that can occur in a community. These three meanings capture the essence of our approach and we translate these below to identify the three minimum requirements of a coactive system. Our contention is that for an agent to effectively engage in joint activity, it must at a minimum have:

1) *Awareness of interdependence in joint activity*
2) *Consideration for interdependence in joint activity*
3) *Capability to support interdependence in joint activity*

We are not suggesting that all team members must be fully aware of the entire scope of the activity, but they must be aware of the interdependence in the activity. Similarly, all team members do not need to be equally capable, but they do need to be capable of supporting their particular points of interdependence. We now address each requirement in more detail.

5.1 Awareness of Interdependence in Joint Activity

In human-machine systems like today's flight automation systems, there is a shared responsibility between the humans and machines, yet the automation is completely unaware of the human participants in the activity. Joint activity implies mutual engagement in a process extended in space and time [22, 30]. Previous work in human-agent interaction has focused largely on assigning or allocating tasks to agents that may know little about the overall goal of the activity or about other tasks on which its tasks may be interdependent. However, the increasing sophistication of human-machine systems depends on a mature understanding of the requirements of interdependence between team members in joint activity.

Consider the history of research and development in unmanned aerial vehicles (UAVs). The first goal in its development was a standard engineering challenge to make the UAV self-sufficient for some tasks (e.g., stable flight, waypoint following). As the capabilities and robustness increased, the focus shifted to the problem of self-directedness (e.g., what am I willing to let the UAV do autonomously). The future directions of UAVs indicate a another shift, as discussed in the Unmanned Systems Roadmap [31] which states that unmanned systems "will quickly evolve to the point where various classes of unmanned systems operate together in a cooperative and collaborative manner..." This suggests a need to focus on interdependence (e.g., how can I get multiple UAVs to work effectively as a team with their operators?). This pattern of development is a natural maturation process that applies to any form of sophisticated automation. While awareness of interdependence was not critical to the initial stages of UAV development, it becomes an essential factor in the realization of a system's full potential. We are no longer dealing with individual *autonomous* actions but with group *participatory* actions [22]. This is a departure from the previous approaches discussed in section 3, with the exception of Collaborative Control [5], which aimed to incorporate all parties into the activity through shared human-agent participation in perceptual and cognitive actions.

5.2 Consideration for Interdependence in Joint Activity

Awareness of interdependence is only helpful if requirements for interdependence are taken into account in the design of an agent's autonomous capabilities. As Clark states, "a person's processes may be very different in individual and joint actions even when they appear identical" [22]. One of Clark's favorite examples is playing the same piece of music as a musical solo versus a duet. Although the music is the same, the processes involved are very different. This is a drastic shift for many autonomous robots, most of which were designed to do things as independently as possible.

In addition to the processes involved being different, joint activity is inherently more constraining than independent activity. Joint activity may require participating parties to assume collective obligations [32] that come into play even when they are not currently "assigned" to an ongoing task. These obligations may require the performance of certain duties that facilitate good teamwork or they may limit our individual actions for the good of the whole. For example, we may be compelled to provide help in certain situations, while at the same time being prevented from hogging more than our share of limited resources. In joint activity, individual participants share an obligation to coordinate; sacrificing to a degree their individual autonomy in the service of progress toward group goals. These obligations should not be viewed as only a burden. While it is true they usually have a cost, they also provide an opportunity.

5.3 Capability to Support Interdependence in Joint Activity

While consideration is about the deliberative or cognitive processes, there is also an essential functional requirement. We have described self-sufficiency as the capability to take care of one's self. Here we are talking about the capability to support interdependence. This means the capability to assist another or be assisted by another. The coactive nature of joint activity means that there is a reciprocal requirement in order for interdependence to be supported, or to put it another way, there is the need for complementary capabilities of those engaged in a participatory action. For example, if I need to know your status, you must be able to provide status updates. If you can help me make navigation decisions, my navigation algorithm must allow for outside guidance. Simply stated, one can only give if the others can take and vice versa. The abilities required for good teamwork require reciprocal abilities from the participating team members.

6   Visualizing the New Perspective

So how does the coactive design perspective change the way we see the agent design problem? In section 3.6, we depicted the two senses of autonomy on two orthogonal axes representing an autonomy-centered plane of agent capabilities. Coactive Design adds a third orthogonal dimension of agent capability: support for interdependence (figure 5).

The *support for interdependence* axis characterizes an agent in terms of its capability to depend on others or be depended on by others in any of the dimensions of autonomy. This axis is specifically about the capability to be interdependent, *not* the need or requirement to *be* dependent which are captured by the other axes. Although we are showing a single set of axes for simplicity, The Coactive Design perspective considers all dimensions [8] as discussed in section 3.5. The take away message is not the support of any particular cognitive model, but instead the concept that there are many aspects to an agent as it performs in a joint activity. Just as Castelfranchi argued that autonomy can occur at any of these "levels" or dimensions, Coactive Design argues that the ability to be *interdependent* exists at each "level" or dimension as well.

As we look at the challenges faced by current autonomous systems from a Coactive Design perspective, we see not only the constraints imposed by interdependence in the system, but also as a tremendous opportunity. Instead of considering the activity an independent one we can think about it as a participatory [22] one. Both the human and the machine *are* typically engaged in the *same* activity. There may be domains where we would like a robot to go on its mission and simply return with a result, but most domains are not like this. We need the agent to have some self-sufficiency and self-directedness, but we remain interdependent as the participatory task unfolds.

Supporting this need provides an opportunity to address some of the current challenges. Figure 5 lists just a few such opportunities. For example, over-trusted robots can be supplemented with human assistance and opaque systems can provide feedback and transparency. In fact, many of the ten challenges [2] of automation, such as predictability and directability apply to this new dimension.

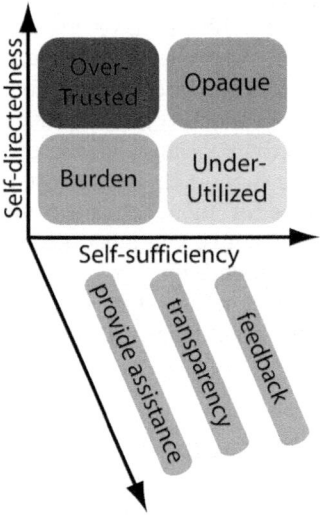

Fig. 5. Support for interdependence as an orthogonal dimension to autonomy and some opportunities this dimension offers

We can now map examples of prior work in autonomy onto this space (table 1). Section 3 describes how previous work was focused on self-sufficiency and self-directedness. Coactive Design presents the unique perspective of the *support for interdependence* dimension which is captured in the two rightmost columns of Table 1: the ability to depend on others and the ability to be depended on by others. The most

Table 1. Scope of concerns addressed by different approaches

Approach	Autonomy-Centered		Teamwork-Centered (Support for Interdependence)	
	Self-sufficiency	Self-directedness	Ability to depend on others	Ability to be depended on
Functional Allocation	✓			
Supervisory Control	✓			
Adjustable Autonomy	✓	✓		
Sliding Autonomy	✓	✓		
Adaptive Autonomy	✓	✓		
Flexible Autonomy	✓	✓		
Mixed Initiative Interaction	✓	✓		
Collaborative Control	✓	✓	✓	
Coactive Design	✓	✓	✓	✓

important innovation of the Collaborative Control [5] approach was in accommodating a role for the human in providing assistance to the robot at the perceptual and cognitive levels. In other words, the robot had the ability to depend on the human for assistance in perception. The key insight of Collaborative Control was that tasks may sometimes be done more effectively if performed jointly. Coactive Design extends this perspective by providing a complement of this type of interdependence, accommodating the possibility of machines assisting people.

7   Initial Experiments

We have begun a series of experiments that relate to the fundamental principle of Coactive Design. Our first domain, Blocks World for Teams (BW4T) [33] was designed to be as simple as possible.

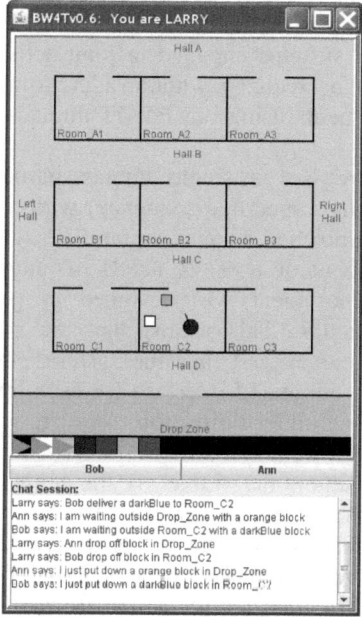

Fig. 6. BW4T game interface

Similar in spirit to the classic AI planning problem of Blocks World, the goal of BW4T is to "stack" colored blocks in a particular order. To keep things simple, the blocks are unstacked to begin with, so unstacking is not necessary. The most important variation on the problem we have made is to allow multiple players to work jointly on the same task. We control the observability between players and the environment. The degree of interdependence that is embedded in the task is represented by the complexity of color orderings within the goal stack. The task environment (figure 6) is composed of nine rooms containing a random assortment of blocks and a drop off area for the goal. The environment is hidden from each of the players, except for the contents of the current room. Teams may be composed of two or more players, each working toward the shared team goal. Players cannot see each other, so coordination must be explicit through the chat window. The task can be done without any coordination, but it is clear that coordination (i.e., the players managing their interdependence) can be beneficial.

7.1 Adding Autonomy without Addressing Interdependence

A common suggestion for how to improve human-agent systems is to increase the level of agent autonomy [34, 35]. This solution is also commonly proposed for future systems [31]. It is true that additional increments of agent autonomy *might*, in a given circumstance, reap benefits to team performance through reduction of human burden. *However, there is a point in problem complexity at which the benefits of autonomy may be outweighed by the increase in system opacity when interdependence issues are not adequately addressed.* The fundamental principle of Coactive Design is that, in sophisticated human-agent systems, the underlying interdependence of participants in joint activity is a critical factor in human-agent system design. Another way to state this is that in human-agent systems engaged in joint activity, the benefits of higher levels of autonomy cannot be realized without addressing interdependence through coordination. Initial experiments using our BW4T domain seem to provide evidence for this claim.

For this experiment, we had a single human participate in a joint activity (collecting colored blocks in a specified sequence) with a single agent player. Both the human and the agent controlled a robot avatar. The agent teammate was directed by the human (i.e. participant or user) at levels of autonomy that varied in each experimental condition. The agent was designed to perform reliably and with reasonably intelligent behavior. This means that the self-directedness is always sufficient for the self-sufficiency and thus the system cannot be over-trusted. This experiment also limited the command interface for each level to the highest possible command set, thus preventing under-utilization. As such, we were looking only at the burdensomeness and opacity of the system.

In our lowest level of autonomy, Level 1, the human made all decisions and initiated all actions for the agent player. In essence, the human was manually controlling two robot avatars. This corresponds to Sheridan's [17] lowest level of autonomy. For Level 2 we automated most actions of the agent. All decisions remained with the human. We expected this automation would be preferred because it was reducing burden without adding opacity. Level 3 had all of the autonomous actions from Level 2 and also added an autonomous decision (i.e., which room to search). This increased opacity in two ways. First, the human is no longer aware of all of the decisions because one of them has been automated. Second, the robot has to make the decision without the same information the human had available when making the decision for the agent. Level 4 added automation of the remaining decision, making the task "fully autonomous." This corresponds to Sheridan's [17] highest level of autonomy.

We expected the burden to reduce from Level 1 to Level 4 and this was confirmed by an exit survey of the participants. However, we expected that as more activity and decision-making were delegated to the agent there would be an increased opacity in the system, reflected in more difficulties in the participants' understanding of what was happening at a given moment. This was also confirmed by an exit survey of the participants. Finally, we expected this increase in opacity would result in reduced user acceptance and poorer team performance. The curves in figure 7a illustrate the general shape of results we expected, with the benefits of reduced human burden being eventually outweighed by the cost of opacity as autonomy increased beyond the inflection point.

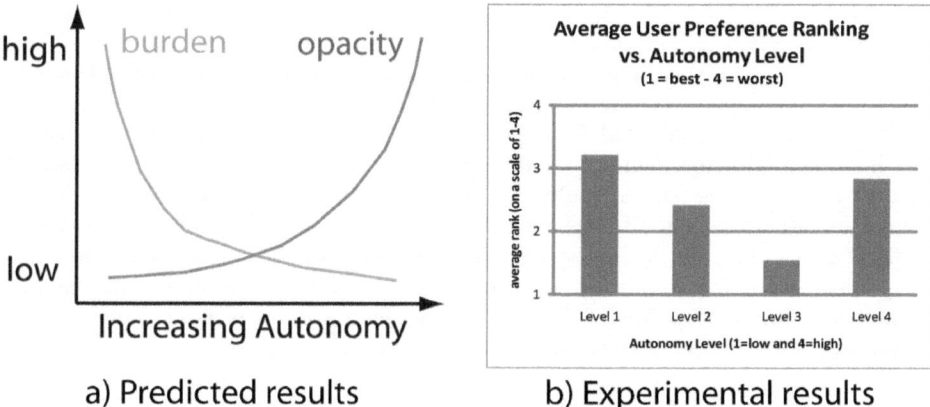

a) Predicted results   b) Experimental results

Fig. 7. a) Hypothetical graph suggesting that the benefits of reduced human burden would eventually by outweighed by the cost of opacity as autonomy increases; b) Experimental results of 24 participants displayed as Average user preference ranking vs. Autonomy level

We ran an initial set of 24 subjects through all four levels (repeated measures) using a Latin Square design. While space prohibits a complete description of these first results here, our results were consistent with our prediction. Figure 7b shows the average rank of all participants for each level of autonomy (rank of 1=best and 4=worst). The predicted inflection point is apparent. Performance, specifically time to complete task had a similar shape, but the variance prohibited achieving significance. While this is a single example in a single task domain, the results are consistent with the hypothesis that the benefits of higher levels of autonomy cannot be realized without addressing interdependence. If the general result holds as we continue our series of experiments, it will be a compelling demonstration of issues that cannot be addressed by autonomy-centered approaches, but can benefit from using the Coactive Design perspective.

7.2 Soft Interdependence Is a Key Factor in Performance

We have also run a pilot study of human-only teams to evaluate interdependence in the Block World for Teams domain. Although a simple domain, it demonstrates the complexity of coordination and interdependence even in the simplest domain. We ran twelve subjects in various team sizes (2, 3, 4, 5, 6, and 8). The subjects were allowed to talk openly to one another. As the activity became more interdependent (more complex ordering of the goal stack), we noted an increase in the number of coordination attempts, as would be expected. We also noted some interesting aspects of the communication. Although only two basic tasks are involved, we observed a wide variety of communications. Of particular interest were the large number of communications that were about *soft interdependencies* and monitoring issues that were related to them. An example of a soft interdependency is the exchange of world state information. Since players could only see the status of their current room, they would exchange information about the location of specific colors. Although the task could clearly be completed without this communication, the importance of this soft interdependence is demonstrated by the frequency of its use. An example of monitoring in support of interdependence issues was when players provided or requested an update as a colored block was picked up. The frequency of both progress updates and world state updates are examples of the importance of addressing *supportive interdependence* in human-agent systems for joint activity. These types of exchanges typically accounted for approximately 60% of the overall communication and increased with the degree of interdependence required for a given problem. A final observation was that not only the amount of communication changed with the degree of interdependence in the task, but the pattern of communication varied as well. For example, during tasks with low interdependence, world state and task assignment were the dominant communications. As interdependence in the task (complexity in the ordering of the goal stack) increased, they both diminished in importance and progress updates became dominant.

8   Discussion

The target for research in Coactive Design is not to support the development of current teleoperated systems or systems struggling with basic self-sufficiency. We are specifically addressing what a human-agent system would look like if it were to fill the more challenging roles of the future. The envisioned roles, if properly performed, have a greater level of interdependence that cannot be addressed solely by adjusting who is in control or who is assigned what task—and necessitate a focus on the coactivity. In contrast to autonomous systems designed to take humans out of the loop, we are specifically addressing the requirements for close and continuous interaction with people. The fundamental principle of Coactive Design provides a new perspective for designers of human-agent systems and gives some initial high-level guidance about what considerations are important. We plan to extend and expand this initial fundamental principle in future work.

In our first experiment, we have tried to demonstrate the issues with taking an autonomy-centered approach. By identifying the interdependence in the system, we can understand that there is a potential inflection point for team effectiveness as autonomy increases. Awareness of this effect and its cause can help designers address the interdependence and improve acceptance and performance, thereby yielding the full potential from autonomous capabilities. We plan to demonstrate this in the future.

We deliberately used a single human and single agent in our first experiment to show that even in the simplest case, our claim is still valid. We expect the effects to be more dramatic in larger teams and teams with higher levels of interdependence. Our demonstration used simple task interdependence, but there are other sources of interdependence including the environment, the team structure, and the team member capabilities. Future work will include developing a better understanding of the different types of interdependence.

We also used perfect autonomy for our experiment to show that even under ideal conditions, our claim is still valid. In real world systems, perfect autonomy will continue to be an elusive goal. This underlying truth necessitates human involvement at some level and accentuates the importance of teamwork. Agent frailties means one will have unexpected events (failures). One cannot overcome failed autonomy with autonomy, but one can possibly do so with teamwork (e.g., Fong's collaborative control [5]). Additionally, Christofferson and Woods [36] describe the "substitution myth": the erroneous notion that automation activities simply can be substituted for human activities without otherwise affecting the operation of the system. Even if frailty were not an issue, the "substitution myth" reminds us that autonomy is not removing something, but merely changing the nature of it. Humans cannot simply offload tasks to the robots without incurring some coordination penalty. This is not a problem as long as we keep in mind that autonomy is not an end in itself, but rather a means to supporting productive interaction [18]. Coactive Design reminds us that interdependence can provide opportunities to counteract these costs.

As agents move toward greater and greater autonomy, several researchers have expressed concerns. Norman states that "the danger [of intelligent agents] comes when agents start wresting away control, doing things behind your back, making decisions on your behalf, taking actions and, in general, taking over [37]." Simply deciding who is doing what is insufficient, because the human will always need to understand a certain amount of the activity. Additionally, humans are typically the desired beneficiaries of the fruits of the robot labor. We are the reason for the system and will always want access to the system. Not only do we want access to understand the system, but we also want to have input to affect it. To paraphrase Kidd [38], it is not merely that human skill is required, but also that human involvement is desired. That involvement means the human-agent system is interdependent.

9 Summary

We have introduced *Coactive Design* as a new approach to address the increasingly sophisticated roles for people and agents in mixed human-agent systems. The fundamental principle of Coactive Design recognizes that the underlying *interdependence* of participants in joint activity is a critical factor in the design of human-agent systems. In order to enable appropriate interaction, an understanding of the potential interdependencies among groups of humans and agents working together in a given situation should be used to shape the way agent architectures and individual agent capabilities for autonomy are designed. We no longer look at the primary problem of the research community as simply trying to make agents more independent through their autonomy. Rather, in addition, we strive to make them more capable of sophisticated interdependent joint activity with people.

References

1. Bradshaw, J.M., Feltovich, P., Johnson, M.: Human-Agent Interaction. In: Boy, G. (ed.) Handbook of Human-Machine Interaction. Ashgate (2011) (in press)
2. Klein, G., Woods, D.D., Bradshaw, J.M., Hoffman, R., Feltovich, P.: Ten challenges for making automation a "team player" in joint human-agent activity. IEEE Intelligent Systems 19(6), 91–95 (2004)

3. Allen, J.E., Guinn, C.I., Horvtz, E.: Mixed-Initiative Interaction. IEEE Intelligent Systems 14(5), 14–23 (1999)
4. Kortenkamp, D.: Designing an Architecture for Adjustably Autonomous Robot Teams. Revised Papers from the PRICAI, Workshop Reader, Four Workshops held at PRICAI 2000, on Advances in Artificial Intelligence. Springer, Heidelberg (2000)
5. Fong, T.W.: Collaborative Control: A Robot-Centric Model for Vehicle Teleoperation. Robotics Institute, Carnegie Mellon University, Pittsburgh, PA (2001)
6. Brookshire, J., Singh, S., Simmons, R.: Preliminary Results in Sliding Autonomy for Coordinated Teams. In: Proceedings of The 2004 Spring Symposium Series (2004)
7. Bradshaw, J.M., Acquisti, A., Allen, J., Breedy, M.R., Bunch, L., Chambers, N., Feltovich, P., Galescu, L., Goodrich, M.A., Jeffers, R., Johnson, M., Jung, H., Lott, J., Olsen Jr., D.R., Sierhuis, M., Suri, N., Taysom, W., Tonti, G., Uszok, A.: Teamwork-centered autonomy for extended human-agent interaction in space applications. Presented at the AAAI 2004 Spring Symposium, March 22-24. Stanford University, CA (2004)
8. Bradshaw, J.M., Feltovich, P., Jung, H., Kulkarni, S., Taysom, W., Uszok, A.: Dimensions of adjustable autonomy and mixed-initiative interaction. In: Nickles, M., Rovatsos, M., Weiss, G. (eds.) AUTONOMY 2003. LNCS (LNAI), vol. 2969, pp. 17–39. Springer, Heidelberg (2004)
9. Castelfranchi, C.: Founding Agents "Autonomy" on Dependence Theory. In: ECAI 2000, pp. 353–357 (2000)
10. Fitts, P.M.: Human engineering for an effective air-navigation and traffic-control system, p. 84, xii. National Research Council, Division of Anthropology and Psychology, Committee on Aviation Psychology, Washington (1951)
11. Sheridan, T.B.: Telerobotics, automation, and human supervisory control, p. 393, xx. MIT Press, Cambridge (1992)
12. Dorais, G., Kortenkamp, D.: Designing Human-Centered Autonomous Agents. Revised Papers from the PRICAI 2000, Workshop Reader, Four Workshops held at PRICAI 2000, on Advances in Artificial Intelligence. Springer, Heidelberg (2000)
13. Dias, M.B., Kannan, B., Browning, B., Jones, E., Argall, B., Dias, M.F., Zinck, M.B., Veloso, M.M., Stentz, A.T.: Sliding Autonomy for Peer-To-Peer Human-Robot Teams. Robotics Institute, Pittsburgh (2008); Myers, K.L., Morley, D.N.: Directing Agent Communities: An Initial Framework. In: Proceedings of the IJCAI Workshop on Autonomy, Delegation, and Control: Interacting with Autonomous Agents, Seattle, WA (2001)
14. Myers, K.L., Morley, D.N.: Human directability of agents. In: Proceedings of the 1st International Conference on Knowledge Capture. ACM, Victoria (2001)
15. Murphy, R., Casper, J., Micire, M., Hyams, J.: Mixed-initiative Control of Multiple Heterogeneous Robots for USAR (2000)
16. Yanco, H.A., Drury, J.L.: A Taxonomy for Human-Robot Interaction. In: AAAI Fall Symposium on Human-Robot Interaction (2002)
17. Parasuraman, R., Sheridan, T., Wickens, C.: A model for types and levels of human interaction with automation. IEEE Transactions on Systems, Man and Cybernetics, Part A 30(3), 286–297 (2000)
18. Goodrich, M.A., Schultz, A.C.: Human-robot interaction: a survey. Found. Trends Hum.-Comput. Interact. 1(3), 203–275 (2007)
19. Stubbs, K., Hinds, P., Wettergreen, D.: Autonomy and common ground in human-robot interaction: A field study. IEEE Intelligent Systems (Special Issue on Interacting with Autonomy), 42–50 (2007)

20. Norman, D.A.: The "problem" of automation: Inappropriate feedback and interaction, not "over-automation". In: Broadbent, D.E., Baddeley, A., Reason, J.T. (eds.) Human Factors in Hazardous Situations, pp. 585–593. Oxford University Press, Oxford (1990)
21. Woods, D.D., Sarter, N.B.: Automation Surprises. In: Salvendy, G. (ed.) Handbook of Human Factors & Ergonomics. Wiley, Chichester (1997)
22. Clark, H.H.: Using language, p. 432, xi. Cambridge University Press, Cambridge (1996)
23. Klein, G., Feltovich, P.J., Bradshaw, J.M., Woods, D.D.: Common Ground and Coordination in Joint Activity. In: William, K.R.B., Rouse, B. (eds.) Organizational Simulation, pp. 139–184 (2005)
24. Thompson, J.D.: Organizations in action; social science bases of administrative theory, p. 192, xi. McGraw-Hill, New York (1967)
25. Feltovich, P.J., Bradshaw, J.M., Clancey, W.J., Johnson, M.: Toward an Ontology of Regulation: Socially-Based Support for Coordination in Human and Machine Joint Activity. In: O'Hare, G.M.P., Ricci, A., O'Grady, M.J., Dikenelli, O. (eds.) ESAW 2006. LNCS (LNAI), vol. 4457, pp. 175–192. Springer, Heidelberg (2007)
26. Malone, T.W., Crowston, K.: The interdisciplinary study of coordination. ACM Comput. Surv. 26(1), 87–119 (1994)
27. Feltovich, P.J., Bradshaw, J.M., Clancey, W.J., Johnson, M., Bunch, L.: Progress Appraisal as a Challenging Element of Coordination in Human and Machine Joint Activity. In: Artikis, A., O'Hare, G.M.P., Stathis, K., Vouros, G.A. (eds.) ESAW 2007. LNCS (LNAI), vol. 4995, pp. 124–141. Springer, Heidelberg (2008)
28. Covey, S.R.: The 7 Habits of Highly Effective People. Free Press, New York (1989)
29. coaction, http://dictionary.reference.com/browse/coactive
30. Sierhuis, M.: "It's not just goals all the way down" – "It's activities all the way down". In: O'Hare, G.M.P., Ricci, A., O'Grady, M.J., Dikenelli, O. (eds.) ESAW 2006. LNCS (LNAI), vol. 4457, pp. 1–24. Springer, Heidelberg (2007)
31. Office of the Secretary of Defense, Unmanned Systems Roadmap (2007-2032)
32. van Diggelen, J., Bradshaw, J.M., Johnson, M., Uszok, A., Feltovich, P.: Implementing collective oblications in human-agent teams using KAoS policies. In: Proceedings of Workshop on Coordination, Organization, Institutions and Norms (COIN), IEEE/ACM Conference on Autonomous Agents and Multi-Agent Systems, Budapest, Hungary, May 12 (2009)
33. Johnson, M., Jonker, C., van Riemsdijk, B., Feltovich, P.J., Bradshaw, J.M.: Joint Activity Testbed: Blocks World for Teams (BW4T). In: Aldewereld, H., Dignum, V., Picard, G. (eds.) ESAW 2009. LNCS, vol. 5881, pp. 254–256. Springer, Heidelberg (2009)
34. Bleicher, A.: The Gulf Spill's Lessons for Robotics. In: IEEE spectrum special report (2010)
35. Jean, G.V.: Duty Aboard the Littoral Combat Ship: Grueling but Manageable in National Defense (2010)
36. Christoffersen, K., Woods, D.D.: How to Make Automated Systems Team Players (2002)
37. Norman, D.A.: The invisible computer: why good products can fail, the personal computer is so complex, and information appliances are the solution, p. 302, xii. MIT Press, Cambridge (1998)
38. Kidd, P.T.: Design of human-centered robotic systems. In: Rahimi, M., Karwowski, W. (eds.) Human-Robot Interaction, pp. 225–241. Taylor & Francis, Abington (1992)

A Probabilistic Mechanism for Agent Discovery and Pairing Using Domain-Specific Data

Dimitris Traskas[1], Julian Padget[2], and John Tansley[1]

[1] CACI Ltd, Andover, UK
{dtraskas,jtansley}@caci.co.uk
[2] Department of Computer Science,
University of Bath, Claverton Down, Bath, UK
jap@cs.bath.ac.uk

Abstract. Agent discovery and pairing is a core process for many multi-agent applications and enables the coordination of agents in order to contribute to the achievement of organisational-level objectives. Previous studies in peer-to-peer and sensor networks have shown the efficiency of probabilistic algorithms in object or resource discovery. In this paper we maintain confidence in such mechanisms and extend the work for the purpose of agent discovery for useful pairs that eventually coordinate to enhance their collective performance. The key difference in our mechanism is the use of domain-specific data that allows the discovery of relevant, useful agents while maintaining reduced communication costs. Agents employ a Bayesian inference model to control an otherwise random search, such that at each step a decision procedure determines whether it is worth searching further. In this way it attempts to capture something akin to the human disposition to give up after trying a certain number of alternatives and take the best offer seen. We benchmark the approach against exhaustive search (to establish an upper bound on costs), random and tabu—all of which it outperforms—and against an independent industrial standard simulator—which it also outperforms. We demonstrate using synthetic data—for the purpose of exploring the resilience of the approaches to extreme workloads—and empirical data, the effectiveness of a system that can identify "good enough" solutions to satisfy holistic organisational service level objectives.

1 Introduction

Agent discovery and pairing in a decentralised multi-agent environment that consists of thousands of agents with different roles and skills and interconnected in various topologies needs to be scalable, efficient, robust and flexible enough to adapt both to changes in requirements and changes in the environment. A number of techniques have been proposed to tackle these challenges; our aim is to demonstrate a simple, effective mechanism that does not require centralised control and maintains reduced communication overheads.

Decentralised multi-agent architectures typically consist of self-organising and co-ordinating agents that do not have any dependencies on a global control system. Information becomes available to agents locally through some form of sensing or messaging and is used to meet the objectives and to satisfy the constraints of the organisation in

M. De Vos et al. (Eds.): COIN 2010 International Workshops, LNAI 6541, pp. 192–209, 2011.

which the agents participate. Such environments are often highly dynamic and agents can join or leave it rapidly for a variety of reasons such as host failure or migration to a different node in the network. They also need to discover and communicate with other agents in order to exploit services that are being made available. The domain of peer to peer networking has inspired us with useful ideas that have been applied to the development of service discovery algorithms [1] [14]. In general service discovery is achieved using pull or push protocols or a combination of the two over structured or unstructured networks. Push-based protocols require the advertisement of available services thus creating unnecessary overhead when demand is low. On the other hand a pull-based approach has the disadvantage of a search over the network but benefits from the elimination of advertisement messages.

In this study we focus on unstructured networks with a pull-based approach that fully utilises information gathered *during* the search. Observations made by the agent while hopping can be used to update or to infer the probability that a subsequent hop will result in reaching a better-suited agent with which to interact. An essential element of this mechanism is an organisational model that exploits available domain-specific data. We use this data to tag agents in the network during an initial bootstrapping and introduction process and create clusters of agents with similar profiles. The result is a form of overlay network that provides useful information to any agent starting a search operation.

A case study from the business domain, specifically the call centre sector, is used to evaluate the technique and generate quantifiable outcomes. The subject of our case-study is the call allocation process—that is how to select the appropriate handler for a call, being essentially a kind of resource discovery problem. Synthetic and empirical data-sets allow us to make useful comparisons with a commercial simulator and with the metrics generated by a real world call centre, while at the same time providing supporting evidence for general results for low-cost resource discovery.

The remainder of this paper is laid out as follows: Section 2 discusses other work related with agent discovery and pairing and Section 3 provides the motivation for our work. In Section 4, we describe the proposed system architecture in detail and in Section 5, we present the case study that we used to validate our theory. In Section 6, we discuss our findings and finally end this paper with our conclusions and future vision in Section 7.

2 Related Work

Service discovery mechanisms are necessarily closely related to the type of networks used. For example unstructured systems characterised by a loose architecture where agent-peers can join, leave or fail at any point are much more resilient, flexible and scalable but have high communication costs during a random search. Our work focuses on such networks and attempts to improve the random search process by employing a probabilistic model. In contrast structured systems hold information about services fixed on certain nodes and use techniques such as distributed hash tables (DHT) [2] for service discovery but suffer from scalability issues.

Common mechanisms encountered in the service discovery literature are agent matchmaking, gossip-based protocols and probabilistic search. Agent matchmaking [22] can be classified into:

- centralised using market bidding mechanisms [21] [20] [18].
- centralised but using a middle agent or broker [12] [6].
- and fully decentralised where agents use local information to form clusters and randomly find useful pairs [15].

The main disadvantages of centralised mechanisms when applied to large scale systems are scalability, robustness and flexible dynamic behaviour. A decentralised matchmaker design is typically preferable and can potentially benefit from a probabilistic approach, as we will shortly demonstrate.

Gossip-based mechanisms are based on probabilistic flooding where an agent sends messages to a certain percentage of its neighbours that it believes they are available [16] [5]. Part of the gossiping approach is the random search of agents which we believe can be improved in a specific problem domain by employing a probabilistic model that utilises any data available.

Probabilistic techniques that have been previously investigated within the context of resource discovery in sensor networks [17] [3] or object searching in peer-to-peer networks [19] [8] seem to offer some of the characteristics we seek. The models employed often use network level information and observations from previous searches to inform the discovery process. The key difference with our work is the use of domain-specific data that allows the discovery of relevant, useful agents while maintaining reduced communication costs. Our objective is to allow agents to discover the best pair possible in order to coordinate towards optimal collective performance. Agent discovery in an application context requires specific problem knowledge which is why we have to ground our experiments in a particular domain in order to demonstrate its effect.

3   Background and Motivation

The past few decades have seen rising consumer demands for more competitive products and services and have increased the need for a more flexible and adaptive business operating model. For many businesses, existing software systems fail to adapt and evolve rapidly while the complexity of their management is becoming a limiting factor in further growth. In an effort to solve these problems business managers choose the reductionist approach; essentially reducing the number of products and services offered or even the size of their customer base under the mantra of focusing on "core business". The desired outcome of this approach is to simplify the processes and systems in place—however reduced performance and profits can also result.

One of the aims of this work is to use the multi-agent paradigm to tackle these challenges and develop software solutions that can operate in highly dynamic environments. Our long term goal is the development of business agent societies which can be characterised by the following:

- closed, scalable and heterogeneous.
- fully decentralised and autonomous.

– distributed across different geographical locations and areas of the business.
– constrained by business rules and policies.

A typical model consists of service providers and service consumers in a closed system where agents are controlled and monitored by the business and where information exchanged can only be true or correct. Within this system the consumer will attempt to locate the provider without having any prior knowledge of location or global system state. Consumers are self-interested and need to discover and pair with a suitable provider so that they can get optimum returns from their specific utility function. The society can be seen as a large search space that contains a great number of provider-consumer pair combinations but with only a few satisfying business constraints and delivering optimum performance. From this perspective the problem is that of optimisation: essentially, how to find the best pair possible with the minimum number of messages. We believe that "best" is not always necessary and for many application domains a "good enough" solution can be adequate as long as the response is timely and overheads are low.

4   System Architecture

This section describes the system architecture for the model used in this study. In the absence of a central control regime we have an heterogeneous society of agents that are fully connected with each other. Agents can join and leave the society over time without significantly affecting processes in place or other interactions. In general the model consists of service consumers and service providers however this does not necessarily imply that a single agent cannot be both or either at different times. Depending on the problem domain agents could potentially change role in response to a changing environment. This dual nature of agents is not part of our investigation but it is something we intend to explore in future work. In a provider-consumer society, we are always going to have consumers searching the network for providers which will result in a successful pairing that enables the completion of an agent's individual goals. Nevertheless this one-sided view might limit the effectiveness of the discovery algorithm and there is no reason that a provider to consumer search would not also work.

One of the fundamental elements of our design is the use of agent-local memory to store useful information such as member addresses, cluster formations, skill distribution or agent availability. Each agent has two types of memory, long term and short term that are used for different purposes. Long term memory is simply a kind of cache with all the unique identifiers of agents keyed by type or skill and used for searching relevant areas of the network. New or withdrawn members are respectively added or removed from this list over time. Short term memory is used during the discovery process to store the recently visited members and cleared when the search terminates. Elements in the short-term memory are ranked by fitness where fitness can be defined as the result of a utility function that relates a given pair of agents. An internal mechanism ensures that the two types of memory are synchronised and updated at the same time when a message arrives with agent membership information.

The model uses a form of a semantic overlay network of skill-based clusters that are updated every time a new agent joins. We use a tagging mechanism like that proposed by Holland [11] where agents are tagged based on their type and grouped in clusters. The clusters allow agents to limit their search and target specific areas of the network without wasting time or messages. There is no limitation to the number of clusters an agent can belong to, since cluster membership depends solely on the number of services that an agent can provide.

There are certain key processes that do not change from one problem domain to another and which we explain in detail below. The messages used in the model can be seen next to each process. Messages have four fields: the sender, the recipient, the subject, and any useful data.

A. Introduction Process [PING]

A new provider or consumer joining the society follows an introduction procedure. On initialisation it will receive a list of all members of the society and start sending *Ping* messages in random order to all other agents in an exhaustive manner; in essence announcing its existence. A list of all members can be retrieved using an address table distributed across a number of host machines. The messages sent contain information that describe the sender and is used by the recipients to classify the new agent. Existing members will examine the information received – specific to a problem domain – and decide if the new agent would be useful to store in local memory or not. Information such as the type of an agent or availability are some examples. If the type of a new member indicates a useful future pairing – relevance of service offered and required – then its unique identifier and all related information get stored in local memory, otherwise it is discarded. For example a service provider who does not have the required skills to provide a service at this current time to a customer agent would not be added in local memory. This process is similar to an agent naming service however we wish to maintain the lack of any dependencies on centralised control systems and structures. It is required to work in a very dynamic environment where agents join and leave all the time. Incorrect information about the clusters does not stop the system operating however it does have an impact on performance because of the limited *visibility* of the agents.

B. Withdrawal Process [WITHDRAWAL]

A consumer agent withdraws from the network when it has accomplished its tasks and a provider when it is time for a break or the end of the working shift. In the case of host migration the agent will have to inform the other agents with an alternative message and thus separate the two distinct events. The withdrawal process is simple and requires a minimal message that is sent to cluster members only. This message does not obstruct or halt any current activity but only updates local memories so that the cluster information within each agent is updated. If a host fails then it is obvious that one or more agents will suddenly disconnect and, as a result, the necessary updates will not be performed. This will only result in temporary delays in the discovery process but under any circumstances stop currently active processes. Communication delays due to host failure or agent failure/migration can also be captured through exception handling mechanisms.

C. Discovery Process [QUERY / QUERYHIT / QUERYREJECT]

The specific requirements of a particular problem domain will ultimately dictate how agents behave. When an agent – either consumer or provider – decides to search the skill clusters for candidate pairs it first checks long term memory. As previously mentioned, skill clusters are stored in long term memory and provide the addresses of any connected agent. Specific tasks require specific skills and thus a search on a single cluster. From a list of potential addresses in the cluster one is picked randomly and a *Query* message sent to it. The message might contain data and that again depends on the specific problem. For every *Query* message a hop counter is incremented to track the number of messages sent. The hop counter is compared to the number of agents that are of interest for a future pairing and the process ultimately stops once that number is reached. There can only be two outcomes from this message:

- *QueryHit*: The *Query* has been successful and the recipient replies to the sender with (domain-specific) information such as waiting time or level of importance. At that point any information sent along with the agent address are stored in short term memory and supplied to the probabilistic decision engine. The result of the decision engine is the probability that a subsequent *Query* will return a better result. If that probability is very low then the agent will stop the search and select the highest ranking agent from short term memory for an *Offer*. If the probability is high then the search will continue.
- *QueryReject*: If the recipient has already formed a pair with someone else or is ready to withdraw from the network then it will send a *QueryReject* reply. On receipt of the reply the originator of this sequence of events will remove the address from short term memory and check if there is anyone else in the list in order to continue the search.

D. Pairing Process [OFFER / ACCEPT / REJECT]

When the decision engine returns with a small probability that the next hop will produce a better pair the search process is stopped and an *Offer* message is sent to the highest ranking agent. The recipient will either *Accept* that offer or *Reject* it.

4.1 Probabilistic Discovery and Pairing

In the decision engine described previously, each agent continuously updates its belief about the state of the world around it, using the messages it receives from other agents. This set of beliefs is then used by each agent when searching for a good pair, in order to estimate whether it is worth continuing the search, or whether further searching is unlikely to produce a better match. This model enables the agent to make an informed choice, by estimating whether the next hop is likely to provide a more suitable pair than the best one it has found so far. The updating of local beliefs is based on a Bayesian framework [4]. Each agent starts off with a prior belief about the state of the system around it which is currently the same for all agents of a given type but as all calculations are purely local, these could easily be made to change from agent to agent. This prior belief is then updated by the agent based on the messages it receives, to give a posterior distribution on the state of the relevant part of the system. As the agent receives more and more information, its probabilistic model reflects the world around it more and more accurately. This updating of prior (before the data) to posterior (after the data) beliefs occurs in a very specific way, according to Bayes' rule:

$$P(H \mid D) = \frac{P(D \mid H)P(H)}{P(D)}$$

where D is the observed data and H is the particular hypothesis being tested by the agent. The prior probability P(H) represents the agent's prior belief in the hypothesis before seeing any data. The model evidence P(D |H) reflects how well a particular hypothesis predicts the data, and the evidence P(D) provides normalisation over all hypotheses. We can see that if we have two hypotheses with equal priors, the hypothesis that predicts the data more accurately will end up with the highest posterior probability, as we would expect.

Suppose that an agent society has one provider and a number of consumers. We also assume that the provider is ready to serve a consumer, and wants to serve the most suitable of the available consumers. Rather than perform an exhaustive search by sending and receiving messages to all consumers, this provider can use its model of the distribution of consumer types to poll a subset of consumers. This provider's initial estimate of the distribution of consumer types is necessarily imprecise, but as more consumers are polled, the accuracy of this estimate improves. This estimate combined with the knowledge of the best consumer seen so far, enables the provider to stop any further hops once it believes, that the probability of the next hop returning a better match than the best one seen so far is sufficiently low. Two main assumptions are required in order to specify this probabilistic inference process fully. The first is the agent's prior belief in the state of the system. This should be as broad a prior as possible if the state of the system can be variable, but may be as informative as desired if the system is more static, and a reasonable guess can be made as to its state without polling many consumers. In this implementation each agent resets its belief each time it goes through a new process of pair discovery. However in a more static environment agents could quite easily retain some information from any previous search and incorporate this into the prior for the next search. The second parameter required is the probability threshold at which each agent stops performing any further hops, and stays with the best pairing found up to that point. This threshold is defined initially at a low level and adjusted accordingly after experimentation with the specific problem. After each hop the agent evaluates the probability that the next hop will return a better solution than the best it has encountered so far. If this probability falls below the threshold searching is terminated and the best solution encountered is selected.

In order to use the probabilistic engine across different domains it is necessary to mine useful information from available data during an initial modelling exercise. Domain knowledge, not necessarily expert, can be exploited in order to make useful observations from the data, which in turn can be used to calculate the probability that a hypothesis may be true. For example across many domains one could use the type of service required and estimate a distribution of consumers waiting in a queue. The question that arises is if this modelling process could become part of the intelligence of an agent however for this study we rely on the modeller.

4.2   Random and Tabu Mechanisms

Given the probabilistic orientation of our research, we have also investigated two other approaches that have produced interesting outcomes. We have experimented with a completely random discovery process where the agent randomly hops from one node to another and decides to stop at random also. Every agent has a given probability of stopping the search after each hop—this is a hypergeometric distribution of the number of hops. When the search is complete short term memory is used to rank the visited agents and make an offer in exactly the same way as with the probabilistic approach. Although there is complete lack of control in the system, experiments conducted with our case study demonstrate interesting results that we briefly discuss in a later section. The other obvious technique is tabu pairing where the agent decides to pair with the first potential candidate. A single *Offer* message is sent and the candidate added in short term memory. If a rejection is received the next candidate will be contacted until the list is exhausted. Our aim with these mechanisms is to explore fully the potential of our design and produce comparisons with the Bayesian model that demonstrate its effectiveness.

5   Call Centre Case Study

Call centres are fundamental to the operation of numerous large organisations, emergency and government agencies and all types of customer service providers [9]. Call centre management and critical aspects of it such as the call routing process which we focus on in this paper, are becoming increasingly complicated for the same reasons mentioned in our motivation section. The term 'call-routing' is probably most commonly associated with telecommunications networks, where the task is to avoid hotspot creation, maximise throughput and minimise latency. However call-routing in call centres is a somewhat different problem that is closer to distributed resource discovery and allocation. Conventional implementations of call-routing in call centres are tightly controlled, centralised systems of asynchronous components, where all the decision-making is embedded in a single element—the call router—that communicates with the call-handlers (typically known as agents in the call-centre literature: here we use the term "handler" to alleviate confusion with the term (software) agent).

It is important to note that our aim with this first study is not necessarily to improve the performance of any of the current call routing algorithms but to demonstrate that a multi-agent system can be adopted effectively in this sector. One of the potential benefits of a decentralised architecture based on agents which can deliver similar performance with current solutions is reduced telephony and maintenance costs. Instead of using a central server that operates in a similar manner with a centralised matchmaker, agents spawned by the customers on mobile or fixed lines would locate the call handlers directly by employing a probabilistic discovery protocol over a peer to peer network. The same base technology could offer improved simulation capabilities and the evaluation of alternative operation models or allow the interconnection of other areas of the business with the call centre.

5.1   A Multi-Agent Approach to Call Routing

During the call routing process a call arrives from the telecommunications network and is ready for allocation by the 'Automatic Call Distributor' (ACD). The ACD processes a set of business rules which determine which call has the highest priority such as the call type or skill, as it is usually referred to in this sector. Another parameter used is handler availability, the resources waiting the longest without work will be at the top of the allocation list excluding those on breaks. A new call is inserted into a queue of calls that are ordered by waiting time and skill priority and when a new resource becomes available the ACD gets notified and begins the allocation process. Customers who wait too long terminate their link with the ACD and their call gets registered as abandoned and removed from the queue. We address the call routing process from a MAS perspective and adopt agents in representing the key elements of it. We have developed a conceptual model of the call centre for our simulations which consists of: (i) the *Call Centre*, (ii) the *Handlers*, (iii) the *Calls* which contain customer information, skill required and time of arrival, (iv) the *Skills* which are the different types of call a handler can process, (v) and finally the *Skill Groups* which are groups of skills call handlers can have; an insurance skill group may consist of motor, home and pet insurance.

For the call allocation process we further developed a multi-agent model based on the concepts described above and where agent *Handlers* use a probabilistic mechanism to discover *Call* agents that have been waiting the longest and have the highest skill priority. A significant difference between our model and the standard industry algorithm, is the allocation of calls to *any* handler irrespective of whether they are the longest waiting. For each customer to be serviced, we spawn a *Call* agent. Any useful information such as time of arrival in the system, type of service required or customer details are contained within the *Call*—this is (some of) the domain-specific data. For simulation purposes we model the abandonment behaviour of customers using a patience-time model. We have implemented this model based on the exponential distribution [13], that is recognised as appropriate for this kind of simulation delay. For each call that joins the network we generate randomised abandonment times using the formula:

$$\text{Time in seconds} = (\log(1 - r) - \sigma)$$

where r is a random number between 0 and 1 and σ is the average patience time. The same model is considered suitable to generate the handling times of agent handlers. With *Calls* being defined as agents in the system, queueing is resolved and managed by the *Call* itself. The core processes of the *Handler* and *Call* are explained below.

5.2   Handler Agent

- *Initialise:* The agent is initialised with shift information and a list of all members of the network.
- *Ping:* The agent sends *Ping* messages to everyone as part of the introduction process. As service providers and consumers can be effectively both we allow all agents to follow this procedure although the information is not used at this stage.
- *Hop:* The agent checks current availability using local time and shift information. If there is no break, then it checks the list of available *Calls* in skill clusters that can be serviced. From the list of *Calls* and skill clusters one is randomly selected and a *Query* message sent and the short term memory is initialised.
- *Query Hit/Query Reject:* If the recipient *Call* is available and has not abandoned or received an offer already it replies with either a *QueryHit* message that contains

the waiting time, or a *QueryReject*. On a *QueryHit* reply the *Handler* adds the *Call* in short term memory and uses the Bayesian inference engine to decide if a further hop is required. If the probability is low then the discovery process ends and an *Offer* message sent to the *Call* that has been waiting the longest and has the highest skill priority. Otherwise the search continues until the list of *Calls* is depleted or the probability of a better pair gets lower than the system defined threshold.

- *On Accept:* If the recipient *Call* is still active and ready for handling it replies with an *Accept* message. The reply triggers the handling process which requires the *Handler* to make a direct connection with the customer and start providing a service.
- *Call Disconnect:* If a *Call* disconnects a *CallDisconnect* message is received and the agents unique address removed from long term memory.

5.3 Call Agent

- *Initialise:* The agent is initialised with customer details, skill priority and time of call arrival.
- *Ping:* Once again *Ping* messages are sent to every member of the society containing skill(s) (required) and time of arrival.
- *Query:* When a *Query* is received the local time and offers from other agents are tested and on success a reply with a *QueryHit* posted, otherwise a *QueryReject*.
- *Offer:* If an *Offer* is made and the agent is still active an *OfferAccept* is sent as a reply otherwise an *OfferReject*.
- *Abandon:* When customer patience has reached the limit the *Call* abandons and the disconnection process begins by sending *CallDisconnect* messages to the society.
- *Call Disconnect:* Same process as with the *Handler* above.

We have implemented an agent-based discrete event simulator to create the agent network required for our call centre simulations. The simulator mimics the characteristics of the Cougaar [10] agent platform in the use of plug-in components—rather than behaviours—to program agent actions and the use of a blackboard-like publish and subscribe mechanism—rather than messaging. The blackboard encourages the use of events for agent interaction and is the primary mechanism for state management and message exchange. In a similar manner our simulator uses events such as the arrival of a new call, or a *QueryHit* to activate agents and a blackboard mechanism to send messages[1]. For simulation purposes, the model required a *Time* update message to wake up every agent and trigger new activity.

The simulation begins by loading a call centre model following that defined earlier and initialising the *Handlers* with shift data. Calls are randomly generated using a predefined call density per interval in a day and a Poisson distribution commonly found

---

[1] This apparently curious approach demands a brief explanation: we developed our own simulator primarily for speed of prototyping. Earlier simulations had been constructed directly in Cougaar, but turn-around time and some concerns about the long-term viability of Cougaar led us to the temporary pragmatic solution described, where the style of agent programming and communication follows the event-driven model that characterises Cougaar, with the aim of returning to the Cougaar framework in due course.

in this domain and added in a list ordered by time of arrival. On every tick a call is removed from the list and a new agent injected into the system with the relevant call information. Time updates are subsequently sent with the time of arrival of the new call and the simulation runs.

5.4   Bayesian Model for Call Discovery

In this implementation all *Handler* agents actively maintain a simple Bayesian model of their immediate environment and use it for optimising the call discovery process. A *Handler* agent needs to track both the distribution of skills and the distribution of waiting times for each skill to get a reasonable picture of the world around it. More specifically, the search is halted when the estimated probability that the next hop would return a better call than the best one seen so far falls below a threshold of 30%, a percentage that we consistently used throughout our experiments after initial testing. During this testing process we experimented with a number of thresholds with the aim to increase the performance of the probabilistic engine during the search and also the performance of the business metrics collected. In the end we found that the threshold of 30% works very well for our probabilistic engine and across a number of call centre models.

Estimate of Call Distribution By Skill. For *NS* skills, the distribution of waiting calls by skill can be described by a categorical distribution, so that for skills S_1 to S_{NS} the probability of a call in the queue being of a particular call type is P_i, where $\sum_{i=1}^{NS} P_i = 1$. An agent needs to estimate this distribution using the observed number of calls n_i for all skills. Assuming a conjugate Dirichlet distribution [7] on the agent's prior belief and using a non-informative Jeffrey's prior [4], we can write the mean prior estimate $P(S_i)$ for P_i as:

$$P(S_i) = \frac{1}{NS}$$

And the mean posterior estimate where N is the total number of calls observed as:

$$P(S_i) = \frac{n_i + \frac{1}{2}}{N + \frac{NS}{2}}$$

This flat prior across the categories could be potentially tailored more accurately if the distribution of skills was known up-front to be non-uniformly distributed.

Estimate of Call Distribution By Waiting Time. An estimate for the mean call waiting time is calculated by each *Handler* agent, for each skill of interest. We follow the common assumption that call waiting times are modelled by an exponential distribution which holds for certain theoretical call centre models. To get an estimate of the mean call time we use a quick short-cut rather than the more rigorous full conjugate distribution formulation (usually using an Inverse Gamma conjugate prior).

Our estimate for the mean posterior waiting time is:

$$t_{EST} = \frac{t_0 + \sum_{j=1}^{ND} t_i}{ND + 1}$$

Where ND is the total number of observed data points. This formulation implies a prior waiting time estimate t_0. As we are assuming an exponential distribution of waiting times, the probability that the waiting time t of the next *Call* agent has been waiting longer than the waiting time t_B of the longest *Call* visited so far is given by:

$$P(t > t_B) = \int_{t_B}^{\infty} P(t|t_{EST})\, dt = \int_{t_B}^{\infty} \frac{1}{t_{EST}} e^{-\frac{t}{t_{EST}}}\, dt$$
$$= e^{-\frac{t_B}{t_{EST}}}$$

Estimating The Probability of a Better Call. We can now calculate the probability P_{next} that the next *Call* queried will be better than the best *Call* seen so far, by combining the probabilities of both the different skills and waiting times:

$$P_{next} = P(SP_{next} > SP_B)$$
$$+ P(SP_{next} = SP_B)$$
$$* P(t_{next} = t_B^{SP_B})$$

This is the probability that either the skill priority SP_{next} of the next call is of a higher priority than the highest seen so far SP_B or that the skill priority will be equal to the best seen so far SP_B and the call waiting time t_{next} will be higher than the best seen so far for that skill type. This estimate can then be directly compared to a threshold value to make a decision about the next action.

5.5 Experiments

For validation purposes we conducted a number of simulation experiments with different scales and using synthetic, and empirical data provided by our sponsor[2]. We compared the performance of the two solutions with that of an industry-standard call centre simulator from our sponsor called Call Centre Workshop (CCW) and actual data provided by one of our clients. CCW is a commercial product used by a significant number of clients from the software, retail, banking, insurance and mobile phone sectors. It is a discrete event simulator which allows users to easily set-up call centre models and alternative routing algorithms. For our experiments we used a set of performance metrics to validate and compare the results that are common in this industry. For space economy reasons we are only presenting Service Level (SL%) which is the percentage of calls answered within a business-specific time frame. This time frame is called

---

[2] CACI Ltd. http://www.caci.co.uk

Telephone Service Factor (TSF) and is usually in the range of 20-30 seconds. SL% can be used to measure intra-day, daily and weekly performance and is normally defined as:

$$SL\% = \frac{\text{Calls Answered before TSF}}{\text{Calls Answered} + \text{Calls Abandoned}} \times 100$$

We also track the total number of messages required for agent discovery—that is, a handler discovering a call. The comparison plots presented in a later section use SL% and message count per interval to measure efficiency in terms of business performance and communication costs. We compare the Bayesian inference model against the standard approach with results from CCW and other techniques such as random, tabu and exhaustive. Our aim is to find the upper and lower limits of the call allocation space and understand where the probabilistic mechanism stands. The exhaustive search goes through every *Call* agent available and as expected this requires the most messages. The tabu search should be at the lower limits of the search using only one message per call and our expectation with the random and probabilistic techniques is to be somewhere in the middle.

For the first experiment we created a synthetic dataset with the aim of testing the agent prototype and allowing all different scenarios to be handled by the agents. The attributes of the model used are summarised in table 1 where (AHT) is Average Handle Time and (APT) Average Patience Time. We run that model for all the different discovery mechanisms and for 10 iterations. During the second phase of the experimentation process we used real customer data. The call centre selected for our experiments is part of one of the UK's leading mobile phone retailers. The client provided us with actual data from one of their main call centres which we use to simulate one day with 560 Handlers, 43,365 incoming calls and 13 different skills. Calls received are considered to be within SL% if they have been answered within 20 seconds from the time of arrival. Skill handling times – time it takes to handle a call – were varied through the day, while customer patience time is drawn from an exponential distribution with a mean value of 180 seconds. For the purpose of this work we set-up a very simple call routing model with no skill priorities and a direct mapping of skills to skill groups. We then loaded the data mentioned above into the agent model and executed the simulation only for 5 runs due to the time it takes to execute the simulation for each of the discovery mechanisms. We compared our results with the actual SL% values which the client's resource planning team calculated after collecting all the raw data stored for that day in the ACD database.

Table 1. Synthetic Model (5 skills, 50 handlers, 7720 calls)

Skills	TSF (secs)	Priority	AHT (secs)	APT (secs)
LOANS	20	1	240	180
MORTGAGES	20	2	240	180
PET INSURANCE	20	2	180	180
MOTOR INSURANCE	20	3	240	180
CREDIT CARD	20	1	240	180

6   Results and Discussion

Below we present comparisons with the metrics produced from our experiments. The graphs in figure 1 show changes in SL% throughout the day as well as query counts for every *Call* agent discovered, for the synthetic model.

As anticipated the synthetic model is over-stretched and agents can hardly cope with the workload. The overall variance in SL% between CCW and the different discovery mechanisms is between 1%-4%. More specifically the probabilistic approach has an average of 46% throughout the day when CCW has 49.5%, random has 45% and finally tabu and exhaustive searches are almost identical at 49%. The significant difference however is in the number of messages. The probabilistic approach requires an average of 300 queries through the day to deliver 46% when exhaustive is at the upper end with 1800 queries on average, random 640 and tabu 310. We believe these results demonstrate that the probabilistic search is efficient while allowing agents to find suitable pairs and contribute towards good global performance.

The real call centre experiments with an actual average SL% through the day of 64% are of greater scale and complexity and show a lot more promise for the probabilistic

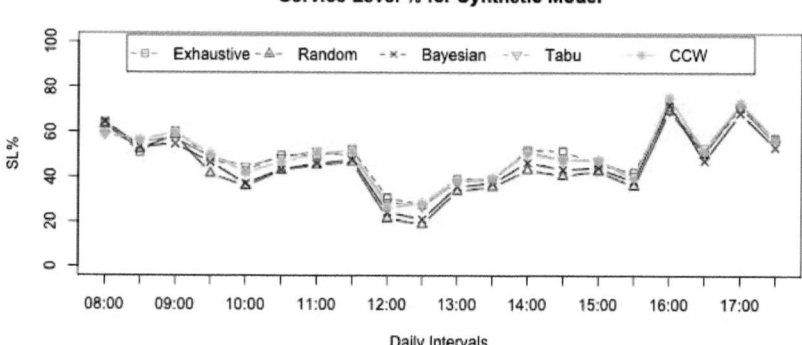

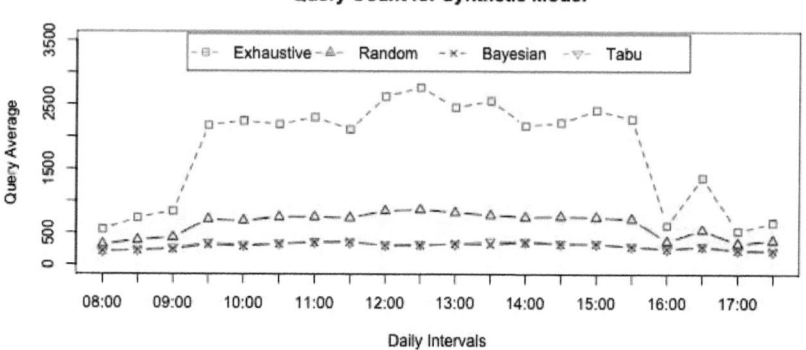

Fig. 1. Service Level and Query Count comparisons for synthetic data experiments

mechanism as shown in figure 2. In figure 3 we demonstrate the variation between the number of calls offered marked as *Actuals* and the number of calls handled by the different techniques.

In this instance the agent prototype that uses the probabilistic search performs at 77% compared to 73% tabu, 76% random and 72% exhaustive. For this study these results are far more important because we are using actual figures from a real world call centre rather than artificially devising the skill sets, the handling times or the number of incoming calls as we did in the earlier synthetic test. There is an important variation of 8%-13% here in performance between actuals and the agent models which can be explained by the different algorithm used for the call allocation process however the two systems follow the same trend. In one case the actual system is assigning calls to the longest available handler using a Router and in the other agent *Handlers* make an informed decision as to which *Call* to handle. The total number of query messages required on average per run are: 40,000 for probabilistic, 41,500 for tabu, 54,000 for random and 102,000 for exhaustive.

We notice that the difference in the number of query messages between the bayesian approach and tabu is greater when using the actual data model rather than the earlier

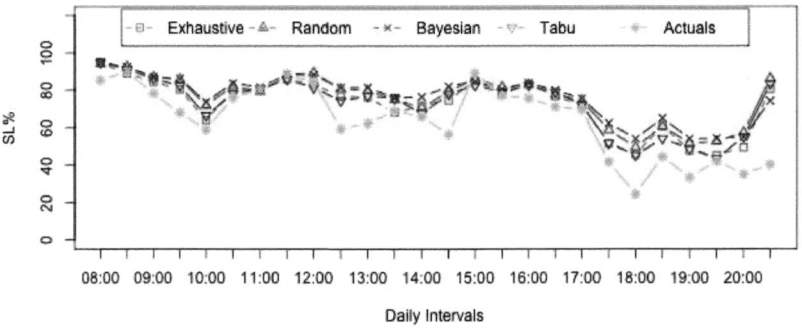

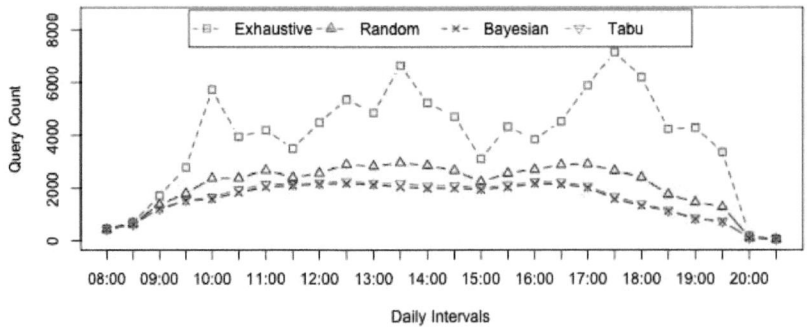

Fig. 2. Service Level and Query Count comparisons for empirical data experiments

Handled vs. Offered for Actuals Model

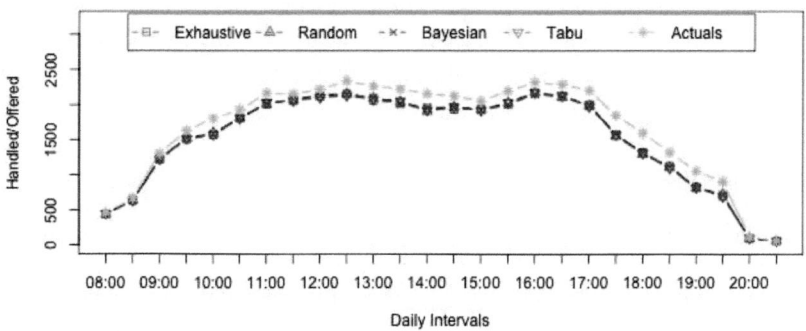

Fig. 3. Handled vs. Offered comparison for empirical data experiments

synthetic test. Tabu although effective does not scale as well as the probabilistic mechanism because of discovery conflicts. During tabu all *Handlers* attempt to handle the same call by choosing an identical candidate from their list and ignore other potentially good pairs. When one of them succeeds the rest start again but once more target the same *Call* agent. This process repeats until all *Calls* are handled but is wasteful in terms of queries required. The random discovery is not as effective as the Bayesian model either; this result was as we anticipated. The *Handlers* do not use any information gathered while hopping from one *Call* to another and just randomly stop at a specific point in time. Nevertheless the technique performs much better than we thought it would and proves that random policies can be equally effective as a much more controlled design.

The results presented in this section confirm that the multi-agent prototypes developed are effective and inspire us to further experimentation. Below we provide a summary of our findings:

– We have shown that a decentralised multi-agent system that uses a probabilistic discovery and pairing mechanism can be applied effectively and shows comparable performance with standard centralised designs. Sometimes it is possible to outperform exhaustive search by employing a Bayesian inference model that can inform decisions. When compared to other techniques such as an exhaustive search, random walk or tabu allocation it shows similar or better performance but with significantly less communication overheads.
– Our solution is simple in principle and efficiently handles task prioritisation and queueing without the use of an agent-mediator or super nodes. Instead it relies on active Consumer / Work / Task agents that can self-manage. The system can host as many types of Consumers as desired without affecting the basic model and discovery process.
– We have demonstrated that it is not necessary to have an architecture with any centralised control structures in place that will dictate how the system operates. Our model has a degree of randomness which allows it to search more efficiently for good pairs of agents that will deliver reasonable performance and follows much more relaxed design principles.

– Finally we have shown that a multi-agent architecture can be used effectively to manage a business process with a real world example from the call centre industry. Agent *Handlers* are capable of discovering customer *Calls* that join the network while trying to adhere to business rules governing skill priority and customer waiting time.

7 Conclusions

We have described a probabilistic discovery and pairing mechanism in which service providers or consumers use available domain-specific data to calculate the probability that the next agent in the search will result in a better match. With lack of global control and by using local information we have shown how agents can inform their decision making by updating a Bayesian inference model. In order to demonstrate the efficiency of the probabilistic mechanism we have applied our ideas to the business domain in the context of call centres. We have developed a decentralised multi-agent prototype to address the call allocation problem and run simulation experiments with synthetic and empirical data. Results show that our approach is at least as effective, when measured by QoS, as current centralised approaches. When compared to multicasting or random walk techniques it demonstrates reduced communication overheads. Agents learn from their observations while hopping and with relatively little messaging manage to discover suitable pairs. Potentially, gossip-based or distributed matchmaking mechanisms that require an initial random search could also benefit from the technique we have outlined.

Future work involves further exploration of the model and its usage in other application domains. We wish to experiment with problems where there is a high number of disconnected and failed agents and measure their impact on the discovery mechanism. Another aspect of this research that interests us is geographical location of agents and how a probabilistic search can use such information to improve pairing. We also plan to improve the Bayesian model using more rigorous conjugate distributions to represent the agent beliefs which would provide a better starting point for the discovery process. Finally we would like to investigate alternative topologies such as scale-free or small-worlds networks and experimentally evaluate designs where *Providers* and *Consumers* both search for each other simultaneously.

Acknowledgements

We wish to thank CACI Ltd for their support and we would like to note that our findings and conclusions do not necessarily reflect those of the sponsor.

References

1. Androutsellis-Theotokis, S., Spinellis, D.: A survey of peer-to-peer content distribution technologies. In: ACM Computing Surveys (CSUR), vol. 36, pp. 335–371. ACM Press, New York (2004) ISSN:0360-0300
2. Balakrishnan, H., Kaashoek, M.F., Karger, D., Morris, R., Stoica, I.: Looking up data in p2p systems. Commun. ACM 46(2), 43–48 (2003)

3. Biswas, R., Thrun, S., Guibas, L.J.: A probabilistic approach to inference with limited information in sensor networks. In: IPSN 2004: Proceedings of the 3rd International Symposium on Information Processing in Sensor Networks, pp. 269–276. ACM, NY (2004)
4. Bolstad, W.M.: Introduction to Bayesian Statistics. Wiley, Chichester (2007) ISBN-978-0-470-14115-1
5. Boyd, S., Ghosh, A., Prabhakar, B., Shah, D.: Randomized gossip algorithms. IEEE Transactions on Information Theory 52(6), 2508–2530 (2006)
6. Czajkowski, K., Foster, I., Karonis, N., Kesselman, C., Martin, S., Smith, W., Tuecke, S.: A resource management architecture for metacomputing systems. In: Feitelson, D.G., Rudolph, L. (eds.) IPPS-WS 1998, SPDP-WS 1998, and JSSPP 1998. LNCS, vol. 1459, pp. 62–82. Springer, Heidelberg (1998)
7. Devroye, L.: Non-uniform random variate generation (1986)
8. Ferreira, R.A., Ramanathan, M.K., Awan, A., Grama, A., Jagannathan, S.: Search with probabilistic guarantees in unstructured peer-to-peer networks. In: P2P 2005: Proceedings of the Fifth IEEE International Conference on Peer-to-Peer Computing, pp. 165–172. IEEE Computer Society, Washington, DC, USA (2005)
9. Gans, N., Koole, G., Mandelbaum, A.: Telephone call centers: a tutorial and literature review. In: Manufacturing And Service Operations Management, pp. 79–141. MSOM (2003)
10. Helsinger, A., Thome, M., Wright, T.: Cougaar: a scalable, distributed multi-agent architecture. In: IEEE International Conference on Systems, Man and Cybernetics, vol. 2, pp. 1910–1917. IEEE, Los Alamitos (2004), ISSN: 1062-922X. ISBN: 0-7803-8566-7. INSPEC Accession Number: 8393468. Digital Object Identifier: 10.1109/ICSMC.2004.1399959.
11. Holland, J.H.: Hidden Order: How Adaptation Builds Complexity. The Perseus Books Group, Cambridge (1995) ISBN-13: 9780201407938
12. Kuokka, D., Harada, L.: Matchmaking for information agents. In: IJCAI 1995: Proceedings of the 14th International Joint conference on Artificial Intelligence, pp. 672–678. Morgan Kaufmann Publishers Inc., San Francisco (1995)
13. Lilja, D.J.: Measuring computer performance: a practitioner's guide. Cambridge University Press, New York (2000)
14. Meshkova, E., Riihijärvi, J., Petrova, M., Mähönen, P.: A survey on resource discovery mechanisms, peer-to-peer and service discovery frameworks. Computer Networks 52(11), 2097–2128 (2008)
15. Ogston, E., Vassiliadis, S.: Local distributed agent matchmaking. In: Batini, C., Giunchiglia, F., Giorgini, P., Mecella, M. (eds.) CoopIS 2001. LNCS, vol. 2172, pp. 67–79. Springer, Heidelberg (2001)
16. Simonton, E., Choi, B.K., Seidel, S.: Using gossip for dynamic resource discovery. In: ICPP 2006: Proceedings of the 2006 International Conference on Parallel Processing, pp. 319–328. IEEE Computer Society, Washington, DC, USA (2006)
17. Stann, F., Heidemann, J.: Bard: Bayesian-assisted resource discovery in sensor networks. Technical report, USC/Information Sciences Institute (July 2004)
18. Sycara, K., Lu, J., Klusch, M., Widoff, S.: Matchmaking among heterogeneous agents on the internet. In: AAAI Spring Symposium on Intelligent Agents in Cyberspace (1999)
19. Tsoumakos, D., Roussopoulos, N.: Adaptive probabilistic search for peer-to-peer networks. In: Proceedings of Third International Conference on Peer-to-Peer Computing (P2P 2003), pp. 102–109 (2003)
20. Veit, D., Weinhardt, C., Müller, J.P.: Multi-dimensional matchmaking for electronic markets. Applied Artificial Intelligence 16(9-10), 853–869 (2002)
21. Vulkan, N., Jennings, N.R.: Efficient mechanisms for the supply of services in multi-agent environments. Decis. Support Syst. 28(1-2), 5–19 (2000)
22. Weiss, G.: Multiagent Systems. The MIT Press, Cambridge (1999)

An Adherence Support Framework for Service Delivery in Customer Life Cycle Management

Leelani Kumari Wickramasinghe[1], Christian Guttmann[1], Michael Georgeff[1],
Ian Thomas[2], and Heinz Schmidt[2]

[1] Department of General Practice
Faculty of Medicine, Nursing and Health Sciences
Monash University, Melbourne, Australia
{leelani.wickramasinghe,christian.guttmann,
michael.georgeff}@med.monash.edu.au
[2] School of Computer Science and Information Technology
RMIT University, Melbourne, Australia
{ian.thomas,heinz.schmidt}@rmit.edu.au

Abstract. In customer life cycle management, service providers are expected to deliver services to meet customer objectives in a manner governed by some contract or agreement. When human agents are involved as contract parties (either as customers or service providers), service delivery failures may occur as a result of changes, inconsistencies, or "deficits" in the mental attitudes of these agents (in addition to other possible changes in the service delivery environment). It may be possible to avoid such failures by monitoring the behavior of the contract parties and intervening to ensure adherence to the contractual obligations. The aim of this paper is twofold: (1) to develop a conceptual framework to model how deficits in mental attitudes can affect service delivery; and (2) to propose an adherence support architecture to reduce service delivery failures arising from such deficits. The conceptual framework is based on Bratman's notion of "future-directed intentions" and Castelfranchi's belief-based goal dynamics. The adherence support architecture introduces the notions of precursor events, mental-state recognition processes, and intervention processes and utilizes the Belief-Desire-Intention (BDI) architecture. A multi-agent implementation is carried out for chronic disease management in health care as a proof-of-concept for a complex customer care management system.

1 Introduction

The aim of Customer Life Ccle Management (CLCM) is to maintain and advance contractual relationships between a customer and service providers, potentially through the entire lifetime of that customer. CLCM has four stages:

1. Providing a customer with a set of services to meet his/her goals, personalised to the circumstances of the customer;
2. Assignment of service providers to provide the services identified in Item 1 above;
3. Maintenance of contractual relationships between the customer and service providers, and among service providers; and

M. De Vos et al. (Eds.): COIN 2010 International Workshops, LNAI 6541, pp. 210–229, 2011.

4. Delivery of services by the service providers in the manner agreed, over time and potentially the entire lifetime of the customer.

The Intelligent Collaborative Care Management (ICCM) Project [1,2] offers a comprehensive architecture for CLCM, in particular, for contracts of which human agents function as contract parties (customers and service providers). In this project, we consider that a customer is provided a number of possibly interrelated services by various service providers in a manner governed by some agreement or contract. The customer has certain goals or objectives that these services are intended to fulfil and the service providers themselves may have certain objectives in delivering the services to the customer. These services are to be delivered over time and potentially the entire lifetime of the customer.

When human agents function as customers and service providers, their unreliable and non-conformance behaviour, may jeopardise CLCM. Humans are goal directed and reason before performing an action or selecting goals to achieve. Human reasoning is a bounded rational process subject to the properties of mental attitudes: beliefs, desires, intentions, plans, emotions etc. In CLCM, changes, inconsistencies, or "deficits" in these mental attitudes may prevent contract parties from performing the required activities, which may then affect:

1. The formation of the contractual arrangements (e.g., service providers forget to respond to agreement formation related requests);
2. The management of these contractual arrangements (e.g., service providers do not know when to communicate contract related data to other parties of the contract); and
3. The delivery of the services according to the contractual arrangements (e.g., a patient forgets to set an appointment with a service provider for the next due visit).

Adherence support mechanisms may assist human agents to maintain and execute contracts as committed. Continuous monitoring and intervention may either reverse the deficits or identify reasons to vary the contract. The ICCM architecture with human contract parties and adherence support requirements is shown in Figure 1. The human parties are modelled as Belief-Desire-Intention (BDI) agents [3,4] because this architecture provides formalisms and representation mechanisms of agents' mental attitudes. (Refer [2] for a detailed description of the ICCM architecture). This paper investigates:

– A conceptual framework to model contract violations arising from deficits in mental attitudes; and
– An architecture for adherence support to reduce contract violations in delivering services.

The conceptual framework is based on Bratman's notion of "future-directed intentions" [5] and Castelfranchi's belief-based goal dynamics [6]. The adherence support architecture with the ongoing monitoring and management processes is based on the following elements:

– precursors: a priori actions, steps or states that may indicate whether the actions of the contract parties are on-track with respect to the contract (e.g., the patient setting an appointment on time to visit a care provider) or likely to go off-track (e.g., very low or very high blood pressure).

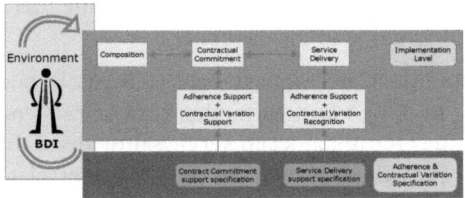

Fig. 1. ICCM architecture: with human contract parties and adherence support requirements

– detection strategies for precursors: mechanisms to detect the occurrence or missing occurrence of such precursors at run-time;
– mental-state recognition processes: processes to identify possible deficit(s) in mental attitudes which may have led to the (non-)occurrences of precursors; and
– intervention processes: strategies to intervene with one or more of the contract parties to reduce the likelihood of the parties violating their obligations.

As seen in Figure 1, the conceptual framework and the adherence support architecture is common to both the contractual commitment stage[1] and the service delivery stage. In this paper, we consider examples and implementation results from the service delivery stage, in which service providers are expected to deliver services as committed and the customer is expected to perform certain required activities to be engaged in the contract. We focus on contracts made in the health care domain, specifically, chronic disease management [7], as an example of a complex, dynamic domain with human contract parties in which precursor recognition, service delivery failure, and adherence support are important elements.

The increasing number of patients with chronic diseases and the associated medical care costs motivated us in focusing on this application area: 7 million Australians [8] and 133 million Americans [9] have a chronic medical condition and 60% of all deaths worldwide are due to chronic diseases. It is estimated that improved adherence to "care plans" (contracts among the care team and the patient) could dramatically reduce health care costs and improve patient outcomes. However, these care plans are usually not followed in practice, and few mechanisms are in place for assisting patients or the care team adhere to the care plan and avoid plan "failures" [10]. We expect our research to provide a framework for better understanding these issues and ultimately lead to mechanisms for assisting patients and their care providers better develop and adhere to care plans.

The paper is organized as follows. A framework to model contract violations due to deficits in mental attitudes is described in Section 2. Section 3 presents an adherence support architecture to reduce contract violations due to such deficits. A multi-agent implementation in chronic disease management as a proof-of-concept is discussed in Section 4. Section 5 relates our work to existing research. Concluding remarks and future work are discussed in Section 6.

---

[1] The contractual commitment stage is additionally based on partially regulated market and negotiation theories and is described elsewhere [2].

2   Framework to Model Contract Violations Due to Deficits in Mental Attitudes

This section investigates a conceptual framework to demonstrate how explicit models of the mental attitudes of the human agents affect service delivery. Humans can be considered as three types of agents: (1) goal-directed agents; (2) rational agents; and (3) planning agents [5]. Out of possibly many desires, that is, objectives or situations that the agent would like to accomplish, humans select one or more than one desire and actively pursuit to achieve it(or them). Such selected desires are termed goals, thus humans exhibit goal-directed behaviour to achieve the selected goal(s). (However, more than one desire is selected only if each of the desire is consistent with all the other desires.) Humans are rational, that is, they deliberate on desires before selecting goals based on the properties of mental attitudes. The selected goals are also termed intentions as the agent is intended to achieve such goals now or in the future. The sequence of actions use to achieve the intentions is termed a plan, thus humans are planning agents.

With respect to CLCM, by forming a contract, the contract parties intend to achieve the obligations specified in the contract within the lifetime of the contract. Each obligation agreed by a contract party is an intention made by the corresponding party at the contract commitment-time prior to the execution-time. There is a time gap between the contract commitment-time and the execution-time. Beliefs are at the core of selecting goals and executing intentions: humans commit to intentions based on beliefs at the commitment time and execute them based on the beliefs at the execution-time. Therefore, the investigation on the conceptual framework is two-facet: (1)selecting goals as future intentions ; and (2) beliefs as the basis for goal selection and execution.

From literature, Bratman's notion of "future-directed intentions" [5] states that humans frequently decide in advance a plan for the future and then use such a plan as a basis for future actions. This concept describes what is possible in between goal selection and intention execution, and why intentions are not always get executed as committed. Future-directed intentions is the basis for goal-directed and deliberative agent architectures such as BDI agent architecture [3,4]. With constructs such as beliefs, desires, intentions and plans, BDI agents aim to depict the reasoning process of humans. We consider future-directed intentions as described in Section 2.1 as a possible concept to address the first phenomenon of the conceptual framework.

The model of belief-based goal dynamics [6] proposes beliefs as the deciding factor for selecting and executing goals. It states that humans commit to obligations based on beliefs that exist at the commitment-time and subsequent execution of the obligations depends on the execution-time beliefs of the agent. Contract parties commit to contractual obligations based on the beliefs that exist at the contract formation time and these beliefs may or may not remain the same until the execution-time. The execution of the obligations depend on the beliefs that exist at the contract execution time. We consider belief-based goal dynamics as described in Section 2.2 as a possible concept to address the last phenomenon of the conceptual framework.

Consolidating future-directed intentions and belief-based goal dynamics, in Section 2.3, we propose three types of deficits in an agent's mental attitudes. This section also discusses the effect of these deficits in realising contractual obligations. The contract shown in Table 1 will be used as the working example throughout the paper.

Table 1. A sample contract

Party's name	Party's type	Obligation	Execution due
Harry Brown	Podiatrist	Examine feet	July, Oct, Jan
Mary John	Optometrist	Check eyes	December
Bob Smith	Patient	Walk 1 km	daily
		Take Diamicron	April, July, Oct

2.1 Future-Directed Intentions

According to Bratman [5], future-directed intentions, which guide the future actions of humans, are two dimensional: (1) volitional, and (2) reasoning centered. The volitional dimension states that if an agent's future-directed intention manages to survive until the time of action, and if the agent senses that the time to perform the action has arrived, and if nothing else interferes with the action, then the agent will execute the action. The reasoning centered dimension considers the roles played by future-directed intentions during the period between the initial formation of intentions and the eventual execution. It involves two reasoning components:

(1) given new information or changes in the agent's expectation, the agent may reconsider future intentions, even though it is expected that the agent settles on future-directed intentions and does not deliberate on them; and
(2) further reasoning from intended ends to the intended means as the agent moves to act on future intentions.

For example, a patient's future-directed intentions (in the form of a "care plan") could include: visit podiatrist in July, visit podiatrist in Oct, ···, visit optometrist in Dec, walk 1km daily, take 1st repeats of the medication (Diamicron) in April, ··· (see Table 1). Subsequent to these commitments, the patient may:

(1) be unaware that the podiatrist appointment is at 10.00am on 1st July 2009 (forgotten or believes to be on another date).
(2) assume his current risk of heart attack is less than that at the time of commitment;
(3) get to know a football match is to be held on an appointment date;
(4) realise he cannot walk more than 0.5 km a day;
(5) discover that the medication (Diamicron) causes severe side effects;
(6) decide not to take medications that have side effects; or
(7) not know how to set an appointment with the podiatrist or optometrist.

The above examples may result in the patient not complying with his care plan, thereby resulting in a service delivery failure (in this case, of the patient). These examples map to the dimensions of future-directed intentions as presented in Table 2.

2.2 Belief-Based Goal Dynamics

In this section, we describe the notion of a contract in terms of belief-based goal dynamics [6] and goal-directed behaviour. In this model, beliefs are proposed as the basis for reasoning about future directed intentions and selecting and executing goals. This

Table 2. Future-directed intentions and examples

Dimension	Sub dimension	Important concept	Applicable Examples
Volitional dimension		Time has arrived to execute the action	Example 1
		Nothing interferes with the intention	Examples 2, 3, 4 and 5
Reasoning centered dimension	Settling on a certain course of actions	New information	Examples 2, 3, 4 and 5
		Change in what the agent wants	Example 6
	Further reasoning be-tween now and time to execute intention	Reason from in-tended end to in-tended means	Example 7

model categorizes beliefs into seven categories: motivating, assessment, cost, incompatibility, preference, precondition and means-end and categorises goal processing into four stages: active, pursuable, chosen and executive. These beliefs affect the goal processing in two ways:

1. Belief types intervene on goal processing at different stages, and
2. Each belief type has a unique effect on the goal.

Prior to execution, a goal gets filtered via four processing stages, depending on beliefs:

Activation stage: motivating beliefs ⇒ active goals
Evaluation stage: assessment beliefs ⇒ pursuable goals
Deliberation stage: cost + incompatibility + preference beliefs ⇒ chosen goals
Checking stage: precondition + means-end beliefs ⇒ executive goals

The obligations shown in Table 1 map to these belief types and goals. In the running example, the obligations: visit podiatrist in July, visit podiatrist in Oct, visit podiatrist in Jan, and so on, are chosen goals (committed goals) for the patient. They are transferred to executive goals based on precondition beliefs and means-end beliefs. For a chosen goal to be part of the checking process, the beliefs on which the goal was deliberated (commitment-time beliefs) have to remain unchanged until the checking stage. Any changes to such beliefs may result in a contract failure. This can be illustrated using the examples mentioned in Section 2.1:

Example (1) corresponds to a missing conditional belief about the appointment time;
Example (2) corresponds to a change in the motivating belief that indicates the risk of heart attack;
Example (3) corresponds to a value belief to be healthy that has changed from a high priority to a lower priority;
Example (4) corresponds to an incompetence belief found at the checking stage;
Example (5) corresponds to an incompatibility belief found at the checking stage;

Example (6) corresponds to a value belief to be healthy changing from a high to a lower priority; and

Example (7) corresponds to a missing means-end belief.

2.3 Deficit Categories

Both the future-directed intentions and the belief-based goal dynamics concepts differentiate between committing to a contract and contract delivery. In this section we identify the deficit types that cause such failures.

Consolidating future-directed intentions and belief-based goal dynamics, the main causes for a breach of contract are:

1. changes to the beliefs on which commitments were made; and
2. changes in agent's expectation/priority from commitment time to execution time.

We summarize such changes into three deficit categories: belief, intention and plan deficits.

Belief Deficit: A belief deficit is said to occur if an agent forgets or does not know when to execute an action, to whom to communicate with to execute an action, or when to execute an action that is necessary for meeting a contractual obligation.

The manner in which belief deficits affects agent behaviour and contractual obligations can be described within the frameworks of Bratman and Castelfranchi. The volitional dimension of practical reasoning requires that, if the agent's future-directed intention manages to survive until the time of action and if the agent senses that the time to perform an action has arrived, the agent will execute the intentions as committed. The belief deficit that occurs when the agent forgets or does not know when to execute an action results in the agent not sensing that the time to perform the action has arrived. A different kind of belief deficit can arise when motivating beliefs change. Belief-based goal dynamics views motivating beliefs as essential for the maintenance of intentions, so that any change to such beliefs could, at a point of re-deliberation, result in the dropping of intentions that were otherwise contractually committed. We class such changes as belief deficits when the motivating belief is no longer true of the real world (or the possible world when the contractual commitment was made); otherwise, we consider the change to be an intention deficit.

Example: The patient intends to visit the podiatrist in July. He is unaware that the appointment is at 10.00am on 1st July (he either has forgotten the date or believes it to be on another day). This example can be formulated as follows.

Let I denote an intention and B a belief.

The patient commits to the plan at time $t0$. The patient's intention at time $t0$ is denoted by I_{to}:

I_{to} (if time = timeOfAppointment(podiatrist)) then
        visit(podiatrist)

Status of the real world at time $t1$ where $t1 > t0$ is

time = 10.00am 01/07/2009

Mental status of the patient at time $t1$ is

I_{t1} (if time = timeOfAppointment(podiatrist)) then
        visit(podiatrist)

If the patient has forgotten the appointment:
$\neg B_{t1}(timeOfAppointment(podiatrist) = 10.00am\ 01/07/2009)$
or, if the patient believes the appointment to be on another day:
$B_{t1}(timeOfAppointment(podiatrist) = 10.00am\ 05/07/2009)$

The patient still intends to visit the podiatrist on 1st July 2009 at 10.00am as committed. That is, the patient has not changed his intention. The fact that he does not know that the visit is on 1st July (or his belief that it is scheduled on another day such as 5th July), however, means that this intention will not trigger the required action. Therefore, while the patient believes he is still consistent with his contractual obligations, the "belief deficit" may result in the patient not realising his obligations in the real world.

We note that there is a difference between forgetting about the appointment and believing it to be on another day. In the former case, the absence of a belief that is a precondition for an existing intention may trigger an action to determine the time of appointment, whereas this would not be so in the latter case. However, at our level of analysis, we class both as belief deficits.

Intention Deficit: An intention deficit arises when an agent drops a committed intention or changes the priority of goals, resulting in a modification or a reordering of intentions so that the agent's behaviour no longer conforms with the contractual obligations.

The volitional dimension of practical reasoning requires that, for a committed intention to get executed, nothing should interfere with the intention. In addition, the reasoning centered dimension allows that, given new information or changes in the agent's expectations, the agent may reconsider future-directed intentions. These events can result in the agent dropping a committed intention or changing the priority of a committed intention.

Similarly, the incompatibility and preference beliefs that were active at the deliberation process should remain the same at the checking stage for the deliberated (committed) intentions to get executed. However, changes in these beliefs after the contractual commitment is made can result in the agent performing another reasoning process (deliberation) before acting on the intention. This subsequent deliberation process can reorder the agent's intentions such that it executes another higher priority intention while dropping the originally committed intention. In addition, belief-based goal dynamics provides that the chosen goals are transferred to executive goals based on preconditions. Therefore, if the preconditions are not satisfied, the agent will drop the chosen goal (committed intention).

Example: The patient chooses to "go to football" rather than "visit a provider" on the day he has the appointment with the provider. At commitment time, the patient may not have a belief about a football match being played on the same date as the appointment date. He acquires this new information after the commitment is made but before the appointment is due. Hence, the patient may reconsider his intention and decides to go to football. From belief-based goal dynamics, this example can be viewed as a change of preference belief after the deliberation is made at the commitment time. The preference belief type that is activated in this case can be an urgency belief that provides an expiry context to the goal of going to football; for example, that it is the last day of football season. As a result, the patient may be persuaded to go to football rather than visit the podiatrist.

Plan Deficit: A plan deficit arises when the agent does not know the means for carrying out an intention or achieving a goal that is necessary for fulfilling the contractual obligations.

Once the commitment or the future-directed intention is made, the party fails to reason from intended end to intended means. According to belief-based goal dynamics, the chosen goal (commitment) fails at the checking stage due to a lack of means-end beliefs. Hence, the chosen goal will not get selected as an executive goal, resulting in a breach of the contract.

Example: The patient intends to set an appointment with the podiatrist. But he does not know how to proceed with setting an appointment. That is, the patient does not have a plan for setting an appointment (e.g., by calling the podiatrist office in a timely way) and thereby cannot determine a means to achieve the desired end.

The mapping between future-directed intentions, belief-based goal dynamics and deficit categories is shown in Table 3.

Table 3. Mapping among future-directed intentions, belief-based goal dynamics and deficit categories

Dimension	Sub dimension	Concept	Mapping belief type	Deficit
Volitional dimension		Time has arrived to execute the action	Motivating beliefs	Belief deficits
		Nothing interferes with the intention	Incompatibility + Preference + Precondition	Intention deficit
Reasoning centered dimension	Settled on a course of action	New information	Incompatibility + Preference + Precondition	Intention deficit
		Change in what I want	Incompatibility + Preference + Precondition	Intention deficit
	Further reasoning between now and time to execute intention	Reason from intended end to intended means	Means-end beliefs	Plan deficit

3   Framework for Adherence Support

In this section, we propose an adherence support architecture to reduce contract violations resulting from the three types of failures described in Section 2.3. Our proactive failure prevention strategy consists of three parts:

- the detection of possible deficits;
- the recognition of the possible deficit type; and
- intervention to eliminate or ameliorate the deficits.

3.1   Detection of Possible Deficits

The detection of possible deficits is carried out with the notions of:

- The execution of an obligation as outlined in the contract usually depends on the successful execution of a priori event(s) or achievement of certain intermediate contract state(s). The occurrence or non-occurrence of these (depending on the way they are defined), a priori events and states can be taken as an indicator of the likelihood of the agent meeting the contractual obligations.
- In this context, a priori events or contract states are called precursors. That is, a precursor is an event, a pattern of events, a state, a pattern of states, or a combination of state and event patterns that has a positive or negative influence over achieving contract obligations as planned.

Each obligation is associated with one or many domain specific precursors. Depending on the way precursors are defined, the occurrence of a favourable precursor indicates that the contract is currently being executed as planned. An unfavourable precursor indicates a possible impending contract violation which may be associated with any deficits in contract parties' mental states.

Precursors are either time dependent (e.g., setting an appointment prior to a provider visit) or time independent (the patient's Systolic blood pressure > 180 or diastolic blood pressure > 110) [11].

Precursor Related Definitions

- Let O denote the set of obligations and P the set of precursors.
- The mapping between an obligation $o \in O$ and a precursor $p \in P$ is usually context dependent and can be represented by a branching tree structure where the context determines the selection of a branch. The context defines the current state of the contract (or the system or the environment).
- We represent obligation to precursor mapping using the notion:
  obligation-precursor-operator: $OPO \subseteq O \times BoolExp \rightarrow P$, which associates an obligation $o \in O$ with one or more boolean expressions $C \in BoolExp$
  and for each of these maps uniquely to a precursor $p = OPO(o, C)$ with $p \in P$.
- An instance of *obligation-precursor-operator* is a triple $< o, C, p >$.

Once OPO is defined, the (non-)occurrences of precursors are detected at execution-time by applying a context sensitive goal-directed algorithm:

```
repeat
    environmentContext := getEnvironmentContext
    precursorsToDetect := selectMatchingPrecursors(environmentContext)
end repeat
```

The function *selectMatchingPrecursors* is of the form:

> *selectMatchingPrecursors(environmentContext)*
>   *let $A = \{\}$*
>   *for each $a, a \in OPO$*
>   *if $(C = environmentContext)$*
>   *let $p \in A$*
>   *return A*

Once the precursors are detected, the next step in failure prevention is to identify the reason for such (non-)occurrences of these precursors.

3.2 Mental-State Recognition to Identify Possible Deficits

If a favourable precursor $P_f, P_f \in P$ occurs, further investigations are not necessary as the P_f indicates that the contract is currently being executed as planned. We define the set of unfavourable precursors as P_{uf} where $P_{uf} \in P$. In the absence of malicious and self-interested contract parties, elements in P_{uf} occur as a result of "deficits" (as defined in this project) in the contract party's mental attitude(s). The corresponding deficits prevent the party from carrying out an action required for the successful completion of the contract.

In general, it is important to be able to recognise the type of deficit (that is, a belief, an intention or a plan deficit) to be able to intervene effectively. This requires techniques to recognise or otherwise characterise the mental state of the non-compliant agent.

Use of observer agents to recognise mental states of the agents under consideration is an existing method for mental-state recognition [12]. Some approaches to observer agent based recognition process are based on the assumptions [12,13,14]:

- observer agent has a correct and complete knowledge of the plans of the agent that it is trying to recognize.
- at any given situation, the observer agent has a small set of plans that it is trying to recognize.

In addition, behaviour monitoring techniques provide strategies to depict mental-states of other agents in the system [15,16]. Intrusive and overhearing are two agent behaviour monitoring approaches adopted in multi-agent systems [17]. The intrusive approach requests the agents to communicate required information and the observer interprets the behaviours using the communicated information [18,15,16,19]. The over-hearing approach observes the messages exchanged among agents and infers the be-haviour using the messages [20].

In our proposed framework, we assign an adherence agent (AA) to each contract party. The role of the AA is, in part, to recognise the mental states of the contract parties. AA's knowledge base includes:

- Obligations of the corresponding contract party;
- Obligation to precursor mappings; and
- Plans to achieve obligations.

AA is designed as an observer agent mentioned above to recognise the mental states of the contract party. As our concern is not with malicious or self-interested contract parties, the AA adopts an intrusive approach to interpret the mental state of the contract party. The algorithm uses by the AA to determine the type of deficit of the contract party is as follows:

```
deficitType = null
contractPartyGoal := getGoal(environmentContext)
if (contractPartyGoal is not obligation)
    contractPartyBeliefs := getBeliefs(environmentContext, obligation)
    for each b, b ∈ contractPartyBeliefs
        if (b is not bc), where bc is the commitment-time belief
            deficitType = BeliefDeficit
    if (deficitType is null)
        planExist := checkExistenceOfPlan(obligation)
        if (planExist)
            deficitType = IntentionDeficit
        else
            deficitType = PlanDeficit
return deficitType
```

At the end of the mental-state recognition process, each AA associates a missing precursor, p to a deficit, d, where d is either a belief, an intention or a plan deficit. Once the deficit is identified, a tailored intervention strategy is applied with the aim to reverse the deficit.

3.3 Intervention to Reduce Deficits

The aim of an intervention is to compensate for any missing favourable precursors, P_f (the missing event(s), state(s) or the pattern of events and states) or to reverse the effect of unfavourable precursors that have occurred, P_{uf}.

Intervention Related Definitions

- Let I denote the set of interventions.
- The mapping between a precursor $p \in P$ and an intervention $i \in I$ is context dependent (similar to the mapping between an obligation to a precursor (Section 3.1)). This mapping is represented by a branching tree structure where the context determines the selection of a branch.
- We present a precursor to an intervention mapping using the notion:
  precursor-intervention-operator: $PIO \subseteq P \times BoolExp \rightarrow I$, which associates a precursor $p \in P$ with one or more conditions $C, C \in BoolExp$
  and for each of these with a unique intervention $i = PIO(p, C)$ where $i \in I$.
- An instance of *precursor-intervention-operator* is a triple $< p, C, i >$.

Once the PIO is defined, the applicable intervention strategy for a detected precursor is obtained by applying the following context sensitive goal-directed algorithm:

applicableIntervention := selectIntervention(precursorDetected, environmentCon-text, deficitType)

The function *selectIntervention* is of the form:

selectIntervention(precursorDetected, environmentContext, deficitType)
   let A = {}
   for each a, a ∈ PIO
      if (p = precursorDetected)
         if (C = environmentContext and deficitType)
            let i ∈ A
   return A

If multiple interventions correspond to a given situation (that is, for given *precursorDetected*, *environmentContext* and *deficitType*), the *selectIntervention* function returns a set with multiple items. In such situations, a single intervention is identified based on the effectiveness and the cost associated with the intervention.

The process of detecting a possible deficit, recognizing the mental state that caused the deficit, and intervening to change the mental state with an aim to prevent the deficit is summarized in the following algorithm.

repeat
   environmentContext := getEnvironmentContext
   precursorsToDetect := selectMatchingPrecursors(environmentContext)
   if (((not(occurred(precursorsToDetect))) and
     (isFavourable(precursorsToDetect))) or
     ((occurred(precursorsToDetect)) and
     (not(isFavourable(precursorsToDetect)))))))
       deficitType := mental-state recognition strategies
       applicableIntervention := selectIntervention(precursorsToDetect,
                            environmentContext, deficitType)
     intervene using applicableIntervention
  end repeat

As depicted in the algorithm, recognition of mental states and intervention are applied only in two situations: (1) non-occurrence of a favourable precursor; or (2) occurrence of an unfavourable precursor.

4   Implementation

A multi-agent implementation was carried out for chronic disease management in health care as a proof-of-concept for a complex customer care management system. The system consists of two types of agents:

– Contract party agent (CPA): Each contract party is assigned a CPA that acts as a personal assistant to the party. Contract parties communicate with the system via the corresponding CPA. Any deficit that occurs in service delivery stage is captured through CPAs; and

- Adherence agent for each contract party (AA): Each CPA has a corresponding AA for adherence support. AAs are implemented according to the theory in Section 3.

In chronic disease management, the customers (patients) and the health care providers (service providers) commit to maintain and deliver services. An example care plan is shown in Table 1. As an example scenario, we discuss in detail the patient's commitment to visit the care providers within the due time frame in this section.

4.1 Service Delivery Specification: Domain-Based Agent Specification

Considering the distinct functionalities associated with the patient and the care providers, we consider two specific CPAs, the $CPA_{patient}$ and $CPA_{careprovider}$. Each CPA is assigned a corresponding Adherence Agent (AA). The service delivery support specification defines the data and processes of $CPA_{patient}$, $CPA_{careprovider}$, $AA_{patient}$ and $AA_{careprovider}$. The AA specification defines the obligations in the care plan, the current state of the obligations and the failure prevention definitions. The specification of the CPAs contains contract obligations as data and processes to perform such obligations and to receive intervening messages and reply to them. In the current implementation, the service delivery support specification is specified as part of the agent code. The agents are implemented using Jason [21], an interpreter for AgentSpeak(L), based on the BDI architecture [4].

To uniquely identify patients and care providers, patients are assigned an Electronic Health Record (EHR) identifier prefix with "c"(for customer) and the health providers are assigned with a unique provider identification number (PIN) prefix with "p" (for provider). Bob (patient) as CPA_{c1}, Harry (podiatrist) as CPA_{p1}, Mary (optometrist) as CPA_{p2}, and the corresponding adherence agents AA_{c1}, AA_{p1} and AA_{p2}.

The care plan obligations of the patient are represented as beliefs of the $CPA_{patient}$:

1. visit(?PIN, ?Month, ?Year)
2. exercise(?Exercise, ?Frequency)
3. renewPrescription(?Medication, ?Month, ?Year)

Examples: visit(p1,07,2009), visit(p1,10,2009), visit(p1,01,2009), visit(p2,12,2009), exercise(walk1km, daily), renewPrescription(Diamicron, 04, 2009), renewPrescription(Diamicron, 07, 2009), renewPrescription(Diamicron, 10, 2009)

Specifications of Care Plan Obligations of $AA_{patient}$: These specifications include

1. All the belief structures of $CPA_{patient}$;
2. The additional beliefs required for the successful execution of the contractual obligations. For example, to visit a provider, the patient has to set an appointment a certain number of days prior to the planned visit. The number of days may vary with the provider. The belief waitingTime(?PIN, ?Days) defines the number of days in advance an appointment has to be set with the provider, ?PIN, e.g., waitingTime(p1, 28); and
3. The current state of the obligations. For example, appointment(?PIN,?Month, ?Year) states that an appointment has been set with the provider, ?PIN for the month, ?Month and the year, ?Year.

Specifications for Failure Prevention: These specifications include obligations to precursor operators (OPO) (Section 3.1), precursor detection strategies, mental-state recognition processes (Section 3.2), and precursors to intervention operators (PIO) (Section 3.3).

Example: Failure Prevention Specification for the Patient's Commitment to Planned Visits
An OPO defines that the patient has to set an appointment with the provider within a specified waiting time:

obligation: visit(?PIN, ?Month, ?Year)
context: waitingTime(?PIN, ?NumberofDays) and
      (= DifferenceinDays(?Month ?Year) ?NumberofDays)
precursor: appointment(?PIN, ?Month, ?Year)

Note: The DifferenceinDays is a function definition which returns the number of days between the current date and the first day of ?Month and ?Year.

Specification for Detecting the above Precursor

goal: CheckForAppointment(?PIN, ?Month, ?Year)
context: waitingTime(?PIN, ?NumberofDays) and
      (= DifferenceinDays(?Month ?Year) ?NumberofDays)
body: if ($\neg$ (appointment(?PIN, ?Month, ?Year) then
      DetectDeficitOfSetAppointment(?PIN, ?Month, ?Year)

The body contains one or many goals required to be executed to achieve the main goal. The main goal *CheckForAppointment* will be a goal for $AA_{patient}$ to execute each day, but the successful execution depends on the context.

Figure 2 is a screen from the implemented framework that corresponds to the beliefs of AA_{c1}. As seen, AA_{c1} has detected the non-occurrence of the precursor, appointment. In the belief base it is shown as a "booking that does not exist".

Specification of Mental-State Recognition Processes (MSRP)
Example MSRPs that define the process to recognise the deficit associated with the patient with regard to the obligation visit(?PIN, ?Month, ?Year) is given below as MSRP1 and MSRP2.

MSRP1
goal: DetectDeficitOfSetAppointment(?PIN, ?Month, ?Year)
context: true
body: RequestWaitingTime(?PIN)

MSRP1 requests the waitingTime for the provider ?PIN from the patient. The patient's response get stored as a belief waitingTimeFromPatient(?PIN, ?Days).

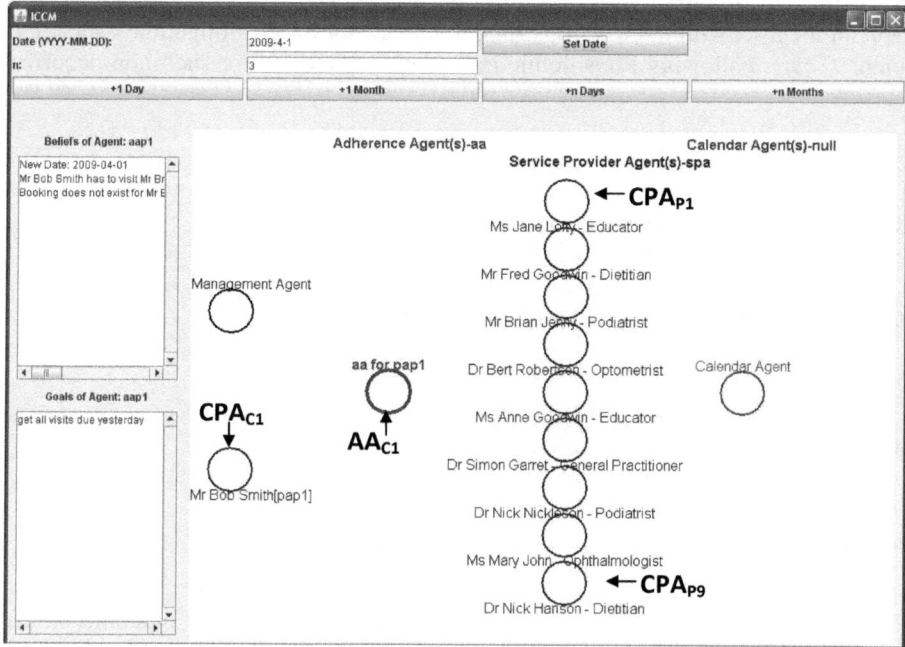

Fig. 2. AA_{c1} has detected the non-occurrence of a precursor that is an appointment. This detection is added to the belief base as a booking that does not exist.

MSRP2
goal: DetectDeficitOfSetAppointment(?PIN, ?Month, ?Year)
context: ?waitingTime(?PIN, ?NumberofDays) and
        waitingTimeFromPatient(?PIN, ?Days) and
        (= ?NumberofDays ?Days)
body: GetRiskLevelFromPatient(heartattack)

MSRP2 requests the heart attack risk level from the patient. The patient's response gets stored as a belief riskLevelFromPatient(heartattack, ?PatientLevel).

The execution outcome of MSRP1 can be that the patient's belief about the waiting time is incorrect:
waitingTimeFromPatient(?PIN, ?Days) and waitingTime(?PIN, ?NumberofDays) and
($\neq$?Days ?NumberofDays) $\rightarrow$ belief deficit.

The execution outcome of MSRP2 can be that the patient's belief on his risk of a heart attack is less than the actual value. This reduced risk may have caused an intention deficit by associating a lower priority to the obligation 'visit provider'. That is,
riskLevelFromPatient(heartattack, ?PatientLevel) and
riskLevel(heartattack, ?ActualLevel) and
($\neq$?PatientLevel ?ActualLevel) $\rightarrow$ change priority $\rightarrow$ intention deficit

Specifications of precursor-intervention-operators (PIO)
An appointment set within the waiting time is a precursor for the obligation visit(?PIN, ?Month, ?Year). Following PIOs define intervention strategies for such non-occurred precursors:

PIO1
precursor: appointment(PIN, ?Month, ?Year)
context: waitingTimeFromPatient(?PIN, ?Days) and
          waitingTime(?PIN, ?NumberofDays) and
          ($\neq$?Days ?NumberofDays)
intervention: remindToSetAppointment(?PIN, ?Month, ?Year)

PIO2
precursor: appointment(PIN, ?Month, ?Year)
context: riskLevelFromPatient(heartattack, ?PatientLevel)
          and riskLevel(heartattack, ?ActualLevel)
          and ($\neq$?PatientLevel ?ActualLevel)
intervention: remindToSetAppointment(?PIN, ?Month, ?Year)
          informCurrentRisk(heartattack, ?ActualLevel)

The selection of a specific PIO for intervention depends on the outcome of the mental-state recognition process. For example, PIO1 is selected for intervention if the

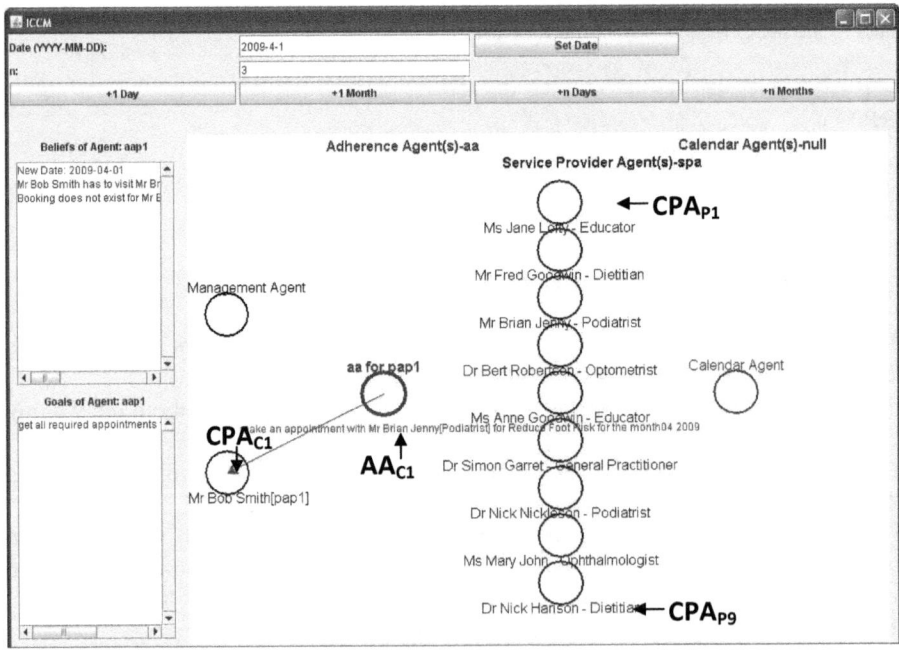

Fig. 3. AA_{c1} informs the CPA_{c1} about the due visit and requests to set an appointment

patient's belief about waiting time is incorrect (refer to the outcome of MSRP1). PIO1 is expected to reverse the belief deficit of the patient. Similarly, PIO2 can be used to reverse an intention deficit associated with the obligation visit(?PIN, ?Month, ?Year). A screen from the implementation which illustrates AA_{c1} intervening CPA_{c1} requesting to set an appointment is shown in Figure 3.

Similar domain-specific failure prevention strategies can be specified for other obligations in chronic disease management such as managing repeat medications and maintaining patient measurements (e.g., blood glucose, blood pressure) within predefined acceptable limits.

5   Related Research

Our aim in this research is to study means for reducing service delivery failures resulting from "deficits" in the mental attitudes of human contract parties. As such, our interest is in predictive monitoring approaches rather than reseach in replanning, plan repair and plan failure recovery, in which remedial actions are considered after a plan failure occurs. Current predictive monitoring frameworks [20] use detection followed by an intervention strategy to avoid contract violations. We argue that when contract parties are autonomous human agents, an intervention does not succeed unless the reason for the possible violation is determined. The reason for the possible violation is encapsulated within the mental attitudes of the agent; that is, the mental state of the contract parties plays a major role here. If the detection and intervention mechanisms ignore the agent's mental state, the intervention may be ineffective. Therefore, for an intervention to be effective, the monitoring framework should capture and interpret the mental attitudes of contract parties. The proposed deficit recognition strategy aims to capture this intermediate layer between detection and recognition.

In addition, the importance of mental-state recognition is already realised in health care. For example, the diabetes management program offered by American Healthways [22] uses the trans-theoretical model of behaviour change [23] to identify patients' readiness for health care interventions. This approach determines how amendable a patient is to making a lifestyle change at a particular point in time, which in turn helps to tailor the selected intervention.

From the perspective of electronic contract formation and management, the CONTRACT project [24] is the most recent and relevant. In this framework, each contract is associated with two types of states: Critical States (CS) and Danger of Violation (DOV) states. CS define the states which are compulsory for the successful execution of contract. That is, at the service delivery stage, if a CS state does not occur, it is identified as a violation of the contract. The DOV states indicate a possible violation of the contract. The DOV states are not explicitly states in the contract. Our definition of precursors (Section 3.1) is similar to the DOV states. The extension in our work is that once a DOV (or absence of a precursor) is identified, we carry out a mental-state recognition process to identify the deficit which prevented the occurrence of the precursor. The mental-state recognition process help to select a tailored and more effective intervention.

6   Conclusions and Future Work

This paper presents the complexities introduced by human contract parties in meeting service delivery objectives in customer life cycle management. It describes the effect of deficits in mental attitudes on the successful delivery of services involving goal-directed agents. It also proposes an adherence support architecture either to reverse such deficits or to identify reasons for revising contractual obligations.

The current implementation uses intrusive behaviour monitoring techniques for mental-state recognition. Due to the fact that intrusive mechanisms heavily depend on agents to communicate all required data, as future work, we aim to use a mix of intrusive and overhearing techniques.

In addition, we are in the process of establishing an understanding of the adherence support architecture through theory and simulations. In doing so, we associate costs and benefits with contract failures and successes, as well as costs associated with precursor recognition, deficit recognition and intervention. We aim to use the theoretical findings to establish general principles of intervention and the simulation to investigate more complex scenarios and other problem domains.

Acknowledgments

The work reported here was supported in part by British Telecom (CT1080050530), the Australian Research Council (LP0774944), the Australian Governments Clever Networks program and the Victorian Department of Innovation, Industry and Regional Development, Department of Health, and Multi Media Victoria. We also gratefully acknowledge the contributions and advice from Dr Simon Thompson and Dr Hamid Gharib of British Telecom and Professor Leon Piterman, Dr Kay Jones, Associate Professor Peter Schattner, and Dr Akuh Adaji of the Department of General Practice, Monash University.

References

1. Wickramasinghe, K., Guttmann, C., Georgeff, M., Gharib, H., Thomas, I., Thompson, S., Schmidt, H.: Agent-based intelligent collaborative care management. In: Proceedings of AAMAS, vol. 2, pp. 1387–1388. IFAAMS (2009)
2. Guttmann, C., Thomas, I., Georgeff, M., Wickramasinghe, K., Gharib, H., Thompson, S., Schmidt, H.: Towards an intelligent agent framework to manage and coordinate collaborative care. In: Proceedings of the First Workshop on Collaborative Agents – REsearch and Development (CARE 2009). LNCS. Springer, Heidelberg (2009) (to appear in 2010)
3. Rao, A.S., Georgeff, M.P.: Modeling rational agents within a BDI-architecture. In: Allen, J., Fikes, R., Sandewall, E. (eds.) Principles of Knowledge Representation and Reasoning (KR), pp. 473–484. Morgan Kaufmann publishers Inc., San Mateo (1991)
4. Rao, A.: Agentspeak(L): BDI agents speak out in a logical computable language. In: Perram, J., Van de Velde, W. (eds.) MAAMAW 1996. LNCS (LNAI), vol. 1038, pp. 42–55. Springer, Heidelberg (1996)
5. Bratman, M.E.: Intentions, Plans, and Practical Reason. Harvard University Press, Cambridge (1987)

6. Castelfranchi, C., Paglieri, F.: The role of beliefs in goal dynamics: Prolegomena to a constructive theory of intentions. Synthese 155(2), 237–263 (2007)
7. Bu, D., Pan, E., Johnston, D., Walkler, J., Adler-Milstein, J., Kendrick, D., Hook, J.A.M., Cusack, C.M., Bates, D.W., Middleton, B.: The value of information technology-enabled diabetes management. In: Healthcare Information and Management System Society (HIMSS) (2007)
8. Chronic disease management (2007) (accessed: November 12, 2007)
9. Anderson, G.F., Wilson, K.B.: Chronic disease in california: Facts and figures (2006)
10. Georgeff, M.: E-health and the Transformation of Healthcare (2007)
11. Diabetes management in general practice. guidelines for type 2 diabetes (2009)
12. Rao, A.: Means-end plan recognition-towards a theory of reactive recognition. In: Proceedings of the Fourth International Conference on Principles of Knowledge Representation and Reasoning, pp. 497–508 (1994)
13. Rao, A.S.: Integrated agent architecture: Execution and recognition of mental-states. In: Zhang, C., Lukose, D. (eds.) DAI 1995. LNCS, vol. 1087, pp. 159–173. Springer, Heidelberg (1996)
14. Rao, A.S., Murray, G.: Multi-agent mental-state recognition and its application to aircombat modelling. In: Proc. Work. Distributed AI (1994)
15. Jennings, N.R.: Controlling cooperative problem solving in industrial multi-agent systems using joint intentions. Artificial Intelligence 75(2), 195–240 (1995)
16. Tambe, M.: Towards flexible teamwork. Arxiv preprint cs/9709101 (1997)
17. Faci, N., Modgil, S., Oren, N., Meneguzzi, F., Miles, S., Luck, M.: Towards a monitoring framework for agent-based contract systems. In: Klusch, M., Pěchouček, M., Polleres, A. (eds.) CIA 2008. LNCS (LNAI), vol. 5180, pp. 292–305. Springer, Heidelberg (2008)
18. Horling, B., Benyo, B., Lesser, V.: Using self-diagnosis to adapt organizational structures. In: Proceedings of the Fifth International Conference on Autonomous Agents, p. 536. ACM, New York (2001)
19. Mazouzi, H., Seghrouchni, A.E.F., Haddad, S.: Open protocol design for complex interactions in multi-agent systems. In: Proceedings of the First International Joint Conference on Autonomous Agents and Multiagent Systems: Part 2, pp. 517–526. ACM, New York (2002)
20. Kaminka, G.A., Pynadath, D.V., Tambe, M.: Monitoring teams by overhearing: A multiagent plan-recognition approach. Journal of Artificial Intelligence Research 17(1), 83–135 (2002)
21. Bordini, R., Huebner, J., Wooldridge, M.: Programming Multi-Agent Systems in AgentSpeak using Jason. Wiley, New York (2006)
22. Pope, J.E., Hudson, L.R., Orr, P.M.: Case study of American Healthways' diabetes disease management program. Health Care Financing Review 27(1), 47 (2005)
23. Prochaska, J.O., DiClemente, C.C.: Toward a comprehensive model of change. In: Treating Addictive Behaviors: Processes of Change, pp. 3–27 (1986)
24. Oren, N., Miles, S., Luck, M., Modgil, S., Faci, N., Alvarez, S., Vazquez, J., Kollingbaum, M.: Contract based electronic business systems theoretical framework. Technical Report D2.2, King's College London (2008)

Norm Diversity and Emergence in Tag-Based Cooperation

Nathan Griffiths[1] and Michael Luck[2]

[1] Department of Computer Science, University of Warwick,
Coventry, CV4 7AL, UK
nathan@dcs.warwick.ac.uk
[2] Department of Informatics, King's College London,
London, WC2R 2LS, UK
michael.luck@kcl.ac.uk

Abstract. In multi-agent systems norms are an important influence that can engender cooperation by constraining actions and binding groups together. A key question is how to establish suitable norms in a decentralised population of self-interested agents, especially where individual agents might not adhere to the rules of the system. It is desirable, in certain situations, to establish multiple co-existing norms within a population to ensure a diversity of norms, for example to give agents alternatives should one norm collapse. In this paper we investigate the problem of norm emergence, and the related issue of group recognition, using tag-based cooperation as the interaction model. We explore characteristics that affect the longevity and adoption of norms in tag-based cooperation, and provide an empirical evaluation of existing techniques for supporting cooperation in the presence of cheaters.

1 Introduction

Multi-agent systems often comprise multiple self-interested agents seeking to achieve tasks that they cannot, or not as easily, achieve alone. In a sense, however, this self-interest suggests that without some other constraining influence, cooperation is unlikely to emerge. Norms provide a source of such influence on agent behaviour, by constraining actions and binding a group together so that cooperation naturally arises. In this view, one key question is how to establish a suitable set of norms. While formally established institutional rules offer a means of doing this in a centralised fashion, such centralised control is often not possible in large dynamic environments. Indeed, as has been recognised elsewhere [5,32], *social norms* are not formal, prescriptive, centrally imposed rules, but often emerge informally through decentralised agent interactions. In this paper, we explore the nature of such social norms and their impact on group formation through empirical analysis, and examine the impact of *cheating* agents: those that fail to comply with norms but seek to enjoy the benefits of the group.

In seeking to investigate these issues, we adopt the *tag-based* approach taken to the problem of *group recognition*, by Riolo, Cohen and Axelrod, who use observable tags as markings, traits or social cues attached to individuals [23].

M. De Vos et al. (Eds.): COIN 2010 International Workshops, LNAI 6541, pp. 230–249, 2011.

Using this approach, Hales and Edmonds have achieved promising results in peer-to-peer settings [14], but these are not resilient when cheaters are introduced, and assume that agents have full control over their links to others, and are able to completely change these links in a single operation. In particular, we need to support cooperation in dynamic environments that may contain cheaters, in which individuals have limited control over their connections.

We view tags as capturing *social norms*: tags are recognised by agents who form groups that share a tag (within their tolerance values). The tag can be seen as an abstraction of a norm that is adopted by the agents who share it, with the group itself being *governed* by that tag, or norm, which binds the group together. This interpretation of norms is rather different from that considered in previous work on norm emergence, which has focused directly on the behaviour of individuals, such that once a behaviour is adopted by a group of agents, the behaviour is said to correspond to a norm. By contrast, in tag-based systems cooperative behaviour is determined by a combination of observable traits, in the form of tags, and tolerance. In changing its tag, an individual alters the nature of its own cooperative actions and the actions of others towards it. The notion of a norm becomes implicit, and results from agents choosing to exhibit similar observable traits, which in turn gives rise to particular behaviour. Individuals may alter their observable appearance in order to influence the manner in which others interact with them, and a particular appearance may come to be correlated with a particular behaviour. In such a setting, adopting a given appearance becomes synonymous with adopting a norm.

Many previous investigations of norm emergence have focused on very small sets of possible actions or states, with the view that the ideal situation is one in which all agents in the population select a common action or state, such as driving on the left. In scenarios such as the Coordination Game, Social Dilemma Game and Prisoner's Dilemma, agents are able to be in one of only two states, and it is with respect to these states that norm emergence is considered [9,10,19,21,27]. Although other scenarios have been explored that contain a wider range of states, such as the language/vocabulary coordination problem [30], the focus has been on obtaining a single common state in the population [25].

In open societies there are typically many possible actions and states from which many possible norms can emerge, and it may not be desirable, or even possible, to converge on a single norm. Many scenarios exist in which it is desirable to establish a selection of norms. For example, in resource allocation we would like a range of resources to be used rather overusing a single resource, and for role adoption it is desirable for agents to adopt different roles to ensure that all the required roles are taken. Such scenarios are exemplified by the *El Farol Bar Problem* [2] in which patrons must decide whether to go to the El Farol Bar, where the utility of attending is high when the bar is not too overcrowded. A high utility is achieved only when people adopt different norms, and attend the bar on different occasions. Multiple norms are also important in situations where an established norm can collapse, since it is desirable for agents to be able to adopt an alternative established norm, rather than having to establish a new norm from scratch. For example, in the case of a monopoly failure the impact is lessened if alternative providers are already established. Tags allow us to investigate this multiplicity of norms, since the range of possible tag values is large and corresponds to the range of possible norms; although we desire sufficient commonality of tags to engender cooperation, we do not require a single tag to be adopted by the entire population. Thus, we are able to investigate norm emergence where many norms are present in the population.

In this paper, we examine the problem of supporting cooperation from the perspective of norm emergence, and evaluate the effect of alternative techniques on norm emergence. Specifically, we investigate our recently proposed techniques for coping with cheaters in tag-based systems [12,13] in terms of the norms that emerge over time. This is a novel interpretation of tag-based cooperation, and allows us to investigate a scenario in which multiple norms co-exist. The key contributions are an evaluation of the characteristics affecting the longevity and size of norm-governed groups in tag-based cooperation, and an increased understanding of the operation and implications of our previously proposed mechanisms for coping with cheaters.

The paper begins with an introduction to tag-based cooperation, followed by the specifics of using *context assessment* and *rewiring* to improve group effectiveness in the presence of cheaters. Then, in Section 4, we present an analysis of our experimental findings, and finally we conclude with a discussion of our results and their more general significance.

2   Background

It has been widely argued that *norms* provide a valuable mechanism for regulating behaviour in decentralised societies [3,11,32]. Through the ongoing behaviour of individuals, norms can emerge that provide coherence and stability, and support cooperation. A common view is that where a group of agents share a particular strategy, behaviour or characteristic, a norm is established [26]. In this paper we investigate factors influencing norm emergence in a population of agents, each of which has a set of neighbours with which it interacts. This abstract environment reflects the form of many real-world settings, such as ad-hoc communication networks or P2P content sharing. We assume that agents know the identity of their neighbours, rather than assuming anonymity of interactions. Although many P2P researchers assume anonymity, this is often introduced as a way of modelling the rarity of repeat interactions between any two individuals. Our formulation is compatible with this view, since we assume that there are very few repeat interactions, yet at some level the identity or location of others must be known, otherwise it is impossible to interact with them. For example, a network address is needed to share content and an identifier is required to forward packets in a communication network. We also assume that agents have limited observations of others and that there is no direct reciprocity, and so we adopt Riolo, Cohen and Axelrod's tag-based approach, introduced below.

Tag-based cooperation has been considered for many years by biologists and social scientists investigating how cooperative societies of selfish individuals might evolve through the recognition of cultural artefacts or traits [1,6,8,15,16]. Simple observable traits, or *tags* [17], can be used as cultural artefacts to engender cooperation without relying on reciprocity [4,23,31]. Existing work on tags, however, has given little consideration to the possibility that some members of the population may be *cheaters* who deviate from the rules of the system, by not cooperating when they should. In this paper, our investigation of norm emergence allows for the possibility of cheaters.

Riolo, Cohen and Axelrod (RCA) propose a tag-based approach to cooperation in which an individual's decision to cooperate is based on whether an arbitrary tag (i.e. observable trait) associated with it, is sufficiently similar to that associated with a potential recipient [23]. The approach is illustrated using a simple *donation scenario* in which each agent acts as a potential donor with a number of randomly selected neighbours. Should an agent opt to donate, it incurs a cost c, and the recipient gains a benefit b (it is assumed that $b > c$), otherwise both receive nothing. Each agent i is initially randomly assigned a tag τ_i and a tolerance threshold T_i with a uniform distribution from $[0, 1]$. An agent A will donate to a potential recipient B if B's tag is within A's tolerance threshold T_A, namely $|\tau_A - \tau_B| \leq T_A$. Agents are selected to act as potential donors in P interaction pairings, after which the population is reproduced proportionally to their relative scores, such that more successful agents produce more offspring. Each offspring is subject to mutation, so that with a small probability a new (random) tag is received or noise added to the tolerance. In relation to norms, the key aspect here is that donation rate is an assessment of the effectiveness of the society and the impact of norms: the greater the effectiveness, the higher the donation rate.

RCA have shown that a high cooperation rate can be achieved with this simple approach. They observe cycles in which a cooperative population is established, which is then invaded by a mutant whose tag is similar (and so receives donations) but has a low tolerance (and so does not donate). Such mutants initially do well, leading to them taking over the population and subsequently lowering the overall rate of cooperation, but eventually the mutant tag and tolerance become the most common and cooperation again becomes the norm [23]. It is important to note that cooperation does not require a single tag to be adopted throughout the population and is achieved where there are subgroups of agents in the population that share different tags, corresponding to subgroups having adopted different norms. As these subgroups evolve they mirror the typical life-cycle of norms: initially a small number of agents adopt the norm; the group then expands as the norm is more widely adopted; over time the norm becomes outdated and alternatives emerge conflicting with the established norm; eventually one of these new norms may replace the previously established norm. Tag-based cooperation, therefore, provides us with a scenario in which to consider the emergence and ongoing evolution of multiple norms within a population.

Hales and Edmonds (HE) apply RCA's approach in a P2P setting, with two main changes [14]. First, a *learning interpretation* of reproduction is adopted, so that each agent compares itself to another in the population at random and adopts the other's tag and tolerance if the other's score is higher (subject to potential mutations) [23]. Second, HE interpret a tag as being an agent's neighbours in the P2P network, i.e. an agent's links to others. In RCA's work each agent is connected to each other agent, with no corresponding notion of neighbourhood. In HE's model, the process of an agent adopting another's tag is equivalent to dropping all of its own connections, and copying the connections of the other agent (and adding a connection to the other agent itself) [14]. Importantly, in our view, this model reflects the formation of groups based on recognition of tags in group members. Since tags, in HE's model, are interpreted as corresponding to an agent's set of neighbours, mutation corresponds to resetting the neighbour list (replacing it with a single neighbour randomly selected from the population). In this paper we use numerical tags, meaning that tag mutation does not affect an individual's set of neighbours. Instead, inspired by HE, we enable agents to rewire their neighbourhood, and so change the set from which potential donors are selected.

Using simulations, HE have shown this approach to be promising in situations where agents are given free reign to rewire the network and replace all of their connections each reproduction. This rewiring is an *all-or-nothing* operation, in that although an agent can adopt a completely new set of neighbours (*replacing* its existing neighbourhood), it cannot *modify* its existing neighbourhood. Our view is that such extreme rewiring, where the neighbourhood topology might completely change with each new generation, is not practicable in all scenarios. For example, in a communication network this would imply that all existing routes become outdated and need to be re-established, while in a content sharing system an agent would lose all information about the content available in its neighbourhood. In this paper we consider a less extreme situation, in which agents are able to rewire a proportion of their neighbourhood.

Both RCA and HE assume that agents do not deviate from the rules of the system, i.e. they assume that there are no cheaters. A *cheater* is an agent that accepts donations, but will not donate to others, even if the rules of the system dictate that it should. We assume that if a cheater reproduces, then its offspring will also cheat. In this paper we assume that the traits embodied by tags are observable to others, meaning that cheaters cannot falsify their tags. To illustrate this assumption, consider a group of agents in which a tag is analogous to wearing a coloured hat. If an agent selects a red hat, then this is visible to all others, and it cannot falsely claim to be wearing a blue hat. In future work we may consider alternative formulations that allow for the potential falsification of tags, such as scenarios in which agents can present a different appearance to different neighbours. The effect of cheaters in standard tag-based cooperation is catastrophic, with the introduction of even a small proportion of cheaters into the population causing cooperation to collapse [12].

Norm emergence has been considered in several other settings. For example, norms can emerge in a Social Dilemma Game when individuals are repeatedly randomly paired [27], and in certain settings can emerge simply by individuals learning based on their own individual histories [29]. In this paper, however, our focus is on using the interpretation of a shared tag as representing a norm to further our understanding of tag-based cooperation.

3   Improving Group Effectiveness

In seeking to examine the impact of cheaters on group formation and norm emergence, we consider a population of agents, each of which has its own tag and a set of connections to n neighbours, such that agents can only interact with their neighbours (although for reproduction we consider the population as a whole). A *random* network topology is used with degree distribution $P(k)$, such that each agent is initially randomly connected to $k = n$ others. Each agent is selected to act as a potential donor in P interaction pairings, with the potential recipient randomly selected from its set of neighbours. As discussed in the previous section we assume that agents know the identity of their neighbours. We assume that a proportion of agents are cheaters and will not cooperate with others even when their tags are within the tolerance threshold. The *donation scenario* and parameter values used by RCA are adopted, such that benefit $b = 1$ and cost $c = 0.1$ [23]. Each agent i is initially assigned an arbitrary tag τ_i and tolerance T_i with uniform distribution from $[0, 1]^1$. We investigate norm emergence in relation to RCA's tag-based approach and two techniques that we have previously proposed for improving cooperation in the presence of cheaters: context assessment [12] and rewiring [13].

3.1   Context Assessment

Our first technique, originally proposed in [12], enables agents to assess their neighbourhood, or group, in terms of how cooperative they perceive their neighbours to be. The donation decision is modified so that an agent's assessment of its neighbourhood context becomes a factor in the decision to donate. Agents are given a fixed length FIFO memory to record the last l donation behaviours observed for each neighbour. When the neighbour donates, an observation value of $+1$ is recorded, and when it does not -1 is recorded. This memory is fairly sparse, since the number of interactions is small compared to the number of agents, and so the overhead incurred is relatively small (2 bits per observation for $n \times P$ observations, where n is the number of neighbours and P the number of pairings).

In order to assess its neighbourhood context, an agent considers each of its n neighbours in turn, and determines the contribution to the context assessment c_i

---

[1] We actually use a lower bound on *tolerance* of 10^{-6} to address Roberts and Sherratt's concerns regarding agents with identical tags being forced to cooperate [24]. This also allows the population to contain non-cooperative agents of the form considered by Masuda and Ohtsuki [20].

of neighbour i, which is simply the proportion of observed interactions in which the neighbour donated, given by:

$$c_i = \begin{cases} \dfrac{\sum_{j=1}^{l_i} \begin{array}{l} o_i^j, \text{ if } o_i^j > 0 \\ 0, \quad \text{otherwise} \end{array}}{l_i}, & \text{if } l_i > 0 \\ 0, & \text{otherwise} \end{cases} \tag{1}$$

where o_i^j represents the j'th observation of neighbour i, and l_i is the number of observations recorded of i's donation behaviour ($l_i < l$). By considering each of its n neighbours, agent A's assessment of its current neighbourhood context C_A is given by:

$$C_A = \frac{\sum_{i=1}^{n} c_i}{n} \tag{2}$$

This context assessment can be used to influence the donation decision. The intuition is that agents 'expect' that by donating they are more likely to receive a future donation from some other (observing) agent, thus binding a group together. However, since the number of interactions is small compared to the number of agents, this is a *weak* notion of indirect reciprocity. An agent's donation to another is unlikely to be directly repaid or directly observed by a third party, and so there is little direct or indirect reciprocity. Instead, context assessment gives an impression of the donation behaviour in a neighbourhood, indicating the likelihood of receiving future donations. An agent's assessment of its neighbourhood context is incorporated into the model by adapting the decision to donate, such that both tolerance and neighbourhood context are considered. Thus, an agent A will donate to B if:

$$|\tau_A - \tau_B| \leq (1 - \gamma).T_A + \gamma.C_A \tag{3}$$

The parameter γ, called the *context influence*, allows us to tune the technique. The context influence is in the range $[0, 1]$, with $\gamma = 0$ making the technique identical to RCA's method, while $\gamma = 1$ causes the donation decision to be determined solely by an agent's assessment of its neighbourhood context.

We adopt a learning interpretation of reproduction, such that after a fixed number of interaction pairings P an agent compares itself to another, randomly selected from the population. If the other agent is more successful, then its tag and tolerance are copied (subject to a small probability of mutation), otherwise the tag and tolerance are unchanged. Note that although an agent's interactions are restricted to its neighbourhood we do not similarly constrain reproduction, and we allow an agent to compare itself against another that is randomly selected from the whole population. Thus, although agents can only donate to (and receive donations from) their immediate neighbours, they can observe the performance of the population at large. If the comparison for reproduction was restricted to an agent's set of neighbours, this would have the effect of structuring the population into (overlapping) sub-groups. In this paper we are concerned with investigating norm emergence within a population as a whole, and so we do not impose such a restriction.

3.2   Rewiring

Our second technique, introduced in [13], enables agents to *rewire* their network neighbourhoods, such that after reproduction an agent removes a proportion λ, called the *rewire proportion*, of connections, and replaces them with connections to new neighbours. This approach is motivated by HE's results, but unlike HE we do not assume that agents can replace *all* of their connections since, as discussed above, this is likely to be impractical in real-world settings. In our mechanism, after reproduction the $n \times \lambda$ worst neighbours are removed and the best (non-duplicate) neighbour from each of the agent's $n \times \lambda$ best neighbours are added. The neighbours are considered in descending rank order and, for each, the best non-duplicate neighbour is added. Additional randomly selected neighbours are added if necessary to prevent the neighbourhood shrinking due to duplication (agents have at most one connection to another given individual, and duplicate connections are meaningless). Other rewiring strategies are of course possible, with alternative criteria for selecting links to remove and add. In [13] we evaluate a small number of alternatives and show that the strategy described above gives reasonable performance.

Connections to remove are determined by ranking each neighbour i using the contribution to the context assessment c_i (defined in Equation 1), with agents having the lowest c_i values being removed. The contribution to the context assessment is also used to determine which connections to add, with an agent asking each of its $n \times \lambda$ best neighbours to recommend their best non-duplicate neighbour. If the c_i values of two or more agents are equal then one is selected arbitrarily. The *rewire proportion* determines the extent to which the network is rewired in each generation. Such rewiring can be thought of as being the result of a simplistic reputation mechanism, since agents update their connections based on the experiences and recommendations of others. However, unlike typical reputation mechanisms, the assessment is based on relatively little information, which is not predicated on repeated encounters or on a notion of (direct or indirect) reciprocity [18,22]. Clearly there is a chance that an agent might ask a cheating neighbour to recommend a new connection, and so be given false or poor information. However, since the approach is to ask the *best* neighbours, the requested agents will be those that have been observed to be cooperative, and we assume that they are likely to give honest information. We consider this issue further in the discussion in Section 5.

Figure 1 illustrates the alternative rewiring approaches, in which circles represent agents, thin solid lines represent existing connections, and dotted and bold solid lines show dropped and new connections respectively. Agent A's original neighbourhood is shown in (a). The results of applying HE's rewiring approach is shown in (b) where A drops all of its connections and adopts those of B. Our rewiring approach is illustrated in (c). If A's neighbours in order of preference are B, C, D, E, F, and 2 neighbours are to be replaced, then connections to E and F will be dropped. If B's neighbours, are D, H, I, G, A and C's neighbours are J, K, L, A, I in preference order, then A will add H from B's neighbourhood (D is already in A's neighbourhood and so not added) and J from C's neighbourhood.

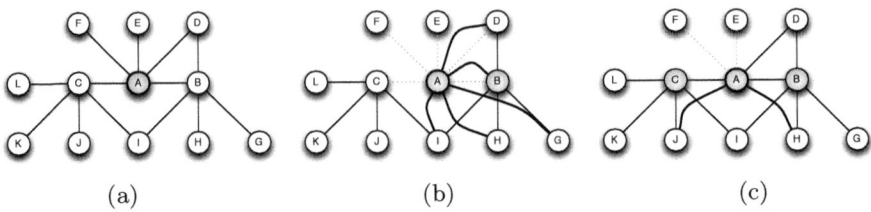

Fig. 1. Rewiring showing (a) the original neighbourhood rewired using (b) HE's method and (c) our rewiring approach

4   Experimental Analysis

Using the PeerSim P2P simulator[2], we have built a simulation that allows us to explore norm emergence using RCA's standard approach, context assessment, and rewiring. The quantitative results presented here are averaged over 10 runs using a population of 100 agents, a neighbourhood size of $n = 10$ (meaning that the population has a degree distribution of $P(k) = 0.1$), with 10 pairings per agent per generation ($P = 10$), and a cheater proportion of 30%. Where context assessment is incorporated a *context influence* of $\gamma = 0.5$ is used, and similarly where rewiring is incorporated we use a *rewire proportion* of $\lambda = 0.5$. After reproduction there is a 0.001 probability of mutating the tolerance of each agent by adding Gaussian noise (with mean 0 and standard deviation 0.01), along with a probability of mutating each agent's tag by selecting a new random value.

We consider two configurations for mutating tags: a *low mutation* rate of 0.001 and a *high mutation* rate of 0.01. The low mutation rate represents a generally stable population in which mutation is simply a small part of the evolutionary process. Conversely, the high mutation rate represents a more dynamic and less stable environment in which there is more significant fluctuation in tags present in the population. Evolutionary approaches, such as tag-based systems, typically use low mutation rates, but in our experiments we use a high rate to simulate a dynamic environment. Since tag mutations are imposed at the beginning of a new generation (with memories of previous interactions having been reset), the mutation of an agent's tag is equivalent to the pre-mutation agent leaving the system and being replaced by a new agent with a new tag, such that the new agent has the same connections and tolerance as the agent being replaced. Thus, using a high tag mutation rate is a simple approximation of a dynamic environment. In Section 5, we discuss the importance of considering a more accurate representation of *churn* (agents leaving and joining the system), but using a high mutation rate gives an indication of the likely performance of the approach in such a setting.

In the remainder of this section we give an overview of the main findings from our simulations, focusing on two main characteristics. First, we consider

---

[2] http://peersim.sourceforge.net/

the *donation rate* defined as the proportion of interactions resulting in a donation in the final generation of the simulation, averaged across the population and across simulation runs. This indicates the effectiveness of the groups that emerge in complying with the norms that establish those groups and govern their maintenance. Second, we consider the *number of unique tags* present in the final generation, again averaged across runs, which indicates the number of norm-governed groups that have been established. Where a group of agents share a tag, or each others' tags are within their tolerance values, we interpret this as recognising a norm that is then established, since those agents will cooperate by donating to each other (provided that they are not cheaters). The number of unique tags indicates the number of such norm-governed groups that are formed, since each tag value corresponds to a tag group. However, it is important to note that this is only a coarse metric since (i) some tags may be adopted only by a single agent with no other agents having a tag and tolerance combination that gives rise to mutual cooperation, in which case there is no norm, and (ii) in some cases where a single agent has adopted a particular tag the tolerance values of this and other agents with similar tags may still give rise to mutual cooperation, and so a norm is established. The role of tolerance in the donation decision significantly increases the complexity of identifying for certain whether a norm is established. In our analysis we take a simple approach by focusing on the number of unique tags, and do not attempt to precisely quantify the number of agents that have tag and tolerance combinations that result in mutual cooperation.

Where there is a low number of unique tags, so that there are few groups, the average number of agents adopting each tag is high, and the groups are larger in size, with the respective norms being more widely adopted, and a reduced likelihood of a tag belonging to a single individual. Conversely, as the number of unique tags (and therefore groups) increases, the average number of agents having adopted each tag (and hence in each group) reduces, so that the corresponding norms are less widely adopted and there is an increased likelihood of a tag being ascribed to a single agent only. Thus, for lower numbers of unique tags there is more significance in them representing groups of agents having adopted

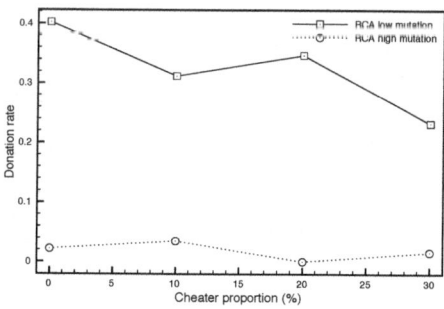

Fig. 2. The effect of cheaters using RCA's standard approach with low and high mutation rates

those tags as norms. Note that this is an informal notion of norm establishment, in comparison to other approaches that have a group leader [7], or explicit strategies emerging rather than simply shared tags [27].

We use a cheater proportion of 30% in our simulations since in stable populations (with a low tag mutation), this is known to have a significant impact on the level of cooperation [12]. Figure 2 shows how the donation rate declines in a stable population (the solid line) as cheaters are introduced using RCA's standard approach (with no context assessment or rewiring). With no cheaters we observe an average donation rate of 40.2% which reduces to 23.2% if 30% of the population are cheating agents. In a dynamic environment (the dotted line), represented by the high mutation rate, we can see that the donation rate is significantly reduced (to an average of 2.4%) regardless of the proportion of cheaters.

4.1   Context Assessment

The base case for our comparisons is RCA's standard approach (without context assessment or rewiring), which with a low mutation rate gives a donation rate of 23.2%, and with a high mutation rate gives a donation rate of 1.5%. The increased dynamism of the environment, represented by the increased mutation rate, has a catastrophic effect on the donation rate, and in turn on group effectiveness. For a donation to occur, agents must share a tag (within their tolerance values). With a low mutation rate, RCA's approach gives an average of 35.8 tags, each shared by 2.8 agents on average. With a high mutation rate, there are 79.2 tags shared by 1.3 agents on average. Thus, with a high mutation rate a large number of tags are adopted by a single agent, as confirmed by the very low donation rate observed (3.2%). In relation to norm emergence, this means that in the low mutation case the resulting norms are on average only adopted by 2.8 agents. In the high mutation case the tag groups do not, on average, correspond to norm emergence since less than two agents adopt each tag. It is not our concern in this paper to attempt to define the number of agents needed for norm emergence, but clearly there must be at least two agents involved.

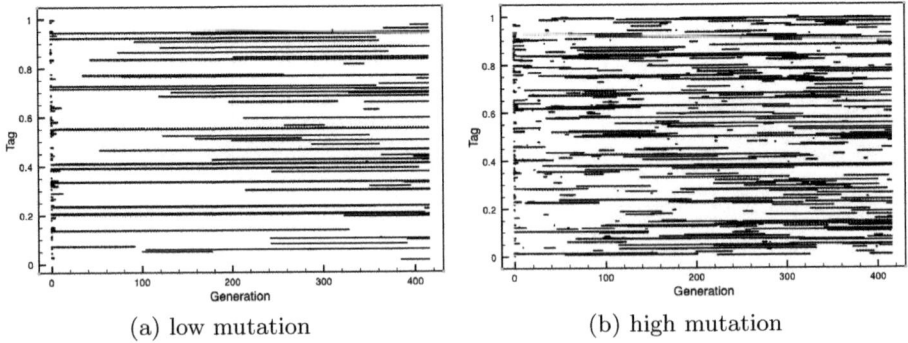

(a) low mutation   (b) high mutation

Fig. 3. Tags with RCA's standard approach using low and high mutation rates

Figure 3 shows the evolution of tags in the population over the duration of a sample simulation run for both low and high mutation settings. Each point represents the presence of a tag in a particular generation, and where a tag persists for several generations the points form a line from the generation in which the tag group is created to the generation in which it collapses. Our numerical results are confirmed by Figure 3 which shows that many more tags are present in the high mutation setting than the low setting. This graphical representation also allows us to observe the formation of norm-based groups. In particular, in the low mutation setting norm-governed groups are established and maintained for many generations, while in the high mutation setting many such groups have very brief durations appearing as points or very short lines. (Note that since the number of unique tags is large in Figure 3(b), many of the points do not represent norm establishment, as discussed above.)

The evolution of tags in the population when using the context assessment technique is shown in Figure 4. Comparing Figures 3 and 4 it is immediately apparent that there are significantly fewer tags present using context assessment than with the standard approach. On average, context assessment in a low mutation setting results in only 3.7 tags (compared to 35.8 with the standard approach) and 12.1 tags (compared to 79.2) for a high mutation rate. Donation rates of 47.5% and 42.9% are obtained for the low and high mutation settings respectively (compared to 20.4% and 3.2%). The reduction in donation rate in the high mutation setting compared to the low mutation setting is less pronounced (approximately 10%) than with the standard approach (where the reduction is approximately 85%). We see this as demonstration that context assessment is more stable in supporting cooperation in dynamic environments than RCA's standard approach. This tells us that norms resulting from context assessment are more widely adopted than with RCA's approach (by 27 and 8.3 agents on average for the low and high mutation rates respectively). Given that these norms are more widely adopted, we would expect an increase in the group effectiveness (as indicated by donation rate achieved), which is indeed the result we observe.

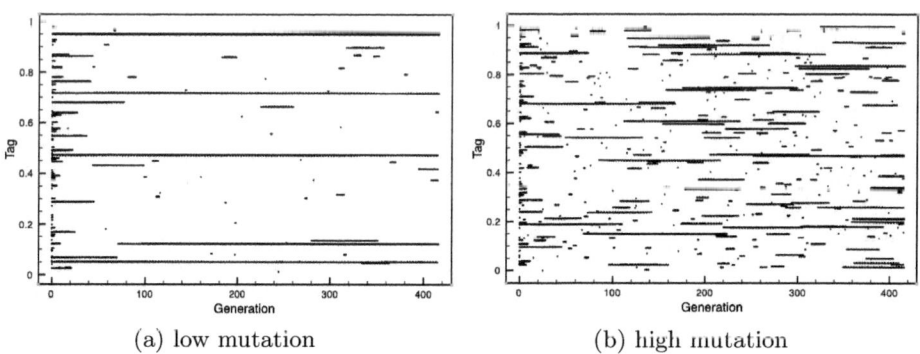

(a) low mutation   (b) high mutation

Fig. 4. Tags with context assessment using low and high mutation rates

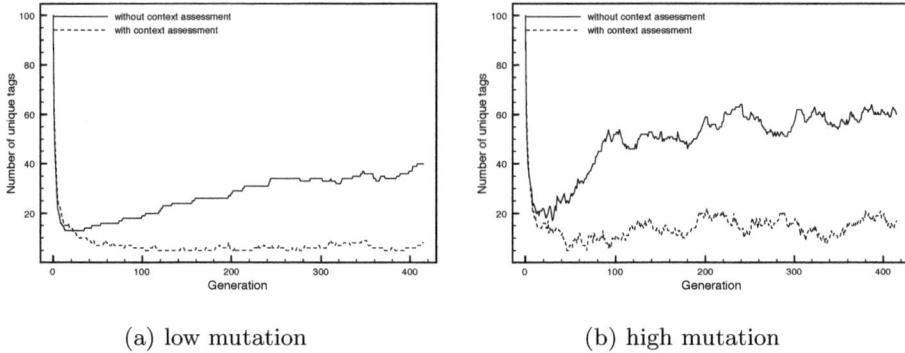

(a) low mutation   (b) high mutation

Fig. 5. Number of unique tags with context assessment using low and high mutation rates

The evolution of the number of unique tags during a sample simulation run for low and high mutation rates is illustrated in Figure 5. In both settings the number of tags is initially very high and is (approximately) equal to the population size since agents are randomly allocated tags. During the first few generations the number of unique tags drops significantly as agents begin to copy tags from their more successful neighbours. As the simulation progresses the number of unique tags then stabilises. From Figure 5 we can see that in addition to context assessment resulting in significantly fewer tags than RCA's approach, the number of tags also stabilises more quickly, meaning that the population reaches a form of convergence. In a stable population (with a low mutation rate) we achieve a quicker convergence using context assessment than without, and the resulting population contains significantly fewer tags. When the mutation rate is high the number of tags increases, as does the extent of the fluctuations over generations (with both approaches having similar fluctuation levels). Thus, dynamism in the population reduces convergence. It is clear that norm-governed groups emerge more quickly using context assessment than with the standard approach, and on average norms are adopted by many more agents. Due to space constraints we do not discuss the effect of memory length in this paper, but in [13] we have shown that it is not a significant factor.

4.2   Rewiring

Rewiring gives similar improvements to context assessment, with donation rates of 57.0% and 49.8% for the low and high mutation settings respectively (both of which are higher than with context assessment). The average number of unique tags is higher than for context assessment, with 11.9 and 16.8 for low and high mutation rates, but is significantly lower than with RCA's approach. The norms that are established are adopted by fewer agents using the rewiring technique than with context assessment, 8.4 (rather than 27) and 6.0 (rather than 8.3) for the low and high mutation rates, although they are still adopted by many more agents than with the standard approach. This result is unexpected, since

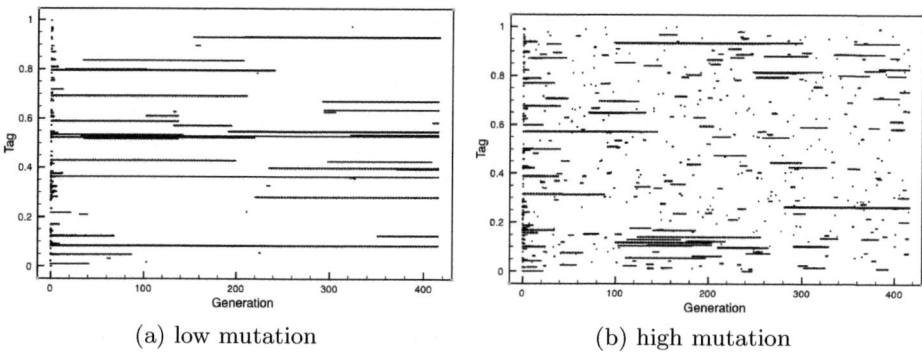

(a) low mutation   (b) high mutation

Fig. 6. Evolution of tags in a population using rewiring with low and high mutation rates

we intuitively expect that a higher donation rate (and therefore higher group effectiveness) would be achieved only when norms are more widely adopted.

The discovery that a higher donation rate can be obtained with smaller groups is potentially very powerful, since in many situations we would like to balance the desire to have widely adopted norms (and few groups) with the desire to ensure that there are several established groups from which agents can select. The widest possible adoption of a norm is where a single norm is adopted by the population in a single group. Conversely, the largest set of norms is obtained where we have a minimum number of agents per tag for norm emergence, giving groups of that size. As mentioned above, we are not concerned with attempting to define a minimum membership, but clearly more than one agent is required, and so the upper bound of the number of norm-governed groups is half the population size. In the donation scenario the motivation behind balancing the level of adoption and number of norms established is that mutations can cause a norm to collapse at any point, and in such cases we would like agents to be able to adopt an alternative norm by joining another tag group. However, this balance is a general issue in many distributed systems, and corresponds to the general view that fostering competition and avoiding monopolies can be beneficial. The question of how many norms or groups is ideal in a particular setting is an open question and requires further investigation.

The evolution of tags in the population using rewiring for sample simulation runs is shown in Figure 6. As is the case with context assessment (Figure 4) there are significantly fewer tags at any point in time than with RCA's approach (Figure 3). As noted above, rewiring results in slightly more tags in any generation than context assessment. Figure 6 also allows us to observe that the duration of a given tag group is generally slightly reduced using rewiring in comparison to context assessment, implying that the norms emerging are less long-lived. In the donation scenario this is not a major concern, since there is little cost to changing tag groups, but more generally there may be a higher cost associated with such a change. It is desirable, in general, for norm-governed groups to be of longer duration as we observe with context assessment, but also for there to be a reasonable number of alternative groups as with rewiring.

4.3   Combining Context Assessment with Rewiring

We have previously shown that combining context assessment and rewiring improves the donation rate [13], and here we observe donation rates of 68.6% and 63.1% for the low and high mutation settings respectively. In terms of norm emergence, a key question is which, if any, of the properties of context assessment (few norms of longer duration) and rewiring (more norms of shorter duration) the combined approach gives. We find that the combined approach results in 4.4 and 10.4 tag groups in the low and high mutation settings, corresponding to adoption by 22.7 and 9.6 agents on average respectively. In the low mutation setting this is similar to context assessment, and we would prefer more norms given our desire to have alternative groups established in case of norm collapse, so that an agent can join an alternative group if their current group collapses. With a high mutation rate, the number of norms is similar to that obtained with rewiring, indicating that there are alternative groups in the event of a norm collapsing. However, the duration of norms and groups is also important in ensuring that alternatives are available.

Figure 7 shows the evolution of tags using a combination of the context assessment and rewiring techniques in sample runs, and we can make two important observations. First, the run for the low mutation rate represents a particularly low number of tag groups, with a single dominant group spanning all generations and a small number of short duration groups appearing. A similar situation can occur when using context assessment alone (although the run in Figure 4 shows an example where this does not occur). We would like to avoid this by ensuring that there are alternative established norms (i.e. tag groups) at any point in time, in case of norm collapse. Second, with a high mutation rate many of the groups established persist for only very short durations. Thus, although there are many groups, avoiding the problem from the low mutation case, we would like them to be of longer duration. It seems, therefore, that while combining context assessment with rewiring increases the donation rate, it does not result

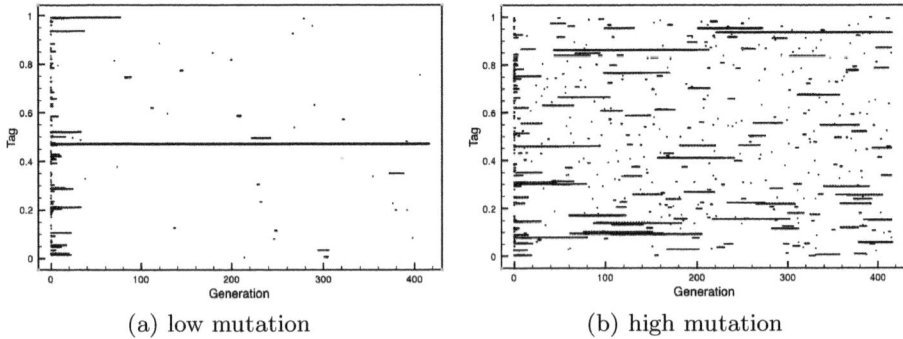

| (a) low mutation | (b) high mutation |

Fig. 7. Evolution of tags using context assessment and rewiring with low and high mutation rates

Table 1. Summary of donation rate, number of tags and size of tag group (number of agents per tag) for the low mutation rate

Approach	Average donation rate	Average number of tags	Average size of tag group
RCA's mechanism	20.4%	35.8	2.8
Context assessment	47.5%	3.7	27
Rewiring	57.0%	11.9	8.4
Context assessment and rewiring	68.6%	4.4	22.7

Table 2. Summary of donation rate, number of tags and size of tag group (number of agents per tag) for the high mutation rate

Approach	Average donation rate	Average number of tags	Average size of tag group
RCA's mechanism	3.2%	79.2	1.3
Context assessment	42.9%	12.1	8.3
Rewiring	49.8%	16.8	6.0
Context assessment and rewiring	63.1%	10.4	9.6

in groups that have the desired characteristics. We would prefer a higher number of norm-governed groups than observed in the low mutation case, to ensure alternative groups are established in case of collapse, and we would prefer more persistence than observed in the high mutation case, to avoid frequent collapses. Thus, although the donation rate is high when using the combined approach, it does not achieve the more generally desired number of norms or persistence.

Context assessment appears to have a significant reduction on the number of norm-governed groups established, and so increases their size, especially with a low mutation rate. Although this results in an increased donation rate (indeed, when combined with rewiring it gives the highest donation rate) suggesting group effectiveness, it also gives reduced diversity in the population. In many settings this is undesirable, since if there is collapse of cooperation in those groups due to the collapse of the respective norms, there are no alternative established groups for agents to join.

4.4   Summary of Results

Our simulations show that both context assessment and rewiring improve group effectiveness (through the donation rate) by the formation of groups of agents sharing a particular tag value, which we can interpret as norm establishment. A summary of the quantitative results is shown in Tables 1 and 2. In both the low and high mutation settings the highest donation rate is achieved when combining context assessment and rewiring. Rewiring gives the second highest rate, followed by context assessment, and finally RCA's approach. In the low mutation setting, context assessment (with and without rewiring) results in a low number of norm-governed groups being established. In the high mutation setting the number of groups established is reduced when context assessment is used in comparison to rewiring alone, but this difference is less significant. A visual analysis of the evolution of tags reveals that norm and group duration is potentially an issue, with each of the techniques discussed resulting in several short duration norm-governed groups being established.

5 Discussion and Conclusions

Interpreting the formation of groups of agents sharing a tag as the emergence of norms allows us to view RCA's approach as facilitating norm emergence. Indeed, it is norm emergence that leads to donations, since only when two or more agents share a tag (within their tolerance) will a donation occur. Unlike many previous investigations on norm emergence, in our model multiple norms can successfully co-exist, and we are not endeavouring to establish a single norm throughout the population. This is important for situations in which multiple established norms are desirable, such as resource allocation and role adoption, as discussed in Section 1. Our previously proposed techniques of context assessment and rewiring to cope with cheaters [12,13] also facilitate norm establishment, and this interpretation enables us to explore their operation. The norms and groups that are formed are more widely adopted (with fewer norms being established) than with RCA's approach. Using context assessment increases adoption, especially in the low mutation setting, but as a result there may be no alternative norm-governed groups available in the event of the collapse of an established norm.

There are four key areas of future work, which aim to broaden the applicability of viewing tags as an abstraction of norms and of the context assessment and rewiring techniques. In particular we aim to (i) further investigate the impact of mutation, (ii) improve our techniques with respect to the persistence and number of established norms, (iii) explore the effects of neighbourhood connection topologies, and (iv) evaluate the approach in more realistic environments.

An increase in mutation rate leads to fewer long lived and fewer widely adopted norms, so that there are more groups, with fewer members, persisting for fewer generations. Norms also emerge with many tag groups and few agents per tag, but only few such norms are widely adopted and long lived, as seen in Figures 4, 6 and 7, where there are few long duration groups. This is the first area of future investigation, to understand how the tag mutation rate, and fluctuations in mutation rate over time, relate to the factors that influence the number and duration of norms, and to investigate whether there is an optimal number of groups in a given configuration.

Using tag-based cooperation to investigate norm emergence allows us to observe the effects of various approaches. In particular, it is through norm establishment (i.e. reducing the number of tags) that the context assessment and rewiring techniques improve group effectiveness, and this interpretation may inform improvements to tag-based approaches. We have shown that tag groups have a similar lifecycle to that observed in more traditional notions of norms: establishment of norms, widening of adoption, and eventual collapse or replacement.

The second area of future work aims to explore this lifecycle in more detail, with a particular focus on improving our techniques to obtain an appropriate number of norms and to increase their persistence. Importantly, since mutation can cause norm collapse it is important to ensure that there are alternative groups. Context assessment (with or without rewiring) is found to reduce the diversity of tags to a low level, and this suggests that further work is needed to develop techniques for coping with cheaters.

The third area of future investigation, and the most significant, is concerned with the network topology that defines agents' neighbourhoods. In our investigations we used a simple random with degree distribution $P(k)$, where k corresponds to the number of neighbours ($k = n$), and observed that cooperation is successfully established. However, such a topology is unlikely to occur in real-world applications, which are more likely to exhibit scale-free or small-world topologies [10]. Further investigation is needed to evaluate our techniques with respect to such topologies, since network topology has been found in other settings to have a significant impact on the emergence of norms and conventions [9,19,25]. Although further investigation is needed, our results show that the tag-based approach has a potentially important difference from other techniques. For example, Pujol *et al.* [21] investigated the impact of network topology on convention emergence, using the example setting of the Highest Cumulative Reward action selection strategy [28] in the Coordination Game. They found that in low clustered environments (such as a random topology like ours) existing conventions are not replaced by newly emergent ones, which differs from our results in the context of tag-based cooperation. We see norms being established, and then being replaced by subsequent norms. More investigation is needed to establish the reason for this difference, but we suspect that it may be connected to our consideration of *multiple* norms, since the Coordination Game only contains two possible states (or norms).

There is a complex relationship between the evolution of tag groups, the number of tags, and the donation rate depending on the particular environment. Our final area of future investigation is to consider more realistic environments. In addition to the issues described above we will investigate techniques to cope with false information provided by malicious neighbours, and will incorporate *churn* into the system, such that agents may leave and join at runtime. By exploring these areas we aim to develop techniques that ensure norm diversity and prolong norm duration in realistic environments.

References

1. Allison, P.D.: The cultural evolution of beneficent norms. Social Forces 71(2), 279–301 (1992)
2. Arthur, W.B.: Inductive reasoning and bounded rationality. The American Economic Review 84(2), 406–411 (1994)
3. Axelrod, R.: An evolutionary approach to norms. American Political Science Review 80(4), 1095–1111 (1986)
4. Axelrod, R., Hammond, R.A., Grafen, A.: Altruism via kin-selection strategies that rely on arbitrary tags with which they coevolve. Evolution 58(8), 1833–1838 (2004)

5. Bicchieri, C.: The Grammar of Society: The Nature and Dynamics of Social Norms. Cambridge University Press, Cambridge (2006)
6. Boyd, R., Richerson, P.J.: The evolution of indirect reciprocity. Social Networks 11(3), 213–236 (1989)
7. Burguillo-Rial, J.C.: A memetic framework for describing and simulating spatial prisoner's dilemma with coalition formation. In: Proceedings of the Eighth International Conference on Autonomous Agents and Multiagent Systems (AAMAS 2009), pp. 441–448 (2009)
8. Dawkins, R.: The Selfish Gene. Oxford University Press, Oxford (1976)
9. Delgado, J.: Emergence of social conventions in complex network. Artificial Intelligence 141(1-2), 171–185 (2002)
10. Delgado, J., Pujol, J.M., Sangüesa, R.: Emergence of coordination in scale-free networks. Web Intelligence and Agent Systems 1(2), 131–138 (2003)
11. Flentge, F., Polani, D., Uthmann, T.: Modelling the emergence of possession norms using memes. Journal of Artificial Societies and Social Simulation 4(4) (2001)
12. Griffiths, N.: Tags and image scoring for robust cooperation. In: Proceedings of the Seventh International Conference on Autonomous Agents and Multiagent Systems (AAMAS 2008), pp. 575–582 (2008)
13. Griffiths, N., Luck, M.: Changing neighbours: Improving tag-based cooperation. In: Proceedings of the Ninth International Conference on Autonomous Agents and Multiagent Systems (AAMAS 2010), pp. 249–256 (2010)
14. Hales, D., Edmonds, B.: Applying a socially inspired technique (tags) to improve cooperation in P2P networks. IEEE Transactions on Systems, Man, and Cybernetics, Part A 35(3), 385–395 (2005)
15. Hamilton, W.D.: The genetical evolution of social behaviour I. Journal of Theoretical Biology 7(1), 1–16 (1964)
16. Hamilton, W.D.: The genetical evolution of social behaviour II. Journal of Theoretical Biology 7(1), 17–52 (1964)
17. Holland, J.H.: Hidden order: How adaptation builds complexity. Addison-Wesley, Reading (1995)
18. Jøsang, A., Ismail, R., Boyd, C.: A survey of trust and reputation systems for online service provision. Decision Support Systems 43(2), 618–644 (2007)
19. Kittock, J.E.: Emergent conventions and the structure of multi-agent systems. In: Lectures in Complex systems: The Proceedings of the 1993 Complex Systems Summer School. Santa Fe Institute Studies in the Sciences of Complexity Lecture, vol. VI, pp. 507–521. Addison-Wesley, Reading (1993)
20. Masuda, N., Ohtsuki, H.: Tag-based indirect reciprocity by incomplete social information. Proceedings of the Royal Society B 274(1610), 689–695 (2007)
21. Pujol, J.M., Delgado, J., Sangüesa, R., Flache, A.: The role of clustering on the emergence of efficient social conventions. In: Proceedings of the Nineteenth International Joint Conference on Artificial Intelligence (IJCAI 2005), pp. 965–970 (2005)
22. Resnick, P., Zeckhauser, R., Friedman, E., Kuwabara, K.: Reputation systems. Communications of the ACM 43(12), 45–48 (2000)
23. Riolo, R., Cohen, M., Axelrod, R.: Evolution of cooperation without reciprocity. Nature 414, 441–443 (2001)
24. Roberts, G., Sherratt, T.N.: Does similarity breed cooperation? Nature 418, 499–500 (2002)

25. Salazar, N., Rodríguez-Aguilar, J.A., Arcos, J.L.: Robust convention emergence through spreading mechanisms. In: Proceedings of the Ninth International Conference on Autonomous Agents and Multiagent Systems (AAMAS 2010), pp. 1431–1432 (2010)
26. Savarimuthu, B.T.R., Purvis, M., Purvis, M.: Social norm emergence in virtual agent societies. In: Proceedings of the Seventh International Conference on Autonomous Agents and Multiagent Systems (AAMAS 2008), pp. 1521–1524 (2008)
27. Sen, S., Airiau, S.: Emergence of norms through social learning. In: Proceedings of the 20th International Joint Conference on Artificial Intelligence, pp. 1507–1512 (2007)
28. Shoham, Y., Tennenholtz, M.: Emergent conventions in multi-agent systems. In: Proceedings of the 3rd International Conference on Principles of Knowledge Representation and Reasoning (KR 1992), pp. 225–231 (1992)
29. Shoham, Y., Tennenholtz, M.: On the emergence of social conventions: modeling, analysis and simulations. Artificial Intelligence 94(1-2), 139–166 (1997)
30. Steels, L.: Self-organising vocabularies. In: Artificial Life V, pp. 179–184 (1996)
31. Traulsen, A.: Mechanisms for similarity based cooperation. The European Physical Journal B - Condensed Matter and Complex Systems 63(3), 363–371 (2008)
32. Villatoro, D., Sabater-Mir, J.: Dynamics in the normative group recognition process. In: Proceedings of the Eleventh Conference on Congress on Evolutionary Computation, pp. 757–764 (2009)

Norm Enforceability in Electronic Institutions?

Natalia Criado[1], Estefania Argente[1], Antonio Garrido[1], Juan A. Gimeno[1],
Francesc Igual[1], Vicente Botti[1], Pablo Noriega[2], and Adriana Giret[1]

[1] DSIC, Department of Information Systems and Computation,
Universitat Politècnica de Valencia
[2] IIIA, Artificial Intelligence Research Institute,
CSIC, Spanish Scientific Research Council
{ncriado,eargente,agarridot,jgimeno,figual,vbotti,agiret}@dsic.upv.es,
pablo@iiia.csic.es

Abstract. Nowadays Multi-Agent Systems require more and more regulation and normative mechanisms in order to assure the correct and secure execution of the interactions and transactions in the open virtual organization they are implementing. The Electronic Institution approach for developing Multi-Agent Systems implements some enforceability mechanisms in order to control norms execution and observance. In this paper we study a complex situation in a regulated environment in which the enforceability mechanisms provided by the current Electronic Institutions implementation cannot deal appropriately with norm observance. The analyzed situation is exemplified with a specific scenario of the *mWater* regulated environment, an electronic market for water-rights transfer. After this example is presented, we extrapolate it to a more generic domain while also addressing the main issues for its application in general scenarios.

1 Introduction

In general, norms represent an effective tool for achieving coordination and co-operation among the members of a society. They have been employed in the field of Multi-Agent Systems (MAS) as a formal specification of a deontic statement that aims at regulating the actions of software agents and the interactions among them. Thus, a *Normative MAS* (NMAS) has been defined in [3] as follows:

> "a MAS organized by means of mechanisms to represent, communicate, distribute, detect, create, modify, and enforce norms and mechanisms to deliberate about norms and detect norm violation and fulfilment."

According to this definition, the norm enforcement problem, faced by this paper, is one of the key factors in NMAS. In particular, this paper faces with the enforcement of norms inside Electronic Institutions (EIs) that simulate real scenarios. EIs [21,24,8] represent a way to implement interaction conventions for agents who can establish commitments in open environments.

M. De Vos et al. (Eds.): COIN 2010 International Workshops, LNAI 6541, pp. 250–267, 2011.
© Springer-Verlag Berlin Heidelberg 2011

When real life problems are modelled by means of EI some of the norms are obtained by giving a computational interpretation to real legislation. In this process we have encountered two main problems:

- *Norm Inconsistency.* Usually the set of laws created by human societies in order to regulate a specific situation are contradictory and/or ambiguous. In particular, there are situations in which there is a general law (*regulative norm* [4]) which is controlled by a local law (*procedural norm* [4]). The problem arises when this local law does not ensure compliance of the more general law. This may be due to the existence of different levels of institutions which are working in the same system [12]. Thus, an elaborated process is necessary in order to determine which norms are active in a specific moment and how they are applied. Traditional methods for implementing norms in EI, which are based on the unambiguous interpretation of norms, are not suitable to overcome this problem.
- *Norm Controlling.* Even in absence of a conflict among norms, there is still the problem of norm controlling. Norm enforcement methods inside EI are based on the observation of these activities controlled by norms. In particular, there are norms whose violation cannot be observed since they regulate situations that take place out of the institution boundaries. Thus, violations are only detectable in presence of a conflict among agents.

In this paper we focus on the enforcement of these norms, which cannot be controlled by traditional techniques. Thus, we address the question of enforceability of non-observable norms inside EIs. In order to make more clear and understandable the problem addressed by this paper, it has been exemplified in the *mWater* scenario [5]. In addition, a first solution for overcoming the *mWater* concrete problem is shown. In particular, we propose the definition of a grievance scene for allowing normative conflicts to be solved within the *mWater* institution. However, this solution can be also extrapolated to generic domains.

This paper is structured as follows: the next section provides background on norm implementation, EIs and the implementation of norms inside EIs. Then a concrete example of the problem addressed by this paper is described. Finally, discussion and future works are described.

2 Background

This section firstly reviews the main methods for ensuring norm compliance in MAS and the techniques that can be employed for implementing these methods. Then, a brief description of the Electronic Institution framework is given, as well as a discussion on how norms are implemented and enforced in this framework.

2.1 Norm Implementation in Multiagent Systems

Norms allow legal issues to be modelled in electronic institutions and electronic commerce, MAS organizations, etc. Most of the works on *norms* in MAS have been proposed from a theoretical perspective. However, several works on norms from an operational point of view have recently arisen, which are focused on giving a computational interpretation of norms in order to employ them in the design and execution of MAS applications. In this sense, norms must be interpreted or translated into mechanisms and procedures which are meaningful for the society [16]. Methods for ensuring norm compliance are classified into two categories: (i) *regimentation* mechanisms, which consist in making the violation of norms impossible, since these mechanisms prevent agents from performing actions that are forbidden by a norm; and (ii) *enforcement* mechanisms, which are applied after the detection of the violation of some norm, reacting upon it.

In a recent work [2], a taxonomy of different techniques for implementing effectively norms is proposed. On the one hand, the regimentation of norms can be achieved by two processes: (i) *mediation*, in which both the resources and communication channels are accessed through a reliable entity which controls agent behaviours and prevents agents from deviating from ideal behaviour; and (ii) *hard-wiring*, assuming that the agents' mental states are accessible and can be modified in accordance with norms. On the other hand, norm enforcement techniques are classified according to both the observer and the enforcer entity. Norms are *self-enforced* when agents observe their own behaviour and sanction themselves. Thus, norm compliance is both observed and enforced without the need of any additional party. In situations in which those agents involved by a transaction are responsible for detecting norm compliance (i.e. *second-party* observability) norms can be enforced by: (i) the *second-party* which applies sanctions and rewards; and (ii) a third entity which is an authority and acts as an *arbiter* or *judge* in the dispute resolution process. In the case of *third-party* observability, two different mechanisms for ensuring norm compliance can be defined according to the entity which is in charge of norm enforcing: (i) *social norms* are defended by the *society* as a whole; (ii) in *infrastructural enforcement* there are infrastructural entities which are authorities in charge of *monitoring* and enforcing norms by applying sanctions and rewards.

2.2   Electronic Institutions

Electronic Institutions (EI) are computational counterparts of conventional institutions [21,24,8]. Institutions are, in an abstract way, a set of conventions that articulate agent interactions [22]. In practice they are identified with the group of agents, standard practices, policies and guidelines, language, documents and other resources —the organization— that make those conventions work. *Electronic Institutions* are implementations of those conventions in such a way that autonomous agents may participate, their interactions are supported by the implementation and the conventions are enforced by the system on all participants. Electronic institutions are engineered as regulated open MAS environments. These MAS are open in the sense that the EI does not control the agents' decision-making processes and agents may enter and leave the EI at their own will. EIs are regulated in four ways. First, agents are capable of establishing and fulfilling commitments inside the institution, and those correspond to commitments in the real world. Second, only interactions that comply with the conventions have any consequence in the environment. Third, interactions are organized as repetitive activities regulated by the institution and, last, interactions, in EIs, are always speech acts.

An EI is specified through: (i) a *dialogical framework* which fixes the context of interaction by defining roles and their relationships, a domain ontology and a communication language; (ii) *scenes* that establish interaction protocols of the agents playing a given role in that scene, which illocutions are admissible and under what conditions; (iii) *performative structures* that, like the script of a play, express how scenes are interrelated and how agents playing a given role move from one scene to another, and (iv) *rules of behaviour* that regulate how commitments are established and satisfied.

The IIIA model has a platform for implementation of EIs. It has a graphical specification language, ISLANDER, in which the dialogical framework, performative structures and those norms governing commitments and the pre- and post- conditions of illocutions are specified [9]. It produces an XML file that is interpreted by AMELI [10], a middleware that handles agent messages to and from a communication language, like JADE, according to the ISLANDER specification [10]. In addition, EIDE [1] includes a monitoring and debugging tool, SIMDEI that keeps track of all interactions and displays them in different modes. There is also a tool, aBuilder, that, from the XML specification, generates, for each role, agent shells that comply with the communication conventions (the decision-making code is left to the agent programmer).

2.3   Norm Implementation in EI

Norm Regimentation. In AMELI, governors filter the actions of agents, letting them only to perform those actions that are permitted by the rules of society. Therefore, governors apply a regimentation mechanism, preventing the execution of prohibited actions and, therefore, preventing agents to violate their commitments.

This regimentation mechanism employed by governors makes use of a formalism based on rules for representing constraints on agent behaviours [14]. This formalism is conceived as a "machine language" for implementing other higher level normative languages. More specifically, it has been employed to enforce norms that govern EIs. The main features of the proposed "machine language" are: (i) it allows for the explicit definition and management of agent norms (i.e. prohibitions, obligations and permissions); (ii) it is a general purpose language not aimed at supporting a specific normative language; (iii) it is declarative and has an execution mechanism. For implementing this rule system, the Jess tool has been employed as an inference engine. Jess allows the development of Java applications with "reasoning" capabilities[1].

In open systems, not only the regimentation of all actions can be difficult, but also sometimes it is inevitable and even preferable to allow agents to violate norms [6]. Reasons behind desirability of norm violations are because it is impossible to take a thorough control of all their actions, or agents could obtain higher personal benefits when violating norms, or norms may be violated by functional or cooperative motivations, since agents intend to improve

---

[1] http://herzberg.ca.sandia.gov/jess/

the organization functionality through violating or ignoring norms. Therefore, all these situations require norms to be controlled by enforcement mechanisms. Next, works on the enforcement of norms inside EI are described.

Norm Enforcement. The enforcement of a norm by an institution requires the institution to be capable of recognizing the occurrence of the violation of the norm and respond to it [16]. Hence, checking activities may occur in several ways: *directly*, at any time, randomly or with periodical checks, or by using monitoring activities; or *indirectly*, allowing agents to denounce the occurrence of a violation and then checking their grievances.

Regarding direct norm enforcement, the institution itself is in charge of both observing and enforcing norms. Thus, in this approach there are infrastructural entities which act as norm observers and apply sanctions when a violation is detected. In [19,13], distributed mechanisms for an institutional enforcement of norms are proposed. In particular, these works propose languages for expressing norms and software architectures for the distributed enforcement of these norms. More specifically, the work described in [19] presents an enforcement mechanism, implemented by the Moses toolkit [18], which is as general (i.e. it can implement all norms that are controllable by a centralized enforcement) and more scalable and efficient with respect to centralized approaches. However, one of the main drawbacks of this proposal is the fact that each agent has an interface that sends legal messages. Since norms are controlled by these local interfaces, norms can be only expressed in terms of messages sent or received by an agent; i.e. this framework does not support the definition of norms that affect an agent as a consequence of an action carried out independently by another agent. This problem is faced by Gaertner et al. in [13]. In this approach, Gaertner et al. propose a distributed architecture for enforcing norms in EI. In particular, dialogical actions performed by agents may cause the propagation of normative positions (i.e. obligations, permissions and prohibitions). These normative propositions are taken into account by the normative level; i.e. a higher level in which norm reasoning and management processes are performed in a distributed manner. In a more recent work, Modgil et al. [20] propose an architecture for monitoring norm-governed systems. In particular, this architecture is formed by trusted observers that report to monitors on states of interest relevant to the activation, fulfilment, violation and expiration of norms. This monitoring system is *corrective* in the sense that it allows norm violations to be detected and reacting to them.

Mixed Approaches. Finally, there are works which employ a mixed approach for controlling norms. In this sense, they propose the usage of regimentation mechanisms for ensuring compliance with norms that preserve the integrity of the application. Unlike this, enforcement is proposed to control norms that cannot be regimented due to the fact that they are not verifiable or their violation may be desirable. In [7] an example on the mixed approach is shown. In particular, this work shows how norms that define the access to the organization infrastructure are controlled, whereas norms controlling other issues such as work domain norms are ignored. In particular, those norms that define permissions and prohibitions related to the access to the organization are regimented through mediation, whereas obligation norms are enforced following the institutional sanction mechanism.

The ORA4MAS [17] is another well known proposal that makes use of a mixed approach for implementing norms. The ORA4MAS proposal defines *artifacts* as first class entities to instrument the organisation for supporting agents activities within it. *Artifacts* are resources and tools that agents can create and use to perform their individual and social activities [23]. Regarding the implementation of norms in the ORA4MAS framework, regimentation mechanisms are implemented in artifacts that agents use for accessing the organization according to the mediation mechanism. Enforcement of norms has been implemented using third party observability, since the detection of norm violations is a functionality provided by artifacts. In addition, norms are enforced by third parties, since there are agents in charge of being informed about norm violations and carrying out the evaluation and judgement of these situations.

However, none of the above mentioned proposals allows norms which regulate activities taking place out of the institution scope to be controlled. In this case, norm compliance is non-observable by the institution and can only be detected when a conflict arises. Thus, in this paper we propose that both a *second-party* and *third-party* can observe non-compliant behaviour and start a grievance process which takes place inside the EI. Therefore, in this paper we face the problem of institutional enforcement of norms based on second-party and third-party observability. Next section provides a concrete instantiation of this problem inside a more specific case-study.

3   A Concrete Sample Scenario in the *mWater* Regulated Environment

In this section we exemplify the problem of non-regimented norm enforcement in EI with *mWater*, a regulated MAS application for trading water-rights within a virtual market. In order to get a good understanding of the overall *mWater* functioning, we first describe the motivation of *mWater* and present a brief overview of its structure. Afterwards, the sample complex situation for norm enforcement in the current *mWater* EI implementation is analyzed.

3.1   *mWater* Overall Description

In countries like Spain, and particularly in its Mediterranean coast, there is a high degree of public awareness of the main consequences of the scarcity of water and the need of fostering efficient use of water resources. Two new mechanisms for water management already under way are: a heated debate on the need and feasibility of transferring water from one basin to another, and, directly related to this proposal, the regulation of *water banks*[2]. *mWater* is an agent-based electronic market of water-rights. Our focus is on demand and, in particular, on the type of regulatory and market mechanisms that foster an efficient use of water while preventing conflicts. The framework is a somewhat idealized version of current water-use regulations that articulate the interactions of those individual and collective entities that are involved in the use of water in a closed basin. The main focus of the work presented in this paper is on the regulated environment, which includes the expression and use of regulations of different sorts: from actual laws and regulations issued by governments, to policies and local regulations issued by basin managers, and to social norms that prevail in a given community of users.

For the construction of *mWater* we follow the IIIA *Electronic Institution* (EI) conceptual model [1]. For the actual specification and implementation of *mWater* we use the EIDE platform.

Procedural conventions in the *mWater* institution are specified through a nested performative structure (Fig. 1) with multiple processes. The top structure, *mWaterPS*, describes the overall market environment and includes other performative structures; *TradingHall* provides updated information about the market and, at the same time, users and trading staff can initiate most trading and ancillary operations here; finally, *TradingTables* establishes the trading procedures. This performative structure includes a scene schema for each trading mechanism. Once an agreement on transferring a water-right has been reached it is "managed" according to the market conventions captured in *AgreementValidation* and *ContractEnactment* scenes. When an agreement is reached, *mWater* staff check whether the agreement satisfies some formal conditions and if so, a transfer contract is signed. When a contract becomes active, other rightholders and external stakeholders may initiate a *Grievance* procedure that may have an impact on the transfer agreement. This procedure is activated whenever any market participant believes there is an incorrect execution of a given norm and/or policy. *Grievance* performative structure includes different scenes to address such grievances or for the disputes that may arise among co-signers. On the other hand, if things proceed smoothly, the right subsists until maturity.

3.2 Complex Scenario: The Registration of Water-Right Transfer Agreements

In *mWater* we have three different types of regulations: (i) government norms, issued by the Spanish Ministry of Environment (stated in the National Hydrological Plan); (ii) basin or local norms, defined and regimented by the basin

---

[2] The 2001 Water Law of the National Hidrological Plan (NHP) —'Real Decreto Legislativo 1/2001, BOE 176' (see www.boe.es/boe/dias/2001/07/24/pdfs/A26791-26817.eps, in Spanish)— and its amendment in 2005 regulates the power of rightholders to engage in voluntary water transfers, and of basin authorities to setup water markets, banks, and trading centers for the exchange of water-rights in cases of drought or other severe scarcity problems.

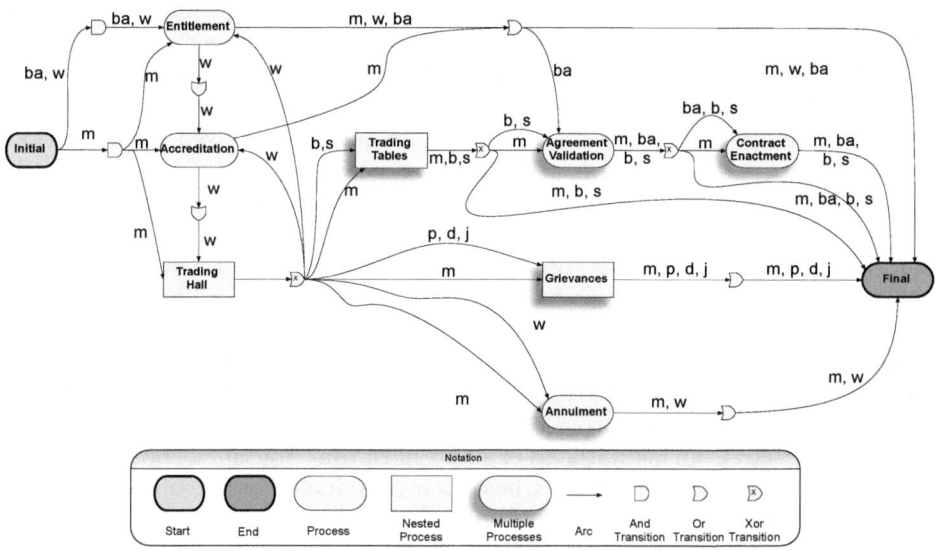

Fig. 1. *mWater* performative structure. Participating Roles: g - Guest, w - Water user, b - Buyer, s - Seller, p - Third Party, m - Market Facilitator, ba - Basin Authority.

authorities; and (iii) social norms, stated by the members of a given user assembly and/or organization. The interplay among different norms from these three groups brings about complex situations in which there are non-regimented norms and, moreover, the non-compliance of the norm is not observable until a conflict appears. A very critical situation for the reliable execution of *mWater* appears when the following norms apply:

Government norm - (N0): A water-user can use a given volume of water from a given extraction point, if and only if he/she owns the specific water-right or has a transfer agreement that endows him/her.

Government norm - (N1): Every water-right transfer agreement must be registered within the fifteen days after its signing and wait for the Basin Authorities' approval in order to be executed.

Local norm - (N2): The registration process of a water-right transfer agreement is started voluntarily by the agreement signing parties.

Social norm - (N3): Whenever a conflict appears, a water user can start a grievance procedure in order to solve it.

Sample situation:
Let's suppose there is a water user A who has a water-right w_1 and wants to sell it. A starts a Trading Table inside the *TradingTables* process (see Fig. 1) in order to sell w_1. The water user B enters the Trading Table and, as a result, there is an agreement Agr_1 between A and B, by which B buys w_1 from A for the period $[t_1, t_2]$, and pays the quantity p_1 for such a transfer. A and B belong to $Basin_x$, in which norms $N1$, $N2$ and $N3$ apply. A and B do not register Agr_1

due to norm $N2$ (in other words, A and B do not go to the Agreement Validation scene of Fig. 1). Since there is no mechanism in $Basin_x$ by which water-right w_1 is blocked from A after its selling (due to Agr_1 is not registered and w_1 is still owned by A in time periods not overlapped with $[t_1, t_2]$), A continues to operate in the market. Afterwards A starts a new Trading Table to sell w_1 for period $[t_3, t_4]$, with $t_1 < t_3 < t_2$ and $t_4 > t_2$ (the new period $[t_3, t_4]$ is overlapped with $[t_1, t_2]$). In this second Trading Table A and C sign Agr_2, by which A sells w_1 to C for the period $[t_3, t_4]$ and C pays p_2 to A. A and C belong to $Basin_x$. In this case C registers Agr_2 in the *Agreement Validation* scene, due to *N1* and *N2*, and obtains the basin approval for executing Agr_2. At time t_3 (the transfer starting time) C attempts to execute Agr_2, but there is no water in the water transportation node, since B is also executing Agr_1. At this moment C has a conflict with B, and in order to solve it he/she has to start a grievance procedure due to *N3* (Grievances performative structure of Fig. 1).

This situation[3] is an instantiated example of the one described above, in which there are non-regimented norms whose non-compliance is not observable and cannot be asserted until the conflict appears. The critical situation comes out due to the compliance procedure for agreement registration and second selling of the same water-right is not coercive.

The current development environment of EI we are using does not provide build-in support for non-coercive processes that are defined by non-regimented norms. Moreover, those situations in which it is not possible to observe the non-compliance of a norm until the resulting conflict appears are not supported either. Nevertheless, there are sample scenarios, like *mWater*, in which this behaviour is required. In the following section we analyze the EI implementation we have devised for this complex scenario.

3.3   Implementation

In this section our approach to solve the previously described complex scenario in *mWater* is described.

In order to include norm *N1* in the current EI implementation of *mWater* we have designed the *Agreement Validation* scene (see Fig. 1) as a successor scene for any Trading Table. When any water user enters this scene, the Market Facilitator verifies the constraint of fifteen days from the agreement statement process related to norm *N1*. If this constraint is satisfied the water-right transfer agreement is forwarded to the Basin Authority who activates a Normative Reasoning process in order to approve, or not, the agreement based on the basin normative regulation. If the agreement gets approved it is published in the Trading Hall in order for every water user of the basin to be informed of the transfer agreement.

---

[3] The scenario presented in this section happens in practice in Spain, due to the impossibility to monitor all the water transfer negotiations that may take place among the different water users. It can be considered as a loophole in the Spanish regulations. Nevertheless we are interested in modeling it due to its complexity and in order to simulate the "real" behaviour of the basin users.

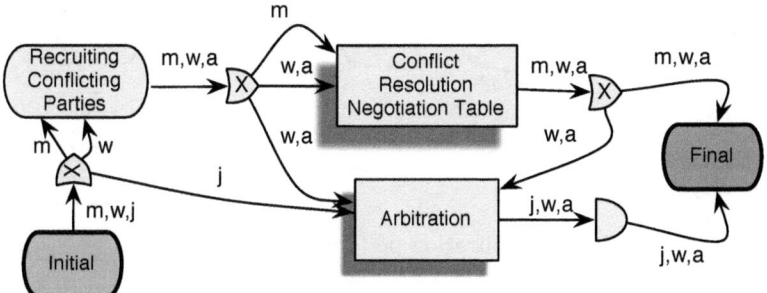

Fig. 2. Grievances performative structure

On the other hand, norm *N2* is automatically included in the *mWater* institution due to the EIDE implementation feature by which no participating agent in the electronic institution can be forced to go to a given scene. For the particular *mWater* example, neither the buyer nor the seller can be forced to go through the transition between the Trading Table scene and the Agreement Validation scene (see Fig. 1). This way, whenever the buyer and/or the seller goes to the Agreement Validation scene he/she starts the scene voluntarily, so norm *N2* is satisfied.

The implementation of norm *N3* requires a specific performative structure, named *Grievances* (Fig. 2), in order to deal with conflict resolution processes.

Finally, the observance of norm compliance is delegated to every water user. Hence, the enforceability of norm *N0* is delegated to every water user.

Fig. 2 shows the different scenes of the complex Grievances performative structure. In this structure any conflict can be solved by means of two alternative processes (these processes are similar to those used in Alternative Dispute Resolutions and Online Dispute Resolutions [26,27]). On the one hand, conflict resolution can be solved by means of negotiation tables (Conflict Resolution Negotiation Table performative structure). In this mechanism a negotiation table is created on demand whenever any water user wants to solve a conflict with other/s water user/s, negotiating with them with or without mediator. Such a negotiation table can use a different negotiation protocol, such as face to face, standard double auction, etc. On the other hand, arbitration mechanisms for conflict resolution can also be employed (Arbitration performative structure). In this last mechanism, a jury solves the conflict sanctioning the offenses.

There are three steps in the arbitration process (see Fig. 3). In the first one, the grievance is stated by the plaintive water user. In the second step, the different conflicting parties present their allegations to the jury. Finally, in the last step, the jury, after hearing the dispute, passes a sentence on the conflict. The difference among the two mechanisms for conflict resolution is that the arbitration process is binding, meanwhile the negotiation is not. In this way if any of the conflicting parties is not satisfied with the negotiation results he/she can activate an arbitration process in order to solve the conflict.

In the previously described complex scenario, when C cannot execute Agr_2 (because there is no water in the water transportation node), C believes that B

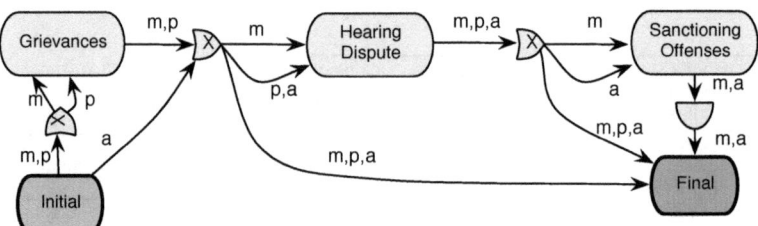

Fig. 3. Arbitration performative structure

is not complying norm *N0*. *C* believes there is a conflict because Agr_2 endows him/her to use the water, and moreover, there is no transfer agreement published in the Trading Hall that endows *B* to do the same. In order to enforce norm *N0* and to execute Agr_2, *C* starts a grievance procedure. In this procedure, water users *C* and *B* are recruited as conflicting parties and *A* as third party because he/she is the seller of w_1 as stated in Agr_2 (Recruiting Conflicting Parties scene of Fig. 2). Let's assume *C* chooses as conflict resolution mechanism arbitration, because he/she does not want to negotiate with *B*. After stating the grievance, *C* and *B* present their allegations to the jury. In this process *B* presents Agr_1 by which he/she believes there is fulfillment of norm *N0*. Nevertheless, in the last arbitration step, by means of a Normative Reasoning function, the jury analyzes the presented allegations and the normative regulations of the basin and deduces that there is an offense. Norm *N1* was not complied by *B* and *A*, and moreover, *A* has sold the same water-right twice for an overlapped time period. In this last step, the jury imposes the corresponding sanctions to *A* and *B*.

Further implementation details. *mWater* is also devised as a simulation tool for helping the basin policy makers to evaluate the behaviour of the market when new or modified norms are applied. *mWater* is implemented by tiers.

We use the typical three-tier architecture defined in software engineering, as depicted in Fig. 4, with the *mWater* electronic institution being executed in background. The persistence layer implements an information model that supports the execution of the EI and it is developed in MySQL, including the different conceptual data required for the market execution, such as basin structure, market structure and all the elements necessary for the conflict resolution process. Fig. 5 shows a fragment of this relational model in which some elements are depicted such as: basin structure, water-right definition, agreement, and conflict resolution table configuration, among others. The business layer includes all the logic of the system, and it is implemented by providing different APIs (Application Programming Interfaces) for querying the database and running the simulation. Fig. 6 shows a snapshot of the *mWater*'s complex scenario implementation running on the AMELI execution environment of EIDE with 3 different agents named as the example 'A', 'B' and 'C'. In each agent window we are able to identify, on the left part, a tree which is labeled with the performative tasks, transitions and scenes where the agent has passed or is staying. Note that the implementation we have devised for this complex situation in *mWater* allows us

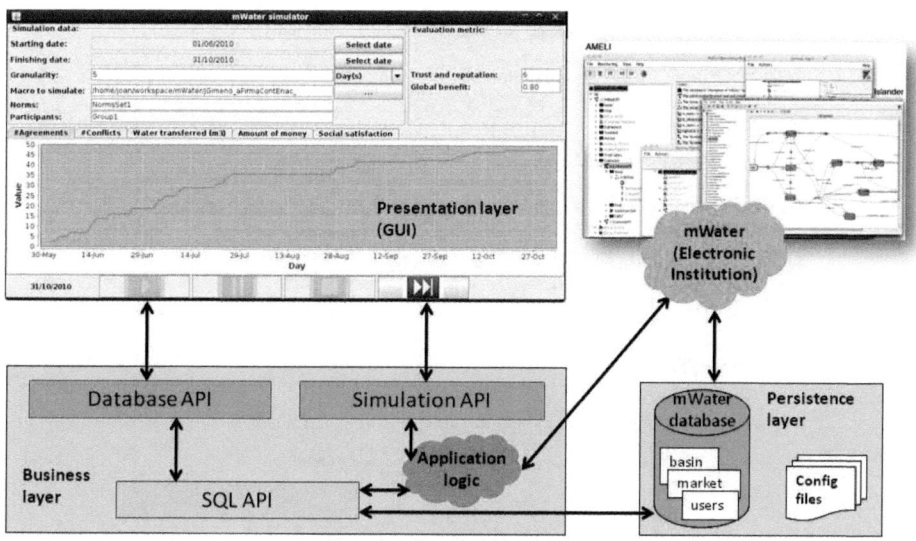

Fig. 4. Architecture of our approach for *mWater* as a simulation tool for decision-taking support

to solve the scenario described above. Moreover, when dealing with this scenario it is also possible to observe the limitations of the current EIDE platform for supporting non-observability and enforceability of non-regimented norms. The implementation of *mWater* we are discussing in this paper is developed with EIDE 2.11[4], and includes all the components described in previous sections. Finally, the presentation layer provides the front-end of the system while gives the user the opportunity to tune some parameters (selection dates, regulation to be applied and water users population) to run the market in a very intuitive way. Additionally, it provides us with very useful (graphical) information that helps stakeholders when taking decisions.

To this end, we are working on defining evaluation functions to measure the performance of the market rather than on the implementation performance itself. However, our tests do not show clear limitations in the the system performance, and the system is fast enough to simulate the market during a whole year in just a few minutes. On the other hand, the functions to measure the performance of the market include now the amount of water transfer agreements signed in the market, volume of water transferred, number of conflicts generated, etc. (see GUI in Fig. 4), but the GUI is open to deal with other indicators. Apart from these straightforward functions we are also working on defining "social" functions in order to asses values such as the trust and reputation levels of the market, or degree of water user satisfaction, among others.

---

[4] Available at http://e-institutions.iiia.csic.es/eide/pub/

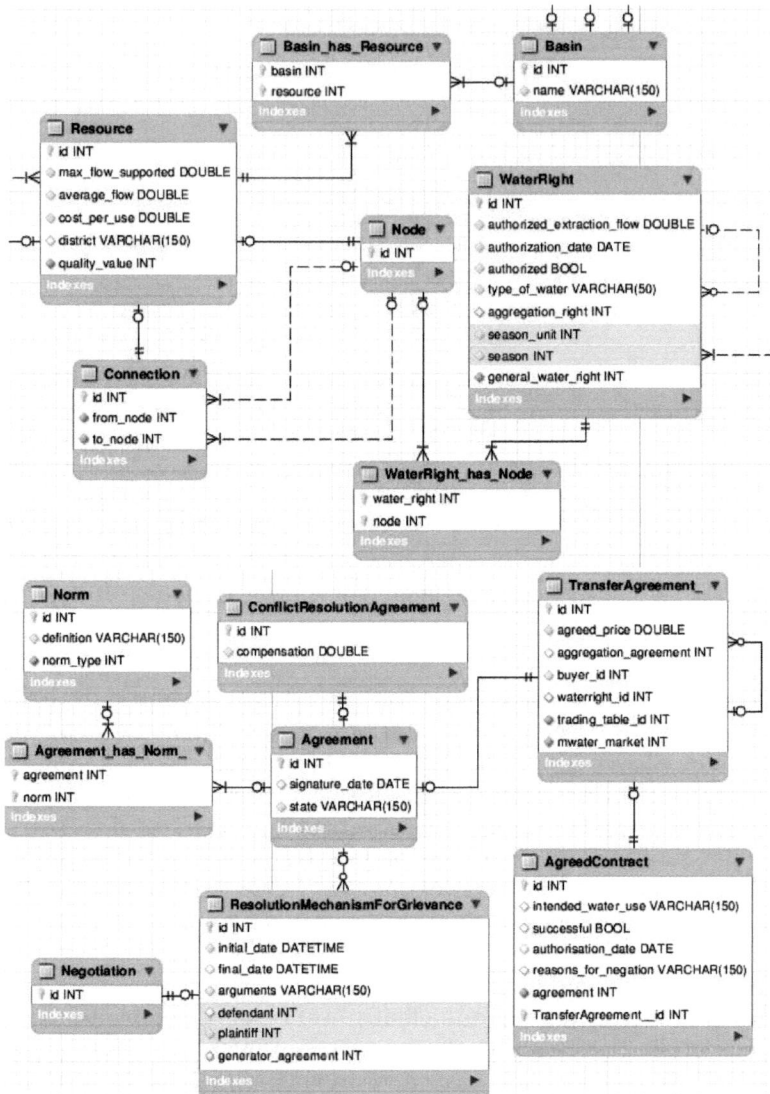

Fig. 5. A fragment of the information model of *mWater*

4   Discussion and Closing Remarks

In real life problems, in many occasions it is difficult or even impossible to check norm compliance, specially when the violation of the norm cannot be directly observable. In other occasions, it is not only difficult to regiment all actions, but it might be preferable to allow agents to violate norms, since they may obtain a higher personal benefit or they may intend to improve the organization functionality, despite violating or ignoring norms. It is clear that from a general

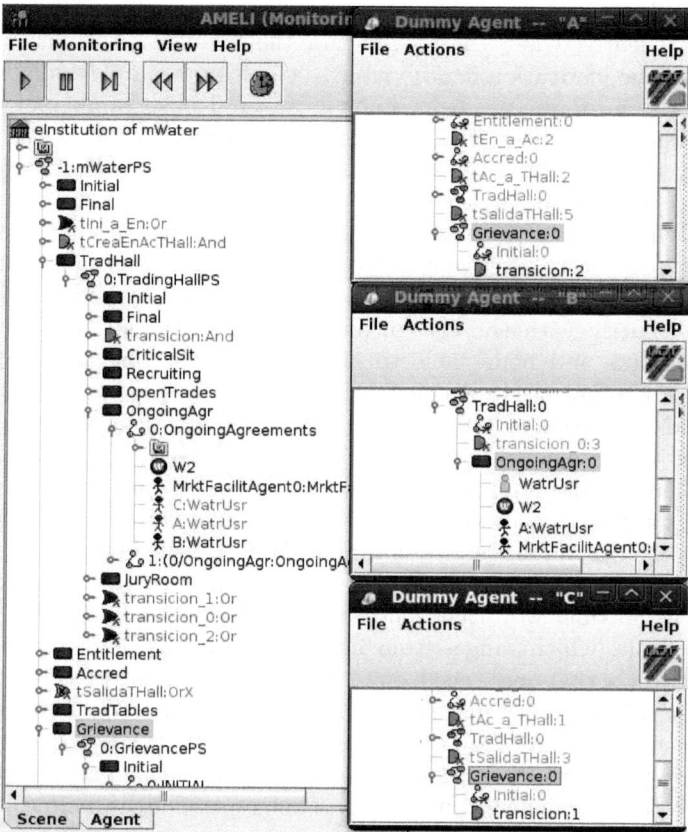

Fig. 6. A snapshot of the *mWater* electronic institution running on AMELI

thought and design perspective of an Electronic Institution, it is preferable to define a safe and trustful environment where norms cannot be violated (i.e. norms are considered as hard constraints), thus providing a highly regimented scenario that inspires confidence to their users. However, from a more flexible and realistic perspective, it is appealing to have the possibility for agents to violate norms for personal gain. Although this is a very realistic attribute that humans can have, it eventually leads to corruption and, consequently, the designer may think to rule it out. But again, from a norm enforceability standpoint it is always a good idea to allow this: it does not only make the environment more open and dynamic, but it also provides a useful tool for decision support. In such a thread, we are able to range the set of norms, from a very relaxed scenario to a very tight one, simulate the institution and the agents' behaviour and, finally, analyze when the global performance —in terms of number of conflicts that appear, degree of global satisfaction or corruption, etc.— shows better, which makes it very interesting as a testbed itself [5]. In all these cases, norm enforcement methods are needed, such as second-party and third-party enforcements.

This paper has highlighted the necessity for norm enforceability in Electronic Institutions. Clearly, when the agents and their execution occur outside the boundaries of the institution it is inviable to count on a simple and efficient way to guarantee a norm-abiding behaviour, as the full observability of the whole execution and environment is rarely possible. In other words, norm violations are perfectly plausible (and unfortunately common) and are only detectable in presence of a conflict among agents.

In our *mWater* scenario, we have proposed an open mechanism that comprises two main principles: (i) the generation of a grievance when one agent detects a conflict, i.e. when an agent denounces the occurrence of a violation; and (ii) an authority entity with the role of arbiter/judge to mediate in the dispute resolution process and being able to apply sanctions. The advantage of this mechanism is twofold. First, it allows different types of grievance, either when it corresponds to the execution of a previous signed (or unsigned) agreement or, simply, when it happens as an occasional event during the habitual execution of the water scenario and its infrastructure use. Second, it provides different ways to deal with grievances, as shown in Fig. 2: (i) in a very formal and strict way by means of an arbitration procedure that relies on a traditional jury, thus applying a *third-party* enforceability mechanism (with an infrastructure enforcement); or (ii) in a more flexible way that relies on the creation of a conflict resolution negotiation table, which ranges from informal protocols (e.g., face to face) to more formal ones that may need one or more mediators. In this last case, a *second-party* enforceability mechanism has been adopted. We have shown that this grievance procedure shows to be effective in the *mWater* scenario. But despite its origin in the water environment, it can be easily extrapolated to any other real problem modelled by using EIs, which represent the main contributions of this paper.

The underlying idea to deal with norm enforcement in generic domains follows a simple flow, but it needs some issues to be clearly defined. First of all, we require a procedure to activate or initiate a new grievance. This can be done from any type of performative structure similar to the *TradingHall* of Fig. 1. This operation requires the identification of the agents that will be involved in the grievance itself, so it is essential for all agents to be uniquely identified; that is, we cannot deal with anonymous agents, which is an important issue. Once the grievance has been initiated, we also require a mechanism for recruiting the conflicting parties. Again, this is related to the agents' identification and the necessity of (perhaps formal) communication protocols to summon all the parties. Note that this step is necessary for any type of dispute resolution, both by negotiation tables and arbitration. And, at this point we have a high flexibility for solving the conflicts, as they can be solved in many ways depending on the type of problem we are addressing at each moment. Analogously to the trading tables that we have in the *mWater* scenario, we can use general or particular tables to reach an agreement and, thus, solving the conflict, no matter the real problem we have. Finally, it is also important to note that reaching an agreement when solving the conflict does not prevent from having new conflicts that appear from such an agreement, being necessary the initiation of a new grievance procedure and repeating all the operations iteratively. Although such new grievances are possible from both the negotiation table and arbitration alternatives, it is common to have situations where the decisions/verdict taken by the arbitration judges are unappealable.

Regarding the limitations of our proposal, the solution provided here is not useful *per se*. In this sense, the solution to the norm enforceability problem in EI is not complete. In particular, this paper focuses on the description of the structure (i.e the *grievance* performative structure) that allows the question of norm enforceability to be solved in case of the *mWater* scenario. However, this structure must be endowed with *arbitration* [15], *trust* [25] and *argumentation* mechanisms [28,11] in order to become a reliable infrastructure for detecting and reacting to non-observable norm violations. Therefore, our current work of research is focused on providing a specification of these mechanisms. In particular, we are working on how the conflict resolution tables can be defined and to come up with specialized protocols for these tables. Hence, our final goal is to be able to integrate this behaviour into a decision support system to be applied to the *mWater* and other scenarios of execution. On a parallel line, we are also working on the development of a simulation tool for the water-right market that allows us to easily range: (i) the type of regulatory and market mechanisms; (ii) the number, type, group of norms and how to reason on them; (iii) the agents' population and their behaviour, in particular the way they are more or less norm-abiding; and (iv) the performance measures to evaluate "social" issues in the market behaviour. This will provide us with very valuable information about the necessity of richer normative regulation and its real impact when different types of water users interact within the market.

Acknowledgements

This paper was partially funded by the Consolider programme of the Spanish Ministry of Science and Innovation through project AT (CSD2007-0022, INGENIO 2010), MICINN projects TIN2008-06701-C03-01 and TIN2009-13839-C03-01 and by the FPU grant AP-2007-01256 awarded to N. Criado. This research has also been partially funded by the Generalitat de Catalunya under the grant 2009-SGR-1434 and Valencian Prometeo project 2008/051.

References

1. Arcos, J., Esteva, M., Noriega, P., Rodriguez-Aguilar, J., Sierra, C.: Engineering open environments with electronic institutions. Engineering Applications of Artificial Intelligence (18), 191–204 (2005)
2. Balke, T.: A taxonomy for ensuring institutional compliance in utility computing. In: Boella, G., Noriega, P., Pigozzi, G., Verhagen, H. (eds.) Normative Multi-Agent Systems, Dagstuhl, Germany. Dagstuhl Seminar Proceedings, vol. 09121. Schloss Dagstuhl - Leibniz-Zentrum fuer Informatik, Germany (2009)

3. Boella, G., van der Torre, L., Verhagen, H.: Introduction to the special issue on normative multiagent systems. Autonomous Agents and Multi-Agent Systems 17(1), 1–10 (2008)
4. Boella, G., van der Torre, L.: Substantive and procedural norms in normative multiagent systems. Journal of Applied Logic 6(2), 152–171 (2008)
5. Botti, V., Garrido, A., Giret, A., Igual, F., Noriega, P.: On the design of mWater: a case study for Agreement Technologies. In: 7th European Workshop on Multi-Agent Systems - EUMAS 2009, pp. 1–15 (2009)
6. Castelfranchi, C.: Formalising the informal? Journal of Applied Logic (1) (2004)
7. Criado, N., Julián, V., Botti, V., Argente, E.: A Norm-based Organization Management System. In: Padget, J., Artikis, A., Vasconcelos, W., Stathis, K., da Silva, V.T., Matson, E., Polleres, A. (eds.) COIN 2009. LNCS, vol. 6069, pp. 19–35. Springer, Heidelberg (2010)
8. Esteva, M.: Electronic Institutions: from specification to development. IIIA PhD Monography 19 (2003)
9. Esteva, M., Rodriguez-Aguilar, J.A., Sierra, C., Garcia, P., Arcos, J.: On the formal specification of electronic institutions. In: Agent Mediated Electronic Commerce, pp. 126–147 (1991)
10. Esteva, M., Rosell, B., Rodriguez-Aguilar, J.A., Arcos, J.L.: Ameli: An agent-based middleware for electronic institutions. In: Proceedings of the Third International Joint Conference on Autonomous Agents and Multiagent Systems, vol. 1, p. 243. IEEE Computer Society, Los Alamitos (2004)
11. Euzenat, J., Laera, L., Tamma, V., Viollet, A.: D2.3.7: Negotiation/argumentation techniques among agents complying to different ontologies. Tech. Report. KWEB/2004/D2.3.7/v1.0 (2006)
12. Fornara, N., Colombetti, M.: Specifying and enforcing norms in artificial institutions (short paper). In: Proc. 7th Int. Conf. on Autonomous Agents and Multiagent Systems (AAMAS 2008), pp. 1481–1484 (2008)
13. Gaertner, D., Garcia-Camino, A., Noriega, P., Rodriguez-Aguilar, J.A., Vasconcelos, W.: Distributed norm management in regulated multiagent systems. In: Proceedings of the 6th International Joint Conference on Autonomous Agents and Multiagent Systems, p. 90. ACM, New York (2007)
14. García-Camino, A., Rodríguez-Aguilar, J.A., Sierra, C., Vasconcelos, W.W.: Norm-oriented programming of electronic institutions. In: Proc. International Conference on Autonomous Agents and Multiagent Systems (AAMAS), pp. 670–672. ACM, New York (2006)
15. Gateau, B., Khadraoui, D.: Arbitration of Autonomous Multimedia Objects with a Multi-Agent System. Proceeding of 2nd Information and Communication Technologies, pp. 3007–3012 (2006)
16. Grossi, D., Aldewereld, H., Dignum, F.: Ubi lex, ibi poena: Designing norm enforcement in e-institutions. In: Noriega, P., Vázquez-Salceda, J., Boella, G., Boissier, O., Dignum, V., Fornara, N., Matson, E. (eds.) COIN 2006. LNCS (LNAI), vol. 4386, pp. 101–114. Springer, Heidelberg (2007)
17. Hübner, J.F., Boissier, O., Kitio, R., Ricci, A.: Instrumenting multi-agent organisations with organisational artifacts and agents. Autonomous Agents and Multi-Agent Systems 20(3), 369–400 (2010)
18. Minsky, N.H., Ungureanu, V.: A mechanism for establishing policies for electronic commerce. In: International Conference on Distributed Computing Systems, vol. 18, pp. 322–331. Citeseer (1998)

19. Minsky, N.H., Ungureanu, V.: Law-governed interaction: a coordination and control mechanism for heterogeneous distributed systems. ACM Transactions on Software Engineering and Methodology (TOSEM) 9(3), 273–305 (2000)
20. Modgil, S., Faci, N., Meneguzzi, F.R., Oren, N., Miles, S., Luck, M.: A framework for monitoring agent-based normative systems. In: Sierra, C., Castelfranchi, C., Decker, K.S., Sichman, J.S. (eds.) AAMAS, pp. 153–160. IFAAMAS (2009)
21. Noriega, P.: Agent-mediated auctions: The fishmarket metaphor. IIIA Phd Monography 8 (1997)
22. North, D.C.: Institutions, institutional change, and economic performance. Cambridge Univ Pr, Cambridge (1990)
23. Omicini, A., Ricci, A., Viroli, M.: Artifacts in the A&A meta-model for multi-agent systems. Autonomous Agents and Multi-Agent Systems 17(3), 432–456 (2008)
24. Rodrıguez-Aguilar, J.A.: On the design and construction of agent-mediated electronic institutions. IIIA Phd Monography 14 (2001)
25. Sabater, J., Sierra, C.: Review on computational trust and reputation models. Artif. Intell. Rev. 24(1), 33–60 (2005)
26. Schultz, T., Kaufmann-Kohler, G., Langer, D., Bonnet, V.: Online dispute resolution: The state of the art and the issues, SSRN http://ssrn.com/abstarct=899079
27. Slate, W.K.: Online dispute resolution: Click here to settle your dispute. Dispute Resolution Journal 56(4), 8–14 (2002)
28. Toulmin, S.: The Uses of Argument. Cambridge Univ Pr, Cambridge (1969)

Initial Steps Towards Run-Time Support
for Norm-Governed Systems

Visara Urovi[1], Stefano Bromuri[1], Kostas Stathis[1], and Alexander Artikis[2]

[1] Department of Computer Science,
Royal Holloway, University of London, UK
{visara,stefano,kostas}@cs.rhul.ac.uk
[2] Institute of Informatics & Telecommunications,
NCSR "Demokritos", Greece
a.artikis@iit.demokritos.gr

Abstract. We present a knowledge representation framework with an associated run-time support infrastructure that is able to compute, for the benefit of the members of a norm-governed multi-agent system, the physically possible and permitted actions at each time, as well as sanctions that should be applied to violations of prohibitions. To offer the envisioned run-time support we use an Event Calculus dialect for efficient temporal reasoning. Both the knowledge representation framework and its associated infrastructure are highly configurable in the sense that they can be appropriately distributed in order to support real-time responses to agent requests. To exemplify the ideas, we apply the infrastructure on a benchmark scenario for multi-agent systems. Through experimental evaluation we also show how distributing our infrastructure can provide run-time support to large-scale multi-agent systems regulated by norms.

Keywords: social interaction, run-time service, GOLEM, event calculus.

1 Introduction

An open multi-agent system [33], such as an electronic market, is often characterized as a computing system where software agents developed by different parties are deployed within an application domain to achieve specific objectives. An important characteristic of this class of applications is that the various parties developing the agents may have competing goals and, as a result, agent developers for a specific party will have every interest to hide their agent's internal state from the rest of the agents in the system. Although openness of this kind may encourage many agents to participate in an application, interactions in the system must be regulated so that to convince skeptical agents that the overall specification of the application domain is respected.

Norm-governed multi-agent systems [21], [2] are open multi-agent systems that are regulated according to the normative relations that may exist between member agents, such as permission, obligation, and institutional power [22], including sanctioning mechanisms dealing with violations of prohibitions and non-compliance with obligations. Although knowledge representation frameworks for specifying such relations exist, these frameworks often focus on the expressive power of the formalism proposed and often abstract away from the computational aspects and experimental evaluation.

M. De Vos et al. (Eds.): COIN 2010 International Workshops, LNAI 6541, pp. 268–284, 2011.

The existing works for representing executable specifications normally do not provide experimental evaluations of multi-agent system deployment over distributed networks. The computational behaviour of many representation frameworks for norm-governed systems is often studied theoretically only, sometimes under simplifying, unrealistic assumptions.

The aim of this paper is to use a specific knowledge representation framework to develop an infrastructure for computing at run-time the physically possible actions, permissions, and sanctions, and eventually the obligations, and institutional powers of the members of a norm-governed system. The need for such an infrastructure is motivated by the observation that agents cannot be expected to be capable of computing these normative relations on their own. Practical reasons for this include (a) computational constraints agents may have (e.g. due to lack of CPU cycles, memory, or battery), and (b) incomplete knowledge agents may have about the application state (e.g. due to a partial view of the environment).

Our run-time infrastructure integrates selected versions of the Event Calculus [25] for describing an open multi-agent system as two concurrent and interconnected composite structures that evolve over time: one representing the physical environment of the open multi-agent system and the other representing the social environment. The focus of our knowledge representation framework and its associated run-time infrastructure is to provide real-time responses to agent requests. The novelty of our approach relies on the ability of our framework to provide a distributed implementation of the Event Calculus for norm governed systems. The advantage here is that by distributing a norm-governed application we can efficiently compute the distributed social and the physical states of the system.

The paper is organised as follows. In Section 2 we introduce a scenario of a norm-governed multi-agent system. We then use this scenario to describe our run-time infrastructure in Section 3, the knowledge representation framework and extensions of this framework to support a social state with norms. In Section 4 we show an experimental evaluation of the approach, followed by a comparison with related work in Section 5. Finally, in Section 6, we summarize our approach and outline plans for future work.

2   The Open Packet World

To exemplify the framework and experiment with the proposed infrastructure we will use the *Packet World* [36]. As seen in Fig. 1(a)(i), a set of agents are situated in a rectangular grid (8 x 8 here) consisting of a number of colored packets (squares) and destination points (circles). Agents (a1, a2, a3, and a4 in Fig. 1(a)(i))) move around the grid to pick colored packets which they must deliver in destinations that match a packet's color. As agents can see only part of the grid at any one time (the square around agent a2 represents the perception range of this agent), they often need to collaborate with each other. Collaboration results in agents forming teams to deliver packets and placing flags in locations for letting other agents know that a particular area has been explored and has no packets left. Also, each agent is powered by a battery that discharges as the agent moves in the grid. The battery can be recharged using a battery charger (situated

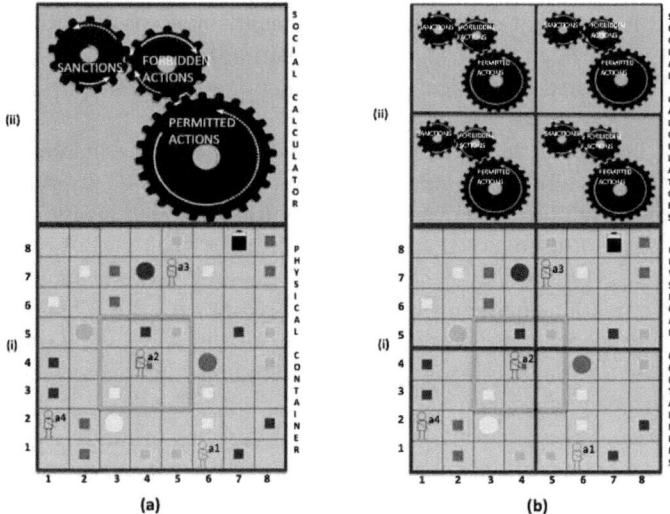

Fig. 1. Open Packet-World as a Norm-Governed System

in location (7,8) of Fig. 1(a)(i))). This charger emits a gradient whose value is larger if the agent is far away from the charger and smaller if the agent is closer to the charger.

We are interested here in a variation of Packet World, which we will refer to as *Open Packet World* (OPW). This variation differs from the original version as follows. We make the scenario competitive by giving points to agents if they deliver packets to appropriate destinations. Agents are now antagonistic and may be developed by different parties. For instance an agent may try to deceive other agents by placing a flag in an area that has packets. As a result of these extensions we introduce norms. Violation of norms results in sanctions. One type of sanction, in this example, is the reduction of points of the violating agent. In this paper we focus on permissions and sanctions.

OPW exhibits a number of features of that make it very appealing for a norm-governed systems test-bed:

- Unlike other practical applications, e.g. electronic markets, it does not require speech acts only but also physical actions, which in turn necessitate the representation of physical possibility in the system. Physical possibility requires the representation of a physical environment whose state should be distinct from the state of the social environment.
- OPW is also convenient from the point of view of experimentation in that we can make the experimental conditions harder by increasing the size of the grid, the number of agents and the number of packets/destinations. Moreover, it is natural to distribute OPW and thus test reasoning frameworks that operate on distributed knowledge bases.
- Because of the intuitive nature of actions taking place in it, OPW can be easily visualized.

3   Run-Time Infrastructure

To experiment with our scenario we use the GOLEM agent platform[1]. GOLEM supports the deployment of *agents* - cognitive entities that can reason about sensory input received from the environment and act upon it, *objects* - resources that lack cognitive ability, and *containers* - virtual spaces containing agents and objects, capturing their ongoing interactions in terms of an *event-based* approach.

A GOLEM container represents a portion of the distributed agent environment and it works as a mediator for the interaction taking place between agents and objects. In general, events in a container can be caused by agents, objects and processes of the agent environment as discussed in [3], [4]. In this paper we focus on the social part of the agent environment which involves events produced mainly by agents. Agents decide what actions to perform according to their goals and to the last environmental state observed. They can modify and observe the state of the environment by using the interface provided by the container to attempt actions in the environment. The containers mediate these actions by performing the necessary updates in the state of the environment.

In this paper we are not concerned with the implementation of agents. Instead, we are concerned with an implementation of a software framework informing the decision-making of agents by computing, on their behalf, the normative positions as they evolve in time. Whether an agent complies with these positions depends entirely on the implementation of the agent. In general, there is a clear separation between the agent code and the code of our software framework. The code presented in the paper belongs entirely to the proposed software framework. A part of that code — the specification of norms and physical possibility — are application-dependent.

3.1   The Open Packet World in GOLEM

The simplest way to model OPW in GOLEM is shown in Fig. 1(a), where we deploy one container representing the world (see Fig. 1(a)(i)) and extend it in a way that contains a social state representing the normative aspects of the system (see Fig. 1(a)(ii)).

Although a single container specification for the original Packet World has been implemented in [3], this container did not have a social state. Here we extend a container with a social state managed by an active object which we call *Social Calculator*. This object computes the agents' permissions and sanctions and publicises this information upon request.

An alternative way to model OPW is to split the physical state of a single container into smaller states that we distribute in different containers. A possible distribution is shown in Fig. 1(b), where we use four 4 x 4 adjacent containers for OPW (see Fig. 1(b)(i)) together with their corresponding Social Calculators (see Fig. 1(b)(ii)). Issues such as distributing the perception range of an agent in different containers (as it is the case with **ag2**) and moving between containers are already described in [4]. Here we show how containers can use a social state to support a norm-governed system.

---

[1] http://golem.cs.rhul.ac.uk

3.2   The Physical State of Containers

To represent the state of a GOLEM container we use the object-based notation of C-logic, a formalism that describes objects as complex terms that have a straightforward translation to first-order logic [5]. The complex term below, for example, represents the state of a 2 x 2 packet world with one agent, one packet, one destination and one battery:

packet_world:c1[
  address ⇒ "container://one@134.219.7.1:13000",
  type ⇒ open,
  grid ⇒ {square:sq1, square:sq2, square:sq3, square:sq4}
  entities ⇒ {picker:ag1, packet:p1, dest:d1, battery:b1}
]

Object instances of this kind belong to classes (e.g. packet_world), are characterized by unique identifiers (e.g. c1), and have attributes (e.g. address). The representation of the 8 x 8 grid of Fig. 1 is similar but larger, i.e. there are more agents, packets, destinations, and squares.

In GOLEM complex instances of objects evolve as a result of events happening in the state of a container. An event happens as a result of entities, such as agents, attempting to act in the environment. For example the assertions:

attempt(e14, 100).
do:e14 [actor ⇒ ag1, act ⇒ move, location⇒ sq3].

describe an attempt e14 at time 100, containing a physical action made by agent ag1 wishing to move to location sq3. In GOLEM, an attempt becomes an event that happens if the attempt is possible:

happens(Event, T) ← attempt(Event, T), possible(Event, T).

Happenings of events cause the state of a container C to evolve over time. To query the value Val of an attribute Attr for an entity Id of container C at a specific time T, we will use the definition:

solve_at(C, Id, Class, Attr, Val, T) ←
    holds_at(C, container, entity_of, Id, T),
    holds_at(Id, Class, Attr, Val, T).

holds_at/5 is defined by the top-level clauses of the *Object Event Calculus* (OEC) [24] and specified as:

holds_at(Id, Class, Attr, Val, T)←
    happens(E, Ti), Ti ≤ T,
    initiates(E, Id, Class, Attr, Val),
    not broken(Id, Class, Attr, Val, Ti, T).

broken(Id, Class, Attr, Val, Ti, Tn)←
    happens(E, Tj), Ti < Tj ≤Tn,
    terminates(E, Id, Class, Attr, Val).

The above definitions utilise a logic programming approach based on negation as failure [8]. They describe how the value Val of an attribute Attr for specific Class instance identified by Id holds at a particular time T, as in the usual Event Calculus [25]. Given an event E, the initiates/5 predicate assigns to the attributes Attr of an object identified by the Id and of class Class a value Val. The terminates/5 predicate has a similar meaning, with the only difference that the event E terminates the value Val of the attribute of an object. The remaining OEC clauses (see [24] for more details) describe how events create instances of C-logic like objects, assign these instances to classes, represent basic hierarchical inheritance where sub-classes inherit attributes from super-classes, destroy complex terms, and terminate single value and multi-valued attributes.

The possible/2 are application dependent rules that specify physical possibility. Below, we show an example of how we use the OEC to express a possible/2 rule in OPW:

```
possible(E, T)←
    do:E [actor ⇒ A, act ⇒ move, location⇒ SqB],
    solve_at(this, A, picker, position, SqA, T),
    adjacent(SqA, SqB),
    not occupied(SqB, T).
```

The above rule states that it is possible for an agent to move to a location SqB if the agent is currently in location SqA, SqA is adjacent to SqB, and SqB is not occupied. The keyword **this** is used here to refer to the identifier of the current container.

3.3   Containers with Social State

We extend GOLEM containers with a social state, formalized as a C-logic structure that has a reference to the physical state, and extends this physical state with social attributes to hold information about (a) any current sanctions imposed on any of the agents and (b) how many points agents have collected so far. An example snapshot of a social state for OPW is shown below:

```
packet_world_social_state: s1 [
    physical_state⇒ packet_world:c1,
    sanctions⇒ {sanction:s1 [agent ⇒ a2, ticket ⇒ 5]},
    records⇒ {record:r1[agent ⇒ a1, points → 35],
                 record:r2[agent ⇒ a2, points ⇒ 25]}
]
```

The term above states that agent a2 has been sanctioned with 5 points. We show the records of two agents only to save space. Agent a1 has collected 35 points, while a2 has collected 25 after the sanction is applied. Sanctions change the points of the agent, and they are stored in the social state to keep a history of all sanctions occurred to the agents during the execution. A social state does not contain explicitly the permitted actions. These are defined implicitly in terms of rules. We write:

```
permitted(Event, T)← not forbidden(Event, T).
```

to state that actions specified in events are permitted only if they are not forbidden. Forbidden actions and the evolution of the social state due to these actions are specified in an application dependent manner. A forbidden/2 rule in OPW can be expressed as follows:

forbidden(E, T) ←
    do:E[actor ⇒ A, act⇒drop, object⇒flag, location⇒SqA],
    solve_at(**this**, Id, packet, position, SqB, T),
    adjacent(SqA, SqB).

states that it is forbidden for an agent A to drop a flag in location SqA if there are packets nearby.

When a forbidden act has taken place, the Social Calculator raises a violation, which results in a sanction.

initiates(E, R, record, points, Points)←
    happens(E,T),
    violation:E[sanction:S [ticket⇒ SanctionPs, agent ⇒ A]],
    solve_at(**this**, R, record, agent, A, T),
    solve_at(**this**, R, record, points, OldPoints, T),
    Points = OldPoints - SanctionPs.

initiates/5 updates the points of agent A as a consequence of receiving a sanction S at time T. This simple example shows how events happening in the physical environment (e.g. dropping a flag in a location of the grid) affect the social state of the application (e.g. through the initiation of a sanction on the agent that dropped the flag). More complex permissions and sanctions are formalized similarly.

Similarly to prohibition and permission, we can also represent a basic form of empowerment. For example, we can express the fact that an agent in a leader role within a team of collaborating agents (here identified by the class instance **team**) is empowered to request a second agent to collect a packet if the second agent is also a member of the same collaboration team. We express this rule as follows:

empowered(E,T)←
    do:E[actor ⇒ A, act⇒collect, agent ⇒B, square ⇒ Sq],
    neighbouring_instance_of(**this**, [], _, Max, TID, team,T),
    solve_at(**this**, TID, team, leader, A, T),
    solve_at(**this**, TID, team, member, B, T).

The above clause states that an agent A, who is a leader in the collaboration team identified as TID, is empowered at time T to request from another agent B of the same team to collect a packet in a square Sq. For a general discussion on empowerment see [22].

Our framework also supports obligations using rules of the form:

obliged(E, T)←
    neighbouring_instance_of(**this**, [], _, Max, TID, team, T),
    solve_at(**this**, TID, team, leader, A, T),
    do:E[actor ⇒ B, act⇒pick, obj⇒ObjId, square ⇒ Sq],
    request:E_j[actor ⇒ A, act ⇒ E],
    happens(E_j, T_j),

$T_j < \mathsf{T}$,
not fulfilled(E, T_j, T),
solve_at(**this**, ObjId, packet, position, Sq, T).

The clause above states that an agent B is obliged at time T to pick a packet in the location Sq if the leader of the team A has requested it before and this has not been done yet, and the packet is still in the location Sq. For our scenario, such rules provide a very basic form of obligations that implicitly persist until they are fulfilled. More complex application scenarios will require more sophisticated treatment of obligations. However, this discussion is beyond the scope of this work.

3.4   Distributing a Norm-Governed Application

One important feature of our knowledge representation framework is that we can distribute the state of a norm-governed application into multiple containers in order to support the parallel evaluation of physical and social states. Distributing a system among multiple containers is not a novel architectural idea; however, the proposed architecture — distributed implementation of the Event Calculus supporting norm-governed systems — is, to the best of our knowledge, novel.

GOLEM supports this feature with the *Ambient Event Calculus* (AEC) [4]. The AEC uses the OEC, described earlier, to query C-logic like objects and their attributes that may be situated in distributed containers. For example, in OPW, we can distribute the grid representing the agent environment into four containers as shown in Fig. 1(b). Every container manages a part of the grid and is defined as a neighbour to the other containers. The neighborhood defines the relationship between the distributed portions of the agent environment and it is used in AEC to perform distributed queries. GOLEM supports also hierarchical representation of the agent environment (where one container contains other sub-containers) for which the interested reader is referred to [4].

The rules bellow specify how we can query the properties of objects in the agent environment:

neighbouring_at(C, Path, Path*, Max, Id, Cls, Attr, Val, T)←
  Max >= 0,
  locally_at(C, Path, Path*, Id, Cls, Attr, Val, T).

neighbouring_at(C, Path, Path*, Max, Id, Cls, Attr, Val, T)←
  holds_at(C, container, neighbour, N, T),
  not member(N, Path),
  Max* is Max - 1,
  append(Path, [C], New),
  neighbouring_at(N, New, Path*, Max*, Id, Cls, Attr, Val, T).

Using the above specification we can query whether an object identified as Id, with class Cls, has an attribute Attr, whose value is Val at time T. In the clause above, Max represents the maximum number (decided at design time) of adjacent neighbors that the distributed query has to consider, Path represents the neighbors visited so far, while Path* represents the resulting path to the neighbor where the query has succeeded.

In particular, the first clause checks whether the object is in the local state of a container. locally_at/8 checks with holds_at/5 to find the object in the container's state, including sub-containers, if any (See [4] for a full definition of locally_at/8). The second clause looks for neighbors. If a new neighbor N is found, this neighbor is asked the query but in the context of a New path and a new Max*.

We are now in a position to customize our representation for distributing the physical and social state by redefining the solve_at/6. The definition below has the effect of changing all the physical and social rules to work with distributed containers:

```
solve_at(C, Id, Class, Attr, Val, T) ←
    neighbouring_at(C, [], _, 1, Id, Class, Attr, Val, T).
```

The [] list above states that the initial path is empty, the underscore '_', that we are not interested in the resulting path, and the number 1 indicates that we should look at all neighbors whose distance is one step from the current container. In this way, we can query all the neighbors of a container in the OPW of Fig. 1(b).

3.5 Implementation Issues

The AEC is implemented on top of OEC [30] which is an object-oriented optimised version of EC. EC has been implemented in many different ways. Mueller [29], for example, has developed an implementation using satisfiability solvers, whereas Farrell et al [13] have developed a Java implementation of EC. The vast majority of EC implementations, however, are in the context of logic programming. We also adopted the logic programming due to the formal and declarative semantics — see [31], for instance, for the benefits of a logic programming EC implementation.

The top-level description of OEC is specified below:

```
holds_at(Obj,Attr,Val,T):-
    object(Obj,Attr,Val,start(E)),
    time(E,T1), T1 =< T,
    not (object(Obj,Attr,Val,end(Evstar)),
        time(Evstar,T2), T2>T1, T2 <T).
```

The main difference between this OEC version and the one discussed earlier is that now we add all new properties that are initiated/terminated as object/4 assertions whenever a new event description is added to the container's state. Time intervals are used to store how the properties of objects change their value in time, which is similar to the approach followed in METATEM [14]. Additionally, the object/4 assertions store the state of the environment distinguishing between objects in the container by their identification Obj. This means that we have a double indexing on the properties of the state, the first one is time and the second one is the identification of the objects that define the state of the container, while in METATEM [14] the indexing is done only in terms of time. We denote the time periods by using start(e1) and end(e2) terms. For example, in OPW the assertions below:

```
time(e1, 2).
time(e2, 7).
object(ag1, position, [3,4], start(e1)).
object(ag1, position, [3,4], end(e2)).
object(ag1, position, [4,4], start(e2)).
```

describe how agent a1 moved to position [3,4] at time 2 and changed it to [4,4] at time 7. We know that the periods in the state of a container are either closed or open intervals which persist into the future. A new event such as e2 either starts a new period of time (i.e. start(e2)) for a conclusion or ends a period of time which was started by another event (i.e. end(e2)). The optimization is obtained now because the new event is either related to the attributes of objects or the class membership, so we do not need to check all the events that have happened, as with the previous OEC version. Our implementation also uses indexing on the arguments of object/4 assertions, so that if the first three arguments are specified, the time to retrieve the term is $O(1)$ (which is typically the case with GOLEM queries).

When we distribute the system in many containers we may have a synchronisation problem due to the different timing in different containers. This issue was already addressed in [4] by applying a precise time protocol between sub and super containers. In this paper we assume that a network of distributed containers, however it is structured, it has always one root container that deals with the synchronisation of the containers.

Another important component of our implementation is that queries to the social and physical environment are executed in parallel. An example of the multi-threaded implementation is shown below for how we implement attempts of agents:

```
attempt(E, T):-
    par([exec(possible(E, T), true), exec(permitted(E,T), R)]),
    add(E, R, T).
```

The above program will be called by an agent that wishes to perform an action specified as an event E. The event provides input to two parallel threads, one executing possible(E,T) (which must succeed i.e. return true) and the other executing permitted(E,T) (which must have result R i.e. return true or false). If the event is concluded possible by the first thread, it will be added in the state of the container using add/3; otherwise, the attempt will fail. If the event is concluded possible by the first thread but not permitted (R=false) by the second thread, then the Social Calculator will be triggered by add/3 to produce a sanction in the social state.

4   Experimental Evaluation

Using OPW, we conducted a number of experiments to evaluate the performance of the system with different configurations. In particular, we measured the performance with a distributed versus centralised deployment of the system to show how the number of entities, the size of the environment and the distribution affect performances. In all experiments, we measured the time to compute whether an action is physically possible and whether an action is permitted. More specifically, we measured the time

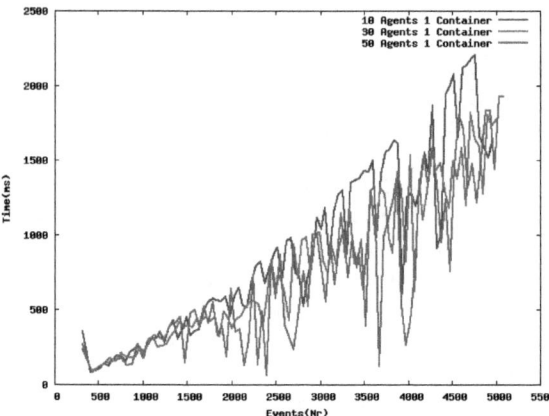

Fig. 2. Time to query the physical and the social state of one container

taken for possible/2 and forbidden/2 rules against an action performed by an agent in the environment. Then we related this time with the number of events produced.

In the first series of tests, we tested OPW in a centralized GOLEM container deployed in an Intel Centrino Core 2 Duo 2.66GHz with 4GB of RAM. The environment was represented by a 40x40 grid and 100 packets were collected by the agents and released into one of the 8 destinations in the grid. We run the first test with 10 agents, the second test with 30 agents and the third test with 50 agents. In all of the runs, the agent "minds" (reasoning components) were deployed in a separate machine and were remotely connected with their "bodies" (action execution components) deployed in the GOLEM container.

Fig. 2 shows three linear curves representing the average time to compute a query in a single GOLEM container with respectively 10, 30 and 50 agents. Since the evaluation of the two states is done concurrently, the curves represent the worst case between the social and the physical state.

All the three curves follow a linear behaviour suggesting that the time to query a GOLEM container grows linearly with the number of events produced in the container. The fluctuations in the curves are explained as follows. The high peaks show the worst case where the attempted action was either impossible or not permitted or both. As we check possible and permitted actions in parallel and we wait for both threads to finish the execution, the time shown is the one that took longer between the two. Alternatively, the lowest peaks show the best case where the attempted action was either possible or permitted or both. As before, the one shown is the one that took longer.

We can represent the time T_c to compute the social and physical state for a centralized container with the following equation:

$$T_c = a * E + t0 \text{ with } a \sim Ne/Na$$

where Ne is the number of entities in the system, Na is the number of active entities performing events, E is the number of events in the system and $t0$ is initial time to register the entities in the container. As the number of agents increases, then Na increases,

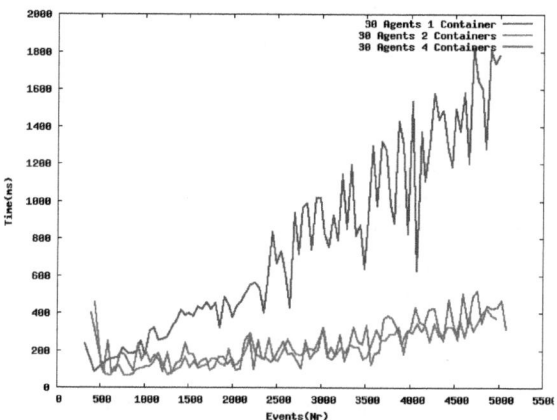

Fig. 3. The effects of distribution

which means that a decreases, which results in better performance. This is due to the fact that OEC is optimized to deal with events indexed by the identifiers of entities in the agent environment. For example, if we have 10 agents, 5000 events, and assuming that all agents perform the same number of events, each time that we call a solve_at/6 predicate (e.g solve_at(c1, ag1, picker, position, [3,4], 100)), the search for the value of an agent attribute will evaluate a maximum of 500 entries (5000/10), while when we have 50 agents and the remaining conditions are the same, the search will evaluate a maximum of 100 entries (5000/50). Of course, if we consider an increasing number of agents, this also means that they produce more events in less time, but it also means that given the same number of changes applied to the environment, the environment responds better with an increasing number of agents. Thus, the environment as supported by GOLEM scales up better in situations when there are many agents rather than few.

In the second series of experiments we distributed the OPW grid (40x40) first into two containers (20x40) and then into four (20x20) different containers. For the distribution of the containers we used an Intel Centrino Core 2 Duo 2.66GHz with 4GB of RAM and an Intel Centrino Core Duo 1.66Ghz with 1GB of RAM. The agents were deployed between the distributed containers and could move from one machine to another by means of the mobility capabilities offered by GOLEM [4].

Fig. 3 shows what happens when we distribute the environment in multiple containers and use AEC to link these containers.

As shown in Fig. 3, with a growing number of events if we increase the number of containers, we improve considerably the performance. In Fig. 3 we show that in a system with a small number of events (0-500), it is better to compute the physical and social state in one container. With a bigger number of events, the experiment shows that we can achieve a big improvement in performance if we distribute in two or four containers instead of one container.

In the distributed version the size of the grid managed by a single container becomes smaller and less complex terms (agents, packets and destinations) are registered in a single container. Between 500 to 3500 events, in average, having four or two containers does not make much difference. However, after 3500 events the performance of the

application with two containers is better from the performance of the application deployed in four containers. This is due to the fact that with less packets on the grid (most
of them after 3500 events have been delivered to the destinations), the agents moving
on the grid are more likely to change containers in search for packets. The smaller the
grid, the bigger the number of times agents try to move from a container to another.
This introduces a distribution cost related to the cost of interactions between containers. For this reason, in the presented experiments there is no improvement when we
change from two to four containers.

In general, the time to compute the physical and social state distributed over many
containers is defined by the equation:

$$T_d = \frac{T_c}{d} + i \times c$$

where T_c is the time to compute the same experiment with a centralised container, d is
number of containers used in the decentralized version, i is the number of interactions
between containers and c is the cost of container interaction. In other words, when we
distribute the agent environment in multiple containers, the time to compute the physical
and the social state is inversely proportional to the number of containers, thus improving
the performance. However, there is an additional delay to compute the physical and
social state which is due to the interactions between the containers.

5   Related Work

There exist several approaches in the literature for executable specifications of norm-
governed systems. Consider, for instance, the 'Law-Governed Interaction' (LGI) [28,
27] framework that has been used to regulate distributed systems. The Moses software
mechanism [26] is an implementation of LGI that employs regimentation devices monitoring the behaviour of agents, blocking the performance of forbidden actions and enforcing compliance with obligations. Laws in Moses are written in pure Prolog or Java.

The Electronic Institution (EI) approach [9, 10, 11] and the AMELI framework [12],
use organisational concepts [18] to model the interaction of the agents. AMELI is an
agent-based middleware for executing a set of normative rules, expressions which impose obligations or prohibitions on communicative actions such as the computation of
the permissions and obligations of the agents at the current state. AMELI deploys governor agents for every external interacting agent and scene manager agents in charge of
maintaining the state of the interactions between agents. One of the differences between
our approach and AMELI is that we handle agent interaction via containers and we do
not use mediating agents, such as AMELI governors. An explicit feature of our approach is that the state of the interaction in the agent environment is easily inspectable,
while in EIs agents need to communicate to build a coherent state. Moreover the EI
approach allows only for permitted actions to happen. It has been argued that regimentation is not always desirable or practical [22]. Therefore, in here we opted for
sanctioning mechanisms as opposed to developing regimentation devices.

In [19] Garcia-Camino et al propose AMELI+, an extended version of the AMELI
framework [12], with a mechanism to handle distribution of norms and possible conflicts [17] that may arise due to normative positions generated from the actions of

agents. The AMELI architecture is extended with additional normative manager agents which together with governor agents and scene manager agents are in charge of the system. AMELI+ is based on a hierarchical structure of agents that deal with the enforcement of norms. These internal agents decide how to update and propagate the changes made in the state of the system to other internal agents interested in these changes. In contrast with our model, AMELI+ defines regimentation mechanisms, while we include a sanction mechanism for prohibited actions. Additionally, the AMELI+ approach requires many internal agents being involved into propagating messages for changes they perform locally. Instead of using internal agents we deploy containers which update the state locally and then use the AEC predicates to perform distributed queries to the containers of the agent environment. Thus we do not need to have additional propagation mechanisms and the same AEC mechanism can be used by the agents to query what is happening in the state of the environment. Moreover, AMELI+ does not support constraints as part of the norm language nor norms include reasoning with properties of the state changing in time.

Several action languages and corresponding software tools have also been employed for specifying and executing norm-governed systems. Fox et al. [16], for example, utilised an automated reasoning tool to execute 'organisational rules' formalised in the Situation Calculus [32]. Farrell et al [13] propose a formalisation of the Event Calculus in XML and apply it to the representation of contracts to facilitate the automated tracking of the contract state. Commitment protocols [7, 15] have been formalised in, among others, the action language $C+$ [20] and various dialects of the Event Calculus. Moreover, the Causal Calculator implementation of $C+$, and the Discrete Event Calculus reasoner [29] have been employed to execute commitment protocols.

Recently, norm-governed systems specifications have been formalised in semantic web languages [34, 23]; furthermore, various automated reasoning tools have been utilised for executing the specifications.

Our logic programming implementation of the Event Calculus has the following benefits. First, it exhibits a declarative semantics whose advantages, compared to procedural semantics, have been well-documented. Second, the Event Calculus offers a formal representation of the agents' actions and their effects. This is in contrast to semantic web languages that offer limited temporal representation and reasoning. Third, the availability of the full power of logic programming, which is one of the main attractions of employing the Event Calculus as the temporal formalism, allows for the development of very expressive social and physical laws. Fourth, we do not have to know from the outset the domain of each variable. Fifth, the OEC and the AEC versions used here provide an efficient and scalable reasoning mechanism, offering the kind of run-time support that is required for norm-governed multi-agent systems. The last point differentiates our work from approaches offering computational support for norm-governed systems. The last three points differentiate our work from other action language implementations.

6   Conclusions and Future Work

We presented a knowledge representation framework with an associated run-time infrastructure that is able to compute, for the benefit of the members of a norm-governed multi-agent system, physically possible and permitted actions at each time, as well as sanctions that should be applied to violations of prohibitions. The presented infrastructure is highly configurable in the sense that it can be appropriately distributed to offer run-time support for large-scale norm-governed systems.

We evaluated the platform based on the OPW scenario and showed that the distributed infrastructure is feasible. The tests showed that distribution can considerably improve the performances of the MAS system and that the distributed topology of the environment depends on the representation of the environment, the number of entities populating it and the number of events they generate.

We specify norms separately from the physical rules governing the environment, to be able to define how agents should interact at a social level. This allows us to have agents in the system that are implemented by different designers and with different strategies. The different agents can query the state of the environment and decide what actions to take exclusively based on their own internal strategy. We found out that the run-time infrastructure simplifies the implementation of the agent reasoning because agents do not need to manage the state of the interactions. Agents can reason about what acts to perform and query the infrastructure if such act is conformant with the social rules defined in the environment.

In addition, for a large norm governed application, there is a significant design decision to be taken for using our approach. This has to do with how we distribute the containers. Namely, how to organise the containers in such a way so bottle necks in evaluating the norms are avoided. In OPW we have found useful to limit the frequency of the distributed queries. In other applications, similar heuristics may be used, however this discussion is out of the scope of the paper as it requires further investigations.

There are various directions of further work. One is to experiment with various techniques, such as those proposed in [6], [1], in order to further improve the temporal reasoning. Two, we aim to perform experiments with larger multi-agent systems in order to determine the extent to which our infrastructure can be used for run-time support. Finally, we aim to extend the game based approach presented in [35] to coordinate the distributed social state of an application in terms of complex games. Different games are governed by different normative relations and complex games use coordination mechanisms to combine normative relations by activating/deactivating one or more games. In this way we will be able to show how to define complex agent interactions and maintain a parallel evaluation between social and physical consequences of the actions performed by agents in the system.

References

1. Artikis, A., Sergot, M., Pitt, J.: A logic programming approach to activity recognition. In: Proceedings of ACM Workshop on Events in Multimedia (2010)
2. Artikis, A., Sergot, M.J., Pitt, J.V.: Specifying norm-governed computational societies. ACM Transactions in Computational Logic 10(1) (2009)
3. Bromuri, S., Stathis, K.: Situating Cognitive Agents in GOLEM. In: Weyns, D., Brueckner, S.A., Demazeau, Y. (eds.) EEMMAS 2007. LNCS (LNAI), vol. 5049, pp. 115–134. Springer, Heidelberg (2008)
4. Bromuri, S., Stathis, K.: Distributed Agent Environments in the Ambient Event Calculus. In: DEBS 2009: Proceedings of the Third International Conference on Distributed Event-Based Systems. ACM, New York (2009)

5. Chen, W., Warren, D.S.: C-logic of complex objects. In: PODS 1989: Proceedings of the Eighth ACM SIGACT-SIGMOD-SIGART Symposium on Principles of Database Systems, pp. 369–378. ACM, New York (1989)
6. Chittaro, L., Montanari, A.: Efficient temporal reasoning in the cached event calculus. Computational Intelligence 12, 359–382 (1996)
7. Chopra, A., Singh, M.: Contextualizing commitment protocols. In: Proceedings of Conference on Autonous Agents and Multi-Agent Systems (AAMAS), pp. 1345–1352. ACM, New York (2006)
8. Clark, K.L.: Negation as failure. In: Logic and Data Bases, pp. 293–322 (1977)
9. Esteva, M., de la Cruz, D., Sierra, C.: Islander: an electronic institutions editor. In: Castelfranchi, C., Johnson, L. (eds.) Proceedings of the First International Conference on Autonomous Agents and Multi-Agent Systems (AAMAS), pp. 1045–1052. ACM Press, New York (2002)
10. Esteva, M., Padget, J., Sierra, C.: Formalizing a language for institutions and norms. In: Meyer, J.-J., Tambe, M. (eds.) ATAL 2001. LNCS (LNAI), vol. 2333, pp. 348–366. Springer, Heidelberg (2002)
11. Esteva, M., Rodríguez-Aguilar, J., Sierra, C., Vasconcelos, W.: Verifying norm consistency in electronic institutions. In: Proceedings of the AAAI 2004 Workshop on Agent Organizations: Theory and Practice, pp. 8–14 (2004)
12. Esteva, M., Rosell, B., Rodriguez-Aguilar, J.A., Ll, J.: Ameli: An agent-based middleware for electronic institutions. In: AAMAS 2004: Proceedings of the Third International Joint Conference on Autonomous Agents and Multiagent Systems, pp. 236–243. IEEE Computer Society, Washington, DC, USA (2004)
13. Farrell, A.D.H., Sergot, M.J., Sall, M., Bartolini, C.: Using the event calculus for tracking the normative state of contracts. International Journal of Cooperative Information Systems 14, 99–129 (2005)
14. Fisher, M., Owens, R.: From the past to the future: Executing temporal logic programs. In: Voronkov, A. (ed.) LPAR 1992. LNCS, vol. 624, pp. 369–380. Springer, Heidelberg (1992)
15. Fornara, N., Colombetti, M.: Formal specification of artificial institutions using the event calculus. In: Multi-Agent Systems: Semantics and Dynamics of Organizational Models. IGI Global (2009)
16. Fox, M., Barbuceanu, M., Grüninger, M., Lin, J.: An organizational ontology for enterprise modeling. In: Prietula, M., Carley, K., Gasser, L. (eds.) Simulating Organizations: Computational Models for Institutions and Groups, pp. 131–152. AAAI Press/The MIT Press (1998)
17. Gaertner, D., Garcia-Camino, A., Noriega, P., Rodriguez-Aguilar, J.A., Vasconcelos, W.: Distributed norm management in regulated multiagent systems. In: AAMAS 2007: Proceedings of the 6th International Joint Conference on Autonomous Agents and Multiagent Systems, pp. 1–8. ACM, New York (2007)
18. García-Camino, A., Noriega, P., Rodríguez-Aguilar, J.: Implementing norms in electronic institutions. In: Proceedings of the Conference on Autonomous Agents and Multi-Agent Systems (AAMAS), pp. 667–673. ACM Press, New York (2005)
19. García-Camino, A., Rodríguez-Aguilar, J.A., Vasconcelos, W.: A distributed architecture for norm management in multi-agent systems. In: Sichman, J.S., Padget, J., Ossowski, S., Noriega, P. (eds.) COIN 2007. LNCS (LNAI), vol. 4870, pp. 275–286. Springer, Heidelberg (2008)
20. Giunchiglia, E., Lee, J., Lifschitz, V., McCain, N., Turner, H.: Nonmonotonic causal theories. Artificial Intelligence 153(1-2), 49–104 (2004)
21. Jones, A., Sergot, M.: On the characterisation of law and computer systems: the normative systems perspective. In: Deontic Logic in Computer Science: Normative System Specification, pp. 275–307. J. Wiley and Sons, Chichester (1993)

22. Jones, A., Sergot, M.: A formal characterisation of institutionalised power. Journal of the IGPL 4(3), 429–445 (1996)
23. Kagal, L., Finin, T.: Modeling communicative behavior using permissions and obligations. Journal of Autonomous Agents and Multi-Agent Systems 14(2), 187–206 (2006)
24. Kesim, F.N., Sergot, M.: A Logic Programming Framework for Modeling Temporal Objects. IEEE Transactions on Knowledge and Data Engineering 8(5), 724–741 (1996)
25. Kowalski, R., Sergot, M.: A logic-based calculus of events. New Gen. Comput. 4(1), 67–95 (1986)
26. Minsky, N.: Law-Governed Interaction (LGI): A Distributed Coordination and Control Mechanism (An Introduction and a Reference Manual) (2005), http://www.moses.rutgers.edu/documentation/manual.pdf (retrieved October 24, 2008)
27. Minsky, N.: Decentralised regulation of distributed systems: Beyond access control (2008) (submitted for publication), http://www.cs.rutgers.edu/~minsky/papers/IC.pdf (retrieved October 24, 2008)
28. Minsky, N., Ungureanu, V.: Law-governed interaction: a coordination and control mechanism for heterogeneous distributed systems. ACM Transactions on Software Engineering and Methodology (TOSEM) 9(3), 273–305 (2000)
29. Mueller, E.: Commonsense Reasoning. Morgan Kaufmann, San Francisco (2006)
30. Nihan, K., Marek, S.: Implementing an object-oriented deductive database using temporal reasoning. J. Database Manage. 7(4), 21–34 (1996)
31. Paschke, A., Bichler, M.: Knowledge representation concepts for automated SLA management. Decision Support Systems 46(1), 187–205 (2008)
32. Pinto, J., Reiter, R.: Temporal reasoning in logic programming: a case for the situation calculus. In: Warren, D. (ed.) Proceedings of Conference on Logic Programming, pp. 203–221. MIT Press, Cambridge (1993)
33. Pitt, J., Mamdani, A., Charlton, P.: The open agent society and its enemies: a position statement and research programme. Telematics and Informatics 18(1), 67–87 (2001)
34. Tonti, G., Bradshaw, J., Jeffers, R., Montanari, R., Suri, N., Uszok, A.: Semantic web languages for policy representation and reasoning: A comparison of kAoS, rei, and ponder. In: Fensel, D., Sycara, K., Mylopoulos, J. (eds.) ISWC 2003. LNCS, vol. 2870, pp. 419–437. Springer, Heidelberg (2003)
35. Urovi, V., Stathis, K.: Playing with agent coordination patterns in MAGE. In: Padget, J.A., Artikis, A., Vasconcelos, W.W., Stathis, K., da Silva, V.T., Matson, E.T., Polleres, A. (eds.) COIN 2009. LNCS, vol. 6069, pp. 86–101. Springer, Heidelberg (2010)
36. Weyns, D., Helleboogh, A., Holvoet, T.: The packet-world: A testbed for investigating situated multiagent systems. In: Software Agent-Based Applications, Platforms, and Development Kits, pp. 383–408. Birkhauser, Basel (2005)

Identifying Conditional Norms in Multi-agent Societies

Bastin Tony Roy Savarimuthu, Stephen Cranefield, Maryam A. Purvis,
and Martin K. Purvis

University of Otago, Dunedin, P.O. Box 56, Dunedin, New Zealand
(tonyr,scranefield,tehrany,mpurvis)@infoscience.otago.ac.nz

Abstract. Most works on norms have investigated how norms are regulated using institutional mechanisms which assume that agents know the norms of the society they are situated in. Few research works have focused on how an agent may infer the norms of a society without the norm being explicitly given to the agent. These works do not address how an agent can identify conditional norms. In this paper we describe a mechanism that an agent can use to identify conditional norms which makes use of our previously proposed norm identification framework. Using park littering as an example, we show how conditional norms can be identified. In addition, we discuss the experimental results on the dynamic addition, modification and deletion of conditional norms.

1 Introduction

Most works on norms in normative multi-agent systems have concentrated on how norms regulate behaviour (e.g. [14, 18]). These works assume that the agent somehow knows (*a priori*) what the norms of a society are. For example, an agent may have obtained the norm from a leader [7] or through an institution that prescribes what the norms of the society should be [1, 31].

Only a few researchers have dealt with how an agent may infer what the norms of a newly joined society are [2, 23]. Recognizing the norms of a society is beneficial to an agent. This process enables the agent to know what the *normative expectation* of a society is. As the agent joins and leaves different agent societies, this capability is essential for the agent to modify its expectations of behaviour, depending upon the society of which it is a part. As the environment changes, the capability of recognizing a new norm helps an agent to derive new ways of achieving its intended goals. Such a norm identification mechanism can be useful for software agents that need to adapt to a changing environment. In open agent systems, instead of possessing predetermined notions of what the norms are, agents can infer and identify norms through observing patterns of interactions and their consequences. For example, a new agent joining a virtual environment such as Second Life [21] may have to infer norms when joining a society as each society may have different norms. It has been noted that having social norms centrally imposed by the land owners in Second Life is ineffective and there is a need for the establishment of community driven norms [29]. When a community of agents determines what the norm should be, the norm can evolve over time. So, a new agent joining the society should have the ability to recognize the changes to the norms. In our previous work we have proposed and experimented with a norm identification

M. De Vos et al. (Eds.): COIN 2010 International Workshops, LNAI 6541, pp. 285–302, 2011.

framework which can be used to identify norms in the society [23–25]. The norm identification framework takes into account the social learning theory [5] that suggests that
new behaviour can be learnt through the observation of punishment and rewards. This
work aims to answer the question of how agents infer conditional norms in a multi-
agent society. Conditional norms are defined as norms with conditions. We distinguish
norms that are not associated with conditions from the ones that have conditions. An
example of a norm without a condition is the norm that prohibits anyone from littering
a public park, i.e. *prohibit(litter)*. An example of a norm with condition is a norm that
prohibits one from littering as long as there is a rubbish bin within x metres from the
agent (e.g. *if (distanceFromBin < 10) then prohibit(litter)*). Software agents should not
only have the ability to identify norms but also the conditions under which these norms
hold.

Identifying conditional norms is important because an agent that has inferred that
another agent gets punished when that agent littered when it was 25 metres away from
the bin may infer that the condition associated with the norm is the distance of 25
metres. But the actual norm could be that no one should litter within 50 metres from the
bin. The utility of the agent can be negatively impacted through a sanction if it litters
30 metres away from a bin. In this case, the agent does not know the correct condition
associated with the norm. Another example of a conditional norm is the tipping norm.
In one society an agent may tip 10% of the bill while in another society an agent might
be obliged to tip 20% of the bill. In this work we are interested in experimenting with
the formation, modification and the removal of conditional norms in the minds of the
agents and the impact of the normative conditions on the utility of the agents.

The paper is organized as follows. Section 2 provides a background on norms and
how the concept of norms is investigated in the field of normative multi-agent systems
(NorMAS). Section 3 provides an overview of our previous work on the norm identification framework. Section 4 describes a mechanism for identifying conditional norms.
Section 5 describes the experiments that we have conducted and the results obtained.
Section 6 provides a discussion on the work that has been achieved and the issues that
can be addressed in the future. Concluding remarks are presented in Section 7.

2 Background

Due to multi-disciplinary interest in norms, several definitions for norms exist [2]. Elster
notes the following about social norms [11]. *"For norms to be social, they must be
shared by other people and partly sustained by their approval and disapproval. They
are sustained by the feelings of embarrassment,anxiety, guilt and shame that a person
suffers at the prospect of violating them. A person obeying a norm may also be propelled
by positive emotions like anger and indignation ... social norms have a grip on the mind
that is due to the strong emotions they can trigger"*.

Based on the definitions provided by various researchers, we note that the social
practices surrounding the notion of a social norm are the following:

- *The normative expectation of a behavioural regularity*: There is a general agreement within the society that a behaviour is *expected* on the part of an agent (or
  actor) by others in a society, in a given circumstance.

- *A norm enforcement mechanism*: When an agent does not follow a norm, it could be subjected to a sanction. The sanction could include monetary or physical punishment in the real world which can trigger emotions (embarrassment, guilt, etc.) or direct loss of utility (e.g. decrease of its reputation score).
- *A norm spreading mechanism*: Examples of norm spreading mechanisms include the notion of advice from powerful leaders, imitation and learning on the part of an agent.

2.1 Normative Multi-agent Systems

The definition of normative multi-agent systems given by the researchers involved in the NorMAS 2007 workshop is as follows [6]. *A normative multi-agent system is a multi-agent system organized by means of mechanisms to represent, communicate, distribute, detect, create, modify and enforce norms, and mechanisms to deliberate about norms and detect norm violation and fulfillment.*

Researchers in multi-agent systems have studied how the concept of norms can be applied to artificial agents. Norms are of interest to multi-agent system (MAS) researchers as they help in sustaining social order and increase the predictability of behaviour in the society. Researchers have shown that norms improve cooperation and collaboration [28, 33]. Epstein has shown that norms reduce the amount of computation required to make a decision [12]. However, software agents may tend to deviate from norms due to their autonomy. So, the study of norms has become important to MAS researchers as they can build robust multi-agent systems using the concept of norms and also experiment on how norms may evolve and adapt in response to environmental changes.

Research in normative multi-agent systems can be categorized into two branches. The first branch focuses on normative system architectures, norm representations, norm adherence and the associated punitive or incentive measures. Several architectures have been proposed for normative agents (refer to [19] for an overview). Researchers have used deontic logic to define and represent norms [16, 35]. Several researchers have worked on mechanisms for norm compliance and enforcement [1, 18].

The second branch of research is related to emergence of norms [15, 27, 28]. Researchers have worked on both prescriptive (top-down) and emergent (bottom-up) approaches to norms. In a top-down approach an authoritative leader or a normative advisor prescribes what a norm of the society should be [32]. In the bottom-up approach, the agents come up with a norm through learning mechanisms [27, 28]. Researchers have used sanctioning mechanisms [4] and reputation mechanisms [10] for enforcing norms.

Many research works assume that norms exist in the society and the focus is on how the norms can be regulated in an institutional setting such as electronic institutions[3]. Very few have investigated how an agent comes to know the norms of the society [2, 23]. We have previously proposed an architecture for norm identification [23, 25]. In this work, we extend our earlier work by incorporating the mechanism for identifying conditional norms. Identifying conditional norms is important because the agent can confidently apply the norm if the conditions associated with the norm are known. This will help the agent not to lose utility by preventing it from applying the norm under wrong conditions.

3   Overview of the Norm Identification Framework

In this section, we provide an brief overview of the norm identification framework that we have proposed and experimented with in earlier works [23–25]. An agent employing this architecture follows a four-step process.

- Step 1: An agent actively perceives the events in the environment in which it is situated.
- Step 2: When an agent perceives an event, it stores the event in its belief base.
- Step 3: Based on recognizing signals (i.e. events that are either rewards or a sanctions), the agent stores them in a "special events" base.
- Step 4: If the perceived event is a special event an agent checks if there exists a norm in its *personal norm* (*p-norm*) base or the *group norm* (*g-norm*) base. An agent may possess some p-norms. A *p-norm* is the personal value of an agent. For example an agent may consider that littering is an action that should be prohibited in a society based on its past experience or preference. This personal value may not be shared by the agents in a society. A *p-norm* may vary across agents, since a society may be made up of agents with different backgrounds and experiences. A *g-norm* is a norm which an agent infers, based on its personnel interactions as well as the interactions it observes in the society. An agent infers g-norms using the norm inference component. The norm inference component of the framework [25] makes use of Candidate Norm Inference (CNI) algorithm. The CNI algorithm uses association rule mining approach to identify sequences of events as candidate norms. The CNI algorithm has two sub-modules to identify prohibition norms [25] and obligation norms [24] respectively.

When a special event occurs an agent may decide to invoke its norm inference component to identify whether a previously unknown norm may have resulted in the occurrence of the special event. In the context of the park-littering scenario, an agent observing a sanctioning event may invoke its norm inference component to find out what events that had happened in the past (or that had not happened in the past) may have triggered the occurrence of the special event. Prohibition norms can be identified by inferring the relevant events that happened in the past [25]. For example an agent may notice that a sanctioning event is always preceded by a littering event. Hence the agent might infer that littering is prohibited in the society. For identifying obligation norms the agent may have to reason about what events that did not happen in the past are the likely reason for a sanction (i.e. not fulfilling an obligation) [24]. For example, an agent may be sanctioned for not tipping a customer in a restaurant. An agent observing the events may infer that the absence of the tipping action is the reason for a sanction. In this work we focus on identifying conditional norms associated with prohibition norms.

The invocation of the norm inference component may result in the identification of a *g-norm*, in which case it is added to the *g-norm* base. An agent, being an autonomous entity, can also decide not to invoke its norm inference component for every occurrence of a special event but may decide to invoke it periodically. When it invokes the norm inference component, it may find a new *g-norm* which it adds to its *g-norm* base. If it does not find a *g-norm*, the agent may change some of its norm inference parameters and repeat the process again in order to find a *g-norm* or may wait to collect more information.

At regular intervals of time an agent re-evaluates the g-norms it currently has, to check whether those norms hold. When it finds that a *g-norm* does not apply (e.g. if it does not find any evidence of sanctions), it deletes the norm from the *g-norm* base. It could be that there are no punishers in the society or all the agents have internalized the norm and are following the norm. Hence, there might be no sanctions in the society. In the case where all agents have internalized the norm and are following the norm, norm deletion on the part of the observer agent may have negative consequence for that agent (i.e. the agent can be sanctioned) in which case it can add the norm again through norm inference.

The next section describes how conditional norms are inferred by an agent. The mechanism for identifying conditional norms is built on top of the norm inference framework.

4   Identifying Conditional Norms

In our framework, when a new agent enters a society it will try to identify the norms that currently hold in that society. Once an agent has identified a norm it may want to identify the context and the exact conditions under which the norm holds. For example, the norm in a public park could be not to litter, i.e. *prohibit (litter)*. It could be that the norm prohibits people from dropping litter in the park as long as a rubbish bin is visible to them (or the rubbish bin is 50 metres away from them). The context here is the rubbish bin and the condition is the distance from the rubbish bin. When an agent identifies the norm in the first instance through observation, it may not know the exact conditions associated with the norm.

Let us assume that an agent upon identifying the norm knows the context of the norm[1]. For example on identifying that littering is prohibited, the agent identifies the presence of the bin as the context. The condition associated with the norm is the distance between the agent and the bin[2]. We call this a contextual condition.

Note that the condition associated with a norm will be specific to the domain under consideration. In the park littering example, the condition can be either one or two-dimensional. For example, the distance between a littering agent and bin is a single dimensional entity. The littering zone can be modelled as a two dimensional entity if it is defined using x and y coordinates (i.e. an agent should not litter within 5 metres from bin's x position and 10 metres from bin's y position). Some researchers have used a two dimensional representation for normative conditions [17, 30]. In this work we have used the distance metric which we call the radius of the non-littering zone.

---

[1] We assume that an agent knows the context based on the past experience or based on the domain knowledge. For example, an agent may know about littering from its past experience.

[2] Proximity or the distance of interaction is a contextual condition in many social norms. For example, two people talking tend to speak in a low voice when they walk past others. Another example is the interpersonal distance norm (i.e. how close you can get to someone while holding a conversation without making him/her uncomfortable). Agents may be aware of the distance based contextual condition from their previous experience.

Algorithm 1. Pseudocode of an agent to identify conditional norm associated with the prohibition of littering

---

Input: Contextual Condition = distance from nearest rubbish bin

1 maxDistanceFromBin = 0, tempDistance = 0 ; /* `maxDistanceFromBin`
   `stores the value of the contextual condition`   */
2 conditionalNormReferralConsidered = true;
3 conditionalNormRecommenders = $\emptyset$;
4 **foreach** *norm inference cycle* **do**
5 $\quad$ Obtain Norms Set (NS) ; /* `By invoking Candidate Norm`
   `Identification algorithm`   */
6 $\quad$ **if** *NS $\neq \emptyset$* **then**
7 $\quad\quad$ **foreach** *norm in NS* **do**
8 $\quad\quad\quad$ **foreach** *punished agent with the visibility threshold* **do**
9 $\quad\quad\quad\quad$ tempDistance = `getDistanceFromNearestBin`;
10 $\quad\quad\quad\quad$ **if** *tempDistance > maxDistanceFromBin* **then**
11 $\quad\quad\quad\quad\quad$ maxDistanceFromBin = tempDistance;
12 $\quad\quad\quad\quad$ **end**
13 $\quad\quad\quad$ **end**
14 $\quad\quad\quad$ **if** *conditionalNormReferralConsidered* **then**
15 $\quad\quad\quad\quad$ conditionalNormRecommenders = `getAgentsFromVicinity`;
16 $\quad\quad\quad\quad$ **foreach** *agent $\in$ conditionalNormRecommenders* **do**
17 $\quad\quad\quad\quad\quad$ **if** *agent.maxDistanceFromBin > maxDistanceFromBin* **then**
18 $\quad\quad\quad\quad\quad\quad$ maxDistanceFromBin = agent.maxDistanceFromBin;
19 $\quad\quad\quad\quad\quad$ **end**
20 $\quad\quad\quad\quad$ **end**
21 $\quad\quad\quad$ **end**
22 $\quad\quad$ **end**
23 $\quad$ **end**
24 **end**

Algorithm 1 shows how an agent identifies the conditional norm of the park. In each norm inference cycle an agent will first identify a set of norms using the norm identification framework [25]. Let us assume that the agent has identified *prohibit(litter)* as the norm which is stored in its Norms Set (NS). For each of the littering agents that were observed to be punished, an agent calculates the distance from the nearest bin to the punished agent using Chebyshev's distance metric [36][3]. The agent finds the radius of the non-littering zone (lines 10-12) and stores it in *maxDistanceFromBin*. The agent can

---

[3] Chebyshev's distance also known as the Chessboard distance is the minimum number of steps required for a King to move from one square of the chessboard to another. In our implementation Chebyshev distance represents the minimum distance between an agent and the nearest bin. Chebyshev distance of length one corresponds to the Moore neighbourhood [34] of size one where an agent in one cell can see all the 8 cells surrounding it.

choose to ask for referral from one or more agents from its vicinity threshold regarding the zone in which littering is prohibited (i.e. *maxDistanceFromBin*). If the referrer's recommended distance is greater than distance observed by the agent the agent increases the distance (lines 14-21).

While Algorithm 1 is specific to the park littering scenario, the generic process of an agent to identify the conditional norm is given in Algorithm 2. Once the agent infers a norm, it will identify the contextual condition. The contextual condition can contain multi-dimensional attributes. For each norm in the norm set (NS), it calculates the value of the contextual condition (line 8). An agent calculates the value for contextual condition based on observing all the punished agents within its visibility threshold.

Algorithm 2. Pseudocode of an agent to identify a conditional norm

---

Input: Contextual Conditions
1 valueOfContextualCondition [] = ∅;
2 conditionalNormReferralConsidered = true;
3 conditionalNormRecommenders = ∅;
4 **foreach** *norm inference cycle* **do**
5   Obtain Norms Set (NS) ; /* By invoking Candidate Norm
    Identification algorithm   */
6   **if** $NS \neq \emptyset$ **then**
7   **foreach** *norm n in NS* **do**
8   valueOfContextualCondition [n] =
            calculateContextualConditionalValue; /* This
            is calculated based on the available data on
            all punished agents within the visibility
            threshold   */
9   **if** *conditionalNormReferralConsidered* **then**
10   conditionalNormRecommenders =
            getAgentsFromVicinity;
11   **foreach** *agent* ∈ *conditionalNormRecommenders* **do**
12   **if** *agent.valueOfContextualCondition is better than
                valueOfContextualCondition* **then**
13   valueOfContextualCondition =
                    agent.valueOfContextualCondition;
14   **end**
15   **end**
16   **end**
17   **end**
18   **end**
19 **end**

The observer agent can optionally ask recommendation from other agents (through referral), on the contextual condition that they have observed (lines 9 and 10). Then, based on the recommendation of other agents it can choose the best value[4] as its value for the contextual condition (lines 11-15).

5   Experiments

In this section we firstly describe the experimental set-up in sub-section 5.1. In the rest of the sub-sections we describe the experiments that were conducted and the results obtained.

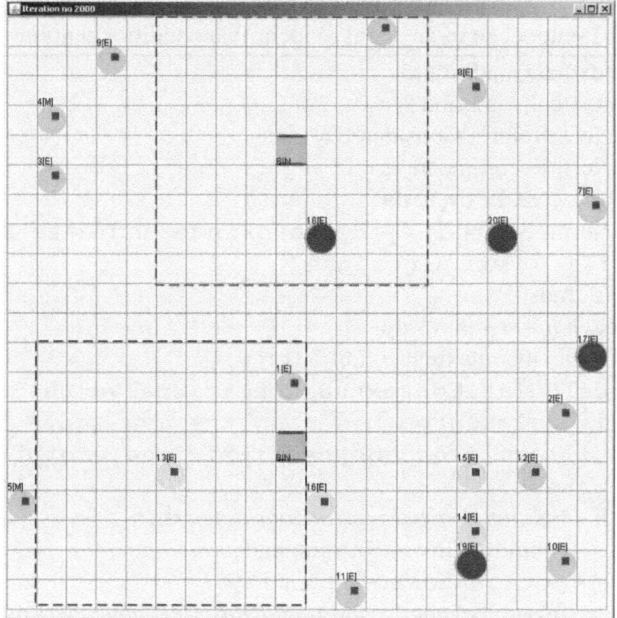

Fig. 1. Snapshot of the simulation of conditional norms

5.1   Experimental Set-Up

We model agents in our virtual society in a two-dimensional space. This virtual environment can be considered as a communal region such as a park shown in Figure 1. The agents explore and enjoy the park by moving around. There are three types of agents in the simulation. They are learning litterers (LL), non-litterers (NL) and non-littering punishers (NLP). There are four possible types of actions defined in the simulation system: *move, eat, litter* and *punish*. The LL agents can *move, eat* and *litter*. The NL agents can *move* and *eat* while the NLP agents can *move, eat* and *punish*. The agents'

---

[4] The logic for choosing the best value of the condition is domain specific. In a domain the best value may correspond to the least numeric value and in another domain it may correspond to the highest value.

movement can be in one of the four directions: up, down, left or right. The agents that are at the edge of the two dimensional space can again re-appear in the opposite side (i.e. a toroidal grid is implemented). The agents are represented as circles using different colours. The LLs are green, the NLs are blue and the NLPs are red. The id and action that an agent currently does appear above the circle.

Each agent has a visibility threshold. The visibility threshold of the agent is governed by a Chebyshev distance [36] of a certain length. An agent can observe actions of agents and the interactions that happen between two agents within its visibility threshold. The dashed square that appears at the bottom of Figure 1 shows the visibility range of agent 13 which is at the centre of the dashed square with a Chebyshev distance of four. All the agents make use of the norm inference component [25] to infer norms. The red squares that appear within the circles represent the identification of a norm. Rubbish bins in the simulation environment appear in orange. The non-littering zone with reference to the bin at the top is given by the dashed square that appears at the top of Figure 1. The radius of the non-littering zone in this case is four.

The simulation parameters that were kept constant for all the experiments are given in Table 1. A sample simulation can be viewed from this link[5].

Table 1. Simulation parameters for identifying conditional norms

Parameters	Values
Grid size	20*20
Total number of agents	20
Number of litterers	12
Number of non-litterers	4
Number of non-littering punishers	4
Visibility threshold	5
Number of rubbish bins	2
radius of non-littering zone (maxDistanceFromBin)	10
Number of referrals (when used)	1

5.2 Experiment 1 - Conditional Norm Identification

The objective of the first experiment is to show that agents in a society infer conditional norms using the proposed mechanism. We also compare the rate of norm establishment in the society with the rate of conditional norm establishment in the society.

Figure 2 shows two lines that represent the proportion of agents with norms and the proportion of agents with conditional norms in a society respectively. It can be seen from Figure 2 that even though the norm has been established in the society[6] in iteration 270, the conditional norm (i.e. the agent should not litter when it is within 10 metres from the bin), is not inferred in the society till iteration number 410. This is because the conditional norm identification process is invoked by an agent after it has found a

---

[5] http://unitube.otago.ac.nz/view?m=iWs217vmy6H

[6] We assume that a norm is established in a society if all the agents (100%) have inferred the norm. Researchers have used different criteria ranging from 35% to 100%[22].

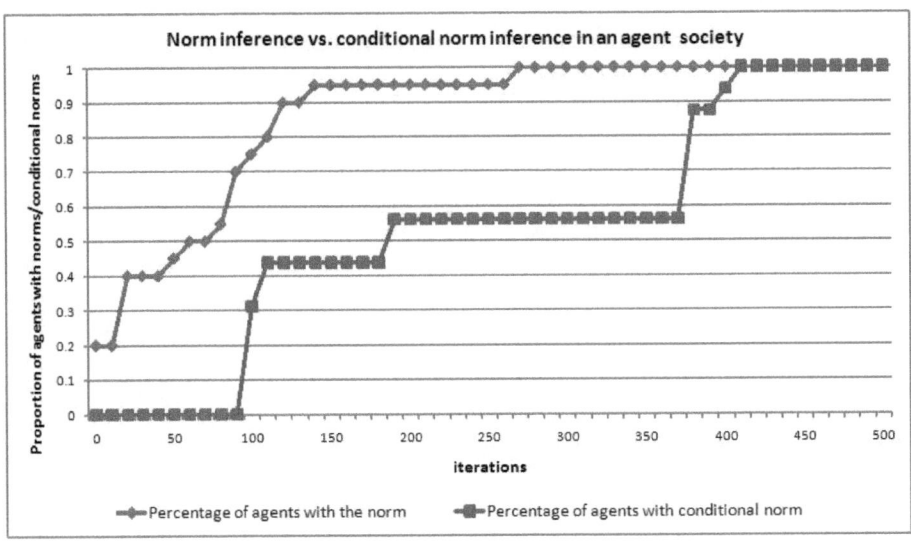

Fig. 2. Conditional norm identification

norm. As the agents interact more and more in the society, they gather more evidence regarding the condition associated with the norm. If the norm does not change, then the correct condition associated with the norm is inferred eventually. When an agent does not infer a norm for certain amount of time or when the norm changes it will remove the norm and its associated conditions from its norms base.

5.3   Experiment 2 - Conditional Norm Identification with and without Referral

An agent can expedite the process of identifying a conditional norm if it asks another agent for its evidence of the normative condition. We call this as the conditional norm referral process. It can be observed from Figure 3 that when the referral is used, the rate of establishment of the conditional norm increases. The agents ask for referral from one other agent in the society. When the number of referees increases, the rate of conditional norm establishment increases. This has also been reported many other works in multi-agent systems[8, 37].

Figure 4 shows the progression of two agents towards the identification of the correct conditional norm (non-littering zone of radius 10) with and without referrals. The progression rates of the two agents are different because of their different paths of travel. If an agent observes more agents on its path, then it has a higher probability of inferring both the norm and the condition associated with the norm. It should be noted that the conditional norm establishment for these two agents improve when the referrals are used.

The two dashed lines in Figure 4 show the radius of the non-littering zone identified by the agents during the simulation. The agent which found the norm first (agent 1, iteration 90) was not the one to find the correct conditional norm first[7]. When agent

---

[7] The correct conditional norm is the non-littering zone of 10 metres.

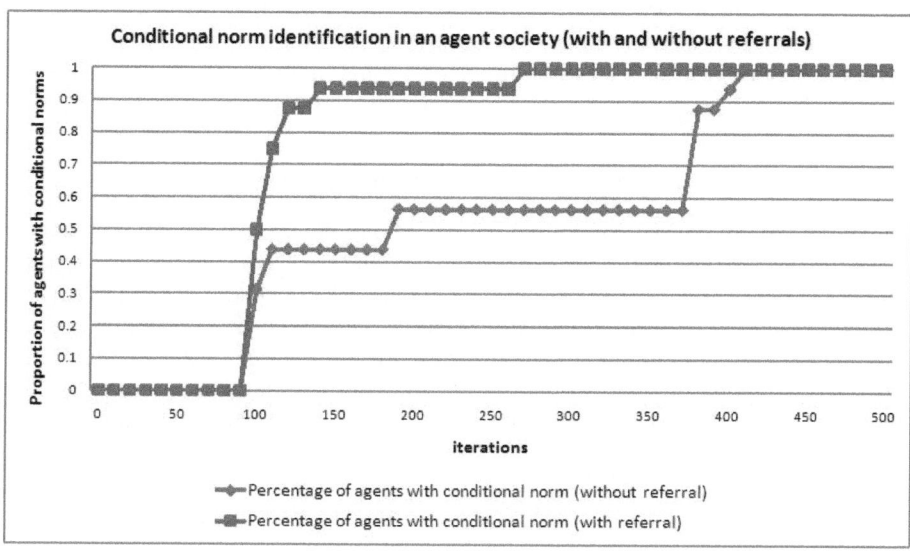

Fig. 3. Rate of norm and conditional norm establishment in an agent society

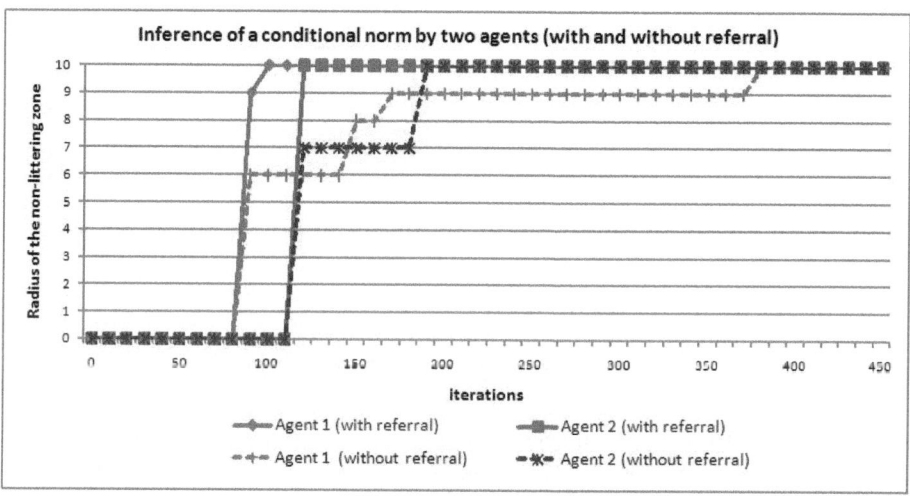

Fig. 4. Rate of conditional norm establishment in two agents with and without referrals

1 found the norm in iteration 90, the non-littering zone identified by the agent was 6 metres (shown using an arrow in the Figure). It found the correct conditional norm in iteration 380. Agent 2, albeit finding the norm second (iteration 110, non-littering zone of radius 7 metres), found the correct conditional norm faster (iteration 190). This again is governed by the number of agents an agent gets to observe (i.e. the path of travel).

The two solid lines show the radius of the non-littering zone identified by the agents when referrals are used. It is interesting to note that when the referral mechanism is used, the agent which found the norm first was also the one that found the normative condition first. This is because once the agent finds the norm it can ask the agents in the vicinity for referral instead of waiting for a long amount of time to find out the maximum distance from the bin from which a violation that was punished occurred.

5.4   Experiment 3 - Dynamic Conditional Norm Identification

An agent should have the ability to dynamically add newly identified norms and remove norms that do not hold. This experiment demonstrates that conditional norms can be added, removed and modified by an agent dynamically depending upon the environmental conditions. The ability to change norms is important for an adaptive agent so that it can flexibly adopt norms. An agent, on identifying a norm, evaluates whether the norm holds at regular intervals of time. If the norm does not hold, it removes the norm from its norm base. When it removes the norm it also removes the condition associated with the norm[8].

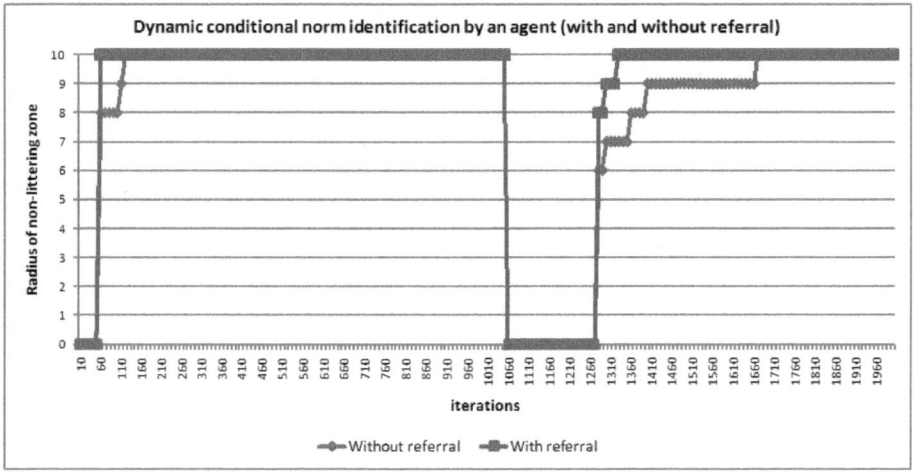

Fig. 5. Dynamic conditional norm identification by an agent

Figure 5 demonstrates that an agent is able to add and remove norms and normative conditions dynamically. Figure 6 demonstrates that agents in our system are able dynamically modify the normative condition. In these experiments, the punishers do not punish from iterations 1000 to 1250. This is to simulate the change in the environment which triggers a norm change. Additionally, having identified a norm, an agent checks for the validity of the norm once again after 5 norm inference cycles (norm inference happens once every 10 iterations). If the norm is found again, then the agent does not delete the norm. If the norm is not found, it removes the norm and the conditions from its norm base.

---

[8] In our previous work [25], we have demonstrated how an agent adds and removes norms dynamically. In this experiment, we show how conditions associated with norms are dynamically added and removed.

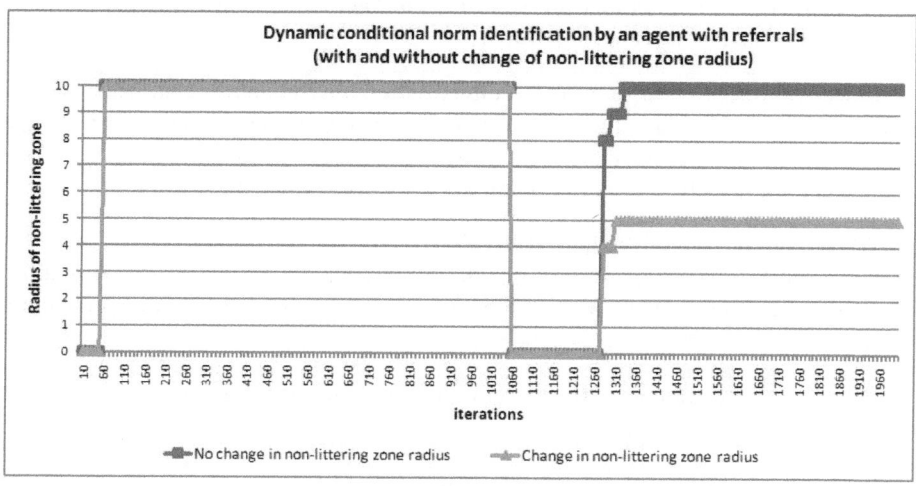

Fig. 6. Dynamic conditional norm identification by an agent

Figure 5 shows two lines that represent an agent adding and removing norms based on changing environmental conditions. The line is red represents the agent using the referral mechanism and the line in blue represents the agent without using the referral mechanism. It can be observed that the agent without using referral identifies a conditional norm in iteration 60, and the correct conditional norm in iteration 120 while it infers the norm faster when it uses referral. In this experiment, when the punishers do not punish, the norm is not inferred for 50 iterations (5 norm inference cycles from iteration 1010 to 1050). So, the agent removes the norm and the conditions associated with the norm (with and without referral) in iteration 1050. The agent that does not use the referral finds a conditional norm again in iteration 1280 and the correct conditional norm in iteration 1670. It can be observed that when the referral is used by the agent it identifies the correct conditional norm earlier (iteration 1330).

Figure 6 shows two lines that represent the identification of different normative conditions under changing environmental conditions (with and without change of non-littering zone) for the same agent. By keeping all the other parameters the same, we varied the radius of the non-littering zone (i.e. the punishment zone for littering). This is to demonstrate that when the radius of the littering zone varies, the agent infers the change. After iteration 1250 all NLP agents punished only those agents that littered within 5 metres from the bin (as opposed to 10 metres which was used in iterations 1 to 1000). It can be observed from the green line in Figure 6 that the agent inferred the new normative condition (radius = 5)[9]. Note that the agent has made use of referral in this experiment. The red line which converges to the littering zone of radius 10 that appears at the top of Figure 6 is the same as the red line shown at the top of Figure 5 which represents the normative behaviour of an agent that uses the referral process.

---

[9] The simulation video can be found at http://unitube.otago.ac.nz/view?m=nQ6y17frCcJ

5.5   Experiment 4 - Comparison of Utility of Agents with and without Conditional Norm Identification

The objective of this experiment is to compare the utility benefits of an agent when it identifies norms with and without conditions. In this experiment, an agent has a utility value which we call the satisfaction level (S) which varies from 0 to 100.

An agent's satisfaction level (S) decreases in the following situations:

- When a litterer is punished, its utility decreases (-1).
- For all agents, littering activity results in the decrease of the utility. This is because each littering activity ruins the "commons" area (-1/number of agents in the society).

An agent's satisfaction level (S) increases (i.e. it gains utility) in the following situation:

- When a litterer litters, it gains utility in a society (+1).

We have experimented with the utility of the agent with and without conditional norm identification. An LL agent is better off by using conditional norm (CN) identification. Once identifying a norm an LL agent may choose to abstain from the action that is being prohibited. In the case of a conditional norm, it learns the exact condition under which it should not violate the norm. By this process, it can improve its utility. It can be observed from Figure 7 that an LL agent's utility increases (greater than 50) when it has identified the conditional norm than just identifying the norm without conditions (less than 50). This is because when the littering agent finds the norm without the normative condition, it abstains from the littering activity which does not lead to an increase in its utility. But, when it identifies the normative condition, it now can litter outside the non-littering zone which results in the increase in its utility.

For an NL agent, when it identified a norm without identifying the condition, the utility initially decreases but then stabilizes to a constant value because when all the agents inferred the norm, there aren't any littering actions in the society. When the NL agent identifies the conditional norm, its utility continues to decrease because whenever an LL agent litters outside the not-to-litter zone, its utility decreases[10]. Similarly, for an LL agent, its utility decreases because of the littering action. However, its net utility increases as it gains from the littering action (i.e. it can litter outside the non-littering zone).

The utilities of NLP agents are not discussed here because we assume these agents have other utility functions for punishing (e.g. a leader who wants to promote a smoother functioning of the society, or an altruistic agent who does not care about its diminishing utility). We note that if non-altruistic punishers are present in the society, then the cost

---

[10] It should be noted that when the utility of an NL agent goes below a certain threshold, it can leave the society, or can become a litterer or become a punisher. This is explored in another work [26]. Additionally, if the parameters of this experiment are varied (for example if the utility gain of a litterer is changed to 0.5 and the utility loss on receiving a punishment is changed to 0.25) the results obtained will be different. The objective here is to show that the conditional norm identification has an impact on the utility of the agents.

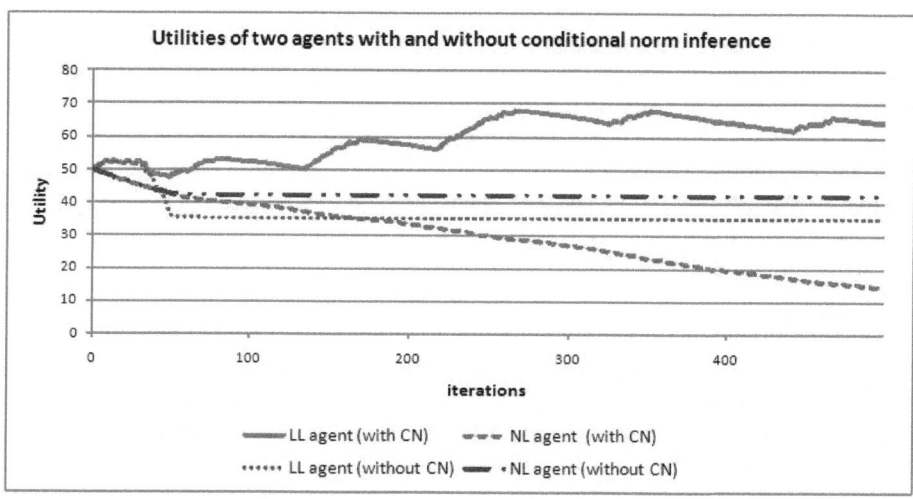

Fig. 7. Utility comparison of two agents

incurred by the non-altruistic punishers will play a role in the establishment of a norm in the society (see [26]). Several other works have investigated the role of punishment costs on norm spreading [13, 20].

6   Discussion

The issue of conditional norm identification has not been dealt with by researchers in the field of normative multi-agent systems. To this end, we have experimented how a conditional norm can be identified by an agent in the context of park-littering. Identifying norms with conditions can be beneficial in several settings. For example, the norm identification architecture can be used to infer norms in Massively Multi-player Online Games (MMOGs). Players involved in massively multi-player games perform actions in an environment to achieve a goal. They may play as individuals or in groups. When playing a cooperation game (e.g. players forming groups to slay a dragon), individual players may be able to observe norms. For example, a dragon can only be slayed if two players are within certain distance from the dragon. An agent that identifies this condition (the distance) will be better-off than an agent that just infers the norm of co-operation (i.e. two players are needed to slay a dragon). The mechanism proposed in this paper can be used to identify norms with conditions. This mechanism can also be used in virtual environments such as Second Life to infer conditional norms.

Another application of identifying conditional norms is in the area of e-commerce. For example, in one society, the norm associated with the deadline for payment (i.e. obligations with deadlines as in [9]) may be set to 120 minutes after winning the item. Depending upon what an agent has observed, agents may have subtly different norms (e.g. one agent may notice that *pay* follows *win* after an average of 80 minutes while another may notice this happens after 100 minutes). Both these agents could still infer the norm but the deadlines they had noticed can be different. This may result in an unstable equilibrium with reference to the norms and hence conflict resolution mechanisms should be used to resolve them [17, 30].

We note that we have modelled and experimented with a simple domain. The number and type of agents can easily be increased and the normative conditions identified can be richer and more complex depending upon the problem domain. However, we believe the main contribution is the mechanism for the identification of conditions associated with norms. We have also shown how an agent can dynamically add, remove and modify conditions associated with the norms.

7 Conclusion

This paper addresses the question of how conditional norms can be identified in an agent society using the norm inference architecture. Identification of conditional norms has been demonstrated in the context of a simple park-littering scenario. The ability of an agent to add, delete and modify a conditional norm has also been demonstrated. It has also been shown that identifying norms with conditions has an impact on the utility of the agents in the society.

References

[1] Aldewereld, H., Dignum, F., García-Camino, A., Noriega, P., Rodríguez-Aguilar, J.A., Sierra, C.: Operationalisation of norms for usage in electronic institutions. In: Proceedings of the Fifth International Joint Conference on Autonomous Agents and MultiAgent Systems (AAMAS 2006), pp. 223–225. ACM Press, New York (2006)
[2] Andrighetto, G., Conte, R., Turrini, P., Paolucci, M.: Emergence in the loop: Simulating the two way dynamics of norm innovation. In: Boella, G., van der Torre, L., Verhagen, H. (eds.) Normative Multi-agent Systems. Dagstuhl Seminar Proceedings, vol. 07122, Internationales Begegnungs- und Forschungszentrum für Informatik (IBFI), Schloss Dagstuhl, Germany (2007)
[3] Arcos, J.L., Esteva, M., Noriega, P., Rodrguez-aguilar, J.A., Sierra, C.: Environment engineering for multiagent systems. Engineering Applications of Artificial Intelligence 18(2), 191–204 (2005)
[4] Axelrod, R.: An evolutionary approach to norms. The American Political Science Review 80(4), 1095–1111 (1986)
[5] Bandura, A.: Social Learning Theory. General Learning Press (1977)
[6] Boella, G., van der Torre, L., Verhagen, H.: Introduction to the special issue on normative multiagent systems. Autonomous Agents and Multi-Agent Systems 17(1), 1–10 (2008)
[7] Boman, M.: Norms in artificial decision making. Artificial Intelligence and Law 7(1), 17–35 (1999)
[8] Candale, T., Sen, S.: Effect of referrals on convergence to satisficing distributions. In: Proceedings of the Fourth International Joint Conference on Autonomous Agents and MultiAgent Systems (AAMAS 2005), pp. 347–354. ACM, New York (2005)
[9] Cardoso, H.L., Oliveira, E.C.: Directed deadline obligations in agent-based business contracts. In: Padget, J.A., Artikis, A., Vasconcelos, W.W., Stathis, K., da Silva, V.T., Matson, E.T., Polleres, A. (eds.) COIN@AAMAS 2009. LNCS, vol. 6069, pp. 225–240. Springer, Heidelberg (2010)
[10] Castelfranchi, C., Conte, R., Paolucci, M.: Normative reputation and the costs of compliance. Journal of Artificial Societies and Social Simulation 1(3) (1998)

[11] Elster, J.: Social norms and economic theory. The Journal of Economic Perspectives 3(4), 99–117 (1989)

[12] Epstein, J.M.: Learning to be thoughtless: Social norms and individual computation. Computational Economics 18(1), 9–24 (2001)

[13] Fehr, E., Fischbacher, U.: Third-party punishment and social norms. Evolution and Human Behavior 25(2), 63–87 (2004)

[14] Gaertner, D., García-Camino, A., Noriega, P., Rodrguez-aguilar, J.A., Vasconcelos, W.W.: Distributed norm management in regulated multi-agent systems. In: Proceedings of the 6th International Joint Conference on Autonomous Agents and Multiagent Systems (AAMAS 2007), Honolulu, Hawaii, pp. 624–631. ACM, New York (2007)

[15] Griffiths, N., Luck, M.: Norm diversity and emergence in tag-based cooperation. In: De Vos, M., et al. (eds.) COIN 2010. LNCS (LNAI), vol. 6541, pp. 230–249. Springer, Heidelberg (2011)

[16] Jones, A.J.I., Sergot, M.: On the characterisation of law and computer systems: The normative systems perspective. In: Deontic Logic in Computer Science: Normative System Specification, pp. 275–307. John Wiley and Sons, Chichester (1993)

[17] Kollingbaum, M.J., Vasconcelos, W.W., García-Camino, A., Norman, T.J.: Managing conflict resolution in norm-regulated environments. In: Artikis, A., O'Hare, G.M.P., Stathis, K., Vouros, G.A. (eds.) ESAW 2007. LNCS (LNAI), vol. 4995, pp. 55–71. Springer, Heidelberg (2008)

[18] López y López, F.: Social Powers and Norms: Impact on Agent Behaviour. PhD thesis, Department of Electronics and Computer Science, University of Southampton, United Kingdom (2003)

[19] Neumann, M.: A classification of normative architectures. In: Proceedings of World Congress on Social Simulation (2008)

[20] Ohtsuki, H., Iwasa, I., Nowak, M.A.: Indirect reciprocity provides only a narrow margin of efficiency for costly punishment. Nature 457(7225), 79–82 (2009)

[21] Rymaszewski, M., Au, W.J., Wallace, M., Winters, C., Ondrejka, C., Batstone-Cunningham, B., Rosedale, P.: Second Life: The Official Guide. SYBEX Inc., Alameda (2006)

[22] Savarimuthu, B.T.R., Cranefield, S.: A categorization of simulation works on norms. In: Boella, G., Noriega, P., Pigozzi, G., Verhagen, H. (eds.) Normative Multi-Agent Systems, Dagstuhl, Germany. Dagstuhl Seminar Proceedings, (09121), pp. 43–62. Schloss Dagstuhl - Leibniz-Zentrum fuer Informatik, Germany (2009)

[23] Savarimuthu, B.T.R., Cranefield, S., Purvis, M.A., Purvis, M.K.: Internal agent architecture for norm identification. In: Padget, J., Artikis, A., Vasconcelos, W., Stathis, K., da Silva, V.T., Matson, E., Polleres, A. (eds.) COIN@AAMAS 2009. LNCS, vol. 6069, pp. 241–256. Springer, Heidelberg (2010)

[24] Savarimuthu, B.T.R., Cranefield, S., Purvis, M., Purvis, M.: A data mining approach to identify obligation norms in agent societies. In: Cao, L., Bazzan, A., Gorodetsky, V., Mitkas, P., Weiss, G., Yu, P. (eds.) ADMI 2010. LNCS, vol. 5980, pp. 43–58. Springer, Heidelberg (2010)

[25] Savarimuthu, B.T.R., Purvis, M.A., Purvis, M.K., Cranefield, S.: Norm identification in multi-agent societies. Discussion Paper 2010/03, Department of Information Science, University of Otago (2010)

[26] Savarimuthu, B.T.R., Purvis, M., Purvis, M.K., Cranefield, S.: Social norm emergence in virtual agent societies. In: Baldoni, M., Son, T.C., van Riemsdijk, M.B., Winikoff, M. (eds.) DALT 2008. LNCS (LNAI), vol. 5397, pp. 18–28. Springer, Heidelberg (2009)

[27] Sen, S., Airiau, S.: Emergence of norms through social learning. In: Proceedings of Twentieth International Joint Conference on Artificial Intelligence (IJCAI 2007), pp. 1507–1512. AAAI Press, Menlo Park (2007)

[28] Shoham, Y., Tennenholtz, M.: Emergent conventions in multi-agent systems: Initial experimental results and observations. In: Proceedings of Third International Conference on Principles of Knowledge Representation and Reasoning, San Mateo, CA, pp. 225–231. Morgan Kaufmann, San Francisco (1992)

[29] Stoup, P.: Athe development and failure of social norms in second life. Duke Law Journal 58(2), 311–344 (2008)

[30] Vasconcelos, W.W., Kollingbaum, M.J., Norman, T.J.: Normative conflict resolution in multi-agent systems. Autonomous Agents and Multi-Agent Systems 19(2), 124–152 (2009)

[31] Vázquez-Salceda, J.: Thesis: The role of norms and electronic institutions in multi-agent systems applied to complex domains. the harmonia framework. AI Communications 16(3), 209–212 (2003)

[32] Verhagen, H.: Simulation of the Learning of Norms. Social Science Computer Review 19(3), 296–306 (2001)

[33] Walker, A., Wooldridge, M.: Understanding the emergence of conventions in multi-agent systems. In: Lesser, V. (ed.) Proceedings of the First International Conference on Multi–Agent Systems, San Francisco, CA, pp. 384–389. MIT Press, Cambridge (1995)

[34] Weisstein, E.W.: Moore neighbourhood (2010),
http://mathworld.wolfram.com/MooreNeighborhood.html

[35] Wieringa, R.J., Meyer, J.-J.C.: Applications of deontic logic in computer science: a concise overview. In: Deontic Logic in Computer Science: Normative System Specification, pp. 17–40. John Wiley & Sons, Inc., New York (1994)

[36] Wikipedia. Chebyshev distance,
http://en.wikipedia.org/wiki/Chebyshev_distance (last accessed on September 15, 2010)

[37] Yolum, P., Singh, M.P.: Emergent properties of referral systems. In: Proceedings of the Second International Joint Conference on Autonomous Agents and MultiAgent Systems (AAMAS 2003), pp. 592–599. ACM, New York (2003)

Using a Two-Level Multi-Agent System Architecture

Jordi Campos[1], Maite Lopez-Sanchez[1], and Marc Esteva[2]

[1] MAiA Deptartment, Universitat de Barcelona
{jcampos,maite}@maia.ub.es
[2] Artificial Intelligence Research Institute (IIIA), CSIC
marc@iiia.csic.es

Abstract. Existing organisational centred multi-agent systems (MAS) regulate agents' activities. Nevertheless, population and/or environmental changes may lead to a poor fulfilment of the system's purposes, and therefore, adapting the whole organisation becomes key. This is even more needed in open MAS, where participants are unknown beforehand, they may change over time, and there are no guarantees about their behaviours nor capabilities. Hence, in this paper we focus on endowing an organisation with self-adaptation capabilities instead of expecting agents to increase their behaviour complexity. We regard this organisational adaptation as an assisting service provided by what we call the *Assistance Layer*. Our abstract Two Level Assisted MAS Architecture (2-LAMA) incorporates such a layer. We empirically evaluate our adaptation mechanism in a P2P scenario by comparing it with the standard BitTorrent protocol. Results provide a performance improvement and show that the cost of introducing an additional layer in charge of system's adaptation is lower than its benefits.

1 Introduction

Developing Multi Agent Systems (MAS) entails the problems of designing a distributed concurrent system plus the difficulties of having flexible and complex interactions among autonomous entities [1]. Organising such systems to regulate agent interactions is a practise that helps to face their complexity [2]. Specially in open MAS, since agents are developed by third-parties, so they may enter or leave the system at any moment and there are no guarantees about their behaviour. To face the derived complexity, some approaches [3,4] use organisation entities as regulative structures. Such an organisation helps designers to predict/regulate the system evolution within certain bounds. The fact that these structures persist with independence of their participants reinforces their role as first-order entities. Moreover, these approaches usually provide an infrastructure to support the enactment of these entities —to create them, to store their specifications, to check if participants fulfil them, etc. In fact, these approaches provide an organisational framework to agents, which minimises the number of possibilities they have to face. This is because agents can construe other participant's behaviour under a certain context.

M. De Vos et al. (Eds.): COIN 2010 International Workshops, LNAI 6541, pp. 303–320, 2011.

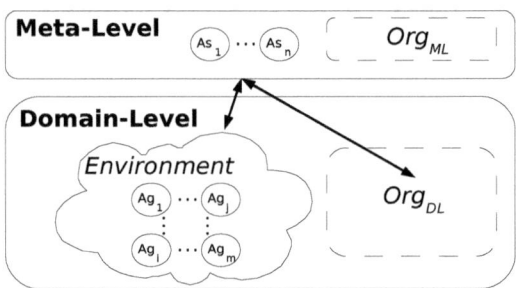

Fig. 1. Meta-level agents (As_i) reason at a higher level of abstraction to update Domain-Level organisation (Org_{DL})

As we previously mentioned, an organisational structure helps to regulate MAS. However, certain environmental or population changes may decrease its performance to achieve goals. Thus, adapting such an organisation is an important topic [5,6,7,8], since it can help to obtain the expected outcomes under changing circumstances. This is motivated by the computational organisational theory, which claims that the best organisation designs are domain and context dependent [9]. Adaptation can be seen as a reconfiguration aspect of autonomic computing, where a MAS is able to reconfigure itself [10].

Concerning such an adaptation, we propose to add a *meta-level* in charge of adapting system's organisation instead of expecting agents to increase their behaviour complexity —see Figure 1. This is specially relevant when dealing with open MAS, since there is no control over participant's implementation. Hence, we cannot expect agents to be endowed with the necessary mechanisms to adapt the organisation when it is not achieving its goals. We regard this adaptation – together with other possible meta-level functionalities– as an assistance to agents that can be provided by MAS infrastructure. Thus, we call our approach Two Level Assisted MAS Architecture (2-LAMA). In order to avoid centralisation limitations such as fault-tolerance or global information unavailability, we propose a distributed *meta-level* composed of several agents. This paper is focused on 2-LAMA's organisational adaptation capabilities. In particular, it focuses on *norm adaptation* —we assume norms are an organisational regulative structure.

Our approach requires domains with organisations that can be dynamically changed. Besides, it is able to deal with highly dynamic environments and even with domains where there is no direct mapping between goals and the tasks required to achieve them —i.e. it is not possible to derive a set of tasks that achieve a certain goal. As an illustration, we present a Peer-to-Peer sharing network (P2P) as a representative case study. In such a network, computers interact to share some data. Furthermore, their relationships change over time depending on network status and participants. We use this scenario to perform an empiric evaluation and compare our approach with standard P2P BitTorrent protocol [11].

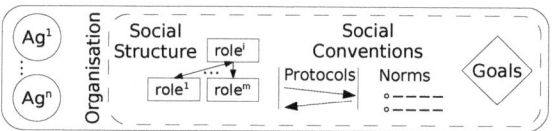

Fig. 2. Organisation's components

Our general model and its application are described in sections 2 and 3. Further, the adaptation process is detailed in section 4. Next, it is compared with BitTorrent in section 5 and with related work in section 6. Finally, section 7 presents the derived conclusions.

2   General Model

Previous section identifies organisations as useful entities to regulate agents' behaviours and facilitate their coordination. In particular, these entities provide a framework that is useful for agent coordination. Besides, there are MAS infrastructures that provide some organisational-related features as domain independent services. Thus, we regard them as *Coordination Support* services [12] that alleviate agent development. These services also include basic coordination elements such as elemental connectivity or agent communication languages. In brief, all these services are devoted to enact agent coordination. In addition to that, we propose an extra set of services that provides an added value by assisting coordination. We propose to add an *Assistance Layer* on top of a regular system in order to provide such coordination assistance services The main contribution of this paper is the proposal of a distributed pro-active service at the Assistance Layer that adapts organisations depending on the system's evolution.

Before provinding an insight into this organisational adaptation service, we detail how we model an organisational structure itself. Usually, organisation-centred MAS provide services that range from establishing the basis for agent communication through individual messages to providing organisational structures. As depicted in Figure 2, we denote one of those organisations as: $Org = \langle SocStr, SocConv, Goals \rangle$, its compoments are detailed next. It has a social structure ($SocStr$) consisting of a set of roles (Rol) and their relationships (Rel). In addition, it has some social conventions ($SocConv$) that agents should conform and expect others to conform. They are expressed as interaction protocols ($Prot$) and/or norms ($Norms$). In more detail, protocols define legitimate sequences of actions performed by agents playing certain roles. Whereas norms delimit agent actions by expressing related permissions, prohibitions or obligations. Notice, that in our case study, the only possible actions are message physical exchanges among agents. Finally, it has some goals ($Goals$) that describe the organisation design purpose —they may differ from participant's individual ones. These goals are expressed as a function over the system's observable

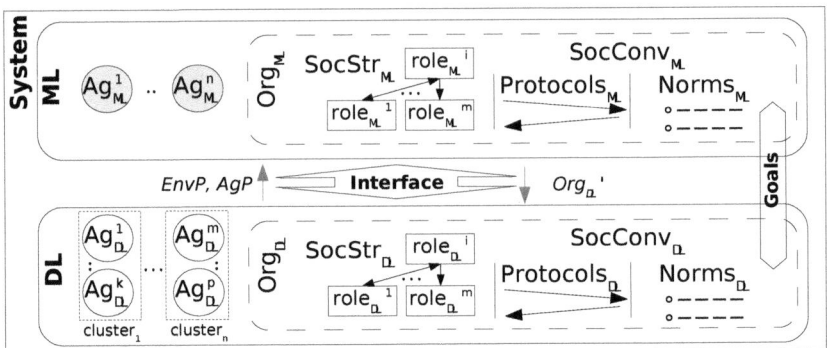

Fig. 3. Two Level Assisted MAS Architecture (2-LAMA)

properties —it may include the reference values they should approach. This way, system performance can be evaluated by using these goals to determine in which degree the system is fulfilling its design objectives.

2.1   Assistance Layer

The Assistance Layer we propose, provides an assistance that may facilitate the enrolment of third-party agents and/or adapt their organisation. This layer provides two main types of services [12]: assisting individual agents to achieve their goals following current social conventions (Agent Assistance); and adapting social conventions to varying circumstances (Organisational Assistance). The former includes services to inform agents about useful information to participate in the MAS (Information Service), to provide justifications about the consequences of their actions (Justification Service), to suggest alternative plans that conform social conventions (Advice Service) and to estimate the possible consequences of certain actions due to current conventions (Estimation Service). The latter, the Organisational Assistance, consists on adapting existing organisations to improve system's performance under varying circumstances. To provide such an adaptation, we propose goal fulfilment as its driving force within the context of a rational world assumption. Hence, the Assistance Layer requires some way (i) to observe system evolution, (ii) to compare it with the organisational goals and (iii) to adapt the organisation trying to improve goal fulfilment. See [12] for further details about all enumerated services.

In order to provide Assistance Layer services, we proposed a Two Level Assisted MAS Architecture (2-LAMA, [13]). The bottom level, we call it domain-level (DL), is composed by agents carrying out domain activities regulated by an organisational structure. On top of it, there is a distributed meta-level (ML) also composed by agents and an organisational structure targeted to provide assistance services to domain-level agents. In between, there is an interface (Int) that communicates both levels as shown in Figure 3. Thus, the whole system can be expressed as: $2LAMA = \langle ML, DL, Int \rangle$. Each level has an organised

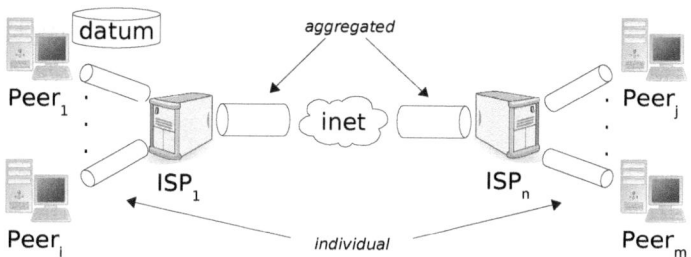

Fig. 4. P2P scenario

set of agents so they are respectively defined as $ML = \langle Ag_{ML}, Org_{ML} \rangle$ and $DL = \langle Ag_{DL}, Org_{DL} \rangle$. Using the interface, the meta-level can perceive environment observable properties ($EnvP$, e.g. date or temperature) and agents observable properties (AgP, e.g. colour or position). Specifically, we assume each meta-level agent ($a_{ML} \in Ag_{ML}$) has partial information about them, so it only perceives a subset of $EnvP$ and AgP —in many scenarios global information is not available. In fact, an a_{ML} has partial information about the subset of domain-level agents it assists. We call this subset of agents a *cluster*, which would be grouped according to a domain criterion —e.g. they could be grouped because interactions among them have lower costs than with other agents. However, an assistant can share part of this information with other meta-level agents in order to provide better assistance services.

3   2-LAMA in a P2P Scenario

Our case study is a Peer-to-Peer sharing network (P2P), where a set of computers connected to the Internet (peers) share some data —see Figure 4. We apply our model to this scenario because it is a highly dynamic environment due to the very nature of the Internet communications. We regard the *overlay network*[1] of current contacted peers as its organisational social structure, which is dynamically updated. Finally, this scenario allows the addition of some *norms* to regulate communications. Overall, it lets us apply our organisational and adaptive autonomic approach.

The performance in this scenario is evaluated in terms of time and network consumptions during the sharing process. Thus, we can define as global goals the minimisation of such measures so that the faster the data is obtained and the less network is consumed, the better for the users. Notice, though, that there is a trade-off between time and network usage. Therefore, although a peer can potentially contact any other peer, it usually contacts just a subset in order to consume less network resources —i.e. overlay network.

---

[1] An overlay network is a network build on top of another one. In the P2P scenario, the base network that connects all peers is the Internet. Then, the network of peers that are really interacting among them is an overlay network on top of the Internet.

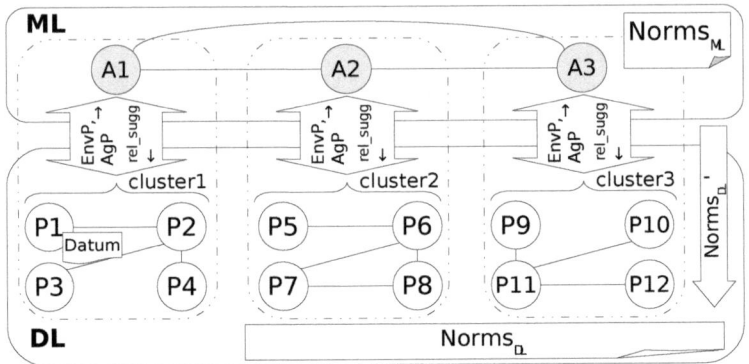

Fig. 5. 2-LAMA in the P2P scenario

Real P2P networks are highly complex, so we try to reduce complexity by assuming some simplifications about the protocol and the underlying network. Specially, we assume information is composed of a single piece of data —accordingly, we say a peer is *complete* when it has that single piece. The rest of this section provides the details of such scenario and our 2-LAMA approach applied to it.

3.1   Architecture in P2P

We model the P2P scenario as a MAS where computers sharing data are participant agents within the domain-level ($Ag_{DL}= P1 \ldots P12$). All of them play a single role $Rol_{DL} = \{peer\}$ within the domain-level organisation (Org_{DL}) —see Figure 5. In addition, we define a type of relationship called *contact* between two agents playing the role peer. Thus, as all agents in domain-level play the role peer, they can establish contact relationships at run-time. These actual relationships form the overlay network mentioned previously. In our model, the meta-level can suggest changes in this net of relationships (*rel_sugg*) taking into account the system's status. Regarding social conventions, peers use the sharing protocol ($Prot_{DL}$) specified below and two norms $Norm_{DL}=\{normBW_{DL}, normFR_{DL}\}$. First norm ($normBW_{DL}$) limits agents' network usage in percentage of its nominal *bandwidth*[2]. This norm can be expressed as: $normBW_{DL} =$"a peer cannot use more than max$_{BW}$ bandwidth percentage to share data". This way, it prevents peers from massively using their bandwidth to send/receive data to/from all other peers. Second norm ($normFR_{DL}$) limits the number of peers to whom a peer can simultaneously send the data. Analogously to previous norm, we define $normFR_{DL} =$"a peer cannot simultaneously send the data to more than max$_{FR}$ peers". The last compoment of domain-level's organisation is its goal ($Goals$). This is that all peers –i.e. all computers sharing data– have the data as soon as

---

[2] The *bandwidth* is the capacity to transfer data over user's network connection. It is expressed as the number of data units that can traverse a communication channel in a time unit. The less is used by the peer, the more is left for other purposes.

Table 1. Protocol messages grouped into subsequent phases and involved levels —only domain-level (DL), only meta-level (ML) or both (Int)

Phase	Level	Protocol Messages
initial	Int	join <hasDatum>
latency	Int	get_lat <peers>, lat <peer> <measure>
	DL	lat_req, lat_rpl
soc.struct.	Int	contact <peers>
handshake	DL	bitfield <hasDatum>
share data	DL	rqst,data,cancel,have,choke,unchoke
	Int	complete, has_datum <peer>
	ML	all_complete, complete_peer <peer>
norms	ML	norm_bw <value>, norm_friends <value>
	Int	norm_updated <norm_id> <new_def>

possible using the minimal network resources. Thus, given some time cost (c_t) and network cost (c_n) metrics, we can define a global goal function that minimises a weighted combination of them: $Goals = min(w_t \cdot c_t + w_n \cdot c_n)$, where ($w_t,w_n$) are the corresponding weights that represent the relative importance of each measure.

In order to provide assistance to the domain-level, we add the meta-level on top of it. This *meta-level* also has a single role $Rol_{ML} = \{assistant\}$. Each agent in $Ag_{ML} = A1 \ldots A3$ assists a disjoint subset of domain-level agents (cluster$\subset$ Ag_{DL}). It does it so by collecting information about them –about agents or their environment– and adapting their local organisation. Its decisions are based on local information about its associated cluster, aggregated information about other clusters –provided by other assistants– and the norms at their level ($Norm_{ML}$). Some examples of local information are latencies ($EnvP$) or which agents have the data (AgP). Information about other clusters come from other assistants —notice that meta-level agents have their own social structure too. Regarding meta-level norms, we consider one that limits the number of domain-level agents to inform about another domain-level agent having the data. More precisely, when an assistant receives the information that one agent in another cluster has become complete, the number of domain-level agents in its cluster it can inform to is limited. In particular, the norm is expressed as $normHas_{ML} =$"upon reception of a complete agent (agent $\notin$ cluster) message, inform no more than max$_{Has}$ agents $\in$ cluster". Finally, we assume assistants are located at Internet Service Providers (ISP) and thus related communications are fast.

3.2 Protocol

Our proposed protocol is a simplified version of the widely used BitTorrent [11] protocol. Table 1 lists all its messages, which follow the sequence detailed next. At the beginning, a domain-level agent (peer) initiates a handshake phase with another one by sending it a bitfield <hasDatum> message. <hasDatum> = [1/0] indicates if it has (1) or has not (0) the data —i.e. it is a *complete* or *incomplete* agent. Notice that in current implementation, the data has only a single piece. In turn, the other agent finishes this handshake phase by replaying with another `bitfield <hasDatum>` message to indicate its status. In case one of these agents have the datum and the other lacks it, the later sends a `rqst` (request) message to the former. Then, the former replies with a message containing the datum. On the contrary, if none of the agents have the datum they will not exchange further messages. However, as soon as one agent receives the datum, it will send a `have` message to these other contacted agents to let them know that its status has changed. In such cases, if they still lack of the datum, they will request it. Additionally, an agent may reply to a request with a `choke` message if it is already serving max_{FR} agents —it means this agent is going to ignore any further message. Later on, when a transmission ends, it sends `unchoke` messages to all choked agents, so they can request the datum again. On the other hand, a requester agent is allowed to get data from two sources simultaneously. This is done –for a short time– in order to compare their effective bandwidth so to choose the fastest source (the other one is discarded with a `cancel` message).

Previous messages are related to communication at domain-level. However, there are other messages related to communication at *meta-level* and among levels. Initially, a new domain-level agent sends its `join <hasDatum>` message to the closest assistant —a domain-level agent measures it latency to all assistants and chooses the one having the smallest latency. Then, the assistant asks the agent to measure its latencies with all other agents in its cluster by sending a `get_lat <peers>` message. The agent measures latencies by exchanging `lat_req/lat_rpl` messages, and informs back the assistant with a `lat <measure>` message. Once an assistant has all latencies among its domain-level agents ($EnvP$) and knows which ones have the datum, it estimates which would be the best social structure —see [13]. Then it suggests the agent relationships by sending `contact <peers>` messages to all the agents in its cluster.

Additionally, when a domain-level agent receives the datum, it also informs its assistant with a `complete` message. Then, at meta-level this assistant informs other assistants with a `complete_peer <peer>` message. For instance, in Figure 5, when P2 receives the datum, it informs A1, which will inform A2 and A3. Next, contacted assistants spread this information towards their domain-level agents –limited by max_{Has}– with a `has_datum <peer>` message —e.g. A2 may inform P6 and P8 that P2 has the datum, if $max_{Has} = 2$. In that moment, informed agents measure their latencies to the new agent and request it, if it is better than any previous source. Finally, when an assistant detects that all domain-level agents in its cluster are complete, it sends an `all_complete` message to other assistants to avoid receiving more `complete_peer` notifications.

Last, the norm adaptation process requires some more messages —see §4. When an assistant wants to update $normBW_{DL}$, it sends a `norm_bw <value>` message to the rest of assistants. Analogously, it would send a `norm_friends <value>` in case of a $normFR_{DL}$ update. Then, when a new value is finally agreed, each *assistant* informs its the domain-level agents in its cluster with a `norm_updated <norm_id> <new_def>` message.

4   Organisational Adaptation

Within our 2-LAMA architecture, the meta-level is able to adapt domain-level's organisation. In particular, we are working on social structure and norm adaptation. The former consists in the meta-level updating domain-level's overlay network as detailed in [13]. The latter is the focus of this paper, and it is described in this section. In brief, norm adaptation proceeds as follows. Initially, assistants collect status information from their cluster domain-level agents but also from other assistants —in a summarised form. Afterwards, they aggregate all this information. Next, they compute their desired values of norm parameters depending on this aggregated information. Finally, they use a voting scheme as a group decision mechanism to choose the actual norm updates before notifying their agents.

The underlying rationale of the norm adaptation process is to align the amount of served data with the amount of received data. Thus, the information collected by each assistant consists of some measures about the agents serving the datum and the ones that lack it. Specifically, they collect the following information:

- srvBW: the sum of the nominal bandwidths of the individual channels of the agents that are serving data.
- rcvBW: the sum of the nominal bandwidth of the individual channels of the agents that are receiving data.
- rcvEffBW: the sum of the effective receiving bandwidth of the agents that are receiving data. It can be smaller than rcvBW when only a few data is served or there is network saturation that delays message transport.
- rcvExpBW: the expected receiving bandwidth. It is estimated using the nominal one (rcvBW) re-scaled by current bandwidth limit (max_{BW}). It is computed to be compared with rcvEffBW. If effective serving bandwidth is limited by a $\text{max}_{\text{BW}} < 100$, the reference receiving bandwidth may be lesser than the nominal one (rcvBW) —since less data is being injected towards receiving agents.
- waiting: the number of agents that do not have the datum and are neither receiving it.

Such information could be collected by each assistant from its agents or by accessing network information. In the former case, assistants would query agents about such information. Thus, this method would require that domain-level agents would report true values —which would be difficult to guarantee in an open MAS. In contrast, we use the latter case, which does not require collaborative agents. In this method, assistants inspect domain-level agent communications to obtain such information by themselves —this requires assistants to have privileges to access network resources, which is acceptable if they are related to ISPs.

Depending on the cost of collecting such information, it may be retrieved continuously or at certain intervals. Also, depending on the cost of applying norm changes, the norm adaptation process may be performed at given intervals.

In the current implementation, this process is performed at a fixed time interval ($\mathtt{adapt_{interv}}$) with an average of these measures along it.

In order to compute the desired norms, an assistant weighs the information it has collected from its cluster with the information provided by other assistants. This way it can give more importance to local information. For instance, $\mathtt{srvBW} = \mathtt{w_L} \cdot \mathtt{srvBW_L} + \sum (\mathtt{w_{R_i}} \cdot \mathtt{srvBW_{R_i}})$, where $\mathtt{srvBW_L}$ stands for the local cluster's measure, $\mathtt{srvBW_{R_i}}$ stands for the remote ones, $\mathtt{w_L}$ stands for the weight of local information, and $\mathtt{w_{R_i}}$ stands for the weight of remote one. Moreover, $\mathtt{w_L} + \sum \mathtt{w_{R_i}} = 1$ and $\nexists \mathtt{w_{R_i}}, \mathtt{w_{R_i}} > \mathtt{w_L}$.

If the local weight is the maximum ($\mathtt{w_L} = 1$), then each assistant computes desired norms taking into account only its cluster status. On the contrary, if this weight is the minimum ($\forall_i \mathtt{w_{R_i}} = \mathtt{w_L}$), then each assistant gives the same importance to local information as to remote one —this is the case in the current implementation. The mid-point is a local weight greater than any remote one ($\forall_i \mathtt{w_{R_i}} < \mathtt{w_L}$) such as an assistant takes its decisions giving more importance to its local cluster, but taking into account the rest of the system.

With this aggregated information each assistant computes its vote for $\mathtt{max_{BW}}$ ($\mathtt{voteBW}$) and $\mathtt{max_{FR}}$($\mathtt{voteFR}$). In the case of $\mathtt{voteBW}$, the vote is the numeric desired value for $\mathtt{max_{BW}}$. Whereas in $\mathtt{voteFR}$, the vote is an action among incrementing $\mathtt{max_{FR}}$ by one ($\mathtt{incr}$), decrementing it by one ($\mathtt{decr}$), keeping the same value ($\mathtt{same}$) or abstaining with a *blank ballot-paper* ($\mathtt{blnk}$) to avoid influencing in new $\mathtt{max_{FR}}$ value. They use the process schematised in Algorithm 1 to compute both votes. This algorithm receives the measures we described plus current norm parameter values. Next, in line 2, some constants are initialised to be used as thresholds in comparisons (their values were empirically tested). Then, the expected receiving bandwidth is computed from the nominal one re-scaled by current bandwidth limit (line 3).

The main decision to choose a $normFR_{DL}$ is related to compare the available bandwidth used to serve ($\mathtt{srvBW}$) to the available bandwidth used to receive ($\mathtt{rcvBW}$). If there is a lack of serving bandwidth (line 6), the suggestion is to decrease the number of friends. This way, server *agents* will be simultaneously serving data to fewer agents, and these transmissions will finish sooner. Afterwards, once these other agents get the datum, there will be more data sources in the system and it will take less time to finish the datum distribution. On the other hand, if there is an excess of serving bandwidth and there are still agents waiting for data (lines 8) then, the assistant can increase the number of friends in order to serve more agents. There is another situation in which there is also an excess of serving bandwidth but there are no agents waiting for data (lines 10). This does not necessarily mean all agents have the datum, but at least the ones lacking it are receiving it from some source. In this case, the assistant uses a blank-ballot paper to let other assistants push for their own interests[3].

---

[3] Notice, though, that the weighting method applied to measures may bring an assistant to this case when no agents in its cluster are waiting for data, but there are still waiting agents in other clusters. In such a case, if there is enough serving bandwidth, it is better to let other assistants choose by themselves the norm parameter values.

Algorithm 1. Adaptation algorithm used by *assistants*

```
00 def adapt( srvBW, rcvBW, rcvEffBW, waiting, maxFR, maxBW ):
01
02   τ = 0.1 ; ε = 0.2
03   rcvExpBW = rcvBW * (maxBW / 100)
04
05   // Adapt maxFR -------------
06   case ( srvBW<(1-τ)*rcvBW ):                    voteFR = decr
07
08   case ( srvBW>(1+τ)*rcvBW && waiting>ε ): voteFR = incr
09
10   case ( srvBW>(1+τ)*rcvBW && waiting<ε ): voteFR = blnk
11
12   other /*srvBW  ≈  rcvBW */:                    voteFR = same
13
14
15   if ( rcvEffBW < (1-τ)*rcvExpBW ):              voteFR = decr
16
17   // Adapt maxBW ------------
18   case (voteFR == decr ∧ maxFR == 1 ):     voteBW = maxBW / 2
19
20   case (voteFR == incr ∧ maxBW < 100):     voteBW = 100
21
22   other                              :     voteBW = maxBW
23
24   return [ voteFR, voteBW ]
```

Finally, if none of the previous cases is true, it means that the serving bandwidth is similar to the receiving one (line 12) then, the vote is for keeping the same norm. This is because if there is no excess of serving bandwidth, the assistant prefers to vote for the same norm instead of just leaving the decision to the rest of assistants.

Despite previous cases, if there is network saturation in the intermediate channels, it is always better to decrease the number of friends. This will reduce the number of data transmissions. Hence, it will cut back network traffic and hopefully network saturation. In order to estimate if there is network saturation, the assistant checks if the effective receiving bandwidth (rcvEffBW) is smaller than the expected one (rcvExpBW). This is a sign that data packets are delayed by the intermediate network because it is saturated. Consequently, as a solution to saturation, the assistant votes for decreasing max$_{FR}$ (line 15).

Regarding the $normBW_{DL}$, it is only decreased in case it is not possible to further diminish the network usage by decreasing the number of friends —since max$_{FR}$ is already 1. In such a case, the assistant votes for dividing max$_{BW}$ by 2 (line 18). This way, server agents will use less bandwidth, which can help to diminish the network saturation. On the contrary, if the bandwidth is previously limited but there is no network saturation —since the assistant chose to increase max$_{FR}$—, then the bandwidth limit can be established again back to 100% (line 20). For the remaining cases, max$_{BW}$ keeps its value (line 22).

After choosing a convenient value for each norm parameter, an assistant sends its votes (vFR, vBW) to the rest of assistants —see norm_bw and norm_friends messages. Then, when assistants receive all the votes, they compute the actual norm parameters. To conclude, they send to their domain-level agents the new norms using the norm_updated message. Notice that the average may provide the same norm parameters values as before, thus no changes would be performed —in practise, it means no update message would be sent. This situation may occur when opposite options are interesting for the same amount of clusters.

Regarding norm updates application, once a domain-level agent receives new norms, it tries to fulfil them. Thus, when an agent receives a $normBW_{DL}$, it adapts its sending ratio and when it receives a $normFR_{DL}$ it also tries to fulfil it. This means that if an agent is serving to less friends than the new max$_{FR}$, it will send unchoke messages to those agents it has previously choked. This may result in new data requests that it will be able to serve. On the contrary, if it was serving to more friends than the new max$_{FR}$, it will cancel some of those data transmissions and send a choke message[4].

5   Empirical Evaluation

In order to test our approach, we have implemented a P2P MAS simulator. This simulator is implemented in Repast Simphony [14] and provides different facilities to execute tests and analyse results. As it simulates both agents and network components, it allows to execute different sharing methods with identical populations and environmental conditions. Thus, we have performed several tests on BitTorrent and 2-LAMA to empirically evaluate the performance of our proposal.

5.1   Sharing Methods

In this work, we compare three different approaches. A single-piece version of the BitTorrent protocol (BT), which is described in [15]. A 2-LAMA approach with social structure adaptation (2L.a) in which assistants update the actual contact relationships among domain-level agents as described in [13]. And a 2-LAMA approach with social structure and the norm adaptation (2L.b) described in this paper.

The BitTorrent implemented protocol (BT) among domain-level agents is very similar to 2-LAMA's since it inspired our approach. In order to make a fair comparison, we adapted BitTorrent to work with a single-piece datum —see [15] for further information. However, it does not have a distributed meta-level but a single agent (*Tracker*) that informs about connected agents. Consequently, agents do not receive any further assistance to share the datum. Instead, they use

---

[4] In the current implementation, an agent does not need to cancel a *friend* if it has already sent more than 75% of the datum to it. This behaviour avoids cancelling data transmissions that will finish really soon.

the algorithms described in [11]. In brief, the main algorithm of an agent having the datum consists in sending `choke` messages to all agents that are interested in it. Then, at certain intervals (`unchoke_interval`), the source agent sends `unchoke` messages to four of the previously choked agents. Next, these agents can request the datum and all of them are served. The selected agents to unchoke are those that were choked most recently. In case two of them were choked at the same time, the one having a larger network bandwidth (`upload_bw`) is selected. In fact, if an agent's interest is older than a defined interval (`aging_period`), its age is ignored and only its agent's `upload_bw` is compared. In addition, in two out of three `unchoke_interval` selection processes, the fourth agent is randomly selected.

Regarding the configuration of our experiments, BitTorrent (BT) uses an `unchoke_interval` of 250 time units (ticks). It is approximately the time required to send four data messages along an average agent link in current topology. Thus, it is the average time that a server agent can invest sending data to four unchoked agents. This is the number of agents that BitTorrent protocol determines that an agent unchokes in an unchoke interval. Accordingly, they use an `aging_period` of 130 ticks to keep the ratio defined by the official protocol. On the other hand, the 2-LAMA experiments (2L.a, 2L.b) have been performed with the following initial norm parameters: `maxHas` $= \infty$, `maxBW` $= 100\%$, `maxFR` $= 3$. These norms lead 2-LAMA approach to a similar initial behaviour as BitTorrent because: `maxHas` $= \infty$ does not restrict communications among clusters, `maxBW` $= 100\%$ does not limit agent communication and `maxFR` $= 3$ is equivalent to the three non-random unchoked agents. This is specially the case because in our current implementation, domain-level agents always fulfil norms[5]. Additionally, for those tests including norm adaptation (2L.b), it has been done at an interval of $\text{adapt}_{\text{interv}} = 50$ time steps.

5.2   Results

In our experiments, we use a packet switching network model to simulate the transport of messages among agents. Figure 6 shows the network topology we use in our simulations. Notice that, as we are interested in having a different communication capacity for each domain-level agent, we place an *individual link* between each agent ($p1..p12$) and its corresponding Internet Service Provider ($ISP_1..ISP_3$ represented by routers $r1..r3$). In 2-LAMA experiments, each ISP has an associated assistant[6] ($a1..a3$) in charge of its connected domain-level agents. In addition, as we want to model simultaneous network usage by different agents, we place an *aggregated link* among each group of agents –i.e. a

---

[5] Otherwise, we could assume there is an infrastructure mechanism at ISPs that detects and filters out messages that exceed the bandwidth limit (`maxBW`), or the simultaneous data messages limit (`maxFR` $= 3$).

[6] Our network model includes a quality of service (QoS) feature that gives more priority to messages among assistants or between assistants and domain-level agents. Thus, communications at meta-level and among levels are faster than communications at domain-level.

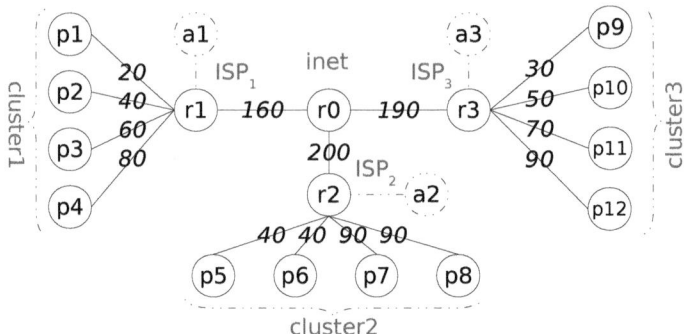

Fig. 6. Network topology

Table 2. Results from BitTorrent (BT), 2-LAMA without norm adaptation (2L.a) and 2-LAMA with norm adaptation (2L.b)

	time	cNet	nHops	nData	cLat	cML
BT	933.3	206182	3.4	11	0	0
2L.a	849.7	345060	3.2	40.1	21600	3749.9
2L.b	811.1	316190	3.0	30.7	21600	6596.0

cluster, those connected to the same ISP– and the Internet (r0). In fact, in Bit-Torrent experiments, there are no assistants at all but a single tracker linked to this r0. Notice that the network topology influences the time required to transmit a message from one agent to another. In particular, this time depends on: message's length, the bandwidths of the traversed links, and the number of simultaneous messages traversing the same links —a link's bandwidth is divided among the messages that traverse it simultaneously. Regarding the former issue, we have used the following message lengths: `piece` messages have 5000 data units, `lat_req` / `lat_rpl` have 150 data units and all the other control messages have a single data unit. Regarding the bandwidths links, Figure 6 shows them as numbers over the edges —we assume upload/download channels are symmetric. Finally, the latter issue, related to simultaneous link usage, is highly dynamic and depends on system's evolution.

We have tested all approaches in the described network topology by varying the agent that initially has the datum. Table 2 shows the results of different evaluation metrics in both approaches: BitTorrent (BT), 2-LAMA with social structure adaptation but no norm adaptation (2L.a) and 2-LAMA with social structure and norm adaptation (2L.b). Figures correspond to the average results for twelve different settings (so that they cover all possible initial datum positions in a single agent).

The evaluation metrics in Table 2 are the following: (1) *time* corresponds to the total time required to spread the datum among all agents; (2) *cNet* is the network cost consumed by all messages —each message cost is computed as its length times the number of links it traverses; (3) *nHops* is the average number of links traversed by each message; (4) *nData* is the total number of sent data messages —they may not be totally transmitted if: a destination agent sends a cancel message to its source or a source stops sending data to fulfil an updated $normFR_{DL}$; (5) *cLat* is the cost of all `lat_req`/`lat_rpl` messages; (6) *cML* is the cost of all messages related with the meta-level —i.e. all messages sent to or by *assistants*.

If we compare the performance of both approaches (BT and 2-LAMA), we see that our proposal requires less time to share the datum. Notice also, that 2-LAMA with social structure and norm adaptation (2L.b) presents shorter times that the version without norm adaptation (2L.a). In general, having better times in 2-LAMA means that the time invested in communicating with meta-level is less than the benefits of having such an additional level. Even more, we expect larger differences in performance when repeating the data sharing among the same P2P agent community since the information collected by our meta-level –e.g. measured latencies– will be used more than once. In fact, in our current 2-LAMA experiments, from 33 up to 56 ticks –depending on the cluster of agents– are invested in measuring latencies.

In contrast, the network cost (*cNet*) is larger in 2-LAMA, although norm adaptation (2L.b) provides the best performance again. Our proposal requires more communication because it initially measures latencies (*cLat*), it has extra communications due to the meta-level (*cML*), and it sends more data messages (*nData*). Specifically, latency measurements (*cLat*) represent up to a 20% of the network cost increment. This measurements are an initialisation phase that could be omitted in subsequent executions. On the other hand, 2-LAMA agents compare data sources by retrieving some data from them. This increases the number of data messages (*nData*) although most of them are cancelled. We expect to minimise this network consumption when dealing with more than one piece of data, since agents could compare sources depending on previous retrieved pieces. Regarding the number of links traversed by messages (*nHops*), our 2-LAMA approach has more local communications –i.e. intra-cluster– than BT. This is convenient because local messages have lower latencies and costs, since they are usually performed in the same cluster.

Furthermore, notice that for the sake of simplicity, we are currently working with a single piece version of all approaches (BT and 2-LAMA). As a consequence, in current BT implementation, the `upload_bw` measure –see §5.1– is taken from the network topology information. Besides, in 2-LAMA implementation, peers receive data simultaneously from more than one source to compare their bandwidths —see §3.2. In contrast, in a multi-piece scenario, these measures could be estimated from previous piece exchanges. This means that BT would require no resources to obtain `upload_bw`, like in current single-piece implementation. But, 2-LAMA would save some network cost —the associated to having simultaneous sources for the same peer. Moreover, the investment of time and network resources during the initial latency phase of 2-LAMA –which is performed only once, see §3.2– would be exploited longer if more pieces were exchanged. In summary, a multi-piece scenario would benefit more 2-LAMA than BT.

Overall, norm adaptation (2L.b) provides the best results despite requiring more assistant communication (*cML*). This stresses the idea that having a meta-level and exploiting its capabilities provides more benefits than the costs it causes.

6 Related Work

Within MAS area, organisation-centred approaches regulate open systems by means of persistent organisations —e.g. Electronic Institutions [3]. Even more, several of these approaches offer mechanisms to update their organisational structures at run-time —e.g. Moise+ [4]. However, most work on adaptation maps organisational goals to tasks and look for agents with capabilities to perform them —e.g. OMACS [5]. Consequently, these approaches cannot deal with scenarios that lack of this goal/task mapping, like our case study. In order to deal with this sort of scenarios, our approach uses norms to influence agent behaviour, instead of delegating tasks. Specifically, our approach uses a norm adaptation mechanism based on social power —see norm taxonomy [16]. In this sense, there are other works that also use the leadership of certain agents (like our assistants) to create/spread norms —e.g. the role model based mechanism [17]. Besides, the most of norm emergence works are agent-centred approaches that depend on participants' implementation and they rarely create/update persistent organisations —e.g. infection-based model [18].

Relating norms and overall system behaviour, is a complex issue that increases its intricacy when there is no control over participant's implementation. In our approach, this task is distributed among a assistant agents which finally reach an agreement about norm updates. Currently, assistants use a voting scheme to agree on actual norms, but they could use some of the other agreement mechanisms present in literature —e.g. using an argumentation protocol [19]. Moreover, currently assistants use an heuristic to take their local decisions, but we are planning to use learning techniques in future work —like in AEI [20].

Finally, regarding our P2P case study, there are some approaches that follow a MAS viewpoint and others that take a network management perspective. For instance, from the former point of view, [21] has a meta-level that enforces norms using a reputation service and offers information about local convention violations. However, agents can only adapt local conventions and meta-level's agents are just individual supervisors. In the latter perspective, Ono [22] tries to promote local communications –those with less latency– without involving ISP whereas P4P [23] involves them. However, they only adapt the social structure and cannot directly update network consumption to balance net capacity and traffic. Above all, our proposal could be empirically compared to these network management approaches, by extending it to multi-piece and replacing our simulator's network component by their precise low-level network simulators.

7 Conclusions

This work proposes an abstract MAS architecture (2-LAMA) to provide *assistance* to its participants. Particularly, this paper regards adapting a MAS organisation to varying circumstances as a type of assistance. It illustrates this approach in a P2P sharing network scenario, providing in-depth details about the adaptation process.

We endow the system with adaptation capabilities instead of expecting the agents to increase their behaviour complexity. Consequently, we propose to add a distributed *Assistance Layer* to improve system's performance by providing new support services to agents. In particular, in our architecture *meta-level* agents perceive information about MAS participants and environment, and are able to adapt the system's organisation.

Our 2-LAMA approach can be applied to domains with highly dynamic environments and no mapping between tasks and goals. It only requires that an organisation-centred MAS with an alterable organisation can be deployed. Such an organisation may include norms in its regulative structures. Moreover, the MAS can be open to third-party agents. As an illustration of all these issues, we introduce a representative case study based on a Peer-to-Peer sharing network. Additionally, to prove 2-LAMA's feasibility empirically, we have performed some experiments which show that the cost of adding our proposed Assistance Layer is lower than the obtained benefit. Specifically, 2-LAMA approach required less time than the original BitTorrent protocol. Even more, our approach results improved when increasing meta-level adaptation capabilities —i.e. when updating norms in addition to social structure adaptations.

As future work, we plan to confront further issues in open MAS such as how the system should react to agents joining or leaving the MAS anytime, or transgressing its organisational restrictions. In fact, we already have preliminary results about norm violations that show how system re-adapts to counter violation side effects. Besides, we are improving meta-level agents to use learning techniques in order to perform the adaptation process.

Acknowledgements. This work is partially funded by IEA (TIN2006-15662-C02-01), EVE (TIN2009-14702-C02-01 / TIN2009-14702-C02-02) and AT (CONSOLIDER CSD2007-0022) projects, EU-FEDER funds, the Catalan Goverment (Grant 2005-SGR-00093) and Marc Esteva's Ramon y Cajal contract.

References

1. Jennings, N., Sycara, K., Wooldridge, M.: A roadmap of agent research and development. Autonomous Agents and Multi-Agent Systems 1(1), 7–38 (1998)
2. Horling, B., Lesser, V.: A survey of multi agent organizational paradigms. The Knowledge Engineering Review 19(4), 281–316 (2004)
3. Esteva, M.: Electronic Institutions: from specification to development. IIIA PhD. 19 (2003)
4. Boissier, O., Gâteau, B.: Normative multi-agent organizations: Modeling, support and control. In: Boella, G., van der Torre, L., Verhagen, H. (eds.) Normative Multi-agent Systems. Dagstuhl Seminar Proceedings, vol. 07122, pp. 1–17. Internationales Begegnungs- und Forschungszentrum für Informatik (IBFI), Schloss Dagstuhl, Germany (2007)
5. Deloach, S.A., Oyenan, W.H., Matson, E.T.: A capabilities-based model for adaptive organizations. Autonomous Agents and Multi-Agent Systems 16(1), 13–56 (2008)

6. Kota, R., Gibbins, N., Jennings, N.: Decentralised structural adaptation in agent organisations. In: AAMAS Workshop on Organised Adaptation in Multi-Agent Systems, Estoril, Portugal, pp. 54–71. Springer, Heidelberg (2009)
7. Sims, M., Corkill, D., Lesser, V.: Automated Organization Design for Multi-agent Systems. Autonomous Agents and Multi-Agent Systems 16(2), 151–185 (2008)
8. Zhang, C., Abdallah, S., Lesser, V.: MASPA: Multi-Agent Automated Supervisory Policy Adaptation. Technical Report 03 (2008)
9. Carley, K.: Computational and mathematical organization theory: Perspective and directions. Computational & Mathematical Organization Theory 1(1), 39–56 (1995)
10. Kephart, J.O., Chess, D.M.: The vision of autonomic computing. IEEE Computer 36(1), 41–50 (2003)
11. BitTorrentInc.: BitTorrent protocol specification (2001), http://www.bittorrent.org/beps/bep_0003.html
12. Campos, J., López-Sánchez, M., Esteva, M.: Assistance layer, a step forward in Multi-Agent Systems Coordination Support. In: Eighth International Conference on Autonomous Agents and Multi-agent Systems, pp. 1301–1302 (2009)
13. Campos, J., López-Sánchez, M., Esteva, M.: Multi-Agent System adaptation in a Peer-to-Peer scenario. In: ACM SAC 209 - Agreement Technologies, pp. 735–739 (2009)
14. North, M., Howe, T., Collier, N., Vos, J.: Repast Simphony Runtime System. In: Agent Conference on Generative Social Processes, Models, and Mechanisms (2005)
15. Campos, J., López-Sánchez, M., Esteva, M., Novo, A., Morales, J.: 2-LAMA Architecture vs. BitTorrent Protocol in a Peer-to-Peer Scenario. In: Artificial Intelligence Research and Development - CCIA 2009, vol. 202, pp. 197–206. IOS Press, Amsterdam (2009)
16. Cranefield, B.S.S.: A categorization of simulation works on norms (2009)
17. Savarimuthu, B.T.R., Cranefield, S., Purvis, M., Purvis, M.: Role model based mechanism for norm emergence in artificial agent societies. In: Sichman, J.S., Padget, J., Ossowski, S., Noriega, P. (eds.) COIN 2007. LNCS (LNAI), vol. 4870, pp. 203–217. Springer, Heidelberg (2008)
18. Salazar-Ramirez, N., Rodríguez-Aguilar, J.A., Arcos, J.L.: An infection-based mechanism for self-adaptation in multi-agent complex networks. In: Brueckner, S., Robertson, P., Bellur, U. (eds.) 2nd IEEE International Conference on Self-Adaptive and Self-Organizing Systems, SASO 2008, pp. 161–170 (2008)
19. Artikis, A., Kaponis, D., Pitt, J.: Dynamic Specifications of Norm-Governed Systems. In: Dignum, V. (ed.) Multi-Agent Systems: Semantics and Dynamics of Organisational Models, pp. 460–479. IGI Global (2009)
20. Bou, E., López-Sánchez, M., Rodríguez-Aguilar, J.A., Sichman, J.S.: Adapting autonomic electronic institutions to heterogeneous agent societies. In: Vouros, G., Artikis, A., Stathis, K., Pitt, J. (eds.) OAMAS 2008. LNCS, vol. 5368, pp. 18–35. Springer, Heidelberg (2009)
21. Grizard, A., Vercouter, L., Stratulat, T., Muller, G.: A peer-to-peer normative system to achieve social order. In: Noriega, P., Vázquez-Salceda, J., Boella, G., Boissier, O., Dignum, V., Fornara, N., Matson, E. (eds.) COIN 2006. LNCS (LNAI), vol. 4386, pp. 274–289. Springer, Heidelberg (2007)
22. Choffnes, D., Bustamante, F.: Taming the torrent: a practical approach to reducing cross-ISP traffic in peer-to-peer systems. SIGCOMM Comput. Commun. Rev. 38(4), 363–374 (2008)
23. Xie, H., Yang, Y.R., Krishnamurthy, A., Liu, Y., Silberschatz, A.: P4P: provider portal for applications. ACM SIGCOMM Computer Communication Review 38(4), 351–362 (2008)

Normative Monitoring: Semantics and Implementation

Sergio Alvarez-Napagao[1], Huib Aldewereld[2],
Javier Vázquez-Salceda[1], and Frank Dignum[2]

[1] Universitat Politècnica de Catalunya
{salvarez,jvazquez}@lsi.upc.edu
[2] Universiteit Utrecht
{huib,dignum}@cs.uu.nl

Abstract. The concept of Normative Systems can be used in the scope of Multi-Agent Systems to provide reliable contexts of interactions between agents where acceptable behaviour is specified in terms of norms. Literature on the topic is growing rapidly, and there is a considerable amount of theoretical frameworks for normative environments, some in the form of Electronic Institutions. Most of these approaches focus on regulative norms rather than on substantive norms, and lack a proper implementation of the ontological connection between brute events and institutional facts. In this paper we present a formalism for the monitoring of both regulative (deontic) and substantive (constitutive) norms based on Structural Operational Semantics, its reduction to Production Systems semantics and our current implementation compliant to these semantics.

1 Introduction

In recent years, several researchers have argued that the design of multi-agent systems (MAS) in complex, open environments can benefit from social abstractions in order to cope with problems in coordination, cooperation and trust among agents, problems which are also present in human societies. One of such abstractions is *Normative Systems*. Research in Normative Systems focuses on the concepts of norms and normative environment (which some authors refer to as *institutions*) in order to provide normative frameworks to restrict or guide the behaviour of (software) agents. The main idea is that the interactions among a group of (software) agents are ruled by a set of explicit norms expressed in a computational language representation that agents can interpret. Although some authors only see norms as inflexible restrictions to agent behaviour, others see norms not as a negative, constraining factor but as an aid that guides the agents' choices and reduces the complexity of the environment, making the behaviour of other agents more predictable.

Until recently, most of the work on normative environments works with norm specifications that are static and stable, and which will not change over time. Although this may be good enough from the social (institutional) perspective, it is not appropriate from the agent perspective. During their lifetime, agents may enter and leave several interaction contexts, each with its own normative framework. Furthermore they may be operating in contexts where more than one normative specification applies. So we need

M. De Vos et al. (Eds.): COIN 2010 International Workshops, LNAI 6541, pp. 321–336, 2011.

mechanisms where normative specifications can be added to the agents' knowledge base at run-time and be practically used in their reasoning, both to be able to interpret institutional facts from brute ones (by using constitutive norms to, e.g. decide if killing a person counts as *murder* in the current context) and to decide what ought to be done (by using regulative norms to, e.g. prosecute the murderer). In this paper we propose to use production systems to build a norm monitoring mechanism that can be used both by agents to perceive the current normative state of their environment, and for these environments to detect norm violations and enforce sanctions. Our basic idea is that an agent can configure, at a practical level, the production system at run-time by adding abstract organisational specifications and sets of counts-as rules.

In our approach, the detection of normative states is a passive procedure consisting in monitoring past events and checking them against a set of active norms. This type of reasoning is already covered by the declarative aspect of production systems, so no additional implementation in an imperative language is needed. Using a forward-chaining rule engine, events will automatically trigger the normative state - based on the operational semantics - without requiring a design on *how* to do it.

Having 1) a direct syntactic translation from norms to rules and 2) a logic implemented in an engine consistent with the process we want to accomplish, allows us to decouple normative state monitoring from the agent reasoning. The initial set of rules we have defined is the same for each type of agent and each type of organisation, and the agent will be able to transparently query the current normative state at any moment and reason upon it. Also this decoupling helps building third party/facilitator agents capable of observing, monitoring and reporting normative state change or even enforcing behaviour in the organisation.

In this paper we present a formalism for the monitoring of both regulative (deontic) and substantive (constitutive) norms based on Structural Operational Semantics (Section 2), its reduction to Production Systems semantics (Section 3) and our current implementation compliant to these semantics (Section 4). In Section 5 we compare with other related work and provide some conclusions.

2   Formal Semantics

In this section we discuss the formal semantics of our framework. First, in section 2.1, we give the semantics of institutions as the environment specifying the regulative and constitutive norms. Then, in section 2.2, we describe the details of how this institution evolves over time based on events, and how this impacts the monitoring process. This formalisation will be used in section 3 as basis of our implementation.

Through this paper, we will use as an example the following simplified traffic scenario:

1. A person driving on a street is not allowed to break a traffic convention.
2. In case (1) is violated, the driver must pay a fine.
3. In a city, to exceed 50kmh counts as breaking a traffic convention.

2.1 Preliminary Definitions

Before giving a formal definition of institutions (see Definition 4), we first define the semantics of the regulative and constitutive norms part of that institution (in definitions 1 and 3, respectively).

We assume the use of a predicate based propositional logic language $\mathcal{L}_O$ with predicates and constants taken from an ontology O, and the logical connectives $\{\neg, \vee, \wedge\}$. The set of all possible well-formed formulas of $\mathcal{L}_O$ is denoted as $wff(\mathcal{L}_O)$ and we assume that each formula from $wff(\mathcal{L}_O)$ is normalised in Disjunctive Normal Form (*DNF*). Formulas in $wff(\mathcal{L}_O)$ can be partially grounded, if they use at least one free variable, or fully grounded if they use no free variables.

In this paper we intensively use the concept of variable substitution. We define a substitution instance $\Theta = \{x_1 \leftarrow t_1, x_2 \leftarrow t_2, ..., x_i \leftarrow t_i\}$ as the substitution of the terms $t_1, t_2, ..., t_i$ for variables $x_1, x_2, ..., x_i$ in a formula $f \in wff(\mathcal{L}_O)$.

We denote the set of roles in a normative system as the set of constants R, where $R \subset O$, and the set of participants as P, where each participant enacts at least one role according to the ontology O.

As our aim is to build a normative monitoring mechanism that can work at real time, special care has been made to choose a norm language which, without loss of expresiveness, has operational semantics that can then be mapped into production systems. Based in our previous work and experience, our definition of *norm* in an extension of the norm language presented in [12]:

Definition 1. *A norm n is a tuple $n = \langle f_A, f_M, f_\delta, f_D, f_w, w \rangle$, where*

- *$f_A, f_M, f_\delta, f_D, f_w \in wff(\mathcal{L}_O), w \in R$,*
- *f_A, f_M, f_D respectively represent the activation, maintenance, and deactivation conditions of the norm, f_δ, f_w are the explicit representation of the deadline and target of the norm, and*
- *w is the subject of the norm.*

In order to create an optimal norm monitor it is important to know which norms are active at each point in time, as only those are the ones that have to be traced (inactive norms can be discarded from the monitoring process until they become active again). The *activation condition* f_A specifies when a norm becomes active. It is also the main element in the norm instantiation process: when the conditions in the activating condition hold, the variables are instantiated, creating a new norm instance[1]. The *target* condition f_w describes the state that fulfills the norm (e.g. if one is obliged to pay, the payment being made fulfills the obligation). The *deactivating condition* f_D defines when the norm becomes inactive. Typically it corresponds to the *target* condition (e.g., fulfilling the norm instance deactivates that instance of the norm), but in some cases it also adds conditions to express other deactivating scenarios (e.g., when the norm becomes deprecated). The *maintenance condition* f_M defines the conditions that, when

---

[1] One main differentiating aspect of our formalisation is that we include variables in the norm representation and we can handle multiple instantiations of the same norm and track them separately.

no longer hold, lead to a violation of the norm. Finally the *deadline* condition f_δ respresents one or several deadlines for the norm to be fulfilled.

An example of a norm for the traffic scenario (*"A person driving on a street is not allowed to break a traffic convention"*) would be formalised as follows

n1 $:= \langle enacts(X, Driver) \wedge is\_driving(X),$
$\neg traffic\_violation(X),$
$\bot,$
$\neg is\_driving(X),$
$is\_driving(X) \wedge \neg traffic\_violation(X),$
$Driver \rangle,$

The activating condition states that each time an event appears where an individual enacting the $Driver$ role drives ('$is\_driving$), then a new instance of the norm becomes active; the maintenance condition states that the norm will not be violated while no traffic convention is violated; this norm has no deadline, it is to apply at all times an individual is driving; the norm instance deactivates when the individual stops driving[2]; the target of this norm is that we want drivers not breaking traffic conventions; finally the subject of the norm is someone enacting the $Driver$ role.

It is important to note here that, although our norm representation does not explicitly include deontic operators, the combination of the activation, deactivation and maintenance conditions is as expressive as conditional deontic statements with deadlines as the ones in [3]. It is also able to express unconditional norms and maintenance obligations (i.e. the obligation to keep some conditions holding for a period of time). To show that our representation can be mapped to conditional deontic representations, let us express the semantics of the norm in definition 1 in terms of conditional deontic statements. Given relations between the deadline and maintenance condition (that is, $f_\delta \rightarrow \neg f_M$, since the maintenance condition expresses more than the deadline alone) and between the target and the deactivation condition (i.e., $f_w \rightarrow f_D$, since the deactivation condition specifies that either the norm is fulfilled or something special has happened), we can formalise the norms of Definition 1 as the equivalent deontic expression (using the formalism of [3]): $f_A \rightarrow [O_w(E_w f_w \leq \neg f_M) \cup f_D]$, where $E_a p$ means that agent a sees to it that (*stit*) p becomes true and U is the CTL* until operator. Intuitively, the expression states that after the norm activation, the subject is obliged to see to it that the target becomes true before the maintenance condition is negated (either the deadline is reached or some other condition is broken) until the norm is deactivated (which is either when the norm is fulfilled or has otherwise expired).

Since we are not reasoning about the (effects of) combinations of norms, we will not go into further semantical details here. The semantics presented in this deontic reduction are enough for understanding the monitoring process that is detailed in the remainder of the paper.

A set of norms is denoted as N. We define as *violation handling norms* those norms that are activated automatically by the violation of another norm:

---

[2] Although the norm is to apply at all times an individual is driving, it is better to deactivate the norm each time the individual stops driving, instead to keep it active, to minimize the number of norm instances the monitor needs to keep track at all times.

Definition 2. *A norm* $n' = \langle f'_A, f'_M, f'_\delta, f'_D, f'_w, w' \rangle$ *is a violation handling norm of* $n = \langle f_A, f_M, f_\delta, f_D, f_w, w \rangle$, *denoted as* $n \rightsquigarrow n'$ *iff* $f_A \wedge \neg f_M \wedge \neg f_D \equiv f'_A$

Violation handling norms are special in the sense that they are only activated when another norm is violated. They are used as *sanctioning norms*, if they are to be fulfilled by the norm violating actor (e.g., the obligation to pay a fine if the driver broke a traffic sign), or as *reparation norms*, if they are to be fulfilled by an institutional actor (e.g. the obligation of the authorities to fix the broken traffic sign).

A norm is defined in an abstract manner, affecting all possible participants enacting a given role. Whenever a norm is active, we will say that there is a *norm instance* $ni = \langle n, \theta \rangle$ for a particular norm n and a substitution instance Θ.

We define the *state of the world* s_t at a specific point of time t as the set of predicates holding at that specific moment, where $s_t \subseteq O$, and we will denote S as the set of all possible states of the world, where $S = \mathcal{P}(O)$. We will call *expansion* $F(s)$ of a state of the world s as the minimal subset of $wff(\mathcal{L}_O)$ that uses the predicates in s in combination of the logical connectives $\{\neg, \vee, \wedge\}$.

One common problem for the monitoring of normative states is the need for an interpretation of brute events as institutional facts, also called constitution of social reality[8]. The use of *counts-as rules* helps solving this problem. Counts-as rules are multi-modal statements of the form $[c](\gamma_1 \rightarrow \gamma_2)$, read as "in context c, γ_1 *counts-as* γ_2". In this paper, we will consider a context as a set of predicates, that is, as a possible subset of a state of the world:

Definition 3. *A counts-as rule is a tuple* $c = \langle \gamma_1, \gamma_2, s \rangle$, *where* $\gamma_1, \gamma_2 \in wff(\mathcal{L}_O)$, *and* $s \subseteq O$.

A set of counts-as rules is denoted as C. Although the definition of counts-as in [8] assumes that both γ_1 and γ_2 can be any possible formula, in our work we limit γ_2 to a conjunction of predicates for practical purposes.

Definition 4. *Following the definitions above, we define an* institution *as a tuple of norms, roles, participants, counts-as rules, and an ontology:*
$I = \langle N, R, P, C, O \rangle$

An example of I for the traffic scenario would be formalised as follows:
$\mathbf{N} := \{\langle enacts(X, Driver) \wedge is\_driving(X),$
$\neg traffic\_violation(X), \bot, \neg is\_driving(X),$
$is\_driving(X) \wedge \neg traffic\_violation(X), Driver\rangle,$
$\langle enacts(X, Driver) \wedge is\_driving(X) \wedge traffic\_violation(X),$
$\top,$
$paid\_fine(X), Driver\rangle\}$
$\mathbf{R} := \{Driver\}, \mathbf{P} := \{Person_1\}$
$\mathbf{C} := \{\langle exceeds(D, 50), traffic\_violation(D), is\_in\_city(D) \rangle\}$
$\mathbf{O} := \{role, enacts, is\_driving, is\_in\_city,$
$exceeds, traffic\_violation, is\_driving, paid\_fine,$
$Person_1, role(Driver), enacts(Person_1, Driver)\}$

2.2 Normative Monitor

In this section we present a formalisation of normative monitoring based on Structural Operational Semantics.

From the definitions introduced in section 2.1, a *Normative Monitor* will be composed of the institutional specification, including norms, the current state of the world, and the current normative state.

In order to track the normative state of an institution at any given point of time, we will define three sets: an instantiation set IS, a fulfillment set FS, and a violation set VS, each of them containing norm instances $\{\langle n_i, \Theta_j \rangle, \langle n_{i'}, \Theta_{j'} \rangle, ..., \langle n_{i''}, \Theta_{j''} \rangle\}$. We adapt the semantics for normative states from [11]:

Definition 5. *Norm Lifecycle: Let* $ni = \langle n, \Theta \rangle$ *be a norm instance, where* $n = \langle f_A, f_M, f_D, w \rangle$, *and a state of the world* s *with an expansion* $F(s)$. *The lifecycle for norm instance* ni *is defined by the following normative state predicates:*

$activated(ni) \Leftrightarrow \exists f \in F(s), \Theta(f_A) \equiv f$
$maintained(ni) \Leftrightarrow \exists \Theta', \exists f \in F(s), \Theta'(f_M) \equiv f \wedge \Theta' \subseteq \Theta$
$deactivated(ni) \Leftrightarrow \exists \Theta', \exists f \in F(s), \Theta'(f_D) \equiv f \wedge \Theta' \subseteq \Theta$
$instantiated(ni) \Leftrightarrow ni \in IS$
$violated(ni) \Leftrightarrow ni \in VS$
$fulfilled(ni) \Leftrightarrow ni \in FS$

where IS *is the instantiation set,* FS *is the fulfillment set, and* VS *is the violation set, as defined above.*

For instance, for norm $n1$, the lifecycle is represented in Figure 1. The maintained state is not represented as it holds in both the activated and fulfilled states. The deactivated state is also not depicted because it corresponds in this case to the Fulfilled state.

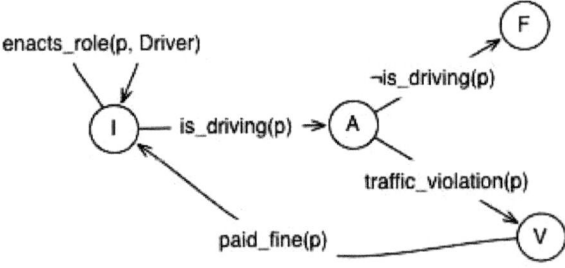

Fig. 1. Lifecycle for norm *n1* in the traffic scenario: (I)nactive, (A)ctivated, (V)iolated, (F)ulfilled

Definition 6. *A Normative Monitor* M_I *for an institution* I *is a tuple* $M_I = \langle I, S, IS, VS, FS \rangle$ *where*

- $I = \langle N, R, P, C, O \rangle$,
- $S = \mathcal{P}(O)$,
- $IS = \mathcal{P}(N \times S \times Dom(S))$,
- $VS = \mathcal{P}(N \times S \times Dom(S))$, *and*
- $FS = \mathcal{P}(N \times S \times Dom(S))$.

Event processed:

$$\frac{e_i = \langle \alpha, p \rangle}{\langle \langle \langle i, s, is, vs, fs \rangle, e_i \rangle, e_{i+1} \rangle \rhd \langle \langle i, s \cup \{p\}, is, vs, fs \rangle, e_{i+1} \rangle} \quad (1)$$

Counts-as rule activation:

$$\frac{\exists \Theta, \exists f \in F(s), \exists \langle \gamma_1, \gamma_2, s_i \rangle \in C, s_i \subseteq s \wedge \Theta(\gamma_1) \equiv f \wedge \Theta(\gamma_2) \notin s}{\langle \langle \langle N, R, P, C, O \rangle, s, is, vs, fs \rangle, e \rangle \rhd \langle \langle \langle N, R, P, C, O \rangle, s \cup \{\Theta(\gamma_2)\}, is, vs, fs \rangle, e \rangle} \quad (2)$$

Counts-as rule deactivation:

$$\frac{\exists \Theta, \exists f \in F(s), \exists \langle \gamma_1, \gamma_2, s_i \rangle \in C, s_i \not\subseteq s \wedge \Theta(\gamma_1) \equiv f \wedge \Theta(\gamma_2) \in s}{\langle \langle \langle N, R, P, C, O \rangle, s, is, vs, fs \rangle, e \rangle \rhd \langle \langle \langle N, R, P, C, O \rangle, s - \{\Theta(\gamma_2)\}, is, vs, fs \rangle, e \rangle} \quad (3)$$

Norm instantiation:

$$\frac{\exists n = \langle f_A, f_M, f_D, w \rangle \in N \wedge \neg \exists n' \in N, n' \rightsquigarrow n \wedge \langle n, \Theta \rangle \notin is \wedge \exists \Theta, \exists f' \in F(s), f' \equiv \Theta(f_A)}{\langle \langle \langle N, R, P, C, O \rangle, s, is, vs, fs \rangle, e \rangle \rhd \langle \langle \langle N, R, P, C, O \rangle, s, is \cup \{\langle n, \Theta \rangle\}, vs, fs \rangle, e \rangle} \quad (4)$$

Norm instance violation:

$$\frac{\begin{array}{c} \exists n = \langle f_A, f_M, f_D, w \rangle \in N \wedge \langle n, \Theta' \rangle \in is \wedge \langle n, \Theta' \rangle \notin vs \wedge \\ \neg(\exists \Theta, \exists f' \in F(s), f' \equiv \Theta(f_M) \wedge \Theta \subseteq \Theta') \wedge NR = \bigcup_{n \rightsquigarrow n'} \langle n', \Theta' \rangle \end{array}}{\begin{array}{c} \langle \langle \langle N, R, P, C, O \rangle, s, is, vs, fs \rangle, e \rangle \rhd \langle \langle \langle N, R, P, C, O \rangle, s, (is - \{\langle n, Theta' \rangle\}) \cup NR, \\ vs \cup \{\langle n, \Theta' \rangle\}, fs \rangle, e \rangle \end{array}} \quad (5)$$

Norm instance fulfilled:

$$\frac{\exists n = \langle f_A, f_M, f_D, w \rangle \in N \wedge \langle n, \Theta' \rangle \in is \wedge \exists \Theta, \exists f' \in F(s), f' \equiv \Theta(f_D) \wedge \Theta \subseteq \Theta'}{\langle \langle \langle N, R, P, C, O \rangle, s, is, vs, fs \rangle, e \rangle \rhd \langle \langle \langle N, R, P, C, O \rangle, s, is - \{\langle n, \Theta' \rangle\}, vs, fs \cup \langle n, \Theta' \rangle \rangle, e \rangle} \quad (6)$$

Norm instance violation repaired:

$$\frac{\exists n, n' \in N \wedge n \rightsquigarrow n' \wedge \langle n, \Theta \rangle \in vs \wedge n \rightsquigarrow n' \wedge \langle n', \Theta \rangle \in fs}{\langle \langle \langle N, R, P, C, O \rangle, s, is, vs, fs \rangle, e \rangle \rhd \langle \langle \langle N, R, P, C, O \rangle, s, is, vs - \{\langle n, \Theta \rangle\}, fs \rangle, e \rangle} \quad (7)$$

Fig. 2. Inference rules for the transition relation $\rhd$

The set Γ of possible configurations of a Normative Monitor M_I is $\Gamma = I \times S \times IS \times VS \times FS$.

However, the definition above does not take into account the dynamic aspects of incoming events affecting the state of the world through time. To extend our model we will assume that there is a continuous, sequential stream of events received by the monitor:

Definition 7. *An event e is a tuple $e = \langle \alpha, p \rangle$, where*

- *$\alpha \in P^3$, and*
- *$p \in S$ and is fully grounded.*

We define E as the set of all possible events, $E = \mathcal{P}(P \times S)$

---

[3] α is considered to be the asserter of the event. Although we are not going to use this element in this paper, its use may be of importance when extending or updating this model.

S. Alvarez-Napagao et al.

Definition 8. *The* Labelled Transition System *for a Normative Monitor* M_I *is defined by* $\langle \Gamma, E, \rhd \rangle$ *where*

- *E is the set of all possible events $e = \langle \alpha, p \rangle$*
- *$\rhd$ is a* transition relation *such that* $\rhd \subseteq \Gamma \times E \times \Gamma$

The inference rules for the transition relation $\rhd$ are depicted in Figure 2.

3 Monitoring with Production Systems

In our approach, practical normative reasoning is based on a production system with an initial set of rules implementing the operational semantics described in Section 2.2. Production systems are composed of a set of rules, a working memory, and a rule interpreter or engine [2]. Rules are simple conditional statements, usually of the form *IF a THEN b*, where *a* is usually called left-hand side (*LHS*) and *b* is usually called right-hand side (*RHS*).

3.1 Semantics of Production Systems

In this paper we use a simplified version of the semantics for production systems introduced in [1].

Considering a set $\mathcal{P}$ of predicate symbols, and an infinite set of variables $\mathcal{X}$, where a fact is a ground term, $f \in \mathcal{T}(\mathcal{P})$, and $\mathcal{WM}$ is the *working memory*, a set of facts, a production rule is denoted `if` p, c `remove` r `add` a, or

$$p, \quad c \Rightarrow r, \quad a,$$

consisting of the following components:

- A set of positive or negative patterns $p = p^+ \cup p^-$ where a pattern is a term $p_i \in \mathcal{T}(\mathcal{F}, \mathcal{X})$ and a negated pattern is denoted $\neg p_i$. p^- is the set of all negated patterns and p^+ is the set of the remaining patterns
- A proposition c whose set of free variables is a subset of the pattern variables: $Var(c) \subseteq Var(p)$.
- A set r of terms whose instances could be intuitively considered as intended to be removed from the working memory when the rule is fired, $r = \{r_i\}_{i \in I_r}$, where $Var(r) \subseteq Var(p^+)$.
- A set a of terms whose instances could be intuitively considered as intended to be added to the working memory when the rule is fired, $a = \{a_i\}_{i \in I_a}$, where $Var(a) \subseteq Var(p)$.

Definition 9. *A set of positive patterns p^+ matches to a set of facts $\mathcal{S}$ and a substitution σ iff $\forall p \in p^+, \exists t \in \mathcal{S}, \sigma(p) = t$. Similarly, a set of negative patterns p^- dismatches a set of facts $\mathcal{S}$ iff $\forall \neg p \in p^-, \forall t \in \mathcal{S}, \forall \sigma, \sigma(p) \neq t$.*

A production rule $p \Rightarrow r, a$ is $(\sigma, \mathcal{WM}')$-fireable on a working memory $\mathcal{WM}$ when p^+ matches with $\mathcal{WM}'$ and p^- dismatches with $\mathcal{WM}$, where $\mathcal{WM}'$ is a minimal subset of $\mathcal{WM}$, and $\mathcal{T} \models \sigma(c)$.

Definition 10. *The application of a* $(\sigma, \mathcal{WM}')$-*fireable rule on a working memory* $\mathcal{WM}$ *leads to the new working memory* $\mathcal{WM}'' = (\mathcal{WM} - \sigma(r)) \cup \sigma(a)$.

Definition 11. *A general production system* $\mathcal{PS}$ *is defined as* $\mathcal{PS} = \langle \mathcal{P}, \mathcal{WM}_0, \mathcal{R} \rangle$, *where* $\mathcal{R}$ *is a set of production rules over* $\mathcal{H} = \langle \mathcal{P}, \mathcal{X} \rangle$.

3.2   Reduction

In order to formalise our Normative Monitor as a production system, we will need to define several predicates to bind norms to their conditions: *activation, maintenance, deactivation*, and to represent normative state over norm instances: *violated, instantiated*, and *fulfilled*. We will also use a predicate for the arrival of events: *event*, and a predicate to represent the fact that a norm instance is a violation handling norm instance of a violated instance: *repair*. For the handling of the DNF clauses, we will use the predicates *holds* and *has_clause*.

Definition 12. *The set of predicates for our production system, for an institution* $I = \langle N, R, P, C, O \rangle$, *is:*

$\mathcal{P}_I := O \cup \{activated, maintained, deactivated,$
$violated, instantiated, fulfilled, event, repair,$
$holds, has\_clause, countsas\}$

The initial working memory $\mathcal{WM}_0$ should include the institutional specification in the form of the formulas included in the counts-as rules and the norms in order to represent the possible instantiations of the predicate $holds$, through the use of the predicate has_clause.

First of all, we need to have the bindings between the norms and their formulas available in the working memory. For each norm $n = \langle f_A, f_M, f_D, w \rangle$, these bindings will be:

$\mathcal{WM}_n := \{activation(n, f_A), maintenance(n, f_M), deactivation(n, f_D)\}$

As we assume the formulas from $wff(\mathcal{L}_O)$ to be in DNF form:

Definition 13. *We can interpret a formula as a set of conjunctive clauses* $f = \{f_1, f_2,$ *..., $f_N\}$, of which only one of these clauses f_i holding true is necessary for f holding true as well:*

$r^h :- has\_clause(f, f') \wedge holds(f', \Theta) \Rightarrow \emptyset, \{holds(f, \Theta)\}$

For example, if $f = (p_1(x) \wedge p_2(y) \wedge ... \wedge p_i(z)) \vee ... \vee (q_1(w) \wedge q_2(x) \wedge ... \wedge q_j(y))$, then the initial facts to be in $\mathcal{WM}_0$ will be:

$\mathcal{WM}_0 := \bigcup_{f' \in f} has\_clause(f, f') = \{has\_clause(f, f_1), ..., has\_clause(f, f_2)\}$

Also, we have to include the set of repair norms by the use of the predicate $repair$, and the counts-as definitions by the use of the predicate $countsas$.

Definition 14. *The initial working memory $\mathcal{WM}_I$ for an institution $I=\langle N, R, P, C, O\rangle$ is:*

$$\mathcal{WM}_I := \bigcup_{n \leadsto n'}^{n \in N} repair(n, n') \qquad \cup$$
$$\bigcup_{n=\langle f_A, f_M, f_D, w\rangle \in N}(\mathcal{WM}_n \cup \mathcal{WM}_{f_A} \cup \mathcal{WM}_{f_M} \cup \mathcal{WM}_{f_D}) \cup$$
$$\bigcup_{c=\langle \gamma_1, \gamma_2, s\rangle \in C}(\{countsas(\gamma_1, \gamma_2, s)\} \cup \mathcal{WM}_{\gamma_1} \cup \mathcal{WM}_s)$$

The rule for the detection of a holding formula is defined as $r_f^{hc} = \lceil f \rceil \Rightarrow \emptyset, \{holds(f, \sigma)\}$, where we denote as $\lceil f \rceil$ the propositional content of a formula $f \in wff(\mathcal{L}_O)$ which only uses predicates from O and the logical connectives $\neg$ and $\wedge$, and σ as the substitution set of the activation of the rule. Following the previous example:

$$r_{f_1}^{hc} = p_1(x) \wedge p_2(y) \wedge ... \wedge p_i(z) \Rightarrow \emptyset, \{holds(f_1, \{x, y, z\})\}$$
$$r_{f_2}^{hc} = q_1(w) \wedge q_2(x) \wedge ... \wedge q_i(y) \Rightarrow \emptyset, \{holds(f_2, \{w, x, y\})\}$$

Similarly as in Definition 14:

Definition 15. *The set of rules R_I^{hc} for detection of holding formulas for an institution $I = \langle N, R, P, C, O\rangle$ is:*

$$R_I^{hc} := \bigcup_{n=\langle f_A, f_M, f_D, w\rangle \in N}\left(\bigcup_{f \in \{f_A, f_M, f_D\}} r_f^{hc}\right) \cup \bigcup_{c=\langle \gamma_1, \gamma_2, s\rangle \in C}\left(\bigcup_{f \in \gamma_1} r_f^{hc}\right)$$

By using the predicate *holds* as defined above, we can translate the inference rules from Section 2.2. Please note that the rules are of the form $p, c \Rightarrow r, a$ as shown in Section 3.1. However, as we only need the c part to create a constraint proposition in the rules for norm instance violation and fulfillment, c is omitted except for these two particular cases.

Definition 16. *Translated rules (see Figure 2)*
Rule for event processing (1):
$r^e = event(\alpha, p) \Rightarrow \emptyset, \{\lceil p \rceil\}$
Rule for counts-as rule activation (2):
$r^{ca} = countsas(\gamma_1, \gamma_2, c) \wedge holds(\gamma_1, \Theta) \wedge holds(c, \Theta') \wedge \neg holds(\gamma_2, \Theta)$
$\Rightarrow \emptyset, \{\Theta(\lceil \gamma_2 \rceil)\}$
Rule for counts-as rule deactivation (3):
$r^{cd} = countsas(\gamma_1, \gamma_2, c) \wedge holds(\gamma_1, \Theta) \wedge \neg holds(c, \Theta') \wedge holds(\gamma_2, \Theta)$
$\Rightarrow \{\Theta(\lceil \gamma_2 \rceil)\}, \emptyset$
Rule for norm instantiation (4):
$r^{ni} = activation(n, f) \wedge holds(f, \Theta) \wedge \neg instantiated(n, \Theta) \wedge \neg repair(n', n)$
$\Rightarrow \emptyset, \{instantiated(n, \Theta)\}$
Rule for norm instance violation (5):
$r^{nv} = instantiated(n, \Theta) \wedge maintenance(n, f) \wedge \neg holds(f, \Theta') \wedge repair(n, n')$,
$\forall \Theta', \Theta' \subseteq \Theta$
$\Rightarrow \{instantiated(n, \Theta)\}, \{violated(n, \Theta), instantiated(n', \Theta)\}$

Rule for norm instance fulfillment (6):

$r^{nf} = deactivation(n, f) \wedge instantiated(n, \Theta) \wedge subseteq(\Theta', \Theta) \wedge holds(f, \Theta'),$
$\Theta' \subseteq \Theta$
$\Rightarrow \{instantiated(n, \Theta)\}, \{fulfilled(n, \Theta)\}$

Rule for norm instance violation repaired (7):

$r^{nr} = violated(n, \Theta) \wedge repair(n, n') \wedge fulfilled(n', \Theta')$
$\Rightarrow \{violated(n, \Theta)\}, \emptyset$

Definition 17. *Following Definitions 13, 15 and 16, the set of rules for an institution* $I = \langle N, R, P, C, O \rangle$ *are:*

$$\mathcal{R}_I := R_I^{hc} \cup \{r^h, r^e, r^{ca}, r^{cd}, r^{ni}, r^{nv}, r^{nf}, r^{nr}\}$$

Definition 18. *The production system* $\mathcal{PS}_I$ *for an institution* I *will be, from Definitions 12, 14 and 17:*

$$\mathcal{PS}_I := \langle \mathcal{P}_I, \mathcal{WM}_I, \mathcal{R}_I \rangle$$

4 Implementation

A prototype of our normative reasoner has been implemented as a DROOLS program. DROOLS is an open-source Object-Oriented rule engine for declarative reasoning in Java [14]. Its rule engine is an implementation of the forward chaining inference Rete algorithm [4]. The use of Java objects inside the rule engine allows for portability and an easier communication of concepts with the reasoning of agents coded in Java.

In DROOLS we can represent facts by adding them to the knowledge base as objects of the class *Predicate*. Predicates are dynamically imported from standardised Description Logic OWL-DL ontologies into Java objects using the tool *OWL2Java*[17], as

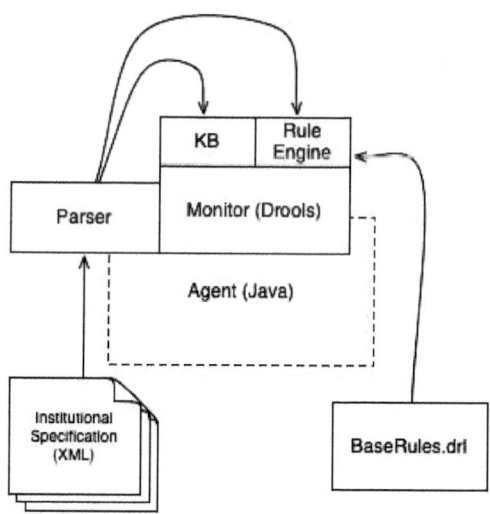

Fig. 3. Architecture of the DROOLS implementation

```
rule "holds"
when
   HasClause(f : formula, f2 : clause)
   Holds(formula == f2, theta : substitution)
then
   insertLogical(new Holds(f, theta));
end

rule "event processed"
when
   Event(a : asserter, p : content)
then
   insertLogical(p);
end

rule "counts-as activation"
when
   CountsAs(g1 : gamma1, g2 : gamma2, s : context)
   Holds(formula == g1, theta : substitution)
   Holds(formula == s, theta2 : substitution)
   not Holds(formula == g2, substitution == theta)
then
   Formula f;

   f = g2.substitute(theta);
   insert(f);
end

rule "counts-as deactivation"
when
   CountsAs(g1 : gamma1, g2 : gamma2, s : context)
   Holds(formula == g1, theta : substitution)
   not Holds(formula == s, theta2 : substitution)
   Holds(formula == g2, substitution == theta)
   f : Formula(content == g2, grounding == theta)
then
   retract(f);
end

rule "norm instantiation"
when
   Activation(n : norm, f : formula)
   Holds(formula == f, theta : substitution)
   not Instantiated(norm == n, substitution == theta)
   not Repair(n2 : norm, repairNorm == n)
then
   insert(new Instantiated(n, theta));
end

rule "norm instance violation"
when
   ni : Instantiated(n : norm, theta : substitution)
   Maintenance(norm == n, f : formula)
   not (SubsetEQ(theta2 : subset, superset == theta)
   and Holds(formula == f, substitution == theta2))
   Repair(norm == n, n2 : repairNorm)
then
   retract(ni);
   insert(new Violated(n, theta));
   insert(new Instantiated(n2, theta));
end

rule "norm instance fulfillment"
when
   Deactivation(n : norm, f : formula)
   ni : Instantiated(norm == n, theta : substitution)
   SubsetEQ(theta2 : subset, superset == theta)
   Holds(formula == f, substitution == theta2)
then
   retract(ni);
   insert(new Fulfilled(n, theta));
end

rule "norm instance violation repaired"
when
   ni : Violated(n : norm, theta : substitution)
   Repair(norm == n, n2 : repairNorm)
   Fulfilled(norm == n2, substitution == theta)
then
   retract(ni);
end

rule "subseteq"
when
   Holds(f : formula, theta : substitution)
   Holds(f2 : formula, theta2 : substitution)
   eval(theta.containsAll(theta2))
then
   insertLogical(new SubsetEQ(theta2, theta));
end
```

Fig. 4. Translation of base rules to DROOLS

subclasses of a specifically designed *Predicate* class. The following shows an example of the insertion of $enacts\_role(p, Driver)$ into the knowledge base to express that p (represented as object p of the domain and instantiating a participant) is in fact enacting the role *driver*:

```
ksession.insert(new Enacts(p, Driver.class));
```

DROOLS programs can be initialised with a rule definition file. However, its working memory and rule base can be modified at run-time by the Java process that is running the rule engine. We take advantage of this by keeping a fixed base, which is a file with fixed contents implementing the rules from Definition 13 and 16, which are independent of the institution, and having a parser for institutional definitions that will feed the rules from Definition 15, which are dependent on the institution (see Figure 3). The institutional definitions we currently use are based on an extension of the XML language presented in [12].

The base rules (see Definitions 13 and 16) has been quite straightforward and the translation is almost literal. The contents of the reusable DROOLS file is shown in Figure 4. The last rule of the Figure is the declarative implementation of the predicate *SubsetEQ* to represent the comparison of substitutions instances $\Theta \subseteq \Theta'$, needed for

```
rule "N1_activation_1"
when
   n : Norm(id == "N1")
   Activation(norm == n, f : formula)
   Enacts(X : p0, p1 == "Driver")
   IsDriving(p0 == X)
then
   Set<Value> theta = new Set<Value>();
   theta.add(new Value("X", X));
   insert(new Holds(f.getClause(0), theta));
end

rule "C1_1"
when
   c : CountsAs(g1 : gamma1)
   Exceeds(D : p0, 50 : p1)
then
   Set<Value> theta = new Set<Value>();
   theta.add(new Value("D", D));
   insert(new Holds(g1.getClause(0), theta));
end
```

Fig. 5. Rules for the traffic scenario

```
ksession.insert(norm1);
ksession.insert(norm2);
ksession.insert(new Repair(norm1, norm2));
ksession.insert(new Activation(norm1, fn1a));
ksession.insert(new Maintenance(norm1, fn1m));
ksession.insert(new Deactivation(norm1, fn1d));
ksession.insert(new HasClause(fn1a, fn1a1));
ksession.insert(new HasClause(fn1m, fn1m1));
ksession.insert(new HasClause(fn1d, fn1d1));
/*          ...same for norm2...          */
ksession.insert(new CountsAs(c1g1, c1g2, c1s));
ksession.insert(new HasClause(c1g1, c1g11));
ksession.insert(new HasClause(c1g2, c1g21));
ksession.insert(new HasClause(c1s, c1s1));
```

Fig. 6. Facts for the traffic scenario

the cases of norm instance violation and fulfillment. In our implementation in *Drools*, substitution instances are implemented as *Set<Value>* objects, where *Value* is a tuple ⟨*String, Object*⟩.

The rest of the rules (see Definitions 15) are automatically generated from the institutional specifications and inserted into the DROOLS rule engine. An example of two generated rules for the traffic scenario is shown in Figure 5.

The initial working memory is also automatically generated by inserting objects (facts) into the DROOLS knowledge base following Definition 14. An example for the traffic scenario is also shown in Figure 6. Please note that this is not an output of the parser, but a representation of what it would execute at run-time.

5   Conclusions and Related Work

The implementation of rule-based norm operationalisation has already been explored in previous research. Some approaches [13,15] directly define the operationalisation of the norms as rules of a specific language, not allowing enough abstraction to define norms at a high level to be operationalised in different rule engine specifications. [5] introduces a translation scheme, but it is bound to Jess by using specific constructs of this language and it does not support constitutive norms. Other recent approaches like [6] define rule-based languages with expressive constructs to model norms, but they are bound to a proper interpreter and have no grounding on a general production system, requiring the use of an intentionally crafted or modified rule engine. For example, in [7,9], obligations, permissions and prohibitions are asserted as facts by the execution of the rules, but the actual monitoring is out of the base rule engine used.

[16] introduces a language for defining an organisation in terms of roles, norms, and sanctions. This language is presented along with an operational semantics based on transition rules, thus making its adoption by a general production system straightforward. Although a combination of counts-as rules and sanctions is used in this language, it is not expressive enough to support regulative norms with conditional deontic statements.

We solve these issues by combining a normative language [12] with a reduction to a representation with clear operational semantics based on the framework in [11] for deontic norms and the use of counts-as rules for constitutive norms. The formalism presented in this paper uses logic conditions that determine the state of a norm (active, fulfilled, violated). These conditions can be expressed in propositional logic at the moment and can be directly translated into *LHS* parts of rules, with no special adaptation needed. The implementation of the operational semantics in a production system to get a practical normative reasoner is thus straightforward. This allows agents for dynamically changing its institutional context at any moment, by *feeding* the production system with a new abstract institutional specification.

Our intention is not to design a general purpose reasoner for normative agents, but a practical reasoner for detecting event-driven normative states. This practical reasoner can then be used as a component not only by normative agents, but also by monitors or managers. Normative agents should deal with issues such as planning and future possibilities, but monitors are focused on past events. For such a practical reasoner, the expressivity of actions languages like $C+$ is not needed, and a simple yet efficient solution is to use production systems, as opposed to approaches more directly related to offline verification or model checking, such as [10].

Mere syntactical translations are usually misleading in the sense that rule language specific constructs are commonly used, constraining reusability [13,5,7]. However, as we have presented in this paper a reduction to a general version of production system semantics, any rule engine could fit our purposes. There are several production system implementations available, some widely used by the industry, such as JESS, DROOLS, SOAR or PROVA. In most of these systems rules are syntactically and semantically similar, so switching from one to the other would be quite simple. As production systems dynamically compile rules to efficient structures, they can be used as well to validate and verify the consistency of the norms. As opposed to [7,9], our reduction ensures that the whole monitoring process is carried out entirely by a general production system, thus effectively decoupling normative state detection and agent reasoning.

DROOLS is an open-source powerful suite supported by JBoss, the community, and the industry, and at the same time it is lightweight enough while including key features that we are or will be using in future work. As an advantage over other alternatives, it includes features relevant to our topic, e.g. event processing, workflow integration. Its OO approach makes it easy to be integrated with imperative code (Java), and OWL-DL native support is expected in a short time.

The monitoring system is available at `http://sf.net/projects/ict-alive` under a GPL license. This implementation is currently being used in use cases with large amounts of events, and we expect to present empirical results of performance as well as an analysis of the algorithmic complexity. A topic that we will cover in more detail in future publications, due to the complexity of the issue on its own and lack of space in this paper, is the addition, modification and removal of normative contexts at run-time. Finally, due to the fact that semantics based on propositional logic can be limiting at a practical level for norm expressivity, as future work we are extending the semantics in order to support, at least, first-order logic norm conditions.

Acknowledgements

This work has been partially supported by the FP7-215890 ALIVE project. J. Vázquez-Salceda's work has been also partially funded by the Ramón y Cajal program of the Spanish Ministry of Education and Science.

References

1. Cirstea, H., Kirchner, C., Moossen, M., Moreau, P.E.: Production Systems and Rete Algorithm Formalisation. Tech. Rep. ILOG, INRIA Lorraine, INRIA Rocquencourt, Manifico (2004)
2. Davis, R., King, J.: An overview of production systems. Tech. rep., Stanford Artificial Intelligence Laboratory, Report No. STAN-CS-75-524 (1975)
3. Dignum, F., Broersen, J., Dignum, V., Meyer, J.J.: Meeting the Deadline: Why, When and How. In: Hinchey, M.G., Rash, J.L., Truszkowski, W.F., Rouff, C.A. (eds.) FAABS 2004. LNCS (LNAI), vol. 3228, pp. 30–40. Springer, Heidelberg (2004)
4. Forgy, C.L.: Rete: A fast algorithm for the many pattern/many object pattern match problem. Artificial Intelligence 19(1), 17–37 (1982)
5. García-Camino, A., Noriega, P., Rodríguez-Aguilar, J.A.: Implementing norms in electronic institutions. In: Proceedings of the Fourth International Joint Conference on Autonomous Agents and Multiagent Systems, Utrecht, Netherlands, pp. 667–673 (2005)
6. García-Camino, A., Rodríguez-Aguilar, J.A., Sierra, C., Vasconcelos, W.: Constraint rulebased programming of norms for electronic institutions. Autonomous Agents and Multi-Agent Systems 18(1), 186–217 (2009)
7. Governatori, G.: Representing business contracts in RuleML. International Journal of Cooperative Information Systems 14(2-3), 181–216 (2005)
8. Grossi, D.: Designing invisible handcuffs: Formal investigations in institutions and organizations for multi-agent systems. Thesis, Universiteit Utrecht (2007)
9. Hübner, J.F., Boissier, O., Bordini, R.H.: A normative organisation programming language for organisation management infrastructures. In: Padget, J., Artikis, A., Vasconcelos, W., Stathis, K., da Silva, V.T., Matson, E., Polleres, A. (eds.) COIN@AAMAS 2009. LNCS, vol. 6069, pp. 114–129. Springer, Heidelberg (2010)

10. Kyas, M., Prisacariu, C., Schneider, G.: Run-time monitoring of electronic contracts. In: Cha, S(S.), Choi, J.-Y., Kim, M., Lee, I., Viswanathan, M. (eds.) ATVA 2008. LNCS, vol. 5311, pp. 397–407. Springer, Heidelberg (2008)
11. Oren, N., Panagiotidi, S., Vázquez-Salceda, J., Modgil, S., Luck, M., Miles, S.: Towards a formalisation of electronic contracting environments. In: Hübner, J.F., Matson, E., Boissier, O., Dignum, V. (eds.) COIN@AAMAS 2008. LNCS, vol. 5428, pp. 156–171. Springer, Heidelberg (2009)
12. Panagiotidi, S., Vázquez-Salceda, J., Alvarez-Napagao, S., Ortega-Martorell, S., Willmott, S., Confalonieri, R., Storms, P.: Intelligent Contracting Agents Language. In: Proceedings of the Symposium on Behaviour Regulation in Multi-Agent Systems (BRMAS 2008) at AISB 2008, Aberdeen, Scotland, vol. 1, p. 49 (2008)
13. Paschke, A., Dietrich, J., Kuhla, K.: A Logic Based SLA Management Framework. In: Proceedings of the 4th Semantic Web Conference (ISWC 2005), Galway, Ireland, pp. 68–83 (2005)
14. Proctor, M., Neale, M., Frandsen, M., Griffith Jr., S., Tirelli, E., Meyer, F., Verlaenen, K.: Drools documentation. JBoss (2008)
15. Strano, M., Molina-Jimenez, C., Shrivastava, S.: A rule-based notation to specify executable electronic contracts. In: Bassiliades, N., Governatori, G., Paschke, A. (eds.) RuleML 2008. LNCS, vol. 5321, pp. 81–88. Springer, Heidelberg (2008)
16. Tinnemeier, N., Dastani, M., Meyer, J.J.: Roles and norms for programming agent organizations. In: Proc. of 8th Int. Conf. on Autonomous Agents and Multiagent Systems (AAMAS 2009), Budapest, Hungary, vol. 1, pp. 121–128 (2009)
17. Zimmermann, M.: OWL2Java (2009), http://www.incunabulum.de/projects/it/owl2java

Learning from Experience to Generate New Regulations

Jan Koeppen[1], Maite Lopez-Sanchez[1], Javier Morales[1], and Marc Esteva[2]

[1] MAiA dept., Universitat de Barcelona
{maite_lopez,jmoralesmat}@ub.edu
[2] Artificial Intelligence Research Institute (IIIA-CSIC)
marc@iiia.csic.es

Abstract. Both human and multi-agent societies are prone to best function with the inclusion of regulations. Human societies have developed jurisprudence as the theory and philosophy of law. Within it, utilitarianism has the view that laws should be crafted so as to produce the best consequences. Following this same objective, we propose an approach to enhance a multi-agent system with a regulatory authority that generates new regulations –norms– based on the outcome of previous experiences. These regulations are learned by applying a machine learning technique (based on Case-Based Reasoning) that uses previous experiences to solve new problems. As a scenario to evaluate this innovative proposal, we use a simplified version of a traffic simulation scenario, where agents move within a road junction. Gathered experiences can then be easily mapped into regular traffic rules that, if followed, happen to be effective in avoiding undesired situations —and promoting desired ones. Thus, we can conclude that our approach can be successfully used to create new regulations for those multi-agent systems that accomplish two general conditions: to be able to continuously gather and evaluate experiences from its regular functioning; and to be characterized in such a way that similar social situations require similar regulations.

1 Introduction

Regulations have been proven to be useful in both human and multi-agent societies. Human societies use regulations within their legal systems. In fact, they have developed Jurisprudence as the theory and philosophy of law, which tries to obtain a deeper understanding of general issues such as the nature of law, of legal reasoning, or of legal institutions[1]. Within it, Normative Jurisprudence is concerned with normative or evaluative theories of law. It tries to answer questions such as "What is the purpose of law?" or "What sorts of acts should be subject to punishment?". Normative Jurisprudence has different schools. Among

---

[1] Jurisprudence definition extracted from Black's Law Dictionary:
http://www.blackslawdictionary.com

M. De Vos et al. (Eds.): COIN 2010 International Workshops, LNAI 6541, pp. 337–356, 2011.

them, Deontology [1] can be described as an ethical theory concerned with duties and rights. On the other hand, Utilitarianism [2] takes the view that the laws should be crafted so as to produce the best consequences. When translating these approaches from human societies to MAS societies, it is obvious that a large number of simplifications have to be taken. Nevertheless, we think that it is still possible to keep and combine their fundamental objectives: to define specific prohibitions, permissions and obligations that promote desired overall system's behaviour for a given MAS society. Thus, the aim of this paper is to define a computational mechanism able to synthesize norms that succeed in the proper regulation of multi-agent societies[2].

We approach this regulation generation problem by learning from the experience of on-going activities within the MAS society. We have chosen Case-Based Reasoning (CBR) as the learning technique to apply. Briefly, CBR solves new problems –i.e., cases– by adapting the solution of similar problems from the knowledge base (which is a compound of solved problems). The selection of this learning technique is somehow inspired in the Anglo-American common law tradition, where judges use legal precedents to make decisions. Hence, using our terminology, we can interpret that judges re*solve* legal *cases* based on the way similar *cases* were previously re*solved*. More specifically, our approach defines a case as a compound of a problem –i.e., a social situation or context– and its associated solution, which in our case corresponds to the regulations that are applied in those contexts. In this manner, the overall learning objective becomes to define cases whose application leads to desired social situations. In CBR, problem description is key, and therefore, we have tested different problem representations that consider global and partial scopes. On the other hand, classical CBR is a supervised learning method that requires an expert to provide the system with correct problem solutions. Nevertheless, we want to generate best regulations without external knowledge, and thus, CBR cannot be directly applied. Instead, we propose to include an exploratory pseudo-random approach so that CBR becomes unsupervised.

Rather than by individual agents in the society, we assume learning to be performed by an independent regulatory authority within the MAS, able to observe and establish its norms. Therefore, we are taking an organizational centered perspective over the MAS as opposed to an agent-centered perspective. The underlying rationale is to restrict the focus of our research. An organizational point of view allows to have learning devoted to finding the best regulations for a whole society and to do it while interactions are taking place. On the contrary, taking an individual centered approach –where learning is performed by individual selfish agents– would also require considering additional aspects such as agreement, trust, uncertainty or communication.

The paper is structured as follows: next section introduces related work. Section 3 describes the tested scenario, section 4 details the learning process, and subsequent section 5 presents its empirical evaluation. Finally, some conclusions and future work are drawn in last Section 6.

---

[2] We assume goals act as a reference that does not evolve.

2   Related Work

Although Artificial Intelligence and Law have been related since a first article from McCarty [3], related research is not usually concerned with machine learning. This is less the case within the MAS area, where some learning techniques have been successfully applied. In fact, Multi-Agent Reinforcement Leaning [4] is quite widely used for individual agent learning. Nevertheless its usage is much more scarce for organizational centered approaches, where an exception is the work by Zhang et al.[5] devoted to improve system's organization. Our work uses CBR as an alternative learning technique, which is also based on system experience, but results in clearer knowledge representations —i.e., cases.

On the other hand, research on norms in multi-agent systems is quite an active area. Just to mention a few works: Boella and van der Torre have done relevant contributions [6] in norm characterization; Campos et al. [7] have proposed norm adaptation methods to specific network scenarios; Artikis et al.[8] have studied the definition of dynamic social conventions (protocols); and Savarimuthu et al. [9], Griffiths and Luck [10], as well as Kota et al. [11] work on norm emergence. Within this area, norm generation has been studied less frequently. Shoham and Tennenholtz [12] focus on norm synthesis by considering a state transition system: they explore the state-space enumeration and state it is NP-complete through a reduction from 3-SAT. Similarly, Hoek et al. [13] synthesize social laws as a model checking problem –again NP-Complete– that requires a complete action-based alternative transition system representation. Following this work, Agotnes and Wooldridge [14] extend the model by taking into account both the implementation costs of social laws and that designer may have multiple (possibly conflicting) objectives, with different priorities. In this setting, the design of social laws become an optimization problem. In our case, CBR has the advantage that, although cases represent the search space, they do not need to be exhaustive, since they can be representatives of a set of similar problems requiring similar solutions. Furthermore, our approach is applied at run-time, being able to generate new norms during the execution of the system (this has the additional advantage of adapting to new situations). An intermediate approach is this of Christelis et al. [15,16], that synthesize generalized norms over general state specifications in planning domains. These domains allow for a local search around declarative specifications of states using planning AI methods. From our point of view, CBR allows the application to a wider range of domains, in particular to those where (i) experiences can be continuously gathered and evaluated, and where (ii) similar social situations require similar regulations (i.e., the continuity solution assumption).

Regarding implementation issues, it might be worth mentioning a related work on system monitoring by Modgil et al.[17] which is able to recognize norm compliance; and another one on traffic domain by Dunkel et al. [18] devoted to managing traffic systems. We have also used a simplified traffic scenario to test our innovative approach empirically.

3   Traffic Scenario

As an initial scenario to evaluate our learning approach, we have chosen a sim-
plification of a traffic scenario. It has been developed as a multi-agent based
simulation model in Repast [19]. This traffic scenario is an orthogonal two-road
junction, where car agents travel along roads towards different destinations. As
Figure 1 shows, the environment has been discretized by means of a square grid
whose cells have the size of a car. Gray (central) cells represent roads and green
(corner) cells correspond to their surrounding non-transitable fields. Each road
lane has a direction of traffic. Agents can join the road from four different entrance points –i.e., four incoming or feeder lanes (see Figure 1 a))– and choose
the exit point, so they decide the route to follow. Time, measured in ticks, is
also discrete. Moreover, cars do have constant speed, so they can only move to
adjacent cells in a single tick. Agent possible actions are stop, move forward,
turn right, or turn left. Nevertheless, cars just turn in the intersection area and
always obey the rules of right side traffic (i.e. they turn right in the first cell of
the intersection whereas left turnings require to further traverse the junction and
turn on the second cell). Furthermore, car agents also follow the social norms
described in section 4 by stopping or moving whenever required.

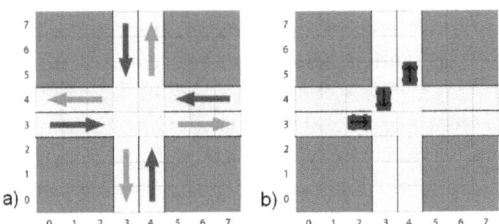

Fig. 1. Orthogonal road junction: a) feeder and exit lines, b)traveling cars

4   Norm Generation through Case-Based Reasoning

Multi-agent systems have been enriched with different regulations –norms, constraints, protocols, etc– with the aim of better organizing the society by restricting both individual behaviours and the way interactions are performed.
In general, regulated societies build their norms as an implicit common agreement, assuming most of their individuals will respect them. Regulations can
come from a norm emergence process or by having a regulatory authority dic-
tating them. Furthermore, they can be created based on previous experiences
or by anticipating situations that may appear. Nevertheless, since the number
of possible outcomes of complex systems is so large, most societies regulate just
those situations that have already occurred so far. This paper focuses on those
regulations that can be established based on the experience of the regular functioning of MAS societies. We assume these societies have regulatory authorities

that gather experiences in an on-going basis. Inspired in jurisprudence used in the Anglo-American common law tradition, we have enriched our MAS with a case based regulatory system. It is in charge of analyzing previous experiences and deciding what (if any) regulations should be applied for specific situation contexts in order to avoid undesired outcomes.

In order to do it, a regulatory authority must be able to first define the goals whose accomplishment guarantees system's performance or its overall desired behaviour. In our traffic scenario, the main goal is to minimize the number of collisions whilst keeping a fluid traffic. This is so because, obviously, if all cars stop, then there will be no collisions at all but cars will not accomplish their individual goals —which most probably will include reaching their destinations. Therefore, we are making an underlying assumption that is that social regulations should guarantee individuals to have enough autonomy so to accomplish their individual goals. Otherwise, punishments should be included to promote norm compliance. In summary, we can somehow interpret that the regulatory authority tries to guarantee basic common agreement about the norms it establishes.

Second, the regulatory authority must have the ability to observe the society in a way that it is able to identify undesired situations —that is, situations where goals are not being accomplished. In our traffic case, both collisions and blockages are main undesired situations.

Afterwards, the regulatory authority should be able to propose regulations that try to prevent undesired situations from being repeated in the future. Prohibitions should be done over those agents' actions that lead to undesired situations. Analogously, obligations can be used to promote desired actions. For example, if we consider our traffic junction, if there is a collision because two cars run on each other, then it is possible to propose a new regulation that prohibits cars to move when they happen to be in the same situation. On the other hand, if no collisions happen when cars traverse the junction it may be useful to create the obligation of keeping moving to prevent blockages. Obviously, deciding which actions should be prohibited or obliged is not a straightforward decision, and that is the reason we introduce automatic learning into the process.

Finally, whenever a new regulation is created and applied on the multi-agent system, the learning process requires the analysis of the consequences of its application. Thus, we need the regulatory authority to observe the society's evolution and to label the experience of applying this new regulation with its subsequent outcome. In this manner, regulatory knowledge is refined in an ongoing basis.

The remaining of this section provides further details of our proposed approach. First subsection specifies the architecture of the MAS applied to the traffic scenario, and subsequent subsections detail the learning process.

4.1   Architecture

Following an organizational centered approach, we assume that the multi-agent system in our traffic scenario consists of a set of external agents that interact

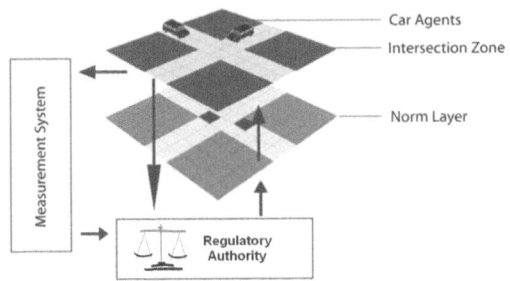

Fig. 2. Traffic scenario architecture

within a road environment together with a regulatory authority (see Figure 2). External agents play a car role; they are able to observe other car agents and to perform certain actions such as join, traverse, and leave the environment. Regarding the regulatory authority, its aim is to promote fluid car traffic flow with as few as possible collisions amongst traffic participants. This authority is constituted by staff permanent agents that perform regulation tasks. From those agents, we highlight the one in charge of defining current norms –we call it norm agent– and the one conducting the learning process —the CBR agent. Nevertheless, there are other staff agents that provide infrastructure services, such as the ones in the tracking system, in charge of obtaining information from the environment; the scene manager, in charge of runtime details; or the monitoring agents, which provide statistical analysis of the overall system operation.

The norm agent uses the regulatory knowledge from the CBR agent to specify the traffic rules that will be applied in the road environment. As a result, it updates a norm layer that is publicly available for the car agents so they become aware of the norms and can thus follow them. Agents conduct this norm updating process continuously, creating new norms when required or applying previously existing ones. The CBR agent will be the one in charge of taking this last decision. Next subsection details how it is performed.

4.2   Unsupervised CBR Cycle

Case-based reasoning is a technique that solves new problems based on past experiences [20]. Experiences are stored in the form of cases, where a case is a description of a problem and its possible solution $Case = \langle probl, sol \rangle$. Cases are stored and maintained in a knowledge base (or case base) for further usage. Briefly, when a new problem is encountered (and thus, it lacks a solution), the CBR process searches for the most similar problem in the case base and adapts its associated solution to solve the current problem. The description of the target problem, together with the provided solution and related information about its performance, constitute a new case that can be in turn stored in the case base. Case performance –i.e., how well the derived solution solved the problem– depends on the continuity of the domain or, in other words, if for the domain it holds that similar problems require similar solutions. This overall process is usually explained in terms of what it is known to be the CBR cycle. It is characterized by four different steps: retrieve, reuse, revise and retain. Before describing them, it is worth mentioning that a case for us is composed of a traffic situation –car distribution–, the regulations –move /not move– that should be applied in such traffic context, and a case performance measure (see subsection 4.3 for further details).

Retrieve: Given a traffic situation description, we first retrieve from our knowledge base the case that is most relevant to solve it. Relevance here is interpreted as similarity, and thus, we search for a case that describes the most similar traffic situation. More specifically, as we will see in next subsection 4.3 a case is considered to be similar to another if it represents the same number of cars and if these cars are located at rotationally equivalent cells. The retrieved case will include the regulations that were applied for its traffic situation and the score of its subsequent applications. Since there are no guarantees that the regulations applied for the case avoid the conflicting situation, the computed score gives a measure of how good these regulations are. Hence, our regulations are empirically evaluated in a continuous manner.

Standard CBR systems are considered as supervised learning methods because they assume there is a pre-existing knowledge base, or that at least, a supervisor can provide solutions for new cases to be learned. Nevertheless, we face an unsupervised learning scenario, since we lack the necessary knowledge to determine the proper traffic rules that should be applied for specific situations. Therefore, it can well be the case that the retrieve phase does not provide any case. In fact, we encounter this situation right at the beginning, since we still lack experience. Hence, if no case has been retrieved, we need to somehow generate a new solution by exploring the space of possible solutions, which in our case means to try different combinations of traffic restrictions (norms). In our current implementation, exploration is performed by randomly assigning stopping/moving restrictions to those cells having cars (avoiding empty cells is an heuristic that prunes the search space). Furthermore, since this pseudo-random solution may not be optimal, we extend the cases to include several alternate solutions (generated in the same way) with a performance measure associated to each of them. The number of possible solutions is bounded in order to differentiate a learning phase –when alternate solutions are built– from a subsequent testing phase —when the case is considered to be learned (i.e., closed) and is applied without adding new solutions. Obviously, this limit in the number of explored solutions prevents us from guaranteeing optimal solutions, but they can still be useful to accomplish the goals of our regulatory authority. Powell et al.[21] have a similar approach to unsupervised CBR that uses reinforcement learning.

In the **reuse** phase, the solution of the retrieved case is mapped to the target problem. This may involve adapting the solution as needed to fit the new situation. In our case, since a case may have more than one associated solution, the one having the best performance results is the one chosen. Reuse is done afterwards by translating the traffic rules of the chosen solution to locations in the new solution that may be rotated if the target problem is a rotated version of the retrieved case.

Afterwards, having mapped the previous solution to the target situation, test the new solution and, if necessary, **revise**. In our traffic scenario this means to dictate the traffic norms to car agents (see previous subsection 4.1), and to observe the outcome of their application in the simulation. In current implementation, the regulatory authority continuously checks if goals are fulfilled by observing each simulation step (tick). Then, it updates the performance measure based on the number of resulting collisions and the number of applied prohibition rules: in order to promote fluid traffic, it penalizes over-regulated solutions —i.e., those abusing from preventing the cars from moving. As a result, the effect of a norm is continuously evaluated as long as the norm is active in the simulation. Although system's goals are two-folded –collision avoidance and fluid traffic– they may have different relevance and, therefore, we use a weighted performance updating formula.

Finally, the cycle ends with the **retain** phase, that consists on the storage the resulting experience in the knowledge base. In our unsupervised CBR scenario this may lead to three different possibilities: i) If a new case was generated, then it will be stored in the case base; ii) If an existing case was retrieved and a new solution for it was generated, then retain becomes an update of the current case; and iii) if the retrieved case was closed –and thus, no solutions were added– the only required update is the performance measure[3]. This will allow the CBR agent to choose among different traffic rules depending on their application outcome. It is worth noticing that for non-deterministic environments, a desirable regulation may become undesirable further in time and become desirable again under changing circumstances. As we can see, this last step enriches the set of stored experiences, and thus it better prepares the system for future encountered problems as far as they satisfy the underlying premise that similar problems have similar solutions.

4.3   Cases and Norms

As we have already mentioned, a case in CBR is generally understood as the description of a problem and its associated solution: $Case = \langle probl, sol \rangle$ where $prob \in StateSpace$ and $sol \in Norms$. Taking into account our traffic domain, a problem description represents one particular traffic situation whereas the solution corresponds to the traffic rules that should be applied for this particular context. The regulatory authority describes traffic situations in terms of the information it gathers from the system (see section 3): empty and occupied cells, and the headings of those cars located at occupied cells. Traffic situations can be described by considering a global point of view or a local perspective. A global scope in the representation will imply a large area of the environment and will contain all cars in the environment, no matter their location. On the

---

[3] Additionally, for all three possibilities we also store/update how many times the case has been applied.

other hand, a local perspective is focused in a narrower environment area and thus, only those cars near the reference point will be considered. A global scope has the advantage that it represents a complete knowledge but the disadvantage of implying a large search space. Regarding the partial scope, although being smaller in its representation size –and thus, search space–, it may fail in representing some important pieces of knowledge. Therefore, as both approaches present pros and cons, we have modeled them both in our particular traffic scenario (see next evaluation section 5 for a comparison). The remaining of this subsection presents them and the associated solutions (norms) they have within our case representation. In fact, depending on the considered scope, norms will be applied to all involved agents –if global scope– or just to the single agent that is acting as reference in the partial representation.

Global scope. When representing a complete traffic situation, the number of possible distributions of cars in the environment becomes high even if just considering the 7×7 example grid in Figure 1. Nevertheless, some simplifications can be taken. First, by assuming that car agents do have basic driving skills it is possible to reduce the size of the environment grid down to the intersection zone (see Figure 3 a)). These skills correspond to basic capacities such as planning a path towards a chosen destination, following this route without leaving the proper road lanes or stopping if a car in front of them in the lane brakes suddenly[4]. Thus, traffic in the feeder and exit lanes (see Figure 1) can be discarded without losing any relevant information. Figure 3 shows how, focusing further on the intersection zone, there are still some cells that can be obviated. These cells correspond to both the field area and the exit lanes, which do not interfere in our simplified traffic. In this manner, the final problem representation can be reduced to 8 cells in the junction area.

The state space (*StateSpace*) we are representing consists thus in 8 cells that can be either empty or occupied by one or several cars. Having more than

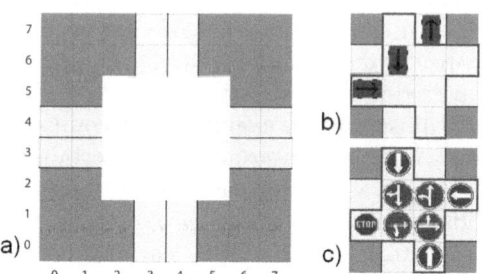

Fig. 3. Global scope junction representation: a) initially discarded cells; b) orthogonal shape representing the problem; and c) applied traffic rules

---

[4] These basic skills may also be modeled as a set of basic norms, but from our point of view regulations should leave some decisions to the agents, whose autonomy can be regulated but should not be overconstrained.

one car in a cell means a collision. Cars in our simulation are removed when colliding, so there is no need to represent this situation (further details can be found in [22]). Furthermore, a car in an occupied cell can have different headings, but due to the traffic flow restrictions, it will only be one for the cells at the junction entrance (the ones of the feeder lanes) or two for the intersection, since two different traffic directions are allowed there. Overall, we have 4 cells with two possible states –i.e., empty or occupied with a fixed heading– and 4 with 3 possible states –empty and occupied with two alternative headings– so that we have $2^4 * 3^4 = 1296$ different possible traffic situations. Finally, we can have situations that represent the same if we apply the appropriated rotation in their representations. Thus, we can further reduce the state space to $1296/4 = 324$ combinations.

Regarding the associated solution ($sol \in Norms$), it represents the same grid area than the problem (see Figure 3 c)) and for each cell, it has a norm that specifies if the car in this location should stop or should keep moving. From a deontic perspective, these traffic rules are represented, respectively, as the obligation of stopping and the prohibition to stop. Thus, the norm agent first considers the solution provided by the CBR agent (see section 4.1) and, afterwards, it applies traffic signs that can be either the stop sign or a direction sign —whose specific direction will correspond to the one of the road cell. Whenever a new conflictive traffic situation occurs, the CBR agent retrieves a single case because cases in the global scope are disjoint. As a consecuence, applied solutions cannot conflict.

Finally, as we have mentioned, we lack the optimal solution ($sol \in Norms$) for each problem ($prob \in StateSpace$) and thus, the learning algorithm explores different candidate solutions. Thus, a case in our global scope representation corresponds in fact to $Case = \langle probl, \{(sol, score)\} \rangle$, where for each problem we have a set of solution-score pairs, and where a solution is a combination of traffic rules and it is associated to information about their application outcome.

Partial scope. As an alternative to use global information, it is also possible to represent situations centered in the point of view of a single agent. Common agent individual perspectives also imply having a limited observation range. Thus, the partial scope reduces the observation area to a subgrid in front of the reference car. Figure 4 illustrates an example that compares the conceptualization of both scopes: for a given global situation at a certain time step we will have as many partial descriptions as involved agents are. Thus following the example in the figure, two different situations –i.e. $prob1, prob2 \in PartialStateSpace$– will be derived. This, in terms of the CBR learning process, means that they will result in two target cases to solve, and therefore, the CBR process will be invoked twice.

As before, problems ($prob \in PartialStateSpace$) are represented by considering empty and occupied cells. The only differences are that their orientation is relative to the reference car and its shape and dimensions, which do not include the cell containing the reference car, are smaller than the global problem representation. Following previous example, we have a rotated 3×1 sub-grid. There, cell states can be 4 (empty, car forward movement, car left turning, and

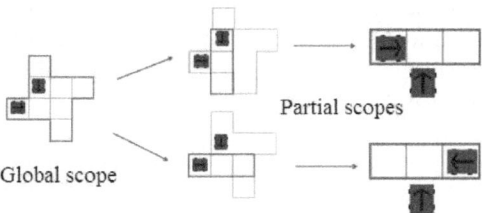

Global scope

Partial scopes

Fig. 4. Case global and partial scopes

car right turning) for those two cells corresponding to the inner junction area
and 2 possible states (empty cell or occupied with a car moving forward) for
the single cell in the junction entrance. Obviously, having a sub-grid implies a
smaller state space ($|PartialStateSpace| < |StateSpace|$) and thus, the number
of possible cases to handle is much smaller ($4^2 * 2 = 32$ in the example). Our implementation allows the definition of different sight range or subgrids –they are
treated as masks over the agent's visibility area– so that they can be empirically
studied.

Once we have defined a problem ($prob \in PartialStateSpace$), its solution
corresponds to the norms that will be applied to the reference agent. In this
manner, cases in our traffic scenario will have a predefined set of two possible
traffic rules: the obligation to stop ($obl(stop)$) and the obligation to keep moving
following the road traffic direction ($proh(stop)$, so that we have a reduced set
of norms: Norms=$\{obl(stop), proh(stop)\}$). Cases in this approach will have a
predefined set of two possible solutions and their associated outcome measure
$Case = \langle probl, \{(obl(stop), scoreStop), (proh(stop), scoreMove)\}\rangle$ and the main
learning task will be to change the score associated to the performance of the
application of both rules ($scoreStop$ and $scoreMove$). Unlike the global scope,
in the partial scope several regulations can be applied given a conflictive traffic
situation. Hence, an applied norm can conflict with another applied norm in the
same simulation step.

Related metrics. Case retrieve and case update phases in our CBR cycle
require the specification of two measures: the distance between two cases and
the score of associated solutions.

Both global and local approaches compute case distance by comparing every
cell in the area (both compared grids have the same size and shape). Differences
between two cells $c_i, c_j \in grid$ are considered to be 1 if their occupancy state is
different:

$dist(c_i, c_j) = 1$ if $state(c_i) \neq state(c_j)$, where
$state(c_k) = \{empty, occupied\_forward, occupied\_right\_turn, occupied\_left\_turn\}$
and $c_i, c_j, c_k \in grid$

Thus, for example, if $state(c_i) = occupied\_forward$ and $state(c_j) = empty$,
then $dist(c_i, c_j) = 1$ and the same distance results if they are occupied with
cars with different headings: $state(c_i) = occupied\_forward$ and $state(c_k) =
occupied_right_turn$ (then $dist(c_i, c_k) = 1$).

The retrieval phase looks for the most similar case in the knowledge base. In our case, the chosen case will be the one for which, if we apply a proper rotation to the retrieved grid, we get a zero distance result when comparing with the grid representing the target problem. Formally:

$$retrieved\_case = argdistance(rotation(grid, \alpha), target\_grid) = 0$$

where $\alpha \in \{0, 90, 180, 279\}$ degrees in our orthogonal environment and $grid$ is the representation of the problem component in the case.

Regarding the scoring computation, we have already said that given a retrieved case with different solutions, the norm agent in the regulatory authority will choose the solution with best application performance. In the global scope, this score update is computed by punishing both the number of collisions (n_col) occurred during the next time step in the simulation as well as the number of stop traffic rules ($obl(stop)$) that were applied (n_stop). Both measures are accordingly weighted so that we have:

$$global\_score = previous\_global\_score + 1 - (w_{col} \cdot n\_col + w_{stop} \cdot n\_stop)$$

Weight values depend on the priority over goals that the regulatory authority has. Our current implementation considers $w_{col} = 5$ and $w_{stop} = 1$ (i.e., a 1 to 5 ratio in the importance of collisions and traffic jams). Otherwise, if both measures (i.e., n_col and n_stop) are zero, the scoring will be increased.

As for the partial scope case, the scoring computation follows the same underlying rationale of punishing norms for leading to collisions but without considering the number of cars that stop, since these norms are related just to one agent.

$$partial\_score = previous\_partial\_score + 1 - w_{col} \cdot n\_col$$

The results shown in subsequent Section 5 consider the weight related to the number of collisions to be $w_{col} = 4$. Nevertheless, it may be worth considering that partial information may lead to different outcomes when applying the same norms to the same partial problem description. In order to deal with this non-deterministic phenomena, it is possible to average the sequence —or a window— of outcomes so to smooth the updating effect.

5   Empirical Evaluation

As we have previously mentioned, we have performed an empirical evaluation of our proposal about regulation generation by developing a multi-agent based simulation of a traffic road junction scenario. The simulator has been implemented over Repast simphony [19] so that its runtime environment interface can be used to enhance the user interface of our simulator. Figure 5 shows the user interface: top toolbar includes the standard simulation buttons such as start, step or stop buttons as well as the time (tick) count; left-side area allows the definition of the setup parameters; middle area shows the actual car simulation; and right-side

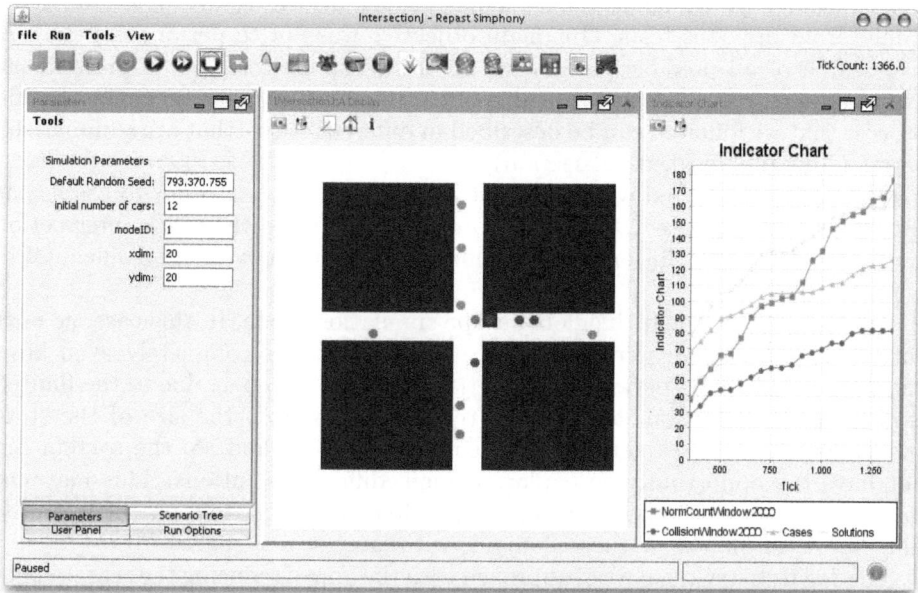

Fig. 5. Traffic simulator in Repast

area is devoted to monitor the evolution of this simulation. Thanks to the setup parameters it is possible to customize current simulation characteristics such as the environment grid dimensions; the maximum number of cars to be simultaneously interacting in the environment; or the learning modality (whose values are 0 if no learning is applied, 1 if a global scope is used in the learning process, and 2 if partial scope). With regards to the actual simulation, cars are represented as circles traversing the two intersecting roads. When cars collide they change their colour to red and disappear. Additionally, a square surrounding a car means that a stop traffic rule has been applied in this specific car position —in the figure example, this specific rule prevents the corresponding car from colliding with the car in front of it. Finally, simulation monitoring shows statistical data about those data that can be useful to follow the evolution of the specified simulation mode. Thus, since the screenshot in figure 5 corresponds to the global scope simulation mode, then the statistical data corresponds to: the number of collisions accumulated during a specific time (tick) window (2000 in the figure); how many stopping rules have been applied for this same period; the total number of cases in the knowledge base; and how many solutions have been explored for this amount of cases.

5.1   Test Design

In addition to the development of the simulator it was necessary to conduct a series of experiments in order to evaluate the learning approach. In fact, these experiments were designed sequentially, guided by the results and intuitions gained from previous tests. Our main objective was not to perform an exhaustive search of all possible parameters in the setup process, but a preliminary exploration that gave us some insights about our learning approach. The specific process that we followed can be described in different steps (that are summarized here and detailed in next subsection).

Obviously, we started with the basic simulation mode, in order to asses that cars behave as expected: they drive properly but, since they lack intersection traffic regulations, collisions in the junction area occur with a significant frequency.

Afterwards, we tested the global scope simulation mode. In this case, as next subsection details, we were not able to avoid collisions completely even after running tests for long periods of time (ticks). This was in part due to the limited exploration capacity but also due to the fact that, given the size of the state space, some rare cases actually happen very scarcely, and so, the system did not have the opportunity to explore enough different solutions. This may not invalidate the global approach for all possible scenarios, but it will certainly limit its performance for those domains with large search spaces.

This led us to try the partial approach with the aim of reducing the search space despite its non-determinism problem. Results there were much more promising, since the system was able to find traffic regulations that further reduced the number of collisions. In addition, it was able to learn them in much shorter periods of time.

Then, by analyzing the resulting regulations, we got the intuition that they could still be described in a shorter way, and thus, we set up a final experiment with cases described by using the minimum amount of information possible.

5.2   Results

Due to the intrinsic randomness of the simulation, all performed tests where repeated five different times[5]. Therefore, all the tables and plots represent figures that correspond to the average over the five resulting series. This section provides the details of these tests by specifying some information that is relevant for the experiments, such as the number of generated cases and associated solutions and the number of collisions. In fact, we take the number of collisions as the metric to evaluate system's performance, and since it requires a finer analysis, we also provide the standard deviation of the values from the repeated experiments.

As for the tests with the global scope, they were performed along a time interval of four thousand ticks. During this time, the system had the opportunity to visit the whole state space —or, in other words, all possible situations were reached. Table 1 shows an excerpt of the averaged results whereas Figure 6 plots the complete series. As it can be observed, first line in the table shows that at

---

[5] CBR learning depends on the order cases are learned. In our case this changes for each new simulation, since the random component on car entrance and route selection may generate traffic situations in different order.

Table 1. Except from the results of the global scope tests

♯ticks	♯cases	♯open cases	♯solutions	$Avg_{2000}(\sharp collisions)$	$\sigma_{collisions}$
100	35	10	40.2	8	2.28
500	79.4	31.4	97.2	38	4.09
1000	104	42.2	140.4	72	5.07
5000	169.4	96.6	213.8	29	7.83
10000	198	113	256	27	8.62
20000	228.4	132.4	329.6	19	5.36
40000	254.4	170.2	345.6	11	1.67

tick number 100, an average number of 35 cases where generated. From those
cases, an average of 10 remain open —which means 25 where already closed—
and an average number of 40.2 solutions where explored so far. Additionally,
the average number of occurred collisions where 8 in this time interval and the
standard deviation of these collisions was 2.28. Collisions are accumulated as
the simulation goes on, nevertheless they tend to happen more scarcely since
the traffic authority improves the norms gradually. Therefore, we provide the
average number of collisions that occurred during a time window of last 2000
ticks. Thus, after this 40000-tick-long period, an average of eleven collisions in a
2000-tick period still occurred. As a consequence, we can state that the learning
process was not much successful in finding the proper set of traffic rules that
prevented cars from colliding.

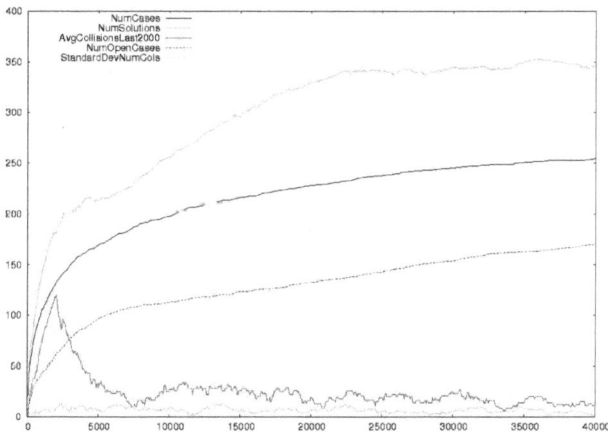

Fig. 6. Global scope results in terms of (averaged) number of: cases, their associated
solutions, open cases, collisions, and the standard deviation of the number of collisions.
Collisions are computed as the average number for last 2000 ticks. X axis corresponds
to the number of simulation ticks.

Table 2. Final number of stops derived from 5 different simulations of the global score. Columns specify the number of solutions that generate zero, one, two or three stops in their norms.

simulation	♯ sol 0 stops	♯ sol 1 stop	♯ sol 2 stops	♯ sol 3 stops
1	226	47	42	40
2	233	53	53	39
3	233	50	41	31
4	233	51	35	33
5	228	48	41	31
Avg	231	50	42	35

Table 3. Excepts from the results of the partial scope tests

♯ ticks	♯ cases	♯ solutions	AvgNumCol2000	σ
100	13.6	27.2	2	2.68
500	22	44	6	4.38
1000	25.2	50.4	10	4.98
5000	28.8	57.6	4	3.35
10000	30.6	61.2	4	4,69
20000	31.4	62.8	4	4.38
40000	31.8	63.6	8	3.58

The explanation of these results for the global scope is two-fold. Firstly, because, despite having encountered possible cases, about 67% of the cases remained open (cases are closed after exploring five different possible solutions). This means that the system learns at slow pace, in part due to the fact that specific traffic situations described as defined by the global scope approach, happen very scarcely and so, the system did not have the opportunity to explore enough different solutions so to learn the best ones. The remaining 33% cases did properly close, and therefore, they were finally assigned a single solution —which corresponds to the one with higher performance score. This leads to the second reason, which is the limited exploration capacity over the set of possible solutions. Table 2 characterises the traffic norms that are active by the end of the simulation period. A total average of 231 norms —which represents about 65% of the total number of norms— corresponded to fluid traffic situations where no stops are added. Accordingly, the remaining 35%, represent norms that cope with problematic situations in the sense that they require the addition of some stopping rules. The number of stops is also related to the number of involved cars. Having more cars imply that there is an increase in the possible combinations in the number and positions of stops to assign. Obviously, having a limited number of chances (5 in our implementation) to explore all possible combinations of traffic rules that can be assigned does not guarantee that the best solution will be found. One may argue that this limit should thus be increased, but it would extend the learning time, where collisions can be generated when applying pseudo-random traffic rules.

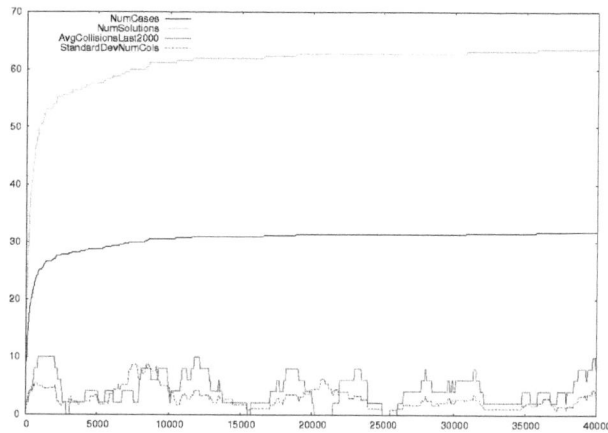

Fig. 7. Partial scope results in terms of (averaged) number of: cases, their associated solutions, collisions —computed as the average number for last 2000 ticks— and their standard deviation. X axis corresponds to the number of simulation ticks.

Having encountered some limitations with the global approach, a second set of experiments with a partial scope were set-up. The main rationale behind this decision was to reduce the size of the search space despite its intrinsic non-determinism problem. The scope was initially defined to be a 3×1 grid (as in Figure 4), so each car was able to see a range of 3 cells wide in front of him. Similarly to previous experiments, Table 3 and Figure 7 show the results of the conducted experiments along 40000 ticks— in this case, though, the concept of open/closed cases is not applicable. As we can see, learning in partial scope is much faster than global scope, since the number of cases stabilizes around 30 after 10000 ticks, much before than the global scope, which tends to more than 250 cases along the whole simulation. Having this small number of cases does not affect the number of collisions. On the contrary, they stay under 10 along the complete simulation period. Obviously, the whole state space was explored and no case could be considered to be rare. In addition to avoiding collisions, we were interested in analyzing the kind of solutions that were found. This is so because a formal translation of an automatically learned case solution into a standard norm specification may be of great interest for many MAS. Thus we analyzed those traffic situations that had an stopping regulation and observed that some grids had in common that the cell located in the front left side of the car position was occupied by another car heading (relatively) eastwards — that is, in the direction of the cell the reference car is steering towards. We can interpret those rules as the authority establishing a "left handside priority" traffic rule. Other grids shared symmetric descriptions codifying the "right handside priority" traffic rule.

Finally, we wanted to further test if the left handside priority rule was enough to avoid collisions in our traffic simulations. Thus, the last test we did was to

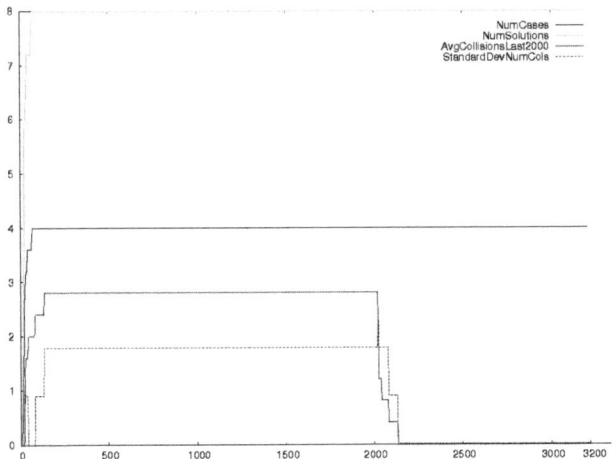

Fig. 8. Single scope results in terms of (averaged) number of: cases, their associated solutions, collisions —computed as the average number for last 2000 ticks— and their standard deviation. X axis is limited to 3500 simulation ticks since values remain constant.

Table 4. Excepts from the results of the single-cell scope tests

♯ ticks	♯ cases	♯ solutions	AvgNumCol2000	σ
20	1.6	3.2	0	0
40	3.6	7.2	1.6	0.89
100	4	8	2.4	0.89
2000	4	8	2.8	1.79
2100	4	8	0.4	0.89
2200	4	8	0	0
3200	4	8	0	0

repeat partial scope experiments with the minimum range of sight for the reference car: a single cell, the one on its left. Obtained results were really satisfactory, since both the convergence time and the number of collisions was further reduced (see Table 4 and Figure 8). From these results, it is possible to argue that the case description in this setting induces the generation of the norm in a straightforward manner, so defining the proper case description may be the underlying problem. Therefore, we do not interpret the positive results obtained with this configuration as the final take-away message. On the contrary, we want to use them as a way that illustrates that learning methods can be used to generate new regulations and that, going a step further, these resulting regulations can be simple enough to be translated into standard traffic rules that can be easily interpreted and followed by external car agents.

6   Conclusions and Future Work

This paper proposes a method to generate new regulations –norms– for multi-agent systems. Specifically, a regulatory authority learns by considering (and exploring) the ones with best application outcome. Learning is based on previous experiences, and corresponds to an unsupervised variation of Case Based Reasoning (CBR). Cases, as defined here, can then be translated to norms, in terms of prohibitions and obligations. We thus claim that this innovative approach can be highly relevant for normative MASs, since, to the best of our knowledge, no general norm generation methods have been established yet.

The paper successfully tests this approach in a simplified traffic scenario. Nevertheless, other scenarios requiring agent coordination –e.g. P2P networks, Robosoccer, etc.– may well benefit from our approach by avoiding (prohibiting) undesired situations –such as network saturation or teammate blocking in previous examples– and promoting (obliging) desired ones. The only requirements[6] are to have monitoring (and evaluating) capabilities as well as continuity in the solution space —i.e., similar social situations require similar regulations. Nevertheless, some undesired situations may appear (e.g, car collisions) as a combination of allowed individual agent actions (e.g., forward driving), thus, norms are required to be more complex than just prohibiting those actions. Context thus becomes necessary. Context, together with its analogy in real Jurisprudence, are the basic rationale of choosing a case representation approach. Nevertheless, we may consider as as future work the application of other learning techniques such as Reinforcement Learning. Additionally, we plan to work on norm violation and norm translation issues.

Acknowledgements. This work is partially funded by EVE (TIN2009-14702-C02-01 / TIN2009-14702-C02-02), AT (CONSOLIDER CSD2007-0022) projects, EU-FEDER funds, and M. Esteva's Ramon y Cajal contract.

References

1. Davis, N.A.: Contemporary deontology. In: Singer, P. (ed.) A Companion to Ethics, pp. 205–218. Blackwell, Malden (1993)
2. Mill, J.S.: Utilitarianism. Parker, Son, and Bourn, London (1863)
3. McCarty, T.: Reflections on Taxman: An Experiment in Artificial Intelligence and Legal Reasoning. Harvard Law Review, 837–93 (1977)
4. Busoniu, L., Babuska, R., de Schutter, B.: A comprehensive survey of multiagent reinforcement learning. IEEE Transactions on Systems, Man, and Cybernetics, Part C: Applications and Reviews 38(2), 156–172 (2008)
5. Zhang, C., Abdallah, S., Lesser, V.: Integrating organizational control into multi-agent learning. In: Aut. Agents and Multiagent Systems, pp. 757–764 (2009)

---

[6] Obviously, the domain has to be discretisable and a learning phase –where some undesired situations may occur– must be acceptable in that domain. Otherwise, as for the traffic scenario, running simulations may be most adequate.

6. Boella, G., van der Torre, L.: Regulative and constitutive norms in normative multiagent systems. In: Proceedings of KR 2004, pp. 255–265 (2004)
7. Campos, J., López-Sánchez, M., Esteva, M.: Multi-Agent System adaptation in a Peer-to-Peer scenario. In: ACM Symposium on Applied Computing - Agreement Technologies Track, pp. 735–739 (2009)
8. Artikis, A., Kaponis, D., Pitt, J.: Dynamic Specifications of Norm-Governed Systems. In: Multi-Agent Systems: Semantics and Dynamics of Organisational Models (2009)
9. Savarimuthu, B., Cranefield, S., Purvis, M., Purvis, M.: Role model based mechanism for norm emergence in artificial agent societies. In: Sichman, J.S., Padget, J., Ossowski, S., Noriega, P. (eds.) COIN 2007. LNCS (LNAI), vol. 4870, pp. 203–217. Springer, Heidelberg (2008)
10. Griffiths, N., Luck, M.: Norm Emergence in Tag-Based Cooperation. In: The Ninth International Workshop on Coordination, Organization, Institutions and Norms in Multi-Agent Systems, pp. 79–86 (2010)
11. Kota, R., Gibbins, N., Jennings, N.: Decentralised structural adaptation in agent organisations. In: AAMAS Workshop Organised Adaptation in MAS (2008)
12. Shoham, Y., Tennenholtz, M.: On social laws for artificial agent societies: off-line design. Journal of Artificial Intelligence 73(1-2), 231–252 (1995)
13. van der Hoek, W., Roberts, M., Wooldridge, M.: Social laws in alternating time: Effectiveness, feasibility, and synthesis. Synthese 1, 156 (2007)
14. Agotnes, T., Wooldridge, M.: Optimal Social Laws. In: Proceedings of he Ninth International Conference on Autonomous Agents and Multiagent Systems, pp. 667–674 (2010)
15. Christelis, G., Rovatsos, M.: Automated norm synthesis in an agent-based planning enviroment. In: Autonomous Agents and Multiagent Systems (AAMAS), pp. 161–168 (2009)
16. Christelis, G., Rovatsoshas, M., Petrick, R.: Exploiting Domain Knowledge to Improve Norm Synthesis. In: Proceedings of he Ninth International Conference on Autonomous Agents and Multiagent Systems, pp. 831–838 (2010)
17. Modgil, S., Faci, N., Meneguzzi, F., Oren, N., Miles, S., Luck, M.: A framework for monitoring agent-based normative systems. In: Autonomous Agents and Multiagent Systems (AAMAS), pp. 153–160 (2009)
18. Dunkel, J., Fernandez, A., Ortiz, R., Ossowski, S.: Event-driven architecture for decision support in traffic management systems. In: IEEE Intelligent Transportation Systems Conf., pp. 7–13 (2008)
19. North, M., Howe, T., Collier, N., Vos, J.: Repast Simphony Runtime System. In: Agent Conf. Generative Social Processes, Models, and Mechanisms (2005)
20. Aamodt, A., Plaza, E.: Case-based reasoning: Foundational issues, methodological variations, and system approaches. AI Commun. 7(1), 39–59 (1994)
21. Powell, J.H., Hauff, B.M., Hastings, J.D.: Evaluating the effectiveness of exploration and accumulated experience in automatic case elicitation. In: Muñoz-Ávila, H., Ricci, F. (eds.) ICCBR 2005. LNCS (LNAI), vol. 3620, pp. 397–407. Springer, Heidelberg (2005)
22. Koeppen, J.F.: Norm Generation in Multi-Agent Systems (master thesis). Univ. of Barcelona (2009)

Controlling Multi-party Interaction within Normative Multi-agent Organizations

Olivier Boissier[1], Flavien Balbo[2,3], and Fabien Badeig[2,3]

[1] Ecole Nationale Supérieure des Mines,
158 Cours Fauriel, 42100 Saint-Etienne, France
Olivier.Boissier@emse.fr
[2] Université Paris-Dauphine - LAMSADE,
Place du Maréchal De Lattre de Tassigny,F-75775 Paris 16 Cedex, France
balbo@lamsade.dauphine.fr
[3] INRETS - GRETIA,
2, Rue de la Butte Verte, 93166 Noisy Le Grand, France
badeig@inrets.fr

Abstract. Multi-party communications taking place within organizations lead to different interaction modes such as (in)direct communication between roles, (in)direct communication restricted to a group, etc. Fully normative organisations need to regulate and control those modes as they do for agents' behaviors. However, this problem is not well addressed in current organisation model proposals. This paper proposes thus to extend the normative organization model $\mathcal{M}$OISE in order to specify such interaction modes. This specification has two purposes: (i) to make the multi-agent organization able to monitor the interaction between the agents, (ii) to make the agents able to reason on these modes as they can do on norms. The paper is focused on the first point. We illustrate with a crisis management application how this extension enlarges the scope of expression of the interaction capabilities and how it has been implemented on the EASI interaction model.

1 Introduction

In a Multi-Agent System (MAS), interaction and organization play key and essential roles. A MAS is often described as composed of agents situated in a shared environment interacting directly or indirectly with each other to execute and cooperate in a distributed and decentralized setting. The behaviors of the agents are often structured along one organization that helps and/or constrains their cooperation schemes within it. Current proposals offer modeling languages usable either by agents either by an organization management system. The latter is dedicated to the regulation and supervision of the agents' execution within the defined organization. Even if some of these models propose some specification to constrain the interactions between the agents, they are limited to the direct communications. However, a wider set of communication between agents exists. For instance, the EASI model[1] [7] proposes an environment-based multi-party

---

[1] Environment as Active Support for Interaction.

M. De Vos et al. (Eds.): COIN 2010 International Workshops, LNAI 6541, pp. 357–376, 2011.
© Springer-Verlag Berlin Heidelberg 2011

interaction model that makes possible to install direct but also indirect and overhearing communications, preserving, if needed, the privacy of the interaction (see [7] for more details). None of existing organisation modeling languages addresses the specification of such communication modes that could be usable within a multi-agent organisation. Having such a feature would bring improvements in the regulation of the system by controlling the way the agents interact with each other. It would also improve the flexibility of the agents within the organisation by making them able to reason on the communication constraints imposed by the organisation in which they evolve.

In this paper, we aim at defining such a specification, focusing on the regulation aspect at the system level. For that, we consider and extend the $\mathcal{M}$OISE Organisational Modeling Language [4]. This language is composed of two independant dimensions – structural and functional - connected to each other by a normative specification. This feature enables to easily extend the model with a new dimension. We validate our proposal on the EASI platform that enacts such communication modes within the MAS. The extended $\mathcal{M}$OISE model is translated into the representation usable by the monitoring facilities offered by the EASI platform. The MAS designer is thus able to use the resulting extended organisation modeling language and to deploy this organisation on the EASI supporting environment. We illustrate the proposal through a crisis management application where different dedicated emergency services are coordinated to solve a crisis situation. This application offers a wide variety of interaction constraints between services involved in the crisis management, given that each service has the possibility to decide on its own which interaction mode to use. We use this application all along the paper to illustrate the components of our proposal.

The paper is organized as follows. In section 2, we present the background of the proposal and motivate our choices. Given that our proposal is dependant of the EASI platform, we describe it as well as the $\mathcal{M}$OISE organisation modeling language in this section. In section 3, we expose how this language has been extended to specify the interaction modes supported by EASI. Section 4 describes how this specification is mapped to the EASI model. In section 5, we illustrate the expressing capabilities of the proposal with different examples issued of a crisis management application. Before conclusion, we compare our proposal to the current related approaches.

2   Background

In the following sections, we introduce first the existing $\mathcal{M}$OISE model and then the EASI platform. Thus the reader will get a complete picture of the context in which we place our proposal.

2.1 $\mathcal{M}$oise

The $\mathcal{M}$OISE framework [6] is composed of an organization modeling language, an organization management infrastructure and organization aware reasoning mechanisms at the agent level. In this paper, we focus on the organization modeling language. Our aim is to use it with the EASI platform in order to specify and regulate the different interaction modes available on this platform (see next section).

The organization modeling language considers the specification of an organization (OS) along three independent dimensions[2]: structural (SS), functional (FS) and normative ($\mathcal{NS}$).

$$OS = \langle SS, FS, \mathcal{NS} \rangle$$

Whereas SS and FS are independent, $\mathcal{NS}$ defines a set of norms binding elements of both specifications. The aim is that the agents enact the behaviors specified in $\mathcal{NS}$ when participating to the organization. The organization modeling language is accompanied by a graphical language (cf. Fig. 1, 2) and XML is used to store the organizational specifications.

Structural Dimension (SS): The structural dimension specifies the *roles*, *groups*, and *links* of an organization. It is defined with the following tuple:

$$SS = \langle \mathcal{R}, \sqsubset, rg \rangle$$

with $\mathcal{R}$ set of the roles, $\sqsubset$, inheritance relation between roles, rg organization root group specification. The definition of this group gives the *compatibility* relations between roles, the maximal and minimal *cardinality* of agents that can endorse roles within the group, the *links* connecting roles to each other (communication, authority, acquaintance) and *sub-groups*. In $\mathcal{NS}$, the role is used to bind a set of constraints on behaviors that the agent commits to satisfy as soon it endorses the role.

To illustrate this SS, let's turn to the crisis application. We define (cf. Fig. 1) two main groups which correspond to the tactical spheres used in a crisis management: decision-making sphere (Decision-making) and operational sphere (Operational). For each of them, we define the roles manager and operator inheriting the generic role role-player. These roles are specialized respectively in coordinator, leader$_D$ for the group Decision-making and leader$_S$ for the subgroups of group Operational. The role coordinator (resp. leader$_D$) can be played by only and only one agent - 1..1 - (resp. several agents - 1..* -). A compatibility link connects the role leader$_D$ to leader$_S$ meaning that any agent playing leader$_D$ will be able to play also the role leader$_S$. Six communication links (cf. l_1 to l_6) have been defined between these roles (e.g. l_1 communication link between coordinator and leader$_D$).

Functional Dimension (FS): The functional dimension is defined by the following tuple:

$$FS = \langle \mathcal{M}, \mathcal{G}, \mathcal{S} \rangle$$

---

[2] In this paper, we will provide the only necessary details in order to globally understand the model as well as the proposed extensions. For further details, readers should refer to http://moise.sourceforge.net/.

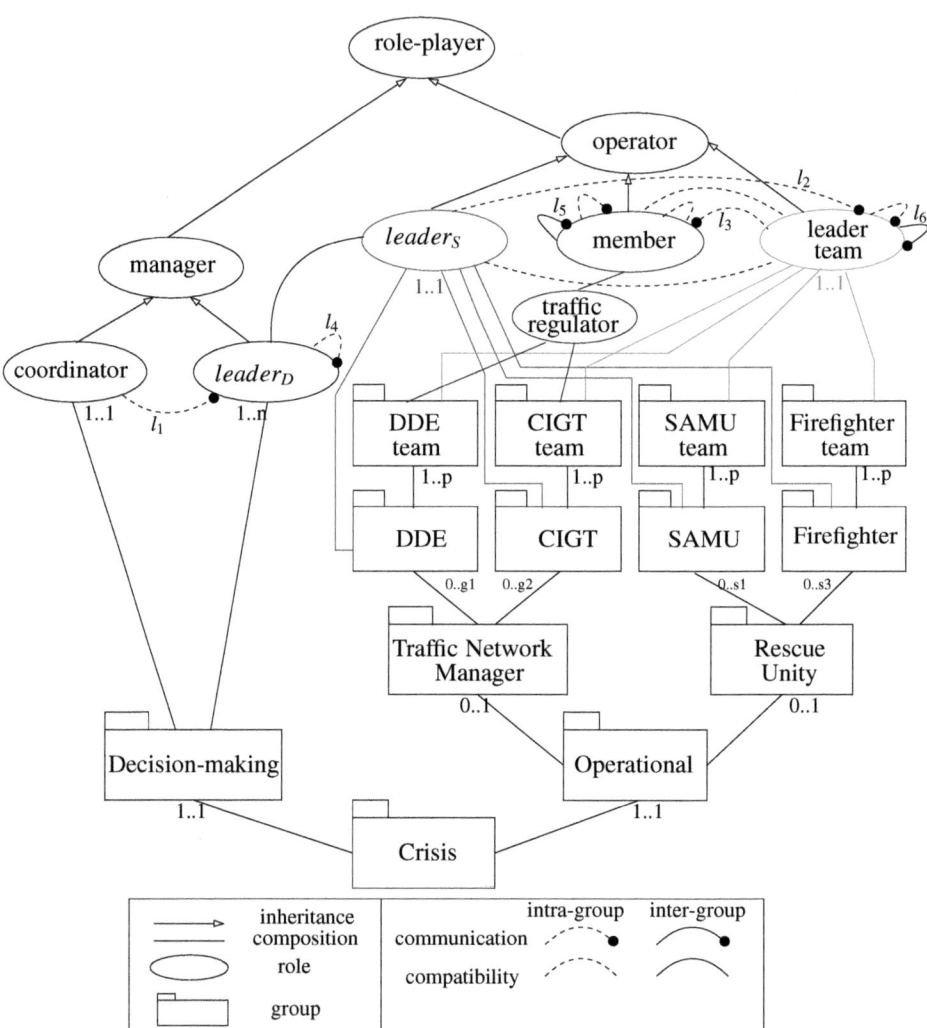

Fig. 1. Partial graphical view of the structural specification for the crisis management application

with $\mathcal{M}$ set of *missions*, consistent grouping of collective or individual goals. A mission defines all the goals an agent commits to when participating in the execution of a social scheme by the way of the roles that they endorse. $\mathcal{G}$ is the set of the *collective or individual goals* to be satisfied and $\mathcal{S}$ is the set of *social schemes*, tree-like structurations of the goals into plans.

Fig. 2 illustrates a social scheme of FS expressing the collective plan for coordinating the decision process within the crisis management application. According to it, agents should aggregate the different information in relation to the crisis situation Refining crisis perception, Safeguarding zone by executing one of the two social schemes (scheme 1 or scheme 2 that are not detailed here) and execute the scheme 3. The different goals are organized into missions.

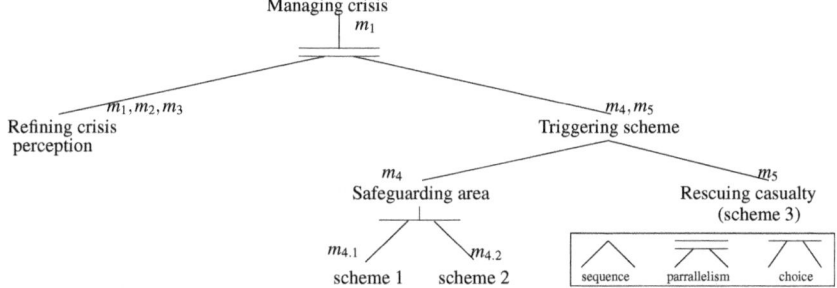

Fig. 2. Graphical view of the social scheme for decision within the crisis management application. Goals are the nodes of the tree. Missions to which the goals are assigned are in italic.

Normative Dimension (NS): The normative dimension $\mathcal{NS}$ defines a set of norms. Each norm has the following expression:

$$norm = \langle id, c, \rho, dm, m \rangle$$

with *id* norm identifier, c activation condition of the norm[3], ρ role concerned by the deontic modality, *dm* deontic modality (obligation or permission), m mission. A normative expression can be read as : "when c holds, any agent playing role ρ has *dm* to commit on the mission m". Within this language, norms are either a *permission*, either an *obligation* for a role to commit to a mission. Goals are indirectly connected to roles since a mission is a set of goals. Interdictions are supposed to exist by default: if the normative specification doesn't have any permission or obligation for a couple mission, role, any agent playing the role is forbidden to commit to mission. A norm becomes in the *active* state (resp. *inactive*) as soon as the condition c holds (resp. doesn't hold). When the norm is active, the deontic expression attached to the norm can be verified. The norm can thus become *fulfilled* or *unfulfilled*.

---

[3] Predicates bearing on the current organization state (e.g. *plays*, *committed*, etc) and/or bearing on particular configurations of the application.

Let's turn again to the crisis management application to give some examples of these norms. For instance, the norm obliging agents playing the role leader$_S$ in the group Traffic Network Management (TNM) to safeguard the zone where the accident took place (mission m_4) is:

$$\langle n_1, c_1, leader_S, obligation, m_4 \rangle$$

where c_1 is $plays(bearer, leader_S, TNM)$. The term *bearer* refers to the agent that will play the role "bearer" in the context of the obligation issued from the instantiation of the norm in the organization entity (see below) and *plays* is a predicate satisfied when the agent plays the leader$_S$ in an instance of group TNM. When the zone is secured, the agents playing the same role within the context of the group Rescue Unity (RU) deploys the intervening scheme (mission m_5) following the norm:

$$\langle n_2, c_2, leader_D, obligation, m_5 \rangle$$

where c_2 is $plays(bearer, leader_S, RU)$.

Organizational Entity (OE): An organizational entity (OE) is defined from the organizational specification OS and a set of agents $\mathcal{A}$ by the following tuple:

$$OE = \langle OS, \mathcal{A}, \mathcal{GI}, \mathcal{SI}, \mathcal{O} \rangle$$

where $\mathcal{GI}$ is the set of concrete groups of the organization, i.e. groups dynamically created from the group specification of the OS, $\mathcal{SI}$ is the set of concrete social schemes dynamically created in the OE from the social schemes specification in the OS and $\mathcal{O}$ is the set of obligations issued from the norms $\mathcal{NS}$ attached to agents of $\mathcal{A}$ whose conditions are satisfied [5].

2.2   Easi

Traditionally, communication involves two interlocutors, the speaker that directs the interaction and the addressee. In such dialogues, the interlocutors know each other. Multi-party communication extends these principles in the sense that several agents are able to hear the same message and that they may have different roles in the communication. All the agents receiving a message are called *recipients*. For example, a "warning" addressed to a group of fire fighters can be also heard by members of the SAMU team. In this case, Fire fighters and members of the SAMU team do not have the same role in the communication act. This difference may affect their reactions. A receiver of a message may be *intended* or not, and if it is, it may be expected to take an *active* part in the conversation, or just to hear *passively* what is exchanged. The speaker can be anonymous, and does not necessarily know *a priori* who will overhear its message, nor their identity, e.g. a public announcement to "agents in the main street ". Finally, hearing a communication may be the result of an initiative of the speaker, (e.g. a multicast decided by the speaker or by the recipient, agents reading voluntarily a blackboard in the crisis management room). The EASI model takes into account all these communication modes. More details can be found in [7].

For cognitive agents, the common point between all these communication modes consists in the *routing* of the messages by identifying *which agent* should obtain *which message* and in *which context*. Solving this problem requires taking into account both sides of the sender and potential receivers. To this aim, EASI manages meta-informations on the MAS (agents, messages, context) in the communication environment and use them to help the agents to interact. The EASI interaction model is thus defined by

$$\langle \Omega, \mathcal{D}, P, \mathcal{F} \rangle$$

where:

- $\Omega = \{\omega_1, ..., \omega_m\}$ the set of entities with $\mathcal{A} \subset \Omega$, $\mathcal{A}$ set of agents, and $MSG \subset \Omega$, MSG set of messages,
- $\mathcal{D} = \{d_1, ..., d_m\}$ set of domain descriptions of the properties,
- $P = \{p_1, ..., p_n\}$ set of properties,
- $\mathcal{F} = \{f_1, ..., f_k\}$ set of filters.

Entity: The entities are the meta-information on the MAS that EASI manages. An entity $\omega_i \in \Omega$ is defined by $\langle e_r, e_d \rangle$ where e_r is a reference to an element of the MAS and e_d is the description of that element. An element of the MAS can be agents ($\mathcal{A}$), messages (MSG) and a reference is its physical address on the platform or other objects such as URL, mailbox, ...

The description e_d is defined by a set of couples $\langle p_i, v_j \rangle$ where $p_i \in P$ and v_j is the value of the property for this entity. Any agent of the MAS has its own processing and knowledge settings. It is connected to the communication environment by the way of its description that it stores and updates in this environment. This description e_d is used for the routing of the informations to the reference e_r.

Property: A property gives an information on an entity. A property $p_i \in P$ is a function : $\Omega \rightarrow d_j \cup \{unknown, null\}$ whose description domain $d_j \in \mathcal{D}$ can be quantitative, qualitative or a finite set of data. The *unknown* value is used when the value of the property cannot be set, and *null* is used to state that the property is undefined in the given description. In order to simplify the notation, only the value of the description domain is given to specify a property.

For instance, in the crisis management application, the properties attached to agents and messages are $id, role, position, subject, sender$ with:

- $id : \Omega \rightarrow N$,
- $role : \Omega \rightarrow \{coordinator, leader_S\}$,
- $position : \Omega \rightarrow N \times N$,
- $subject : \Omega \rightarrow \{alert, demand\}$,
- $sender : \Omega \rightarrow N$.

An agent a can have the following description $\{\langle role, coordinator \rangle\}$ and an agent b $\{\langle role, leader_S \rangle, \langle position, (10, 20) \rangle\}$ and a message m $\{\langle subject, alert \rangle, \langle position, (15, 20) \rangle\}$.

Filter: A filter identifies the entities according to their description (e_d) and realizes the interaction between the concrete objects (e_r). A filter $f_j \in \mathcal{F}$ is a tuple $f_j = \langle f_a, f_m, [f_C], n_f \rangle$ where n_f is the filter name and:

- $f_a : \mathcal{A} \to \{T, F\}$ is an assertion that identifies the receiving agents (*which agent*),
- $f_m : MSG \to \{T, F\}$ is an assertion that identifies the concerned messages (*which message*),
- $f_C : \mathcal{P}(\Omega) \to \{T, F\}$ is an optional set of assertions identifying other entities of the context (*which context*).

Each agent $?r$ (a $'?'$ preceedings a letter denotes a variable) whose description validates f_a receives in its mailbox the message $?m$ that satisfies f_m if there exists a set of entities in the $?c$ such that f_C is true. A filter is therefore valid for any tuple $\langle ?r, ?m, [?c] \rangle$ with $?r \in \mathcal{A}, ?m \in MSG$, and $?c \subset \Omega$.

Let's turn to the crisis management application to illustrate these filters. For instance, the filter $Fe = \langle f_{ae}, f_{me}, f_{ce}, ne \rangle$ installs the routing of the communication as follows ($' = '$ is the comparison operator, ne is the filter name):

- Agents playing the role leader$_D$, situated at the place where the crisis initiated:

$$f_{ae} : [role(?r) = leader_D] \land [position(?r) = (0, 0)]$$

- should receive messages whose subject is "alert":

$$f_{me} : [subject(?m) = alert] \land [sender(?m) = ?ide]$$

- sent by agent playing the role coordinator:

$$f_{ce} : [id(?e) = ?ide] \land [role(?e) = coordinator]$$

In this example, the description of the message sender ($?e$) that is identified thanks to the property *sender* in the message belongs to the context.

Agents who want to send or receive a message, (i) update their description in the communication platform and (ii) add (resp. retract) dynamically in (resp. from) the environment filters that involve them. Thus the environment supports simultaneously direct interaction (including dyadic, broadcast, multi-cast and group communication) and indirect interaction (including mutual-awareness and overhearing). If the filter is added by the future receiver of the message then the interaction is indirect: the agent that deposits the filter defines which message it wants to receive. If the filter is added by the message sender before it sends its message then the interaction is direct: the agent that deposits the filter defines which agent it wants to contact.

According to the state of the different descriptions within the environment, the triggered filters enable the routing of the messages in the different interaction modes towards the corresponding targets. Even if EASI offers an advanced communication management by identifying precisely the interaction context, it cannot be used by the agents to reason on the causes of the interaction. For instance, the filter Fe, introduced above, permits the routing of messages according to its expression but the reasons of the setting of this filter is not expressed within EASI. For Fe, the choice of the communication mode may depend on the relations between the roles coordinator and leader$_D$: the *coordinator* sends messages to *leaders* (direct mode) for dedicated messages whereas the *leaders* listen to all the messages issued from the *coordinator* (indirect mode). Using this knowledge, an agent could reason on the current interactions. For instance, the coordinator may choose a direct interaction to handle certain informations and indirect interaction for others. The leaders can deduce the importance of the informations according to the filter used to receive informations. The explicit specification of communications within an organizational model would help the agents to relate communication filters to the reasons that cause the use of such a communication channel.

3   Extending $\mathcal{M}$oise with Communication Modes

In order to clearly specify the interaction modes that are used in EASI at the organisation level, we are going to enrich and extend the organization modeling language of $\mathcal{M}$OISE with a new dimension. This new dimension is called *communication mode specification* (noted $\mathcal{CS}$). It is dedicated to expressing the communication modes that will be used within the organization. As the other $\mathcal{M}$OISE dimensions, we keep it independent of SS and FS. We use the same principle to connect it to these dimensions and enrich the normative specification accordingly. The communication modes are thus connected to the structure and functioning of the organization by the way of norms. Those norms will be made accessible to the agents when interacting with other agents of the organization.

The new $\mathcal{M}$OISE organization specification is thus defined with the following 4-uple:

$$OS = \langle SS, FS, \mathcal{CS}, \mathcal{NS} \rangle$$

with $\mathcal{CS}$ communication modes specification and $\mathcal{NS}$ the modified normative specification. We detail these two components in what follows.

3.1   Communication Modes Specification (CS)

The specification $\mathcal{CS}$ is composed of the set of communication modes $cm \in \mathcal{CS}$ considered in the organization. A communication mode cm is defined as:

$$cm = \langle type, direction, protocol \rangle$$

with

- *type*, the type of the communication mode (*direct* or *indirect*),
- *direction*, the message transmission direction (*unidirectional* or *bidirectional*),

  protocol, the interaction protocol that is used. The values of this last variable correspond to the name of the different interaction protocols that the designer wishes to be used and deployed in the organization (e.g. $FIPA_{REQUEST}$, *Publish_Subscribe*, ...).

As we will see below, a communication mode qualifies the communication link defined in the structural specification between roles. The communication link is directed from the *initiator* of the communication - source of the link - to the *participant* - target of the link -. Therefore, a link can be considered as:

- a unidirectional channel, letting circulate messages in only one direction,
- a bidirectional channel, letting circulate messages in both directions from the initiator to the participant and inversely.

Orthogonal to these two directions, we consider the direct and indirect interaction models proposed within EASI.

In the crisis management application, we define, for instance, the two following communication modes $cm_{d,b}$ and $cm_{i,u}$:

$$cm_{d,b} = \langle direct, bidirectional, FIPA_{REQUEST} \rangle$$
$$cm_{i,u} = \langle indirect, unidirectional, PublishSubscribe \rangle$$

where $cm_{d,b}$ is used to directly ask for information whereas $cm_{i,u}$ is used to provide informations to agents that will consult it when they want.

3.2 Communication Norms

In order to bind communication link and communication mode as defined in $\mathcal{CS}$ by making explicit the deontic modalities attached to their use, we generalize the writing of the norms described in the $\mathcal{NS}$ of $\mathcal{M}$OISE initial version, with the following expression:

$$norm = \langle id, c, \rho, dm, object \rangle$$

where id is norm identifier, c the activation condition, ρ the role on which the deontic modality bears, dm the deontic modality (obligation or permission), $object$ the subject of the norm.

Object of a norm: The object of a norm $object$ is defined as the two following expressions:

$$object = do(m) | use(l, cm, \alpha)$$

- $do(m)$ in the case where a mission m has to be executed - initial case considered in $\mathcal{M}$OISE,
- $use(l, cm, \alpha)$ in the case where the communication mode cm should be used for the link l in the context α.

Context: The context α defines the constraints bearing on the different entities involved in the interaction using this communication link. When α's status is T (true), the link is usable in any situation.

Before defining the context expression, we have first to introduce the following functions:

- $initiator : \mathcal{O} \rightarrow A$, that returns the agent involved as initiator in the communication link defined in the object of the obligation issued from the norm,
- $participant : \mathcal{O} \rightarrow A$, that returns the agent involved as participant in the communication link defined in the object of the obligation issued from the norm,

- $org : A \rightarrow \mathcal{P}(OC)$, that returns the subset of organisational descriptions OC coming from the participation of an agent to the organization.

The organisational description is managed by the EASI platform (see Sec. 4.1). For instance $org(initiator(n_j))$ enables the access to the organizational context attached to the description of the agent initiating the communication in the context of the instantiated norm n_j in which it is involved. An organisation description $oc_i \in OC$ is defined by:

$$oc_i = \langle ig : g, r, m, go \rangle$$

where

- $ig \in \mathcal{IG}$, ig is a group instance, concrete group created from the group specification g defined in the SS of the organization.
- $g \in \{rg\} \cup rg.subgroups$,
- $r \in \mathcal{R}$,
- $m \in \mathcal{M}$,
- $go \in \mathcal{G}$.

The parameter rg and the sets $\mathcal{R}$, $\mathcal{M}$, $\mathcal{G}$ are defined in the organization specification (cf. Sec. 2.1).

Having introduced all the necessary components, let's turn now to the definition of the context expression α. It is a conjunction of boolean expression where each boolean expression tests the satisfaction of an organisational pattern (op) on the organisational description of the participants concerned by the norms. An organisational pattern op is an organisational description as defined above

$$op = \langle ig : g, r, m, go \rangle$$

where the term of such expressions can refer to entities of the organisation or be let undefined, using the symbol '_' denoting that the value is not a consraint in the choice of the tuples. For instance, in the crisis management application, the expression $\langle \_ : DDE, \_, m_2, \_ \rangle$ defines an organizational pattern such that the concrete group must be of type DDE and the mission is m_2 whatever are the values for roles and goals.

Example: In order to illustrate the different norms that can be defined to constrain the communication modes available in the organisation, let's turn to our application of crisis management. Let's consider the communication link l_1 used by the agents playing the role coordinator towards agents playing the role leader_D (cf. Fig. 1). Given the normative specification that we have defined, it is possible to bind to it the communication mode $cm_{i,u}$ defined above, by writing the following norm:

$$n_1 = \langle n_1, c_1, coordinator, obligation, use(l_1, cm_{i,u}, T) \rangle$$

with $c_1 : committed(m_1)$ to express that l_1 ought to be used by agents playing the role coordinator when they are committed to the mission m_1. No particular context is attached to the use of the communication mode $cm_{i,u}$.

We can also attach to this link another communication mode $cm_{d,b}$, by defining a new norm n_2 :

$$n_2 = \langle n_2, c_2, coordinator, obligation, use(l_1, cm_{d,b}, \alpha_2) \rangle$$

with $c_2 : committed(m_4)$ and a context α_2 stating that the communication on the link l_1 takes place for the sending of messages to agents belonging to group CIGT (Center of the Ingineering and Management of the Traffic):

$$\alpha_2 : [\langle\_ : CIGT, \_, \_, \_\rangle \in org(participant(n_2))]$$

The link l_1 can also be bound to the same constraints but for communication in the context α_3 stating the sending of messages from the agent playing role coordinator to agent belonging to group TNM:

$$n_3 = \langle n_3, c_2, coordinator, obligation, use(l_1, mc_{d,b}, \alpha_3) \rangle$$

where c_2 is defined as above and α_3 is defined as:

$$\alpha_3 : \langle\_ : TNM, \_, \_, \_\rangle \in org((participant(n_3))$$

4   Mapping $\mathcal{M}$oise on the Easi Platform

In order to test and validate our proposal we use the EASI platform that supports the different communication modes that we have defined. As presented in Sec. 2.2, the main constructs used by EASI to manage these communication modes, are the properties of agents, messages on one hand and filters on the other hand. In this section, we present how we generate filters for the communication environment from the specifications expressed with the organization modeling language as defined above. These filters are based on the basic definition they have in EASI and are extended to handle informations on the organization defined with the OML. These informations are stored in the description of the entities that are managed by the EASI platform in order to be accessible to the filters. In this section, we introduce the necessary properties for describing agents, messages and organisation entity in the communication environment. Then we describe how we generate filters from the communication norms as defined in the $\mathcal{M}$OISE OML.

4.1   Properties

In order to make EASI able to manage specifications of the organisation as defined with the $\mathcal{M}$OISE OML, it is necessary to incorporate in the description of an agent and of a message some descriptions of the current organisation in which agents execute and messages are exchanged. Given the definition of an entity in section 2.2, we define the following properties that are accessible in the environment for each type of entity.

Agent Properties: The description of an agent is at least composed of the id and org properties, where:

- id returns the identifier of the agent ($id : A \rightarrow ID_A$ with ID_A set of agent identifiers),
- org is the function defined above, returning the subset of organizational descriptions coming from the participation of the agent to the organization ($org : A \rightarrow \mathcal{P}(OC)$ with OC set of organization descriptions).

For instance, in the crisis management application, the agent a described by $org(a) = \{\langle g1 : Decision\_making, leader_D, m_2, b_2\rangle, \langle g2 : DDE, leader_S, m_1, b_1\rangle\}$, belongs to the group $g1$ of type Decision-making and to a group $g2$ of type DDE, in which it plays respectively role leader$_D$, committed to mission m_2, trying to achieve goal b_2 and the role leader$_S$, committed to the mission m_1 trying to achieve the goal b_1.

This agent minimal description is managed in two different ways:

- a non intrusive method where the agent doesn't master the informations that describe it in the EASI platform. The properties being related to the organization are handled by the organization management infrastructure itself.
- an agent based method where the agent deposits itself the information in the EASI platform. Those information may be specific properties related to the internal state of the agents. For instance, a property $availability$ returning the availability of an agent in the platform may be managed and deposit by the agent itself.

Message Properties: In the same way, we specialize the description of a message given in Sec. 2.2 with the following set of minimal properties $sender, receiver, subject$, reception context rc, sending context sc where:

- $sender : MSG \rightarrow ID_A$,
- $receiver : MSG \rightarrow \mathcal{P}(ID_A) \cup \{unknown\}$,
- $subject : MSG \rightarrow D_{subject} \cup \{unknown\}$, with $D_{subject} = G \cup R \cup \{expression\}$, $expression$ is a string,
- $rc : MSG \rightarrow OC \cup \{unknown\}$ being the reception context,
- $sc : MSG \rightarrow OC \cup \{unknown\}$ being the sending context.

Using these properties, the sender gives informations on the organizational context in which the interaction takes place. For a message, each of these properties can receive a value or the value $unknown$. The more the sender specifies values of properties, the more precise will be the filter that can be used for the routing. We impose that the property $sender$ doesn't get a value $unknown$ in order to avoid anonymous messages. Given these different properties and playing with them, it is possible to obtain a routing ranging from indirect interaction, based on only the identifier of the sender, to one, focused on a subset of receivers ($receiver$) in a particular organizational context (rc), with a sender being in a given organizational context (sc) and the message with a particular content ($subject$).

The sender can also decide to define *patterns* for conditioning the routing along different organizational contexts. To this aim, it can use the same boolean expressions that are used for defining the context α of a norm (see previous section).

For instance, the message mes_1 described below means that the sender whose identifier is a_1 and having the goal b_2 (sending context) sends a message to the agents a_2 and a_4. In this case, the processing of the message is not constrained by the organizational states of the participating agents. They only have to be trying to achieve the organizational goal b_2.

$$mes_1 : \langle\langle sender, a_1\rangle, \langle receiver, \{a_2, a_4\}\rangle, \langle subject, demand\rangle, \langle rc, \langle \_ : \_, \_, \_, b_2\rangle\rangle,$$
$$\langle sc, \langle \_ : \_, \_, \_, b_2\rangle\rangle\rangle$$

For the sender a_1, these are only possibilities since the routing of the message depends on the filters that are installed in the communication environment.

In fact, according to the filters that are installed in it, the routing of the message can lead to different situations: interaction as intended by the sender, no interaction or interaction not intended by the sender. For instance, the agent a_2 can receive the message although it doesn't have the goal b_2 in the case there exists a filter enabling the reception of messages from the agent a_1, whatever are the values for the properties of the message.

In each message is stored the organizational context of its sending in order to enable the agents to filter them. An agent can thus choose to receive messages or to route them according to their organizational contexts without being imposed their use. Moreover, this definition of messages enables to consider the evolution of the organization state. Thus, a message kept in the environment can still be received by an agent in case of change of the organization state. For instance, an agent can be interested by any message whose receiving context concerns a role that it just endorsed. It is useful to keep an history of the past interaction to better understand the current situation. Another advantage is to avoid that a message is missed because it has been sent before the agent has endorsed the role. In order to avoid a risk of confusion between messages, a property related to the time value of their emission or related to their life time can be added to the message description. This choice belongs to the system designer and is out of the scope of this paper.

4.2   From Communication Norms to Environment Filters

The activation of a norm for a communication link leads to the generation and addition of a filter in the environment. This filter is called *normative filter*. It corresponds to the exact translation of the norm as it is instantiated by the organization management system. Thanks to the organization management system, the agents are aware of the norm activation. Besides to the normative filters, the communication environment contains also filters set by the agents according to their activity in the system. In case of direct interaction, the sender knows that it can reach the agents identified as receiver in the norm. In case of indirect interaction, the receiver knows that it can receive messages identified in the norm.

A normative filter uses all the possible informations coming from the organizational specification and routes a message according to its *sc* and *rc* properties. The property *receiver* is not used in the generation process of a normative filter since it requires that the sender knows the identifiers of the agents. This is a too strong hypothesis. The same way, since the routing comes from the activation of a norm, the filter cannot constrain the subject of the message (*subject*) except additional conditions in the norms (context α of the object of the norm). The filter identifies a state of the context corresponding to the interaction. It is identical in the direct and indirect cases. We then propose a *generating pattern* that will be specialized for each activated communication norm.

Access to the organizational specification: Let's first introduce some definitions and notations. We define the predicate $achieves_\alpha$ that is automatically generated from the constraints expressed in the context α of the object of a norm. This predicate checks that the context is satisfied given the initiator, participant, message and entity descriptions in the environment, given α:

$$achieves_\alpha : A \times MSG \times A \times \mathcal{P}(\Omega) :\rightarrow \{T, F\}$$

In order to access to the different features of a communication link from the structural specification, we use pointed notation. $l_j.initiator$ (resp. $l_j.participant$) is used to access to the source role (resp. target) of the link l_j, and $l_j.group$ to access to the group in which l_j is defined.

Given the previous definitions, we are able now to express the generic normative filter $f_{n_k}(?p, ?m, \{?i, C\})$ for the receiver $?p$ of the message $?m$ sent by $?i$ in the context C. This filter is generated from the activated norm n_k as soon as it is activated. The object of the norm bears on the communication link l_j. The filter is composed of the following assertions: f_a that identifies the receiver of the message $?p$ according to its organizational context, f_m that identifies the message $?m$ according to its organizational context and f_c that identifies the organizational context of the sender and the constraints α of the norm n_k.

$f_a : \langle [org(?p) \ni \langle ?x : l_j.group, l_j.participant, \_, \_ \rangle] \rangle$
$f_m : \langle [sender(?m) = id(?i)] \wedge$
$\qquad [sc(?m) = \langle ?y : l_j.group, l_j.initiator, \_, \_ \rangle] \wedge$
$\qquad [rc(?m) = \langle ?x : l_j.group, l_j.participant, \_, \_ \rangle] \rangle$
$f_C : \langle [org(?i) \ni \langle ?y : l_j.group, l_j.initiator, \_, \_ \rangle] \wedge achieves_\alpha(?p, ?m, ?i, C) \rangle$

Example: Let's consider again the norm n_2 of the crisis management application:

$$\langle n_2, committed(m_4), coordinator, obligation, use(l_1, cm_{d,b}, \alpha_2) \rangle$$

with $\alpha_2 : [\langle \_ : CIGT, \_, \_, \_ \rangle \in org(participant(n_2))]$.

The interaction is a direct and bidirectional one (cf. $cm_{d,b}$ of n_2) and the *participant* (the role $leader_D$ according to the link l_1) must belong to the group $CIGT$. The sending agent deposits the first message. The two necessary filters have been generated and added thanks to the activation of n_2. The normative filter generated for n_2 for the interaction from initiator to participant is $f_{n_2}(?p, ?m, \{?i, C\})$ where :

$f_a : \langle [org(?p) \ni \langle ?x : Decision\_making, leader_D, \_, \_ \rangle]$
$f_m : \langle [sender(?m) = id(?i)] \wedge$
$\quad [sc(?m) = \langle ?y : Decision\_making, coordinator, \_, \_ \rangle] \wedge$
$\quad [rc(?m) = \langle ?x : Decision\_making, leader_D, \_, \_ \rangle]$
$f_C : \langle [org(?i) \ni \langle ?y : Decision\_making, coordinator, \_, \_ \rangle] \wedge$
$\quad [org(?p) \ni \langle \_ : CIGT, \_, \_, \_ \rangle] \rangle$

The normative filter from the participant to the initiator is $f_{n_{2b}}(?i, ?m, \{?p, C\}) :^4$, where:

$f_a : \langle [org(?i) \ni \langle ?x : Decision\_making, coordinator, \_, \_ \rangle]$
$f_m : \langle [sender(?m) = id(?p)] \wedge$
$\quad [sc(?m) = \langle ?y : Decision\_making, leader_D, \_, \_ \rangle] \wedge$
$\quad [rc(?m) = \langle ?x : Decision\_making, coordinator, \_, \_ \rangle]$
$f_c : \langle [org(?p) \ni \langle ?y : Decision\_making, leader_D, \_, \_ \rangle] \wedge$
$\quad [org(?p) \ni \langle \_ : CIGT, \_, \_, \_ \rangle] \rangle] \rangle$

This way, for two agents participating to the same concrete group, the message sent by the initiator agent a_1 processed by the filter f_{n_2} will have the following description:

$$\langle \langle sender, id(a_1) \rangle, \langle rc, \langle g1 : Decision\_making, coordinator, \_, \_ \rangle \rangle,$$
$$\langle sc, \langle g1 : Decision\_making, leader_D, \_, \_ \rangle \rangle \rangle$$

The message sent by the participant agent a_2, processed by $f_{n_{2b}}$ will have the following description:

$$\langle \langle sender, id(a_2) \rangle, \langle rc, \langle g1 : Decision\_making, leader_D, \_, \_ \rangle \rangle,$$
$$\langle sc, \langle g1 : Decision\_making, coordinator, \_, \_ \rangle, \rangle$$

With these two filters, a communication channel has been created between agents having the roles coordinator and responsible in the group CIGT. The interaction model EASI has make possible to elaborate these filters. The MOISE model has made possible its use.

5   Example

In this section, we illustrate and discuss the expressing capabilities of our proposal going back to the interaction modes attached to the communication link l_1 issued of the communication norms n_1, n_2, n_3 in the crisis management application described in the paper.

---

[4] We continue to use the variable $?p$ for the participant in the interaction and $?i$ for the initiator given that the agent which is identified by the variable $?i$ who receives the message sent by $?p$.

- $\langle n_1, c_1, coordinator, obligation, use(l_1, cm_{i,u}, T) \rangle$ with $c_1 : committed(m_1)$
- $\langle n_2, c_2, coordinator, obligation, use(l_1, cm_{d,b}, \alpha_2) \rangle$ with $c_2 : committed(m_4)$
  and $\alpha_2 : \langle \_ : CIGT, \_, \_, \_ \rangle \in org(participant(n_2))$
- $\langle n_3, c_3, coordinator, obligation, use(l_1, cm_{d,b}, \alpha_3) \rangle$ with $c_3 : committed(m_4)$
  and $\alpha_3 : \langle \_ : TNM, \_, \_, \_ \rangle \in org((participant(n_3))$

On these three norms, the differences bear on the *activation conditions* of the norm c_x, the *communication mode* $cm_{x,y}$ and the communication *context* specified in the object.

The norm n_1 whose activation condition bears on the management of the crisis (mission m_1) is activated during all the crisis management. The norms n_2 and n_3 are not active since the agents on which the norms bear are committed on the mission m_4.

The predicate $achieves_\alpha$ of the normative filter f_{n_1} generated from the norm n_1 is always true ($\alpha_1 = T$). According to this norm, all the agents playing the role leader$_D$ (target of link l_1) must consult the informations set available by any agent playing the role coordinator. The norm n_2 imposes a direct interaction in the context of mission m_4 so that the coordinator is able to get informations on the state of the transportation network. According to this norm, any agent playing the coordinator role can reach any agent playing the role leader$_D$ (target of link l_1) and being a member of concrete group of type CIGT. The normative filter f_{n_2} described in the previous section expresses these constraints. For the same mission m_4, the coordinator requires information on the available ressources in the services TNM. The normative filter f_{n_3} resulting from the activation of norm n_3, enables the coordinator to reach any leader of each traffic network management service (TNM).

In our example, if the missions m_1, m_4 are under examination, the normative filters corresponding to the three norms are simultaneously present in the environment. From the point of view of the agent playing the role coordinator, it means that it can route messages directly to the agents who are leader$_D$ in groups of type CIGT (n_2) and broaden their demand to agents playing the role leader$_D$ in the groupes of type TNM (n_3) given its needs.

Let's turn to the agents playing the role leader$_D$ in the group Decision-making. If involved in the role leader$_S$ within the groups CIGT and TNM (let's notice that this situation is possible thanks to the compatibility link between both roles), the agents will receive the requests from the agent playing the role coordinator and will be able to know that this is a direct interaction issued from the coordinator. The agents will be able to answer to this agent by using the normative filter created in case of bidirectionnal interaction. Thanks to norm n_1, every agent playing the role leader$_D$ will receive the messages sent by the agents playing the role coordinator via the filter f_{n_1}, building a common and shared knowledge (indirect interaction). According to their processing activity, the agents will be more or less aware of these messages.

Given the norms that we have defined above in the organisation specification, we can envision easily to change the interaction channels between the agents. Where the $\mathcal{M}$OISE normative dimension $\mathcal{NS}$ enables to specify the interaction behavior within the organization, the EASI model using the translation method described in the previous section enables to dynamically install the corresponding interaction channels between the agents situated in the organisation. In our example, it is possible to assess the consequences of the information sharing between the agents thanks to the use of the norm n_1. According to the presence of this norm n_1 in $\mathcal{NS}$ or not, information will be shared or not between the agents. In this last case, the coordinator interacts in a separate way with the leaders within the groups CIGT and TNM thanks to the norms n_2 and n_3. Moreover, if the *communication context* of the norm n_1 is changed to α_2 then it is possible to test that the coordinator shares the information only with the leaders in CIGT group and leaders in the TNM group. Let's stress that the consequences of these different interaction scenario within the same organization can be assessed without changing the agent implementation.

This short example that we can't detail more, shows the richness of expressiveness of the interaction modes and the modularity made possible by combining EASI and MOISE as described in this paper.

6   Related Work

To our knowledge, there doesn't exist a similar support to interaction enabling, for the same communication, to consider simultaneously the direct and indirect interaction modes.

Considering related works to the indirect interaction, the general principle consists in the use of a shared data space that is integrated or not to the environment [8]. In this approach, the tuples that are deposit by the sender in the shared space are compared to patterns expressing the needs of the receivers. These works are focused on the accompanying coordination language and don't consider, at any moment, the organization or the state of the agents.

Dealing with the direct interaction model, several works propose to use an organizational structure in order to manage the communications. In [1], the agents are organised in a hierarchy where each level knows the skills of the agents belonging to the lower level in order to make possible for the sender, a routing of the messages according to the skills. However, it is not an organizational model that is usable by the agents. In the AGR model [3], the organization constrains the interactions according to the groups to which the agents participate. It supports a routing of the message according to the organizational model (group, role). However, the only interaction mode is the direct one and the agents don't have access to an explicit description of the different specifications.

Normative organization models have been proposed in the literature in order to regulate and control the communication between agents. However the specifications address the interaction protocols, i.e. the coordination of the interaction instead of interaction modes. The only considered interaction mode is the direct one (e.g. ISLANDER [2]). They don't consider the interaction at the level addressed in this paper.

7   Conclusions

In this paper, we have proposed a specification of interaction modes between agents within an organization. For that aim, we have extended and enriched the organization modeling language of the $\mathcal{M}$OISE framework. We have also shown how the specifications have been used to generate and to configure dynamically the communication environment supported by the EASI platform. We have illustrated the use of this proposal in a crisis management application.

In the future, we intend to extend the considered interaction modes to over-hearing. We will also consider the communication between groups by extending the scope of communication to groups by enriching and modifying the structural specification of $\mathcal{M}$OISE. Thanks to these new primitives in the organization specification, we can turn to the development of reasoning mechanisms at the agent level to make agents able to reason on the interaction modes that they can use within the organization.

Acknowledgement

We would like to thank D. Trabelsi, H. Hadioui and J.F. Hübner for the fruitful discussions about the content of this paper.

References

1. Bensaid, N., Mathieu, P.: A hybrid architecture for hierarchical agents. In: Veram, B., Yao, X. (eds.) Proceedings of the 1997 International Conference on Computational Intelligence and Multimedia Applications (ICCIMA 1997), pp. 91–95. Watson Ferguson & Co (1997)
2. Esteva, M., Rodriguez-Aguiar, J.A., Sierra, C., Garcia, P., Arcos, J.L.: On the formal specification of electronic institutions. In: Dignum, F., Sierra, C. (eds.) Proceedings of the Agent-mediated Electronic Commerce. LNCS (LNAI), vol. 1191, pp. 126–147. Springer, Berlin (2001)
3. Ferber, J., Gutknecht, O.: A meta-model for the analysis and design of organizations in multi-agents systems. In: Demazeau, Y. (ed.) Proceedings of the 3rd International Conference on Multi-Agent Systems (ICMAS 1998), pp. 128–135. IEEE Press, Los Alamitos (1998)
4. Hübner, J.F., Sichman, J.S., Boissier, O.: A model for the structural, functional, and deontic specification of organizations in multiagent systems. In: Bittencourt, G., Ramalho, G.L. (eds.) SBIA 2002. LNCS (LNAI), vol. 2507, pp. 118–128. Springer, Heidelberg (2002)
5. Hübner, J., Boissier, O., Bordini, R.: A normative organisation programming language for organisation management infrastructures. In: Padget, J., Artikis, A., Vasconcelos, W., Stathis, K., da Silva, V., Matson, E., Polleres, A. (eds.) COIN@AAMAS 2009. LNCS, vol. 6069, pp. 114–129. Springer, Heidelberg (2010)
6. Hübner, J., Boissier, O., Kitio, R., Ricci, A.: Instrumenting multi-agent organisations with organisational artifacts and agents. Autonomous Agents and Multi-Agent Systems 20, 369–400 (2010)

7. Saunier, J., Balbo, F.: Regulated multi-party communications and context awareness through the environment. Journal on Multi-Agent and Grid Systems 5(1), 75–91 (2009)
8. Tummolini, L., Castelfranchi, C., Ricci, A., Viroli, M., Omicini, A.: "Exhibitionists" and "Voyeurs" do it better: A shared environment for flexible coordination with tacit messages. In: Weyns, D., Van Dyke Parunak, H., Michel, F. (eds.) E4MAS 2004. LNCS (LNAI), vol. 3374, pp. 215–231. Springer, Heidelberg (2005)

Author Index

GPSR Compliance

The European Union's (EU) General Product Safety Regulation (GPSR) is a set of rules that requires consumer products to be safe and our obligations to ensure this.

If you have any concerns about our products, you can contact us on ProductSafety@springernature.com

In case Publisher is established outside the EU, the EU authorized representative is:

Springer Nature Customer Service Center GmbH
Europaplatz 3
69115 Heidelberg, Germany

Batch number: 09473985

Printed by Printforce, the Netherlands